T4-ACT-290

Under the editorship of

Wayne C. Minnick

The Florida State University

MR. GLADSTONE INTRODUCING THE SECOND HOME RULE BILL, 1893

BRITISH PUBLIC ADDRESSES 1828–1960

EDITED BY

JAMES H. McBATH

WALTER R. FISHER

University of Southern California

HOUGHTON MIFFLIN COMPANY · BOSTON

NEW YORK · ATLANTA · GENEVA, ILL. · DALLAS · PALO ALTO

PR
1322
.M3

COPYRIGHT © 1971 BY HOUGHTON MIFFLIN COMPANY

The selections reprinted in this book are used by permission of and special arrangement with the proprietors of their respective copyrights. All rights reserved. No part of this work may be reproduced or transmitted in any form or by any means, electronic or mechanical, including photocopying and recording, or by any information storage or retrieval system, without permission in writing from the publisher.

Printed in the U.S.A.

Library of Congress Catalog Card Number: 72-141902

ISBN: 0-395-04852-4

CONTENTS

Preface ix

Acknowledgments xii

ONE   BRITAIN AS AN IMPERIAL POWER

Lord Palmerston
"'CIVIS ROMANUS SUM' SPEECH"   Commons, June 25, 1850   5

John Bright
"ON THE FOREIGN POLICY OF ENGLAND"   Birmingham
October 29, 1858   23

William E. Gladstone
"PRINCIPLES OF FOREIGN POLICY"   West Calder
November 27, 1879   39

John R. Seeley
"TENDENCY IN ENGLISH HISTORY"   Cambridge University, 1882   50

Joseph Chamberlain
"IMPERIAL PREFERENCE"   Birmingham, May 15, 1903   60

Harold Macmillan
"THE WIND OF CHANGE"   Cape Town, February 3, 1960   75

TWO   CONSTITUTION AND PARLIAMENTARY REFORM

Lord John Russell
"REFORM OF PARLIAMENT"   Commons, March 1, 1831   87

Thomas B. Macaulay
"FOR THE REFORM BILL"   Commons, March 2, 1831   110

Sir Robert Peel
"AGAINST THE REFORM BILL"   Commons, March 3, 1831   120

Robert H. Lowe
"AGAINST THE EXTENSION OF DEMOCRACY"   Commons
March 13, 1866   138

John Stuart Mill
"REPRESENTATION OF THE PEOPLE"   Commons, April 13, 1866   154

H. H. Asquith
"The Commons and Constitutional Change" Commons
July 24, 1911   162

Earl Curzon, Earl of Halsbury, Marquess of Lansdowne, Viscount Morley, and Earl of Rosebery
"Debate on the Parliament Bill" Lords, August 9–10, 1911   169

THREE   ECONOMIC POLICY AND SOCIAL CHANGE

Richard Cobden
"Corn Laws and Agricultural Distress" Commons
March 13, 1845   189

Benjamin Disraeli
"Against Repeal of the Corn Laws" Commons
May 15, 1846   211

David Lloyd George
"The Budget and the People" Limehouse, London
July 30, 1909   233

Stanley Baldwin
"Industrial Peace" Commons, March 6, 1925   243

Hugh Gaitskell
"Labour Politics and Democratic Socialism" Blackpool
November 28, 1959   250

FOUR   RELIGIOUS AND POLITICAL LIBERTY FOR IRELAND

Richard Lalor Sheil
"Religious Toleration" Penenden Heath, Kent
October 24, 1828   269

Daniel O'Connell
"Speech at Tara" Tara Hill, Ireland, August 15, 1843   288

Charles S. Parnell
"The Irish Land Question" Ennis, Ireland
September 19, 1880   296

William E. Gladstone
"The First Home Rule Bill" Commons, June 7, 1886   301

H. H. Asquith, Sir Edward Carson, and John Redmond
"Debate on the Government of Ireland Bill" Commons
April 11, 1912   321

FIVE FAITH, REASON, AND KNOWLEDGE

John Henry Cardinal Newman
"Christianity and Scientific Investigation"
Catholic University of Ireland, Dublin, 1855 — 361

Thomas Huxley
"Science and Culture" Mason College, Birmingham
October 1, 1880 — 376

Matthew Arnold
"Literature and Science" Cambridge University
June 14, 1882 — 388

Alfred North Whitehead
"Technical Education and Its Relation to Science
and Literature" London, January 5, 1917 — 403

C. P. Snow
"The Two Cultures" Cambridge University, May 7, 1959 — 417

SIX POLITICS AND PARTY PRINCIPLES

Benjamin Disraeli
"Conservative and Liberal Principles" Crystal Palace
London, June 24, 1872 — 431

Lord Randolph Churchill
"Trust the People" Birmingham, April 16, 1884 — 441

J. Keir Hardie
"Socialist Commonwealth" Commons, April 23, 1901 — 451

John Maynard Keynes
"Am I A Liberal?" Liberal Summer School, Cambridge
August 1, 1925 — 456

Winston S. Churchill
"The Conservative Programme" BBC Broadcast
June 4, 1945 — 464

Clement R. Attlee
"The Labour Programme" BBC Broadcast, June 5, 1945 — 471

SEVEN WORLD WARS AND UNSTABLE PEACE

David Lloyd George
"Appeal to the Nation" London, September 19, 1914 — 483

Winston S. Churchill
"Blood, Toil, Tears, and Sweat" Commons, May 13, 1940 — 493

viii

Winston S. Churchill
"BE YE MEN OF VALOUR"   BBC Broadcast, May 19, 1940   495

Winston S. Churchill
"DUNKIRK: 'A MIRACLE OF DELIVERANCE' "   Commons
June 4, 1940   498

Winston S. Churchill
"THEIR FINEST HOUR"   Commons, June 18, 1940   506

Winston S. Churchill
"NEVER IN THE FIELD OF HUMAN CONFLICT"   Commons
August 20, 1940   514

Aneurin Bevan
"CHANGE THE DIRECTION OF THE WAR"   Commons
July 2, 1942   524

Clement R. Attlee
"A COMMON ENDEAVOUR"   Westminster, London
January 10, 1946   536

Winston S. Churchill
"THE SINEWS OF PEACE"   Westminster College
Fulton, Missouri, March 5, 1946   541

Research Materials   553

Ministries, 1828–1960   564

Biographical Sketches   572

ILLUSTRATIONS

"GLADSTONE INTRODUCING THE SECOND HOME RULE BILL"
February 13, 1893   ii
   Courtesy of the Radio Times Hulton Picture Library
"FOR QUEEN AND EMPIRE"   June 19, 1897   2
"THE REFORM JANUS"   May 5, 1860   84
"THE SEVEN LEAGUE BOOTS"   March 7, 1846   186
"THE LIVE SHELL"   January 30, 1886   266
"MAN IS BUT A WORM"   *Almanack* for 1882   358
"POLITICAL PARROTS"   December 3, 1881   428
   Reproduced from *Punch* by permission of The Huntington
   Library, San Marino, California
"CONQUERING THE HOUSE"   *Time and Tide*, June 1, 1940   480
   Reproduced by permission of Vicky and *Time and Tide*

PREFACE

This volume is a comprehensive collection of authentic texts of British speeches given between 1828 and 1960. Meant to complement the classic work of Chauncey Goodrich, *Select British Eloquence*, it also seeks to provide examples of persuasion that "not only awaken" a "love of genuine eloquence," but also "initiate the pupil in those higher principles which (whether they are conscious of it or not) have always guided the great masters of the art." The purpose of *British Public Addresses, 1828–1960* is to present speeches that reveal significant elements in the emergence of contemporary British ideas and ideals, to offer grist for the mill of the scholar and student, whether biographer, historian, political scientist, or rhetorical critic and theorist.

This collection differs from Goodrich's volume not only in the period covered, but also, and more importantly, in organization, selection of speeches, choice of sources, recording of texts, and basic assumption of how the book should be used. First, it offers (except in a few instances) full text-tested speeches organized around seven issues: Britain as an Imperial Power; Constitution and Parliamentary Reform; Economic Policy and Social Change; Religious and Political Liberty for Ireland; Faith, Reason, and Knowledge; Politics and Party Principles; World Wars and Unstable Peace. Second, it emphasizes the continuing dialogue and debate of spokesmen trying to win support for rival views of truth, justice, and wisdom on enduring questions of public philosophy and program. Third, each speech is fully annotated, so that the reader may comprehend it as did well-informed members of the original audience. Assuming that why and how one studies public discourse is the province of the individual scholar or the principal concern of teachers and students in seminar investigation, we have presented only brief commentaries on speakers and none on speeches. We have attempted to satisfy a widely acknowledged need by providing primary speech texts and research materials—the indispensable resources for the work of the scholar, teacher, and student, regardless of particular interest or critical bias.

In selecting issues and speeches, an attempt was made to focus on questions that excited the mind of the times and hold continuing interest for students of great men, public decision making, the history of ideas, and the theory and practice of rhetorical transactions. The speakers are foremost advocates of the views they express.

The first step in selecting addresses for this anthology was a canvass to determine those usually studied in British Public Address courses. That list was expanded and refined by consulting works in speech, history, literature, religion, education, and politics to discover the most vital and lasting public statements of the period 1828–1960. As a result, many addresses included in this collection appear for the first time in a modern anthology: for instance, the speeches of John R. Seeley, John Stuart Mill, John Henry Cardinal Newman, Thomas Huxley, Matthew Arnold, J. Keir Hardie, Alfred North Whitehead, and C. P. Snow; the political broadcasts of Churchill and Attlee in 1945; Aneurin Bevan's criticism of the war effort; Robert Lowe's argument against a broader franchise; Hugh Gaitskell's statement on democratic socialism; and Harold Macmillan's speech on colonialism. The debates on the Parliament Bill in 1911 and the Government of Ireland Bill in 1912 also are new to an anthology. Other speeches appear in their most authoritative versions; for example, Richard Sheil's address at Penenden Heath; Daniel O'Connell's speech at Tara (published in a short-lived Dublin newspaper); Macmillan's "The Wind of Change" taken from the Cape Town, South Africa, account from which other reports were drawn; Attlee's remarks to the United Nations recorded in its official journal; and speeches on parliamentary reform printed in the *Mirror of Parliament*, a more reliable source for its time than *Hansard*.

The basic criterion of selection was *rhetorical significance*: whether examination of the speech would contribute to the theory of effectiveness, reveal or confirm standards of excellence, in public address. In general, speeches were selected if they evoked immediate or long-range response to an issue or idea of historical import; if they were an authentic expression of one side of a controversial public issue, reflecting the interaction of speaker, audience, and occasion; if they represented the speaker and his position fairly, providing insight into his conception of the problem and his values in approaching its resolution; and, if the speaker was a leading spokesman for an idea, issue, or movement.

Speech texts were chosen on the basis of whether they were the fullest statement, the earliest copy, or the most original version. The source of each text is indicated. The few deletions in the speeches are marked by ellipses if the omission is insignificant. If the omission is extensive, the missing content is provided by a synopsis. We have modified some paragraphing for the convenience of the reader. Obvious misprints and misspellings have been corrected. We have also taken the liberty of changing punctuation to improve the flow or meaning of key passages. For the most part, however, the conventions of the period and culture in spelling and capitalization have not been disturbed.

Speeches may be studied for various reasons and in a variety of ways. A speech expresses a speaker's sense of himself, his sense of his subject, his sense of those to whom he speaks, and a sense of the time and place in which he speaks. Hence, a speech may be profitably criticized from any humanistic perspective. It may be examined as an interaction of author and his expression; as one man's attempt to cope with the "truth" of a matter, with the tension between wisdom and expediency, and with the translation of thought into action; as a response to a rhetorical situation; and as a datum in the building of communication theory. One may analyze speeches for their biographical significance, for what they reveal about public address as a force in the making of history, and for their value in ascertaining the mind of a man, era, culture, or movement. One may also read speeches as a literary genre, to understand how words help to create the fictions men live by. These critical tasks ultimately ask the student of speeches to know all there is to know about how man uses and is used by symbols of inducement.

Such complete knowledge is impossible to attain, of course; one works toward the ideal, hoping to come closer to it as time goes on. As indicated earlier, it is assumed that this enterprise is best pursued by the individual scholar or the teacher and his students. The collection provides reliable materials to help advance independent and seminar study. In addition to the documented speeches, a bibliography is appended that identifies titles most relevant to problems raised in this volume. For more convenient use, it is classified according to major issues.

The bibliography is limited primarily to the period 1828 to the present, but earlier materials are included if they throw light on ideas being discussed. References were selected that provide specific factual information, that lead to other sources for study, and that furnish the corpus of past scholarship basic to understanding the rhetorical context of speeches. Biographies and autobiographies, editions of diaries and letters, collections of speeches, books by speakers, and works of contemporary fiction are omitted; these conventional materials are readily located. The appendix also contains a table of Ministries of the period and a biographical resume of each speaker included in the volume.

An anthology of historic addresses is sometimes viewed as a museum of artifacts, a collection of eloquent utterances of men long dead and irrelevant to the business of contemporary life. It has been our intention, however, not to preserve speeches merely to be read and admired, but to offer material that will stimulate useful theory and criticism now and in the future. As Alfred North Whitehead declared, "If the past is irrelevant to the present, the present is irrelevant to the future."

James H. McBath
Walter R. Fisher

ACKNOWLEDGMENTS

We wish to recognize those who have generously granted permission to include a number of works still under copyright:

Clement R. Attlee, "The Labour Programme." Permission of the British Broadcasting Corporation and The Rt. Hon. Earl Attlee.

Winston S. Churchill, "Be Ye Men of Valour." Permission of *The Times*.

Winston S. Churchill, "The Conservative Programme." Permission of the British Broadcasting Corporation and the Estate of Sir Winston S. Churchill.

Winston S. Churchill, "The Sinews of Peace." Permission of The New York Times Company and the Estate of Sir Winston S. Churchill.

Hugh Gaitskell, "Labour Politics and Democratic Socialism." Permission of the Labour Party.

David Lloyd George, "The Budget and the People." Permission of the First Beaverbrook Foundation.

John Maynard Keynes, "Am I a Liberal?" Permission of the *New Statesman*, London.

Harold Macmillan, "The Wind of Change." Permission of *The Cape Argus*.

C. P. Snow, "The Two Cultures." Permission of the Cambridge University Press.

Alfred North Whitehead, "Technical Education and its Relation to Science and Literature." Permission of E. A. Maxwell, Keeper of the Records, Queens' College, Cambridge.

We also would like to express our appreciation to the Controller of Her Majesty's Stationery Office for permission to make extensive use of official publications under Crown Copyright.

This work required the assistance of many people and the use of a variety of library resources. We are grateful to all who have aided our efforts, especially the staff of the Reference Room at The Huntington Library, the staff of the Reading Room of the British Museum, and Miss Helen Azhderian and the staff of the Reference Department, University of Southern California Library. We also want to thank Miss Minnette Gersh and Mr. Paul Hribar, our research assistants, for their contributions to this book.

"FOR QUEEN AND EMPIRE!!"

1

Britain as an Imperial Power

Lord Palmerston

"*Civis Romanus sum*' Speech"
Commons, June 25, 1850

Sir, anxious as many Members are to deliver their sentiments upon this most important question, yet I am sure they will feel that it is due to myself, that it is due to this House, that it is due to the country, that I should not permit the second night of this debate to close without having stated to the House my views upon the matters in question and my explanation of that part of my conduct for which I have been called to account.

When I say that this is an important question, I say it in the fullest expression of the term. It is a matter which concerns not merely the tenure of office by one individual, or even by a government; it is a question that involves principles of national policy and the deepest interests as well as the honour and dignity of England. I cannot think that the course which has been pursued and by which this question has assumed its present shape is becoming those by whose act it has been brought under the discussion of Parliament, or such as fitting the gravity and the importance of the matters which they have thus led this House and the other House of Parliament to discuss. For if that party in this country imagine that they are strong enough to carry the Government by storm and to take possession of the citadel of office, or if, without intending to measure their strength with that of their opponents, they conceive that there are matters of such gravity connected with the conduct of the Government that it becomes their duty to call upon Parliament solemnly to record its disapprobation of what has passed, I think that either in the one case or in the other that party ought not to have been contented with obtaining the expression of the opinion of the House of Lords, but they ought to have sent down their resolution for the consent and concurrence of this House; or at least those who act with them in political co-operation here should themselves have proposed to this House to come to a similar resolution. But be the road

---

* This text is taken from *Hansard's Parliamentary Debates*, Third Series, Vol. CXII, cols. 380-444.

what it may, we have come to the same end, and the House is substantially considering whether they will adopt the resolution of the House of Lords or the resolution which has been submitted to them by my honourable and learned Friend the Member for Sheffield.[1]

Now, the resolution of the House of Lords involves the future as well as the past. It lays down for the future a principle of national policy which I consider totally incompatible with the interests, with the rights, with the honour, and with the dignity of the country; and at variance with the practice not only of this but of all other civilised countries in the world. Even the person who moved it was obliged essentially to modify it in his speech. But none of the modifications contained in the speech were introduced into the resolution adopted by the other House. The country is told that British subjects in foreign lands are entitled—for that is the meaning of the resolution—to nothing but the protection of the laws and the tribunals of the land in which they happen to reside. The country is told that British subjects abroad must not look to their own country for protection, but must trust to that indifferent justice which they may happen to receive at the hands of the government and tribunals of the country in which they may be.

The House of Lords has not said that this proposition is limited to constitutional countries. The House of Lords has not said that the proposition is inapplicable not only to arbitrary and despotic countries, but even to constitutional countries where the courts of justice are not free, although these limitations were stated in the speech. The country is simply informed by the resolution as it was adopted that so far as foreign nations are concerned, the future rule of the Government of England is to be that in all cases and under all circumstances, British subjects are to have that protection only which the law and the tribunals of the land in which they happen to be may give them.

Now, I deny that proposition; and I say it is a doctrine on which no British Minister ever yet has acted and on which the people of England never will suffer any British Minister to act. Do I mean to say that British subjects abroad are to be above the law or are to be taken out of the scope of the laws of the land in which they live? I mean no such thing; I contend for no such principle. Undoubtedly, in the first instance, British subjects are bound to have recourse for redress to the means which the law of the land affords them, when that law is available for such purpose. That is the opinion which the legal advisers of the Crown have given in numerous cases, and it is the opinion on which we have founded our replies to many applications for our interposition in favour of British subjects abroad.

. . . . .

[1] John Arthur Roebuck.

I say, then, that if our subjects abroad have complaints against individuals or against the government of a foreign country, if the courts of law of that country can afford them redress, then, no doubt, to those courts of justice the British subject ought in the first instance to apply; and it is only on a denial of justice or upon decisions manifestly unjust that the British Government should be called upon to interfere. But there may be cases in which no confidence can be placed in the tribunals, those tribunals being, from their composition and nature, not of a character to inspire any hope of obtaining justice from them. It has been said, "We do not apply this rule to countries whose governments are arbitrary or despotic, because there the tribunals are under the control of the government and justice cannot be had; and, moreover, it is not meant to be applied to nominally constitutional governments where the tribunals are corrupt." But who is to be the judge in such a case whether the tribunals are corrupt or not? The British Government, or the government of the state from which you demand justice?

I will take a transaction that occurred not long ago as an instance of a case in which, I say, the people of England would not permit a British subject to be simply amenable to the laws of the foreign country in which he happened to be. I am not going to talk of the power of sending a man arbitrarily to Siberia nor of a country the constitution of which vests despotic power in the hands of the sovereign. I will take a case which happened in Sicily, where not long ago a decree was passed that any man who was found with concealed arms in his possession should be brought before a court-martial, and if found guilty, should be shot. Now, this happened. An innkeeper of Catania was brought before a court-martial, accused under this law by some police officers who stated that they had discovered in an open bin in an open stable in his inn-yard a knife, which they denounced as a concealed weapon. Witnesses having been examined, the counsel for the prosecution stated that he gave up the case, as it was evident there was no proof that the knife belonged to the man or that he was aware it was in the place where it was found. The counsel for the defendant said that such being the opinion of the counsel for the prosecution, it was unnecessary for him to go into the defence, and he left his client in the hands of the court. The court, however, nevertheless pronounced the man guilty of the charge brought against him, and the next morning the man was shot.

Now, what would the English people have said if this had been done to a British subject? And yet everything done was the result of a law, and the man was found guilty of an offence by a tribunal of the country.

I say, then, that our doctrine is that in the first instance, redress should be sought from the law courts of the country; but that in cases where redress cannot be so had—and those cases are many—to confine a British subject to that remedy only would be to deprive him of the protection which he is entitled to receive.

Then the question arises, how does this rule apply to the demands we have made upon Greece?

[*After reviewing the origins of Britain's relations with Greece and his handling of specific cases prior to 1850, Palmerston states his view of the Finlay and Pacifico affairs.*]

Then I come to the case of Mr. Finlay. It is said that he is "a cannie Scot," that he speculated in land, buying in the cheapest and wishing to sell in the dearest market. His land was taken by the King of Greece for purposes of private enjoyment. Nobody will deny that it is fitting the Sovereign of Greece should have a palace; and if it was necessary to take Mr. Finlay's ground for its site or for the garden attached to it, Mr. Finlay himself made no objection to that. All that Mr. Finlay wanted was to be paid for his land. It is said that Mr. Finlay bought his land at a very cheap rate. That was a matter with which the Greek Government had nothing to do; they had only to pay Mr. Finlay what was the value of the land at the time when they took it from him.

The conduct of the Greek Government in Mr. Finlay's case was very different from that of Frederick the Great in a similar case towards one of his subjects, a man of humble rank. This man refused to sell to his sovereign a little bit of ground on which a windmill stood, the ground being necessary for the completion of a magnificent plan of a residence for the monarch. The conduct of the King of Prussia was very different from that of the King of Greece. The King of Prussia, though a conqueror in the field and the absolute monarch of a great country, respected the rights of a subject however humble and not only left the monument of the independence of his subject standing in the midst of his ornamented grounds but used to point to it with pride, feeling that it was a proof that though he was great and powerful, he knew how to respect the rights of the meanest. For fourteen long years Mr. Finlay was driven from pillar to post, put off with every sort of shuffling and evasive excuse, and deprived of compensation for his land unless he would take what was wholly inadequate.

In 1843 came a revolution. Till 1843 the Greek Government had continued arbitrary, the King declining, under the circumstances I have mentioned, to grant a constitution. In 1843 the patience of the Greeks was exhausted. They rose in Athens and extorted by force that which had been refused to reason. When the Constitution was granted, courts of justice were established which were not indeed independent, because the judges were liable not only to be removed from one court to another, but to be entirely dismissed at the will of the Sovereign; still, in 1843 there were courts to which Mr. Finlay might, as it has been stated, have applied. But they had no competence with respect to events which had happened before their creation. Mr. Finlay, therefore, had no remedy. But I have heard it most triumphantly, distinctly, positively asserted that this case exhibits the bad faith of the English Government, for that at the time when Mr. Wyse[2] made his demands on the Greek Government, we and he knew that the case of Mr. Finlay was absolutely, finally, and conclusively settled. No such thing. That is an assertion absolutely, finally, and conclusively at variance with the truth.

There had been an agreement made for arbitration in this case, and a most curious sample it affords of the manner in which things are carried on in Greece. Mr. Finlay said, "I will submit my claim to arbitration." "By all means," was the reply of the Greek Government; "you shall name one arbiter and we another." But Mr. Finlay has been described as "a cannie Scot," and looking far into the future, he foresaw a possibility which might have struck a man even not so far north that the two arbiters might differ, and he suggested that an umpire should be appointed. The Greek Government said, "You are quite right. We see how it is, and we will appoint one." But Mr. Finlay, being a sensible man, did not like to submit his case to a tribunal where there would be two to one against him, and so he declined that arbitration. The Greek Government then gave up this unreasonable proposal, which they had made just as if it had been quite a matter of course, and a commission of arbitration was agreed upon consisting of two respectable people and an umpire properly appointed. If that arbitration had gone on and the money awarded by it had been paid, Mr. Finlay's case would have been absolutely, finally, and conclusively settled. But by the law of Greece, arbiters so appointed must pronounce an award within three months or, if they don't, then the arbitration falls and drops to the ground. The commissioners could not make their award without certain documents, which could only be furnished by an officer of the Greek Government. This officer, by some unfortunate accident, did not furnish them, and the arbitration fell to the ground by efflux of time.

Therefore, when Baron Gros[3] came to inquire into the matter, he found this case just as it had been when Mr. Finlay first made his complaint. Baron Gros said to Mr. Finlay, "Why, your claim is settled." "Settled? No," said Mr. Finlay. "Why, have you not received your money?" "Not a farthing; and I don't know what amount I am to receive." In short, his case was exactly in the same state in which it was before the arbitration had been agreed to.

That was a case in which we made no specific demand. The only specific demand was that Mr. Finlay should receive whatever the value of his land

[2] Sir Thomas Wyse, Minister to Athens.
[3] French envoy sent to Athens to mediate between England and Greece.

should be found to be. We fixed no sum; we were unable to fix any; and the sum he received afterwards was the amount which the two arbiters, one named by Mr. Finlay, the other by the Greek Government, were prepared to award, splitting the difference between their respective estimates. I don't think that in that case the claim was either doubtful in justice or exaggerated in amount.

Then we come to the claim of M. Pacifico—a claim which has been the subject of much unworthy comment. Stories have been told involving imputations on the character of M. Pacifico; I know nothing of the truth or falsehood of these stories. All I know is that M. Pacifico, after the time to which those stories relate, was appointed Portuguese consul, first to Morocco and afterwards at Athens. It is not likely that the Portuguese Government would select for appointments of that kind a person whose character they did not believe to be above reproach. But I say with those who have before had occasion to advert to the subject that I don't care what M. Pacifico's character is. I do not and cannot admit that because a man may have acted amiss on some other occasion and in some other matter, he is to be wronged with impunity by others.

The rights of a man depend on the merits of the particular case, and it is an abuse of argument to say that you are not to give redress to a man because in some former transaction he may have done something which is questionable. Punish him if you will—punish him if he is guilty—but don't pursue him as a Pariah through life.

What happened in this case? In the middle of the town of Athens, in a house which I must be allowed to say is not a wretched hovel, as some people have described it—but it does not matter what it is, for whether a man's home be a palace or a cabin, the owner has a right to be there safe from injury—well, in a house which is not a wretched hovel, but which in the early days of King Otho was, I am told, the residence of the Count Armansperg, the Chief of the Regency—a house as good as the generality of those which existed in Athens before the Sovereign ascended the throne—M. Pacifico, living in this house, within forty yards of the great street, within a few minutes' walk of a guard-house where soldiers were stationed, was attacked by a mob. Fearing injury when the mob began to assemble, he sent an intimation to the British Minister, who immediately informed the authorities. Application was made to the Greek Government for protection. No protection was afforded. The mob, in which were soldiers and gendarmes who, even if officers were not with them, ought from a sense of duty to have interfered and to have prevented plunder—that mob—headed by the sons of the Minister of War, not children of eight or ten years old, but older—that mob for nearly two hours employed themselves in gutting the house of an unoffending man, carrying away or destroying every single thing the house contained, and left it a perfect wreck.

Is not that a case in which a man is entitled to redress from somebody? I venture to think it is. I think that there is no civilised country where a man subjected to such grievous wrong, not to speak of insults and injuries to the members of his family, would not justly expect redress from some quarter or other. Where was he to apply for redress at Athens? The Greek Government neglected its duty and did not pursue judicial inquiries or institute legal prosecutions as it might have done for the purpose of finding out and punishing some of the culprits. The sons of the Minister of War were pointed out to the Government as actors in the outrage. The Greek Government were told to "search a particular house, and that some part of M. Pacifico's jewels would be found there." They declined to prosecute the Minister's sons or to search the house. But it is said M. Pacifico should have applied to a court of law for redress. What was he to do? Was he to prosecute a mob of 500 persons? Was he to prosecute them criminally or in order to make them pay the value of his loss? Where was he to find his witnesses? Why, he and his family were hiding or flying during the pillage to avoid the personal outrages with which they were threatened. He states that his own life was saved by the help of an English friend. It was impossible, if he could have identified the leaders, to have prosecuted them with success.

But what satisfaction would it have been to M. Pacifio to have succeeded in a criminal prosecution against the ringleaders of that assault? Would that have restored to him his property? He wanted redress, not revenge. A criminal prosecution was out of the question, to say nothing of the chances, if not the certainty, of failure in a country where the tribunals are at the mercy of the advisers of the crown, the judges being liable to be removed and being often actually removed upon grounds of private interest and personal feeling. Was he to prosecute for damages? His action would have lain against individuals and not, as in this country, against the hundred. Suppose he had been able to prove that one particular man had carried off one particular thing or destroyed one particular article of furniture; what redress could he anticipate by a lawsuit, which, as his legal advisers told him, it would be vain for him to undertake? M. Pacifico truly said, "If the man I prosecute is rich, he is sure to be acquitted; if he is poor, he has nothing out of which to afford me compensation if he is condemned."

The Greek Government having neglected to give the protection they were bound to extend and having abstained from taking means to afford redress, this was a case in which we were justified in calling on the Greek Government for compensation for the losses, whatever they might be, which M. Pacifico had suffered. I think that claim was founded in justice. The amount we did not pretend to fix. If the Greek Government had admitted the principle of the claim and had objected to the account sent in by M. Pacifico—if they had said, "This is too much, and we think a less sum sufficient"—that would have been a question open to discussion and which our Ministers, Sir E. Lyons at first, or Mr. Wyse afterwards, would have been ready to have gone into, and no doubt some satisfactory arrangement might thus have been effected with the Greek Government. But the Greek Government denied altogether the principle of the claim. Therefore, when Mr. Wyse came to make the claim, he could not but demand that the claim should be settled or be placed in train of settlement, and that within a definite period, as he fixed it, of twenty-four hours.

Whether M. Pacifico's statement of his claim was exaggerated or not, the demand was not for any particular amount of money. The demand was that the claim should be settled. An investigation might have been instituted, which those who acted for us were prepared to enter into, fairly, dispassionately, and justly.

M. Pacifico having from year to year been treated either with answers wholly unsatisfactory or with a positive refusal or with pertinacious silence, it came at last to this, either that his demand was to be abandoned altogether or that, in pursuance of the notice we had given the Greek Government a year or two before, we were to proceed to use our own means of enforcing the claim. "Oh! but," it is said, "what an ungenerous proceeding to employ so large a force against so small a power!" Does the smallness of a country justify the magnitude of its evil acts? Is it to be held that if your subjects suffer violence, outrage, plunder in a country which is small and weak, you are to tell them when they apply for redress that the country is so weak and so small that we cannot ask it for compensation? Their answer would be that the weakness and smallness of the country make it so much the more easy to obtain redress. "No," it is said, "generosity is to be the rule." We are to be generous to those who have been ungenerous to you, and we cannot give you redress because we have such ample and easy means of procuring it.

Well, then, was there anything so uncourteous in sending to back our demands a force which should make it manifest to all the world that resistance was out of the question? Why, it seems to me on the contrary that it was more consistent with the honour and dignity of the Government on whom we made those demands that there should be placed before their eyes a force which it would be vain to resist and before which it would be no indignity to yield. If we had sent merely a frigate and a sloop of war or any force with which it was possible their forces might have matched, we should have placed them in a more undignified position by asking them to yield to so small a demonstration. Therefore, so far from thinking that the amount of the force which happened to be on the spot was any aggravation of what is called the indignity of our demand, it seems to me that the Greek Government, on the contrary, ought rather to have considered it as diminishing the humiliation, whatever it might be, of being obliged to give at last to compulsion that which had been so long refused to entreaty.

Well, then, however, did we in the application of that force either depart from established usage or do anything that was unnecessarily pressing on the innocent and unoffending population of Greece? I say the innocent and unoffending population, because it was against the Government and not against the nation that our claim for redress was directed. The courses that may be pursued in cases where wrong is done by one government towards the subjects of another are various. One is what is commonly called "reprisals," that is, the seizing something of value and holding it in deposit until your demands are complied with; or if you fail in that and don't choose to resort to other methods, applying that which you have seized as a compensation for the wrong sustained. That is one method. Another is the modified application of war—such as a blockade—a measure frequently adopted by the governments of maritime states when they demand redress for injuries. Last come actual hostilities. Many instances of such measures have been quoted in this debate as having been adopted by the governments of other countries, especially by the French Government, when they have had a demand to make for injuries sustained by their subjects; and, by the by, when people complain of the peremptory manner in which our demand was made and the shortness of the time allowed for consideration, I wish to call to the recollection of honourable Gentlemen what was done by the French squadron no longer ago than 1848.

There was an insurrection at Naples, in May, 1848. The great street of the town was filled with barricades, and the troops had to force those barricades. To do that, they were obliged to occupy the houses right and left in order to turn those defences; and as they forced one house after another and passed on from house to house, they neglected to leave any guards behind them. They were followed by the *lazzaroni*,[4] and the houses were plundered. Some French people whose shops were thus rifled complained to the French Minister and to the French Admiral—there being then a French squadron before the port of Naples. The French Admiral, Admiral Baudin, quite cut out Sir W. Parker,[5] and being applied to by those French citizens, he sails up the bay, lays his ships broadside to in front of the palace, and writes a note to the Government to say that he has been called on by his countrymen to protect them; and he adds—that letter being dated half-past one on the 17th of May—that unless by three o'clock of that very day he obtains a satisfactory assurance—a satisfactory assurance that his countrymen shall be efficiently protected, reserving, he says, for future discussion their claims for compensation—but:

> ... unless in one hour and a half I get, on board this ship, a satisfactory assurance that they shall be efficiently protected, I shall land the crews of my fleet, and will take care of them myself.

[4] Homeless idlers of Naples who lived by chance or begging.
[5] Admiral Sir William Parker, in charge of the fleet of fifteen line-of-battleships which was used to block Greek shipping following unsuccessful attempts to negotiate British claims.

Well, then, I say that Sir W. Parker acted with the greatest moderation in enforcing our demands. He began with reprisals, not with a blockade, wishing to avoid all unnecessary interruption to the commerce of other countries. But he made reprisals in a way which I believe has not often been adopted. The Government was the offending party, and he took possession of vessels belonging to the Government. Now, that is not the usual plan, and for very good reasons.

Vessels belonging to governments are armed. They may feel it to be their duty to defend themselves. To seize armed vessels would therefore probably lead to bloodshed; and reprisals are generally effected by seizing merchant vessels belonging to the country on whom the demand is made. But the disparity of force being so great on this occasion, Sir W. Parker began by seizing the few armed vessels belonging to the State. He then gave the Government time to reflect upon that demonstration. It was not attended to. Even then he did not immediately proceed to make reprisals upon merchant vessels. He first laid an embargo upon them. He gave notice that he had placed a lien upon them and that they must not quit their ports. That failed; then he took merchant vessels, but only a limited number, and placed them under the custody of his fleet, avoiding to subject commerce in general to any greater degree of restraint than was unavoidably necessary for the execution of his instructions. It has been said that we seized upon fishing boats and interrupted the coasting trade. I don't believe that. On the contrary, I believe that the embargo did not extend to fishing boats or to vessels of small tonnage employed in the coasting trade of the country.

Well, Sir, in that state of things, the French Government offered us their good offices and mediation. We readily and cheerfully accepted their good offices. We accepted them by a note of the 12th of February, which has been laid on the table and in which we distinctly stated the grounds and conditions on which and the extent to which those good offices were accepted.

There could be no mistake between the English and French Governments upon that point. We took as our precedent the course that was pursued in the sulphur questions at Naples when M. Thiers was Minister. In that case, we stated that reprisals would be suspended the moment any French Minister on the spot declared himself authorised to negotiate. In the present case we went further and said that the moment the good offices of France were officially offered and officially accepted, we would send out instructions that the further making of reprisals should be suspended. In both cases we said we could not release the ships that had been detained because by so doing we should give up the security which we held in our hands against the offending government.

It has been stated that a misunderstanding arose between the Governments of France and England in the course of the mediation, good offices, or whatever it may be called. I cannot say that there was any misunderstanding between M. Drouyn de Lhuys[6] and myself, because it will be seen from his own despatches laid before the French Chamber that he clearly understood the conditions on which the good offices of France were accepted. He repeatedly states that England gives up none of her demands —that is to say, that she gives up none of the principles of her demands— and that the only questions which the French negotiator is competent to discuss are those which do not involve the negation of the principles of our demands. Well, what were those questions? They were only the amount of money to be given to Mr. Finlay and to M. Pacifico, but not the question whether those gentlemen were to receive anything or nothing.

Then the question arose between us, what were the circumstances under which the good offices were to cease, and coercive measures were to be resumed? And it was distinctly understood on my part, as well as on that of M. Drouyn de Lhuys, that Mr. Wyse was not to take upon himself to determine when Baron Gros' mission had failed; and that it was only when Baron Gros should have announced that his mission had ceased that Mr. Wyse was to resume coercive measures. It was further agreed between us, and especially on the 9th of April, that if a difference of opinion arose between Baron Gros and Mr. Wyse on those points which Baron Gros was competent to discuss, Mr. Wyse was not to stand out absolutely on his difference, and that if he did not find it possible to give way, he was, instead of saying, "Now, Baron Gros, your mission is at end," to refer home for further instructions. It is said that it was wrong of me not to have sent out to Mr. Wyse information of that understanding come to on the 9th of April with M. Drouyn de Lhuys. Well, but in the first place I had already sent to Mr. Wyse on the 25th of March instructions which, if acted on in the spirit in which they were written, would render such a reference home altogether unnecessary. And they did render such reference home altogether unnecessary; because at last, when Baron Gros and Mr. Wyse came to the point of difference as to the amount of money to be paid, and Baron Gros said, "I would counsel the Government of Greece to pay 150,000 drachmas," while Mr. Wyse said he was ready to accept 180,000 drachmas, Mr. Wyse at last, much more prudently than if he had referred this difference home and had exposed Greek commerce to the restraint to which a continuance of the *status quo* would have subjected it for a whole month, said, "I will, if other things are agreed to, come down to your amount—I will waive my own opinion, and accept the sum you are willing to recommend the Greek Government to give." Therefore practically, I say, and in the result, the case did not arise to which those instructions could have applied.

Those instructions, if they had reached Mr. Wyse, would not have applied to the difference which did arise between him and Baron Gros; for that

[6] French Minister in London.

difference was this—it turned upon the claims of M. Pacifico. Baron Gros, on the 16th of April, was willing to recommend to the Greek Government to take an engagement to investigate the claims of M. Pacifico in regard to the destruction of his Portuguese documents; and to pay him whatever might be the amount which, upon investigation, he might prove to be entitled to on that account; and to make a deposit of 150,000 drachmas as a pledge for the good faith with which they would execute that engagement. The only difference between Baron Gros and Mr. Wyse upon that occasion was that Baron Gros proposed that the deposit, which they had both agreed should consist of shares of the Bank of Athens, should be left in the Bank of Athens; whereas Mr. Wyse required that it should be deposited either in the Bank of England or, if the Greek Government preferred it, in the Bank of France. That seemed to be a difference that might be easily settled. But on the 22nd of April, Baron Gros altered his opinion. He retracted his opinion upon that point and stated that later information from Portugal had convinced him that M. Pacifico's claim in reference to the destruction of his Portuguese documents was wholly unfounded. Baron Gros said he would no longer consent to recommend the Greek Government to enter into any engagement to pay anything to M. Pacifico on that account. He would agree to an investigation, but only provided that Portugal and not the Greek Government should pay what might turn out to be due. But this was a point which Baron Gros was not competent to discuss. This new view of his would have been a negation of the principle upon which one of our claims rested; and there being a difference of that kind between Mr. Wyse and Baron Gros, Mr. Wyse had no occasion to refer for fresh instructions for he had received detailed instructions from me in a despatch, dated the 25th of March, sufficient to guide his conduct upon that point.

Baron Gros then withdrew from the negotiation, and that withdrawal was officially communicated not only to Mr. Wyse, but to the Greek Government also. On the 24th, however, he received a despatch from General Lahitte giving an account of the conversation which had passed between me and M. Drouyn de Lhuys on the 9th; an account, by the way, which was not quite accurate, because it made me say that if any difference arose between Baron Gros and Mr. Wyse, Mr. Wyse should refer home for instructions; whereas all that I agreed to was that such reference should be made in the case of irreconcileable difference between them as to the amount of money to be paid by the Greek Government for those claims, in regard to which we had not specified fixed sums; that is to say, for Mr. Finlay's land and for M. Pacifico's losses of furniture and goods at Athens. Baron Gros then proposed to withdraw the note by which he had announced officially the cessation of his functions, and he asked that his draft of arrangement, together with Mr. Wyse's draft, should be referred to London for decision.

An impression has gone abroad that on that occasion (the 24th) Baron Gros received and communicated to Mr. Wyse not merely an account of the conversation between me and M. Drouyn de Lhuys on the 9th of April, but an account of the essential bases and an announcement of the expected arrival of the draft of convention which had been proposed to me by M. Drouyn de Lhuys for the first time on the 15th, discussed on the 16th, agreed to on the 18th, and sent off on the 19th; and Mr. Wyse is greatly blamed by many persons, both here and in France, upon the assumption that—whereas Baron Gros had informed him on the 24th of April that the English and French Governments had come to an agreement as to the essential bases of the convention to be signed between England and Greece, and had moreover told him that the convention itself would shortly be received at Athens—yet nevertheless, with this knowledge of the facts, he renewed coercive measures and compelled the Greek Government to yield to his own demands. This assertion, so far as Mr. Wyse is concerned, is positively untrue. It is totally and wholly untrue. He received no communication from Baron Gros on the 24th and none earlier than the 2nd of May relative to the draft of the convention agreed upon in London. Whether Baron Gros received the information or not on the 24th by the *Vauban*, I leave to be settled between him and his Government. The explanations of General Lahitte would indeed lead to the inference that he did not.

The statement to which I refer was made by "our own correspondent" of *The Times*. I may say in passing that one person who has spoken on this subject elsewhere has had the substance of his speech claimed publicly by the *Morning Herald* as a compilation from its leading articles; and another has obviously been more indebted to *The Times* than to the blue books for the statements on which he has founded his assertions. But the correspondent of *The Times* stated distinctly, and upon that statement public opinion in this country has been formed, that Baron Gros did inform Mr. Wyse on the 24th that he had received by the *Vauban* a statement announcing the London convention, and that in spite of that information, Mr. Wyse resumed coercive measures. I understand that the French Government say that this is an entire mistake; that no information respecting the convention could have been communicated to Mr. Wyse on the 24th, because Baron Gros did not receive any by the *Vauban*, which arrived on that day. The complaint, therefore, against Mr. Wyse, come from what quarter it may—and I have no doubt it was sincerely believed at the moment it was made—that complaint can no longer be maintained and is withdrawn.

With respect to the other complaint—that I did not write to Mr. Wyse an account of what had passed on the 9th of April—the simple reason why I did not was that he was already in possession of instructions which were sufficient; that I could not have written till the 17th; and that on the

15th another arrangement was proposed which provided an immediate settlement on the spot and which therefore rendered any further reference to me by him out of the question. But it was said that if the French Government could have sent information to Baron Gros by the *Vauban,* why could not we have sent at the same time similar information to Mr. Wyse? Why, solely because we were in London and the French Government was in Paris, and that if a steamer had been despatched by us from Portsmouth, it could not have got round to Athens so soon as a steamer despatched by the French Government from Marseilles or Toulon. But as I have said, the convention of the 15th having been agreed to, all further reference to me by Mr. Wyse was rendered unnecessary, because that convention was to be presented as an ultimatum to the Greek Government by the British and French diplomatic agents.

And when it is said that those demands of ours on the Greek Government were so much repudiated by the Governments of Russia and of France, and that by putting forward those claims we ran the risk of involving this country in a war with those powers, I must be permitted to say that, with respect to Russia, the despatch of Count Nesselrode[7] to Baron Brunow[8] of the 19th of February totally negatives that assertion. In that despatch, Count Nesselrode admits that he was aware as long ago as 1847 that our patience might be exhausted and that we might have recourse to coercive measures against Greece to enforce our claims; and he says, moreover, that if lately, when we determined to enforce our claims, we had asked Russia to give us her assistance, she would have endeavoured to persuade the Greek Government to come to an amicable settlement with us; and if the efforts of Russia to that effect had been unsuccessful, Russia could not then have expected that we should indefinitely postpone coercive measures out of deference to her.

With respect to France, the much-talked-of convention of the 19th of April was to be recommended by France to Greece in a way which made its acceptance pretty certain; and in that convention there was at once a full acknowledgment of the principle of all our demands and of the amount which we thought it just and right to require. I am sorry that the convention did not arrive before the other settlement took place, but that was not the fault of our negotiator. It was not he who put an end to Baron Gros' functions, but Baron Gros himself. Baron Gros formally and officially withdrew from the negotiation, and that by a written communication, not addressed to Mr. Wyse alone, but to the Greek Government also.

But it is said he was willing to retract it, and that on the 24th of April he wrote to Mr. Wyse to say: "Send me back my note, and I will give you back yours." Now, to this Mr. Wyse said:

---

[7] Count Karl Robert von Nesselrode, Russian Minister of Foreign Affairs.
[8] Baron Ernst Phillip von Bronnow, Ambassador to Great Britain.

I cannot exactly do what you wish, but I have another proposal to make to you. You ask me to refer to England and to maintain the *status quo* till I get an answer; but to keep the Greek vessels in custody till that answer arrives would subject Greek commerce to great inconvenience. Instead of this, I propose that if the Greek Government will send me 180,000 drachmas, with a letter stating that that sum is in satisfaction of all our claims excepting M. Pacifico's claim on account of the loss of his Portuguese documents, I will—

Do what? Refer home? No. Continue the *status quo?* No.

—I will immediately release all the Greek merchant vessels. I will only retain the few Government vessels as a pledge, leaving the wording of the apology in the case of the *Fantome*, and the compensation for the loss sustained by M. Pacifico by the destruction of his Portuguese documents to be settled by future discussion.

The effect of that arrangement would have been that the points on which Mr. Wyse and Baron Gros differed would have been left open for future discussion; that coercive measures, as far as Greek commerce was concerned, would have been entirely suspended; the convention of London of the 19th of April would have arrived in time; but the Greek Government indeed would, by that convention, have had to pay probably a larger sum than the 180,000 drachmas. But what was Baron Gros' answer to that? He said on the 24th: "I have withdrawn from the negotiation, and I cannot therefore officially transmit to the Greek Government your proposal." Therefore, it was not merely by his official notes of the 22nd of April to Mr. Wyse and M. Londos[9] that Baron Gros withdrew from the negotiation, for he repeated his withdrawal in answer to this proposition; but he intimated, in a private letter, that he had made it known to the Greek Government. "Tomorrow, the 25th," he said, "I believe you will have, before five o'clock of the afternoon, your letter and your money."

Now, was Mr. Wyse in a hurry to resume coercive measures? Did he catch at the first moment at which he might have been authorised to resume hostilities? Far from it. He waited from the 22nd to the 24th, and from the 24th till five o'clock on the afternoon of the 25th, and it was not till after that hour had passed—at which Baron Gros had led him to expect that he would receive from the Greek Government an acceptance of his conciliatory proposal—it was not till that hour had passed without any communication arriving that he announced, through the British Consul, that the embargo would again be established. It is plain, therefore, that Mr. Wyse did not put an end to Baron Gros' functions or show any impatience to renew coercive measures. Baron Gros himself put an end to

---

[9] Representative of the Greek Government.

his own functions, in spite of Mr. Wyse's repeated entreaties that he would not do so; and when Baron Gros had formally withdrawn, Mr. Wyse, instead of at once resuming coercive measures, made another and a very conciliatory proposal; but Baron Gros' answer to this was a renewed declaration that he had withdrawn from the negotiation and that his official functions had ceased.

Since then, negotiations have taken place between the Governments of England and France, which, I am happy to say, have been brought at last to a satisfactory conclusion. We are ready to accept such parts of the proposed convention as are still applicable to what remains to be done. Having received and distributed to the claimants the 180,000 drachmas, we don't insist upon the difference between that sum and the sum that was to be required by the convention. The apology written by M. Londos is retained and cannot be returned to him, in order that instead of it, he may send us the one proposed by M. Drouyn de Lhuys. The only thing, therefore, that remains to be settled is the investigation of the claims of M. Pacifico on account of the loss of his Portuguese documents. With regard to these claims, by the arrangement of the 27th of April, a material security was given in the shape of a pecuniary deposit. The convention, of which I had drawn up the details, contained on that point a diplomatic guarantee instead of a substantial guarantee; for it was a convention to be ratified by the two sovereigns, providing that a commission of arbitration should be named by the three governments to investigate that claim, while by Mr. Wyse's arrangement this investigation was to be made not by a commission, but by the British and Greek Governments jointly. We are perfectly ready to substitute the one arrangement for the other if the Greek Government choose to adopt it; but we do not intend to urge it upon them if they do not. If they prefer the arrangement of the convention, we are prepared to conclude a convention to that effect, superseding the corresponding part of the arrangement which was concluded at Athens.

There is, however, one point in Mr. Wyse's arrangement which was not included in the draft of the convention, because it applies to circumstances of which we were not aware at the time when the convention of London was framed. Mr. Wyse exacted an engagement on the part of the Government of Greece that they should not put forward nor support, if put forward by others, any claims for compensation arising from losses or injuries consequent upon the coercive measures to which we had recourse. The motive of Mr. Wyse for requiring that engagement was that he understood the Government of Greece had been collecting and beating up for claims of that kind, which they meant to put forward to a very large amount. We attach no value to that engagement as bearing in any manner whatever upon the validity of any such claims. Such claims can have no just foundation whatever; and if they were put forward by the Greek Government or by other persons supported by the Greek Government, our answer could only be: "These claims have no foundation in right or reason, and we utterly and entirely reject them." But the value of that arrangement was that by shutting the door against such claims, it prevented the Greek Government from raising discussions which might interrupt the good understanding and friendly relations between the two countries. The British Government are willing, instead of that engagement, to accept the good offices of the French Government, whose good offices with the Government of Greece under existing circumstances have some value, and who will advise the King of Greece not to put forward any such unfounded claims. France, therefore, will advise the King of Greece not to bring forward or to support any such claims, and with that advice we shall be content.

Thus terminates all difference between the Governments of England and France in regard to these matters; and I believe that if it had not been for discussions which are now taking place in the French Assembly, the distinguished individual who represents the French Government at this Court might have been present to hear the debate of tonight. So much, then, with regard to the affairs of Greece and the course which we have pursued in regard to them. . . .

[*Palmerston goes on to justify his actions in the case of the islands of Sapienza and Cervi, and England's relations with Belgium, Portugal, Spain, France, Switzerland, and Italy.*]

I believe I have now gone through all the heads of the charges which have been brought against me in this debate. I think I have shown that the foreign policy of the Government, in all the transactions with respect to which its conduct has been impugned, has throughout been guided by those principles which, according to the resolution of the honourable and learned Gentleman the Member for Sheffield, ought to regulate the conduct of the Government of England in the management of our foreign affairs. I believe that the principles on which we have acted are those which are held by the great mass of the people of this country. I am convinced these principles are calculated, so far as the influence of England may properly be exercised with respect to the destinies of other countries, to conduce to the maintenance of peace, to the advancement of civilization, to the welfare and happiness of mankind.

I do not complain of the conduct of those who have made these matters the means of attack upon Her Majesty's Ministers. The government of a great country like this is undoubtedly an object of fair and legitimate ambition to men of all shades of opinion. It is a noble thing to be allowed to guide the policy and to influence the destinies of such a country; and, if ever it was an object of honourable ambition, more than ever must it be so at the moment at which I am speaking. For while we have seen, as stated by the right honourable Baronet the Member for Ripon,[10] the political earthquake rocking Europe from side to side—while we have seen thrones shaken, shattered, levelled; institutions overthrown and destroyed; while in almost every country of Europe the conflict of civil war has deluged the land with blood, from the Atlantic to the Black Sea, from the Baltic to the Mediterranean—this country has presented a spectacle honourable to the people of England and worthy of the admiration of mankind.

We have shown that liberty is compatible with order; that individual freedom is reconcilable with obedience to the law. We have shown the example of a nation in which every class of society accepts with cheerfulness the lot which Providence has assigned to it, while at the same time every individual of each class is constantly striving to raise himself in the social scale—not by injustice and wrong, not by violence and illegality—but by persevering good conduct and by the steady and energetic exertion of the moral and intellectual faculties with which his Creator has endowed him. To govern such a people as this is indeed an object worthy of the ambition of the noblest man who lives in the land; and therefore I find no fault with those who may think any opportunity a fair one for endeavouring to place themselves in so distinguished and honourable a position. But I contend that we have not in our foreign policy done anything to forfeit the confidence of the country. We may not, perhaps, in this matter or in that, have acted precisely up to the opinions of one person or of another—and hard indeed it is, as we all know by our individual and private experience, to find any number of men agreeing entirely in any matter on which they may not be equally possessed of the details of the facts and circumstances and reasons and conditions which led to action. But, making allowance for those differences of opinion which may fairly and honourably arise among those who concur in general views, I maintain that the principles which can be traced through all our foreign transactions, as the guiding rule and directing spirit of our proceedings, are such as deserve approbation. I therefore fearlessly challenge the verdict which this House, as representing a political, a commercial, a constitutional country, is to give on the question now brought before it; whether the principles on which the foreign policy of Her Majesty's Government has been conducted and the sense of duty which has led us to think ourselves bound to afford protection to our fellow subjects abroad are proper and fitting guides for those who are charged with the Government of England; and whether, as the Roman, in days of old, held himself free from indignity when he could say, "*Civis Romanus sum*," so also a British subject, in whatever land he may be, shall feel confident that the watchful eye and the strong arm of England will protect him against injustice and wrong.

---

[10] Sir James R. Graham.

John Bright

"On the Foreign Policy of England"*
Birmingham, October 29, 1858

The frequent and far too complimentary manner in which my name has been mentioned tonight and the most kind way in which you have received me have placed me in a position somewhat humiliating, and really painful; for to receive laudation which one feels one cannot possibly have merited is much more painful than to be passed by in a distribution of gratitude to which possibly one might lay some claim.

If one-twentieth part of what has been said is true, if I am entitled to any measure of your approbation, I may begin to think that my public career and my opinions are not so un-English and so anti-national as the best of those who presume to be the best of our public instructors have sometimes assumed. [*Cheers.*] How, indeed, can I any more than any of you be un-English and anti-national? Was I not born upon the same soil? Do I not come of the same English stock? Are not my family committed irrevocably to the fortunes of this country? Is not whatever property I may have depending as much as yours is depending upon the good Government of our common fatherland? [*Hear, hear.*] Then how shall any man dare to say to any one of his countrymen, because he happens to hold a different opinion on questions of great public policy, that therefore he is un-English and is to be condemned as anti-national? [*Cheers.*] There are those who would assume that between my countrymen and me and between my constituents and me there has been and there is now a great gulf fixed, and that if I cannot pass over to them and to you, they and you can by no possibility pass over to me.

Now, I take the liberty here in the presence of an audience as intelligent as can be collected within the limits of this island and of those who have the strongest claims to know what opinions I do entertain relative to certain

---

* The text is taken from *The Times*, October 30, 1858, p. 9.

great questions of public policy to assert that I hold no views—that I have never promulgated any views—on those controverted questions with respect to which I cannot bring as witnesses in my favour and as fellow-believers with myself some of the best and most revered names in the history of English statesmanship. [*Hear, hear.*]

About 120 years ago the Government of this country was directed by Sir Robert Walpole, a great Minister, who for a long period preserved the country in peace and whose pride it was that during those years he had done so. Unfortunately, toward the close of his career, he was driven by faction into a policy which was the ruin of his political prospects.

Sir Robert Walpole declared, speaking of the question of war as affecting this country, that nothing could be so foolish, nothing so mad, as a policy of war for a trading nation. [*Hear, hear.*] And he went so far as to say that any peace was better than the most successful war. [*Hear, hear.*]

I do not give you the precise language of the Minister, for I speak only from memory; but I am satisfied I am not misrepresenting him in what I have now stated.

Come down fifty years nearer to our own time and you find a statesman not long in office but still held in the affections of all persons of Liberal principles in this country, and in his time representing fully the sentiments of the Liberal Party—Charles James Fox. [*Cheers.*] Mr. Fox, referring to the policy of the Government of his time, which was one of constant interference in the affairs of Europe and by which the country was continually involved in the calamities of war, said that although he would not assert or maintain the principle that under no circumstances could England have any cause of interference with the affairs of the continent of Europe, yet he would prefer the positive policy of non-interference and of perfect isolation rather than the constant intermeddling to which our recent policy had subjected us, and which brought so much trouble and suffering upon the country. [*Hear, hear.*] In this case also I am not prepared to give you his exact words, but I am sure that I fairly describe the sentiments which he expressed.

Come down fifty years later, and to a time within the recollection of most of us, and you find another statesman, once the most popular man in England and still remembered in this town and elsewhere with respect and affection. I allude to Earl Grey. [*Cheers.*] When Earl Grey came into office for the purpose of carrying the question of Parliamentary Reform, he unfurled the banner of "peace, retrenchment, and reform," and that sentiment was received in every part of the United Kingdom by every man who was or had been in favour of Liberal principles as the pronouncement of the commencement of a new era which should save this country from many of the calamities of the past. [*Hear.*]

Come down still nearer, and to a time that seems but the other day, and you find another Minister, second to none of those whom I have mentioned—the late Sir Robert Peel. [*Cheers.*] I observed the conduct of Sir Robert Peel from the time when he took office in 1841; I watched his proceedings particularly from the year 1843,[1] when I was in the House of Commons, up to the time of his lamented death; and during the whole of that period, I venture to say his principles, if they were to be discovered from his conduct and his speeches, were precisely those which I have held and which I have always endeavoured to press upon the attention of my countrymen. [*Cheers.*] If you have any doubt upon that point, I would refer you to that last, that most beautiful, that most solemn speech, which he delivered with an earnestness and a sense of responsibility as if he had known he was leaving a legacy to his country.[2] [*Hear, hear.*] If you refer to that speech, delivered on the morning of the very day on which occurred the accident which terminated his life, you will find that its whole tenor is in conformity with all the doctrines that I have urged upon my countrymen for years past with respect to our policy in foreign affairs. [*Hear, hear.*] When Sir Robert Peel went home just before the dawn of day upon the last occasion that he passed from the House of Commons, the scene of so many of his triumphs, I have heard from what I think a good authority that after he entered his own house he expressed the exceeding relief which he experienced at having delivered himself of a speech which he had been obliged reluctantly to make against a Ministry which he was anxious to support, and he added, "If I am not mistaken, I have made a speech of peace." [*Hear, hear.*]

Well, if this be so, if I can give you four names like these—if there were time I could make a longer list of still eminent, if inferior, men—I should like to know why I, as one of a small party, am to be set down as teaching some new doctrine which is not fit for my countrymen to hear, and why I am to be assailed in every form of language as if there was one great department of Governmental affairs on which I was incompetent to offer any opinion to my countrymen. [*Hear, hear.*]

But leaving the opinions of individuals, I appeal to this audience, to every man who knows anything of the views and policy of the Liberal Party in past years, whether it is not the fact that, up to 1832 and indeed to a much later period, probably to the year 1850, those sentiments of Sir Robert Walpole, of Mr. Fox, of Earl Grey, and of Sir Robert Peel, the sentiments which I in humbler mode have propounded, were not received unanimously by the Liberal Party as their fixed and unchangeable creed? [*Hear, hear.*] And why should they not? Are they not founded upon reason? Do not all statesmen know, as you know, that upon peace, and peace alone, can be based the successful industry of a nation, and that by successful industry alone can be created that wealth which, permeating all classes of the people, not confined to great proprietors, great merchants, and great

[1] The year Bright entered Parliament.
[2] Peel spoke against Palmerston's *Civis Romanus sum* foreign policy on June 28, 1850.

speculators, not running in a stream merely down your principal streets, but turning fertilising rivulets into every by-lane and every alley, tends so powerfully to promote the comfort, happiness, and contentment of a nation? [*Cheers.*] Do you not know that all progress comes from successful and peaceful industry, and that upon it is based your superstructure of education, of morals, of self-respect among your people, as well as every measure for extending and consolidating freedom in your public institutions? [*Cheers.*] I am not afraid to acknowledge that I do oppose—that I do utterly condemn and denounce—a great part of the foreign policy which is practised and adhered to by the Government of this country. [*Hear, hear.*]

You know, of course, that about 170 years ago there happened in this country what we have always been accustomed to call "a glorious revolution"—a revolution which had this effect: that it put a bit into the mouth of the monarch, so that he was not able of his own free will to do, and he dared no longer attempt to do, the things which his predecessors had done without fear. But if at the revolution the monarchy of England was bridled and bitted, at the same time the great territorial families of England were enthroned [*Hear, hear*]: and from that period until the year 1831 or 1832 —until the time when Birmingham politically became famous—those territorial families reigned with an almost undisputed sway over the destinies and the industry of the people of the United Kingdom. [*Hear, hear.*] If you turn to the history of England from the period of the revolution to the present, you will find that an entirely new policy was adopted, and that while we had endeavoured in former times to keep ourselves free from European complications, we now began to act upon a system of constant entanglement in the affairs of foreign countries, as if there were neither property nor honours nor anything worth striving for to be acquired in any other field. The language coined and used then has continued to our day. Lord Somers, in writing for William III,[3] speaks of the endless and sanguinary wars of that period as wars "to maintain the liberties of Europe." There were wars "to support the Protestant interest," and there were many wars to preserve our old friend "the balance of power." [*A laugh.*]

We have been at war since that time, I believe, with, for, and against every considerable nation in Europe. We fought to put down a pretended French supremacy under Louis XIV. We fought to prevent France and Spain coming under the sceptre of one monarch, although, if we had not fought, it would have been impossible in the course of things that they should have become so united. We fought to maintain the Italian provinces

---

[3] Lord John Somers served as Lord Chancellor of England and headed the junta, including Wharton, Oxford, Halifax, and Charles Spencer, that governed England during the early years of Queen Anne's reign. He is reported to have written the speech delivered by William III on September 30, 1701.

in connection with the house of Austria. We fought to put down the supremacy of Napoleon Bonaparte; and the minister who was employed by this country at Vienna after the great war, when it was determined that no Bonaparte should ever again sit on the Throne of France, was the very man to make an alliance with another Bonaparte for the purpose of carrying on a war to prevent the supremacy of the late Emperor of Russia.[4] So that we have been all around Europe and across it over and over again, and after a policy so distinguished, so pre-eminent, so long-continued, and so costly, I think we have a fair right—I have, at least—to ask those who are in favour of it to show us its visible result. [*Hear, hear.*] Europe is not at this moment, so far as I know, speaking of it broadly and making allowance for certain improvements in its general civilisation, more free politically than it was before. [*Hear, hear.*] The balance of power is like perpetual motion or any of those impossible things which some men are always racking their brains and spending their time and money to accomplish. [*A laugh.*]

We all know and deplore that at the present moment a large number of the grown men of Europe are employed and a larger portion of the industry of Europe is absorbed to provide for and maintain the enormous armaments which are now on foot in every considerable Continental state. [*Hear, hear.*] Assuming, then, that Europe is not much better in consequence of the sacrifices she has made, let us inquire what has been the result to England, because, after all, that is the question which it becomes us most to consider. [*Hear, hear.*] I believe that I understate the sum when I say that, in pursuit of this will-o'-the-wisp (the liberties of Europe and the balance of power), there has been extracted from the industry of the people of this small island no less an amount than £2,000,000,000 sterling. I cannot imagine how much £2,000,000,000 sterling is, and therefore I shall not attempt to make you comprehend it.

I presume it is something like those vast and incomprehensible astronomical distances with which we have been lately made familiar; but, however familiar, we feel that we do not know one bit more about them than we did before. [*A laugh.*] When I try to think of that sum of £2,000,000,000 sterling there is a sort of vision passes before my mind's eye. I see your peasant labourer delve and plough, sow and reap, sweat beneath the summer's sun, or grow prematurely old before the winter's blast. I see your noble mechanic with his manly countenance and his matchless skill toiling at his bench or his forge. I see one of the workers in our factories in the north, a woman—a girl it may be—gentle and good, as many of them are, as your sisters and daughters are—I see her intent upon the spindle, whose revolutions are so rapid that the eye fails altogether to detect them, or repeating the alternating flight of the unresting shuttle. I turn again to

---

[4] Probably George Hamilton Gordon, Earl of Aberdeen.

another portion of your population, plunged in mines, forgets that the sun was made, and I see a man who digs from the secret chambers of the earth the elements of the riches and greatness of his country. When I see all this, I have before me a mass of produce and of wealth which I am no more able to comprehend than I am that £2,000,000,000 sterling of which I have spoken, but I behold in its full proportions the hideous error of your governments, whose fatal policy consumes in some cases a half, never less than a third, of all the results of that industry which God intended should fertilise and bless every home in England, but the fruits of which are squandered in every part of the surface of the globe, without producing the smallest good to the people of England. [*Cheers.*]

We have, it is true, some visible results that are of a more positive character. We have that which some people call a great advantage—the national debt—a debt which is now so large that the most prudent, the most economical, and the most honest have given up all hope, not of its being paid off, but of its being diminished in amount.

We have, too, taxes which have been during many years so onerous that there have been times when the patient beasts of burden threatened to revolt—so onerous that it has been utterly impossible to levy them with any kind of honest equality, according to the means of the people to pay them. [*Hear.*] We have that, moreover, which is a standing wonder to all foreigners who consider our condition—an amount of apparently immovable pauperism which to strangers is wholly irreconcilable with the fact that we, as a nation, produce more of what should make us all comfortable than is produced by any other nation of similar numbers on the face of the globe. [*Hear.*] Let us likewise remember that during the period of those great and so-called glorious operations on the continent of Europe every description of Home Reform was not only delayed, but actually crushed out of the minds of the great bulk of the people. There can be no doubt whatever that in 1793, England was about to realise political changes and reforms such as did not appear again until 1830, and during the period of that war, which now almost all men agree to have been wholly unnecessary, we were passing through a period which may be described as the dark age of English politics; when there was no more freedom to write or speak or politically to act than there is now in the most despotic country of Europe. [*Cheers.*]

But, it may be asked, did nobody gain? If Europe is no better and the people of England have been so much worse, who has benefited by the new system of foreign policy? What has been the fate of those who were enthroned at the revolution, and whose supremacy has been for so long a period undisputed among us? Mr. Kinglake, the author of an interesting book on Eastern travel,[5] describing the habits of some acquaintances that

---

[5] *Eothen; or Traces of Travel Brought Home from the East* (London, 1800).

he made in the Syrian deserts, says that the jackals of the desert follow their prey in families like the place-hunters of Europe. [*A laugh.*] I will reverse, if you like, the comparison, and say that the great territorial families of England, which were enthroned at the revolution, have followed their prey like the jackals of the desert. [*Cheers and laughter.*] Do you not observe at a glance that as from the time of William III, by reason of the foreign policy which I denounce, wars have been multiplied, taxes increased, loans made, and the sums of money which every year the Government has to expend augmented, and so the patronage at the disposal of Ministers must have increased also, and the families who were enthroned and made powerful in the legislation and administration of the country must have had the first pull at and the largest profit out of that patronage? [*Hear, hear.*] There is no actuary in existence who can calculate how much of the wealth, of the strength, of the supremacy of the territorial families of England has been derived from an unholy participation in the fruits of the industry of the people, which have been wrested from them by every device of taxation and squandered in every conceivable crime of which a government could possibly be guilty. [*Cheers.*]

The more you examine this matter the more you will come to the conclusion which I have arrived at, that this foreign policy, this regard for the "liberties of Europe," this care at one time for "the Protestant interests," this excessive love for "the balance of power," is neither more nor less than a gigantic system of outdoor relief for the aristocracy of Great Britain. [*Great cheering and laughter.*] I observe that you receive that declaration as if it were some new and important discovery. In 1815, every Liberal in England whose politics, whose hopes, and whose faith had not been crushed out of him by the tyranny of the time of that war was fully aware of this and openly admitted it, and up to 1832 and for some years afterward, it was the fixed and undoubted creed of the great Liberal Party. [*Hear, hear.*] But somehow all is changed. We who stand upon the old landmarks, who walk in the old paths, who would conserve what is wise and prudent [*Hear, hear*], are hustled and shoved about as if we were come to turn the world upside down. [*Hear, hear.*] The change which has taken place seems to confirm the opinion of a lamented friend of mine, who, not having succeeded in all his hopes, thought that men made no progress whatever, but went round and round like a squirrel in a cage. [*A laugh.*] The idea is now so general that it is our duty to meddle everywhere, that it really seems as if we had pushed the Tories from the field, expelling them by our competition.

I should like to lay before you a list of the treaties which we have made, and of the responsibilities under which we have laid ourselves with respect to the various countries of Europe. I do not know where such an enumeration is to be got, but I suppose it would be possible for antiquaries and men of investigating minds to dig them out from the recesses of the Foreign

Office and perhaps to make some of them intelligible to the country. I believe, however, that if we go to the Baltic we shall find that we have a treaty to defend Sweden, and the only thing which Sweden agrees to do in return is not to give up any portion of her territories to Russia. Coming down a little south, we have a treaty which invites us, enables us, and perhaps, if we acted fully up to our duty with regard to it, would compel us to interfere in the question between Denmark and the duchies. If I mistake not, we have a treaty which binds us down to the maintenance of the little Kingdom of Belgium, as established after its separation from Holland. We have numerous treaties with France. We are understood to be bound by treaty to maintain constitutional government in Spain and Portugal. If we go round into the Mediterranean, we find the little Kingdom of Sardinia, to which we have lent some millions of money and with which we have entered into important treaties for preserving the balance of power in Europe. If we go beyond the Kingdom of Italy and cross the Adriatic, we come to the small Kingdom of Greece, against which we have also a nice account that will never be settled [*a laugh*], while we have engagements to maintain that respectable but diminutive country under its present constitutional government. Then, leaving the Kingdom of Greece, we pass up the eastern end of the Mediterranean, and from Greece to the Red Sea, wherever the authority of the Sultan is more or less admitted, the blood and the industry of England are pledged to the permanent sustentation of the "independence and integrity" of the Ottoman Empire. [*Hear, hear.*]

I confess that as a citizen of this country wishing to live peaceably among my fellow-countrymen and wishing to see my countrymen free and able to enjoy the fruits of their labour, I protest against a system which binds us in all these networks and complications from which it is impossible that we can gain one single inch of advantage for this country. [*Cheers.*] It is not all glory, after all. Glory may be worth something, but it is not always glory. We have had within the last few years despatches from Vienna and from St. Petersburg, which, if we had not deserved them, would have been very offensive and not a little insolent. We have had the Ambassador of the Queen expelled summarily from Madrid, and we have had an Ambassador expelled almost with ignominy from Washington. We have blockaded Athens for a claim which was known to be false. We have quarrelled with Naples, for we chose to give advice to Naples which was not received in the submissive spirit expected from her, and our Minister was therefore withdrawn. Not three years ago, too, we seized a considerable kingdom in India, with which our Government had but recently entered into the most solemn treaty, which every lawyer in England and in Europe, I believe, would consider binding before God and the world. We deposed its monarch; we committed a great immorality and a great crime, and we have reaped an almost instantaneous retribution in the most gigantic and sanguinary revolt which probably any nation ever made against its conquerors. Within the last few years we have had two wars with a great empire[6] which, we are told, contains at least one-third of the whole human race. The first war was called, and appropriately called, the Opium War. No man, I believe, with a spark of morality in his composition, no man who cares anything for the opinion of his fellow-countrymen, has dared to justify that war. [*Cheers.*] The war which has just been concluded, if it has been concluded, had its origin in the first war; for the enormities committed in the first war are the foundations of the implacable hostility which it is said the inhabitants of Canton bear to all persons connected with the English name. Yet, though we have these troubles in India—a vast country which we know not how to govern—and a war with China—a country with which, though everybody else can remain at peace, we cannot—such is the inveterate habit of conquest, such is the insatiable lust for territory, such is, to my thinking, the depraved, unhappy state of opinion of the country on this subject, that there are not a few persons—Chambers of Commerce, to wit—in different parts of the Kingdom (though I am glad to say it has not been so with the Chamber of Commerce at Birmingham) who have been urging our Government to take possession of a province of, perhaps, the greatest island in the Eastern seas[7]—a possession which must at once necessitate increased estimates and increased taxation and which would probably lead us into one of the most merciless and disgraceful wars with the half-savage tribes who inhabit those islands. [*Cheers.*]

I will not dwell upon that question. The gentleman who is principally concerned in it is at this moment, as you know, stricken down with affliction, and I should be ashamed of myself if I were to enter here into any considerable discussion of the case which he is urging upon the public; but I say that we have territory enough in India; and if we have not troubles enough there, if we have not difficulties enough in China, if we have not taxation enough, by all means gratify your wishes for more; but I hope that whatever may be the shortcomings of the Government with regard to any other questions in which we are all interested—and may they be few!—they will shut their eyes, they will turn their backs obstinately from adding in this mode or in any mode to the English possessions in the East. [*Cheers.*] I suppose that if any ingenious person were to prepare a large map of the world, as far as it is known, and were to mark upon it in any colour that he liked the spots where Englishmen have fought and English blood has been poured forth and the treasure of England squandered, scarcely a country, scarcely a province of the vast expanse of the habitable globe, would be undistinguished.

---

[6] The Opium War of 1839 and the Lorcha Arrow War of 1856 with the Chinese.
[7] Japan.

Perhaps there are in this room—I am sure there are in the country—many persons who hold a superstitious traditionary belief that somehow or other our vast trade is to be attributed to what we have done in this way, that it is thus we have opened markets and advanced commerce, that English greatness depends upon the extent of English conquests and English military renown. But I am inclined to think that with the exception of Australia, there is not a single dependency of the Crown which, if we come to reckon what it has cost in war and protection, would not be found to be a positive loss to the people of this country. Take the United States, with which we have such an enormous and constantly increasing trade. The wise statesmen of the last generation, men who your school histories tell you were statesmen ruled over by a monarch who they tell you was a patriotic monarch, spent £130,000,000 of the fruits of the industry of the people in a vain—happily a vain—endeavour to retain the Colonies of the United States in subjection to the Monarchy of England.

Add up the interest of that £130,000,000 for all this time, and how long do you think it will be before there will be a profit on the trade with the United States which will repay the enormous sum we invested in a war to retain those States as Colonies of this Empire? It never will be paid off. [*Cheers.*] Wherever you turn, you will find that the opening of markets, developing of new countries, introducing cotton cloth and calico with cannon balls, are vain, foolish, and wretched excuses for wars, and ought not to be listened to for a moment by any man who understands the multiplication table or who can do the simplest sum in arithmetic. [*Hear.*]

Since the "glorious revolution," since the enthronisation of the great Norman territorial families, they have spent in wars and we have worked for about £2,000,000,000. The interest on that is £100,000,000 per annum, which is three or four times as much as the whole amount of your annual export trade from that time to this.

Therefore, if war had provided you with a trade, it would have been at an enormous cost; but I think it is by no means doubtful that your trade would have been no less in amount and no less profitable, had peace, harmony, and justice been inscribed on your flag instead of conquest and the love of military renown. [*Cheers.*] But even in this year, 1858—we have got a long way into the century—we find that within the last seven years our public debt has greatly increased. Whatever be the increase of our population, of our machinery, of our industry, of our wealth, still our national debt goes on increasing. Although we have not a foot more territory to conserve or an enemy in the world who dreams of attacking us [*cheers*], we find that our annual military expenses during the last twenty years have risen from £12,000,000 to £22,000,000.

Some people believe that it is a good thing to pay a great revenue to the state. Even so eminent a man as Lord John Russell is not without a delusion of this sort. [*A laugh.*] His Lordship, as you have heard, while speaking of me in the most flattering and friendly terms, says he is unfortunately obliged to differ from me sometimes; therefore I suppose there is no particular harm in my saying that I am sometimes obliged to differ from him. Some time ago he was a great star in the Northern Hemisphere, shining not with unaccustomed but with his usual brilliancy at Liverpool. He made a speech, in which there was a great deal to be admired, to a meeting composed, it was said, to a great extent of working men; and in it he stimulated them to a feeling of pride in the greatness of their country and in being citizens of a state which enjoyed a revenue of £100,000,000 a year, which included the revenues of the United Kingdom and of British India. But I think it would have been far more to the purpose if he could have congratulated the working men of Liverpool on this vast Empire being conducted in an orderly manner, on its laws being well administered and well obeyed, its shores sufficiently defended, its people prosperous and happy, on a revenue of £20,000,000. The State, indeed, of which Lord John Russell is a part, may enjoy a revenue of £100,000,000, but I am afraid the working men can only be said to enjoy it in the sense in which men not very choice in their expressions say that for a long time they have enjoyed "very bad health." [*A laugh.*]

I am prepared to admit that it is a subject of congratulation that there is a people so great, so free, and so industrious that it can produce a sufficient income out of which £100,000,000 a year, if need absolutely were, could be spared for some great and noble purpose; but it is not a thing to be proud of that our Government should require us to pay that enormous sum for the simple purposes of government and defence.

Nothing can by any possibility tend more to the corruption of a government than enormous revenues. [*Cheers.*] We have heard lately of instances of certain joint-stock institutions with enormous capital collapsing suddenly, bringing disgrace upon their managers and ruin upon hundreds of families. A great deal of that has arisen not so much from intentional fraud as from the fact that weak and incapable men have found themselves tumbling about in an ocean of bank-notes and cash, and they appear to have lost all sight of where it came from, to whom it belonged, and whether it was possible by any maladministration ever to come to an end of it. That is absolutely what is done by governments. You have read in the papers lately some accounts of the proceedings before a commission appointed to inquire into some alleged maladministration with reference to the supply of clothing to the army, but if anybody had said anything in the time of the late Government about any such maladministration, not one of those great statesmen, of whom we are told we ought always to speak with so much reverence, but would have got up and declared that nothing could be more admirable than the system of book-keeping at Weedon, nothing more economical than the manner in which the War Department spent the money provided by public taxation. But we know that it is not so.

[*Cheers.*] I have heard a gentleman—one who is as competent as any man in England to give an opinion about it—a man of business, and not surpassed by anyone as a man of the world—declare, after a long examination of the details of the question, that he would undertake to do everything that is done not only for the defence of the country, but for many other things which are done by your navy, and which are not necessary for that purpose, for half the annual cost that is voted in the estimates. [*Cheers.*]

I think the expenditure of these vast sums and especially of those which we spend for military purposes leads us to adopt a defiant and insolent tone towards foreign countries. We have the freest press in Europe and the freest platform in Europe, but every man who writes an article in a newspaper and every man who stands on a platform ought to do it under a solemn sense of responsibility. Every word he writes, every word I utter, passes with a rapidity of which our forefathers were utterly ignorant to the very ends of the earth; words become things and acts, and they produce on the minds of other nations effects which a man may never have intended. Take a recent case—take the case of France. I am not expected to defend and I shall certainly not attack the present Government of France.

The instant that it appeared in its present shape, the Minister of England conducting your foreign affairs, speaking ostensibly for the Cabinet, for his Sovereign, and for the English nation, offered his congratulations, and the support of England was at once accorded to the recreated French Empire. Soon after this, an intimate alliance was entered into between the Queen of England, through her Ministers, and the Emperor of the French.

I am not about to defend the policy which flowed from that alliance, nor shall I take up your time by making any attack upon it. An alliance was entered into and a war was entered into. English and French soldiers fought on the same field, and they suffered, I fear, from the same neglect. They now lie buried on the bleak heights of the Crimea, and, I suppose, except by their mothers, who do not soon forget their children, I suppose they are mostly forgotten. I have never heard it suggested that the French Government did not behave with the most perfect honour to this Government and this country all through these grave, momentous transactions; but I have heard it stated by those who must know that nothing could be more honourable, nothing more just, than the conduct of the French Emperor to this Government throughout the whole of that struggle. More recently, when the war in China was begun by a government which I have condemned and denounced in the House of Commons, the Emperor of the French sent his ships and troops to co-operate with us, but I never heard that anything was done there to create a suspicion of a feeling of hostility on his part towards us. The Emperor of the French came to London, and some of those powerful organs that have since taken the line of which I am complaining did all but invite the people of London to prostrate themselves under the wheels of the chariot which conveyed along our streets the revived Monarchy of France. The Queen of England went to Paris, and was she not received there with as much affection and as much respect as her high position and her honourable character entitled her to? [*Cheers.*]

What has occurred since? If there was a momentary unpleasantness, I am quite sure that every impartial man will agree that under the peculiarly irritating circumstances of the moment, there was at least as much forbearance shown on one side of the Channel as on the other. Then we have had much said lately about a naval fortification recently completed in France, which has been more than 100 years in progress, and which was not devised by the present Emperor of the French nor by his will.

For 100 years great sums had been spent on it, and at last, like every other great work, it was brought to an end. The English Queen and others were invited over, and many went who were not invited. And yet in all this we are told that there is something to create extreme alarm and suspicion; we, who have never fortified any places; we, who have not a greater than Sebastopol or Gibraltar; we, who have not an impregnable fortress at Malta, who have not spent the fortune of a nation almost in the Ionian Islands; we, who are doing nothing at Alderney!—in fact, there never was a nation so perfectly guiltless of preparing to do anything to anybody! There are few persons who at some time or other have not been brought into contact with a poor unhappy fellow-creature who has some peculiar delusion or suspicion pressing on his mind. I recollect a friend of mine going down from Derby to Leeds in the train with a very quiet and respectable-looking gentleman sitting opposite to him. They had both been staying at the Midland Hotel, and they began talking about it. All at once the gentleman said, "Did you notice anything particular about the bread at breakfast?" "No," said my friend, "I did not." "Oh! but I did," said the poor gentleman, "and I am convinced there was an attempt made to poison me, and it is a very curious thing that I never go to a hotel without I discover some attempt to do me mischief." The unfortunate man was labouring under one of the greatest calamities which can befall a human creature. But what are we to say of a nation which lives under a perpetual delusion that it is going to be attacked—a nation which is the most combined on the face of the earth, with little less than 30,000,000 people all united under a government which, though we intend to reform it, we do not the less respect [*cheers*], and which has mechanical power and wealth to which no country offers any parallel? There is no causeway to Britain; the free waves of the sea flow day and night forever round her shores, and yet there are people going about with whom this hallucination is so strong that they do not merely discover it quietly to their friends, but they write it down in double-leaded columns, in leading articles—nay, some of them actually get up on platforms and proclaim it to hundreds and thousands of their fellow-countrymen. [*Laughter.*] I should like to ask you whether these delusions are to last forever, whether this policy is to be the perpetual policy of England, whether these results are to go on gathering and gathering until there come, as come there must inevitably, some dreadful catastrophe on our country.

[Bright noted the "revolutions" in public opinion regarding reform, protection, colonial government, and criminal law, and then returned to the theme of comparing England with Rome.]

... I do not think that examples taken from pagan, sanguinary, bloodthirsty Rome are proper models for the imitation of a Christian country, nor would I limit my hopes of the greatness of England even to the long duration of 800 years. [*Cheers.*]

But what is Rome now? The city is dead. A poet has described her as "the lone mother of dead empires." Her language even is dead. Her very tombs are empty; the ashes of her most illustrious citizens are dispersed, for "the Scipios' tomb contains no ashes now." Yet I am asked—I, who am one of the Legislators of a Christian country—to measure my policy by the policy of ancient and pagan Rome!

I believe there is no permanent greatness to a nation except it be based upon morality. [*Cheers.*] I do not care for military greatness or military renown. I care for the Constitution of the people among whom I live. [*Cheers.*] There is no man in England who is less likely to speak irreverently of the Crown and Monarchy of England than I am; but crowns, coronets, mitres, military display, the pomp of war, wide colonies, and a huge empire are, in my view, all trifles, light as air, and not worth considering, unless with them you can have a fair share of comfort, contentment, and happiness among the great body of the people. [*Cheers.*] Palaces, princely castles, great halls, showy mansions do not make a nation. The nation in every country dwells in the cottage [*cheers*]; and unless the light of your constitution can shine there, unless the beauty of your legislation and the excellence of your statesmanship are printed there in the feelings and condition of the people, rely upon it, you have yet to learn the duties of government. [*Great cheering.*]

I have not, as you have observed, pleaded that this country should remain without adequate and scientific means of defence. [*Hear, hear.*] I acknowledge it to be the duty of your statesmen, acting upon the known opinions and principles of ninety-nine out of every hundred persons in the country, at all times, with all possible moderation, but with all possible efficiency, to take steps which shall preserve order within and on the confines of your Kingdom. [*Cheers.*] But I shall repudiate and denounce the expenditure of every shilling, the engagement of every man, the employment of every ship, which has no object but intermeddling in the affairs of other countries, and endeavouring to extend the boundaries of an empire which is already large enough to satisfy the greatest ambition, and I fear is much too large for the highest statesmanship to which any man has yet attained. [*Cheers.*]

The most ancient of profane historians has told us that the ancient Scythians were a very warlike people, and that they elevated an old scimitar upon a platform as a symbol of Mars, and to Mars alone, I believe, they built altars, and to this scimitar they offered sacrifices of horses and cattle, the main wealth of the country. I often ask myself whether we are at all advanced in one respect beyond those Scythians. What are our contributions to Church, to education, to morality, to religion, to justice, and to civil government, when compared with the wealth we expend in sacrifices to the old scimitar? [*Cheers.*] Two nights ago I addressed in this hall a vast assembly composed to a great extent of your countrymen who have no political power, who are at work from the dawn of the day to the evening, and who have therefore humble means of informing themselves on these great subjects. Now I am privileged to speak to a somewhat different audience. You represent those of your great community who have a more complete education, who have on some points greater intelligence, and in whose hands reside the power and influence of the district. I am speaking, too, within the hearing of those whose gentle nature, whose finer instincts, whose purer minds have not suffered as some of us have suffered in the turmoil and strife of life. You can mould opinion, you can create political power; you cannot think a good thought on this subject and communicate it to your neighbours, you cannot make these points, points of discussion in your social circles and more general meetings, without affecting sensibly and speedily the course which the Government of your country will pursue. [*Cheers.*]

May I ask you, then, to believe, as I do most devoutly believe, that the moral law was not written for men alone in their individual character, but that it was written as well for nations, and for nations great as this of which we are citizens. If nations reject and deride that moral law, there is a penalty which will inevitably follow. It may not come at once, it may not come in our lifetime; but rely upon it, the great Italian is not a poet only, but a prophet, when he says:

> The sword of heaven is not in haste to smite,
> Nor yet doth linger.[8]

We have experience, we have beacons, we have landmarks enough. We know what the past has cost us, we know how much and how far we have

---

[8] The lines are from Dante's *Paradiso*.

wandered, but we are not left without a guide. It is true we have not, as an ancient people had, Urim and Thummim—those oracular gems on Aaron's breast—from which to take counsel, but we have the unchangeable and eternal principles of the moral law to guide us, and only so far as we live by that guidance can we be permanently a great nation, or our people a happy people. [*Loud and continous cheers.*]

William E. Gladstone

"Principles of Foreign Policy"*
West Calder, November 27, 1879

In addressing you today, as in addressing like audiences assembled for a like purpose in other places of the country, I am warmed by the enthusiastic welcome which you have been pleased in every form to accord to me. I am, on the other hand, daunted when I think, first of all, what large demands I have to make upon your patience; and secondly, how inadequate are my powers and how inadequate almost any amount of time that you can grant me to set forth worthily the whole of the case which ought to be laid before you in connection with the coming election.

[*Gladstone first addresses himself to the "subject of agricultural distress" and economic policies, and then he moves to the problem of foreign affairs.*]

There was a saying of a great and ancient Greek orator, who unfortunately very much undervalued what we generally call the better portion of the community—namely, women. He made a very disrespectful observation, which I am going to quote not for the purpose of concurring with it, but for the purpose of an illustration. Pericles, the great Athenian statesman, said with regard to women, their great merit was to be never heard of. [*Laughter.*] Now, what Pericles said of women I am very much disposed to say of foreign affairs. Their great merit would be to be never heard of. [*Laughter and loud cheers.*] Unfortunately, instead of being never heard of they are always heard of, and you hear almost of nothing else. And I cannot promise you that you will be relieved from this everlasting din, because the consequences of meddling with foreign affairs are consequences which will for some time necessarily continue to trouble you, and they have found their way to your pockets in the shape of increased taxation.

Gentlemen, with this apology I ask you again to come with me beyond the seas; and as I wish to do justice, I will tell you what I think to be the

---
* The text is taken from *The Times*, November 28, 1879, p. 10.

right principles of foreign policy; and then, as far as your patience and my strength will permit, I will at any rate for a short time illustrate those right principles by some of the departures from them which have taken place of late years. [*Cheers.*] I give you, Gentlemen, what I think are the right principles of foreign policy.

The first thing is this: to foster the strength of the Empire by just legislation and by economy at home [*cheers*], thereby producing two great elements of national power—namely, wealth, which is the physical element, and union and contentment, which are moral elements [*cheers*]; and to reserve the strength of the Empire, to reserve the expenditure of that strength, for great and worthy occasions. [*Cheers.*] That is my first principle.

My second principle of foreign policy is this: that its aim ought to be to preserve to the nations of the world—and especially, were it but for shame, when we recollect the sacred name we bear as Christians, especially for the Christian nations of the world—the blessings of peace. [*Cheers.*] That is my second principle. Even, Gentlemen, when you do a good thing you may do it in so bad a way that you may entirely spoil its beneficial effects; and if we were to act the apostles of peace in such a way as to convey to the minds of other nations that we thought ourselves more entitled to an opinion on that subject than they are, or if we were to deny their rights, we should destroy the value of this doctrine.

. . . . .

... My third sound principle is this: to take care to cultivate and maintain to the utmost the concert of Europe, to keep the powers of Europe together. And why? Because in keeping them all in union together you neutralize and fetter and bind up the selfish aims of each. [*Cheers.*] I am not here to flatter England or any of the great powers. They may have selfish aims, as, unfortunately, they in late years have too sadly shown; and we too have selfish aims. But common action is fatal to selfish aims. Common action for a common object is the only way in which you can unite together the great powers of Europe to obtain objects connected with the common good of all. [*Cheers.*] These are three of my points.

My fourth point is that you should avoid needless and entangling engagements. You may boast about and brag about them; you may say that you are increasing the consideration of England in the eyes of Europe; you may say that an Englishman may now hold up his head [*laughter*]; you may say he is not now in the hands of a Liberal Ministry who thought nothing but about pounds, shillings, and pence. But what does all this come to? It comes to this, that you are increasing your engagements without increasing your strength; and if you increase engagements without increasing strength, you diminish strength [*cheers*]—you reduce the Empire and do not increase it; you render it less capable of performing its duties, and you render it an inheritance less precious to hand on to future generations. [*Cheers.*]

My fifth principle, Gentlemen, is this: to acknowledge the equal rights of all nations. You may sympathise with one nation more than another—you must sympathise in certain circumstances with one nation more than another. You sympathise most with those nations, as a rule, with which you have the nearest connexion in language and blood, in religion or other circumstances which at the time seem to give the strongest claim to sympathy. But in point of right all are equal; and you have no right to set up a system under which one is to be placed under moral suspicion or espionage, or made the constant subject of invective. If you do that, and especially if you claim for yourself a pharisaical superiority, then I say you may talk about your patriotism as you please, but you are a misjudging friend of your country and are undermining the basis of esteem and respect of others for your country. You are in reality inflicting serious injury upon it. [*Cheers.*] I have given you, Gentlemen, five principles of foreign policy, and I will give you a sixth [*laughter and cheers*], and then I have done.

The sixth is that in my opinion the foreign policy—subject to all the limitations I have described—the foreign policy of England should always be inspired by the love of freedom. [*Cheers.*] There should be a sympathy with freedom, a desire to give it a scope founded not upon visionary ideas, but upon the long experience of many generations within the shores of this happy isle. In freedom you lay the firmest foundation both of loyalty and of order, the firmest foundation for the development of individual character, and the best protection for the happiness of the nation at large. [*Cheers.*] In the foreign policy of this country the name of Canning ever will be honoured, the name of Russell ever will be honoured, the name of Palmerston ever will be honoured, by those who recollect the erection of the Kingdom of Belgium and the union of the disjoined provinces of Italy. It is that sympathy—not a sympathy with disorder, but, on the contrary, founded on the deepest and most profound love of order—it is that sympathy which, in my opinion, ought to be the very atmosphere in which the Foreign Secretary of England ought to live and move.

Gentlemen, it is impossible for me to say more today [*cheering; "Go on"*] than to attempt a very slight illustration of those principles. I have put myself in a position in which no one is entitled to tell me—you will bear me out in what I say—that I simply object to the acts of others and lay down no rules of action myself. I am not only prepared to show what are the rules of action that, in my judgment, are right rules; I am prepared to apply them, nor will I shrink from their application. I will take, Gentlemen, the name which most of all others is associated with suspicion and with alarm and with hatred in the minds of Englishmen. I will take the name of Russia and at once will tell you what I think about Russia, and how I am prepared as a member of Parliament to proceed with anything that respects Russia. You have heard me denounced sometimes, I believe, as a Russian spy [*laughter*], sometimes as a Russian agent [*laughter*], sometimes, perhaps, as a Russian tool [*laughter*]—titles not very desirable. But, Gentlemen, when you go to evidence, the worst thing that I have ever seen quoted out of any speech or writing of mine about Russia is this: that I did one day say or write these terrible words—I recommended Englishmen to imitate Russia in her good deeds. [*Laughter.*] Was not that terrible? [*Laughter.*] I cannot recede from it. I think we ought to imitate Russia in her good deeds [*cheers*], and if the good deeds are few I am sorry for it; but not less on that account should we be disposed to imitate them when they come. [*Cheers.*] I will now tell you, Gentlemen, what I think about Russia.

I make it one of my charges against the Foreign Policy of the Government[1] that while they have completely estranged from this country the feelings of a nation of 80 millions—for that is the number of the subjects of the Russian Empire—while, I say, Her Majesty's Government have contrived to completely estrange the feelings of that nation, they have aggrandized Russia in two ways which I will state with perfect distinctness. They have augmented her territory. Before the European powers met at Berlin, Lord Salisbury met with Count Schouvaloff,[2] and Lord Salisbury agreed that unless he could convince them by his arguments in the Congress at Berlin he would support the restoration to the despotic power of Russia of that country north of the Danube which at that moment constituted a portion of the free State of Roumania. Why, Gentlemen, what had been done by the Liberal Government, which, it was said, looked at nothing but pounds, shillings, and pence? The Liberal Government had driven Russia back from the Danube. Russia, which was a Danubian power before the Crimean war, lost its position on the Danube through the Crimean war; and the Tory Government, which has been incensing and influencing you against Russia, yet, notwithstanding, by binding itself beforehand to support its restoration to that country, aggrandized the power of Russia in Armenia, to which I would not refer were it not for a very strange circumstance. You know that an Armenian province was given back to Russia after the war, but I own I have less feeling or objection to that. I from the first objected vehemently and in every form to granting territory on the Danube to Russia and carrying back a population from a free state to a despotic state. As to a transfer of the Armenian people from the Government of Turkey to Russia, I must own that I look upon it with much greater equanimity. I have no fear of the territorial extension of Russia in Asia. I think they are old women's fears [*laughter*]; at any rate I do not wish to encourage her aggressive tendencies in Asia or anywhere

---

[1] Disraeli Ministry.
[2] Pëtr Andreevich Shuvalov, Russian ambassador to Great Britain from 1874 to 1879.

else. It may probably be that there is some benefit attending the transfer of a portion of Armenia from Turkey to Russia.

But there is a very strange fact. You know that portion of Armenia includes the port of Batoum. Lord Salisbury has lately stated to the country that by the Treaty of Berlin the port of Batoum is to be only a commercial port, and if the Treaty of Berlin stated that it was to be only a commercial port it could not be made into an arsenal, and that fact would be very important. But happily, Gentlemen, although treaties are concealed from us nowadays [*laughter*], the Treaty of Berlin is an open instrument. We can consult it for ourselves, and when we consult the Treaty of Berlin we find it states that Batoum shall be essentially a commercial port, but not that it shall be only a commercial port. Why, Gentlemen, Leith is an essentially commercial port, but there is nothing to prevent the people of this country, if in their wisdom or in their folly they should think fit, from constituting Leith into a great naval arsenal or naval fortification. But there is nothing to prevent the Emperor of Russia, while leaving to Port Batoum a character that shall be essentially commercial, from joining another character that is not in the slightest degree excluded by the treaty and making it as much as he pleases a port of military defence. [*Hear, hear.*] Therefore I challenge the assertion of Lord Salisbury, and, as Lord Salisbury is fond of writing letters to *The Times* [*laughter*] and of bringing the Duke of Argyll[3] to book, he perhaps will be kind enough to write another letter to *The Times* and tell in what clause of the Treaty of Berlin he finds it written that the port of Batoum shall be only a commercial port. [*"Hear" and laughter.*]

With respect to Russia, I take two views of the position of Russia. The position of Russia in Central Asia I believe to be one that has in the main been forced upon her against her will. She has been compelled—and this is the impartial opinion of the world—she has been compelled to extend her frontier southwards in Central Asia by causes in some degree analogous, but certainly more stringent and imperative, than the causes which have commonly led us to extend far more importantly our frontier in India. And I think it much to the credit of the late Government, much to the honour of Lord Clarendon and Lord Granville, that when we were in office we made a covenant with Russia under which Russia bound herself to exercise no influence or interference whatever in Afghanistan, while on the other hand making known our desire that Afghanistan should continue free and independent, and that both the powers acted with uniform strictness and fidelity upon those engagements till the day when we were removed from office. [*Cheers.*] But Russia has another position, her position in respect to Turkey, and here it is that I have complained of the Government for aggrandizing the power of Russia. On this point it is that I most complain.

[3] George Douglas Campbell, author of *The Eastern Question* (London, 1879).

The policy of Her Majesty's Government was a policy of repelling and repudiating the Slavonic populations of Turkey in Europe and of declining to make England the advocate of their interests. Nay, more; she became in their view the advocate of interests opposed to theirs—not, indeed, a decided advocate of Turkey; and now the Turks are full of loud complaints —and complaints, I must say, not unjust—that we lured them on to their ruin; that we gave them the impression we should support them; for our Ambassadors, Sir Henry Elliot and Sir Austin Layard, both of them said we had the most vital interests in Turkey; and the Turks thought if we had vital interests in Turkey, we should certainly defend them, and were thereby lured on to a ruinous and destructive war with Russia. [*Cheers.*] By our conduct we repelled them from us and made our name odious among them, though they had every disposition to sympathise with us and every disposition to confide in us; for they are a people desirous of freedom and desirous of self-government, with no aggressive views, but hate the idea of being absorbed in a huge despotic empire like the Empire of Russia. [*Cheers.*] But when they found we and the other powers of Europe under our unfortunate guidance declined to become in any manner their champions in defence of the rights of life or property and of female honour; when they found there was no call which could find its way to the heart of England through its Government or to the hearts of the other powers; and that Russia alone was able and disposed to fight for them—why, naturally they said, "Russia is our friend." We have done everything in our power to drive these people into the arms of Russia. If Russia has an aggressive disposition in the direction of Turkey, and I think it probable she may have, then it is we who have laid the ground upon which Russia may make her march to the south; we who have taught the Bulgarians, the Servians, the Roumanians, and the Montenegrins that there is one power in Europe and only one which is ready to support in act and by the sword her professions of sympathy with the oppressed populations of Turkey. That power is Russia; and how can you blame these people if under such circumstances they are disposed to say, "Russia is our friend?" But why did we make them say it? Simply because of the policy of the Government, not because of the wishes of our people. [*Cheers.*] Gentlemen, that is the most dangerous form of aggrandizing Russia. If Russia is aggressive anywhere, it is by movements towards the south, by schemes for acquiring the command of the Straits of Constantinople, and there is no way by which you can jointly so much assist her in giving reality to these designs as by inducing and disposing the populations of those provinces who are now in virtual possession of them to look upon Russia as their champion and friend, to look upon England as their disguised, perhaps, but yet their real and effective enemy. [*Cheers.*]

I have said that I think it not unreasonable either to believe or at any rate to admit it to be possible that Russia has aggressive designs in the

East of Europe. I do not mean immediate aggressive designs. I do not believe that the Emperor of Russia is a man of aggressive schemes of policy. But looking at the question in the long run—looking at what is happening, looking at what may happen in ten or twenty years, in one or two generations—it is highly probable that under such circumstances, Russia may develop some aggressive tendencies towards the south.

Perhaps you may say that I am here guilty of the same conduct towards Russia which I have but just now deprecated, because I say that we ought not to adopt a method of condemning anybody without cause or of setting up exceptional principles in proscription of the acts of any particular nation. I will explain in a moment the principles on which I act, the grounds on which I form my judgment. I look on the geographical position of Russia relative to Turkey, I look on the comparative strength of the two empires, I look at the importance of the Dardanelles and the Bosphorus as an exit and channel for the military and commercial marines of Russia into the Mediterranean, and what I say to myself is this: if the United Kingdom were in the same position relative to Turkey which Russia holds upon the map of the globe, I feel quite sure that we should be very apt to entertain and execute aggressive designs. Gentlemen, I will go further, and I will frankly own to you that I believe if we, instead of happily inhabiting these islands, had been in the position of the Russian people, we should have eaten up Turkey long ago. [*Loud laughter and cheers.*] Consequently, in saying that Russia ought to be vigilantly watched in every quarter, I am only applying to her the rule which in parallel circumstances I feel convinced ought to be applied and should be justly applied in judgment upon our own country.

Gentlemen, there is only one other point upon which I would say a few words, though there are a great many points on which I have a great many words to say somewhere or other. [*Laughter and cheers.*] Of all the principles of foreign policy which I have enumerated, that to which I attach the greatest value is the principle of the equality of nations, because without recognition of that principle there is no such thing as public right, and without public international right there is no other instrument for settling the transactions of mankind except material force. Consequently, the principle of equality among nations lies, in my opinion, at the very basis and root of all Christian civilisation, and when that principle is compromised or abandoned, with it must depart our hopes of tranquillity and of progress for mankind. [*Cheers.*] I am sorry to say, Gentlemen, that I feel it my absolute duty to make this charge against the foreign policy under which we have lived for the last two years, since the resignation of Lord Derby. [*Cheers.*] It has been a foreign policy, in my opinion, wholly or to a perilous extent unregardful of public right, and it has been founded upon the basis of a false, I think an arrogant and a dangerous, assumption, although I do not question its being made conscientiously and for what was believed to be for the advantage of the country; an untrue, arrogant, and dangerous assumption that we were entitled to assume to ourselves some dignity which we should be entitled to withhold from others, and to claim on our part authority to do things which we would not permit to be done by others. [*Cheers.*] For example, when Russia was going to the Congress of Berlin, we said, "Your treaty of San Stefano is of no value; it is an act between you and Turkey; but we insist upon it, the whole of your treaty of San Stefano must be submitted to the Congress of Berlin, that they may judge how far to open it in each and every one of its points, because the concerns of Turkey are the common concerns of the powers of Europe, acting in concert."

Having asserted that principle to the world, what did we do? These two things. Secretly, without the knowledge of Parliament, without even the forms of official procedure, Lord Salisbury met Count Schouvaloff in London, and agreed with him upon the terms on which the two powers together should be bound in honour to one another to act upon all the most important points when they came before the Congress at Berlin. Having alleged against Russia that she should not be allowed to settle Turkish affairs with Turkey because they were but two powers, and because those affairs were the affairs of Europe—having done that, I say, they got Count Schouvaloff into a private room, and there, on the part of England and Russia, they also being but two powers, they settled a large number of the most important of these affairs, in utter contempt and degradation of the very principle for which Her Majesty's Government had been contending for months before—that principle for which they asked Parliament for a vote of £6,000,000, that principle for the sake of which they spent these £6,000,000 in needless and mischievous armaments. [*Cheers.*] What we would not allow Russia to do with Turkey because of the rights of Europe, we did with Russia in contempt of the rights of Europe. [*Loud cheers.*] Nor was that all; that was done on the last days of May, 1878, and the document was published, made known to the world, made known to the Congress of Berlin, to its infinite astonishment if I am not greatly misinformed.

But this was not all. Nearly at the same time we performed the same operation in another quarter. [*Laughter.*] We objected to a treaty between Russia and Turkey as having no authority, though that treaty was made in the light of day—namely, the Treaty of San Stefano. And what did we do? We went, not in the light of day, but in the darkness of the night—not in the knowledge and cognisance of other powers, all of whom had the faculty and means of watching all along and preparing to take their own objections and shaping their own policy—not in the light of day but in the darkness of night, we sent our ambassador in Constantinople to the Minister of Turkey, and there he framed—even while the Congress of Berlin was sitting to determine those matters of common interest—he framed that which is too famous—or rather too notorious, shall I say?—the Anglo-Turkish Convention.

Gentlemen, it is said and said truly that truth beats fiction. That what happens in fact from time to time is of a character so daring and so strange that if a novelist were to imagine it and put it on his pages the whole world would reject it on account of its impossibility; and that is the case with the Anglo-Turkish Convention. For who would have believed it possible that we should assert before the world the principle that Europe only could deal with the affairs of the Turkish Empire, should ask Parliament for £6,000,000 to support us in asserting that principle, should send Ministers to Berlin who declared that unless that principle was acted upon they would go to war with the material that Parliament had placed in their hands, and should at the same time be concluding a separate agreement with Turkey under which these matters of European jurisdiction and the whole matter were settled with the worthless bribe of the possession and administration of the island of Cyprus? [*Laughter.*] I said, Gentlemen, "the worthless bribe" of the island of Cyprus, and that is the truth. [*Cheers.*] It is worthless for our purposes and worse than worthless for our purposes—not worthless in itself, but an island of resources, an island of natural capabilities, provided they are allowed to develop themselves in the course of circumstances without violent or unprincipled methods of action. [*Hear.*] But Cyprus was not thought to be worthless by those who accepted it as a bribe. On the contrary, you were told that it was to secure the road to India. You were told that it was to be an arsenal very cheaply made, but more valuable than Malta. You were told that it would revive trade [*laughter*]; and multitudes of companies were formed that sent agents and capital to Cyprus, and some, I fear, grievously burnt their fingers there. [*Laughter.*] I am not going to dwell on that now. What I have in view is not the particular merits of Cyprus but the illustrations that I have given you—in the case of the agreement of Lord Salisbury with Count Schouvaloff, and in the case of the Anglo-Turkish Convention—of the manner in which we have asserted for ourselves the principles that we had denied to others—namely, the principle of over-riding the European authority of the Treaty of Paris and taking the matters which that treaty gave to Europe into our own separate jurisdiction. [*Cheers.*]

Now, Gentlemen, I am sorry to find that what I call the pharisaical assertion of our own superiority has found its way alike into the practice and seemingly into the theories of the Government. I am not going to assert anything which is not known, but the Prime Minister has stated there is one day in the year—viz., the 9th of November, the Lord Mayor's day—on which the language of sense and truth is to be heard amid the surrounding din of idle rumours, generated and fledged in the brains of irresponsible scribes. I don't agree, Gentlemen, in panegyric of November. I am much more apt to compare the 9th of November, with regard to some of the speeches which have lately been made upon that day, with another day of the year well known to British tradition, and that other day in the year is the 1st of April. [*Cheers and laughter.*] But, Gentlemen, on that day the Prime Minister—speaking out, I do not question for a moment, his own sincere opinions—made what I think one of the most unhappy and ominous allusions ever made by a Minister of this country. He quoted certain words usually rendered as "Empire and liberty"—words of a Roman statesman, words describing the state of Rome—and he quoted them as words which were capable of legitimate application to the position and circumstances of England. I join issue with the Prime Minister upon that subject, and I affirm that nothing can be more fundamentally unsound, more practically ruinous, than the establishing of a Roman analogy for the guidance of British policy. What was Rome? Rome was, indeed, an imperial state—a state having a mission to subdue the world, but a state whose very basis it was to deny equal rights, to proscribe the existence of other nations. In that, Gentlemen, was the Roman idea. It has been forcibly illustrated in three lines in the translation of Virgil by our great poet Dryden, which are as follows:

> But Rome, 'tis thine alone with awful sway,
> To rule mankind and make the world obey;
> Disposing peace and war thine own majestic way.[4]

[*Cheers.*] We are told to fall back on this example. No doubt the word "Empire" was qualified with the word "Liberty"; but what did the two words "Liberty" and "Empire" mean in the Roman mouth? They meant simply this: "liberty for ourselves, Empire over the rest of mankind." [*Cheers.*]

I do not think, Gentlemen, that this Ministry or any other Ministry is going to place us in the position of Rome. What I object to is the revival of the idea. I care not how feeble, I care not, from a philosophic or historic point of view, how ridiculous the attempt at this revival may be, I say it indicates an intention, I say it indicates a frame of mind, and that frame of mind, unfortunately, I find has been consistent with the policy of which I have given you some illustrations—a policy of denying to others the right that we claim ourselves. [*Cheers.*] No doubt, Gentlemen, Rome may have had its work to do and Rome did its work, but modern times brought about a different state of things. Modern times have established a sisterhood of nations, equal, independent, each of them built upon that legitimate foundation which public law afforded to every nation living within its own borders and seeking to perform its own affairs. But if one thing more than another has been detestable to Europe it has been the appearance upon

---

[4] From Dryden's translation of the *Aeneid*.

the stage from time to time of men who, even in the times of the Christian civilisation, have been thought to aim at universal dominion. It was this aggressive disposition on the part of Louis XIV, King of France, that led your forefathers, in a cause not immediately their own, freely to spend their blood and treasure in a struggle against a method of policy which, having Paris for its centre, seemed to aim at universal dominion.

It was the very same thing a century and a half later. It was the charge launched, and justly launched, against Napoleon that under his dominion France was not content even with her extended limit, but Germany and Italy and Spain, apparently without any limit to this pestilent and pernicious process, were to be brought under the dominion or influence of France, and national equality was to be trampled underfoot and national rights denied. For that reason England in the struggle almost exhausted herself, greatly impoverished her people, brought upon herself and Scotland too the consequences of a debt that nearly crushed her energies, and poured forth her best blood without limit in order to resent and put down these intolerable pretensions. It is but in a pale and weak and almost despicable miniature that such ideas are now set up, but you will observe the poison and the mischief lie in the principle and not in the scale.

And that principle, which I say has been compromised by the action of the Ministry, and which I call upon you and upon all who choose to hear my voice to vindicate when the day of election comes [*cheers*], is that sound and sacred principle that nations are knitted one to another in the bonds of right, a bond without distinction of great or small; that there is equality between them, the same sacredness defending the narrow limits of Belgium as attaches to the extended frontiers of Russia, of Germany, or of France; and I say that he who by act or word brings that principle into peril or disparagement, however honest his intentions may be, places himself in the position of one inflicting—I will not say intending to inflict, for I ascribe nothing of the sort—inflicting injury upon his own country and endangering the best and most fundamental interests of Christian society. [*Loud cheers.*]

John R. Seeley

"Tendency in English History"[*]
Cambridge University, 1882

It is a favourite maxim of mine that history, while it should be scientific in its method, should pursue a practical object. That is, it should not merely gratify [one's] curiosity about the past, but modify his view of the present and his forecast of the future. Now if this maxim be sound, the history of England ought to end with something that might be called a moral. Some large conclusion ought to arise out of it; it ought to exhibit the general tendency of English affairs in such a way as to set us thinking about the future and divining the destiny which is reserved for us. The more so because the part played by our country in the world certainly does not grow less prominent as history advances. Some countries, such as Holland and Sweden, might pardonably regard their history as in a manner wound up. They were once great, but the conditions of their greatness have passed away, and they now hold a secondary place. Their interest in their own past is therefore either sentimental or purely scientific; the only practical lesson of their history is a lesson of resignation. But England has grown steadily greater and greater, absolutely, at least, if not always relatively. It is far greater now than it was in the eighteenth century; it was far greater in the eighteenth century than in the seventeenth, far greater in the seventeenth than in the sixteenth. The prodigious greatness to which it has attained makes the question of its future infinitely important and at the same time most anxious, because it is evident that the great colonial extension of our State exposes it to new dangers, from which in its ancient insular insignificance it was free.

The interest of English history ought therefore to deepen steadily to the close, and since the future grows out of the past, the history of the past of England ought to give rise to a prophecy concerning her future. Yet our popular historians scarcely seem to think so. Does not Aristotle say that a drama ends, but an epic poem only leaves off? English history, as it is

[*] This text is taken from John R. Seeley, *The Expansion of England: Two Courses of Lectures* (London, 1883), pp. 1–16.

popularly related, not only has no distinct end, but leaves off in such a gradual manner, growing feebler and feebler, duller and duller towards the close, that one might suppose that England, instead of steadily gaining in strength, had been for a century or two dying of mere old age. Can this be right? Ought the stream to be allowed thus to lose itself and evaporate in the midst of a sandy desert? The question brings to mind those lines of Wordsworth:

> It is not to be thought of that the flood
> Of British freedom, which to the open sea
> Of the world's praise, from dark antiquity
> Hath flowed 'with pomp of waters unwithstood,'
> Roused though it be full often to a mood
> Which spurns the check of salutary bands,
> That this most famous stream in bogs and sands
> Should perish, and to evil and to good
> Be lost for ever—[1]

Well! This sad fate which is "not to be thought of" is just what befalls if not the stream itself of British freedom, yet the reflexion of it in our popular histories.

Now suppose we wish to remedy this evil, how shall we proceed? Here is no bad question for historical students at the opening of an academic year, the opening perhaps to some of their academic course. You are asked to think over English history as a whole and consider if you cannot find some meaning, some method in it, if you cannot state some conclusion to which it leads. Hitherto, perhaps you have learned names and dates, lists of kings, lists of battles and wars. The time comes now when you are to ask yourselves, "To what end?" For what practical purpose are these facts collected and committed to memory? If they lead to no great truths having at the same time scientific generality and momentous practical bearings, then history is but an amusement and will scarcely hold its own in the conflict of studies.

No one can long study history without being haunted by the idea of development, of progress. We move onward, both, each of us, and all of us together. England is not now what it was under the Stuarts or the Tudors, and in these last centuries, at least, there is much to favour the view that the movement is progressive, that it is toward something better. But how shall we define this movement, and how shall we measure it? If we are to study history in that rational spirit, with that definite object which I have recommended, we must fix our minds on this question and arrive at some solution of it. We must not be content with those vague flourishes which the old

---

[1] The lines are from "National Independence and Liberty."

school of historians, who according to my view lost themselves in mere narrative, used to add for form's sake before winding up.

Those vague flourishes usually consisted in some reference to what was called the advance of civilisation. No definition of civilisation was given; it was spoken of in metaphorical language as a light, a day gradually advancing through its twilight and its dawn towards its noon; it was contrasted with a remote, ill-defined period called the dark ages. Whether it would always go on brightening, or whether, like the physical day, it would pass again into afternoon and evening, or whether it would come to an end by a sudden eclipse, as the light of civilisation in the ancient world might appear to have done, all this was left in the obscurity convenient to a theory which was not serious, and which only existed for the purpose of rhetorical ornament.

It is a very fair sample of bad philosophising, this theory of civilisation. You have to explain a large mass of phenomena about which you do not even know that they are of the same kind—but they happen to come into view at the same time; what do you do but fling over the whole mass a *word* which holds them together like a net? You carefully avoid defining this word, but in speaking of it you use metaphors which imply that it denotes a living force of unknown, unlimited properties, so that a mere reference to it is enough to explain the most wonderful, the most dissimilar effects. It was used to explain a number of phenomena which had no further apparent connexion with each other than that they happened often to appear together in history; sometimes the softening of manners, sometimes mechanical inventions, sometimes religious toleration, sometimes the appearance of great poets and artists, sometimes scientific discoveries, sometimes constitutional liberty. It was assumed, though it was never proved, that all these things belonged together and had a hidden cause, which was the working of the spirit of civilisation.

We might no doubt take this theory in hand and give it a more coherent appearance. We might start with the one principle of freedom of thought and trace all the consequences that will follow from that. Scientific discoveries and mechanical inventions may flow from it, if certain other conditions are present; such discoveries and inventions coming into general use will change the appearance of human life, give it a complicated, modern aspect; this change then we might call the advance of civilisation. But political liberty has no connexion with all this. There was liberty at Athens before Plato and Aristotle, but afterwards it died out; liberty at Rome when thought was rude and ignorant, but servitude after it became enlightened. And poetical genius has nothing to do with it, for poetry declined at Athens just as philosophy began, and there was a Dante in Italy before the Renaissance, but no Dante after it.

If we analyse this vague sum-total which we call civilisation, we shall find that a large part of it is what might be expected from the name—that is, the result of the union of men in civil communities or states—but that another part is only indirectly connected with this and is more immediately due to other causes. The progress of science, for example, might be held to be the principal factor in civilisation, yet, as I have just pointed out, it by no means varies regularly with civil well-being, though for the most part it requires a certain *modicum* of civil well-being. That part of the human lot "which laws or kings can cause or cure" is strictly limited. Now history may assume a larger or a narrower function. It may investigate all the causes of human well-being alike; on the other hand, it may attach itself to the civil community and to the part of human well-being which depends on that. Now, by a kind of unconscious tradition, the latter course has more usually been taken. Run over the famous histories that have been written; you will see that the writers have always had in view, more or less consciously, states and governments, their internal development, their mutual dealings. It may be quite true that affairs of this kind are not always the most important of human affairs. In the period recorded by Thucydides the most permanently important events may have been the philosophical career of Socrates and the artistic career of Phidias, yet Thucydides has nothing to say of either, while he enlarges upon wars and intrigues which now seem petty. This is not the effect of any narrowness of view. Thucydides is alive to the unique glory of the city he describes; how else could he have written φιλοκαλοῦμεν μετ' εὐτελείας καὶ φιλοσοφοῦμεν ἄνευ μαλακίας?[2] Nay, so far as that glory was the result of political causes, he is ready to discuss it, as that very passage shows. It is with purpose and deliberation that he restricts himself. The truth is that investigation makes progress by dividing and subdividing the field. If you discuss everything at once, you certainly get the advantage of a splendid variety of topics, but you do not make progress; if you would make progress, you must concentrate your attention upon one set of phenomena at a time. It seems to me advisable to keep history still within the old lines, and to treat separately the important subjects which were omitted in that scheme. I consider therefore that history has to do with the State, that it investigates the growth and changes of a certain corporate society, which acts through certain functionaries and certain assemblies. By the nature of the State, every person who lives in a certain territory is usually a member of it, but history is not concerned with individuals except in their capacity as members of a state. That a man in England makes a scientific discovery or paints a picture is not in itself an event in the history of England. Individuals are important in history in proportion not to their intrinsic merit, but to their relation to the State. Socrates was a much greater man than Cleon, but Cleon has a much greater space in Thucydides. Newton was a greater

---

[2] The quotation is from Pericles' "Funeral Oration for the Athenian Soldiers": "We cultivate refinement without extravagance and knowledge without effeminacy."

man than Harley, yet it is Harley, not Newton, who fixes the attention of the historian of the reign of Queen Anne.

After this explanation you will see that the question I raised—"What is the general drift or goal of English history?"—is much more definite than it might at first sight appear. I am not thinking of any general progress that the human race everywhere alike, and therefore also in England, may chance to be making, nor even necessarily of any progress peculiar to England. By England I mean solely the state or political community which has its seat in England. Thus strictly limited, the question may seem to you perhaps a good deal less interesting; however that may be, it certainly becomes much more manageable.

The English State, then—in what direction and towards what goal has that been advancing? The words which jump to our lips in answer are "Liberty," "Democracy"! They are words which want a great deal of defining. Liberty has, of course, been a leading characteristic of England as compared with Continental countries, but in the main, liberty is not so much an end to which we have been tending as a possession which we have long enjoyed. The struggles of the seventeenth century secured it—even if they did not first acquire it—for us. In later times there has been a movement towards something which is often called liberty, but not so correctly. We may, if we like, call it democracy; and I suppose the current opinion is that if any large tendency is discernible in the more recent part of English history, it is this tendency, by which first the middle class and then gradually the lower classes have been admitted to a share of influence in public affairs.

Discernible enough no doubt this tendency is, at least in the nineteenth century, for in the eighteenth century only the first beginnings of it can be traced. It strikes our attention most because it has made for a long time past the staple of political talk and controversy. But history ought to look at things from a greater distance and more comprehensively. If we stand aloof a little and follow with our eyes the progress of the English State, the great governed society of English people, in recent centuries, we shall be much more struck by another change, which is not only far greater but even more conspicuous, though it has always been less discussed, partly because it proceeded more gradually, partly because it excited less opposition. I mean the simple obvious fact of the extension of the English name into other countries of the globe, the foundation of Greater Britain.

There is something very characteristic in the indifference which we show towards this mighty phenomenon of the diffusion of our race and the expansion of our state. We seem, as it were, to have conquered and peopled half the world in a fit of absence of mind. While we were doing it—that is, in the eighteenth century—we did not allow it to affect our imaginations or in any degree to change our ways of thinking; nor have we even now ceased to think of ourselves as simply a race inhabiting an island off the northern coast of the Continent of Europe. We constantly betray by our modes of speech that we do not reckon our Colonies as really belonging to us; thus if we are asked what the English population is, it does not occur to us to reckon in the population of Canada and Australia. This fixed way of thinking has influenced our historians. It causes them, I think, to miss the true point of view in describing the eighteenth century. They make too much of the mere Parliamentary wrangle and the agitations about liberty, in all which matters the eighteenth century of England was but a pale reflexion of the seventeenth. They do not perceive that in that century the history of England is not in England but in America and Asia. In like manner, I believe that when we look at the present state of affairs and still more at the future, we ought to beware of putting England alone in the foreground and suffering what we call the English possessions to escape our view in the background of the picture.

Let me describe with some exactness the change that has taken place. In the last years of Queen Elizabeth, England had absolutely no possessions outside Europe, for all schemes of settlement, from that of Hore in Henry VIII's reign to those of Gilbert and Raleigh, had failed alike. Great Britain did not yet exist; Scotland was a separate kingdom, and in Ireland the English were but a colony in the midst of an alien population still in the tribal stage. With the accession of the Stuart family commenced at the same time two processes, one of which was brought to completion under the last Stuart, Queen Anne, while the other has continued without interruption ever since. Of these the first is the internal union of the three kingdoms, which, though technically it was not completed till much later, may be said to be substantially the work of the seventeenth century and the Stuart dynasty. The second was the creation of a still larger Britain comprehending vast possessions beyond the sea. This process began with the first charter given to Virginia in 1606. It made a great advance in the seventeenth century; but not till the eighteenth did Greater Britain in its gigantic dimensions and with its vast politics first stand clearly before the world. Let us consider what this Greater Britain at the present day precisely is.

Excluding certain small possessions, which are chiefly of the nature of naval or military stations, it consists besides the United Kingdom of four great groups of territory, inhabited either chiefly or to a large extent by Englishmen and subject to the Crown, and a fifth great territory also subject to the Crown and ruled by English officials, but inhabited by a completely foreign race. The first four are the Dominion of Canada, the West Indian Islands, among which I include some territories on the continent of Central and Southern America, the mass of South African possessions of which Cape Colony is the most considerable, and fourthly, the Australian group, to which, simply for convenience, I must here add New Zealand. The dependency is India.

Now what is the extent and value of these possessions? First, let us look at their population, which, the territory being as yet newly settled, is in many cases thin. The Dominion of Canada with Newfoundland had in 1881 a population of rather more than four millions and a half, that is, about equal to the population of Sweden; the West Indian group rather more than a million and a half, about equal to the population at the same time of Greece; the South African group about a million and three quarters, but of these much less than a half are of European blood, the Australian group about three millions, rather more than the population of Switzerland. This makes a total of ten millions and three quarters, or about ten millions of English subjects of European and mainly English blood outside the British Islands.

The population of the great dependency India was nearly a hundred and ninety-eight millions and the native states in India which look up to England as the paramount power had about fifty-seven millions in addition. The total makes a population roughly equal to that of all Europe excluding Russia.

But of course it strikes us at once that this enormous Indian population does not make part of Greater Britain in the same sense as those ten millions of Englishmen who live outside of the British Islands. The latter are of our own blood, and are therefore united with us by the strongest tie. The former are of alien race and religion, and are bound to us only by the tie of conquest. It may be fairly questioned whether the possession of India does or ever can increase our power or our security, while there is no doubt that it vastly increases our dangers and responsibilities. Our Colonial Empire stands on quite a different footing; it has some of the fundamental conditions of stability. There are in general three ties by which states are held together, community of race, community of religion, community of interest. By the first two our Colonies are evidently bound to us, and this fact by itself makes the connexion strong. It will grow indissolubly firm if we come to recognise also that interest bids us maintain the connexion, and this conviction seems to gain ground. When we inquire then into the Greater Britain of the future, we ought to think much more of our Colonial than of our Indian Empire.

This is an important consideration when we come to estimate the Empire not by population but by territorial area. Ten millions of Englishmen beyond the sea—this is something; but it is absolutely nothing compared with what will ultimately, nay, with what will speedily, be seen. For those millions are scattered over an enormous area, which fills up with a rapidity quite unlike the increase of population in England. That you may measure the importance of this consideration, I give you one fact. The density of population in Great Britain is 291 to the square mile; in Canada it is not much more than one to the square mile. Suppose for a moment the Dominion of Canada peopled as fully as Great Britain, its population would actually be more than a thousand millions. That state of things is no doubt very remote, but an immense increase is not remote. In not much more than half a century the Englishmen beyond the sea—supposing the Empire to hold together—will be equal in number to the Englishmen at home, and the total will be much more than a hundred millions.

These figures may perhaps strike you as rather overwhelming than interesting. You may make it a question whether we ought to be glad of this vast increase of our race, whether it would not be better for us to advance morally and intellectually than in mere population and possessions, whether the great things have not for the most part been done by the small nations, and so on. But I do not quote these figures in order to gratify our national pride. I leave it an open question whether our increase is matter for exultation or for regret. It is not yet time to consider that. What is clear in the meantime is the immense importance of this increase. Good or bad, it is evidently the great fact of modern English history. And it would be the greatest mistake to imagine that it is a merely material fact, or that it carries no moral and intellectual consequences. People cannot change their abodes, pass from an island to a continent, from the fiftieth degree of north latitude to the tropics or the Southern Hemisphere, from an ancient community to a new colony, from vast manufacturing cities to sugar plantations, or to lonely sheepwalks in countries where aboriginal savage tribes still wander, without changing their ideas and habits and ways of thinking, nay, without somewhat modifying in the course of a few generations their physical type. We know already that the Canadian and the Victorian are not quite like the Englishman; do we suppose, then, that in the next century, if the Colonial population has become as numerous as that of the mother country, assuming that the connexion has been maintained and has become closer, England itself will not be very much modified and transformed? Whether good or bad, then, the growth of Greater Britain is an event of enormous magnitude.

Evidently, as regards the future it is the greatest event. But an event may be very great and yet be so simple that there is not much to be said about it, that it has scarcely any history. It is thus that the great English Exodus is commonly regarded as if it had happened in the most simple, inevitable manner, as if it were merely the unopposed occupation of empty countries by the nation which happened to have the greatest surplus population and the greatest maritime power. I shall show this to be a great mistake. I shall show that this Exodus makes a most ample and a most full and interesting chapter in English history. I shall venture to assert that during the eighteenth century it determines the whole course of affairs, that the main struggle of England from the time of Louis XIV to the time of Napoleon was for the possession of the New World, and that it is for want of perceiving this that most of us find that century of English history uninteresting.

The great central fact in this chapter of history is that we have had at different times two such Empires. So decided is the drift of our destiny towards the occupation of the New World that after we had created one Empire and lost it, a second grew up almost in our own despite. The figures I gave you refer exclusively to our second Empire, to that which we still possess. When I spoke of the ten millions of English subjects who live beyond the sea, I did not pause to mention that 100 years ago we had another set of colonies which had already a population of three millions, that these colonies broke off from us and formed a federal state, of which the population has in a century multiplied more than sixteenfold, and is now equal to that of the mother country and its Colonies taken together. It is an event of prodigious magnitude not only that this Empire should have been lost to us, but that a new state, English in race and character, should have sprung up, and that this state should have grown in a century to be greater in population than every European state except Russia. But the loss we suffered in the secession of the American Colonies has left in the English mind a doubt, a misgiving, which affects our whole forecast of the future of England.

For if this English Exodus has been the greatest English event of the eighteenth and nineteenth centuries, the greatest English question of the future must be what is to become of our second Empire and whether or no it may be expected to go the way of the first. In the solution of this question lies that moral which I said ought to result from the study of English history.

It is an old saying to which Turgot[3] gave utterance a quarter of a century before the Declaration of Independence—"Colonies are like fruits which cling to the tree only till they ripen." He added, "As soon as America can take care of herself, she will do what Carthage did." What wonder that when this prediction was so signally fulfilled, the proposition from which it had been deduced rose, especially in the minds of the English, to the rank of a demonstrated principle! This no doubt is the reason why we have regarded the growth of a second Empire with very little interest or satisfaction. "What matters," we have said, "its vastness or its rapid growth? It does not grow for us." And to the notion that we cannot keep it we have added the notion that we need not wish to keep it, because, with that curious kind of optimistic fatalism to which historians are liable, the historians of our American war have generally felt bound to make out that the loss of our Colonies was not only inevitable, but was even a fortunate thing for us.

Whether these views are sound, I do not inquire now. I merely point out that two alternatives are before us, and that the question, incomparably

---

[3] Anne Robert Jacques Turgot, Baron de l'Aulne, French statesman and economist. His most famous work, said to have influenced Adam Smith, was *Réflexions sur la formation et la distribution des richesses* (Paris, 1766).

the greatest question which we can discuss, refers to the choice between them. The four groups of Colonies may become four independent states, and in that case two of them, the Dominion of Canada and the West Indian group, will have to consider the question whether admission into the United States will not be better for them than independence. In any case, the English name and English institutions will have a vast predominance in the New World, and the separation may be so managed that the mother country may continue always to be regarded with friendly feelings. Such a separation would leave England on the same level as the states nearest to us on the Continent; populous, but less so than Germany and scarcely equal to France. But two states, Russia and the United States, would be on an altogether higher scale of magnitude, Russia having at once, and the United States perhaps before very long, twice our population. Our trade too would be exposed to wholly new risks.

The other alternative is that England may prove able to do what the United States does so easily, that is, hold together in a federal union countries very remote from each other. In that case England will take rank with Russia and the United States in the first rank of state, measured by population and area, and in a higher rank than the states of the Continent. We ought by no means to take for granted that this is desirable. Bigness is not necessarily greatness; if by remaining in the second rank of magnitude we can hold the first rank morally and intellectually, let us sacrifice mere material magnitude. But though we must not prejudge the question whether we ought to retain our Empire, we may fairly assume that it is desirable after due consideration to judge it.

With a view to forming such a judgment, I propose in these lectures to examine historically the tendency to expansion which England has so long displayed. We shall learn to think of it more seriously if we discover it to be profound, persistent, necessary to the national life, and more hopefully if we can satisfy ourselves that the secession of our first Colonies was not a mere normal result of expansion, like the bursting of a bubble, but the result of temporary conditions, removable and which have been removed.

Joseph Chamberlain

"Imperial Preference"*
Birmingham, May 15, 1903

Mr. Chairman, Ladies and Gentlemen—I thank you from the bottom of my heart for the warmth of your welcome, for the assurance, which is always delightful to me, of your continued confidence and support. I am proud of being the representative of West Birmingham, of an essentially working-class constituency. I have ventured before now in the House of Commons to claim that I represented more labour than any other Labour representative ["*Hear, hear*" *and cheers*]; and I do not think the less of that position, because I believe that I represent labour in no narrow and selfish sense. I represent labour as it constitutes the majority of the people of this country, and as it is characterized by the virtues and the qualities that have made this country what it is—by labour, that is, which thinks not of itself as a class opposed to any other class in the community, but as responsible for the obligations of the country and the Empire to which it belongs, and as participators in all that concerns the prosperity and the welfare of the whole. [*Hear, hear.*]

It is now two months since I returned home from a voyage which will always be one of the most memorable incidents of my life [*hear, hear*]; but I have not forgotten—I shall never forget—that my constituents and fellow-citizens sent me forth to make a great experiment encouraged by their good wishes and by the most splendid and inspiring demonstration that was ever accorded to any public man. [*Cheers.*] It was to me also a matter of greatest gratification that when I returned the first to greet me on these shores was a deputation from you, my friends and constituents, assuring me of your welcome home and of your congratulations; and during the interval between those two events I was constantly reminded of you. I could come to no great city in South Africa, hardly to any village, but always it seemed to me I was cheered by the presence and the enthusiasm of Birmingham men [*cheers*], proud to recall their connexion with our city

---
* The text is taken from *The Times*, May 16, 1903, p. 8.

and anxious to prove that neither time nor distance had lessened their affection for their old home. [*Cheers.*] I go back often to my old associations; I think of the time when I entered upon public life, thanks to the support of those who in St. Paul's Ward sent me to the Town Council of Birmingham; and amongst all my recollections there is none of which I am prouder than of the fact that I was permitted at that time to co-operate with men, our then leaders, most of whom have passed away, but who have left behind them an imperishable legacy, who have impressed upon us and instilled into our lives that intense feeling of local patriotism which makes it the duty of every Birmingham man at home and abroad to maintain and to raise the reputation of the city from which he came.

On my return, as is right and proper, I am called upon to make my first political speech to my constituents. [*Cheers.*] You will excuse me if I am a little out of touch. [*Laughter.*] It is true that in South Africa I did a deal of talking; but I am bound to say that my party weapons are a little rusty. When I was in South Africa it was not of our controversial politics that I was speaking; and for a considerable period my whole mind was turned towards the problems connected with the birth of a new nation in South Africa, and, above all, to the question of how it was possible to reconcile the two strong races who were bound to live together there as neighbours, and who, I hope, will live together as friends. [*Cheers.*] In connexion with that, I had to think also of how this new nation would stand, how these races would be concerned in the future of the Empire which belongs to both of them, Dutch and English—great people with many virtues in common, but still with great differences. Who would wish that the traditions of either should be forgotten, that their peculiarities should disappear? And yet we have to make of them a united nation. Here in the United Kingdom we have different races but one people. It would be rather difficult, I imagine, that an Englishman should feel exactly the same in regard to, let us say, Bannockburn[1] as a Scotsman would do [*a laugh*]; yet both Scotch and English may equally be proud of having had their full part in Waterloo or Trafalgar. Why should it not be the same, I ask, of the Dutchman that he should not forget any of the traditions of which he may justly be proud, that he should not abandon any of the peculiarities or prejudices of his race any more than I would ask it of any Briton? But my confident hope and belief is that in the future both these representatives of different races will be able to co-operate and to create for themselves a common existence in which they may have a common pride. It is, therefore, to the Empire with all that that means that I look to produce that union in South Africa which we all desire to achieve. [*Cheers.*]

---

[1] Battle fought on June 24, 1314. A small force of Scotsmen defeated an English army. Scotsmen regard the battle as the "culmination of the War of Independence."

But you will understand that in the absorbing preoccupation of these thoughts in a work which strained every nerve and which filled every waking moment, I had no time to keep myself abreast of purely party politics in this country. I am still under the glamour of this new experience. [*Laughter.*] My ideas even now run more on these questions which are connected with the future of the Empire than they do upon the smaller controversies upon which depend the fate of by-elections [*laughter*] and sometimes even the fate of governments. When you are 6,000 miles away from the House of Commons, it is perfectly extraordinary how events and discussions and conflicts of opinion present themselves in different—I think I may even say in truer—proportion. You are excited at home about an Education Bill[2] [*laughter*], about temperance reforms [*loud laughter*], about local finance. Yes, I should be if I had remained at home. But these things matter no more to South Africa, to Canada, to Australia than their local affairs matter to you; and, on the other hand, everything that touches Imperial policy, everything which affects their interests as well as yours, has for them, as it ought to have for us, a supreme importance. Our Imperial policy is vital to them and vital to us. Upon that Imperial policy and what you do in the next few years depends that enormous issue whether this great Empire of ours is to stand together, one free nation, if necessary, against all the world [*Hear, hear*], or whether it is to fall apart into separate states, each selfishly seeking its own interest alone, losing sight of the commonweal, and losing also all the advantages which union alone can give.

I came here, as I have said, after an experience which seems to me now almost a dream, and I find that here it has not been Imperial but local questions which were filling the minds of the people of this country. The political meteorologist had been at work [*laughter*], and had been predicting in the course of a few short months an entire change in the situation, had been predicting disaster and confusion to the Unionist Party. Meanwhile, there seemed to me to be on the part of the Opposition an unseemly exultation. They were occupied greedily apportioning out the spoils of the victory which they anticipated [*laughter*], just as the Boers before the war were casting lots for the farms which they expected to wrest from their British possessors. When I inquired what had happened to suggest the depression on the one side and the elation on the other, I was told that a reaction was in progress [*laughter*]; that the Education Bill had caused many persons to leave the Unionist Party; that caves were being formed; that younger members of the Party, tired of the monotony of a loyal support, had sought a freer and more strenuous life as troglodytes, political troglodytes, in the caves of their selection. Yet we found, however, even at the commencement that very few occupied the same cave. I was told that

---

[2] Balfour's Education Act of 1902.

the by-elections were going against the Government; I was told that the constituencies were prepared to forgive the pro-Boers their want of patriotism and the Little Englanders their want of courage, and that they were now ready to give to Home Rule and the Newcastle programme[3] a new chance. [*Laughter.*] Well, it may be that I am less sensible to sudden emotion since I returned from my travels in South Africa. The calm which is induced by the solitude of the illimitable veld may have affected my constitution. [*Laughter.*] At any rate, I was not moved by those depressing statements. I was not brought to think that my countrymen were so inclined to rapid change. I was not induced to believe the by-elections were of this excessive importance; and when I came to examine the particular elections from which so much was anticipated, when I found that in one of them the Liberal Party, so-called [*laughter*], had gained a supporter in a gentleman who proposed to hand back the Transvaal to the Boers [*laughter*], and, at the same time, had gained another supporter in a gentleman who professed himself to be a sincere Imperialist thoroughly convinced of the justice of the war—when I found that Sir Wilfrid Lawson[4] declared that he came to Parliament in order to confiscate the property of every publican, and that Dr. Hutchinson[5] came to Parliament determined to give compensation to every publican [*laughter*]—and that all of these were going to join the Liberal Party [*laughter and cheers*], it seemed to me that the combination was not so terrible. And while I was prepared to congratulate Sir Henry Campbell-Bannerman[6] on the flexibility of adaptation which his followers displayed; while I was disposed to say, as of Cleopatra, "age cannot wither nor custom stale her infinite variety" [*laughter*], I was not prepared unduly to excite myself as to the prospect of the Government and its supporters.

There must be ups and downs in politics. I have had now a long experience, and I will safely predict of any government that if it endeavours honestly to grapple with the great problems of its time it will lose a certain amount of support. You cannot deal with any domestic question and find an absolutely united party to support it; and the more bold your policy, the more drastic the changes which you propose to bring about, the more certain it is that you will pay the price, for the time at any rate, in the votes of a certain number of those whose support you greatly value. Well, but that is the business of the Government. Under ordinary circumstances the business of the Government is to spend itself doing what it thinks to be right. And, let me say, in all seriousness, that if I were assured that the main lines of our Imperial and national policy, those things which touch our

[3] Comprehensive set of reform policies adopted by the Liberal Party in October, 1891.
[4] Lawson was a strong Gladstonian who applied the term "jingo" to the more blustering followers of Disraeli.
[5] Sir Charles F. Hutchinson, Member for Sussex.
[6] With Lord Morley, Campbell-Bannerman, who served as Prime Minister from 1905 to 1908, led Liberals who opposed the Boer War.

existence, were assured, if I could tell that there was that continuity in foreign and Colonial policy which I have known to exist in past times, I for one should be very willing indeed to allow to my political opponents their chance in their turn to try their hands at the difficult domestic problems with which we have to deal. After eight years of such strenuous work as seldom falls to the lot of a politician, I can say for myself, and I believe I can say for all my colleagues, that I would rejoice if I could be relieved, at all events for a time, and if I could occupy instead of the post of a prominent actor the much more easy and less responsible post of universal critic.

But what do I want in order to face the future not only without regret, but with absolute relief and rejoicing? I want to know that the Party which would take our place has frankly abandoned that disastrous policy of Home Rule [*Hear, hear*], which would begin by the disruption of the United Kingdom and which would end in the disruption of the Empire [*Hear, hear*]; for, believe me, it is borne in upon me now more than ever, you cannot weaken the centre without destroying all that depends upon the centre. If you want an Empire you must be strong and united at home. [*Hear, hear.*] If separation begins here, take my word for it, it will not stop here. The Empire itself will be dissolved into its component atoms. If I could believe, however, that our opponents had frankly abandoned Home Rule—if Sir Henry Campbell-Bannerman, as the leader of the Party, should divest himself of that curious antagonism to everything British [*"Hear, hear" and laughter*] which makes him the friend of every country but his own—if I thought that his followers were animated by that broader patriotism by which alone our Empire can be held together, then, indeed, I would be the first to sing *nunc dimittis*.[7] [*Hear, hear.*] But this assurance is wanting. [*Hear, hear.*] I have read with care and interest all the speeches that have been made by the leaders of the Liberal Party; and in none of them do I find a frank acceptance of that national and Imperial policy which I believe at the present time is the first necessity of a united kingdom. As long as that is the case, however anxious I may be personally for rest, I confess I cannot look forward without dread of handing over the security and existence of this great Empire to the hands of those who have made common cause with its enemies [*Hear, hear*], who have charged their own countrymen with methods of barbarism [*Hear, hear*], and who apparently have been untouched by that pervading sentiment which I found everywhere where the British flag floats and which has done so much in recent years to draw us together.

I should not require to go to South Africa in order to be convinced that this feeling has obtained deep hold on the minds and hearts of our children beyond the seas. It has had a hard life of it. This feeling of Imperial

---

[7] "Now, spread the word."

patriotism was checked for a generation by the apathy and the indifference which were the characteristics of our former relations with our Colonies. It was discouraged by our apparent acceptance of the doctrines of the Little Englanders, of the provincial spirit which taught us to consider ourselves alone and to regard with indifference all that concerned those, however loyal they might be, who left these shores in order to go to our Colonies abroad. But it was never extinguished. The embers were still alight. And when in the late war[8] this old country of ours showed that it was still possessed by the spirit of our ancestors, showed that it was still prepared to count no sacrifice that was necessary in order to maintain the honour and the interests of the Empire that was committed to its charge, then you found a response from your brethren, your children across the seas, a response such as has not been known before, that astonished the world by a proof, an undeniable proof, of affection and regard. [*Cheers.*] I have said that that was a new chapter, the beginning of a new era. Is it to end there? ["*No.*"] Is it to end with the end of the war, with the termination of the crisis that brought it forth? Are we to sink that with the old policy of selfish isolation, which went very far to dry and even to sap the loyalty of our Colonial brethren? I do not think so. I think these larger issues touch the people of this country. I think they have awakened to the enormous importance of a creative time like the present, taking advantage of the opportunities that are offered in order to make permanent what has begun so well. Remember, we are a kingdom, an old country. We proceed here upon settled lines. We have our quarrels and our disputes and we pass legislation which may be good or bad, but which, at any rate, can be altered; but we go towards an object which is sufficiently defined. We know that whatever changes there may be, whatever meandering of the current, at all events the main stream ultimately reaches its appointed destination. That is the result of centuries of constitutional progress and freedom, but the Empire is not old. The Empire is new, the Empire is in its infancy. Now is the time when we can mould that Empire and when we and those who live with us can decide its future destinies.

Just let us consider what that Empire is. I am not going tonight to speak of those millions, hundreds of millions, of our Indian and native fellow-subjects for whom we have become responsible. It is upon us that the obligation lies to give them good government and in every way to promote their development and prosperity; and some day it might be worth my while, and it might be possible for me to discuss with you, to confer with you upon all the important questions which such an enormous obligation imposes. But tonight I put that aside, and I consider only our relations to our own kinsfolk, to that white British population that constitutes the majority in the great self-governing Colonies of the Empire. What is our

[8] The Boer War.

position in regard to them? Here in the United Kingdom there are some forty millions of us; outside there are ten millions of men either directly descended from ancestors who left this country or more probably men who themselves in their youth left this country in order to find their fortunes in our possessions abroad. Now how long do you suppose that this proportion of population is going to endure? How long are we going to be four times as many as our kinsfolk abroad? The development of those Colonies has been delayed by many reasons—partly, as I think, by our inaction, partly by the provincial spirit which we have not done enough to discourage, that spirit which attaches undue importance to the local incidents and legislation of each separate state and gives insufficient regard to the interests of the whole—but mainly probably by a more material reason, by the fact that the United States of America has offered a greater attraction to British emigration. But that has changed. The United States of America with all their vast territory are filling up; and even now we hear of thousands and tens of thousands of emigrants leaving the United States of America in order to take up the fresh and rich lands of our Colony of Canada. And it seems to me to be not at all an impossible assumption that before the end of the present century we may find that our population, our fellow-subjects beyond the seas, may be as numerous as we are at home.

I want you to look forward. I want you to consider the infinite importance of this not only to yourselves but to your descendants. Now is the time when you can exert influence. Do you wish that if these ten millions become forty millions they shall still be closely, intimately, affectionately united to you? [*Cheers.*] Or do you contemplate the possibility of their being separated, going off each in his own direction under a separate flag? Think what it means to your power and influence as a country; think what it means to your position among the nations of the world; think what it means to your trade and commerce. I put that last. The influence of the Empire is the thing I think most about; and that influence I believe will always be used for the peace and civilisation of the world. [*Hear, hear.*] But the question of trade and commerce is one of the greatest importance. Unless that is satisfactorily settled, I for one do not believe in a continued union of the Empire. I am told—I hear it stated again and again by what I believe to be the representatives of a small minority of the people of this country, those whom I describe, because I know no other words for them, as "Little Englanders"—I hear it stated by them, what is a fact, that our trade with those countries is much less than our trade in foreign countries; and therefore it appears to be their opinion that we should do everything in our power to cultivate that trade with foreigners and that we can safely disregard the trade with our children. Now, Sir, that is not my conclusion. [*Cheers.*] My conclusion is exactly the opposite. [*Renewed cheers.*]

Look into the future. I say it is the business of British statesmen to do everything they can, even at some present sacrifice, to keep the trade of the Colonies with Great Britain [*cheers*], to increase the trade, to promote it, even if in doing so we lessen somewhat the trade with our foreign competitors. ["*Hear, hear*" *and cheers.*] Are we doing everything at the present time to direct the patriotic movement which I see not only here, but through all the Colonies, in the right channel? Are we, in fact—by our legislation, by our action—are we making for union or are we drifting to separation? That is a critical issue. In my opinion the germs of a federal union that will make the British Empire powerful and influential for good beyond the dreams of anyone now living—the germs of that union are in the soil; but it is a tender and delicate plant and requires careful handling. [*Hear, hear.*]

I wish you would look back to our history. Consider what might have been, in order that you may be influenced now to do what is right. Supposing, when self-government was first conceded to these Colonies, the statesmen who gave it had had any idea of the possibilities of the future. Do you not see that they might have laid broad and firm the foundations of an Imperial edifice of which every part would have contributed something to the strength of the whole? But in those days the one idea of statesmen was to get rid of the whole business. They believed that separation must come. What they wanted to do was to make it smooth and easy; and none of these ideas which subsequent experience has put into our minds appears ever to have been suggested to them. By their mistakes and their neglect our task has been made more difficult—more difficult, but not impossible. [*Hear, hear.*] There is still time to consolidate the Empire. We also have our chance, and it depends upon what we do now whether this great idea is to find fruition or whether we will for ever and ever dismiss it from our consideration and accept our fate as one of the dying empires of the world.

Now, what is the meaning of an empire? What does it mean to us? We have had a little experience. We have had a war—a war in which the majority of our children abroad had no apparent direct interest. We had no hold over them, no agreement with them of any kind; and yet at one time during this war, by the voluntary decision of these people, at least 50,000 Colonial soldiers were standing shoulder to shoulder with British troops, displaying a gallantry equal to their own and the keenest intelligence. [*Loud cheers.*] It is something for a beginning; and if this country were in danger—I mean if we were, as our forefathers were, face to face some day, Heaven forfend, with some great coalition of hostile nations—then, when we had with our backs to the wall to struggle for our very lives, it is my firm conviction that there is nothing within the power of these self-governing Colonies they would not do to come to our aid. I believe their whole resources in men and in money would be at the disposal of the mother country in such an event. Well, as I say, that is something—that is something which it is wonderful to have achieved, which it is worth almost any sacrifice to maintain.

So far as personal sacrifices are involved, risking your life and encountering every hardship, the Colonies did their duty in the late war. If it came to another question, the question of the share they bore in the pecuniary burden which the war involved, well, I think they might have done more. [*Hear, hear.*] I did not hesitate to tell my fellow-subjects in the colonies of South Africa, whether in the new colonies or in the old ones, that though they had done much, they had not done enough, they had left substantially the whole burden on the shoulders of the mother country; and that in the future, if they valued Empire and its privileges, they must be prepared to take a greater share of the obligations. [*Hear, hear.*] If I had been speaking in Australia or in Canada I would have said the same thing [*Hear, hear*], and perhaps I should have been inclined to say it even in stronger terms; and, if I may judge by the reception of my utterances in South Africa, I should give no offence by this frank speaking. [*Hear, hear.*] There is something, however, to be remembered on behalf of our Colonies, and that is that this idea of a common responsibility is altogether a new one, and we have done nothing to encourage it. It is presented to them in the light of a new tax, and people have an extraordinary way of regarding a new tax with a suspicion [*laughter*], and even with dislike. [*Hear, hear.*] But what happened? I spoke in Natal, and the people of Natal responded by taking upon their shoulders a burden which for a small colony was considerable, and which they had thought of placing upon ourselves. I spoke in the Transvaal; and the representatives of every class in the Transvaal, and none more enthusiastically than the working people, took upon themselves a burden of £80 per head of the white population, a burden which, indeed, the riches of the country justified, but which was something altogether in excess of any similar obligation placed upon any other country in the world. [*Hear, hear.*] I spoke in Cape Colony, and only in Cape Colony, owing to the division of opinion which has prevailed there, I neither expected nor asked for a contribution towards the war. I do expect—I do not know whether I shall be disappointed—but I do expect in the time to come Dutch and English will both feel, as the Empire belongs to them as well as to us, bound towards the future expenditure of the country to contribute more liberally than they have done in the past. Well, all have done something; and, to my mind, it is a great thing to get the principle accepted; and I think it depends upon us whether in future the application of this principle should be made with greater liberality or whether, as I have said, we are all to fall back each to care for himself and "the devil take the hindmost." [*Laughter.*]

Sir, my idea of British policy, I mean the policy of the United Kingdom, is that here, at the beginning of things, at the beginning of this new chapter, we should show our appreciation, our cordial appreciation, of the first step to be taken by our Colonies to show their solidarity with us. Every advance which they make should be reciprocated. We should set ourselves a great example of community of interest, and, above all, that community of sacrifice on which alone the Empire can permanently rest. I have admitted that the Colonies have hitherto been backward in their contributions towards Imperial defence. They are following their own lines. I hope they will do better. But in the meantime they are doing a great deal, and they are trying to promote this union which I regard as of so much importance in their own way and by their own means.

And first among those means is the offer of preferential tariffs. [*Cheers.*] Now, that is a matter which at the present moment is of the greatest possible importance to every one of you. It depends upon how we treat this policy of the Colonies—not a policy inaugurated by us, but a policy which comes to us from our children abroad—it depends upon how we treat it, whether it is developed in the future or whether it is withdrawn as being non-acceptable to those whom it is sought to benefit. The other day, immediately after I left South Africa, a great conference[9] was held for the first time of all the colonies in South Africa, the new colonies as well as the old. Boers and the Dutch were represented as well as the British. And this conference recommended the other legislatures of the different colonies to give to us, the mother country, preference upon all dutiable goods of 25 per cent. [*Cheers.*] Last year at the Conference of Premiers, the representatives of Australia and New Zealand accepted the same principle. They said in their different colonies there might be some difference of treatment; but so far as the principle was concerned they pledged themselves to recommend to their constituents a substantial preference in favour of goods produced in the mother country. Now, that again is a new chapter in our Imperial history; and again I ask is it to end there? In my opinion, these recommendations and these pledges will bear fruit just in proportion as you show your appreciation of them; and they will depend largely upon the experience of Canada, which has been their precursor in a similar movement.

Canada is the greatest, the most prosperous of our self-governing Colonies. At the present time it is in the full swing of an extraordinary prosperity, which, I hope—I believe—will lead to a great increase in its population, its strength, its importance in the constellation of free nations which constitutes the British Empire. Canada is of all our Colonies the most backward in contributing to common defence; but Canada has been the most forward in endeavouring to unite the Empire by the other means of strengthening our commercial relations and by giving to us special favour and preference. If we appreciate this action properly it seems to me that

---

[9] Intercolonial Conference held at Bloemfontein in March, 1903. A Customs Union was established for South Africa and policies were forged which would allow for free intercolonial exchange of produce and goods.

not only is it certain that every other Colony of the Empire will necessarily and in due time follow this example, but Canada herself and the other Colonies also, as the bonds are drawn closer, as we become more and more one people united by interest as well as by sentiment, will be more and more ready to take its fair share in these burdens of defence to which I have referred.

Now, what has Canada done for us? Let me say, however, before I come to that that my policy which I wish to make clear to you is not to force our Colonies—that is hopeless; they are as independent as we are—but to meet everything they do. If they see a way of drawing the Empire together, let us help them in that, even if they may not be prepared to join us in some other way from which we think the same result would be achieved. But let us be prepared to accept every indication on their part of this desire. Let us show we appreciate it, and believe me it will not be long before all will come into line; and the results which follow will be greater than perhaps it would be prudent now to anticipate. Well, I say, what has Canada done for us? Canada in 1898 freely, voluntarily of her own accord, as a recognition of her obligations to the mother country, as a recognition especially of the fact that we were the greatest of the free markets open to Canadian produce, gave us a preference on all dutiable goods of 25 per cent. In 1900 she increased that preference, also freely of her own accord, to 33.3 per cent. [*Cheers.*]

I have had occasion to point out that the results of this great concession have been to a certain extent in some respects disappointing. The increase in our trade with Canada has been very great, but it has not increased largely out of proportion to the increase of the trade between Canada and other countries; but this remains true, that whereas before these concessions the trade of this country with Canada was constantly reducing, getting less and less, that reduction had been stayed and the trade has continually increased. [*Hear, hear.*] And to put it in a word, the trade between our Colony of Canada and the mother country, which was £6,500,000 in 1897-1898, is now carried on at a rate of probably a good deal more; but at all events I will say, to be safe, of £11,000,000 sterling in the present year [*cheers*], and the increase is chiefly in textile goods, cotton, woollen, and goods of that kind, and in manufactures of hardware and iron and steel. At the same time, whereas the percentage of the total trade had fallen from 40 per cent, I think, or at all events from a large percentage, to 23.5 per cent in these last two years, it has been gradually climbing up again and it has now reached for the present year 26.5 per cent.

Well, that is an important result; but the Ministers of Canada when they were over here last year made me a further definite offer. They said: "We have done for you as much as we can do voluntarily and freely and without return. If you are willing to reciprocate in any way, we are prepared to reconsider our tariff with a view of seeing whether we cannot give you further reductions, especially in regard to those goods in which you come into competition with foreigners, and we will do this if you will meet us by giving us a drawback on the small tax of 1*s*. which you have put upon corn." That was an offer which we had to refuse. I must say that, if I could treat matters of this kind solely in regard to my position as Secretary of State for the Colonies, I should have said, "That is a fair offer; that is a generous offer from your point of view, and it is an offer which we might ask our people to accept." But, speaking for the Government as a whole, not in the interests of the Colonies, I am obliged to say that it is contrary to the established fiscal policy of this country, and that we hold ourselves bound to keep an open market for all the world even if they close their markets to us [*laughter*], and that, therefore, so long as that is the mandate of the British public, we are not in a position to offer any preference or favour whatever even to our own children. We cannot make any difference between those who treat us well and those who treat us badly. ["*Shame.*"] Yes; but that is the doctrine which I am told is the accepted doctrine of the free-trader; and we are all free-traders. ["*No, no*" *and laughter.*] Well, I am. [*Loud laughter.*] I have considerable doubt whether the interpretation of free trade which is current amongst a certain limited section is the true interpretation. [*Hear, hear.*] But I am perfectly certain that I am not a protectionist. But I want to point out that if the interpretation is that our only duty is to buy in the cheapest market without regard to whether we can sell, if that is the theory of free trade which finds acceptance here and elsewhere, then in pursuance of that policy you will have to forgo the advantage of a reduction, a further reduction, in duty which your great Colony of Canada offers to you manufacturers of this country; and you may lose a great deal more, because in the speech which the Chancellor of the Exchequer,[10] the Minister of Finance as he is called in Canada, made to the Canadian Parliament the other day, which he has just sent me, I find he says that if we are told definitely Great Britain, the mother country, can do nothing for us in the way of reciprocity we must reconsider our position and reconsider the preference that we have already given.

Well, these are big questions, and this particular question is complicated in a rather unexpected manner. The policy which prevents us from offering an advantage to our Colonies prevents us from defending them if they are attacked. Now I suppose you and I are agreed that the British Empire is one and indivisible. [*Cheers.*] You and I are agreed that we absolutely refuse to look upon any of the states that form the British Empire as in any way excluded from any advantage or privilege to which the British Empire is entitled. We may well, therefore, have supposed an agreement of this kind by which Canada does a kindness to us a matter of family agreement

---

[10] William Stevens Fielding.

concerning nobody else; but unfortunately Germany thinks otherwise. There is a German Empire. The German Empire is divided into states—Bavaria and, let us say, Hanover, Saxony, and Würtemberg. They may deal between themselves in any way they please. As a matter of fact, they have entire free trade among themselves. We do not consider them separate entities; we treat the German Empire as a whole. We do not complain because one state gives an advantage to another state in that Empire and does not give it to all the rest of the world. But in this case of Canada, Germany insists upon treating Canada as though it were a separate country, refuses to recognise it as a part of one Empire, entitled to claim, as I have said, the privileges of that Empire, regards this agreement as being something more than a domestic agreement; and it has penalised Canada by placing upon Canadian goods an additional duty.

Well, now, the reason for that is clear. The German newspapers very frankly explain that this is a policy of reprisal, and that it is intended to deter other colonies from giving to us the same advantage. Therefore, it is not merely punishment inflicted by Germany upon Canada, but it is a threat to South Africa, to Australia, and to New Zealand; and this policy, as a policy of dictation and interference, is justified by the belief that we are so wedded to our fiscal system that we cannot interfere, that we cannot defend our Colonies, and that in fact any one of them which attempts to establish any kind of special relations with us does so at her own risk and must be left to bear the brunt of foreign hostility. In my mind that is putting us in a rather humiliating position. [*Hear, hear.*] I do not like it at all. I know what will follow if we allow it to prevail. It is easy to predict the consequences. How do you think that under such circumstances we can approach our Colonies with appeals to aid us in promoting the union of the Empire, or ask them to bear a share of the common burden? Are we to say to them, "This is your Empire, take pride in it, share its privileges?" They say: "What are its privileges? The privileges appear to be if we treat you as relations and friends, if we show you kindness, we give you preference; you who benefit by our action can only leave us alone to fight our own battles against those who are offended by our action." Now, is that free trade? ["*No.*"] I am not going further tonight. ["*Go on.*"] My object is to put the position before you; and above all, as I have just come home from great colonies, I want you to see these matters as they appear to our Colonial fellow-subjects. There is no doubt what they think, and there is no doubt of what great issues hang upon their decision.

I said just now, is this free trade? No, it is absolutely a new situation. [*Cheers.*] There has been nothing like it in our history. It was a situation that was never contemplated by any of those whom we regard as the authors of free trade. What would Mr. Bright, what would Mr. Cobden, have said to this state of things? I do not know. It would be presumptuous to imagine; but this I can say. Mr. Cobden did not hesitate to make a treaty of preference and reciprocity with France [*Hear, hear*], and Mr. Bright did not hesitate to approve his action; and I cannot believe if they had been present among us now and known what this new situation was, I cannot believe that they would have hesitated to make a treaty of preference and reciprocity with our own children. [*Loud and prolonged cheers.*]

Well, you see the point. You want an Empire. [*Hear, hear.*] Do you think it better to cultivate the trade with your own people or to let that go in order that you may keep the trade of those who, rightly enough, are your competitors and rivals? I say it is a new position. I say the people of this Empire have got to consider it. I do not want to hasten their decision. They have two alternatives before them. They may maintain, if they like, in all its severity the interpretation—in my mind an entirely artificial and wrong interpretation—which has been placed upon the doctrines of free trade by a small remnant of Little Englanders of the Manchester school[11] who now profess to be the sole repositories of the doctrines of Mr. Cobden and Mr. Bright. They may maintain that policy in all its severity, although it is repudiated by every other nation and by all your own Colonies. In that case they will be absolutely precluded either from giving any kind of preference or favour to any of their Colonies abroad or even protecting their Colonies abroad when they offer to favour us. That is the first alternative. The second alternative is that we should insist that we will not be bound by any purely technical definition of free trade, that, while we seek as one chief object free interchange of trade and commerce between ourselves and all the nations of the world, we will nevertheless recover our freedom, resume that power of negotiation, and, if necessary, retaliation [*loud cheers*], whenever our own interests or our relations between our Colonies and ourselves are threatened by other people. [*Cheers.*]

I leave the matter in your hands. I desire that a discussion on this subject should be opened. The time has not yet come to settle it; but it seems to me that for good or for evil this is an issue much greater in its consequences than any of our local disputes. [*Hear, hear.*] Make a mistake in legislation, yet it can be corrected; make a mistake in your Imperial policy, it is irretrievable. You have an opportunity; you will never have it again.

I do not think myself that a General Election is very near [*laughter*]; but, whether it is near or distant, I think our opponents may perhaps find that the issues which they propose to raise are not the issues on which we shall take the opinion of the country. [*Cheers.*] If we raise an issue of this kind, the answer will depend not upon petty personal considerations, not upon temporary interests, but upon whether the people of this country really have it in their hearts to do all that is necessary, even if it occasionally goes against their own prejudices, to consolidate an Empire which can

---

[11] The reference is probably to "pro-Boers" such as Campbell-Bannerman, Lloyd George, and John Morley.

only be maintained by relations of interest as well as by relations of sentiment. For my own part I believe in a British Empire, in an Empire which, although it should be its first duty to cultivate friendship with all the nations of the world, should yet, even if alone, be self-sustaining and self-sufficient, able to maintain itself against the competition of all its rivals; and I do not believe in a Little England which shall be separated from all those to whom it would in the natural course look for support and affection, a Little England which would then be dependent absolutely on the mercy of those who envy its present prosperity, and who have shown they are ready to do all in their power to prevent its future union with the British races throughout the world. [*Loud and continued cheers.*]

Harold Macmillan

"The Wind of Change"*
Cape Town, February 3, 1960

It is a great privilege to be invited to address the members of both Houses of Parliament in the Union. It is a unique privilege to do so in 1960, just half a century after the Parliament of the Union came to birth. I am most grateful to you all for giving me this opportunity, and I am especially grateful to your Prime Minister[1] who invited me to visit your country and who arranged for me to address you here today. This tour of Africa—the first ever made by a British Prime Minister in office—is now, alas, near its end. But it is fitting that it should culminate in the Union Parliament here in Cape Town—in this historic city so long Europe's gateway to the Indian Ocean and the East.

In the Union, as in all the other countries I have visited, my stay has been all too short. I wish it could have been possible for me to spend longer here, to see more of your beautiful country and to get to know more of your people. But in the past week I have travelled many hundreds of miles and met many people from all walks of life. I have been able to get at least some idea of the great beauty of South Africa's countryside, with its farms and forests, mountains and rivers, and the clear skies and wide horizons of the veld. I have seen some of the great and thriving cities. I am most grateful to your Government for all the trouble they have taken to enable me to see so much in so short a time. Some of the younger members of my staff have told me that it has been a heavy programme, but I can give the assurance that my wife and I have enjoyed every moment of it. Wherever we have gone, in town or in country, we have been received in a spirit of friendship and affection, which has warmed our hearts. And we value this the more because we know that it is an expression of your goodwill, not only to ourselves, but to all the people of Britain.

---

* This text is taken from *The Cape Argus* (Cape Town, South Africa), February 3, 1960, pp. 1–2, a fuller version than that supplied by *The Times*, February 4, 1960, p. 15.

[1] Dr. H. F. Verwoerd.

It is a special privilege for me to be here in 1960, when the people are celebrating what I may call the golden wedding of the Union. At such a time it is natural and right that the people should pause to take stock of their position—to look back at what you have achieved, to look forward to what lies ahead.

In the fifty years of nationhood, the people of South Africa have built a strong economy founded on a healthy agriculture and thriving and resilient industries. During my visit I have been able to see something of the mining industry on which the prosperity of the country is so firmly based. I have seen the Iron and Steel Corporation and visited the Council for Scientific and Industrial Research at Pretoria. These two bodies in their different ways are symbols of a lively, forward-looking, and expanding economy. I have seen the great city of Durban with its wonderful port, and the skyscrapers of Johannesburg standing where, seventy years ago, there was nothing but the open veld. I have seen, too, the fine cities of Pretoria and Bloemfontein. This afternoon I hope to see something of your wine-growing industry, which so far I have admired only as a consumer. [*Laughter.*]

No one could fail to be impressed with the immense material progress which has been achieved. All this accomplished in so short a time is a striking testimony to the initiative, energy, and skill of your people. We in Britain are proud of the contribution we have made to this remarkable achievement. Much of it has been financed by British capital. According to a recent survey made by the Union Government, nearly two-thirds of the overseas investment outstanding in the Union at the end of 1956 was British. That is after two staggering wars which have bled our economy white. But that is not all. We have developed trade between us to our common advantage, and our economies are now largely interdependent. You export to us raw materials and food—and, of course, gold—and we in return send you consumer goods and capital equipment. We take a third of all your exports and we supply a third of all your imports. This broad, traditional pattern of investment and trade has been maintained in spite of the changes brought about by the development of our two economies.

It gives me great encouragement to reflect that the economies of both our countries, while expanding rapidly, have yet remained interdependent and capable of sustaining one another. If you travel round this country by train you will travel on South African rails made by Iscor; but if you prefer to fly you can go in a British Viscount. Here is true partnership; living proof of the interdependence between nations. Britain has always been your best customer, and as your new industries develop we believe we can be your best partners, too.

In addition to building this strong economy within your own borders, you have also played your part as an independent nation in world affairs. As a soldier in World War I and as a Minister in Sir Winston Churchill's

Government in the Second, I know personally the value of the contribution which your forces made to history in the cause of freedom. I know something too of the inspiration which General Smuts brought to us in Britain in our darkest hours. Again, in the Korean crisis, you played your full part. Thus, in the testing times of war or aggression your statesmen and your soldiers have made their influence felt far beyond the African continent.

In the period of reconstruction when Dr. Malan was your Prime Minister, your resources greatly assisted the recovery of the sterling area in the post-war world. Now in the no less difficult tasks of peace, your leaders in industry, commerce, and finance continue to be prominent in world affairs. Today, your readiness to provide technical assistance to the less well-developed parts of Africa is of immense help to the countries that receive it. It is also a source of strength to your friends in the Commonwealth and elsewhere in the Western world. You are collaborating in the work of the Commission for Technical Co-operation in Africa South of the Sahara, and now, in the United Nations Economic Commission for Africa. Your Minister of External Affairs[2] intends to visit Ghana later this year. All this proves your determination as the most advanced industrial country of the continent to play your part in the new Africa of today.

As I have travelled through the Union I have found everywhere, as I expected, a deep pre-occupation with what is happening to the rest of the African continent. I understand and sympathise with your interest in these events and your anxiety about them.

Ever since the break-up of the Roman Empire one of the constant facts of political life in Europe has been the emergence of independent nations. They have come into existence over the centuries in different forms with different forms of government. But all have been inspired with a keen feeling of nationalism, which has grown as the nations have grown. In the twentieth century, and especially since the end of the war, the processes which gave birth to the nation states of Europe have been repeated all over the world. We have seen the awakening of national consciousness in peoples who have for centuries lived in dependence on some other power. Fifteen years ago this movement spread through Asia. Many countries there, of different races and civilisations, pressed their claim to an independent national life. Today the same thing is happening in Africa.

The most striking of all the impressions I have formed since I left London a month ago is of the strength of this African national consciousness. In different places it takes different forms, but it is happening everywhere. The wind of change is blowing throughout the continent. Whether we like it or not, this growth of national consciousness is a political fact. We must all accept it as a fact. Our national policies must take account of it.

[2] E. H. Louw.

Of course, you understand this better than anyone. You are sprung from Europe, the home of nationalism. And here in Africa you have yourselves created a free nation, a new nation. Indeed, in the history of our times yours will be recorded as the first of the African nationalisms. And this tide of national consciousness which is now rising in Africa is a fact for which you and we and the other nations of the Western world are ultimately responsible. For its causes are to be found in the achievements of Western civilisation, in the pushing forward the frontiers of knowledge, the applying of science to the service of human needs, in the expanding of food production, in the speeding and multiplying of the means of communication, and, above all, spreading education.

As I have said, the growth of national consciousness in Africa is a political fact and we must accept it as such. This means, I would judge, that we must come to terms with it. I sincerely believe that if we cannot do so, we may imperil the precarious balance between East and West on which the peace of the world depends.

The world today is divided into three main groups. First, there are what we call the Western powers. You in South Africa and we in Britain belong to this group, together with our friends and Allies in other parts of the Commonwealth, in the United States of America, and in Europe. We call it the free world. Secondly, there are the communists: Russia and her satellites in Europe, and China, whose population will rise by 1970 to the staggering total of 800 million. Thirdly, there are those parts of the world whose people are at present uncommitted either to communism or to our Western ideas. In this context we think first of Asia and of Africa.

As I see it, the great issue in this second half of the twentieth century is whether the uncommitted peoples of Asia and Africa will swing to the East or to the West. [*Mr. Macmillan said this thumping his desk in emphasis.*] Will they be drawn into the communist camp? Or will the great experiments of self-government that are now being made in Asia and Africa, especially within the Commonwealth, prove so successful and by their example so compelling that the balance will come down in favour of freedom and order and justice? The struggle is joined, and it is a struggle for the minds of men. What is now on trial is much more than our military strength or our diplomatic or administrative skill. It is our way of life.

The uncommitted nations want to see before they choose. What can we show them to help them choose aright? Each of the independent members of the Commonwealth must answer that question for itself. It is a basic principle of our modern Commonwealth that we respect each other's sovereignty in matters of internal policy. At the same time we must recognise that in this shrinking world in which we live today, the internal policies of one nation may have effects outside it. We may sometimes be tempted to say to each other: "Mind your own business." But in these days I would expand the old saying so that it runs: "Mind your own business, of course, but mind how it affects my business, too."

Let me be very frank with you, my friends. What governments and parliaments in the United Kingdom have done since the last war in according independence to India, Pakistan, Ceylon, Malaya, and Ghana, and what they will do for Nigeria and other countries now nearing independence—all this, though we take full and sole responsibility for it, we do in the belief that it is the only way to establish the future of the Commonwealth and of the free world on sound foundations. All this, of course, is also of deep and close concern to you. For nothing we do in this small world can be done in a corner or remain hidden. What we do today in West, Central, and East Africa becomes known tomorrow to everyone in the Union, whatever his language, colour, or traditions.

Let me assure you in all friendliness that we are well aware of this, and that we have acted and will act with full knowledge of the responsibility we have to you and to all our friends. Nevertheless, I am sure you will agree that in our own areas of responsibility we must each do what we think right. What we British think right derives from a long experience both of failure and success in the management of these affairs. We have tried to learn and to apply the lessons of both. Our judgment of right and wrong and of justice is rooted in the same soil as yours—in Christianity and in the rule of law as the basis of a free society.

This experience of our own explains why it has been our aim, in the countries for which we have borne responsibility, not only to raise the material standards of living, but to create a society which respects the rights of individuals—a society in which men are given the opportunity to grow to their full stature, and that must in our view include the opportunity to have an increasing share in political power and responsibility; a society, finally, in which individual merit, and individual merit alone, is the criterion for a man's advancement, whether political or economic. Finally, in countries inhabited by several different races, it has been our aim to find means by which the community can become more of a community and fellowship can be fostered between its various parts.

This problem is by no means confined to Africa. Nor is it always a problem of a European minority. In Malaya, for instance, though there are Indian and European minorities, Malays and Chinese make up the great bulk of the population, and the Chinese are not much fewer in numbers than the Malays. Yet these two peoples must learn to live together in harmony and unity, and the strength and future of Malaya as a nation will depend on the different contributions which the two races can make.

The attitude of the United Kingdom Government towards this problem was clearly expressed by the Foreign Secretary,[3] speaking at the United

[3] Selwyn Lloyd.

Nations General Assembly on the 17th of September last year. These were his words:

> In those territories where different races or tribes live side by side, the task is to ensure that all the people may enjoy security and freedom and the chance to contribute as individuals to the progress and well-being of these countries. We reject the idea of any inherent superiority of one race over another. Our policy, therefore, is non-racial; it offers a future in which Africans, Europeans, Asians, the peoples of the Pacific, and others with whom we are concerned will all play their full part as citizens in the countries where they live, and in which feeling of race will be submerged in loyalty to new nations.

I have thought you would wish me to state plainly and with full candour the policy for which we in Britain stand. It may well be that, in trying to do our duty as we see it, we shall sometimes make difficulties for you. If this proves to be so, we much regret it. But I know that, even so, you would not ask us to flinch from doing our duty. You too will do your duty as you see it.

I am well aware of the peculiar nature of the problems with which you are faced here in the Union. I know the differences between your situation and that of most of the many other states in Africa. You have here some three million people of European origin. This country is their home. It had been their home for many generations. They have no other. The same is broadly true of Europeans in Central and East Africa. In most other African states those who have come from Europe have come to work, to contribute their skills, perhaps to teach; but not to make a home. That is quite a different problem. The problems to which you as Members of the Union Parliament have to address yourselves are very different from those which face the parliaments of countries with homogeneous populations. Of course, I realize these are hard, difficult, and sometimes baffling problems.

It would be surprising if your interpretation of your duty did not sometimes produce very different results from ours in terms of Government policies and actions. As a fellow member of the Commonwealth we have always tried to give South Africa our support and encouragement, but I hope you will not mind my saying frankly that there are some aspects of your policies which make it impossible for us to do this without being false to our own deep convictions about the political destinies of free men, to which in our own territories we are trying to give effect. I think we ought, as friends, to face together—without seeking to apportion credit or blame—the fact that in the world of today this difference of outlook lies between us.

I said that I was speaking as a friend. I can also claim to be speaking as a relation. For we Scots can claim family connexions with both the great European sections of your people, not only with the English-speaking people, but with the Afrikaans-speaking people. This is a point which hardly needs emphasis in Cape Town, where you can see every day the statue of that great Scotsman, Andrew Murray. His work in the Dutch Reformed Church, in the Cape, and the work of his son in the Free State, was among Afrikaans-speaking people. There has always been a very close connexion between the Church of Scotland and the Church of the Netherlands. The Synod of Dort plays the same great part in the history of both. Many aspirants to the ministry of Scotland, especially in the seventeenth and eighteenth centuries, went to pursue their theological studies in the Netherlands. I think Scotland can claim to have repaid its debt to South Africa. I am thinking particularly of the Scots in the Free State, not only the younger Andrew Murray but also the Robertsons, the Frasers, the McDonalds, families who have been called "the Free State clans," who became burgers of the old Free State and whose descendants still play their part there.

But, though I count myself a Scot, my mother was an American. And the United States provides a valuable illustration of one of the main points which I have been trying to make today. The population of America, like yours, is a blend of many different strains, and, over the years, most of those who have gone to North America have gone there to escape conditions in Europe which they found intolerable. The Pilgrim Fathers were escaping from persecution as Puritans—the Marylanders were escaping from persecution as Catholics. Throughout the nineteenth century a stream of immigrants flowed across the Atlantic to escape from the poverty in their home lands. And in the twentieth century the United States has provided asylum for the victims of political oppression in Europe. Thus for the majority of its inhabitants, America has been a place of refuge— a place to which people went because they wanted to get away from Europe.

It is not surprising, therefore, that for many years a main objective of American statesmen, supported by the American public opinion, was to isolate themselves from Europe; and with their great material strength and the vast resources open to them, this might have seemed an attractive and a practical course. Nevertheless, in the two world wars of this century, they have found themselves unable to stand aside. Twice their manpower in arms has streamed back across the Atlantic to shed its blood in those European struggles from which their ancestors thought they had escaped by emigrating to the New World. And when the second war was over, they were forced to recognise that in the small world of today isolationism is out of date and more than that offers no assurance of security.

The fact is that in this modern world no country, not even the greatest, can live for itself alone. Nearly 2,000 years ago, when the whole of the civilised world was comprised within the confines of the Roman Empire, St. Paul proclaimed one of the great truths of history: "We are all members one of another."[4] During this twentieth century that eternal truth has taken on a new and exciting significance. It has always been impossible for the individual man to live in isolation from his fellows—in the home, the tribe, the village, or the city. Today it is impossible for nations to live in isolation from one another.

What Dr. John Donne said of individual men 300 years ago is true today of my country, your country, and every other country in the world:

> Any man's death diminishes me,
> Because I am involved in mankind.
> And therefore never send to know
> For whom the bell tolls:
> It tolls for thee.[5]

All nations now are interdependent one upon another. This is generally recognised in the Western world, and I hope that in due course the countries of communism will recognise it too.

It was certainly with that thought in mind that I took the decision to visit Moscow about this time last year. Russia has been isolationist in her time and still has tendencies that way, but the fact remains that we must live in the same world with Russia and we must find a way to do so. I believe that the initiative which we took last year has had some success, although grave difficulties may arise. Nevertheless, I think nothing but good can come out of extending contacts between individuals, contacts in trade, and from the exchange of visitors.

The members of the Commonwealth feel particularly strongly the value of interdependence. They are as independent as any countries in this shrinking world can be, but they have voluntarily agreed to work together. I certainly do not believe in refusing to trade with people just because you dislike the way they manage their internal affairs at home. Boycotts will never get you anywhere. Here I would like to say, in parenthesis, I deprecate the attempts which are being made in Britain today to organise a consumer boycott of South African goods. [*Hear, hear.*]

I and my colleagues in the United Kingdom Government deplore this proposed boycott and regard it as undesirable from every point of view. It can only have serious effects on Commonwealth relations and trade and be to the ultimate detriment of others than those against whom it is aimed. It has never been the practice of any Government in the United Kingdom, of whatever complexion, to undertake or support campaigns of this kind designed to influence the internal policies of another Commonwealth country. I and my colleagues recognise that there may be differences between them, in their institutions or in their internal policies, and membership

---

[4] Romans 12:5.
[5] "Devotions, XVII."

does not imply either the wish to express a judgment on these matters or the need to impose a stifling uniformity.

It is, I think, a help that there has never been a question of any rigid constitution for the Commonwealth. Perhaps this is because we have got on well enough in the United Kingdom without a written constitution and tend to look suspiciously at them. Whether that is so or not, it is quite clear that a rigid constitutional framework for the Commonwealth would not work. At the first of the stresses and strains which are inevitable in this period of history, cracks would appear in the framework and the whole structure would crumble. It is the flexibility of our Commonwealth institutions which gives them their strength.

The independent members of the Commonwealth do not always all agree on every subject. It is not a condition of their association that they should do so. On the contrary, the strength of our Commonwealth lies largely in the fact that it is a free association of free and independent sovereign states, each responsible for ordering its own affairs, but cooperating in the pursuit of common aims and purposes in world affairs.

Moreover, these differences may be transitory. In time, they may be resolved. Our duty is to see them in perspective against the background of our long association. Of this, at any rate, I am certain. Those of us who, by the grace of the electorate, are temporarily in charge of affairs in my country and in yours have no right to sweep aside on this account the friendship that exists between our two countries. For this is the legacy of history. It is not ours alone to deal with as we wish.

We must face the differences. But let us try to see beyond them down the long vista of the future. I hope—indeed I am confident—that in another fifty years we shall look back on the differences that exist now between us as matters of historical interest. For as time passes and one generation yields to another, human problems change and fade. Let us remember these truths. Let us resolve to build, not to destroy. And let us remember always that weakness comes from division, and strength comes from unity.

THE REFORM JANUS.

2

Constitution and Parliamentary Reform

Lord John Russell

"Reform of Parliament"*
Commons, March 1, 1831

I rise, Sir, with feelings of the deepest anxiety to bring forward a question which, unparalleled as it is in importance, is as unparalleled in difficulties. Nor is my anxiety in approaching this question lessened by reflecting that on former occasions I have brought this subject before the consideration of the House. For if, on other occasions, I have invited the attention of the House of Commons to this most important subject, it has been upon my own responsibility—unaided by any one—and involving no one in the consequences of defeat. And although in most instances my projects of reform have been entirely frustrated, I have sometimes been gratified with partial success. But the measure which I have now to bring forward is a measure not of mine, but of the Government, in whose name I appear; it is the deliberate measure of the whole Cabinet, unanimous upon this subject; it has only been reserved to me to place it before the House as their measure, and in redemption of the solemn pledge which they have given to their Sovereign, to Parliament, and to the country. It is, therefore, with the greatest anxiety that I venture to explain their intentions to this House on a subject the interest of which is shewn by the crowded audience who have assembled here; but still more by the deep interest which is felt by millions out of this House, who look with anxiety, with hope, and with expectation, to the result of this day's debate. I am sure it will not be necessary for me to say more to do away with the notion which the honourable and learned Member opposite[1] has endeavoured to excite, that this question, not being brought forward by a Member of the Cabinet, is not the measure of the King's Ministers. I assure the House that what I am about to propose is a measure that they have determined on; but

---

* The text is taken from the *Mirror of Parliament*, III (1831), 555–562. Published by John Henry Barrow, the *Mirror* is the most authoritative source for Parliamentary debates in the period 1828–1842.

[1] Probably Horace Twiss, Member for Newport. Russell refers frequently to Sir Robert Peel, leader of the Tory opposition, as "the right honourable Baronet."

though I cannot say that it is one of my originating, neither can I pretend that I have been kept in ignorance of its nature. The measure itself, after the noble Lord[2] who is at the head of the Government had framed it in his mind and communicated it to his colleagues in the Cabinet, was explained to me, and I have been ever since consulting individually or collectively with the Members of that Cabinet on the subject. I only wish that the noble Lord to whom I have alluded could have been permitted by any law of Parliament to have explained this measure in his own clear and intelligible language; but, as that is impossible, I trust that the House will favour me with its indulgence while I perform the task of laying before it the details of the measure—inadequately, I fear, but with a most sincere and earnest prayer for its efficiency and success.

Much cavil has been raised upon an expression used by the noble Lord to whom I have before alluded that he would endeavour to frame such a measure as would satisfy the public mind without endangering the settled institutions of the country. Some persons have said that one part of the settled institutions of the country was composed of the close and rotten boroughs; but all must be convinced, I think, that the close and rotten boroughs were not what was intended by his Lordship. "But can you," say this party, "pretend to satisfy the public mind without shaking the settled institutions of the country?" We are of an opinion the reverse of what is expressed in this question. We think that attempting to satisfy the public mind will not endanger the institutions of the country, but that not to attempt to satisfy it would most certainly endanger them. We are of opinion that these institutions rest, as they have always hitherto done, upon the confidence and the love of Englishmen—and that they must continue to rest on the same foundation; and while we desire not to comply with extravagant demands, at the same time we are anxious to bring forward such a measure as every reasonable man may be satisfied should pass into a law. We wish to place ourselves between the two hostile parties —not agreeing with those who assert that no reform is necessary, not following in the path with others who declare that some particular reform will alone be satisfactory to the people, or wholesome in its effect upon the state of the representation in this House; but, placing ourselves between the abuses we wish to amend and the convulsion we hope to avert, we have chosen that which we trust will prove firm and steadfast ground.

It will not be necessary, on this occasion, that I should go over the ground which has frequently before been gone over for arguments in favour of a change in the state of the representation; but it is due to the House that I should state shortly the points on which the reformers rest their case. In the first place, then, the ancient Constitution of our country declares that no man shall be taxed for the support of the State who has

---

[2] Lord Grey, Prime Minister and leader of the Whigs.

not consented, by himself or his representative, to the imposition of these taxes. The well-known statute *De tallagio non concedendo*[3] repeats the same language; and, although some historical doubts have been thrown upon it, its legal meaning has never been disputed. It includes "all the freemen of the land" and provides that each county should send to the Commons of the realm two knights, each city two citizens, and each borough two burgesses. In the first instance, about 120 places sent representatives, and some thirty or forty others occasionally enjoyed the privilege, which was discontinued or revived as they rose or fell in the scale of wealth and importance. There is no doubt, therefore, that at that early period the House of Commons did represent the people of England; there is no doubt, likewise, that the House of Commons, as it now subsists, without entering into the history of the alterations it has from time to time undergone, does not represent the people of England. Therefore, if we look to the question of right, the reformers have right in their favour. Then, if we consider what is reasonable, we shall find a similar result. On any view of the case, then, it will be impossible to keep the constitution of the House as it exists at present.

We have heard—as who has not?—of the fame of this country—that in wealth it is unparalleled, in civilisation unrivalled, and in freedom unequalled in the history of the empires of the world. Now suppose a foreigner well acquainted with these facts were told that in this most wealthy, most civilised, and most free country, the representatives of the people—the guardians of her liberties—were chosen only every six years. Would he not be very curious and very anxious to hear in what way that operation was performed? Would he not be anxious to know the way in which this great and wise nation selected the Members who were to represent them, and upon whom depended their fortunes and their rights? Would not such a foreigner be much astonished if he were taken to a green mound and informed that it sent two Members to the British Parliament? If he were shewn a stone wall, and told that it also sent two Members to the British Parliament? Or, if he were walked into a park without the vestige of a dwelling and told that it, too, sent two Members to the British Parliament? But if he were surprised at this, still more would he be astonished if he were carried into the North of England, where he would see large flourishing towns, full of trade and activity, vast magazines of wealth and manufactures, and were told that these places sent no representatives to Parliament. But his wonder would not end here; he would be astonished if he were carried to such a place as Liverpool (there can be no sufficient reason for not naming it by way of illustration) and there told that he might see a specimen of a popular election and, at the same time, witness the most barefaced scenes of the grossest bribery and corruption. Would

---

[3] The document by which Edward I renounced the right of arbitrary taxation (tallage). The principle of no taxation without consent was reaffirmed by a statute in 1340.

he not be indeed surprised when he had seen all I have described that representatives so chosen could possibly perform the functions of legislators?

I say, then, that if we appeal to reason, the reformers have reason on their side. It may be said by the opponents of a change, "We agree that, in point of right, the House of Commons does not represent the people, and that, in point of reason, nothing can be more absurd than the constitution of such a body; but government is a matter of practise and worldly wisdom—of experience of life; and as long as the House of Commons enjoys the respect of the people, it would be unwise to change the system." In this argument I must confess there is much weight; and so long as the people did not answer the appeals of the friends of reform (among whom I was always one), I felt that the argument was not to be resisted. But what is the case at this moment? The whole people call loudly for reform. That confidence, whatever it was, which formerly existed in the constitution of this House, exists no longer—it is completely at an end. Whatever may be thought of particular acts of this House, I repeat that the confidence of the country in the construction and constitution of the House of Commons is gone, and gone forever. I will say more—I will say that it would be easier to transfer the flourishing manufactures of Leeds and Manchester to Gatton and Old Sarum than to re-establish confidence and sympathy between this House and those whom it calls its constituents. I end this argument, therefore, by saying that if the question be one of right, right is in favour of reform; if it be a question of reason, reason is in favour of reform; if it be a question of policy and expediency, policy and expediency are in favour of reform.

I come now to the most difficult part of the subject—the explanation of the measure which, representing the Ministers of the King, I am about to propose to the House. Those Ministers have thought, and in my opinion justly thought, that it would not be sufficient to propose a measure which should merely lop off some excrescences or cure some notorious defects, but would still leave the main battle to be fought hereafter. They have thought that no half measures would be sufficient—that no trifling, no paltering with reform could give stability to the Crown, strength to the Parliament, or satisfaction to the country. Let us look, then, at what have been the chief complaints of the people; and in my mind there is much difference between complaints of grievances and propositions of remedy. We ought to look with deference to the opinions of the people on a matter of grievance; but, with regard to remedies, I should endeavour to discover, in communication with my friends, the relief that ought to be afforded.

The chief grievances of which the people complain are these: first, the nomination of Members by individuals; second, the elections by close corporations; third, the expense of elections. With regard to the first—the nomination by individuals—it may be exercised in one of two ways: either over a place containing scarcely any inhabitants and with a very extensive right of election, or over a place of wide extent and numerous population, but where the franchise is confined to a very few residents. Gatton is an example of the first and Bath of the second. At Gatton the right is popular, but there is nobody to exercise it; at Bath the inhabitants are numerous, but very few of them have any concern in the result of an election. We have addressed ourselves to both these evils because we have thought it essential to apply a remedy to both; but they must, of course, be dealt with in different ways. With regard to boroughs where there are scarcely any inhabitants and where the elective franchise is such as to enable many individuals to give their voices in the choice of Members for this House, it would be evidently a mere farce to take away the right from the person exercising it and to give it to the borough; and the only reform that can be justly recommended is to deprive the borough of its franchise altogether. I am perfectly aware that in making this proposition we are proposing a bold and decisive measure. I am perfectly aware and I should myself vote upon that persuasion that on all ordinary occasions, rights of this kind ought to be respected. For no trifling interest—for no small consideration—ought they to be touched or injured; but I perfectly remember an occasion on which the right honourable Baronet opposite proposed a great and important measure to this effect. Two years ago the right honourable Baronet, standing here as a Minister of the Crown, proposed the measure of Catholic Emancipation. It was accompanied by another measure for the disfranchisement of 200,000 unoffending freeholders who had broken no law, corrupted no right, but exercised their privilege, ignorantly, perhaps, but independently, and according to the best light they could obtain from their consciences.

Now, if I am about to quote his words, it is not because I think he is bound to be consistent. On great questions of this kind, men must act as the interests of the country demand; but I beg the House to recollect that he stood here as the servant of the Crown, representing the Ministry which has gone out of office, and declaring in their name what principles ought to bind Parliament in the decision of a great question at an important crisis. I remember he told us that on fit occasions the House was bound to step beyond its ordinary rules, and that it did so on the discussion of the Union —of the Septennial Act and some others. To avoid great dangers by extraordinary remedies, the House has not unfrequently disregarded the common rules that govern its proceedings. The right honourable Gentleman then brought forward his measure and at once met the objection to which I have referred, and in a few words: "I admit at once," said he, "the full force of the objection which will be urged against that part of the measure I propose, by which the existing right of voting is taken away from the freeholder. No doubt it is a vested right, but it is a right that differs in its character from the rights of property and other strictly private rights. It is a public trust given for public purposes, to be touched, no doubt, with great caution and reluctance; but still which we are competent to touch, if the public interest manifestly demands the sacrifice."

Such were the sentiments of the right honourable Gentleman—sentiments, be it observed, in which the House agreed—and never was any measure carried through the House with more general approbation. Shall we say, then, that this principle is to be maintained when the poor peasantry of Ireland are concerned, but that when it touches the great and the wealthy, we are not to venture to treat the question as the public interest demands? Shall we at once deprive the freeholder of Ireland of that right which he merely exercised as the Constitution gave it to him, and shall we be afraid to touch the right of the noble Proprietor of Gatton who returns two Members to Parliament although he derived no such power from the Constitution? Shall we say that a strictly constitutional, a strictly legal right shall be abolished because the convenience, the necessity of the country demands it—and that a right which is mere usurpation, with no sanction of law and supported only by usage, shall be respected and left untouched, though the public interest requires and the public voice demands its abolition? Shall we make this glaring distinction between rich and poor, high and low, disfranchise the peasant and prop the fortunes of the Peer? The plan we propose is, therefore, to meet the difficulty in point as the Duke of Wellington and his colleagues met that of 1829, only our measures will have the effect of disfranchising a number of boroughs instead of a number of voters.

It would be a task of extreme difficulty, if not of utter impossibility, to ascertain the exact proportion of the wealth, trade, extent, and population of a given number of places, and we have, therefore, been governed by what is manifestly a public record—I mean the Population Returns of 1821—and we propose that every borough which in that year had less than 2,000 inhabitants should altogether lose the right of sending Members to Parliament. The effect of this will be utterly to disfranchise sixty boroughs. But we do not stop here. As the honourable Member for Boroughbridge[4] would say, we go *plus ultra*. We find that there are forty-seven boroughs of only 4,000 inhabitants, and these we shall deprive of the right of sending more than one Member to Parliament. We likewise intend that Weymouth, which at present sends four Members, shall, in future, only send two. The abolition of sixty boroughs will occasion 119 vacancies, to which are to be added forty-seven for the boroughs allowed to send only one Member, and two of which Weymouth will be deprived—making in the whole 168 vacancies. That, I believe, is the whole extent to which Ministers propose to go. But, as I have already said, we do not mean to allow that the remaining boroughs should be in the hands of select corporations—that is to say, of a small number of persons to the exclusion of the great body of

---

[4] Sir Charles Wetherell, whose borough was to be disfranchised.

the inhabitants who have property and interest in the place. It has been a point of great difficulty to decide to whom the franchise should be extended. Although it is a much-disputed question, yet I believe it will be found that in ancient times every inhabitant householder resident in a borough was competent to vote for Members of Parliament. As, however, this arrangement excluded villeins and strangers, the franchise always belonged to a particular body in every town; that the voters were persons of property is obvious from the fact that they were called upon to pay subsidies and taxes. Two different courses seem to have prevailed in different places. In some, every person having a house and being free was admitted to a general participation in the privileges formerly possessed by burgesses; in others the burgesses became a select body and were converted into a kind of corporation, more or less distinct—more or less exclusive—of the rest of the inhabitants. These differences, the House will be aware, have led to those complicated questions of right which we are every week called upon to decide.

I think no one will deny that our Election Committees often have before them the most vexatious, the most difficult, and, at the same time, the most useless questions that men can be called upon to decide. Originally these points were decided in this House by the prevalence of one Party or of another; they are now determined more fairly, but still the determinations are all founded upon the iniquity of some Party. I contend that it is important to get rid of these complicated rights—of these vexatious questions—and to give to the real property and to the real respectability of the different cities and towns the right of voting for Members of Parliament. The first distinction that naturally occurred as forming a proper class of voters was that pointed out by the Bill of the right honourable Baronet opposite, for persons qualified to serve on juries. But, upon looking into this qualification, we found that in Edinburgh, Liverpool, Manchester, and other important places, although it certainly would give an extended constituency, it would still be too limited for the number of the inhabitants. On the other hand, in small boroughs it would have the evil of confining the elective franchise to a very few persons indeed. According to the returns from the Tax Office—which, I admit, are not entirely to be depended upon —ten, seven, three, and even one would be the number of persons in some towns rated for a house of £20 a year. Therefore we saw, if we took this qualification, we should be creating new close boroughs and confining the elective franchise instead of enlarging it; we therefore propose that the right of voting should be given to householders paying rates for houses of the yearly value of £10 and upwards. Whether he be the proprietor or whether he only rent the house, the person rated will have the franchise upon certain conditions hereafter to be named. At the same time it is not intended to deprive the present electors of their privilege to vote, provided they be resident.

With regard to non-residents, we are of opinion that they introduce so much expense, are the cause of so much bribery, and occasion such manifold and manifest evils that they ought not to be permitted to retain their votes. At the same time, I do not believe that we are inflicting even upon this class any injury, for nearly all, either in one place or in another, will possess a franchise in the great mass of householders. With regard to resident voters, we propose that they should retain their right during life, but that no vote should be allowed hereafter, excepting on the condition I have before stated, that the person claiming the right must be a householder to the extent of £10 a year.

I shall now proceed to the manner in which we propose to extend the franchise in counties. The Bill I wish to introduce will give all copyholders to the value of £10 a year, qualified under the right honourable Gentleman's Bill to serve on juries, a right to vote for the return of Knights of the Shire; it also provides that leaseholders for not less than twenty-one years whose leases have not been renewed within two years shall enjoy the same privilege—

SIR ROBERT PEEL: What amount of rent will be necessary to give the right?

LORD JOHN RUSSELL: The right will depend upon a lease for twenty-one years where the annual rent is £50. It will be recollected that when speaking of the numbers disfranchised, I said that 168 vacancies would be created. We are of opinion that it would not be wise or expedient to fill up the whole number of those vacancies. After mature deliberation we have arrived at the conclusion that the number of Members at present in the House is inconveniently large. I believe there is no honourable Gentleman who was a Member of the House before the Union with Ireland who will not agree that the facility of getting through business has since been greatly diminished. Besides, it is to be considered when this Parliament is reformed, as I trust it will before long, there will not be such a number of Members who enter Parliament merely for the sake of the name and as a matter of style and fashion. It is not to be disputed that some Members spend their money in foreign countries and never attend the House at all, to a certain degree to the inconvenience of those who do attend to their public duties. A few, I know, for two or three years together have never attended in their places; and, at the end of a Parliament, I believe there is generally found an instance or two of individuals who, having been elected, have never appeared at the Table even to take the oaths. But it is obvious that whenever a Member has a certain number of constituents watching his actions and looking to his votes in order that the people's money be not given for purposes inconsistent with the people's interests, his attendance will be much more regular. Therefore, when we are proposing a great change by cutting off a number of Members, the effect will be to facilitate public business to the manifest advantage of the country.

CONSTITUTION AND PARLIAMENTARY REFORM

We propose, then, to fill up a certain number of the vacancies but not the whole of them. We intend that seven large towns should send two Members each, and that twenty other towns should send one Member each. The seven towns which are to send two Members each are the following:

Manchester and Salford
Birmingham and Aston
Leeds
Greenwich, Deptford, and Woolwich, forming a district
Wolverhampton, Bilston, and Sedgeley, combined
Sheffield
Sunderland and the Wearmouths

The following are the names of the towns each of which, it is proposed, should send one Member to Parliament:

Brighton
Blackburn
Macclesfield
South Shields and Westoe
Warrington
Huddersfield
Halifax
Gateshead
Whitehaven, Workington, Harrington
Kendal
Bolton
Stockport
Dudley
Tynemouth and North Shields
Cheltenham
Bradford
Frome
Wakefield
Kidderminster
Walsall

It is well known that a great portion of the metropolis and its neighbourhood, amounting in population to 800,000 or 900,000, is scarcely at all represented; we propose, therefore, to give eight Members to those who are thus unrepresented by dividing them into the following districts:

Districts	Population
Tower Hamlets	283,000
Holborn	218,000
Finsbury	162,000
Lambeth	128,000

The two large populous parishes of Marylebone, which, no doubt, are entitled to be represented—at least, as much entitled to it as Boroughbridge—are included in one of the districts I have named. Next we propose an addition to the Members for the larger counties—a species of reform always recommended, and which, I believe, Lord Chatham was among the first to advocate. Those counties contain a variety of interests and form an admirable constituency; in some, as in Staffordshire, there is a large manufacturing population better represented in this way than perhaps in any other; and as county Members have unquestionably the most excellent class of constituents, they form of themselves a most valuable class of representatives. The Bill I shall beg leave to introduce will give two additional Members to each of the twenty-seven counties where the inhabitants exceed 150,000. Everybody will expect that Yorkshire, divided into three Ridings—the East, the West, and the North—should have two Members for each Riding; and the other counties to which this additional privilege will be given are the following:

Chester	Wilts	Salop
Derby	Warwick	Stafford
Durham	Cumberland	Sussex
Gloucester	Northampton	Nottingham
Lancaster	Cornwall	Surrey
Norfolk	Devon	Northumberland
Somerset	Essex	Leicester
Suffolk	Kent	Southampton
	Lincoln	Worcester

I now proceed to another part of the measure. I spoke at first of the evils connected in the minds of the people with the power of nomination by individuals, and with the power of election by a few persons in very small and close corporations. The remedies I have detailed are pointed against these defects. I now beg leave to direct the attention of the House to that part of the plan which relates to the expense of long-protracted polls and which, while it removes that evil, also greatly facilitates the collection of the sense of the elective body. The names of electors are to be enrolled and the disputes regarding qualification in a great measure avoided. We propose that all electors in counties, cities, towns, or boroughs shall be registered, and for this purpose machinery will be put in motion very similar to that in the Jury Act—that is to say, at a certain period of the year (I now speak of boroughs), the parish officers and churchwardens are to make a list of the persons who occupy houses of the yearly value of £10. This list of names will be placed on the church doors, we will suppose in September; and in the following month, October, the returning officer will hold a sort of trial of votes where claims made and objections stated will be considered and decided. When this process has been gone through, the returning officer will declare the list complete, and on the 1st of December in every year the list will be published; every person who chooses will obtain a copy of it, and it will be the rule to govern electors and elections for the ensuing year. We intend that during that ensuing year every person shall be entitled to vote whose name is in the list, and that no question shall be asked but as to his identity and whether he has polled before at the same election. These regulations are extremely simple and will prevent all those contentious, vexatious, and noisy scenes now so often witnessed regarding disputed votes. The means of ascertaining who are electors being thus easy, there is no reason why the poll should be kept open for a week, as in some cases, or for eight days, or as in some places for a longer period. It is proposed that, nearly according to the present law, booths shall be erected in the different parishes so that the whole poll may be taken in two days. For my own part, I would say that the time may come when the machinery will be found so simple that every vote may be given in a single day; but in introducing a new measure it is necessary to allow for possible defects in the working of the machinery. Attempts might be made to obstruct the polling, and we therefore recommend two days, in order that no voter may be deprived of the opportunity of offering his suffrage. I think the sense of the electors in any town may be taken in two days. As to counties, the matter may be somewhat more difficult. We propose, in the same manner, that the churchwardens should make out a list of all persons claiming the right to vote in the several parishes and that these lists shall be affixed to the church doors. A person to be appointed (say a barrister of a certain standing) by the Judge of Assize shall go an annual circuit within a certain time after the lists have been published, and he will hear all claims to vote and objections to voters. Having decided who are entitled to exercise the privilege, he shall sign his name at the bottom of the list and shall transmit it to the Clerk of the Peace. The list will then be enrolled as the roll of the freeholders of the county for the ensuing year.

With respect to the manner of proceeding at elections, we have it in view to introduce a measure which can hardly fail to be an improvement of the present system. Everybody knows and must have lamented the enormous expense to which candidates are put in bringing voters to the poll. In Yorkshire, without a contest, it has cost upwards of £100,000 to bring the electors to the poll. In Devonshire the electors are obliged to travel forty miles over hard cross-roads, which occupies one day; the next is consumed in polling, and the third in returning home—the whole a manifest source of vast expense and most inconvenient delay. We propose, therefore, that the poll shall be taken in separate districts, those districts to be arranged according to circumstances by the magistrates at quarter-sessions. The counties will be divided into districts with this arrangement, that they shall not be changed for two years. The formation of those districts will give an opportunity of more readily taking the votes when an election occurs. The Sheriffs shall hold the election on a certain day, and if it should happen that a poll be demanded, they shall adjourn the election to the day next but one. The poll shall then be kept open for two days so as to enable all the persons qualified under the several Acts of Parliament to give their votes. On the third day the poll shall be closed, and on the sixth day the returning officer will make his return according to the number who have polled for the several candidates. It will be so arranged that no voter shall have to travel more than fifteen miles to give his vote. At the same time it is not proposed that the number of polling places in one county shall exceed fifteen, as the multiplication of places for receiving the votes would give rise to great inconvenience and perhaps leave an opening for abuses. We propose that each large county shall be divided into two districts returning each two Members to Parliament. The adjusting the division of the counties will, I have no doubt, be a matter of some difficulty. I propose that His Majesty shall nominate a Committee of the Privy Council to determine the direction and extent of the districts into which each county shall be divided. Those Privy Councillors, I need not say, will be persons known to the House and to the country. They will be known persons, responsible for the discharge of that duty. In some of the boroughs to which the right of representation is left and will be continued, the number of electors is exceedingly small. We shall, therefore, insert in the Bill which we propose to submit to Parliament a clause giving power to the Commissioners nominated under the Bill authority to enable the inhabitants of the adjoining parish or chapelry rated at £10 a year to take part in the elections, when the number of electors in such borough shall be below 300, for the purpose of adding to the number of voters. That these are extensive powers I shall not attempt to deny. But, as the difficulty exists, it is our duty to consider how it may be overcome. How it is to be met His Majesty's Ministers do not know, otherwise than by committing the power to persons known and responsible to Parliament and to the nation and appointed by the Royal Proclamation. If any honourable Gentleman stands up in his place and says that the powers which we propose to give to the Committee of the Privy Council are too great, I will only ask him: if it be granted that the business is to be done, that the objects for which we propose the Committee are proper and useful, can he suggest any better and more effectual mode of doing it? If any Gentleman in the House will suggest a mode more safe, more constitutional, His Majesty's Ministers will have no difficulty in adopting that mode and waiving their own, their only object being to advance the interest of the people, to which every other consideration ought to yield.

There is but one other thing which I am aware of that I have yet to state with regard to the representation of England. In all those new towns to which we propose to give the right of sending Members to Parliament, all persons who are in them entitled by their property to vote shall be excluded from the right to vote for the representatives of the county. At the same time that the towns shall have themselves a proper share in the representation, having their own proper representatives chosen by themselves, I do not intend that they shall interfere with the representation of the counties. At the same time it is not intended to interfere with the franchise of those freeholders in towns who are at present entitled to vote.

I believe I have now concluded the statement of all the alterations which are intended to be made in the representation of England. With respect to the right of the 40s. freeholders in counties, I do not think that there should be any alteration, for I consider that they are a class of persons eminently qualified to have the trust of electors committed to them. By the smallness of the property which constitutes their qualification, they are especially calculated to give the representation that large and extended basis which it is most desirable that it should have. ["*Name the boroughs disfranchised.*"]

I now come to the list of places to be disfranchised. It is proposed to take away the right of electing Members to serve in Parliament from all towns which do not contain 2,000 inhabitants. With respect to some of these, the franchise, perhaps, has been properly exercised and might be left without disadvantage; and it was at first a question whether we should not still allow some of them to send each one Member; but, on consideration, we thought it better to avoid all chance of an imputation of partiality. We therefore determined to fix upon the number of 2,000 inhabitants and thereby leave no doubt that in their disfranchisement we were not influenced by partiality, by prejudice, or by a wish to favour some particular interests. I shall read the lists of the boroughs to be disfranchised upon this principle:

Aldborough, York	Hedon	Queenborough
Aldborough, Suffolk	Heytesbury	Reigate
	Higham Ferrers	Romeny
Appleby	Hindon	St. Mawes
Bedwin	Ilchester	St. Michael's, or
Beeralston	East Looe	St. Mitchel's,
Bishop's Castle	West Looe	Cornwall
Bletchingley	Lostwithiel	Saltash
Boroughbridge	Ludgershall	Old Sarum
Bossiney	Malmesbury	Seaford
Brackley	Midhurst	Steyning
Bramber	Milborne Port	Stockbridge
Buckingham	Minehead	Tregony
Callington	Newport, Cornwall	Wareham
Camelford	Newton, Lancashire	Wendover
Castle Rising		Weobly
Corfe Castle	Newton, Isle of Wight	Whitchurch
Dunwich		Winchelsea
Eye	Okehampton	Woodstock
Fowey	Orford	Wootton Bassett
Gatton	Petersfield	Yarmouth, Isle of Wight
Haslemere	Plympton	

In all, sixty boroughs to be disfranchised.

I will now read the second list of the boroughs which will be allowed to return one Member of Parliament each:

Amersham	Helston	Rye
Arundel	Honiton	St. Germains
Ashburton	Huntingdon	St. Ives
Bewdley	Hythe	Sandwich
Bodmin	Launceston	Sudbury
Bridport	Leominster	Shaftesbury
Chippenham	Liskeard	Tamworth
Clitheroe	Lyme Regis	Thetford
Cockermouth	Lymington	Thirsk
Dorchester	Maldon	Totness
Downton	Marlborough	Truro
Droitwich	Marlow	Wallingford
Evesham	Morpeth	Westbury
Grimsby	Northallerton	Wilton
East Grinstead	Penryn	Wycombe
Guildford	Richmond	

In the whole, forty-seven boroughs.

JOHN W. CROKER: What is to be the number of Members in this House?

LORD JOHN RUSSELL: Of that, hereafter. With regard to the addition of certain towns to boroughs in their immediate vicinity, or more properly, the extension of the elective franchise to towns in the neighbourhood of boroughs, I may mention that it is intended to add Holyhead to Beaumaris; Bangor to Carnarvon; Wrexham to Denbigh; Holywell and Mold to Flint; Llandaff and Merthyr Tydvil to Cardiff; Welshpool, Llanvilling, and three other places which returned Members to Parliament formerly, but which were disfranchised by a decision of the House of Commons, I believe in the time of Sir Horace Walpole, to Montgomery; St. David's, Fishguard, and Newport to Haverfordwest; Milford to Pembroke; Presteign to Radnor; and we further propose that a new district of boroughs should be erected, consisting of Swansea, Cowbridge, Laugharn, and three other places, which shall have the privilege of returning one Member to Parliament. That is the only additional Member which it is proposed to add to the representation of Wales.

I now come to the representation of Scotland; and if the representation of England wants reform, certainly the same thing may be said in a stronger manner, and with additional reason, as regards the representation of Scotland. If we have close boroughs in England, we have also popular elections and, in some degree, popular representation in many of those boroughs, but in Scotland there is not a vestige of popular representation. Indeed, there is no such thing known in that country as a popular election;

consequently, the wealth, the respectability, and the intelligence for which the inhabitants of that country are so distinguished are virtually unrepresented. In the counties of Scotland there are 3,253 persons who appear on the lists as qualified to vote, but, from various causes, a number of those electors cannot vote; so that the whole number of electors by which the county Members of Scotland are returned does not exceed 2,340 persons.

I shall not enter into the details of the manner in which the right of voting is obtained in the counties of Scotland. I shall only mention that the right is, in many instances, obtained by an authority distinct from that derived from the possession of land. Formerly it was connected with the possession of land, but when persons sold land, they were in the practice of retaining in their own hands that superiority which gave them the right of voting. Latterly proprietors of land have sold the superiority, which is often purchased for corrupt purposes by persons who are altogether unconnected with the counties in which they have votes. This has been so much the case that I thought it necessary to procure a return shewing the proportion of the number of persons holding landed property and possessing votes in the counties in Scotland, a few extracts from which I shall read to the House. I find that in Ayrshire there are 308 electors and that only 105 of these possess any landed property in the county. In Bute, out of the nineteen electors only two are landed proprietors. In Kinross, of twenty-seven voters eighteen only are possessors of land. In Ross and Cromarty there are twenty-nine electors, and only eight of these possess landed property; and in the county of Lanark there are 224 electors, of which number ninety-eight only are landed proprietors. This is the state of the representation in the counties of Scotland; and this state of the representation, I conceive, is not fair as regards the landed proprietors.

If I hear anyone object to this measure on the ground that it tends to deprive the landowner in Scotland of his fair and legitimate influence or of any right which he now possesses, I shall refer to this return, for I conceive that it presents a complete answer to any such objection. I consider that it affords decisive evidence that the franchise is not in the landowner. What I propose in the counties of Scotland is that everyone possessing what is called the *dominium utile*, or what we should call a beneficial interest in lands or houses to the amount of £10 per annum in the nature of a freehold or copyhold, shall be entitled to a vote. We propose, likewise, that leaseholders in possession and having a written lease for a term of nineteen years or over that of the rent of £50 shall be entitled to vote, with this qualification—that the lease has not been renewed within two years previous to the election at which they vote. We have fixed on nineteen years, for it is the custom in Scotland to give leases for nineteen years more generally than for twenty-one, as in England. This class of voters will be placed very much on the same footing as they are placed in this country, and nearly the whole of the details of the measure as applicable to England are likewise applicable to Scotland.

We propose also one or two arrangements respecting the representation of the counties in Scotland. For instance, it is intended that Selkirk should be joined with Peebles, and that those two counties, both very being small, should return only one Member. Dumbarton and Bute, Elgin and Nairne, Ross and Cromarty, Orkney and Shetland, and Clackmannan and Kinross, with certain additions, to do the same. The remaining twenty-two counties each singly to return one Member. We also propose that Edinburgh should have two Members, Glasgow two, and that Aberdeen, Paisley, Dundee, Greenock, and Leith (with the addition of Portobello, Musselburgh, and Fisherrow) should each singly return one Member. We propose that the East Fife district of burghs should no longer return any, but that it should be thrown into the county. The remaining thirteen districts of burghs we propose should each return one Member, with these variations—that Kilmarnock shall take the place of Glasgow in the district of burghs to which Glasgow formerly belonged; that Peterhead shall take the place of Aberdeen; and that Falkirk shall be added to the districts of Lanark, Linlithgow, Selkirk, and Peebles.

As to the right of voting in the boroughs and towns of Scotland, it will be founded on the principle of property arising from the occupation of houses rented or rated to taxes at not less than £10 a year. The manner in which the eligibility of electors is to be ascertained in Scotland is very similar to the manner proposed in England—namely, by a registry of the names. In Scotland, however, there will be advantages and facilities afforded because there are already proper officers in that country perfectly competent to fulfill the duties which that system imposes. With these several alterations, Scotland will have fifty Members instead of forty-five. The elections for the burghs are to continue, but not in the same way as at present. It is proposed that the election should no longer remain in delegates or town councils appointed by self-elected corporations, but all the persons who have a right to vote will vote in their own persons; and the number voting in the whole district will be summed up by the returning officer who, according to the sum of the whole number of votes, will return the Members.

I now proceed to Ireland, where a reform in the representation, though necessary, will be more simple than those proposed with respect to the representation of England and Scotland. At the time of the Union, little more than thirty years ago, the representation of Ireland was entirely remodelled, and therefore in that country we do not find small and decayed boroughs sending representatives as is the case in England. Yet there are many of the boroughs in Ireland in which the franchise is held by only a small number of persons who are not qualified by property to return the representatives. I propose that the inhabitants of those boroughs should have the right of voting for a representative in the same manner as in England, although such right is to be ascertained differently. I propose that property or occupancy of a house or land to the value of £10 per annum should give every man a vote who resides in a borough. I am convinced that this arrangement will be attended with the greatest benefit to Ireland. I know that the people of that country have suffered the greatest inconvenience and injury, owing to the political rights being in the hands of a few. Not long since, I brought before the House a case arising in the borough of Wexford. The merchants of that town, it appeared, were totally excluded from all political rights, and the dues they paid on goods shipped by them for the English coast amounted to £2,000 per annum, which charges they would not have been subject to if they had been free of the corporation. I am convinced, therefore, that this enlargement of the franchise in Ireland will tend to promote industry and encourage trade, and I hope that country will make such a progress before many years that we shall hear of no other agitation in it but that caused by the bustle of increasing business and wealth. There are three towns in Ireland which have grown into great commercial importance and to which we propose to give an additional representative. Those towns are Belfast, Limerick, and Waterford, all of which at present send one Member. Ireland, therefore, will send three in addition to the number of 100 representatives which she now sends. Ireland and Scotland likewise obtain some advantage from the number of Members cut off and not to be supplied from the English representation. As regards the number of representatives, therefore, the relative importance of Ireland and Scotland is increased by this measure. In those countries, therefore, I apprehend this measure will afford great satisfaction.

I now proceed to state the result of these changes on the numbers in this House.

NICHOLAS P. LEADER: You have not mentioned what is proposed as the qualification for voters in counties.

LORD JOHN RUSSELL: The arrangement as to elections is to be the same as in England. The county elections must be concluded within six days from the time of their commencement, as in England, and all persons at present entitled to vote will continue to have that right. I think there is no other alteration of any importance as regards Ireland.

Having gone through the several alterations proposed in England, Wales, Scotland, and Ireland, I now come to the result:

Number of Members belonging to this House	658
Number to be disfranchised	168
Number remaining	490

Additional Members for Scotland	5
Additional Members for Ireland	3
Additional Member for Wales	1
Additional Members for the metropolis	8
New Members for large towns in England	34
Additional Members for counties in England	55
Total additional Members	106
Members now of the House	490
Total	596

Making a decrease of sixty-two Members in the total number of representatives

I will now state the number of additional persons who will be entitled to votes for counties, towns, and boroughs under this Bill:

	Persons
The number in towns and boroughs in England, already sending Members, will be increased by	110,000
The electors of new towns (in England) sending Members I estimate at	50,000
Electors in London who will obtain the right of voting	95,000
Increase of electors in Scotland	60,000
In Ireland, perhaps	40,000
Increase in the counties of England (at least)	100,000

These numbers, at least, will be entitled to vote, and upon the whole I calculate that under this Bill there will be added at least 500,000 persons to the number now exercising the right of sending Members to this House. Be it remembered, too, in addition to the number added to our constituents, that every one added is connected with the country by property. All the electors, having themselves a valuable stake in the country, are interested parties, upon whom we may confidently depend to come forward in the event of any future struggle to support the House, the Parliament, and the Throne in carrying that struggle to a successful issue. I think it more than probable that the proposed extension of the elective franchise will be of itself a great incentive to industry and good conduct amongst all classes and in all the transactions of life. When an individual knows that by being rated to a certain amount he insures the right of voting for a Member to represent him in Parliament, and that his name will be placed in the list of electors, he will find in that circumstance a reason for being frugal and punctual in his payments and for preserving a character amongst his neighbours. When adding a large number to our constituents, therefore, I conceive that we shall be adopting a measure calculated to promote both their physical and moral improvement.

Having gone through the different heads of alteration and reform proposed, perhaps it will be considered that I ought to notice certain points which are looked to with great interest by the most zealous advocates for reform, but which are not included in the proposed measure. In the first place, then, I have to state that there is no provision in this Bill for shortening the duration of Parliament. That is a subject which has been much considered, but upon the whole, without stating the opinion of His Majesty's Ministers on it, I may observe that it was thought better to leave that matter to be brought forward as a separate question than to bring it in at the end of a Bill affecting franchises and matters of local reference, separate and essentially different from any question concerning the duration of Parliament. Without saying to what opinion His Majesty's Ministers incline on this point, I may say that they consider it of the utmost importance not to burden this measure with any other, but to reserve it by itself, leaving it to any other Member at any time that may be considered fitting to introduce the question and to make it the subject of future consideration. For my own part, I can only say that whilst I am fully of opinion that the constituents should have a proper control over their representatives, I cannot but think it would be extremely inexpedient to make the duration of Parliaments so short that the Members would be engaged in a perpetual canvass. I am apprehensive that a too-frequent appeal to the opinions of their constituents would lead to a want of that due deliberation and of that decision with freedom which should always appertain to legislators. Nor do I think these frequent appeals to the constituency consistent with that confidence which it behooves the people of a great nation to repose in their representatives, at least to a certain point. Where that point should end I shall not say, but whenever the question is brought forward I shall be prepared to deliver my sentiments on it fully and freely. At present, all I can say on it is that His Majesty's Ministers have no measure to propose altering the duration of Parliaments. If they provide good and sufficient constituents and a popularly-elected representation, their object in this measure will be gained, and they have thought it better not to embarrass a measure having so great an object with another question having its own doubts and difficulties and obstacles, and attended by full as many of those as that measure which they now propose.

There is another question, likewise, which has excited a vast deal of interest in the country and of which no mention is made in this Bill. I mean the vote by ballot. I have no doubt that the ballot has much to recommend it as a mode of election. More ingenious arguments never fell under my eye on any subject than I have seen in favour of the ballot; but, at the same time, I am bound to say that I hope this House will pause before it sanctions the motion which the honourable Member for Bridport[5]

[5] Henry Warburton.

is to make and adopts the mode of voting by ballot. The honourable Member for Bridport holds that the ballot affords the only security for the independence of the elector. If, upon the whole, the ballot is in favour of the constituent body by securing voters from corruption—yet it must be admitted that it gives a cover to much fraud and falsehood and gives a scope to many bad passions—if it would prevent bad influence from overcoming good, I conscientiously believe that it would also prevent good influence from overcoming bad. But be this as it may, I think even if the ballot were introduced, it would be very doubtful whether the people of this country, accustomed as they are to the right of voting openly, would ever resort to such a mode or that they would ever dream it necessary to avail themselves of the secrecy which belongs to the ballot. I am bound to say, moreover, that this is in my mind one of the strongest objections to the ballot—that it does appear to me of all things the most doubtful whether there ought to be any class or description of persons, connected in any manner with the representation of the country, possessing power wholly of an irresponsible character. Now the ballot would place an irresponsible power in the hands of all persons entitled to vote. I know that men of rank and wealth are in favour of that measure. I know that men of enthusiastic minds are in favour of a measure by which they suppose all influence over the electors would be removed. But I am not satisfied that the electors should not be subject to that influence which the several classes of the community exercise over each other—which the Crown exercises over the Peers, the Lords over the Commons, and the people over their representatives. Sir, I do not wish that any man in the country should possess an irresponsible power, knowing that man's mind is liable to be clouded by every variety of error and to be swayed by every ruling passion.

I will now say a few words to the probable objections that may be made to any change of our representative system. The first great objection to any plan of this kind is that it overturns what is old; but, Sir, I contend that we act more in accordance with the principles of our ancestors in conceding than in refusing reform. They said that Old Sarum should have representatives on the same grounds on which we now say give representatives to Manchester and to other large towns. I remember, indeed, that Mr. Burke said in one of his speeches that the House of Commons was, at that time, constituted on the same principle as ever, because the same places continued to send representatives. But, Sir, I wonder that a man of Mr. Burke's powers of mind could argue in that manner. He might as well have said that the Roman Empire in the time of Augustus was governed on the same principle as in the time of the Republic, because the names of their magistrates and the externals of their power were the same. Because Old Sarum sent Members to Parliament in the reign of Edward III when it had a population to be benefited by it, we follow the principles of our ancestors by taking away that franchise now that it has no population and bestowing it where there is a population. We have been told as another objection that merchants and lawyers and men of genius who have obtained seats in this House by means of those close boroughs will, if they are abolished, be no longer able to do so. I very much doubt the correctness of that proposition. I cannot believe that any reform we can make will prevent wealth, learning, and wit from having great influence, although, no doubt, their possessors may be at more trouble to make it available; but still, in populous towns, they will, as now, have their proper influence.

My right honourable Friend, the Attorney-General,[6] is an illustrious instance out of many, that in populous towns lawyers and persons of eminence will be elected to contribute to the deliberations of this House that varied information and extensive knowledge which, I must confess, are of the utmost importance to us. I may be told again, Sir, that this Bill will destroy the power of the aristocracy; but that I deny. I say that wherever the aristocracy are residing on their estates beneficially exercising the large power they possess, receiving their neighbours with hospitality, relieving the poor with charity, it is not in human nature that such an aristocracy should not have great influence with those who are to elect the Members to serve their country in Parliament. Though, therefore, such an aristocracy may not have the direct nomination of boroughs, it will always be able to hold as much influence as it ought to have in the election of the Members of this House; but if it be meant that this Bill will destroy the influence of an aristocracy which does not live among the people— which knows not the people—which cares nothing for the people—an aristocracy which seeks only for honours, without desert—for places, without duties—for pensions, without service—then, I say, for such an aristocracy I have no sympathy and that the sooner its influence is carried away with the corruption in which it has thriven, the better it will be for the country—the better it will be for every wholesome and invigorating influence. Language has been held upon this subject which I hope I shall not hear in this House. A call has been made—a sort of summons has gone forth to those who are connected with the aristocracy—to make a stand against the just request of the people to be represented in their own Commons House. It has even been said that that party could, by its own numerical strength, defeat any attempted sedition.

Sir, the question is not one of sedition or of numerical strength, but whether, without some larger measure of reform, we can carry on the affairs of the country with the confidence and support of the people. If you cannot, it may be a question of whether you can resist reform; but it is no question whatever that there must either be a reform or that the British Constitution must perish. This House, even in its unreformed state, has had nothing to look to but the confidence, support, and sympathy of

[6] Sir James Scarlett, who had been returned for Malton.

the nation. It is quite clear that if you refuse reform, that sympathy and confidence will in future be withheld. I ask you, then, whether, when the Ministers of the Crown are convinced that reform is necessary—when they, serving a Gracious Master, who has permitted them to lay these propositions before the House—when they come forward to declare they think reform essential and indispensable—when the people out of doors, by multitudes of petitions, by millions of voices, are calling for the same thing—I ask whether the House of Commons will say, "We alone are the judges of our own purity—we despise the propositions of the Minister of the Crown—we despise the warning voice of the people whom we profess to represent, and will keep our power anyhow, against all remonstrance, against all petitions, and take our chance of the dreadful consequences." Sir, I apply in my turn to the aristocracy of England. My own opinion is that the gentlemen of England, in every great crisis of the country, have never been found wanting; that when it was engaged in war against a national enemy they were always the foremost; that when burdens were to be supported, they were as ready to support them as the rest of their fellow-subjects. And I now ask them, when a great sacrifice is to be made, whether they will shew their generosity—whether they will evince their public spirit—whether, for the future, they will identify themselves with the people—whether they will give to the Throne stability, to the Parliament strength, to the country peace.

Whatever may be the result of this proposition, the King's Ministers will feel that they have done their duty. They have hitherto proceeded on the line of their duty in a straightforward course, neither seeking for the support of a particular class, nor courting the approbation of the multitude. Whenever the line of their duty has led them against the popular feelings, they have not hesitated to encounter them. By a firm and vigorous execution of the law, the disturbances which prevailed in parts of England at their accession to office have been set at rest—I trust permanently—by a firm and vigorous execution of laws passed before they came into power. The agitation of the Sister Kingdom[7] will, I trust, subside into peace. At all events, in neither of these instances can Ministers be accused of bending to popular clamour, or seeking to ingratiate themselves with the multitude to obtain its transient favour. I think, therefore, that they have a right to be believed when they come forward with a measure of effectual reform and say that they do not so for any sinister purpose of their own. Interested as they are—as all must be—in the future welfare and prosperity of the country, do they think that this measure will tend to promote that future welfare and secure that future prosperity; and above all, do they think that it is the only way calculated to ensure permanency to that Constitution which has so long been the admiration of foreign

---

[7] Disturbances in Ireland arising from the issue of Catholic Emancipation.

nations, on account of its popular spirit? But that admiration cannot be made to exist much longer, unless by an infusion of new popular spirit you shew that you are determined not to be the representatives of small classes or particular interests, but that you will form a body, which representing the people—which springing from the people—which sympathizing with the people, can fairly call upon the people to support any future burdens, and to struggle with any future difficulties you may have to encounter, confident that those who ask them so to do are united heart and hand with them, and look only like themselves to the glory and welfare of England.

I now conclude, Sir, with moving for leave to bring in a Bill "for amending the state of the representation in England and Wales."

Thomas B. Macaulay

"For the Reform Bill"*
Commons, March 2, 1831

Sir, I confess I am glad to see that the measure of Reform proposed by His Majesty's Ministers has given such general satisfaction, and that it is only opposed by those who are opposed to all reform. My apprehension with respect to any plan of reform was that its greatest risk would arise from disunion—disunion amongst the reformers themselves. When I knew that there were so many systems of reform before the public, that almost every man had his own system, I feared that an adherence to individual theories and opinions might have been found a great obstacle to any general plan; I confess, therefore, that it is with no slight satisfaction that amongst the reformers themselves, the plan has as yet met with no opposition. For myself, I can only say that so far as I have been able to consider the proposition of the noble Lord during the last twenty-four hours, I think it a great, noble, and comprehensive measure—a medicine most skilfully prepared for removing a dangerous distemper—a plan excellently contrived for uniting and knitting together all orders in the State. The honourable Baronet[1] has observed that Ministers proceeded on two principles which he deems incongruous. I, on the contrary, think that they acted on one plain and distinct principle, and that was that it was necessary to give weight in the representation of this country to the middle classes and to do it by means that would produce a change as little violent as possible in the institutions of the country. [*Hear, hear.*]

Sir, I understand the meaning of that cheer, but I adhere to my proposition. It is made a matter of complaint that this measure has not assumed

---

* This text is from the *Mirror of Parliament*, III (1831), 595–598. Macaulay revised the speech for *Hansard's Parliamentary Debates* and his "Speeches" in *Miscellaneous Works of Lord Macaulay*. Some revised versions bear little resemblance to what Macaulay said on the evening of March 2. The speech also was reported, in third person, by *The Times*, March 3, 1831, p. 4, whose reporter complained, "The unexampled rapidity with which the greater part of it was delivered rendered a more detailed account absolutely impossible."

[1] Sir John Walsh, the preceding speaker.

a more symmetrical form. I am glad that it wants that symmetry, because it keeps the classes distinct and does not proceed on the rule-of-three principle which was adopted in the United States. I certainly do not think that the same form of representation which is fit for this country would answer every other. In my opinion, there are countries where the people are so happily circumstanced that the best form of representation would be by universal suffrage. I believe if the labouring classes here were always employed, if wages were high, and children considered as a blessing and not as a burden to the country—in that case I would, without feeling any great apprehension, give to the whole body the right of suffrage. I know that the Americans possess that right and use it well; and I do not think that in head or heart they are in any respect superior to our own people.

I know that the great body of the labouring classes are reduced to a state of considerable distress; and we all know what effect distress has on the minds of people even better educated and of sounder judgments than the labouring classes: distress makes men credulous and irritable; and it is, therefore, on that ground principally that I never can consent to an extension of suffrage of which property is not to be the basis. Sir, I support this measure because I am opposed to universal suffrage; I support it because I look with horror on the thought of anything in the shape of revolution; and I support it because I believe that it is the best security against all possibility of revolution.

A great deal has been said about the employment of threats and intimidation. I do not think that any have been used. When Lord Castlereagh[2] came down to this House and enforced his proposition for the suspension of the *Habeas Corpus* by alluding to the possibility of popular tumults arising —when he enforced his arguments in favour of the Six Acts[3] by the same observation—no one then thought of assuming that a reference to the possibility of such an occurrence was either threat or intimidation. So I refer to the present state of the country as a reason for granting reform; I do not refer to it as a threat. I feel great alarm for the fate of the country, which will be endangered, I will not say if this measure be rejected, but unless some similar measure be passed. I do not threaten the House, but am discharging my duty to my country and to the House in stating soberly as a reason and not as a threat my firm and sincere conviction that unless some measure be adopted for admitting the middle classes to an

---

[2] The *Hansard* version reports "Lord Londonderry" instead of "Lord Castlereagh." It is puzzling why Macaulay revised his reference for *Hansard* since Robert Stewart, Second Marquess of Londonderry, took the title Viscount Castlereagh in 1796, and was obviously better known as Castlereagh.

[3] Repressive measures enacted by Parliament in 1819 to deal with public protest. They concerned procedures for bringing cases to trial, prohibition of meetings for military exercises, issuance of search warrants for arms, regulation of public meetings, seizure of seditious literature, and extension of taxation to all periodical publications.

effective share of the representation, the institutions of this country will be exposed to great danger. I support the measure not merely as a measure of reform, but as a measure of conservation. If the House wish to exclude revolution, this measure is necessary; and it must be adopted as a means of safety for a desired end. If it be said that property and intelligence are the basis of a representative government, it is only by means of intelligence, it is only by means of property, that such a government can be preserved. If property and intelligence ought to govern the country, if it be necessary to keep out the mass that property and intelligence should be represented, why now compel them to side with the multitude and join the enemies of order? Are the times such that the cause of good government can spare one of its natural allies? If I wished to set before the House in the strongest light the evils of the present system of representation, I should refer to the northern part of this city. If I had that foreigner who has been introduced first into the debate by the noble Lord who opened it and has been subsequently used by almost every speaker—if I had that foreigner and wished to make him fully sensible on the peculiar evils of our system, I would conduct him to that great city which lies to the north of Oxford Street and the west of Russell Square. There I would shew him a city that exceeds in size the capitals of many kingdoms and is even superior in intelligence and knowledge to any city on the face of the globe. I would there shew him long lines of interminable streets and spacious squares filled with well-built magnificent houses, inhabited by opulent and intelligent men, some of the first citizens of the State. I would shew that stranger the magnificent shops, the splendid apartments. I should like to carry him to the palaces that stretch along each side of the Regent's Park, and I would tell him that the rental of these palaces and houses exceeds the rental of all Scotland at the time of the Union; and then I would tell that stranger that all this wealth and intelligence were unrepresented!

I should not refer him to Leeds, or Birmingham, or Sheffield, or other great towns unrepresented, or point out to him that Edinburgh or Glasgow, the chief cities of Scotland, had only the shadows of representation. It would be quite sufficient to shew him that the immense, wealthy, populous, and intelligent district which I have mentioned was without a representative. Sir, the principle of the property tax, I believe, was that no income below £150 should be taxed; but I very much doubt, if I were to include the whole of the parties assessed to that tax, I should find one-half of them having votes for representatives in Parliament. Indeed, I am convinced that it would not be beyond the mark to state that one-fiftieth of the property of the Kingdom only is represented, the other forty-nine parts being wholly without representatives. Ours, then, Sir, is not a government on the principle of property; it is only a government on some fragments of property, and, as applicable to present circumstances, I should say that no principle whatsoever presided over its formation.

But the honourable Member for Oxford[4] asks us to shew the time in which our Constitution was better than it now is. Sir, we are not here to decide upon what it was, but to make it what it ought to be. We do not sit here as antiquarians but as legislators. Our Constitution might at some former time have been worse than it is; that is not the question; it is our duty to suit it to the circumstances of the present time. If in its form it has stood still, the population, the wealth, and the intelligence of the country have been continually advancing. The noble Lord[5] has openly and manfully stated that the borough which he represents is the same now as in the time of Edward I. Does the noble Lord, however, consider the great difference between the state of the country at that period and at the present time? Does he consider the change that has since taken place, that what were then small hamlets or villages have since become great towns, equal in wealth and population to some of the largest cities; and that the population of England, which at that time did not exceed two millions, has since then increased to more than seven times that amount? Sir, I have great respect for the wisdom of our ancestors; but my deference to it will not lead me to adopt a system wholly unsuited to the present altered state of the country.

In one thing, however, our ancestors were wise; they acted for their own times. It never entered their heads to give four Members to York as well as to London because York had been the capital of the kingdom in the time of Constantius Chloris; nor did they refuse to give representives to a town with 100,000 inhabitants because that town stood on the site where only a few hovels existed in the thirteenth century. Our Constitution, such as it is, has had great inroads made upon it from time to time. At one time it was put aside by the lawless violence of pirates; at another it was encroached upon by domestic tyrants; but yet by the Constitution, as it was originally established, the commonalty alone had a right to raise taxes; that was guaranteed by Magna Charta; so was the freedom from arbitrary arrests; though these principles were frequently violated not by the people but by the despotic conduct of monarchs. Great changes have taken place in every part of society since the period to which the noble Lord and the honourable Baronet referred; new property and new modes of acquiring it have been since called into existence; society has assumed a different form; cities have dwindled into villages, and obscure villages have risen to the rank of cities, and places not known in the remote period referred to have now risen to station and opulence, far greater than London was in the time of the Plantagenets. The form, however, of the original Constitution still remains applicable to certain parts; but as the form continues, the spirit departs; it is new wines in the old bottles; they are unfit for it; they burst. I repeat, then, Sir, that we must not adhere to what

[4] Sir Robert Harry Inglis. Inglis had responded to Russell's speech on the previous day.
[5] Viscount Stormont, Member for Aldborough.

our ancestors did but must do what under similar circumstances it is probable they would have done. We must accommodate ourselves to the changes which have taken place in society. All history is full of such changes.

Sir, when the honourable Member for Oxford describes this measure as revolutionary, is he not aware that society is always in a state of revolution, and that institutions must be changed to correspond with it? The political history of the world cannot be opened without finding numerous instances of such changes, without finding some new interest coming into existence. It is at first weak and is trampled on; then it grows strong and presses on those who resist it; and it is only when such resistance is made that we find those struggles commence which have convulsed nations. Such was the struggle between the plebeians and patricians at Rome; such the struggle between the Romans and their Italian neighbours; and such, in more modern times, was the struggle between the American Colonies and the mother country. Such was the struggle in Ireland between the Catholics and Protestants, till the former were released from their servitude; such, too, is the struggle now going on in Jamaica between the free men of colour and the aristocracy of the skin; and such is the struggle now making between the middle classes of England and the aristocracy—the aristocracy of gentlemen, merely, not distinguished for talent or genius, and who, by withholding from the wealth and intelligence of the middle classes that which they concede to the pot-wallopers, have made themselves absurd and contemptible in the eyes of Europe.

The honourable Member for Oxford says that the great unrepresented cities have their interests as well taken care of as if they were represented, and that his vote is given as much with a view to the interest of Manchester as of Oxford. This is the old doctrine of virtual representation; I confess that I cannot understand the reasoning of those who stand up for virtual representation and will not give real representation because it is noxious. I cannot comprehend how that power, which is virtually so beneficial, should be, when directly exercised, so injurious; if the influence be good, virtually exercised, it must be good when directly exercised. If there be an evil in change as change, there is also an evil in discontent as discontent. This is the strong part of the case of those who oppose the measure. It is said that the system works well. Sir, I deny that the system works well as regards the people of England, though it may work well for a few people in this House. Is that a good system which is approved by no other 658 men in the kingdom? If you were to select that number by lot from the shopkeepers or middle classes in any part of the country, you could not attempt to persuade them that the present system of representation is a perfect one without the risk of being hooted by them for such an attempt. Sir, I am not defending this feeling. I am only arguing upon it as a fact, and if the people do believe that the present system is bad, it is no slight proof of its being so. However, I will not press this point further. I know it must be unpopular to state to any assembly that they have acted ill; besides, it will raise a number of questions as to all the great transactions for nearly the last hundred years. One thing, however, we see—that we are popular—and from that fact I argue. There are many circumstances which tend to render the representation unpopular. It is the theory of the Constitution that property should be represented; the practice is opposed to that theory. Sir, I am convinced the people of England do not forget what is due to the privileges of their Sovereign or of the other House. They desire not a reform of that kind nor was it desired, except by a few crazy radicals, whom the very boys point at in derision as they walk the streets.

Who, then, is it that desire reform? I say the people of England. The state of the House of Commons it is which creates its unpopularity, and for a good reason: because *corruptio optimi est pessima*.[6] Burke very properly describes the House of Commons as a check not on but for the people. If instead of being a check for it has become a check on, it cannot be surprised that it should be unpopular. "If the salt has lost its savour, wherewith shall it be salted?" If the check for the people be corrupted, how will they be able to keep other evils in check? Sir, I repeat it is not from any feeling of disloyalty to the King or dislike of the aristocracy that the people desire reform; they have nothing to fear from the hereditary aristocracy as long as they keep within their proper sphere. We are told that this desire of innovation has sprung from the recent proceedings in France and Belgium. Sir, I have read history very falsely if this feeling has sprung from any such cause. The plague of discontent is not the growth of a day, and if we examine into this, it will be found that it is a chronic and deep-seated malady. The present discontent has been growing through two generations. The Legislature has tried every means in its power to put an end to it. It has called new laws into operation; it has altered or abrogated old. What, indeed, has it not done? Is it to be supposed that any probable measure of cure should escape the subtlety of Burke or the sagacity of Windham? Was not every species of coercion tried by Lord Londonderry?[7] Have not laws been passed to put down public meetings and to enthral the press? And is not the evil still in existence, and is it not increasing from day to day? What have we not done to palliate it? And what more palliatives can we try? What further palliatives have we?

Under these circumstances, the Government proposes to adapt the system of representation to the present state of the country, which the noble Lord[8] seems to regard with horror, as if the system that is several centuries old was adapted to the political feelings and rights of the people of this day. The measure is a practical measure, adapted to the wants of the country.

[6] "Corruption of the best is worst".
[7] See footnote 2.
[8] Stormont.

It is founded on the good practical principle of giving to the middle classes political power. It is calling into alliance with the ordinary principles of good government all the intelligence of the middle classes. I congratulate the Ministry on their standing or falling by such a measure. If I were in their place, I would rather fall with such a system of representation than stand on any other question. The honourable Member for Oxford has stated one objection, which, if it were well founded, would be an attack on other parts of the Constitution. The honourable Member told the House that a reformed House of Commons could not exist for ten years without pulling down the Throne and destroying the House of Lords. It was impossible, the honourable Member said, that the property and intelligence of the middle classes could be adequately represented without the result being to pull down the majesty of the Throne and the dignity of the aristocracy.

Sir, if the honourable Baronet could imbue this House—if he could imbue the public mind—fully with this opinion, he would do more to injure the aristocracy and the monarchy in public estimation than anything which had ever been done by their greatest enemies. Nothing ever said or written by Tom Paine could be so injurious. [*Hear, hear.*]

Sir, honourable Members who give those cheers seem to look upon monarchy and aristocracy as the end of government and not the means; I view them as the means and not the end. If the Bill shall produce a republic by improving the representation—though I am convinced it will have no such effect—if what the honourable Member for Oxford says be true, if giving the great body of the intelligent and middle classes a share in the Government will lead to the destruction of the aristocracy and the demolition of the Throne, what does that imply but that these two are opposed to the welfare of the nation? It will not bear an argument to assert that admitting the middle classes to a share of the representation will subvert the Government of the King and the Peers. If that be the only objection to the measure, there is no ground whatever for opposing it.

Another great objection which I have heard to the plan of the noble Lord is that it will shut out from men of great talent and ability the means of making their talents available to the service of their country, as they now can by means of the boroughs proposed to be disfranchised. This argument is, I think, as little founded in fact as that which has been urged with respect to the case of the death of the King in the rebellion preceding the Commonwealth. The fact that men of talents have often and do still make their way to this House by means of these boroughs is by no means a conclusive argument in favour of the present system. Every system of government that can be devised has its happy accidents—men of great ability come into power under every system—and I have no doubt that if it were determined that the representation of the people should be confined to the 100 tallest men in the country, some of them would be found to be men excelling in qualifications for their functions. If the first

100 names on the *Court Guide* were chosen for that purpose, or if 100 gentlemen of tawny complexion were selected, the same thing would occur; and these happy accidents would form quite as just a ground for preferring any of these modes of election as the one to which I am alluding does for the present mode.

The sovereign who once owed his kingdom to the neighing of his horse happened to prove a great and good monarch; but does that form a ground for preferring that mode of choosing a king? In ancient Athens the choice of magistrates was by lot, and many eminent and good men were thus brought into power; but that forms no ground for preferring a choice of magistrates by lot. It happened on one occasion that Socrates was by lot called to preside in an assembly, where his presence contributed to defeat a most unjust measure; but no one will contend that the lot was a fair mode of selecting officers of great trust. This country is, happily, not depending on one or two great men, and whatever may be the means selected for their admission into power, men of ability will find their way. They may not be the same men as would come in under the borough system, but they will be men of talents, and no one man is indispensably necessary. Sir, a great nation needs no one individual. Let us give the country good institutions and we will be sure to find good and great men.

Some honourable Members have said the measure attacks property; and the honourable Member for Newport[9] has compared it to the proceedings which took place at the close of the reign of Charles II for disfranchising the cities and boroughs. I am rather surprised at this, because the noble Lord who brought in the Bill anticipated this argument and reminded the House of a recent case which should have prevented the honourable Member from saying one word. If the franchise be property, as a noble Lord[10] said, which is not to be taken away without compensation —if, as the honourable Gentleman said, it is not to be withdrawn but after a judicial investigation, after proof of guilt, after some crime has been fully established, what must be said to the disfranchisement of the forty-shilling freeholders, which, on this doctrine, was a flagitious robbery? They were all at once deprived of their rights without any charge, without having been guilty of any crime, without having been heard, and without a thought of compensating them for their loss. If the franchise at Louth be a property, is it not also a property at Waterford? And should it be taken away in the latter case, where no crime could be imputed? It may be said, indeed, that it was a crime in the Catholic freeholders of Clare to elect the present honourable Member for Waterford[11] for the county. But then, I ask, why punish the Protestant freeholders of Louth for the crime of the Catholic freeholders of Clare?

[9] Horace Twiss.
[10] Earl of Darlington, Member for Saltash.
[11] Daniel O'Connell.

Sir, there is one more circumstance to which I will allude. Every one, I believe, of the honourable Members who have spoken on the other side has said that His Majesty's Ministers had at some former time opposed Parliamentary Reform. It is not for me to defend those who are so well able to defend themselves; I will only say that I firmly believe that the country will not think the worse of them nor value their services the less because they have shewn themselves capable of learning by experience that they have profited by their observation and are no longer opposed to what they and many others see is an inevitable change. I only wish that other persons would learn a similar lesson. Is it possible that they who now despise this lesson can forget the humiliating lesson they were taught not long ago by an obstinate resistance to a measure which was rendered inevitable by the progress of society? Is it possible that they who now arrogantly censure others do not recollect that they were then obliged to surrender what they strove in vain to defend?

In May, 1827, I was in this House, though I had not a seat in it at that time, and I then heard the right honourable Baronet[12]—of whom I wish to speak with all due respect—I then heard that right honourable Baronet, who had just before quitted office, demand of the Government of that day what it meant to do with respect to the Test and Corporation Acts and Parliamentary Reform; and then the right honourable Baronet stated that he should give to these questions his decided opposition. Such was the case four years ago, and how stands the case now with these three great questions? The Test and Corporation Acts have been repealed. By whom? By the Ministers who succeeded Mr. Canning. The penal laws against the Catholics have been repealed. By whom? By the Ministers who succeeded Mr. Canning. There remains the question of Parliamentary Reform; and whoever beholds the signs of the times, the important signs that are hourly manifested, must be convinced, that unless the question of Parliamentary Reform be speedily settled, unless the great body of the middle classes of the people obtain some share in the representation, unless their affections for our institutions be restored, there is great hazard of our being exposed to the most fearful dangers. I cannot believe that any person versed in political affairs and reading these signs can believe that the present system of representation can continue to the year 1860.

What is it, then, I ask, for which you are to wait? Is it merely to shew that you have not profited by experience? Do you wait to defer the measure to a period when, as it was seen on another great question, you can no longer refuse it with safety, or concede it with grace? Do you wait for the time when men shall come into the Ministry with cries of "No reform" and become reformers, as they had come with cries of "No popery" and then become emancipators? Do you wait until public resolution becomes

---

[12] Sir Robert Peel.

irresistible? Do you wait for more disturbances—for a larger mass of discontent? Do you wait for a more organised system of agitation than that of the "Corn Exchange"—for a collection of a fund more formidable than the "rent?"[13] Do you wait for more skillful agitators, who may again divide with the Cabinet the Government of the country? Or do you wait for that worst of all resources in a conflict with public opinion—the fidelity of the military? Do you want to have the scenes of 1827[14] acted over again? Do you remember the restrictions laid on the expression of the public mind in one part of the Kingdom; and how that mind found an outlet still more dangerous than if it had still been unrestrained? Have you forgotten the history of Ireland, where the Catholics were indulged in rebellion because they were denied justice?

Sir, there are signs abroad, and none can see them with his eyes and hear them with his ears and not feel it his duty to stand between them and the dangerous results which may be anticipated. Now, then, I say, is the time to concede Reform, not as a measure of revolution, but of conservation. Now, when the crash of the proudest throne in Europe, which has fallen in a struggle with public opinion, is still sounding in our ears; now, when one of our decayed palaces affords an ignominious asylum to the descendant of forty kings;[15] now, while yet the heart of England is sound—while the national feelings of attachment to old associations are yet retained, bound as it were to the honour and character of the country, but which may too soon pass away—now is the accepted time, now is the day of salvation; now is the moment when the great debt due from the aristocracy to the people should be paid, and which, if paid, will never be forgotten by those whose prosperity it will ensure. Let me then implore you to take counsel, not from prejudice or party, but from the history of past events, the knowledge of what is passing around you. It is yet time to save the country from risk—to save the multitude from its own ungovernable power and passion—to save it from that danger to which even a few days might expose it and the country.

Sir, I earnestly hope that those who resist this measure of reform may not end their days in unavailing regrets that they had not taken a different course; earnestly do I pray that they may not feel those regrets amidst riot, confiscation, and massacre—amidst that wreck of the institutions of the country which can only lead to the entire dissolution of social order.

---

[13] "Rent" was the term used for voluntary contributions of one shilling a year raised by the Catholic Association for Daniel O'Connell's campaign fund. The fund, collected outside the doors of churches in Ireland, reached £15,000 by 1825.

[14] When Canning became Prime Minister in 1827, Wellington, Peel, and four other Tories resigned from the cabinet; they distrusted Canning's liberal views on Catholic emancipation. But public pressure forced Wellington, Canning's successor, reluctantly to introduce legislation to permit Roman Catholics to sit in Parliament.

[15] The deposed French monarch Charles X was in exile at Holyrood Palace in Edinburgh.

Sir Robert Peel

"Against the Reform Bill"[*]
Commons, March 3, 1831

Sir, I must begin by assuring my noble Friend[1] that the part of his speech in which he adverted to the delicacy and difficulty of his personal situation in this debate appeared to me wholly unnecessary; for if my noble Friend had not thought it right to explain the grounds which have induced him to adopt a different course from that which he pursued on a former occasion, still I, for one, should not have drawn any unfavourable conclusion from his silence or joined in the taunts of which he has complained. I have been placed in the same situation with my noble Friend.[2] I, too, have found it necessary, from a regard to the interests of the country, to adopt a different course from that which I had long conscientiously followed; and I ought, therefore, to be the last man in this House who would refuse to put an indulgent construction on the language or to join in harsh conclusions with respect to the motives of public men. I never can allow it to be supposed that public men have not higher and nobler motives for their public conduct that the paltry desire to retain place; and the character of my noble Friend, therefore, even if he had been silent, would have proved to me a sufficient guarantee for the rectitude of his intentions.

Having thus imitated that generous courtesy which prevails in more deadly combats than that in which I am about to engage—having shaken hands with my noble Friend and disclaimed all personal hostility—I trust I shall now be excused if I descend into the arena and with perfect freedom apply myself to the speech of my noble Friend. At the moment when we were anxiously waiting for a vindication of the measure before the House—at the moment when we wanted to know not what popular opinion demanded from us, but what we were practically to gain from the adoption of the measure of the noble Lord—at that moment the noble Lord had thought fit to enter into an invidious comparison of the merits

---

[*] The text is from the *Mirror of Parliament*, III (1831), 644–650.
[1] Lord Palmerston.
[2] The reference probably is to Peel's reversal of stand on Catholic Emancipation.

of the late and the present Administrations, and the greater part of his speech was composed not of the arguments which the House so greatly desiderated, but of sarcastic allusions to the conduct and opinions of the late Administration, connected with an attempt—not a very successful one, I admit—to magnify the deeds of the present Government at the expense of that Government which was lately honoured with His Majesty's confidence. My noble Friend says that if there had not been a change in the Government, the same results, and especially with reference to Ireland, would not have taken place. In that opinion I am much disposed to concur. No Party hostility shall ever prevent me from doing justice whenever justice should be done, or bestowing praise wherever praise ought to be bestowed. I approve the course of the present Home Department; I admire the conduct of the noble Marquess now at the head of the Irish Government;[3] ever since he has re-assumed that office, I have seen nothing in his conduct but what entitles him to praise. I believe, too, that there is some truth in what has been said by my noble Friend, that had the late Administration been in office, they would not have been able to effect what has been effected there by the present Administration. But should we have had the same assistance? Should we, if at a period of great excitement, if amid a loud and general demand for retrenchment, we had produced estimates of increased extent—should we have found all Party considerations yield to a feeling for the public service; or had we resorted to measures of extreme coercion, should we have found a united and generous disposition in all parts of the House to supply the executive Government with the means of defeating whatever efforts might be made to disturb the public tranquillity? Sir, I will not enter into any comparison of the merits of the two Administrations.

. . . . .

I now come to the tremendous question before the House; but before I approach the consideration of it, I must give vent to feelings of pain and humiliation, which I cannot adequately express. I am asked, I will not say to make a revolution in the country, but, as was properly said by the honourable Member for Callington,[4] to substitute for the present a different Constitution; and I am not invited to do this after a calm and dispassionate inquiry, but to take this hasty step by an appeal to motives, which, if I permitted them to influence me, would brand me with disgrace. I am desired—expressly and repeatedly desired—not to subject my fears to my judgment, but my judgment to my fears; to defer to authority which I cannot recognise; and to consult my own personal interest, by averting the threatened penalty of a dissolution.

[3] Marquess of Anglesey.
[4] Alexander Baring.

I would ask why the King's name is introduced in this discussion. Why has it been stated day after day to the country that this plan has received the particular sanction of the King? As to the reference that has been made to the discussion on the Catholic question, the cases have no similarity. On that occasion it had been publicly stated that the measure had not the sanction of the King, and the Ministers had then no alternative but to declare that the measure was brought forward with the sanction of the King. But when a measure like this is introduced by the Administration—when the King's consent must be presumed—when it is not called in question by the Administration—is it necessary, day after day, in both Houses of Parliament and in the public press, to state that this measure has received the approbation of His Majesty, and not only the approbation but the written sanction of the King? I assume that such is the fact. But granting the fact, it is no imputation on my profound respect and loyalty towards His Majesty if I disregard that circumstance; and if, admitting that the noble Lord's plan has the sanction of the King, I nevertheless as a Member of Parliament exercise my judgment as unreservedly upon the question as if that sanction had not been so indefatigably proclaimed. But, Sir, I regret on other grounds that it has been thought necessary by the friends of the measure, day after day, to introduce the name of the King in connexion with it. I will not now discuss the right or the expediency of the sweeping disfranchisement that is proposed. But I am sure it will be granted to me that the great measure is at least one of harshness towards a number of corporate bodies of proved loyalty to the Crown suddenly called upon to sacrifice privileges of which they have been long and justly proud. Why hold out to those bodies His Majesty as the approver, almost as the especial author, of the plan by which these privileges are to be invaded? I had thought the King was the fountain of grace and favour; but it now seems as if his Ministers shrunk from their proper share of their own acts and transferred to their Sovereign the odium of this plan of disfranchisement, if it is to be received. I do not think that it is right or decent to aggravate the injury which the corporate bodies of this country are to sustain, by telling them that it is inflicted at the instigation and by the hand of their King.

I have further to complain of the menace of dissolution which has been thrown out by some Members of His Majesty's Government. I will not stop to inquire whether or not it is probable that that menace will have any effect. For myself, I care not for it; for I should be unworthy of a seat in this House if I were to permit myself to be influenced by it. Dissolve Parliament if you will; I care not much whether I am returned again or retire altogether into the obscurity of private life; but if I did feel any extreme anxiety on this head, I would go to my constituents with your Bill in my hand, and I would put forward, as my especial claim for a renewal of their confidence, my determined opposition to its enactments. I will go to a community which consisted in 1811 of between 7,000 and 8,000 persons; I will go to a borough which, whatever may have been the case in 1821, in 1831 contains above 4,000 souls; and I will tell my constituents—400 or 500 in number, many of them not paying a rent of £10 but entitled to vote as resident householders paying church and poor rates—I will tell them that to this Bill, brought in without proof or even argument of its necessity so far as it concerns them, I opposed myself to the utmost extent of my power. I will tell them that I did my utmost to preserve to them the privilege they at present enjoy, and which the humblest of them never abused by the solicitation or acceptance of a bribe. Those constituents received me with kindness at the time when I was subjected to the indignity of expulsion elsewhere for doing what I conceived to be an act of duty—an act beneficial to the country, but especially beneficial to that Church of whose interests I was bound to be the guardian.[5] Shortly after I lost that proud distinction to which I have just adverted, my present constituents received me; and I will not, till some better reasons are brought forward, repay their kindness by being a party to their disfranchisement.

Sir, another and a still more alarming menace has been thrown out by the advocates of the Bill. I am told by them that the alternative before me is the adoption of that Bill or civil commotion. I am to be deterred from forming a deliberate judgment on a most important public question by the prophetic visions of massacre and confiscation. Such were the words used last night by the honourable Member for Calne.[6] Let me ask the friends of the Bill why I am to allow myself to be scared by this intimation. Why may I not form the same deliberate judgment on this Bill which you who have introduced it formed on the Bill which was introduced last year by a noble Lord?[7] By your opposition to that Bill you did not imply that you were opposed to all reform; you merely implied that you objected to that Bill. It is the same with me in this case. Again, on the same principle on which you who support the Bill reject the application of the people for vote by ballot, why am not I at liberty to reject your Bill? Why am I to yield to popular clamour and violence when the noble Lord opposite has not yielded to them? We were told last night that if we rejected this proposition, we, the individual Members who so rejected it, would be held responsible for the consequences. "We will shift from our own shoulders," say His Majesty's Ministers, even at this early period of the agitation they foresee, "the responsibility of having provoked it. We have proved our incapacity to govern, but we will shew you our capacity to destroy and hold you responsible if you obstruct us." Oh no, for on their heads shall be the responsibility of this mad proceeding. I, for one, utterly disclaim it. For

---

[5] Peel relinquished his seat for Oxford University to give the electorate an opportunity to respond to his stand on Catholic Emancipation. The voters elected Robert H. Inglis; and Peel was returned for the pocket borough of Westbury.

[6] See Thomas B. Macaulay's speech, pages 110–119.

[7] Marquess of Blandford, Member for Woodstock.

what can I be made responsible? Was it I who raised the stormy waves of the multitude? Was it I who manifested my patriotism by exerting all my powers to excite the people to discontent with the existing Constitution? Did I taunt the people with their indifference to reform, with having closed their ears to "the voice of the charmer, charm he never so wisely," with having lived in the lazy enjoyment of practical good and disregarded the promises of visionary improvement? Was it I who called for the pension list of the Privy Council for the express purpose of holding up the Members of that Council to public indignation? Did I draw invidious comparisons between a great naval commander and the civilians who presided over the department of the Admiralty? Did I ever doom to public obloquy that hopeless First Lord who should be so grasping of emolument as to include in his own estimates £5,000 per annum for his own salary? Did I, at a moment when the events of Paris and Brussels had caused great public excitement, when various causes were conspiring to agitate the public mind, did I express my misplaced admiration of the conduct of assembled thousands who were supposed to have flaunted in the face of their King the emblem of a foreign revolution? Sir, if there be men who, having thus excited the passions of the people and spurred their lazy indifference, bring forward the question of reform at a time when all prudential considerations, whether with reference to foreign or to domestic topics, ought to have forbidden such a step—if, I say, disappointment should follow their rash undertaking, I will never, while I have a voice in this House, allow them to hold me or any other individual Member of the House responsible for the consequences of their infatuation.

I am told that an appeal will be made to the people. I beg not to be included among those who are charged with making any one observation disparaging to the middle classes of society in this country. I repudiate that sentiment, sprung myself, as I am, from those classes and proud of my connexion with them. So far am I from underrating their intelligence or influence that I tell you this—you who talk of appealing to the people—that unless these middle classes shall shew more prudence, more judgment, and more moderation than their rulers, I shall despair of the destinies of my country. There are happy indications, however, which induce me to think that the confidence which I repose in the prudence, the moderation, and the judgment of the middle classes of society has not been misplaced. You have all heard what the noble Lord opposite, the Chancellor of the Exchequer,[8] said with respect to the supposed exhibition of a tri-coloured flag at the Palace of St. James's; but have you also heard the indignant refutation of that charge which was laid on your Table by a portion of the middle classes of society? So far from thinking that it was becoming to wave under the windows of their Sovereign the memento of a fallen dynasty

---

[8] Viscount Althorp.

—so far from thinking that it was decent, that it was consistent with the patriotic feelings of Englishmen to prefer any foreign standard to a flag which

> ... has braved for a thousand years
> The battle and the breeze[9]

—these people, these middle classes of society, presented an address to this House in which, so far from accepting the vindication which had been offered for their conduct in the supposed use of the tri-coloured flag, they stated "that they felt themselves much aggrieved by certain observations and misrepresentations made on the 9th instant, which conveyed a charge of a most foul and disgraceful nature and an approach even to the foul crime of treason." Sir, so far were they from intending to express any approbation "of the beautiful days of Paris" that they assured the House that the flag they so unfortunately displayed "was nothing more than four specimens of silk, of different colours, of curious workmanship, curiously sewed together, and manufactured expressly for the occasion by Messrs. Lee and Bousfield, of Cheapside." I may say, then, Sir, that from this expression of just indignation and this natural explanation of their quadri-colour flag, the middle classes of this country, notwithstanding the bribe of power by which it is attempted to cajole them, have too much of self-denial and too much of good sense to wish to invade that admirable Constitution under which they, of all classes, have especially flourished.

If I must appeal not to the reason and calm judgment of this House, but to some extrinsic and higher authority—the feelings and wishes of the people—why, then I have nothing to hope for but that, before the people of England approve of this Bill, they will listen to a calm and temperate appeal in behalf of what the noble Lord calls, with somewhat of cruel mockery, the old English Constitution. I hope they will consider that the constitution of a government is a matter of extreme delicacy and importance, and that it is a most complex machine, not to be judged of by the examination of any isolated part which may be put forward for the purpose of exciting abhorrence; but that they will take a comprehensive view not only of the structure as a whole, but of its practical effects. It was well said by Mr. Canning, whose language, however, I will not attempt to quote, that in judging of any form of government, we should bring to the consideration of it the same caution, the same distrust in our own knowledge, with which we should pronounce upon some mighty and complex piece of mechanism. There may be detached movements that we do not comprehend—movements which, to the superficial and ignorant, may seem not only useless, but pernicious—but surely we must not condemn them if there be harmony in the working of the whole machine, and if its object be completely effected. "Look," said Mr. Canning, "at the frame of man—

[9] The lines are from Thomas Campbell's "Ye Mariners of England."

it is fearfully and wonderfully made! yet this frame of a created being so 'noble in reason!'—so 'infinite in faculty'—in apprehension so 'like a God'[10]—has parts, and performs functions which, if they are to be separately regarded, provoke feelings of abhorrence and disgust."

Sir, let the people recollect that the writers of ancient times—who existed upwards of a thousand years ago and could have no partiality for the British Constitution—that mere speculative writers, discussing *a priori* the various forms of government, either despaired altogether of the formation of such a Constitution as ours or described it as the most perfect of all. Can there, by possibility, be a better description of the British Constitution than that contained in the words of Cicero: "*Statu esse optimo constitutam rempublicam*"—I do not know whether I quote the words correctly—"*quæ ex tribus generibus illis regali, optimo, et populari, modice confusa.*"[11] Another eminent writer of antiquity (Tacitus) speaking of forms of government says that all forms of government must consist either of king, noble, or the people, or a combination of all these elements, the practicability of which he doubts: "*Cunctas nationes et urbes populus aut primores, aut singuli regunt. Delecta ex iis et constituta reipublicæ forma, laudari facilius quam evenire; vel, si evenit, haud diuturna esse potest.*"[12] Such, Sir, are the dicta of great writers on the abstract question of the modes of government. The British Constitution has been made a subject of praise by every writer who has touched upon the question. I have heard quotations from Mr. Canning, from Mr. Burke, and from other great men now no more, in assertion of the excellence of the British Constitution, but to these I will not refer, for I have a higher and a living authority on the same subject. I will venture to say that if the House will permit me to substitute it for my own imperfect praise, I will read to it one of the most beautiful panegyrics on the English Constitution, and more especially on the Constitution of this House, that wisdom and truth have ever produced. The author of this panegyric is the noble Member for Tavistock,[13] alas! too, the author of a proposal fatal to the object of his praise. Sir, in quoting this speech, I beg that the noble Lord who now proposes to lay violent hands on what was once the theme of his warmest admiration will not imagine that I am about to upbraid him with inconsistency on account of his having altered his opinion. If he has changed his opinion, I am sure it is from a sense of duty; but change that opinion as he may, he cannot gainsay the eternal truths which he himself has put upon record in language worthy to convey them. Sir, it was in the year 1819, on a motion

[10] From *Hamlet* (Shakespeare), II, ii.
[11] "A state is constituted with the best arrangement, which is appropriately combined of the three types of government: monarchy, aristocracy, and democracy" (*Republic* I.45).
[12] "The people or the nobility or individuals rule every nation and city; a form of government selected and blended from these types can more easily be commended than effected, or if it is effected, it cannot endure" (*Annals* IV.33).
[13] Lord John Russell.

which was brought forward for reform in Parliament, that the noble Lord made the speech which I am about to quote.[14] The question put to him was this: "Why not disfranchise also the unconvicted boroughs?" What was the answer of the noble Lord?

> To this [says he] I answer that I do not by any means maintain that the resolutions I now propose comprise all the amendments that can be made in the frame of this House. Whenever a specific proposition is made, I shall be ready to give it all my attention and, if I can approve of it, to adopt it. But I do not, at present, I confess, see any rule by which any unconvicted borough can be disfranchised without disfranchising the whole.

He goes on to say, "We then arrive at what is called a reform upon a principle, or the re-construction of the entire House of Commons." Therefore, Sir, I have the authority of the noble Lord himself for this explanation of the character and effect of his present proposal, that it is neither more nor less than an entire re-construction of the House of Commons. Says the noble Lord:

> We then arrive at what is called a reform upon principle, or the re-construction of the entire House of Commons. Now, Sir, I will not dwell upon the arguments which are generally used to repel such a proposition; arguments resting chiefly upon the advantage of admitting men of talent into this House by means of the close boroughs; and on the danger that an assembly of popular delegates would overthrow the two other branches of the Legislature. But I cannot forget that these arguments have been urged not, as some out of doors endeavour to persuade the people, by borough-mongers anxious to defend their own vile interests, but by some of the greatest, the brightest, and the most virtuous men whom this country ever produced. I cannot say, however, that I give entire credit to these arguments, because I think that in political speculation the hazard of error is immense and the result of the best formed scheme often different from that which has been anticipated. But for this very reason I cannot agree to the wholesome plans of reform that are laid before us. We have no experience to guide us in the alterations which are proposed, at least none that is encouraging. There is, indeed, the example of Spain. Spain was formerly in the enjoyment of a free constitution; but in the course of the fifteenth century many of the towns fell into the hands of the nobility, who, instead of influencing the election of Members to Cortes (the practise so much reprobated in this House), prevented their sending Members at all. The consequence was that when a struggle took place between the King and Cortes, the aristocracy, feeling no common interest with the representative body, joined the Crown and destroyed forever the liberties of their country. The Constitution of this country is not written down like that of some of our neighbours. I know not where to look

[14] The lengthy quotation that follows is from Russell's speech of December 14, 1819. Peel quoted Russell's remarks accurately.

for it, except in the division into King, Lords, and Commons and in the composition of this House, which has long been the supreme body in the State. The composition of this House by representatives of counties, cities, and boroughs I take to be an intimate part of our Constitution. The House was so formed when they passed the *Habeas Corpus* Act—a law which, together with other wise laws, Mr. Cobbett himself desires to preserve, although, with strange inconsistency, whilst he cherishes the fruit, he would cut the down the tree. This House was constituted on the same principle of counties, cities, and boroughs when Montesquieu pronounced it to be the most perfect in the world. Old Sarum existed when Somers and the great men of the Revolution established our Government. Rutland sent as many Members as Yorkshire when Hampden lost his life in defence of the Constitution. Are we then to conclude that Montesquieu praised a corrupt oligarchy? That Somers and the great men of that day expelled a King in order to set up a many-headed tyranny? That Hampden sacrificed his life for the interests of a borough-mongering faction? No! The principles of the construction of this House are pure and worthy. If we should endeavour to change them altogether, we should commit the folly of the servant in the story of Aladdin who was deceived by the cry of "New lamps for old." Our lamp is covered with dirt and rubbish, but it has a magical power. It has raised up a smiling land, not bestrode with overgrown palaces, but covered with thickset dwellings, every one of which holds a freeman enjoying equal privileges and equal protection with the proudest subject in the land. It has called into life all the busy creations of commercial prosperity. Nor, when men were wanting to illustrate and defend their country, have such men been deficient. When the fate of the nation depended upon the line of policy she should adopt, there were orators of the highest degree placing in the strongest light the argument for peace and war. When we were engaged in war, we had warriors ready to gain us laurels in the field or to wield our thunders on the sea. When again we returned to peace, the questions of internal policy, of education of the poor, and of criminal law found men ready to devote the most splendid abilities to the welfare of the most indigent class of the community!

And then, exclaims the noble Lord, with just and eloquent indignation at the thought:

And, Sir, shall we change an instrument which has produced effects so wonderful for a burnished and tinsel article of modern manufacture? No! Small as the remaining treasure of the Constitution is, I cannot consent to throw it into the wheel for the chance of obtaining a prize in the lottery of Constitutions.

Now, Sir, I think I have fulfilled my promise, that I would present the House with as just and beautiful a panegyric on the British Constitution, as able and prudent a warning against the danger of tampering with it, as practical wisdom ever uttered. Let it not be forgotten that this speech was delivered in the year 1819—a period when the internal state of the country was such that almost every page of your debates teems with the proofs of internal disorder. There was a Seizure of Arms Bill, a Blasphemous Libel Bill, a Seditious Meetings Prevention Bill, a Newspaper Stamp Duty Bill, and a Bill to prevent Training and Exercise, each following the other in sad succession. Why, Sir, there might be in 1819—when these six Acts of coercion were necessarily introduced—there might be in the circumstances of the time some justification for the measure of reform. The Member for Calne might then have said with some plausibility, "You have exhausted every measure of restraint; try now the measure of reform." But it is strange to hear that argument used in 1831, when every one of the coercive measures of 1819 has been blotted from the Statute Book. Now, Sir, allow me to ask the noble Lord in his own emphatic language, "What cause should now induce me to exchange the old lamp for a burnished and tinselled article of modern manufacture?"

I could not have proposed reform as a Minister of the Crown. I deprecated the agitation of such a question at the instance of the Crown. But having left office, and being reduced to the station of a private individual, I was then at liberty to take other views of this subject. I have to balance this danger of moderate reform against the monstrous evil of perpetual change in the executive Government of this country; and I do not hesitate to avow that there might have been proposed certain alterations in our representative system, founded on safe principles, abjuring all confiscation, and limited in their degree, to which I would have assented. I see a smile on the faces of some honourable Gentlemen opposite. I am speaking with the utmost unreserve and sincerity. I never conferred upon this point, upon my honour, with any individual whatever. I am not stating this as an indication of any other plan which I have to propose. I am stating the course which I should take as a private individual, having a deeper interest in the prosperity of this country than any that I could possibly have in a return to office. In this plan, which proceeds upon so extensive a principle, amounting, in fact, to a reconstruction—to use the words of the noble Lord himself—of this House, I cannot concur; and I so wholly despair of modifying its provisions in any way that when the time shall come, I shall have no alternative than to give my positive dissent to the proposed measure. I do this because I am wholly dissatisfied with it. Having listened attentively to the plan, I am wholly unconvinced by the arguments of the noble Lord.

Really, I fear, I am wearying the House; but the subject is of such immense importance that it constitutes an apology even for unseasonable length. Let me then address myself to the arguments of the noble Lord. They are arguments which, if good for anything, will not constitute this as the final change. We must proceed further. The noble Lord said—with some inconsiderate frankness, as I think—that he found the Constitution of this country in the 25th of Edward I and the statute "*De tallagio non concedendo.*" The Constitution of England in the reign of Edward I! And what did he find there? That no taxes could be imposed without the consent of the whole commonalty of the realm; and therefore, says the noble Lord, "if this be a question of right, as I contend it is, the right is on the side of the reformer." These are the noble Lord's own words; but if it be a question of right and if the right be on the side of the reformer, why, I would ask, does the noble Lord limit the franchise to particular districts and particular classes? Why confine the privilege of voting to those who rent a house rated at £10 a year?

The law knows no distinction in this respect between the contributors to the support of the State. Yet the noble Lord not only refuses the right of voting to persons rated at less than £10, but he also disfranchises many who contribute to the public taxes and who now possess the privilege of suffrage. I conceive the noble Lord's plan to be founded altogether upon an erroneous principle. Its great defect, in my opinion, is that to which an objection has been urged with great force and ability by the honourable Member for Callington. The objection is this—that it severs all connexion between the lower classes of the community and the direct representation in this House; and that I think a fatal objection—that it should be proposed in these times that every link between the representative and the constituent body should be separated, as regards the lower classes. I think it an immense advantage that there is at present no class of people, however humble, which is not entitled to a voice in the election of representatives. I think this system would be defective if it were extended further; but at the same time I consider it an inestimable advantage that no class of the community should be able to say they are not entitled in some way or other to a share in the privilege of choosing the representatives of the people in this House. Undoubtedly, if I had to choose between two modes of representation and two only, and if it were put to me whether I would prefer that system which would send the honourable Member for Windsor or that which would return the honourable Member for Preston, I should, undoubtedly, prefer that by which the honourable Member for Windsor would be returned; but I am not in this dilemma and am at perfect liberty to protest against a principle which excludes altogether the Member for Preston. I think it an immense advantage that the class which includes the weavers of Coventry and the pot-wallopers of Preston has a share in the privileges of the present system.

The individual right is limited and properly limited within narrow bounds; but the class is represented. It has its champion within your walls, the organ of its feeling, and the guardian of its interests. But what will be the effect of cutting off altogether the communication between this House and all that class of society which is above pauperism, and below the arbitrary and impassable line of £10 rental which you have selected? If you were establishing a perfectly new system of representation and were unfettered by the recollections of the past and by existing modes of society, would it be wise to exclude altogether the sympathies of this class? How much more unwise, when you find it possessed from time immemorial of the privilege, to take the privilege away and to subject a great, powerful, jealous, and intelligent mass of your population to the injury—aye, and to the stigma of entire, uncompensated exclusion! Well, but, says my noble Friend,[15] "our plan at least does this—it cures that anomaly, that absurdity of the present system, which gives to voters the right of voting for places where they do not reside." My noble Friend is shocked that men who have or who may acquire the right of voting for places in which they do reside should enjoy the right of voting for other places from which they are habitually absent. Well, Sir, this at least must be admitted, that my noble Friend is liberal in thus consenting to the disfranchisement of a great majority of his own constituents, the non-resident Masters of Arts of Cambridge.

LORD PALMERSTON: They will still continue to vote; the rule of non-residence will not apply to universities.

SIR ROBERT PEEL: Not apply to the universities! Every non-resident voter in England to be disfranchised, except non-resident Masters of Arts! And do you think that the disfranchised class will acquiesce in the reason and justice of this exception? Why may not the non-resident voter of Norwich, who cannot find employment in the place of his nativity—who is earning an honest subsistence in London—why may not he plead just as good a reason for his absence from his town, where he is now entitled to vote, as the non-resident clergyman of Cambridge or Oxford? And mark the difference. The latter will almost certainly acquire, under this very Bill, the right of voting for a district in which he does reside; the former may probably never be able to acquire it. To the one you give a new right of voting and also continue to him the possession of the old one; while to the latter you give no new right, and yet you deprive him, for a reason which equally applies to both—namely, non-residence—of the privilege of which he is now possessed. And this is your notion of justice and conciliation!

A word more as to the disfranchisement of non-resident voters. One of the loudest complaints we now hear is directed against the influence exercised over voters by their landlords. We have petition after petition pointing to what has occurred at Newark and Stamford as one of the strongest proofs of the defective state of our representative system. What is the effect of your Bill? It is to confine the right of voting to a class the great majority of which must be tenants subject to the influence of their landlords, and to deprive of the right of voting that class whose right accrues from their being freemen of a corporation on account of birth or servitude—who are all liable, as others are, to the temptation of bribery—but who

[15] Lord Palmerston.

possess an inalienable right of voting not acquired by and in no way dependent on the will of the aristocracy.

These considerations, Sir, however important, are but subordinate when compared with the changes which must take place in the practical working of the Constitution. In defence of it, we have frequently referred with exultation to the names of those men who were indebted for their first return to Parliament to some borough of comparative insignificance, and who, had that avenue not been open, might probably have never had the opportunity of distinguishing themselves in the public service. This argument has been met, in the course of this debate, by two observations. The first fell from the Member for Westminster,[16] the second from the Member for Calne. Says the Member for Westminster—and the remark comes with a bad grace from a man of his ability—"I admit that the small boroughs return frequently very able men, but I think we have had too much ability; we have suffered much from the talents of able men; and I want a system of representation which will give us honest, rather than able men." I reply, first, that it is absurd to suppose that the man of ability will be less honest than the man of no ability; and, secondly, that any system which tended to exclude from this House men of the first ability of their day would be a great practical evil. If the average of the talent and general acquirements of this House should even be below the general average of society, this House would sink in public estimation, and the distrust in our opinions and judgments would very rapidly spread downwards from the class of persons more enlightened than ourselves to the great mass of society. The second observation to which I have referred fell from the Member for Calne. He, too, admits that men of first-rate ability have occasionally owed their entrance into Parliament to small boroughs. "But then," says he—and says very justly—"we must judge of every human contrivance not by its accidents but by its tendencies. No plan of selections," says he, "could be hit upon which would not give you occasionally able men; take the hundred tallest men that you meet in the streets; you will probably have some able men among the number." The cheers with which this remark was followed were so encouraging that the honourable Gentleman proceeded to illustrate his arguments by various other instances. "Take," says he, "the first hundred names in the *Court Guide*—adopt any other principle of selection that you will—occasionally and accidentally able men will be ensured by it."

Now, Sir, I am content to try the merits of our present representative system by the honourable Member's own test. I repeat with him that it is by tendencies and not by accidents that we are to judge of its merits. For the purpose of submitting those merits to that test, I wrote down this morning the names of those distinguished men who have appeared in this

[16] John C. Hobhouse. Bankes, Hobhouse, Baring, and Palmerston had spoken earlier the same night, just before Peel's address.

House during the last forty or fifty years as brilliant lights above the horizon, and whose memory, to quote the expression of Lord Plunkett, has had buoyancy enough to float down to posterity on the stream of time. I made this selection of these men, in the first instance, without a thought of the places they severally represented. I looked to their ability and their fame alone. If I have omitted any, their names may be added, but I believe the list I shall read will contain all the names that are of the highest eminence. It includes the names of Dunning, Lord North, Charles Townsend, Burke, Fox, Pitt, Lord Grenville, Sheridan, Windham, Perceval, Lord Wellesley, Lord Plunkett, Canning, Huskisson, Brougham, Horner, Romilly, Tierney, Sir William Grant, Lord Liverpool, Lord Castlereagh, Lord Grey.

I will now read the names of the places for which they were respectively returned, on their first entrance into public life: Dunning was returned for Calne, Lord North for Banbury, Burke for Wendover, Charles Townsend for Saltash, Pitt for Appleby, Fox for Midhurst, Lord Grenville for Buckingham, Sheridan for Stafford, Windham for Norwich, Lord Wellesley for Beeralston, Perceval for Northampton, Plunkett for Midhurst, Canning for Newton, Huskisson for Morpeth, Brougham for Camelford, Romilly for Queenborough, Horner for Wendover, Lord Castlereagh for the County of Down, Tierney for Southwark, Sir William Grant for Shaftesbury, Lord Grey for Northumberland, Lord Liverpool for Rye.

These are the names of, I believe, the most distinguished men of the times in which they lived. They are twenty-two in number. Sixteen on first entering public life were returned for boroughs, every one of which, without exception, the noble Lord proposes to extinguish. Some few of these distinguished men owed, it is true, their first return to a more numerous body of constituents. Mr. Sheridan was first returned for Stafford, Mr. Windham for Norwich, Lord Castlereagh for the County of Down, Mr. Tierney for Southwark, Lord Grey for Northumberland. But it is equally true that for some cause or other, either the caprice of popular bodies or the inconvenience of Ministers of the Crown sitting for populous places, in every one of these cases the honour of the populous place is relinquished for the repose of the small borough. Mr. Sheridan quits Stafford for Ilchester, Mr. Windham takes refuge in Higham Ferrers, Mr. Tierney prefers Knaresborough to Southwark, Lord Castlereagh rejects Down for Orford, and Lord Grey consoles himself for the loss of Northumberland by appealing, with success, to the electors of Tavistock.

Now, then, I have applied your own test—I have looked not to accidents but to tendencies—and I ask you whether the tendency of the present system of representation is not to secure to distinguished ability a seat in the public councils? But after all this question must be determined by a reference to still higher considerations. The noble Lord has pointed out the theoretical defects in our present system of representation—he has appealed to the people—he has desired them to accompany him to the green mounds of Old Sarum and the ruined niches of Midhurst. I, too, make my appeal to that same people. I ask them, when they have finished poring over the imputed blots in their form of government, when they have completed their inspection of the impurities of Old Sarum and Gatton and Midhurst, I ask them to elevate their vision—*os homini sublime dedit*[17]—to include within their view a wider range than that to which the noble Lord would limit them. I ask them to look back upon a period of 150 years—to bear in mind that their Constitution, in its present form, has so long endured—and I ask them, where among the communities of Europe do you find institutions which have afforded the same means of happiness, and the same security for liberty? I conjure them to bear in mind the result of every attempt that has hitherto been made to imitate our own institutions. In France, in Spain, in Portugal, in Belgium, the utmost efforts have been made to establish a form of government like ours; to adjust the nice balance between the conflicting elements of royal, aristocratical, and popular power; to secure the inestimable blessings of limited monarchy and temperate freedom. Up to this hour these efforts have signally failed—I say not from what causes or through whose fault—but the fact of their failure cannot be denied. Look beyond the limits of Europe and judge of the difficulties of framing new institutions for the government of man. If power can be so safely entrusted to the people—if they are so competent to govern themselves, such enlightened judges of their own interests—why has it happened that up to this hour every experiment to establish and regulate popular control over executive government has, with one single exception, failed? Where are the happy republics of South America? What has obstructed their formation? What has prevented the people from exercising the new power conferred upon them to the advancement of their own interest, and the confirmation of their own liberties?

Let us beware how we are deluded by the example of the single successful experiment—how we conclude that because the form of government in the United States is more popular than own own that it would be safe, therefore, to make ours more popular than it is. The present form of the American Government has not endured more than forty years. It dates its institution not from the establishment of American independence but from the year 1789. Even within that period, the spirit of that Government has undergone a change. It is not the same as it was at its original formation; its constant tendency has been towards the establishment of a more pure and unmixed democracy. If I were to grant that it is a form of government constantly tending towards improvement—that it is calculated permanently to guarantee vigour in war and internal repose, and to meet all the growing wants of a great nation—still the circumstances of the two countries are so totally different that no inference could be drawn from

---

[17] "He gave man a face looking upward" (Ovid, *Metamorphoses* I.85).

the success of such a form of government in the United States in favour of the application of its principles to this country. The boundless extent of unoccupied land in the United States—the absence of all remote historical recollections—of an ancient monarchy—a powerful aristocracy—an Established Church—the different distribution of property in the two countries—are all circumstances essentially varying the character of the institutions suitable to each country.

We should do well to consider, before we consent to the condemnation of our own institutions, what are the dangers which menace states with ruin or decay. Compare our fate with that of other countries of Europe during the period of the last century and a half. Not one has been exempt from the miseries of foreign invasion; scarcely one has preserved its independence inviolate. In how many have there been changes of the dynasty or the severest conflicts between the several orders of the state? In this country we have had to encounter severe trials and have encountered them with uniform success. Amid foreign wars, the shock of disputed successions, rebellion at home, extreme distress, the bitter contention of parties, the institutions of this country have stood uninjured. The ambition of military conquerors—of men endeared by success to disciplined armies—never have endangered and never could endanger the supremacy of the law or master the control of public opinion.

These were the powerful instruments that shattered with impunity the staff of Marlborough and crumbled into dust the power of Wellington. What is the character of the armies which they have led to victory? The most formidable engines that skill and valour could direct against a foreign enemy; but in peace, the pliant, submissive instruments of civil power. "Give us," says the Member for Waterford,[18] "give us for the repression of outrage and insurrection the regular army, for the people respect it for its courage and love it for its courteous forbearance and patience and ready subjection to the law." And what, Sir, are the practical advantages which we are now promised as the consequence of the change we are invited to make—as the compensation for the risk we must incur? Positively not one. Up to this hour, no one has pretended that we shall gain anything by the change, excepting, indeed, that we shall conciliate the public favour. Why, no doubt, you cannot propose to share your power with half a million of men without gaining some popularity—without purchasing by such a bribe some portion of goodwill. But these are vulgar arts of government; others will outbid you, not now, but at no remote period; they will offer votes and power to a million of men, will quote your precedent for the concession, and will carry your principles to their legitimate and natural consequences. On all former occasions, some inducements were held out to us to embark on this perilous voyage. We used to be told that

[18] George T. Beresford. Daniel O'Connell also represented the County of Waterford.

we should acquire new securities against ruinous wars—as if every war, according to the express admission of Mr. Fox up to the time at which he was speaking, and every subsequent war had not been the war of the people. We used to be told that great retrenchment, great reduction of taxes, must inevitably follow reform; but we are told this no longer, since a reforming Government has found it necessary to increase the public expenditure in the very year in which they propose reform.

But reform is necessary for the purpose of curtailing the influence of the Crown in this House. Some say that through the influence of the Crown, others that through the influence of the aristocracy, bad Ministers are kept in office against the wishes and interests of the people, and that this is effected through the means of enormous patronage and for the purpose of sharing in its spoils. The influence of the Crown, indeed! The power of the Peerage to maintain unpopular Ministers against the public opinion! And this is gravely said at the time when you have had five different Administrations in four years; five Prime Ministers in rapid succession, from Lord Liverpool to Lord Grey. I lament—deeply lament—the time which has been chosen for the introduction of this measure. It is brought forward at a period of great excitement, when men are scarcely sober judges of the course which it is fitting to pursue. This has been always the case with reform; it has been uniformly brought forward, either at the times of domestic calamity or when the agitations of other states had infected us with extravagant and temporary enthusiasm for what was considered the cause of liberty. Look at the great periods of commercial or agricultural distress. You will almost invariably find reform in Parliament proposed as the panacea for distress, and finding favour just so long as the distress has endured. If you find a debate on Parliamentary Reform, be assured that "some dire disaster follows close behind."

Look again at the political struggles in other states. They never have occurred without suggesting to us the necessity of Parliamentary Reform. In 1782, shortly after the great contest in North America and the establishment of an independent and popular government in the United States, Mr. Pitt brought forward the question of Parliamentary Reform. It remained dormant altogether from 1785 to 1790. The revolution in France had then commenced, and Mr. Flood, who brought forward the question in 1790, appealed to the example of France as a powerful reason for adopting reform at home. He dwelt on the shame of England in being behind any other country in the race for liberty, and prophesied that France was about to establish a popular and therefore a pacific government—abjuring all wars and all aggressions because they were contrary to the interests of the people. We fortunately waited a short period and found that his prophecies were not very accurately fulfilled. In 1820, revolutions took place in Italy, in Spain, and in other parts of the Continent. In 1821, we had a motion for reform; and the author of that motion, the present Lord Durham, then Mr. Lambton, hailed the events that had occurred on the

Continent as the auspicious dawn of liberty abroad and improvement here. He said, speaking of the force of public opinion:

> Where its power and justice are acknowledged, as in Spain, the prospect is most cheering. We see disaffection instantaneously quelled—venerable and rotten abuses reformed—superstition eradicated—and the monarch and the people united under a Constitution which alike secures the privileges of the one and the liberties of the other. May I not, then, consistently hail the rising of this star in what was once the most gloomy portion of the European horizon, as a light to shew us the way through all our dangers and difficulties—as a splendid memorial of the all-conquering power of public opinion?[19]

Again we waited, and again I ask, was the star that appeared in Spain that steady light by which it was fitting that our steps should be guided? Or was it the return of an eccentric comet, shedding disastrous light and "perplexing nations with the fear of change?"

We are arrived at 1831 and reform is again proposed, whilst the events of the last year in Paris and Brussels are bewildering the judgment of many and provoking a restless, unquiet disposition, unfit for the calm consideration of such a question. I, too, refer to the condition of France, and I hold up the revolution in France not as an example, but as a warning to this country. Granted that the resistance to authority was just; but look at the effects—on the national prosperity, on industry, on individual happiness—even of just resistance. Let us never be tempted to resign the well-tempered freedom which we enjoy in the ridiculous pursuit of the wild liberty which France has established. What avails that liberty which has neither justice nor wisdom for its companions—which neither brings peace nor prosperity in its train?

It was the duty of the King's Government to abstain from agitating this question at such a period as the present—to abstain from the excitement throughout this land of that conflict (God grant it may be only a moral conflict!) which must arise between the possessors of existing privileges and those to whom they are to be transferred. It was the same duty of the Government to calm, not to stimulate, the fever of popular excitement. They have adopted a different course: they have sent through the land the firebrand of agitation, and no one can now recall it. Let us hope that there are limits to their powers of mischief. They have, like the giant enemy of the Philistines, lighted three hundred brands and scattered through the country discord and dismay; but God forbid that they should, like him, have the power to concentrate in death all the energies that belong to life, and to signalise their own destruction by bowing to the earth the pillars of that sacred edifice, which contains within its walls according even to their own admission "the noblest society of freemen in the world."

[19] From Lambton's speech of April 17, 1821.

Robert H. Lowe

"Against the Extension of Democracy"[*]

Commons, March 13, 1866

Sir, in the course of a long and illustrious career this House of Commons has gathered into its hands a very large proportion of the political power of the country. It has outlived the influence of the Crown; it has shaken off the dictation of the aristocracy; in finance and taxation it is supreme; it has a very large share in legislation; it can control and unmake, and sometimes nearly make, the executive Government. Probably, when the time shall arrive that the history of this nation shall be written as the history of that which has passed away, it may be thought that too much power and too much influence were concentrated and condensed in this great assembly, and that England put too much to hazard on the personal qualifications of those who sit within these walls. But, Sir, in proportion as the powers of the House of Commons are great and paramount, so does the exploit of endeavouring to amend its Constitution become one of the highest and noblest efforts of statesmanship. To tamper with it lightly, to deal with it with unskilled hands, is one of the most signal acts of presumption or folly.

When we speak of a Reform Bill, when we speak of giving the franchise to a class which has it not, of transferring the electoral power from one place to another, we should always bear in mind that the end we ought to have in view is not the class which receives the franchise, not the district that obtains the power of sending Members to Parliament, but that Parliament itself in which those Members are to sit, and for the sake of constituting which properly those powers ought alone to be exercised. To consider the franchise as an end in itself—to suppose that we should confer it on any one class of persons because we think them deserving, that we should take it away from one place because it is small, or give it to another

---

[*] The text is from *Hansard's Parliamentary Debates*, Third Series, Vol. CLXXXII, cols. 142–164.

because it happens to be large—is in my opinion to mistake the means for the end. The franchise is an enormous advantage to this country—we are naturally enamoured of it; but when we look upon it in the light which I have just mentioned and regard the conferring of it as the ultimate effort of statesmanship, as a matter of Reform, we, it appears to me, fall into the same error as the man would do who, having found that money had contributed much to his pleasure when young and to his power in middle life, should, when he was approaching the close of his days—when pleasure could charm him no more, and power was no longer within his grasp—turn his attention from the end to the means, and terminate by loving money for its own sake.

I mention this because I have, I think, some right to complain of my right honourable Friend the Chancellor of the Exchequer[1] for the manner in which he introduced the great subject under discussion to the notice of the House. The Chancellor of the Exchequer told us, in substance, that he feared he had much to say to the House, and that he would not, therefore, take up our time by entering into the arguments or reasons in favour of a revision of our electoral system or the extension of the electoral franchise. Now, Sir, I wish to speak on this matter with perfect temper and good humour; but I cannot help believing that my right honourable Friend will be of opinion that in taking the course I have just mentioned he did not deal altogether respectfully with the House. It is not right that a great assembly like this should be called upon to entertain a proposition of the very utmost moment, touching most nearly a most vital part of our Constitution—effecting, in fact, if carried into law, an immense re-distribution of political power and an enormous alteration in the constituencies of the country—it is not right, I say, that such a proposition should be introduced to us without having the reasons which induced the Government to lay such a proposition before us stated by the Minister by whom it is introduced, so that we may have something to guide us in estimating his scheme and the principles upon which it is based.

For my own part, I am not very particularly wedded to anything just because it exists, and I am quite prepared to follow experience and expediency as my guide in political matters wherever they may lead me. I have no prejudice in favour of the existing state of things. I care not, as far as any feelings or prejudices of my own are concerned, what the amount of the franchise is, or what the place in which Parliamentary power is vested. These are questions I am free to consider, because I wish to be guided by experience and induction, which, from their very nature, are always open to new light, from whatever quarter it may come, and by which everything is repudiated which savours in any degree of dogmatism. If, therefore, I complain of my right honourable Friend the Chancellor of

---

[1] William E. Gladstone, who spoke on March 12.

the Exchequer in this matter, it is not because I am not willing to give the best consideration in my power to any proposal which the Government may make with the view of improving the Constitution of this House; but although I am perfectly ready to entertain such a question, I do think it is but fair to existing institutions to say that the burden of proof is in their favour—that the presumption is in favour of that which is until it is removed by some argument which shows that that can be replaced by something better.

The way in which the Chancellor of the Exchequer proposed this great change without condescending to offer a word depreciatory of the present system points out its faults and suggests remedies for them, leads to the conclusion that he assumed the burden of proof to be in the opposite direction to that which I have indicated, and that the defenders of the Constitution are bound to answer in the first instance the arguments of the innovators instead of waiting until the latter have made out their case. I, for one, deprecate that spirit of innovation which assumes that what exists is wrong and introduces a proposal which distinctly calls upon us to pull down the noble work of our forefathers before a single word is said to show why we should assail it. The Chancellor of the Exchequer found plenty of time to deal with a great many subjects much less important. He discussed with the utmost sagacity and felicity the difference between "annual value" and "gross estimated rental," while he was eloquent in distinctions—in which we could not all follow him—with respect to compound householders, tenants of flats, lodgers, and other abstruse personalities. But, although he ably entered into all these matters, and with a detail which reminds me more of a speech on the Budget than on Reform, he did not find—so pinched was he for time—a moment to say a single word why the Constitution under which we have lived so long might not be left to us a little longer.

Passing from that subject, I will state in a few words to the House all that I deem it to be necessary to address to them with respect to the Bill which the right honourable Gentleman asks leave to introduce. This Bill proposes, in short, to increase the whole electors of the country, whom he estimates at 900,000, by 400,000—that is to say, nearly one-third. ["*One-half.*"] Yes, one-half of the present constituency, but only one-third of that which will exist if the Bill passes into law. That is, nearly one-half of the existing number, and one-third of what the number would be. He proposes to make in the counties 171,000 new electors and in the boroughs 204,000, the latter being almost altogether derived from the single class of persons renting at £10 or under £10. It will be almost entirely so, but there may be some slight difference—144,000 are absolutely and the rest pretty nearly so.

With regard to the county franchise, I have only one observation to make. The proposition of the Chancellor of the Exchequer will very much enlarge the electoral area, enormously increase the expense of elections, and create a great re-distribution of political power. That may be right or it may be wrong, but before we pass it we should be told the reason why. Then coming to the boroughs, the case is much more serious. The right honourable Gentleman opposed the voters in counties as being of the middle class to the voters in boroughs as being of the working class; and, according to the right honourable Gentleman's showing, if this Bill passes, we are to have 330,000 voters in the constituencies belonging to the working class and 360,000 in the constituencies not working men. That is the system he proposes for our adoption. This leads us to a very grave consideration, because not only the statement of the right honourable Gentleman but the statistics laid before the House show that the number of persons belonging to the working class already admitted to the franchise is 126,000, or about one-fifth of the whole amount of electors. That is a most grave and momentous fact. Look what it proves. It proves in the first place that the Government were entirely mistaken as regards the main ground on which they introduced the present measure. The main ground they put forth for bringing in the Bill—until they came to bring it in, when they thought it expedient to put forth no ground at all—was that the best of the working class were excluded from the franchise. The authority on which I make this statement is an authority which no one can dispute—it is a work on the English Government and Constitution issued by Lord Russell twice in the course of last year, once in the spring and again in the autumn.[2] This is a passage from the Preface to the work—"But may there not be still improvements?" (in the Reform Bill, the noble Lord means)—and this is the answer he gives:

> Each of the last four Ministries have been willing to add as it were a supplement to the Reform Act. For my part, I should be glad to see the sound morals and clear intelligence of the working classes more fully represented. They are kept out of the franchise, which Ministers of the Crown have repeatedly asked for them, partly by the jealousy of the present holders of the suffrage and partly by a vague fear that by their greater numbers they will swallow up all other classes. Both those obstacles may be removed by a judicious modification of the proposed suffrage.

That proves most clearly that in the opinion of Lord Russell as expressed last autumn, the best of the working classes had not the franchise. Is that true? Take the right honourable Gentleman's own statistics in your hands and compare them with that Preface. Can you reconcile them? No, for they are absolutely irreconcilable. It is quite clear that Earl Russell wrote under a delusion which was shared in by every gentleman who used the

[2] The reference is to "An Essay on the History of the English Government and Constitution, from the Reign of Henry VII to the Present Time."

argument and that I believe comprehended almost every gentleman on the Treasury Bench. He was under the delusion that we all more or less shared in and believe: that the working classes were excluded from the franchise and that there was a sharp line drawn at the £10 franchise, above which the working men could not penetrate. That being the whole proposition which the noble Lord put forward with respect to Reform, and that being proved to be founded upon a mistake, I want to know upon what principle it is that the Government—having received the statistics which my noble Friend the Member for Haddingtonshire[3] advised them to obtain, showing that these people, for the sake of whom they asked for a Reform Bill, were already represented— I want to know why they now go on at all with a Bill in respect of the representation of the people. Surely this was worth explaining. We could have perfectly understood it if these statistics had not been there; my right honourable Friend would have told us at once that it was to enfranchise the working men; but these facts being as they are, my right honourable Friend says absolutely nothing, but assumes that this House is going to entertain a proposition without knowing in the least what his adhesion to it in his own mind is based upon or what reason there is for asking the House to accede to it.

These statistics prove a little more. They prove a thing for saying which I have been greatly reproved—that the franchise was, in fact, in the power to a great extent of the working classes. I have been reviled in the best and in the worst of English for the statement, and nobody has taken me to task more severely than the noble Lord whose Preface I have read, because he has introduced a fresh series of paragraphs into his Preface to the last edition merely for the purpose of castigating me for saying anything so unkind and so untrue as that the franchise was in their power. All I can say is if it is not in their power, how did they get there? These statistics prove something more still, and what is also very well worth the notice of the Government. It is this—I do not apprehend we have any statistics to show us when it was that this great increase in the constituencies took place, but I think no one who knows the history of this country can doubt that it is owing to the great expansion of everything during the last twenty or thirty years. We know the causes at work which produced the expansion, but are they permanent or are they transient? The first cause was undoubtedly the discovery of gold in California and Australia, and the consequent depreciation of the precious metals gave an apparent increase of prices both in wages and in commodities. This led to higher rents and to higher wages—though I do not wish to embarrass the subject by going into figures. Another cause which kept up the rate of wages was the great emigration which took place, and is still taking place, from Ireland. Another cause was the vast extension in our trade and commerce, making labour

---

[3] Lord Elcho.

every day more and more in demand. Therefore, I am not wrong, I think, in considering that these causes which have existed hitherto have their efficacy by no means spent, and what we have a right to look at is that the process of spontaneous enfranchisement that has been going on since the passing of the Reform Bill will go on hereafter, and probably with re-doubled vigour. We have to build upon an admission—I cannot extract many principles from the Chancellor of the Exchequer's speech, but it is impossible to manipulate figures and statements without implying something —and one thing that he laid down was that he did not wish to see the working classes in a majority in the constituencies in this country; at least, he said he did not much care himself, but for the sake of weaker brethren he would not like to see that. And therefore he rejected—with a bitter pang no doubt—the £6 franchise and took the £7, because the £6 would have given 428,000, which would have been a clear majority of 362,000, whereas the £7 franchise gives 330,000, which leaves a very small majority the other way.

But it must be remembered that we are not speaking for a year or two but for the future, and I would ask the House: what are the prospects of the constituencies—what are the chances that the principle which the Chancellor of the Exchequer could not screw his nerves up to face would remain inviolate? Is it not certain that in a few years from this the working men will be in a majority? Is it not certain that causes are at work which will have a tendency to multiply the franchise—that the £6 houses will become the £7 ones, and the £9 houses will expand to £10? There is no doubt an immense power of expansion; and therefore, without straining anything at all, it is certain that sooner or later we shall see the working classes in a majority in the constituencies.

Look at what that implies. I shall speak very frankly on this subject, for having lost my character by saying that the working man could get the franchise for himself, which has been proved to be true, and for saying which he and his friends will not hate me one bit the less, I shall say exactly what I think. Let any Gentleman consider—I have had such unhappy experiences, and many of us have—let any Gentleman consider the constituencies he has had the honour to be concerned with. If you want venality, if you want ignorance, if you want drunkenness and facility for being intimidated; or if, on the other hand, you want impulsive, unreflecting, and violent people, where do you look for them in the constituencies? Do you go to the top or to the bottom?

It is ridiculous for us to allege that since the Reform Bill the sins of the constituencies or the voters are mainly comprised between £20 and £10. But then it has been said the £10 shopkeepers and lodging-house keepers and beerhouse keepers are an indifferent class of people; but get to the artizan, and there you will see the difference. It is the sort of theory the ancients had about the north wind. The ancients observed that as they went further to the north the wind got colder. Colder and colder it got the further they went, just as the constituencies get worse and worse the nearer you approach £10. They reasoned in this way: if it is so cold when you are in front of the north wind, how very warm it would be if you could only get behind it. And therefore they imagined for themselves a blessed land we have all read of, where the people, called the Hyperboreans, were always perfectly warm, happy, and virtuous, because they had got to the other side of the north wind. It is the same view that my right honourable Friend takes with respect to the £10 franchise—if you go a little lower you get into the virtuous stratum. We know what those persons are who live in small houses—we have had experience of them under the name of "freemen"—and no better law, I think, could have been passed than that which disfranchised them altogether.

The Government are proposing to enfranchise one class of men who have been disfranchised heretofore. This class, dying out under one name, the Government propose to bring back under another. That being so, I ask the House to consider what good we are to get for the country at large by this reduction of the franchise. The effect will manifestly be to add a large number of persons to our constituencies of the class from which if there is to be anything wrong going on we may naturally expect to find it. It will increase the expenses of candidates—it will enormously increase the expenses of management of elections, even supposing that everything is conducted in a legitimate and fair manner—and it will very much increase the expenses of electioneering altogether. If experience proves that corruption varies inversely as the franchise, you must look for more bribery and corruption than you have hitherto had. This will be the first and instantaneous result.

Then, there is another which I wish to point out to honourable Gentlemen on this side of the House—their own experience will bear me out if they would frankly admit it—and that is that by a singular retribution of Providence the main mischief will fall on the promoters of this Bill. A great many of these new electors are addicted to Conservative opinions; I do believe the franchise of the Government, if carried, will displace a number of most excellent Gentlemen on this side and replace them with an equal number of Gentlemen from the other side of the House. But all this is merely the first stage. The first stage, I have no doubt, will be an increase of corruption, intimidation, and disorder, of all the evils that happen usually in elections. But what will be the second? The second will be that the working men of England, finding themselves in a full majority of the whole constituency, will awake to a full sense of their power. They will say, "We can do better for ourselves. Don't let us any longer be cajoled at elections. Let us set up shop for ourselves. We have objects to serve as well as our neighbours, and let us unite to carry those objects. We have machinery; we have our trades unions; we have our leaders all ready. We have the power of combination, as we have shown over and over again; and when we have a prize to fight for we will bring it to bear with tenfold more force than ever before." Well, when that is the case—when you have a Parliament appointed, as it will be, by such constituencies so deteriorated—with a pressure of that kind brought to bear, what is it you expect Parliament to stop at? Where is the line that can be drawn?

The right honourable Gentleman has said to us that he does not pledge Government to any re-distribution of seats, but if the Government should bring it forward he thinks this Parliament might be kept alive in order to effect that re-distribution. I am very much obliged to my right honourable Friend; but for my part I think Parliamentary life would not be worth preserving on those terms. Look at the position Parliament will occupy. As long as we have not passed this Bill we are masters of the situation. Let us pass the Bill, and in what position are we? That of the Gideonites—hewers of wood and drawers of water, rescued for a moment from the slaughter that fell on the other Canaanites in order that we may prepare the Bill for re-distribution, with a threat hanging over our heads that if we do not do the work we shall be sent about our business and make way for another Parliament.

. . . . .

The House must remember that Members of Parliament have thrown on them another duty than that of merely representing the people. It has been ever since the Revolution of 1688, and if we do not destroy the conditions under which the arrangement subsists, it will continue to be the happy lot of this country that the leading offices of the executive Government have only approached it through the vestibule of the House of Commons. If you form your House solely with a view to numbers, solely with a view to popular representation, whatever other good you obtain you will destroy the element out of which your statesmen must be made. You will lower the position of the executive Government and render it difficult, if not impossible, to carry on that happy union between the two powers which now exists. The Reform Bill of 1832 has certainly invigorated our legislation; but it may be a question whether it has been equally efficient in invigorating our executive Government.

And here, if I have not already trespassed too much on the indulgence of the House, I would just pause to inquire what reasons can possibly be alleged—the Government have given us none—for bringing in this Bill at all. It is that it is demanded out of doors? The working classes have gone very wisely, as I myself would go, ten miles to hear the honourable Member for Birmingham;[4] but have they demanded this Bill? Has there been any

[4] John Bright.

energy in the demand for such a franchise as this? There have been meetings at St. Martin's Hall and elsewhere, but the resolutions have always been for universal suffrage. ["*No, no!*"] Almost uniformly they have spoken very disrespectfully of the honourable Member for Leeds[5] and his proposition. Have any petitions been presented for this Bill? The last account I heard of the petitions was that four had been presented; how many more are there? Those who met in St. Martin's Hall have spoken out. Mr. Odger[6] moved the first resolution, but what he said he wanted was an Act of Parliament to keep up wages. There was another man, a mason, I think, who soared to a higher degree of patriotism and asked, "Why don't you pass an Act of Parliament to make Ireland happy at once?" I therefore conclude that there is no very overwhelming pressure for Reform from that quarter yet.

Is it from the constituencies the pressure comes? Why, I have read a passage from Lord Russell's letter in which he says that it is on account of the selfishness of the constituencies that the working men are kept out. That is, in other words, the constituencies are not favourable to Reform. Well, is it from the Members of this House? There, again, I call the same witness. The noble Earl said to a deputation which went to him with very extreme views on the subject of Reform, "I agree with you in most of what you have said; but I anticipate the greatest difficulty from the House of Commons." Lastly—and owing to the delicacy of the question I would not put it, only the public interests require that I should do so—is it from the Cabinet? There, again, I call on Lord Russell, because the honourable Gentleman the Member for Birmingham asserted at a meeting that on the occasion of receiving a deputation or on some other occasion he found the noble Lord as ardent as possible for Reform, but that he told him he had immense difficulties to deal with in his Cabinet.

MR. BRIGHT: I do not know whether the right honourable Gentleman was at that meeting; but I say that there is not a word of truth in the statement. Lord Russell has never said one word to me that would in any way inform me what the opinion of any Member of his Cabinet was. I have no recollection of having said anything such as the right honourable Gentleman alleges. If he is quoting anything that he has read, it is something which I never said—something which was incorrectly reported.

MR. LOWE: I have no wish to persevere in attributing anything to the honourable Gentleman which he denies having said. What I have quoted I read in *The Star*, though, of course, I am quoting from memory. I take in *The Star* when I want any information about the honourable Member.

Well, now, let us come to reason on the thing. It is said that it is in deference to public opinion this Bill is brought in. It is not because the

---

[5] Edward Baines, who introduced bills for lowering the borough franchise to £6 in 1861, 1864, and 1865.

[6] George Odger was secretary of the London Trades Council.

working man is excluded. I have shown that. But the Chancellor of the Exchequer says that honourable Gentlemen on both sides have entered this House committed to Reform. Now, this is a question of high morality, and I wish honourable Gentlemen to turn this matter seriously in their minds. I apprehend that any Gentleman who enters this House does not enter it as the Member for any particular borough or county, but as a representative of the whole country; and he enters it bound by an obligation which no promise he has given can add to or take away from one jot or tittle. That obligation is that to the best of his ability he will honestly do his duty to the country. Well, then, if a Gentleman finds himself hampered by pledges which touch his honour, there is always a course open to him to take. If he has got into a situation incompatible with honour, he should get out of it. If he remain in it he will be in that position described by one of our greatest poets:

> His honour in rooted dishonour stood,
> And faith unfaithful made him falsely true.[7]

I hope, therefore, whatever may be the fate of this question, we shall not hear that honourable Gentlemen are pledged to act contrary to their consciences and to do what they believe will be injurious to their country.

I have now very little more to add in respect of the reasons for introducing this measure. I find nothing so difficult as to get a Reformer to assign his reasons. The plan is to assume that there are reasons. Bring in the Bill *solvitur ambulando*—by walking into the subject. In the arguments put forward on this subject we very seldom hear a Gentleman take it up and argue it from the beginning, so as to show us why we should have Reform at all. I do not now say we should not have it; but I say that you should not argue the Reform question as if the franchise were a boon which you had at your disposal and of which you should make an equal distribution. You should not deal with it as if it were the Banda and Kirwee prize money[8] which you were going to distribute. Is it a consideration of that kind which should form part of the political system of a great empire? In fact, we have *a priori* grounds of all kinds alleged. But the franchise is not to be given on an *a priori* principle of justice. This is not a question to be decided *a priori*, or on what a Gentleman can evolve from the depths of his inner consciousness. It is a question of practical experience of the working of our laws—one as to the best machinery we can have for the work we have to do.

I can well understand how such notions get root among the people. When the common people are told that there is anything to be got, they think that, as in the administration of justice, there should be equality to all. They think the Government ought to distribute everything equally,

---

[7] The lines come from Alfred Lord Tennyson's "Lancelot and Elaine."
[8] Parliament had for several years been considering conflicting claims of army officers over distribution of booty from the capture of Banda and Kirwee in India.

as if something was to be divided between co-partners. But that is an entire misunderstanding of the real business of a government. Government does not deal with justice. It deals with expediency. The object is to construct the best machinery for the purpose to which it is to be applied. We may violate any law of symmetry, equality, or distributive justice in providing the proper machinery to enable us to do what is required of us. That being so, I will now state what I think the Government really ought to have done, and which it has not done. As this Bill, though it works on the constituencies, really is a Bill to alter the Constitution of the House and to redistribute power in the House, I say it is the bounden duty of the Government to begin their inquiries by a minute examination of the state of this House—to see wherein it has succeeded and wherein it has failed. When that is done, let them still further improve what they find good, if they can do so, and remedy what they find to have failed.

It is the duty of the Government, like any other physicians, to study the case with which they have to deal. If they do otherwise they are acting like a physician who spends his time in mixing drugs and sharpening lancets and never takes the trouble to see what is the matter with his patient. As the Government do not appear to have conducted such an examination as I have suggested, perhaps we may with advantage do a little in this way for ourselves. I have the most unfeigned respect and veneration for this House, and therefore I should not wish to see its Constitution altered without good grounds; but let us try to do what is the most difficult of all things—let us endeavour to acquire self-knowledge; let us try "to see ourselves as others see us." This House has been called the "mirror of the nation," as if the nation had nothing to do but look at this House in order to see itself as in a looking-glass. Now, I want the House to look at itself in this mirror. I think, then, we may say without self-praise that this House holds—not only in England, but throughout the whole world—a position far above that ever held by any other deliberative assembly that ever existed. It is more respected all over the world, its debates are more read, and they exercise more influence on mankind than those of assemblies infinitely more popular. Ought we not to be proud, then, of the position which this House occupies in the body politic of nations?

Well, I think I may go further, and say that the functions which it has principally to discharge—those of finance—it has discharged with greater success than any other deliberative assembly. Of course it is not perfect; nothing human is. I dare say there are people who think that the votes for the army and navy are outdoor relief for the aristocracy, that the Church is in the same category, and so forth; but the majority of the people of this country are satisfied that the finances are managed by the House in a manner creditable both to the House and the nation. If I go further, it must be said of this House that it never has been deaf to any appeal for the protection of the humbler classes. I know there is a clamour that the poor man is not represented in this House. But can anyone say that the interests of the poor are neglected here? Look to the debates we have had on the cases of poor women who have been removed in steamers from this country to Ireland.[9] In this House immediate attention is given to everything affecting the poor. It is impossible to find a remedy always, but such cases always receive attention. I will not say what this House has done in legislation; I said it last year, and I will not repeat it. But I think I may say this House is a very orderly assembly—one of the most orderly of deliberative assemblies. When we go to other places—and indeed we need not go further than a place not 100 miles from us, we find that the House of Commons will bear comparison with any other assembly for the regularity of its proceedings. It is independent also. Whatever may have happened 100 years ago, no one will say that there is any personal corruption in the House of Commons now. It is industrious, too. We labour more hours and get through a greater amount of business than any other assembly in the world. These are great merits.

I want to know, will the Bill which the Government have proposed leave all these things as it finds them? Will the constituencies in their altered character have no influence on the House? As the polypus takes its colour from the rock to which it affixes itself, so do the Members of this House take their character from the constituencies. If you lower the character of the constituencies, you lower that of the representatives and you lower the character of this House. I do not want to say anything disagreeable, but if you want to see the result of democratic constituencies, you will find them in all the assemblies of Australia and in all the assemblies of North America.

But this House, like all human institutions, possesses imperfections, and I will point out one or two of them. In the first place, a great change has been operating since the year 1832 which no one has noticed but which, I think, ought to have been taken into consideration. That change is this, that the House of Commons is now much nearer its constituents and much more influenced by them than it was before. In old days when a man left his constituents there was a great gulf between him and them, but now the constituents have a second function in addition to electing their Members. They can communicate with them by railway and by telegraph, and sometimes it has happened that the vote of a Member has been changed in the course of a debate by a telegram received from his constituents. A measure is sometimes proposed but not fully gone into, and the local press, although insufficiently informed on the question, takes it up and argues upon it, and the result is that the constituents make up their mind on the subject before they have heard the real issue to be raised, and they force their conclusions on their representatives though these may be far better in-

---

[9] Commons recently had discussed charges of hardship and mistreatment suffered by Irish paupers who were, as the Poor Law directed, being deported from England to Ireland.

formed. The less informed tribunal, therefore, acquires more influence than it should over the superior and better informed tribunal. These are small blots, perhaps, but they are worth mentioning, because I want to ask whether more democratic constituencies would be inclined to give their Members more freedom than they have at present. Would they be more tolerant of the opinions of the honest and able man who does not follow the whim of the moment? Would they be more patient, more tolerant, and more inclined to respect real dignity and consistency of character than they are now?

. . . . .

I think, then, that I have shown that such a Bill as the Government intends to bring in, while it would not in any degree alleviate any of the faults which I have taken the liberty with all respect to point out in the Constitution of this House, would aggravate every one of them, and there is not a single merit described in this imperfect sketch which it would not injuriously affect. Now, I want the Chancellor of the Exchequer to show us how this measure would work in regard to this House. My sketch is imperfect and possibly may be entirely erroneous, but let the Government make their sketch or theory upon the subject. Let them tell us what are the faults in the House of Commons, and how the present measure will remedy those faults; but let them not fling the measure on the table and say that we must adopt it without hearing one single reason in favour of or against a state of things which has existed so long and so happily.

It has been said, indeed, that precisely the same arguments have been used now as were used in 1832; but you must remember that to make a good argument two things are requisite—first, that the principle itself be sound, and secondly that the fact corresponds to the fact which it assumes. Now, the arguments against Reform in 1832 were excellent, only they did not correspond to the facts of the case. The question which honourable Gentlemen beg in representing the two cases as parallel is, are the facts of the case now the same as they were in 1832? Well, Sir, that is a question I am not going to enter into; but I may just point out this, that in 1832 the controversy was perfectly defined. The question was, did the system then existing work well or not? One side maintained that it did work well, the other contended that it did not; and the country decided very rightly, as I, for one, think, that it did not. But that is not the controversy now. It is now admitted that the system does work well; and the controversy now is, ought we not still to alter it? Take, for instance, a very clever letter signed "H," which appeared in *The Times* of yesterday. In reply to the question what good a Reform Bill could be expected to accomplish, the writer said:

> I am quite willing, for the sake of this argument, to answer "none." Nevertheless, I reply, even if that be so, the passing of a Reform Bill is a positive advantage

—simply, as I suppose, because Gentlemen are, as they call themselves, "committed." That is, for the sake of preserving our consistency, we are to do that which we know to be injurious to the best interests of the country. You must also make this distinction between the present time and 1832. The grievances that were complained of in 1832 were practical grievances. Do not believe for a moment that the House of Commons was reformed simply on account of the anomalies of the system. The House of Commons was reformed because the public mind was revolted by things which they thought bad in the legislation and government of the country, and seized upon those anomalies as the weapons to abate the nuisance. That, being a practical grievance, has been redressed, and led for a certain time to a settlement of the question. But, Sir, nobody ever settles a question by remedying a mere theoretical grievance, and that is just the grievance we have now to deal with.

My right honourable Friend the Chancellor of the Exchequer told us in his speech, as one great inducement to pass his Bill, that we should find in it a complete settlement of the question, and that he hoped that impracticable persons—I do not know whether I was one to whom he referred—if for no other reason would be induced to give their assent to the Bill because it would be a settlement of the question. Settlement? What significance does the right honourable Gentleman attach to that word? He stated that you are to go on with this Bill for twelve nights in this Session, and if you cannot pass it in twelve nights, it is to be left to the charities of private Members, and those charities are, we know, very cold. Thus, probably, the measure might go over this year and begin over again next year, and when we have disposed of it we are to be refreshed by a Franchise Bill for Scotland and a Franchise Bill for Ireland, about which we were told that the information was rather than not in a state of preparation. Then, when we have done with the three Franchise Bills, three Re-distribution Bills are to follow; and even then we shall not be out of the wood, because there is to be also a Boundaries Bill, one of the most difficult and irritating subjects which can be imagined—and after that we are to come to a Registrat'on Bill, which is also a matter of great difficulty. We have now reckoned up eight measures, and there is one more yet, enough to make any man shudder to think of, and that is an Anti-corruption Bill. So that the prospect of a settlement which the right honourable Gentleman holds out is that we are to begin *de novo* with the whole of our electoral system and to go through the whole of it in measures which, according to his own enumeration, amount at least to nine; and that he holds out as a settlement, so that if we will pass this Bill we may possibly, if we behave well, employ ourselves in going through this amount of work. That, however, is not my idea of a settlement, and I am quite sure that in addition to that there are unsettling causes which the right honourable Gentleman did not tell us of.

Supposing the Bills are passed—as they will be passed, if at all—in mere deference to numbers at the expense of property and intelligence, in deference to a love of symmetry and equality—at least that is the name under which the democratic passion of envy generally disguises itself, and which will only be satisfied by symmetry and equality—I feel convinced that when you have given all the right honourable Gentleman asks, you will still leave plenty of inequalities, enough to stir up this passion anew. The grievance being theoretical and not practical will survive as long as practice does not conform to theory; and practice will never conform to theory until you have got to universal suffrage and equal electoral districts. I say, therefore, that there is no element of finality in this measure, and though, as I have before said, I am perfectly willing to consider anything that may be brought forward, I crave leave to say that I shall consider the guidance of my own vote and conduct with reference to its influence on the good or bad working of the House of Commons, and not with reference to any theories about the ideal of good government, which, according to one great thinker, consists in everybody having a share in it—just as I suppose his ideal of a joint-stock company is one in which everybody is a director.

Well, Sir, the right honourable Gentleman, who had not time to give us a reason for introducing the Bill, found time to give us a quotation; and it was a quotation of a very curious kind, because, not finding in his large classical *repertoire* any quotation that would exactly describe the state of perfect bliss to which his Bill would introduce us, he was induced to take the exact contrary and make a quotation to show us what his Bill was not.

Scandit fatalis machina muros,
Fœta armis,[10]

he exclaimed, "and that," he added, "is not my Bill." Well, that was not a very apt quotation; but there was a curious felicity about it which he little dreamt of. The House remembers that among other proofs of the degree in which public opinion is enlisted in the cause of Reform is this—that this is now the fifth Reform Bill that has been brought in since 1851. Now, just attend to the sequel of the passage quoted by the right honourable Gentleman. I am no believer in *sortes Virgilianæ*, and the House will see why in a moment:

O Divum domus Ilium, et inclyta bello
Mœnia Dardanidum! Quater ipso in limina portæ
Substitit, atque utero sonitum quater arma dedêre.[11]

[10] "The deadly machine, abounding in weapons, scales the walls" (Virgil. *Aeneid* II. 237–238).

[11] "O Ilium, home of the gods and walls of the Dardanians that are famous in war! Four times on the very threshold of the gate [the Trojan horse] stopped and four times arms rattled in its belly" (Virgil, *Aeneid* II. 241–243).

But that is not all:

> *Instamus tamen immemores, cæcique furore,*
> *Et monstrum infelix sacratâ sistimus arce.*[12]

Well, I abominate the presage contained in the last two lines; but I mix my confidence with fear. The intentions and actions of the new Parliament are as yet hidden by the veil of the future. It may be that we are destined to avoid this enormous danger with which we are confronted, and not, to use the language of my right honourable Friend, be fated to compound with danger and misfortune. But, Sir, it may be otherwise; and all I can say is, that if my right honourable Friend does succeed in carrying this measure through Parliament, when the passions and interests of the day are gone by I do not envy him his retrospect. I covet not a single leaf of the laurels that may encircle his brow. I do not envy him his triumph. His be the glory of carrying it; mine of having to the utmost of my poor ability resisted it.

---

[12] "Yet we press on, heedless and blind with madness, and we place the ill-omened monster within the holy citadel" (Virgil, *Aeneid* II. 244–245).

John Stuart Mill

"Representation of the People"*
Commons, April 13, 1866

. . . . .

We are, I dare say, as sincerely desirous as the noble Mover of the amendment[1] that family and pocket boroughs should be extinguished and the inordinate political influence of a few noble and opulent families abridged. We are, I believe, as anxious to curtail the power which wealth possesses, of buying its way into the House of Commons and shutting the door upon other people, as the wealthiest gentleman present. But though we are quite orthodox on these great points of Conservative Parliamentary Reform—and look forward with delight to our expected co-operation with Gentlemen on the opposite benches in the congenial occupation of converting them from theories into facts—we yet think that a measure of enfranchisement like this Bill—moderate, indeed, far more moderate than is desired by the majority of Reformers, but which does make the working classes a substantial power in this House—is not only a valuable part of a scheme of Parliamentary Reform, but highly valuable even if nothing else were to follow. And as this is the only question among those raised on the present occasion which seems to me in the smallest degree worth discussing, I shall make no further apology for confining myself to it.

Sir, measures may be recommended either by their principle or by their practical consequences; and if they have either of these recommendations, they usually have both. As far as regards the principle of this measure, there is but little to disagree about; for a measure which goes no farther

---

* The speech is from *Hansard's Parliamentary Debates*, Third Series, Vol. CLXXXII, cols. 1253–1263.

[1] The amendment, introduced on April 12 by the Earl of Grosvenor, was ingeniously worded to appeal to all those who saw their interests threatened by political change: "That this House ... is of the opinion that it is inexpedient to discuss a Bill for the reduction of the Franchise in England and Wales until the House has before it the entire Scheme contemplated by the Government for the amendment of the representation of the people." Disraeli and Lowe encouraged Grosvenor to introduce this amendment so that the scope of discussion would be greatly expanded.

than this does not raise any of the questions of principle on which the House is divided; and I cannot but think that the right honourable Baronet,[2] in introducing those questions, has caused the debate to deviate somewhat from its proper course. If it were necessary to take into consideration even all the reasonable things which can be said pro and con about democracy, the House would have a very different task before it. But this is not a democratic measure. It neither deserves that praise, nor, if honourable Members will have it so, that reproach. It is not a corollary from what may be called the numerical theory of representation. It is required by the class theory, which we all know is the Conservative view of the Constitution—the favourite doctrine not only of what are called Conservative Reformers, but of Conservative non-Reformers as well. The opponents of Reform are accustomed to say that the Constitution knows nothing of individuals but only of classes. Individuals, they tell us, cannot complain of not being represented, so long as the class they belong to is represented. But if any class is unrepresented or has not its proper share of representation relatively to others, that is a grievance.

Now, all that need be asked at present is that this theory be applied to practise. There is a class which has not yet had the benefit of the theory. While so many classes, comparatively insignificant in numbers and not supposed to be freer from class partialities or interests than their neighbours, are represented, some of them, I venture to say, greatly over-represented in this House, there is a class, more numerous than all the others, and therefore, as a mere matter of human feeling, entitled to more consideration—weak, as yet, and therefore needing representation the more, but daily becoming stronger and more capable of making its claims good—and this class is not represented. We claim, then, a large and liberal representation of the working classes, on the Conservative theory of the Constitution. We demand that they be represented as a class, if represented they cannot be as human beings; and we call on honourable Gentlemen to prove the sincerity of their convictions by extending the benefit of them to the great majority of their countrymen.

But honourable Gentlemen say the working classes are already represented. It has just come to light, to the astonishment of everybody, that these classes actually form 26 per cent of the borough constituencies. They kept the secret so well—it required so much research to detect their presence on the register—their votes were so devoid of any traceable consequences—they had all this power of shaking the foundations of our institutions, and so obstinately persisted in not doing it—that honourable Gentlemen are quite alarmed and recoil in terror from the abyss into which they have not fallen. Well, Sir, it certainly seems that this amount of enfranchisement of the working classes has done no harm. But if it has not done harm, perhaps

[2] Sir E. Bulwer-Lytton, the preceding speaker.

it has not done much good either, at least not the kind of good which we are talking about.

A class may have a great number of votes in every constituency in the kingdom and not obtain a single representative in this House. Their right of voting may be only the right of being everywhere outvoted. If, indeed, the mechanism of our electoral system admitted representation of minorities; if those who are outvoted in one place could join their votes with those who are outvoted in another; then, indeed, a fourth part, even if only of the borough electors, would be a substantial power, for it would mean a fourth of the borough representatives. Twenty-six per cent concentrated would be a considerable representation, but 26 per cent diffused may be almost the same as none at all. The right honourable Baronet has said that a class, though but a minority, may, by cleverly managing its votes, be master of the situation, and that the tenant farmers in Hertfordshire can carry an election. They may be able to decide whether a Tory or a Whig shall be elected; they may be masters of so small a situation as that. But what you are afraid of is lest they should carry points on which their interest as a class is opposed to that of all other classes—on which if they were only a third of the constituency, the other two-thirds would be against them. Do you think they would be masters of such a situation as that? Sir, there is no known contrivance by which in the long run a minority can outnumber a majority—by which one-third of the electors can outvote the other two-thirds. The real share of the working classes in the representation is measured by the number of Members they can return —in other words, the number of constituencies in which they are the majority—and even that only marks the extreme limit of the influence which they can exercise, but by no means that which they will. Why, Sir, among the recent discoveries, one is that there are some half-dozen constituencies in which working men are even now a majority; and I put it to honourable Gentlemen, would anybody ever have suspected it? At the head of these constituencies is Coventry. Are the Members for Coventry generally great sticklers for working-class notions? It has, I believe, been observed that these Gentlemen usually vote quite correctly on the subject of French ribbons, and as that kind of virtue comes most natural to Conservatives, the Members for Coventry often are Conservative. But probably that would happen much the same if the master manufacturers had all the votes. If, indeed, a tax on power looms were proposed and the Members for Coventry voted for it, that might be some indication of working-class influences; though I believe that the working men even at Coventry have far outgrown that kind of absurdities.

Even if the franchise were so much enlarged that the working men, by polling their whole strength, could return by small majorities 200 of the 658 Members of this House, there would not be fifty of that number who would represent the distinctive feelings and opinions of working men or would be, in any class sense, their representatives. And what if they had the whole 200? Even then, on any subject in which they were concerned as a class, there would be more than two to one against them when they were in the wrong. They could not succeed in anything, even when unanimous, unless they carried with them nearly a third of the representatives of the other classes; and if they did that, there would be, I think, a very strong presumption of their being in the right. As a matter of principle, then, and not only on liberal principles but on those of the Conservative Party, the case in favour of the Bill seems irresistible.

But, it is asked by my right honourable Friend the Member for Calne,[3] what practical good do we expect? What particular measures do we hope to see carried in a reformed House which cannot be carried in the present? If I understand my right honourable Friend correctly, he thinks we ought to come to the House with a Bill of indictment against itself—an inventory of wrong things which the House does and right things which it cannot be induced to do—and when, convinced by our arguments, the House pleads guilty and cries "*Peccavi*,"[4] we have his permission to bring in a Reform Bill. Sir, my right honourable Friend says we should not proceed on *a priori* reasoning but should be practical. I want to know whether this is his idea of being practical. For my part, I am only sorry it is not possible that in the discussion of this question special applications should be kept entirely out of view; for if we descend to particulars and point out this and that in the conduct of the House which we should like to see altered, but which the House, by the very fact that it does not alter them, does not think require alteration, how can we expect the House to take this as a proof that its Constitution needs Reform? We should not at all advance our cause, while we should stir up all the most irritating topics in the domain of politics.

. . . . .

Ought the debate on a Reform Bill to consist of a series of discussions on points similar to this, and a hundred times more irritating than this? Is it desirable to drag into this discussion all the points in which anyone may think that the rights or interests of labour are not sufficiently regarded by the House? I will ask another question. If the authors of the Reform Bill of 1832 had foretold (which they scarcely could have done, since they did not themselves know it), if they had predicted that through it we should abolish the Corn Laws—that we should abolish the Navigation Laws[5]—that we should grant free trade to all foreigners without reciprocity

[3] Robert Lowe.
[4] "I have sinned."
[5] The Navigation Act of 1651 required that no goods might be imported from Asia, Africa, or America except in English ships and that importation from Europe was restricted to English ships and those of the country producing the goods. The Act was repealed in 1849.

—that we should reduce inland postage to a penny—that we should renounce the exercise of any authority over our colonies—all which things have really happened—does the House think that these announcements would have greatly inclined the Parliament of that day towards passing the Bill? Whether the practical improvements that will follow a further Parliamentary Reform will be equal to these the future must disclose; but whatever they may be, it is already certain that they are not at the present time regarded as improvements by the House, for if the House thought so, there is nothing to hinder it from adopting them.

Sir, there is a better way of persuading possessors of power to give up a part of it; not by telling them that they make a bad use of their power—which, if it were true, they could not be expected to be aware of—but by reminding them of what they are aware of—their own fallibility. Sir, we all of us know that we hold many erroneous opinions, but we do not know which of our opinions these are, for if we did they would not be our opinions. Therefore, reflecting men take precautions beforehand against their own errors, without waiting till they and all other people are agreed about the particular instances; and if there are things which, from their mental habits or their position in life, are in danger of escaping their notice, they are glad to associate themselves with others of different habits and positions, which very fact peculiarly qualifies them to see the precise things which they themselves do not see. Believing the House to be composed of reasonable men, this is what we ask them to do. Every class knows some things not so well known to other people, and every class has interests which are more or less special to itself, and for which no protection is so effectual as its own. These may be *a priori* doctrines—but so is the doctrine that a straight line is the shortest distance between two points; they are as much truths of common sense and common observation as that is, and persons of common sense act upon them with the same perfect confidence. I claim the benefit of these principles for the working classes. They require it more than any other class. The class of lawyers or the class of merchants is amply represented, though there are no constituencies in which lawyers or merchants form the majority. But a successful lawyer or merchant easily gets into Parliament by his wealth or social position, and once there, is as good a representative of lawyers or merchants as if he had been elected on purpose; but no constituency elects a working man or a man who looks at questions with working men's eyes. Is there, I wonder, a single Member of this House who thoroughly knows the working men's view of trades unions or of strikes and could bring it before the House in a manner satisfactory to working men? My honourable Friend the Member for Brighton,[6] if anyone; perhaps not even he. Are there many of us who so perfectly understand the subject of apprenticeships, let us say, or of the

---

[6] James White, Radical M.P.

hours of labour, as to have nothing to learn on the subject from intelligent operatives? I grant that, along with many just ideas and much valuable knowledge, you would sometimes find pressed upon you erroneous opinions —mistaken views of what is for the interest of labour; and I am not prepared to say that if the labouring classes were predominant in the House, attempts might not be made to carry some of these wrong notions into practise. But there is no question at present about making the working classes predominant. What is asked is a sufficient representation to ensure that their opinions are fairly placed before the House and are met by real arguments addressed to their own reason by people who can enter into their way of looking at the subjects in which they are concerned.

In general, those who attempt to correct the errors of the working classes do it as if they were talking to babies. They think any trivialities sufficient; if they condescend to argue, it is from premises which hardly any working man would admit; they expect that the things which appear self-evident to them will appear self-evident to the working classes. Their arguments never reach the mark, never come near what a working man has in his mind, because they do not know what is in his mind. Consequently, when the questions which are near the hearts of the working men are talked about in this House—there is no want of goodwill to them, that I cheerfully admit—everything which is most necessary to prove to them is taken for granted. Do not suppose that working men would always be unconvincible by such arguments as ought to satisfy them.

It is not one of the faults of democracy to be obstinate in error. An Englishman who had lived some years in the United States lately summed up his opinion of the Americans by saying, "They are the most teachable people on the face of the earth." Old countries are not as teachable as young countries, but I believe it will be found that the educated artizans, those especially who take interest in politics, are the most teachable of all our classes. They have much to make them so; they are, as a rule, more in earnest than any other class; their opinions are more genuine, less influenced by what so greatly influences some of the other classes—the desire of getting on; and their social position is not such as to breed self-conceit. Above all, there is one thing to which, I believe, almost everyone will testify who has had much to do with them and of which even my own limited experience supplies striking examples: there is no class which so well bears to be told of its faults—to be told of them even in harsh terms, if they believe that the person so speaking to them says what he thinks and has no ends of his own to serve by saying it. I can hardly conceive a nobler course of national education than the debates of this House would become if the notions, right and wrong, which are fermenting in the minds of the working classes, many of which go down very deep into the foundations of society and government, were fairly stated and genuinely discussed within these walls.

It has often been noticed how readily in a free country people resign themselves even to the refusal of what they ask, when everything which they could have said for themselves has been said by somebody in the course of the discussion. The working classes have never yet had this tranquillising assurance. They have always felt that not they themselves, perhaps, but their opinions, were prejudged—were condemned without being listened to. But let them have the same equal opportunities which others have of pleading their own cause—let them feel that the contest is one of reason and not of power—and if they do not obtain what they desire, they will as readily acquiesce in defeat or trust to the mere progress of reason for reversing the verdict as any other portion of the community. And they will, much oftener than at present, obtain what they desire. Let me refer honourable Gentlemen to Tocqueville, who is so continually quoted when he says anything uncomplimentary to democracy that those who have not read him might mistake him for a enemy of it instead of its discriminating but sincere friend. Tocqueville says that, though the various American legislatures are perpetually making mistakes, they are perpetually correcting them, too; and that the evil, such as it is, is far outweighed by the salutary effects of the general tendency of their legislation, which is maintained, in a degree unknown elsewhere, in the direction of the interest of the people.[7] Not that vague abstraction, the good of the country, but the actual, positive well-being of the living human creatures who compose the population. But we are told that our own legislation has made great progress in this direction—that the House has repealed the Corn Laws, removed religious disabilities, and got rid of I know not how many more abominations. Sir, it has; and I am far from disparaging these great reforms, which have probably saved the country from a violent convulsion. As little would I undervalue the good sense and good feeling which have made the governing classes of this country capable of thus far advancing with the times. But they have their recompense—*habes pretium, cruci non figeris*.[8] Their reward is that they are not hated, as other privileged classes have been. And that is the fitting reward for ceasing to do harm—for merely repealing bad laws which Parliament itself had made.

But is this all that the Legislature of a country like ours can offer to its people? Is there nothing for us to do but only to undo the mischief that we or our predecessors have done? Are there not all the miseries of an old and crowded society waiting to be dealt with—the curse of ignorance, the curse of pauperism, the curse of disease, the curse of a whole population born and nurtured in crime? All these things we are just beginning to look at—just touching with the tips of our fingers—and by the time two or three more generations are dead and gone, we may perhaps have discovered how to keep them alive and how to make their lives worth having.

[7] The reference is to Alexis de Tocqueville's *De la démocratie en Amérique* (Paris, 1850).
[8] "You have your price, you will not be crucified."

I must needs think that we should get on much faster with all this, the most important part of the business of Government in our days, if those who are the chief sufferers by the great chronic evils of our civilisation had representatives among us to stimulate our zeal, as well as to inform us by their experience. Of all great public objects, the one which would be most forwarded by the presence of working people's representatives in this House is the one in which we flatter ourselves we have done most—popular education.

And let me here offer to my right honourable Friend the Member for Calne, who demands practical arguments, a practical argument which I think ought to come home to him. If those whose children we vote money to instruct had been properly represented in this House, he would not have lost office on the Revised Code.[9] The working classes would have seen in him an administrator of a public fund, honestly determined that the work for which the public paid should be good, honest work. They are not the people to prefer a greater quantity of sham teaching to a smaller quantity of real teaching at a less expense. Real education is the thing they want, and as it is what he wanted, they would have understood him and upheld him. I have myself seen these services remembered to his honour, even at this moment of exasperation, by one of the leaders of the working classes. And, unless I am mistaken—it is not my opinion alone—very few years of a real working-class representation would have passed over our heads before there would be in every parish a school rate and the school doors freely open to all the world; and in one generation from that time England would be an educated nation. Will it ever become so by your present plan, which gives to him that hath, and only to him that hath? Never. If there were no reason for extending the franchise to the working classes except the stimulus it would give to this one alone of the Imperial works which the present state of society urgently demands from Parliament, the reason would be more than sufficient.

These, Sir, are a few of the benefits which I expect from a further Parliamentary Reform; and as they depend altogether upon one feature of it, the effective representation of the working classes, their whole weight is in favour of passing the present Bill, without regard to any Bills that may follow. I look upon a liberal enfranchisement of the working classes as incomparably the greatest improvement in our representative institutions which we at present have it in our power to make; and as I should be glad to receive this greatest improvement along with others, so I am perfectly willing to accept it by itself. Such others as we need, we shall, no doubt, end by obtaining, and a person must be very simple who imagines that we should have obtained them a day sooner if Ministers had encumbered the subject by binding up any of them with the present Bill.

[9] Lowe resigned as vice-president of the Education Committee (1859–1864) after the House passed a motion censuring the Committee.

H. H. Asquith

"The Commons and Constitutional Change"*
Commons, July 24, 1911

[*On July 24, Prime Minister Asquith proposed to outline the Liberal Government's response to the Lords' continued opposition to the Parliament Bill. As he rose to speak in a crowded Commons, he was greeted with jeers by diehard Tories who knew the announcement he would make. "Divide, divide," was a dominant chant, but interspersed with it were shouts of "Traitor," "You've disgraced your office," and "Who killed the King?" For nearly three-quarters of an hour, Asquith stood, unable to make connected sentences heard by the House.*

Mrs. Asquith, in the Ladies Gallery, passed down a note to Sir Edward Grey: "They will listen to you, so for God's sake defend him from the cats and the cads." At last Asquith, a consummate parliamentarian, gave up his attempt to speak. Never before in the history of Parliament had a Prime Minister been refused a hearing. "It was," reported Winston Churchill to the King, "a squalid, frigid, organized attempt to insult the Prime Minister."]

In offering the advice which the Government think it right at this juncture to tender to the House, I must once more recall the facts, familiar as they are, which from a Parliamentary point of view place this Bill in an almost unique category.

The principle upon which it is founded and the main lines upon which it is drawn were affirmed and approved by the House of Commons as far back as the year 1907. At the General Election in the year 1910, which followed rejection by the House of Lords of the Budget, this principle took its place in the forefront of party controversy, was debated upon every platform, and became the predominant issue of the election. In the new House of Commons, resolutions embodying all or almost all its detailed provisions were carried by large majorities, the Bill itself was introduced,

---

* Asquith supplied this copy of his intended remarks to *The Times*, July 25, 1911, p. 13. The *Hansard* report, as might be expected, is brief and disjointed.

and no one doubts that, but for the death of the King and the temporary truce which ensued, it would have been passed in that Session through all its stages and sent to another place. The Conference which followed proved that with the best will and the most strenuous efforts a settlement by agreement was impossible. The Bill was then presented to the House of Lords and was laid aside in favour of an alternative scheme put forward by Lord Lansdowne on behalf of the responsible leaders of the Opposition, and of which the novel and at the same time the governing (so far as conflicts between the two Houses are concerned) principle was the introduction and application of the referendum. Another General Election followed in December, 1910. The people now had before them on the one hand this Bill itself in all its details, both principle and machinery; on the other hand, the counter-proposals of the Opposition, which, especially in regard to the referendum, were vigorously defended on the one side and as vigorously attacked on the other in every constituency in the country. What was the result? A majority for the Government of sixty in Great Britain, of 120 in the United Kingdom as a whole.

In a word, it is true to say of this Bill, in a sense in which it would not be true of any Bill in our Parliamentary history, that it was the main issue of two elections, and that by no form of referendum that could be devised could the opinion of the electorate upon it have been more carefully ascertained or more clearly pronounced.

The Bill was approved, as I have said, both as to its principle and as to its machinery. That is important, because, as I shall show in a moment, the main purpose and effect of the amendments made in the House of Lords is, in regard to matters of the greatest importance, to set that machinery aside, and to replace it by a new and, as I think, a worse edition of the very expedient which the electors, when consulted, deliberately rejected.

It is a mistake, indeed it is a misrepresentation, to allege that the Government have shown themselves indisposed to accept changes consistent with the main principle and purpose of the Bill. On the contrary, in Committee here, on Clause 1, we consented to amendments containing the clause to public Bills, excluding all matters that dealt only with local taxation, and amplifying and rendering more precise the enumeration of the classes of Bills which alone were to be entitled to the relatively privileged position conferred by the clause. In the same spirit, in Clause 2 we accepted amendments to protect its machinery against possible, though as we thought most improbable, risks of abuse. If the amendments made by the House of Lords were of the same or a similar class; if they were—as I see they are strangely described by a most reverend prelate,[1] who on this occasion seems to have lost touch with the realities of the situation—"safeguarding" amendments; if they were not, in fact—whatever may have

---

[1] The Archbishop of Canterbury, in his speech in the House of Lords on July 20.

been their intention—the substitution for the Bill in its main features of the alternative repudiated less than a year ago by the electorate, we should have been prepared to ask the House even now to give them respectful consideration.

Let me make good in a few words the description I have just given of the general effect of the Lords' amendments. Their most novel feature is undoubtedly the creation of a new tribunal which is to be, in effect, predominant over the House of Commons in matters of finance and over both Houses in all legislative matters which the tribunal holds to be at once of great gravity and insufficiently considered by the electorate. And how is this junta to be composed? It is, in its latest form—an improvement, I admit, due to Lord St. Aldwyn, on the original proposal—to consist of the Lord Chancellor, the Speaker, the Lord Chamberlain, Chairmen of Ways and Means, a Lord of Appeal chosen by and from persons who have held high judicial office, and a member of this House appointed by the Speaker.

Just consider the functions which, for the first time, it is proposed—for I do not suggest that anyone had the courage to submit this part of the scheme to the electorate—to entrust to such a body. Take, first, finance. It is not a question merely of associating with the Speaker some two or three men of experience for the purpose of considering whether the Bill does or does not fall within any of the categories set out in Clause 1. That is a very different matter. I believe that in the course of our debates, when we were settling the specific enumeration of Bills which alone were to be deemed to be Money Bills—so as to avoid the possible abuse of tacking—I described as their general qualification that their governing and not merely their incidental purpose should be financial. But as the House will remember, I was most careful throughout to make it clear that the only safe way of dealing with such a matter was to eschew general language, and to describe specifically, and with precision, what Bills were, and what were not, to be deemed of a financial character. The House of Lords, seizing upon my phrase and using it for the very purpose which I deprecated, propose that this Joint Committee can, at their discretion, remove from the uncontrolled jurisdiction of the House of Commons any Bill if, in their opinion, the governing purpose of the Bill or any portion of it is such as to bring it within the category of general legislation.

I do not hesitate to say that there is not a single one of the great Budgets of the last seventy years which might not conceivably and even plausibly be brought within the ambit of these words. If we were to assent to any such proposal—and it is not a question of language but of substance—we should be deliberately putting the House of Commons, by Act of Parliament, in a lower and weaker position as regards finance than it has occupied for 200 years. A strange result, indeed, of the emphatic condemnation by the electors of the rejection of the Budget of 1909.

But even more serious, and, with all respect, I must say more grotesque, are the functions assigned to the junta under the celebrated Lansdowne amendment to Clause 2.[2] That amendment begins by excluding absolutely from the operation of the clause Bills affecting the existence of the Crown or the Protestant Succession; no one is likely to use the Parliament Bill for such a purpose. It goes on to another specific exclusion—that of measures establishing national parliaments, assemblies, or councils with legislative powers in any part of the United Kingdom. Why, one may ask, is this of all forms of Constitutional or organic change the one selected for express mention? What, for example, of the Established Church or of franchise and redistribution, or of a change in the number and composition of the Second Chamber itself? I believe that some noble Lords, whose hatred and fear of Home Rule does not wholly blind them to other possible developments in the field of political emancipation, ventured to put these questions or some of them. They were referred for reassurance to Subsection C, which empowers the Joint Committee on reference to exclude from the normal working of Clause 2 any measure of any kind provided in their opinion it raises an issue of great gravity (whatever that means) and the judgment of the country has not been sufficiently (whatever that means) ascertained. And what is to happen then? Why, the measure in question is to be submitted for approval to the electors in manner to be hereafter provided by Act of Parliament.

This, Sir, is the proposal which is deliberately put forward by the Opposition late in the eleventh hour of this Constitutional controversy, and, as the Archbishop solemnly assures us, for the purpose of safeguarding our Bill against possible abuse. Just see what in practise it would mean. A Bill is brought in, say, for Welsh disestablishment. It is passed by the House of Commons in three successive Sessions, at least two years having elapsed between the date of its Second Reading in the first and its passing in the third of those Sessions. Under those conditions it would, notwithstanding rejection by the House of Lords by virtue of Clause 2, pass automatically on to the Statute Book. But under the Lansdowne amendment all that the House of Lords has to do is to carry a resolution requiring a reference to the Joint Committee which must thereupon be assembled. And then these six gentlemen are solemnly to meet together and determine—and remember their determination, the determination of this wholly irresponsible body, is final and conclusive in all Courts of Law— they are to go through the farce of appearing to determine whether a Bill, passed in three successive Sessions through the House of Commons against the House of Lords, in their opinion raises an issue of great gravity, and whether, some three years before, the judgment of the country had or had not been "sufficiently ascertained." And what then? The measure

[2] For Lansdowne's discussion of this amendment in Lords, see *The Times*, July 21, 1911, p. 12.

(say a measure for Welsh disestablishment) is to go separately to a referendum to the electors of the United Kingdom in manner to be hereafter provided by Act of Parliament. By what sort of an Act of Parliament? In the meantime, the whole of this Bill is to be hung up. Nowhere and at no time has such a proposal been put forward in the whole domain of Constitutional experiment. Is this what the electors voted for last December?

No, Sir, these amendments, taken as a whole, amount to a rejection of our Bill. What would happen if they were to be incorporated in the measure? When you have a Unionist majority in both Houses, the whole thing becomes a dead letter. Matters remain exactly as they are. Measures of the utmost gravity and most far-reaching effect may be passed in defiance of public opinion over the heads of the electorate. You live in fact under unchecked and undiluted single-chamber government. But, with a Liberal government in power, you would have a House of Commons fettered beyond all its predecessors in the control of finance, and in all cases where an irresponsible and non-representative body independent of both Houses should so determine, every deadlock will be settled and settled only by a referendum *ad hoc*. In other words, the Bill in its present form is a direct contradiction and a flat negation of the decision of the country.

What, then, ought to be done, and in particular what ought to be the attitude of this House in the situation so created? We tried—the leaders on both sides tried—to settle this controversy last year by conference and agreement. That attempt, unhappily, came to nothing. Lord Lansdowne tells us that there are some, at all events, of the amendments which the Lords have introduced into the Bill which in their view are so essential that they would certainly not be prepared to recede from them in substance so long as they remained free agents. I assume, of course, that this language refers to amendments like his own, and I have to say in reply on behalf of the Government, and I believe on the majority of the House of Commons, that to such amendments we cannot and shall not see our way to accede.

We have, therefore, come to the conclusion, and thought it courteous and right to communicate that conclusion in advance to leaders of the Opposition, that unless the House of Commons is prepared to concede these essential points there is only one Constitutional way of escape from what would otherwise be an absolute deadlock. It is the method of resort to the Prerogative which is recognised by the most authoritative exponents of Constitutional law and practise, by writers such as Erskine May, Bagehot, and Dicey, when, as is here the case, the House of Commons must be presumed to represent on the matter in dispute the deliberate decision of the nation. But it is not necessary to rely on the *dicta* of text writers, however eminent. For the precedent of 1832 is what the lawyers call a case precisely in point. As we are accused by ignorant people of being responsible for a *coup d'état*, or at any rate of an unprecedented breach in the practise of the Constitution, I think it is worth while to go in some little detail into the history of that transaction:

> Duke of Wellington defeated. Lord Grey office, late in 1830.
> No Reform Bill before country at previous elections.
> 1831. March 1: Bill introduced.
> March 22: Second Reading carried by majority of one.
> April 18: On General Gascoyne's amendment, Government defeated in this House by majority of eight. They at once advised King to dissolve.
> 1831. May: General Election.
> July 6: Second Reading Commons; majority, 136. Went up to Lords.
> October 8: Second Reading rejected (House of Lords), forty-one. No second Dissolution, but Parliament prorogued and Bill re-introduced in Commons. Passed through all stages there, and went up to Lords a second time.
> 1832. May 6: Second Reading in Lords; majority, nine.
> May 7: Lyndhurst's amendment (on going into Committee). It was at this stage that Ministers asked the Sovereign to authorise them, if necessary, to use the Royal Prerogative of creation. William IV refused, and Lord Grey resigned.
> After ten days: abortive attempt of Lyndhurst and Wellington to form Government (Peel standing aloof).
> May 17: Grey recalled, King giving written consent "to create such number of Peers as will be sufficient to ensure passing of Reform Bill." Lord Grey announced in House of Lords that he had now confident security of passing Reform Bill unimpaired in its principles and in all its essential details.

The Bill was carried without its being necessary to resort to Prerogative. But everyone knows that it would not have been carried unless Lord Grey had requested and the King had consented to the exercise to any extent that might be necessary of the power of creation. Lord Grey was attacked, as I am now, for advising an unconstitutional course. This is what he said in reply:

> (May 17, 1832)—We were under the necessity of offering the advice to create as many new Peers as would carry the measure of Reform through this House unmutilated in any of its essential provisions, or resign our offices. Now I say that under these circumstances the advice to create new Peers was required. The noble and learned Lord says that it was not Constitutional; but I say that it was Constitutional and I can refer him to books of authority on the subject in which it is distinctly asserted that one of the uses of vesting the prerogative of creating new Peers in the Crown is to prevent the possibility of the recurrence of those evils which must otherwise result from a permanent collision between the two Houses of Parliament; and this danger was rendered imminent by the opposition made to the Reform Bill by the noble Lords on

the other side of the House. And, I ask, what would be the consequences if we were to suppose that such a prerogative did not exist, or could not be Constitutionally exercised? The Commons have a control over the power of the Crown by the privilege, in extreme cases, of refusing the Supplies, and the Crown has, by means of its power to dissolve the House of Commons, a control upon any violent and rash proceedings on the part of the Commons; but if a majority of this House [House of Lords] is to have the power whenever they please of opposing the declared and decided wishes both of the Crown and the people, without any means of modifying that power, then this country is placed entirely under the influence of an uncontrollable oligarchy. I say that if a majority of this House should have the power of acting adversely to the Crown and the Commons, and was determined to exercise that power without being liable to check or control, the Constitution is completely altered and the Government of this country is not a limited monarchy; it is no longer, my Lords, the Crown, the Lords, and Commons, but a House of Lords—a separate oligarchy—governing absolutely the others. On these grounds we tendered that advice to His Majesty which we were well justified by the spirit and by the letter of the Constitution in tendering; nay, more, which, under the circumstances, it was our imperative duty to tender, considering the consequences that were likely to result from the failure of the measure.[3]

We cannot then doubt, Sir, that the advice we have tendered to the Crown—and which the Crown has accepted—is warranted by Constitutional principles, and that we are following in spirit and almost to the letter the precedent set by the great Whig statesman of 1832. I need hardly add that we do not desire to see the Prerogative exercised and that we trust that the necessity for its exercise may be avoided. There is nothing derogatory or humiliating to a great party in admitting defeat. No one asks them to accept that defeat as final. They have only to convince their fellow-countrymen that they are right and we are wrong and they can repeal our Bill. Believing, as we do, that the chances of a satisfactory issue may thereby be improved, I do not propose today to ask the House to take any action in regard to the Lords' amendments, but in due course to adjourn this debate.

---

[3] *Hansard's Parliamentary Debates*, Third Series, Vol. XII, cols. 1005–1006.

Earl Curzon, Earl of Halsbury, Marquess of Lansdowne, Viscount Morley, and Earl of Rosebery

"Debate on the Parliament Bill"[*]

Lords, August 9-10, 1911

THE MARQUESS OF LANSDOWNE: . . . I am haunted by my apprehension of the spectacle which will be presented not only to this country, but to the whole civilised world and to the rest of the British Empire, if the threat of His Majesty's Government is carried into effect. Can the noble Viscount[1] tell us of any country in which any exhibition approaching to it has ever been seen? Some of us who have had an interest in foreign affairs know how much of the respect which our country commands abroad is due to the stability of our institutions and to the respect in which our Parliamentary system is held. What, I ask, will be thought of our Parliamentary system and of the stability of our institutions when 300 or 400 or 500 Peers—I do not care which—are created for the express purpose of voting down one of the two Chambers of the Legislature? We should have exclaimed and poured forth volumes of ridicule and contempt if such a thing had happened in the Republic of Venezuela under the Presidency of President Castro, and that is what we are asked to contemplate as likely to happen in this country and to this House.

I shall perhaps be told that the spectacle will be every whit as degrading if the Peers are not actually made and if this House yields to the threat that Peers will be made. I shall be told that the infamy remains, although it will be kept out of sight. I shall be told that it is bad for political morality that these things should be hid away and that it is much better that the thing should be done and a salutary shock administered to public opinion. But I take leave to say that to my mind it makes an immense difference whether this outrage has been merely contemplated or whether it has been actually accomplished. The moral guilt of the criminals would no doubt

---

[*] The debate is taken from *Parliamentary Debates (Official Report)*, Fifth Series, Vol. IX, cols. 888–900, 1003–1007, 1064–1072.

[1] Viscount Morley.

be the same, but if it is not actually accomplished, then, at any rate, the British Government will not have added to our history a piece of what I can only call stupendous political corruption. If it is not accomplished, 500 English Gentlemen will not have taken their seats in this House upon conditions which I can only describe as humiliating and disgraceful. If it is not accomplished, this House, with all its historic traditions, will not have sustained the most outrageous affront which could be offered to it. And finally, the Sovereign will not have been required to lend himself to a transaction which is already agitating the minds of all those who are devoted to the Monarchy and which will, beyond all question, disfigure the annals of the new reign. To my mind it is not inconsistent with the honourable traditions of this House, not inconsistent with patriotism, not inconsistent with the self-respect which we owe to ourselves, that these considerations should be carefully weighed by your Lordships. With some of us, indeed, they weigh so heavily that we are ready to face all the misrepresentation, all the abuse, which has been levelled against us, and even —what is worst of all—the interruption of old political friendships rather than face the consequences which we apprehend; and we say that in our belief the country even now—a great number of the people now and a much greater number as time goes by—will recognise that our patriotism is as much above suspicion and our sincerity fully as transparent as that of those who differ from us.

My Lords, I may be told that all this time I have been waving a mere bogey in the face of your Lordships' House, that I have been talking of an overwhelming creation of Peers, and that there is no question of an overwhelming creation of Peers. Some noble Lords seem to think that all that is contemplated is a pleasant little addition to the composition of this House—a little reinforcement which will perhaps have the effect of enlivening our debates and promoting a greater abundance of repartee from the Benches on the other side. If, however, it be true, if it were ever true, that all we are threatened with is a small creation of Peers, I would ask this question: "To whom do you owe it that it is so?" When my noble and learned Friend[2] started on his crusade he made it his business to collect as large a number of recruits as he could gather to his standard. But supposing we had all followed his example, His Majesty's Government would have had at once to create the whole of their 400 or 500 Peers in order to outnumber us, and if the necessity of that large creation has in any way become less, surely there should be some gratitude to those who have been instrumental in bringing about that result.

But I must ask, in passing, whether, if that really represents the feeling of my noble and learned Friend, if he desires to have, let us say, fifty or

[2] Earl of Halsbury, leader of the "Ditchers," pledged to resist the Parliament Bill to the end.

sixty Peers, but strongly objects to having 500 or 600, it is not fair to point out that those who follow him are in the delightful position of getting all the glory while we save him from the risk of the calamity he does not wish to incur and obtain all the ridicule and vituperation. But there is a much more serious aspect of the case. Are the noble Lords who hold these views satisfied that the only danger that we have to anticipate is a small creation of Peers? I should very much like to know upon what foundation that belief is grounded. One noble Member of this House is reported to have said the other day that he was quite ready to rise from the ditch with a little mud on his clothes rather than have collars round our necks. I hope the noble Lord will be grateful to those who saved him from getting a great deal more mud and from perhaps breaking his bones into the bargain; but is he quite sure that he will get off with only a little mud? I believe nothing of the sort.

It was said by the Home Secretary[3] in the House of Commons two nights ago that the creation of Peers which His Majesty's Government have in view is a creation of 400 or 500. And last night a most remarkable statement was made by Lord Crewe. Lord Crewe warned us that when the creation of Peers took place, no regard would be had by His Majesty's Government to the newspaper list of Peers or to the division lists. He said they were not relevant to the question at all, and that His Majesty's Government would assume that all combinations had ceased and come to an end. I will tell the House how I interpret these words, and I would ask the noble Viscount to correct me if I am wrong. I understand that His Majesty has promised a creation of Peers sufficient to ensure the passing of this Bill in its House of Commons shape. There is no doubt about that. The number necessary for this purpose must necessarily be an indefinite number, and what I gather is that the pledge given to His Majesty's Government is a pledge which, beyond all question, covers the creation of any number of Peers which, as the result of the calculations made by the Government or of their inability to make any calculations at all, His Majesty's Government may choose to demand in order to prevent a further miscarriage of the Bill. Is that the correct interpretation of the words of the noble Marquess?

VISCOUNT MORLEY: I am not at all averse to answering any plain question, but I believe the noble Marquess and your Lordships will feel that to ask a question of that kind across the Table of the House without any notification upon so delicate and important a matter is rather going beyond Parliamentary practise.

MARQUESS OF LANSDOWNE: I merely put to the noble Viscount what I believe to the ordinary reader is the obvious interpretation of the words

[3] Winston S. Churchill.

used in this House last night by the noble Marquess. I am sure that I am not misleading your Lordships when I say that if this Bill is thrown out it will be a case not of a small but of a large creation of Peers. And to use Lord Crewe's words:

> I venture to say that anybody who tells you a different story has either been misled himself as to the facts of the case or has a purpose to serve in making the statement.

In these circumstances, some of us are disposed to consider that the wiser course for this House to adopt is to recognise that the Prime Minister's letter to Mr. Balfour and the speech made by Lord Crewe last night are conclusive on this point. We believe that in the face of these facts we shall be wise to desist from opposition which can only be futile, and that when the moment comes for dividing on these amendments, it will be better that we should withdraw from this House, leaving the modest battalion commanded by the noble Viscount in occupation of the field. We should, in this event, assume no responsibility whatever for the measure. We should desist from our opposition only because we are profoundly convinced that further resistance would be absolutely useless, and we should have the Bill passed over our heads every bit as effectually as if 300 or 400 Peers were to come down to this House to outvote us.

My Lords, what is the alternative course? It is a course which implies divided counsels; Peers on this side of the House voting in groups and sections, one man going into a particular Lobby because another man has chosen to go into another Lobby; the public puzzled and distracted; the action of those who have abstained from voting misunderstood; because obviously, if courage and heroism are claimed by one side, by implication cowardice and want of courage are imputed to the other side. Finally, we shall have the invasion of new Peers—and after all, that is the pity of it—we shall have the Parliament Bill without our amendments all the same. I cannot hesitate between these two courses. If I believed that these proceedings were going to be the end of this Constitutional struggle, if I thought that nothing lay beyond the debate which will finish tonight or tomorrow, then I would join my noble and learned Friend's standard and have one good fight before the end came. But, my Lords, in our view this is not the end. This is the beginning of a struggle which may last for many years and of which some of us who are here tonight may not see the end. It is a struggle which we shall pursue with unrelenting energy so long as life and health and spirit are given to us. We may be worsted in this encounter, but we are not going to be annihilated, and when our turn comes it will be our business to rebuild upon the ruins of the Constitution which you have wrecked a new Constitution more appropriate to the spirit of the age in which we live. In that great task we shall want all our resources, all our fighting strength, and above all a united party. It is because I hope that in this great struggle your Lordships' House will play an honourable and momentous part that I do not want to see it now weakened and discredited by such a use of the Royal Prerogative as that for which His Majesty's Government have now, in our opinion, most improperly, obtained the consent of the Crown.

EARL OF HALSBURY: My Lords, I would not have intervened so early in this debate but for one or two observations which have fallen from my noble Friend and which call at once for an explanation from me. My noble Friend has spoken of a crusade which I have initiated. I can assure him upon my honour that I never spoke to one single person on the subject until a large number of Peers came to wait upon me, after a speech which I made in this House, and suggested that we should agree in regard to our action. So far from entering into a crusade against my noble Friend or any of those who think with him, I had no idea that what I had said would have any effect or would meet with so enthusiastic an agreement on the part of such a large number of friends of my own. So much for the personal point.

.   .   .   .   .

But a more important matter is that which we are supposed to be discussing at this moment—namely, the question of the consideration of the Commons' amendments. The proposition that this House should be overborne by the creation of a number of Peers has been described in language I will not attempt to imitate; but what strikes me is that there is one thing we must clear our minds upon. Is there any bargain that if the Parliament Bill is passed the Peers will not be created? I think we must deal in the open if we are to have this question discussed, and also with respect to the number. Is there any guarantee that the operation is not to be repeated next year? How have you got rid of the degrading condition of things which my noble Friend has eloquently described by staying out of the House and allowing a Bill to be passed which has been denounced over and over again in language which no one can exceed in violence? I say nothing about courage, about the necessity of something like principle as distinguished from tactics; but what is to happen? If you say that this Parliament Bill is simply a question of delay for a couple of years and of securities, then what is to happen? Is this bogey, as I will call it, of the Royal Prerogative to be brought out every time there is a difference of opinion between the two Houses? What are you doing now? You are making something like a transaction with the other side in politics to do that which you yourselves have denounced over and over again as an improper thing to do. If there is a bargain that no Peers are to be made, I want to know whether that bargain goes any further. How long is the bargain, if there is one, to last? Is there any Royal Prerogative Suppression Bill to be brought forward after this measure? What is there left of power to this House without the amendments of my noble Friend? Everyone knows that there is no power in it.

. . . . .

I confess that I was a little surprised when I heard myself denounced and those who have been acting with me, as if we were disloyal to our own side. ["*No, no.*"] I do not know, but some of the language used by the noble Marquess certainly points to something of that kind. I am glad, however, to hear it disclaimed; but the noble Marquess will allow me, I hope, to say that when he is dealing in that way with friends and colleagues, I should have thought it to be a little more appropriate to take care that he was not so misunderstood.

MARQUESS OF LANSDOWNE: I did not use a single word or make a suggestion of what my noble Friend has said. I am incapable of harbouring any such thought regarding him, and I venture to prophesy that if he will look at my speech tomorrow he will find no sentence conveying that idea.

EARL OF HALSBURY: I assume then that I was mistaken. Even if I had not the high opinion which I have of the noble Marquess, one would always accept, of course, an explanation made by one gentleman to another under a misapprehension. I leave that topic altogether.

I wish to say something about the temptation which is offered to us to allow the Bill to pass. For my part I do not and will not draw any distinction between the responsibility of a person who votes for it and a person who abstains from voting. It seems to me that upon a question of principle, if I believed a thing to be wrong, I ought to do my best to prevent it. The temptation given to us is that we must allow the Bill to pass, and then, forsooth! agitate, until we get the country to take our view. Thus we are told that we shall be satisfied that we have saved this House from degradation. Have we? Is it saving this House from degradation when that which is admitted to be so degrading to it is yielded to as a threat? I ask those who yield to it as a threat—are they very much better than those who strive to the best of their ability to resist that threat to the end? I cannot help thinking that that rather savours of the spirit of "Stand aside; I am holier than thou." I do not understand those who will walk out of the House and allow that to be done which they think wrong because they think they will gain a little time.

I myself certainly will not yield to the threat. Let the Government take the responsibility of introducing 400 or 500 Peers—I care not how many—in the circumstances that my noble Friend has pointed out and then let him shield himself by saying, "And you forced them to do it." I never heard such an extraordinary argument in my life. It is as if a highwayman came and said, "Give me your watch or I cut your throat," and if you did not give him your watch that you are the author of your own throat being cut. I deny that because one may resist to the best of his ability what was believed to be a wrong, therefore he was responsible for the wrong being done. The contention is so absurd that everyone would laugh in your face if you advanced it. I have no more to say on this part of the case. The abuse, the contempt, and the epithets heaped on those with whom I have been associated are greater than I have ever heard or read. I speak particularly of some of the organs of public opinion, forsooth! who profess to give guidance and who take the other side. I have nothing more to say, except that nothing in the world will induce me to vote for a Bill or to abstain from not voting against a Bill which I believe to be wrong and immoral and a scandalous example of legislation.

. . . . .

EARL OF ROSEBERY: My Lords, I certainly did not come here tonight with any intention of speaking, and I shall not trouble your Lordships for more than a minute. But the speech of my noble Friend opposite,[4] important and weighty as it is and wholly convincing as I think it is, on the point at issue in the Division tonight does raise one or two more issues than perhaps he contemplated. The misfortune of this debate is that it is almost impossible to keep the name of the Sovereign out. I do not think the charge brought by my noble Friend Lord St. Aldwyn is completely valid as against His Majesty's Ministers.[5] I do not think they were bound to advise the Sovereign in November to send for Mr. Balfour or Lord Lansdowne. I think there is only one instance, perhaps, on record of such a thing being done, and that was when Lord Melbourne went to Brighton in 1834 and laid on the Sovereign all the discredit of dismissing him, when, as a matter of fact, he had practically advised that course. I do not think anybody can maintain sincerely that it was the duty of His Majesty's Government, with a large majority in the House of Commons, to send for any other personages to form a Government. But my noble Friend must remember that the circumstances were extremely exceptional.

I venture to say that, great as the noble Viscount's knowledge of Constitutional history is, he will never find that any Minister went to any Sovereign to ask for a third Dissolution in the course of their tenure of office—a second in the course of a single year. That, to my mind, is a circumstance of exceptional gravity. Deep as the waters may be in which we find ourselves tonight—and on my part I think they are as deep as the Pacific Ocean—we cannot overlook that grave consideration: going to a

---

[4] Morley.
[5] Lord St. Aldwyn earlier had asked the question: "Is it not a fact that by permission of His Majesty's Ministers ... His Majesty had the opportunity of consulting Lord Lansdowne and Mr. Balfour, and why could they have not given him the same opportunity last November?" (col. 1002).

young and inexperienced King four or five months on the Throne to ask him for a third Dissolution, a second within the year, and accompanying that demand, as I understand the case—and this part of the case is wrapped in some obscurity—with a request for a contingent guarantee, before they had read their Bill, perhaps, even once in the House of Commons, that should that Bill not meet with acceptance in the House of Lords, there should be an immense creation of Peers. Deep as our waters may be, I venture to say that we cannot exaggerate the enormous gravity of the position brought about by the Government at that time. That was the true Constitutional crisis. I think myself it would have been open to the Sovereign to say that before he acceded to so enormous a demand he should be allowed to take counsel with ex-Ministers and not be left entirely in the hands of His Majesty's Government, an *ex parte* body pleading their own cause with one who was hitherto unversed in such affairs. But that is all history. It does give an unpleasant savour to the whole of this transaction. No words that I can use—and I do not mean to use any such words—would exaggerate the effect that such a transaction would produce on any impartial and thinking man in this country.

Now I come to a far more important point, the announcement that the noble Viscount has categorically made this evening.[6] I confess I am not very well qualified to advise your Lordships as to rejecting a measure supported by two General Elections. I am not a good adviser, because ever since I have been in this House, some forty-three years, I have always been under the impression, though I was as jealous of the honour of this House as any member of it, that it was not a political instrument that was capable of achieving the purposes which its leaders thought it capable of producing. I never thought it was an instrument that could be used for rejecting what might even appear to be the will of the people without causing an exasperation and a reaction pre-eminently dangerous to the fortunes of this House. For taking that line on more than one occasion I have been reproached with cowardice in this House, and if I continued to sit here I might again make myself liable to that charge; but it is my conviction that an unreformed, hereditary House of Lords is wholly unfitted to resist great popular movements, and that is why all the time I have been in this House I have endeavoured to further the cause for Reform. I do not think that this House is a body that could resist a cause or a measure supported by two General Elections.

I think there is a great deal to be said about these General Elections. We swallow them rather too easily. The Government sometimes gives one

---

[6] Morley had announced that the Government's intention to create new peers was not an empty threat: "If the Bill should be defeated tonight His Majesty would assent to a creation of Peers sufficient in number to guard against any possible combination of the different Parties in opposition by which the Parliament Bill might be exposed a second time to defeat" (col. 999).

account of these General Elections and sometimes another, and never the same. The first General Election was on the Budget and not on the House of Lords. We have been told, and I am willing to accept it, that the second election was on the House of Lords, but if that were so, how could it give a mandate for Irish Home Rule? It either was an election, a referendum as complete as could be had on the question of the House of Lords, and therefore confined to that particular object, or it was a General Election of the usual kind in which the House of Lords figured for one thing, Irish Home Rule for another, cheap food for another, and so forth. There is another point affecting these General Elections which I think has a considerable bearing on the case. They were elections both fought on the part of the Government under the most enormous bribe that has ever been given to the people of the country. Thirteen million pounds a year were to be awarded in exchange for no consideration whatever in old-age pensions to the great masses of the country, who were naturally under the influence of that boon when they came to vote at the poll. I therefore think that these General Elections are questionable in more than one respect; but we must recognise that they have taken place, and that the measure has come up with that support.

Now, how do we find ourselves? We find ourselves chiefly divided on this [the Opposition] side of the House in arguing not against the propositions of the Government, but on the best method of dealing with those propositions. I have tried as hard as I can to convince myself that I could do what is a congenial thing to everybody in our position, when an act of degradation and disability is aimed at us, to resist it with my noble and learned Friend[7] as long as Widdrington fought upon his stumps.[8] But I cannot see more than one side of this question. You must admit that whichever side of the Opposition prevails tonight the Bill must pass. No one denies that. I see that my noble and learned Friend denied it last night, but he was speaking legally. He could delay it for forty-eight hours; he might delay it for a week.

EARL OF HALSBURY: I said more than that.

EARL OF ROSEBERY: How long?

EARL OF HALSBURY: Until next Session.

EARL OF ROSEBERY: My noble Friend has all the sanguineness of youth.

EARL OF HALSBURY: It is all very well for my noble Friend to turn it off in that way. I want to know as a matter of fact whether, if we insist upon our amendments and we prevail, the Bill is dead or not.

EARL OF ROSEBERY: The Bill is temporarily dead; but there could be a Prorogation tomorrow and the Bill could be passed rapidly through all its

[7] Halsbury.
[8] Squire Widdrington (or Witherington) is the knight mentioned in *The Ballad of Chevy Chase*, one of the oldest of English ballads: "For when his legs were smitten off, he fought upon his stumps."

stages. What is a month in the Constitutional history of this country? What is a month in the future of the House of Lords? We acknowledge on both sides that within a month, or six weeks if you like, the Bill must pass.

EARL OF HALSBURY: Do not say we all admit it. We do not.

EARL OF ROSEBERY: My noble Friend does not admit it; but I think the general sense of the House is that, after what has passed, this Bill must come into law before the 31st of December. Let me give that latitude. The only difference between the two sections of the Opposition, who loathe and detest this Bill with equal hatred, is whether it shall pass with some enormous creation of Peers, such as has just been announced by the noble Viscount, to control the future conduct of this House, or whether it shall pass without the scandal of such a Constitutional strain as that. That is the victory at which my noble and learned Friend aims. Is it worth while, simply for the purpose of further degrading and weakening this House, to insist upon these futile amendments? I read with great interest a letter from the noble and gallant Field-Marshal[9] in *The Times* yesterday. It was as noble and gallant as himself; but it was conducted on the principle which has done enormous injury in this discussion—the principle of military analogy. My noble and gallant Friend conducted his military analogy with complete success. But there is no analogy between the two cases. If he does want a military analogy, let me put this case to him. Would he, if he were in command of an army, as he has so often been, be willing to obtain a slight victory in a skirmish at the beginning of a war on condition that his whole army should be flattened out next day by the enemy? That is the point.

My Lords, this is no subject for recrimination. It is the most solemn moment the House of Lords has had to face in my lifetime or in that of many men much older. By a wise concession to the feeling of the people, under the guidance of a leader whom no one ever dared to accuse of cowardice, the Duke of Wellington, the House of Lords preserved its existence for eighty years, when without that concession it would not have had three years of life. That is one example. We stand now at the parting of the ways. Whatever happens, I recognise for my part that nothing can ever restore the House of Lords. After the Second Reading of the Bill to which we were compelled reluctantly to yield our assent, the House of Lords as we have known it disappeared. It is possible that if this Bill be allowed to go through tonight there may still be a considerable balance of party which may be of great use in opposing the Government, and which I was glad to see my noble Friend the noble Viscount wished to see unimpaired. There will still be a force left in this House to oppose and even sometimes to thwart the dangerous measures of the Government. If this Bill be allowed to pass, Europe and the Empire will be spared the sight of a scandal which

---

[9] Earl Roberts.

may go far to weaken the hold of the centre of the Empire on its component parts, and we shall be left, at any rate, with a certain amount of vitality without the strain on the Constitution involved in the creation of hundreds of Peers; whereas, on the other hypothesis, we shall be left with no power at all, flattened out completely, with an addition of hundreds of Peers, added to this House under, I must be allowed to say, a most degrading franchise, and the ruin of this ancient Constitutional assembly will be as complete as its worst enemies could desire.

. . . . .

EARL CURZON OF KEDLESTON: My Lords, I shall not intrude for any length of time between yourselves and the Division that you are anxious to take, and in the few moments which I may occupy I could not hope—and if I could hope I should not attempt—to add anything that is new to this debate. It may, however, be permissible for me, on behalf of that large section on this side of the House with which I am acting, to say one or two words in conclusion before your Lordships proceed to a Division, by way of summing up the case as it appears to stand in the opinion of the noble Marquess[10] and those who act with him.

It has been brought against us more than once in this debate that it has been a debate of rather a domestic character. Nobody regrets that more than myself. There is a difference between noble Lords who sit on this side of the House, and I rather agree with Lord Plymouth that the difference is not one of procedure alone, but that principles are involved. I have not said one word in this controversy against the sincerity, integrity, and conscientiousness of any man, whichever way he is going to vote, and I hope my noble Friends will make an equal concession to those who, taking their fortunes in their hands, are going to do what they regard as an odious and distasteful thing, rather than see this House involved in what they conceive to be not only a great danger, but its certain and ultimate ruin. I ask noble Lords to concede to them what they claim for themselves.

From this discussion surely there emerge two salient facts. First, that enforced with so much emphasis by my noble Friend Lord Rosebery this afternoon—that there is no getting away from the fact that this Bill is going to pass. The action of Lord Halsbury and his friends may retard its passage into law for a few days or at most a few weeks, but they cannot prevent its ultimate passage. We have reached a point at which it must be admitted that the powers of effectual resistance have gone from us. We cannot force a General Election. I do not know that my noble Friends who sit behind me would force one if they could. That, at any rate, is a solution of the question to which I for one am not prepared at the present moment

[10] Lansdowne.

to refer. That is the first feature of the present situation—that the Bill is going to pass. If your Lordships throw it out tonight, there will be a sharp and swift resurrection of the Bill, and nothing can prevent it from being placed on the Statute Book at most in a few weeks from the present date. I wish it were not so.

The second point is that it has emerged from the discussion for the first time with absolute clearness tonight that if the Prerogative of the Crown is to be used for a creation of Peers it will be, to use the words of the noble Viscount, a prompt and large creation of Peers sufficient in number to overcome any combination of forces on this side of the House that might be brought against this Bill. [*Hear, hear.*] I do not join in those "Hear, hears." I think it is one of the most deplorable things that has ever happened in the history of this House. I am not now concerned to question or to characterise its morality. I am only concerned to describe it as an impending fact. For a long time a number of my noble Friends on this side of the House have cherished what I have told them was an illusion—that if there were a creation of Peers it would be slight, small, and insignificant. They declined to change their opinion even in the face of the statement of the Home Secretary in the other House[11] and of the practical endorsement of it by the noble Marquess, Lord Crewe. Even then the scales did not fall from the eyes of several of my noble Friends, and they said that Lord Crewe had thrown over his colleague in the House of Commons. Is it not perfectly certain, after the words of the noble Viscount, Lord Morley, which I need not recapitulate, that if the Bill is thrown out there is going to be a creation of Peers so large—I do not pause to inquire whether it is to be 300, 400, or 500—as to alter altogether the composition of this House, to destroy the House of Lords as we have known it, and to upset the Constitution of this country? Is not that the second great salient fact that emerges from our proceedings this evening?

May I ask this question of my noble Friends who are about to vote? Supposing that by your votes you defeat the Government and force such a creation, what good will you do to yourselves, to your Party, to the Constitution, to the country, or to anyone concerned? I know that you are animated by motives wholly dissociated from personal feeling. You are acting in the public interest. I ask you, therefore, in the public interest, what is it you are going to effect? You are not going to stop the Bill being passed within a few days or weeks. That is conceded. The noble and learned Earl[12] attaches more importance to the interval of a few weeks than I do. It does not seem to me that your operations tonight can succeed in doing any more than arrest the passage into law of this Bill for a short time. Then are you going to make the Government contemptible in the eyes of the country? I wish you were. I truly think that nothing more ridiculous—

[11] Churchill.
[12] Halsbury.

more open to the charge of contempt—could be imagined than this creation of Peers; but at the bottom of my heart I cannot help thinking that the country—I am not speaking of our Party in the country but the great mass of the electorate—so far from believing that His Majesty's Government had resorted to an action which is ridiculous, would say that the Peers, who had twice stood out against His Majesty's Government and been defeated, were finally being hoisted with their own petard. I do not say that that would be a just thing for the electorate to say, but it is a very likely thing to be said; and so far from thinking that ridicule would fall on the shoulders where it ought to fall—on those of noble Lords opposite—I think it might conceivably recoil on the heads of noble Lords on this side of the House.

My noble Friends have been very strong on the point that this action which they hope to take is necessary to convince the country of the seriousness of this revolution. I pay my noble Friends the compliment of saying that the whole of their action during the past fortnight—their speeches, their letters, their resolutions—have not been without effect in convincing the country of the existence of a revolution. I pay them that compliment. But if they think that the country is likely to be brought more face to face with revolution because 400 or 500 gentlemen are going to troop into this House and sit on the Benches opposite, I respectfully differ from them. I would ask noble Lords for a moment to contemplate the positive consequences of the action which they propose to take. If you succeed tonight in defeating the Government and compelling the creation of a large number of Peers, is it not clear that you will be making an enormous and gratuitous addition to the power for mischief of the Party opposite? A noble Lord[13] last night used this metaphor—that noble Lords on this side of the House who were taking such a line of action were committing suicide on the doorstep of their opponents. I think my noble Friends to whom I am appealing would be doing much worse than that. They would be presenting a regiment, an army, to the enemy in the campaign upon which we are about to enter.

Then I come to the point on which Lord St. Levan touched just now—the exceedingly difficult and delicate point of Party allegiance. Do not let any of your Lordships who are going to give this vote conceal from yourselves the fact that you are giving a vote against the definite advice of the trusted leaders of your Party. I believe that the sentiments which have been expressed by more than one noble Lord who has spoken from these Benches of personal and devoted attachment to the noble Marquess are genuine sentiments. I believe they are echoed by every man who sits in this House and who has had the privilege of sitting here under his able, his courteous, his attractive leadership. But, my Lords, I cannot

---

[13] Lord Newton.

help remembering what Lord Salisbury said in the debate last night. He said, "The country only understands deeds; it utterly despises words." I cannot conceal from myself the fact that these protestations, genuine as I believe them to be, of loyalty and devotion to my noble Friend, are accompanied by a reluctance to accept his advice upon the present occasion. I think that is greatly to be deplored. The position is a difficult one. I do not desire to press it for more than it is worth, but at least I do ask noble Lords on this side of the House to bear in mind that those of them who are going to take this action are taking it in opposition of the advice of their leaders, not only in this House but in the other House of Parliament.

There is one other point to which I allude with some diffidence after what was said by the Duke of Norfolk this evening. The noble Duke, in what, if I may say so, was a most cogent and powerful speech, made effective use of the proposition that great reluctance ought to be felt by anyone on an occasion of this sort in bringing in the name of the King. I accept that. The name of the King has been brought into the matter not by us. We have not utilised it to extract any Party advantage, even if that had been possible. We regret that the name of the Sovereign has been introduced, but in this matter the position of the Sovereign cannot be altogether eliminated. There is no noble Lord who heard the noble Marquess, Lord Crewe, address us two nights ago who cannot have been assured of the fact that in November last and again in July, the position of the Sovereign, confronted with the pressure that was put upon him, must have been painful, anxious, embarrassing, and almost, to use Lord Crewe's words, odious. If that be so, is it not absolutely certain that whatever may have been the feelings of the Sovereign—and we have been told what they were—when these matters were placed before him, ten times more painful, more anxious, more embarrassing must it be to the Sovereign to have, as almost the first act after his Coronation in a reign that we hope will be happy and glorious, to give his assent to the actual introduction into your Lordships' House of a number of Peers that would destroy the character of this assembly and pull down the pillars of the Constitution. I hope I have not made an unfair use, even by implication, of the name of the Sovereign.

One last point. We are all Members of the House of Lords. We have reached it by different avenues, some of us by descent, some of us by election, some of us by service; but I believe there is no man who sits in this House, not even the latest recruit to it, who does not when he comes within these walls acquire some measure of inspiration, some idea that this House is the centre of a great history and of noble traditions—the idea that he is part of an assembly that has wrought and is capable of doing in the future great and splendid service to this country. I have those feelings. I cannot contemplate with satisfaction anything which must effect the pollution—perhaps that is too strong a word—the degradation of this House, and I ask your Lordships to pause before you not only acquiesce in, but precipitate or facilitate, a course of procedure with regard to this House which cannot but have the effect of covering it with ridicule and of destroying its power for good in the future.

There is only one other appeal I would like to make. My noble Friends who sit behind me and whom I have been to a large extent addressing are a small minority of the whole House; they are a minority of the Party to which they belong. I do not say this in an invidious sense. I state it as a matter of fact. They are a minority in numbers, though I do not say that they have not in their ranks some of the most distinguished members of your Lordships' House. It is open to that minority, in the Division which is about to take place, to adopt an action which their numbers alone or even their ability alone would hardly entitle them to take. I perhaps have put it not very well. What I mean is that it is in the power of 80 or 90 or 100 Members of your Lordships' House tonight, by the vote which you are going to give to dictate an action to the whole of the House. All I want is that your Lordships should clearly realise the responsibility you are assuming in this matter, because it may be that by a small majority, a majority of two or three or four of that small minority, you may impose upon the Government a course of action which may have a profound effect on the whole future of this country. I do not suppose a more momentous Division will ever have taken place in the House of Lords. It is possible that as a result of this Division 400 Peers may be created. If that is done, the Constitution is gone as we have known it. We start afresh to build up a new Constitution. God knows how we shall do it. We may do it with success or with failure. Let us realise what is before us—

MARQUESS OF BRISTOL: It is because 400 Peers are going to run away tonight.

EARL CURZON OF KEDLESTON: I would sooner run away with the Duke of Wellington than stand with the noble Lord.

MARQUESS OF BRISTOL: I would rather fight with Nelson at Copenhagen than run away with the noble Earl.

EARL CURZON OF KEDLESTON: I do not wish to get involved in a controversy with the noble Lord. My appeals, I am afraid, would be useless if directed to him. They were only intended to ask Members of your Lordships' House who are about to vote to carefully weigh in you own minds the vast interests that are at stake; to ponder, before you give your vote, the consequences that must ensue; and to be very careful indeed before you register a vote which, whatever may be your emotions at this moment, when you look over it calmly, I do not say tomorrow but a month, three months, or six months hence, you may find has wrought irreparable damage to the Constitution of this country, to your own Party, and to the State.

EARL OF HALSBURY: My Lords, I would have been quite content to join in the cry of "Divide!" which greeted the conclusion of the noble

Earl's speech, but I cannot allow the oration to which we have just listened to remain without an answer. A great deal of what the noble Earl has said has been in the nature of an exhortation to us to do our duty and think carefully. Did it ever occur to the noble Earl that others besides himself have been considering our duty and do not require his exhortation to consider the supreme importance of the matter in which we are engaged? I can assure him that I have thought very deeply on the subject. Nothing could be more repugnant to my feelings than to be obliged to vote against the wishes of my noble Friend the Leader of the Opposition. Not only the noble Earl but others also—I think I may include the Episcopal Bench—seem to consider that for the first time in our lives we are encountered with the broad proposition that we should do our duty.

A good many of the observations that were made by Lord Curzon have been traversed over and over again and I do not propose to go through them, but there are one or two remarks I should like to make upon what the noble Earl said. I noticed that a misrepresentation—unconscious, no doubt—of something which I said has been twice repeated. I am stated to have said that this was a question of tactics. I never said anything of the sort in that connexion. What I did say was that the only thing which divided us on this side of the House was a question of tactics. Noble Lords who do not agree with us on the question of tactics are as determined as we are on the question of principle. But there is a matter which they have not discussed at all, apparently—that is, what will be the condition of this House if this Bill passes? That is one of the things which have been entirely omitted. One would suppose that the subject on which we are now engaged is the question of leaving us in the position in which we were. But this Bill is a Bill which destroys the independence of this House absolutely, and when we talk about this being only a question of tactics we get entangled into the question of discussing our Party loyalty; but that has nothing to do with the broad question of principle here, which is, are we or are we not to give our assent to a Bill which will destroy this chamber as a legislative chamber altogether? That is the question we have to consider, and that seems to me to be a question of principle.

Let me make another observation. I am not one of those who regard this as a question to be treated jocosely. I do not think that the destruction of this historic House, with all its traditions, with all its powers, and with all the benefits it has conferred on this country, is a thing to be treated as the climax of fun. It seems to me that that is beneath the dignity of the discussion in which we are engaged and somewhat degrading to the dignity of the House. When pictures are presented to us and we are asked, in language which perhaps is more appropriate to the pulpit than to this discussion, to consider whether five months or six months hence we will regard our action as right or wrong, I confess that the only question which I would consider under such circumstances would be whether I believed

I was doing right at the time; whether I was right in declaring over and over again in the course of the discussion of this destructive Bill that the amendments which the noble Marquess the Leader of the Opposition moved with such convincing logic and great eloquence were absolutely essential, and whether I was to abandon them at the last minute. Looking back, I should not care what the result was if I did that which I believed to be right. I am prepared to leave the final decision of the rightness or wrongness of it to a higher tribunal.

Earl of Rosebery: My Lords, I am going to make the shortest and perhaps the most painful speech of my life. We have had an exhortation from the noble and learned Earl to do our duty. I have never supported the amendments. I have never even been present in the House when they were brought forward. I have bitterly opposed the Bill of the Government. But the question now narrows itself into whether we should insist upon an amendment which I have never thought would greatly mitigate the operation of this Bill. I certainly cannot risk the danger to which we are liable to be exposed by insisting upon it now. In a recent letter to the press I urged the House of Lords to abstain from voting on this question. I hold still that that is a position which I should greatly prefer. I cannot conceive a more painful position than being obliged to vote apparently for a Bill which is abhorrent to me as it practically abolishes the only second chamber which exists without substituting anything in its place. Happily that is not exactly the position I occupy tonight, because the strict question is whether we shall insist upon an amendment with which I personally do not agree. Therefore I have not the least hesitation in saying, profoundly painful as it is, that I shall think it my duty to follow the Government into the Division Lobby.[14]

---

[14] The motion, "that this House do not insist upon the said amendments," passed 131–114.

THE SEVEN-LEAGUE BOOTS;

OR, DEATH OF GIANT MONOPOLY.

3

Economic Policy and Social Change

Richard Cobden

"Corn Laws and Agricultural Distress"*
Commons, March 13, 1845

Sir, I am relieved upon the present occasion from any necessity for apologising to the other side of the House for the motion which I am about to submit. It will be in the recollection of honourable Members that a fortnight before putting this notice upon the book I expressed a hope that the matter would be taken up by some honourable Member opposite. I do not think, therefore, that in reply to any observations that I may have to make upon the question, I shall hear as I did last year an expression that the quarter from which this motion came was suspicious. I may also add, Sir, that I have so framed my motion as to include in it the objects embraced in both the amendments which are made to it; I therefore conclude that having included the honourable Gentlemen's amendments,[1] they will not now feel it necessary to press them. Sir, the object of this motion is to appoint a select Committee to inquire into the present condition of the agricultural interests, and, at the same time, to ascertain how the laws regulating the importation of agricultural produce have affected the agriculturists of this country. As regards the distress among farmers, I presume we cannot go to a higher authority than those honourable Gentlemen who profess to be the farmers' friends and protectors. [*Hear.*] I find it stated by those honourable Gentlemen who recently paid their respects to the Prime Minister that the agriculturists are in a state of great embarrassment and distress. I find that one Gentleman from Norfolk (Mr. Hudson) stated that the farmers in that county are paying their rents, but paying them out of capital and not profits. I find Mr. Turner, of Upton, in Devonshire, stating that one-half of the smaller farmers in that county are insolvent, and that the others are

---

* The text is from *The League*, March 15, 1845, pp. 388–391. It is a fuller version than that reported in *Hansard's Parliamentary Debates*, Third Series, Vol. LXXVIII, cols. 785–810.

[1] A. Stafford O'Brien, North Northamptonshire, and Edmund Wodehouse, Norfolk East, Conservatives who believed that an inquiry would vindicate protection.

rapidly falling into the same condition; that the farmers with larger holdings are quitting their farms with a view of saving the rest of their property; and that unless some remedial measures are adopted by this House, they will be utterly ruined. [*Hear.*]

The accounts which I have given you of those districts are such as I have had from many other sources. I put it to honourable Gentlemen opposite whether the condition of the farmers in Suffolk, Wiltshire, and Hampshire is anything better than that which I have described in Norfolk and Devonshire? [*Hear, hear.*] I put it to county Members whether, taking the whole of the South of England from the confines of Nottinghamshire to the Land's End, whether, as a rule, the farmers are not now in a state of the greatest embarrassment? [*Hear, hear.*] There may be exceptions, but I put it to them whether, as a rule, that is not their condition in all parts? Then, Sir, according to every precedent in this House, this is a fit and proper time to bring forward the motion of which I have given notice. [*Hear, hear.*] I venture to state that had his Grace of Buckingham possessed a seat in this House, he would have done now what he did when he was Lord Chandos[2] —have moved this resolution which I am now about to move.

The distress of the farmer being admitted, the next question which arises is, what is its cause? [*Hear, hear.*] I feel a greater necessity to bring forward this motion for a Committee of inquiry because I find great discrepancies of opinion among honourable Gentlemen opposite as to what is the cause of the distress among the farmers. In the first place there is a discrepancy as to the generality or locality of the existing distress. I find the right honourable Baronet at the head of the Government[3] saying that the distress is local, and he moreover says it does not arise from legislation. The honourable Member for Dorsetshire[4] declares, on the other hand, that the distress is general, and that it does arise from legislation. [*Hear, hear.*]

I am at a loss to understand what this protection to agriculture means, because I find such contradictory accounts given in this House by the promoters of that system. For instance, nine months ago, when my honourable Friend the Member for Wolverhampton[5] brought forward his motion for the abolition of the Corn Laws, the right honourable Gentleman then the President of the Board of Trade,[6] in replying to him, said that the last Corn Law had been most successful in its operations. He took great credit to the Government for the steadiness of price that was obtained under that

---

[2] On February 21, 1834, the Marquess of Chandos moved a "revision of taxes" to relieve "the distressed condition of the agricultural interest."

[3] Sir Robert Peel.

[4] George Bankes.

[5] Charles P. Villiers, one of the League's most effective spokesmen, advocated repeal on June 25, 1844. His motion was defeated 124–328. Beginning in March, 1838, several years before Cobden entered Parliament, Villiers annually introduced a motion for abolition of the Corn Laws.

[6] William E. Gladstone.

law. I will read you the quotation, because we find these statements so often controverted. He said:

> Was there any man who had supported the law in the year 1842 who could honestly say that he had been disappointed in its working? Could anyone point out a promise or a prediction hazarded in the course of the protracted debates upon the measure which promise or prediction had been subsequently falsified?

Now, recollect that the right honourable Gentleman was speaking when wheat was 56*s*. per quarter, and that wheat is now 45*s*. [*Hear.*] The right honourable Baronet at the head of the Government says, "My legislation has had nothing to do with wheat being at 45*s*. a quarter"; but how are we to get over the difficulty that the responsible Member of Government at the head of the Board of Trade, only nine months ago, claimed merit for the Government having kept up the price of wheat at 56*s*.? [*Hear, hear.*] These discrepancies themselves between the Government and its supporters render it more and more necessary that this question of protection should be inquired into. I ask, what does it mean? The price of wheat is 45*s*. this day. I have been speaking to the highest authority in England upon this point—one who is often quoted by this House—within the last week, and he tells me that with another favourable harvest, he thinks it very likely that wheat will be 35*s*. a quarter. [*Hear.*] What does this legislation mean, or what does it purport to be, if you are to have prices fluctuating from 56*s*. down to 35*s*. a quarter, and probably lower? [*Hear, hear.*] Can you prevent it by the legislation of this House? That is the question. There is a great delusion spread abroad amongst the farmers, and it is the duty of this House to have that delusion dissipated by inquiring into the matter. [*Hear.*]

Now, there are these very different opinions on one side of the House, but there are Members upon this side representing very important interests, who think that farmers are suffering because they have this legislative protection. There is all this difference of opinion. Now, is not that a fit and proper subject for your inquiry? I am prepared to go into a select Committee and to bring forward evidence to show that the farmers are labouring under great evils—evils that I would connect with the Corn Law, though they are evils which appear to be altogether dissociated from it. The first great evil under which the farmer labours is the want of capital. [*Hear.*] No one can deny that. I do not mean at all to disparage the farmers. The farmers of this country are just the same race as the rest of us, and, if they were placed in a similar position, theirs would be as good a trade; I mean that they would be as successful men of business as others; but it is notorious as a rule that the farmers of this country are deficient in capital, and I ask, how can any business be carried on successfully where there is a deficiency of capital?

I take it that honourable Gentlemen acquainted with farming opposite would admit that £10 an acre on an arable farm would be a sufficient amount of capital for carrying on the business of farming successfully. [*Hear.*] I will take it, then, that £10 an acre would be a fair capital for an arable farm. I have made many inquiries upon this subject in all parts of the Kingdom, and I give it you as my decided conviction that at this present moment farmers do not average £5 an acre capital on their farms. [*Hear, hear.*] I speak of England, and I take England south of the Trent, though of course there are exceptions in every county; there are men of large capital in all parts, men farming their own land; but, taking it as a rule, I hesitate not to give my opinion—and I am prepared to back that opinion by witnesses before your Committee—that as a rule, farmers have not upon an average more than £5 an acre capital for their arable land. Only think what an evil this is! I have given you a tract of country to which I may add all Wales; probably twenty millions of acres of cultivatable land. I have no doubt whatever that there are £100 millions of capital wanting upon that land. What is the meaning of farming capital? There are strange notions about this word "capital." It means more manure, a greater amount of labour, a greater number of cattle, and larger crops. Fancy a country in which you can say there is a deficiency of one-half of all those blessings which ought to, and might, exist there, and then judge what the condition of labourers wanting employment and food is. [*Hear, hear.*]

But you would say capital would be invested if it could be done with profit. I admit it; that is the question I want you to inquire into. How is it that in a country where there is a plethora of capital, where every other business and pursuit is overflowing with money, where you have men going to France for railways and Pennsylvania for bonds, embarking in schemes for connecting the Atlantic with the Pacific by canals, railways in the valley of the Mississippi, and sending their money to the bottom of the Mexican mines—while you have a country rich and overflowing, ready to take investments in every corner of the globe—how is it, I say, that this capital does not find its employment in the most attractive of all forms—upon the soil of this country? [*Hear, hear.*] Admitting this evil, with all its train of evil consequences, what is the cause of it? The cause is notorious, it is admitted by your highest authorities; the reason is there is not security for capital in land. Capital shrinks instinctively from insecurity of tenure; and you have not in England that security which would warrant men of capital investing their money in the soil.

Now, is not this a matter worthy of consideration, how far this insecurity of tenure is bound up with that protective system with which you are so enamoured? Suppose it can be shown that there is a vicious circle—that you have made politics of Corn Laws and that you want voters to maintain them; that you very likely think that the Corn Laws are your great mine of wealth, and therefore you must have a dependent tenantry that you may have their votes at elections to maintain this law in this House. Well, if you will have dependent voters, you cannot have men of spirit and capital. [*Hear.*] Then your policy reacts upon you. If you have not men of skill and capital, you cannot have improvements and employment for your labourers. Then comes round that vicious termination of the circle—you have pauperism, poor-rates, county-rates, and all the other evils of which you are now speaking and complaining. Now, Sir, I like to quote from the highest authority upon that side of the House. I will just state to you what is the opinion of the honourable Member for Berkshire[7] upon this subject. When speaking at a meeting of the Agricultural Society, he says:

> He knew this country well, and he knew that there was not a place from Plymouth to Berwick in which the landlords might not make improvements; but when the tenant was short of money, the landlord generally would be short of money, too. [*Hear.*] But he would tell them how to find funds. There were many districts where there was a great superfluity not only of useless but of mischievous timber, and if they would cut that down which excluded the sun and air and fed on the soil and sell it, they would benefit the farmer by cutting it down, and they would benefit the farmer and the labourer too by laying out the proceeds in under-draining the soil. [*Cheers.*] There was another mode in which they might find money. He knew that on some properties a large sum was spent in the preservation of game. [*Cheers.*] It was not at all unusual for the game to cost £500 or £600 a year; and if this were given up, the money would employ 100 able-bodied labourers in improving the property. [*Cheers.*] This was another fund for the landlords of England to benefit the labourers and the farmers at the same time.

Now, there is another authority—a very important member of your Protection Society—Mr. Fisher Hobbes—who thus speaks at a meeting of the Colchester Agricultural Association:

> Mr. Fisher Hobbes was aware that a spirit of improvement was abroad. Much was said about the tenant farmers doing more. He agreed they might do more; the soil of the country was capable of greater production; if he said one-fourth more he should be within compass. [*Hear, hear.*] But that could not be done by the tenant farmer alone; they must have confidence [*loud cheers*]; it must be done by leases [*renewed cheers*]; by draining; by extending the length of fields; by knocking down hedgerows and clearing away trees which now shielded the corn.

I will quote a still higher authority. Lord Stanley,[8] at a late meeting at Liverpool, said:

---

[7] Philip Pusey, a close friend of Peel and Gladstone, was a founder and president of the Royal Agricultural Society of England.
[8] Stanley was a protectionist leader in the House of Lords.

I say, and as one connected with the land I feel myself bound to say it, that a landlord has no right to expect any great and permanent improvement of his land by the tenant unless that tenant be secured the repayment of his outlay, not by the personal character or honour of his landlord, but by a security which no casualties can interfere with—the security granted him by the terms of a lease for years.

Now, Sir, not only does the want of security prevent capital flowing into the farming business, but it actually deters from the improvement of the land those who are already in the occupation of it. [*Hear.*] There are many men, tenants of your land, who could improve their farms if they had a sufficient security and they have either capital themselves or their friends could supply it; but with the absence of leases and the want of security, you are actually deterring them from laying out their money upon your land. They keep everything the same from year to year. You know that it is impossible to farm your estates properly unless a tenant has an investment for more than one year. A man ought to be able to begin a farm with at least eight years before him before he expects to see a return for the outlay of his money. You are therefore keeping your tenants-at-will at a yearly kind of cultivation, and you are preventing them carrying on their cultivation in a proper way. Not only do you prevent the laying out of capital upon your land and disable the farmers from cultivating it, but your policy tends to make them servile and dependent, so that they are actually disinclined to improvement, afraid to let you see that they can improve, because they are apprehensive that you will pounce upon them for an increase of rent. [*Hear.*] I see the honourable Member for Lincolnshire[9] opposite, and he rather smiled at the expression when I said that the state of dependence of the farmers was such that they were actually afraid to appear to be improving their land. [*Hear, hear.*] Now, that honourable Gentleman the Member for Lincolnshire, upon my honourable Friend's[10] motion for agricultural statistics last year, made the following statement:

> It was most desirable for the farmer to know the actual quantity of corn grown in this country, as such knowledge would ensure steadiness of prices, which was infinitely more valuable to the agriculturist than fluctuating prices. But to ascertain this there was extreme difficulty. They could not leave it to the farmer to make a return of the quantity which he produced, for it was not for his interest to do so. If in any one or two years he produced four quarters per acre on land which had previously grown but three, he might fear lest his landlord would say, "Your land is more productive than I imagined, and I must therefore raise your rent." The interest of the farmers, therefore, would be to underrate and to furnish low returns.

[9] Robert A. Christopher.
[10] T. Milner Gibson, Member for Manchester. Gibson's motion and Christopher's statement were made on April 18, 1844.

Now, here is a little evidence of the same kind, which I find at a meeting of the South Devonshire Agricultural Association. The Rev. C. Johnson said:

> He knew it had been thought that landlords were ready to avail themselves of such associations on account of the opportunity it afforded them for diving into their tenants' affairs and opening their eyes. [*Hear.*] An instance of this occurred to him at a recent ploughing match, where he met a respectable agriculturist whom he well knew, and asked him if he was going to it. He said, "No." "Why?" Because he did not approve of such things. This *why* produced another *why*, and the man gave a reason *why*. Suppose he sent a plough and man, with two superior horses, the landlord at once would say, "This man is doing too well on my estate," and increase the rent.

Now, I ask honourable Gentlemen here—the landed gentry of England—what a state of things is that when upon their own testimony respecting the farming capitalists in this country the farmers dare not appear to have a good horse—they dare not appear to be growing more than four quarters instead of three? [*"Hear, hear" and cheers from Mr. Christopher.*] The honourable Member cheers, but I am quoting from his own authority. I say this condition of things, indicated by those two quotations, brings the tenant farmers—if they are such as these Gentlemen describe them to be—it brings them down to a very low point of servility. In Egypt the landlords take the utmost grain of their corn from the tenants, who bury it beneath their hearths of stone in their cottages and will suffer the bastinado rather than they will tell how much corn they grow. Our tenants are not afraid of the bastinado, but they are terrified at a rise of rent. [*Cheers.*] This is the state of things amongst the tenant farmers farming without leases. That I take to be the condition of a great portion of the tenant farmers in this country. In England leases are the exception and not the rule. [*Hear, hear.*] But even when you have leases in England—where you have leases or agreements—I doubt whether they are not in many cases worse tenures than where there is no lease at all, the clauses being of such an obsolete and preposterous character as to defy any man to carry on the business of farming under them profitably. I do not know whether the honourable Member for Cheshire is here, but if so I will read him a passage from an actual Cheshire lease, showing what kind of covenants farmers are called on to perform:

> To pay the landlord £20 for every statute acre of ground, and so in proportion for a less quantity, that shall be converted into tillage, or used contrary to the appointment before made; and £5 for every cwt. of hay, thrave of straw, load of potatoes, or cartload of manure, that shall be sold or taken from the premises during the term; and £10 for every tree fallen, cut down, or destroyed, cropped, lopped, or topped, or willingly suffered so to be; and £20 for any servant or other person so hired or admitted as to gain a settlement

in the township; and £10 per statute acre, and so in proportion for a less quantity, of the said land, which the tenant shall let off or underlet. ["*Hear, hear*" *from the Ministerial side*.] Such sums to be paid on demand after every breach, and in default of payment to be considered as reserved rent, and levied by distress and sale as rent in arrear may be levied and raised. And to do six days' boon team work whenever called upon; and to keep for the landlord one dog, and one cock or hen; and to make no marlpit without the landlord's consent first obtained in writing, after which the same is to be properly filled in; nor to allow any inmate to remain on the premises after six days' notice; nor to keep or feed any sheep except such as are used for the consumption of the family.

Now, what is such an instrument as that? I will tell you. It is a trap for the unwary man, it is a barrier against men of intelligence and capital, and it is a fetter to the mind of any free man. No man could farm under such a lease as that, or under such clauses as it contains. [*Hear, hear*.] I perceive that the honourable Member for the rape of Bramber[11] is cheering. I will by and by allude to one of the honourable Member's own leases. [*Hear, hear*.] You will find in your own leases, though there may not be a stipulation for cocks and hens and dogs and probably team work, yet that there are almost as great absurdities in every lease and agreement you have. ["*Hear, hear*" *and laughter*.] What are those leases? Why, they are generally some old antediluvian dusty remains which some lawyer's clerk takes out of a pigeonhole, and merely writes out for every fresh incoming tenant—a thing which seems to have been in existence for a hundred years. You tie them down by the most absurd restrictions; you do not give men credit for being able to discover any improvement next year and the year after, but you go upon the assumption that men are not able to improve, and you do your best to prevent them doing so. [*Hear*.]

Now, I do not know why we should not in this country have leases for land upon similar terms to the leases of manufactories or any "plant" or premises. I do not think that farming will ever be carried on as it ought to be until you have leases drawn in the same way as a man takes a manufactory and pays perhaps £1,000 a year for it. I know people who pay £4,000 a year for manufactories to carry on their business, and at fair rents. There is an honourable Gentleman near me who pays more than £4,000 a year for the rent of his manufactory. What covenants do you think he has in his lease? What would he think if it stated how many revolutions there should be in a minute of the spindles, or if they prescribed the construction of the straps or the gearing of his machinery? Why, he takes his manufactory with a schedule of its present state—bricks, mortar, and machinery

---

[11] Sir Charles Burrell, later referred to as "the honourable Baronet the Member for Shoreham." *Hansard* omits this allusion to Bramber, one of the six Norman divisions (known as "rapes") of the County of Sussex.

—and when the lease is over, he must leave it in the same state, or else pay a compensation for the dilapidation. [*Hear, hear.*] The right honourable Gentleman the Chancellor of the Exchequer[12] cheers that statement. I want to ask his opinion respecting a similar lease for a farm. I am rather disposed to think that the Anti-Corn Law Leaguers will very likely form a joint-stock association and have none but free-traders in the body, that we may purchase a joint-stock estate and have a model farm [*"Hear, hear" and laughter*], taking care that it shall be in one of the rural counties, one of the most purely agricultural parts of the country, where we think there is the greatest need of improvement—perhaps in Buckinghamshire [*laughter*]; and there shall be a model farm, homestead, and cottages; and I may tell the noble Lord the Member for Newark[13] that we shall have a model garden, and we will not make any boast or outcry about it. But the great object will be to have a model lease. [*Cheers and laughter.*] We will have as the farmer a man of intelligence and capital.

I am not so unreasonable as to tell you that you ought to let your land to men who have not a competent capital or are not sufficiently intelligent; but I say select such a man as that; let him know his business and have sufficient capital, and you cannot give him too wide a scope. We will find such a man and will let him our farm; there shall be a lease precisely such as that upon which my honourable Friend takes his factory. There shall be no single clause inserted in it to dictate to him how he shall cultivate his farm; he shall do what he likes with the old pasture. If he can make more by ploughing it up he shall do so; if he can grow white crops every year—which I know there are people doing at this moment in more places than one in this country [*Hear, hear*]—or if he can make any other improvement or discovery, he shall be free to do so. We will let him the land, with a schedule of the state of tillage and the condition of the homestead, and all we will bind him to will be this: "You shall leave the land as good as when you entered upon it. [*'Hear, hear' from both sides of the House.*] If it is in an inferior state it shall be valued again, and you shall compensate us; but if it is in an improved state it shall be valued and we, the landlords, shall compensate you." [*Hear, hear.*] You think there must be something very difficult about this and that it will be impossible to be done; but it is not. We will give possession of everything upon the land, whether it be wild or tame animals; he shall have the absolute control. There shall be no game and no one to sport over his property. Take as stringent precautions as you please to compel the punctual payment of the rent; take the right of re-entry as summarily as you please if the rent is not duly paid; but let the payment of rent duly be the sole test as to the well-doing of the tenant; and

---

[12] Henry Goulburn, Member for Cambridge University. Appointed to Peel's second cabinet in 1841, Goulburn remained a staunch supporter of Peel as the Prime Minister's policy on Corn Laws underwent change.

[13] Lord John Manners, a Tory friend of Disraeli.

so long as he can pay the rent and do it promptly, that is the only test you need have that the farmer is doing well; and if he is a man of capital, you have the strongest possible security that he will not waste your property while he has possession of it. [*Hear.*]

I have sometimes heard honourable Gentlemen opposite say, "It is all very well for you to preach up leases, but there are many farmers who do not want them. We have asked them, and they will not take them." [*Hear, hear.*] The honourable Gentleman cheers that remark; but what does it argue? That by that process which my honourable Friend the Member for Lincolnshire has described—that degrading process by which you have rendered those tenants servile, hopeless, and dejected, so that they have not the spirit of men when they are carrying on their business. Now, hear what Professor Low[14] states, he being, as you are aware, a professor of agriculture. He says:

> The argument has again and again been used against an extension of leases that the tenants themselves set no value upon them; but to how different a conclusion ought the existence of such a feeling amongst the tenantry of a country to conduct us! The fact itself shows that the absence of leases may render a tenantry ignorant of the means of employing their own capital with advantage, indisposed to the exertions which improvements demand, and better contented with an easy rent and dependent condition than with the prospect of an independence to be earned by increased exertion.

Whilst you have a tenantry in the state described or pictured by the honourable Member for Lincolnshire, what must be the state of the population? Your labourers can never be prosperous when the tenants are depressed. Go through the length and breadth of the land, and you will find that where capital is in the greatest abundance and capitalists are most intelligent, there you will invariably find the working classes most prosperous and happy; and on the other hand, show me an impoverished and enfeebled tenantry—go to the north of Devonshire, for instance, and show me a tenantry like that—and there you will find a peasantry sunk into the most hopeless and degraded condition. [*Hear.*]

Now, Sir, I have mentioned a deficiency of capital as being the primary want amongst farmers. I have stated the want of security in leases as the cause of the want of capital; but you may still say, "You have not connected this with the Corn Laws and the protective system." I will therefore read the opinion of an honourable Gentleman who sits, I believe, upon this side of the House, and I wish he may give us an opinion upon the subject in this debate; it is in a published letter of Mr. Hayter,[15] who, I know, is himself an ardent supporter of agriculture. He says:

---

[14] Probably David Low, professor of agriculture at the University of Edinburgh, a leading authority on the management of agricultural property.

[15] William G. Hayter, Member for Wells, was a successful farmer and a free-trader. He later served as "whip" in the Liberal Governments of Derby, Aberdeen, and Palmerston.

ECONOMIC POLICY AND SOCIAL CHANGE 199

The more I see of and practise agriculture, the more firmly am I convinced that the whole unemployed labour of the country could, under a better system of husbandry, be advantageously put into operation; and moreover, that the Corn Laws have been one of the principal causes of the present system of bad farming and consequent pauperism. Nothing short of their entire removal will ever induce the average farmer to rely upon anything else than the Legislature for the payment of his rent, his belief being that all rent is paid by corn and nothing else than corn; and that the Legislature can, by enacting Corn Laws, create a price which will make his rent easy. The day of their (the Corn Laws) entire abolition ought to be a day of jubilee and rejoicing to every man interested in land.

Now, Sir, I do not stop to connect the cause and effect in this matter, and inquire whether your Corn Laws or your protective system have caused the want of leases and capital. I do not stop to make good my proof, and for this reason: that you have adopted a system of legislation in this House by which you profess to make the farming trade prosperous. I show you, after thirty years' trial, what is the condition of the agriculturists; I prove to you what is the state of farmers and also of the labourers, and you will not contest any one of those propositions. I say it is enough, having had thirty years' trial of your specific, for me to ask you to go into Committee to see if something better cannot be devised. [*Cheers.*] I am going to contend, independent of protection and Corn Law, that free trade in corn would be more advantageous to farmers—and with them I include labourers—than restriction; to oblige the honourable Member for Norfolk, I will take with them also the landlords; and I contend that free trade in corn and grain of every kind would be more beneficial to them than to any other class of the community. I should have contended the same before the passing of the late tariff; but now I am prepared to do so with tenfold more force. [*Hear.*]

What has the right honourable Baronet done? He has passed a law to admit fat cattle at a nominal duty. Some foreign fat cattle were selling in Smithfield the other day at about £15 or £16 per head, paying only about 7.5 per cent duty; but he has not admitted the raw material out of which these fat cattle are made. Mr. Huskisson[16] did not act in this manner when he commenced his plan of free trade. [*Hear.*] He began by admitting the raw material before he permitted the manufactured article; but in your case you have commenced at precisely the opposite end and have allowed free trade in cattle instead of that upon which they are fattened. I say, give free trade in that grain which goes to make the cattle. [*Hear.*] I contend that by this protective system the farmers throughout the country are more injured than any other class in the community. I would take, for instance, the

[16] William Huskisson, Member for Liverpool.

article of seeds, beginning with clover seed. The honourable Member for North Northamptonshire put a question the other night to the right honourable Baronet at the head of the Government. He looked so exceedingly alarmed that I wondered what the subject was which created the apprehension. He asked the right honourable Baronet whether he was going to admit clover seed into this country. I believe clover seed is to be excluded from the schedule of free importation. Now, I ask for whose benefit is this exception made? I ask the honourable Gentleman the Member for North Northamptonshire whether those whom he represents—the farmers of that district of the county—are, in the large majority of instances, the great sellers of clover seed. [*Hear, hear.*] I will undertake to say they are not. How many counties in England are there which are benefited by the protection of clover seed? [*Hear.*] I will take the whole of Scotland. If there be any Scotch Members present, I ask them whether they do not in their country import the clover seed from England. They do not grow it. I undertake to say that there are not ten counties in the United Kingdom which are interested in the exportation of clover seed out of their own borders. [*Hear.*] Neither have they any of this article in Ireland. But yet we have clover seed excluded from the farmers, although they are not interested as a body in its protection at all.

Again, take the article of beans. There are lands in Essex where they can grow them *alternately*. I find that beans come from that district to Mark Lane, and I believe also that in some parts of Lincolnshire and Cambridgeshire they do the same; but how is it with the poor lands of Surrey or the poor down land of Wiltshire? Take the whole of the counties. How many of them are there which are exporters of beans or send them to market? You are taxing the whole of the farmers who do not sell their beans for the pretended benefit of a few counties or districts of counties where they do. [*Hear.*] Mark you, where they can grow beans on the stronger and better soils, it is not in one case out of ten that they grow them for the market. They may grow them for their own use; but where they do not cultivate beans, send them to market, and turn them into money, those farmers can have no interest whatever in keeping up the money price of that which they never sell. [*Hear.*] Take the article of oats. How many farmers are there who ever have oats down on the credit side of their books as an item upon which they rely for the payment of their rents? [*Hear.*] The farmers may, and do generally, grow oats for feeding their own horses; but it is an exception to the rule—and a rare exception too—where the farmer depends upon the sale of his oats to meet his expenses. [*Hear.*] Take the article of hops. You have a protection upon them for the benefit of the growers in Kent, Sussex, and Surrey; but yet the cultivators of hops have no protection in articles which they do not themselves produce. [*Hear.*]

Take the article of cheese. Not one farmer in ten in the country makes his own cheese, and yet they and their servants are large consumers of it. But what are the counties which have the protection in this article? Cheshire, Gloucestershire, Wiltshire, part of Derbyshire, and Leicestershire. Here are some four or five dairy counties having an interest in the protection of cheese: but recollect that those counties are peculiarly hardly taxed in beans and oats, because in those counties where they are chiefly dairy farms, where they are most in want of artificial food for their cattle. There are the whole of the hilly districts; and I hope my honourable Friend the Member for Nottingham[17] is here, because he has a special grievance in this matter: he lives in Derbyshire, and very commendably employs himself in rearing good cattle upon the hills, but he is taxed for your protection for his oats, Indian corn, and anything which he wants for feeding them. [*Hear.*] He told me only the other day that he should like nothing better than to give up the protection on cattle if they would only let him buy a thousand quarters of black oats for the consumption of his stock. [*Hear, hear.*] Take the whole of the hilly districts and the down county of Wiltshire; the whole of that expanse of downs in the south of England; take the Cheviots, where the flock-masters reside, or the Grampians in Scotland; and take the whole of Wales without exception—they are not benefited in the slightest degree by the protection on these articles; but on the contrary, you are taxing the very things they want. They require provender as abundantly and cheaply as they can get it. [*Hear.*] Allowing a free importation of food for cattle is the only way in which those counties can improve the breed of thin stocks and the only manner in which they can ever bring their land up to anything like a decent state of fertility. I will go farther and say that farms with thin soil—I mean the stock farmers, which you will find in Hertfordshire and Surrey, farmers with large capitals, arable farmers—I say those men are deeply interested in having a free importation of food for their cattle because they have thin poor land. The land of its own self does not contain the means of its over-increased fertility; and the only way is the bringing in an additional quantity of food from elsewhere, that they can bring up their farms to a proper state of cultivation.

I have been favoured with an estimate made by a very experienced clever farmer in Wiltshire—probably honourable Gentlemen will bear me out when I say a man of great intelligence and skill and entitled to every consideration in this House. I refer to Mr. Nathaniel Atherton, Kington, Wilts. That Gentleman estimates that upon 400 acres of land he could increase his profits to the amount of £280, paying the same rent as at present, provided there was a free importation of foreign grain of all kinds. He would buy 500 quarters of oats at 15s., or the same amount in beans or peas at 14s. or 15s. a sack, to be fed on the land or in the yard; by which he would grow additional 160 quarters of wheat and 230 quarters barley, and gain an increased profit of £300 upon his sheep and cattle. His plan embraces the

[17] Thomas Gisborne, Radical M.P., a member of the Anti-Corn Law League.

employment of an additional capital of £1,000; and he would pay £150 a year more for labour. I had an opportunity, the other day, of speaking to a very intelligent farmer in Hertfordshire—Mr. Lattimore, of Wheathampstead. [*Hear.*] Very likely there are honourable Gentlemen here to whom he is known. I do not know whether the noble Lord the Member for Hertford[18] is present, because if so, he will no doubt know that Mr. Lattimore stands as high in Hertford market as a skillful farmer and a man of abundant capital as any man in the county. [*Hear.*] He is a Gentleman of most unquestionable intelligence: and what does he say? He told me that last year he paid £230 enhanced price on his beans and other provender which he bought for his cattle—£230 of enhanced price in consequence of that restriction upon the trade in foreign grain, amounting to 14s. a quarter on all the wheat he sold upon his farm. Now, I undertake to say in the names of Mr. Atherton of Wiltshire and Mr. Lattimore of Hertfordshire that they are as decided advocates for free trade in grain of every kind as I am. [*Hear.*] I am not now quoting merely solitary cases.

I told honourable Gentlemen once before that I have probably as large an acquaintance among farmers as anyone in the House. I think I could give you from every county the names of some of the first-rate farmers who are as ardent free-traders as I am. [*Hear.*] I requested the secretary of this much-dreaded Anti-Corn Law League to make me out a list of the farmers who are subscribers to that association, and I find there are upwards of 100 in England and Scotland who subscribe to the League Fund, comprising, I hesitate not to say, the most intelligent men to be found in this Kingdom. [*Cheers.*] I myself went into the Lothians, at the invitation of twenty-two farmers there, several of whom were paying upwards of £1,000 a year rent. I spent two or three days among them, and I never found a body of more intelligent, liberal-minded men in my life. Those are men who do not want restrictions upon the importation of corn. [*Hear.*] They desire nothing but fair play. They say, "Let us have our Indian corn, Egyptian beans, and Polish oats as freely as we have our linseed cake, and we can bear competition with any corn growers in the world." [*Hear.*] But by excluding the provender for cattle and at the same time admitting the cattle almost duty free, I think you are giving an example of one of the greatest absurdities and perversions of nature and common sense which ever was seen. We have heard of great absurdities in legislation in commercial matters of late. We know that there has been such a case as sending coffee from Cuba to the Cape of Good Hope in order to bring it back to England under the law; but I venture to say that in less than ten years from this time people will look back with more amazement in their minds at the fact that while you are sending ships to Ichaboe to bring back the guano, you are passing a law to exclude Indian corn, beans, oats, peas,

---

[18] Probably Viscount Grimston.

and everything else that gives nourishment to your cattle, which would give you a thousand times more production than all the guano of Ichaboe. [*Loud cheers.*]

Upon the last occasion when I spoke upon this subject, I was answered by the right honourable Gentleman the President of the Board of Trade. He talked about throwing poor lands out of cultivation and converting arable lands into pasture. I hope that we men of the Anti-Corn Law League may not be reproached again with seeking to cause any such disasters. My belief is—and the conviction is founded upon a most extensive inquiry among the most intelligent farmers, without stint of trouble and pains—that the course you are pursuing tends every hour to throw land out of cultivation and make poor lands unproductive. [*Hear.*] Do not let us be told again that we desire to draw the labourers from the land in order that we may reduce the wages of the work people employed in factories. I tell you that if you bestow capital on the soil and cultivate it with the same skill as manufacturers bestow upon their business, you have not population enough in the rural districts for the purpose. [*Hear.*] I yesterday received a letter from Lord Ducie[19] in which he gives precisely the same opinion. He says if we had the land properly cultivated there are not sufficient labourers to till it. What is the fact? You are chasing your labourers from village to village, passing laws to compel people to support paupers, devising every means to smuggle them abroad to the Antipodes if you can get them there; why, you would have to chase after them and bring them back again if you had your land properly cultivated. I tell you honestly my conviction that it is by these means and these only that you can avert very great and serious troubles and disasters in your agricultural districts.

Sir, I remember, on the last occasion when this subject was discussed, there was a great deal said about disturbing an interest. It was said that this inquiry could not be gone into because we were disturbing and unsettling a great interest. I have no desire to under-value the agricultural interest. I have heard it said that they are the greatest consumers of manufactured goods in this country; that they are such large consumers of our goods that we had better look after the home trade and not think of destroying it. But what sort of consumers of manufactures think you the labourers can be with the wages they are now getting in agricultural districts? Understand me: I am arguing for a principle that I solemnly believe would raise the wages of the labourers in the agricultural districts. I believe you would have no men starving upon 7s. a week if you had abundant capital and competent skill employed upon the soil.

But I ask, what is this consumption of manufactured goods that we have heard so much about? I have taken some pains and made large inquiries as to the amount laid out in the average of cases by agricultural labourers

---

[19] The Earl of Ducie, a leading agriculturist, who strongly supported free trade.

and their families for clothing; I probably may startle you by telling you that we have exported in one year more goods of our manufactures to Brazil than have been consumed in a similar period by the whole of your agricultural peasantry and their families. You have 960,000 agricultural labourers in England and Wales, according to the last census. I undertake to say they do not expend on an average 30s. a year on their families, supposing every one of them to be in employ. I say manufactured goods, excluding shoes. I assert that the whole of the agricultural peasantry and their families in England and Wales do not spend £1,500,000 per annum for manufactured goods, in clothing and bedding. And with regard to your exciseable and duty-paying articles, what can the poor wretch lay out upon them, who out of 8s. or 9s. a week has a wife and family to support? [Hear.] I undertake to prove to your satisfaction—and you may do it yourselves if you will but dare to look the figures in the face [loud cheers]—I will undertake to prove to you that they do not pay upon an average each family 15s. per annum, that the whole of their contributions to the revenue do not amount to £700,000. Now, is not this a mighty interest to be disturbed? I would keep that interest as justly as though it were one of the most important; but I say when you have by your present system brought down your agricultural peasantry to that state, have you anything to offer for bettering their condition, or at all events to justify resisting an inquiry? [Hear.]

On the last occasion when I addressed this House,[20] I recollect stating some facts to show that you had no reasonable ground to fear foreign competition; those facts I do not intend to reiterate, because they have never been contradicted. [Hear, hear.] But there are still attempts made to frighten people by telling them, "If you open the ports to foreign corn you will have corn let in here for nothing." One of the favourite fallacies which is now put forth is this: "Look at the price of corn in England and see what it is abroad. You have prices low here, and yet you have corn coming in from abroad. Now, if you had not 20s. duty to pay, what a quantity of corn you would have brought in, and how low the price would be!" This statement arises from a fallacy—I hope not dishonestly put forth in not understanding the difference between the real and the nominal price of corn. The price of corn at Dantzic now is nominal; the price of corn when it is coming in regularly is a regular price—that is the real price. Now, go back to 1838: in January of that year the price of wheat at Dantzic was nominal; there was no demand for England; there were no purchasers except for speculation, with the chance, probably, of having to throw the wheat into the sea; but in the months of July and August, when apprehensions arose of a failure of our harvest, then the price of corn in Dantzic rose instantly, sympathising with the markets in England; and at the end of the year, in

---

[20] Cobden made this point in the debate on Villiers' motion the previous year.

December, the price of wheat at Dantzic had doubled the amount at which it had been in January. And during the three following years, when you had a regular importation of corn from Dantzic, during all that time, by the averages laid upon the table of this House, wheat at Dantzic averaged 40s. Wheat at Dantzic was at that price during the three years 1839, 1840, and 1841. [*Hear.*] Now, I mention this just to show the fact to honourable Gentlemen, and to entreat them that they will not go and alarm their tenantry by this outcry of the danger of foreign competition. You ought to be pursuing a directly opposite course—you ought to be trying to stimulate them in every possible way—by showing that they can compete with foreigners, that what others can do in Poland they can do in England.

I have an illustration of the case with reference to a society of which the honourable Member for Suffolk was chairman. We have lately seen a new light spreading amongst agricultural gentlemen. We are told the salvation of this country is to arise from the cultivation of flax. There is a National Flax Society, of which Lord Rendlesham is the president. This flax society state in their prospectus—a copy of which I have here, purporting to be the first annual report of the National Flax Agricultural Improvement Association—after talking of the Ministers holding out no hope from legislation, they avow their inability to meet the difficulty; and then the report goes on to state that upon these grounds the National Flax Society call upon the nation for its support, on the ground that they are going to remedy the distresses of the country. Now, I observe that Mr. Warnes[21] was paying a visit in Sussex. I take a lively interest in what is going on in that county. I observe Mr. Warnes paid a visit to Sussex, and he attended an agricultural meeting at which the honourable Baronet the Member for Shoreham presided. After the usual loyal toasts, the honourable Baronet proposed the toast of the evening: "Mr. Warnes and the cultivation of flax." [*Laughter.*] The right honourable Baronet was not aware, I dare say, that he was then furnishing a most deadly weapon to the lecturers of the Anti-Corn Law League. We are told you cannot compete with foreigners unless you have a high protective duty. You have a high protective duty on wheat, amounting at this moment to 20s. a quarter. A quarter of wheat at the present time is just worth the same as one cwt. of flax. On a quarter of wheat you have a protective duty against the Pole and Russian of 20s.; upon the one cwt. of flax you have a protective duty of 1d. [*loud cheers*]; and yet I did not hear a murmur from honourable Gentlemen opposite when the right honourable Baronet proposed to take off that protective duty of 1d. totally and immediately. ["*Hear*" *and laughter*].

But we are told that English agriculturists cannot compete with foreigners and especially with that serf labour that is to be found somewhere up the Baltic. Well, but flax comes from the Baltic, and there is no protective duty.

---

[21] John Warnes, founder of the National Flax Society.

[*Renewed cheers.*] We are told that you may admit some other things. Honourable Gentlemen say we have no objection to raw materials where there is no labour connected with them; but we cannot contend against foreigners in wheat, because there is such an amount of labour in it. Why, there is twice as much labour in flax as there is in wheat [*cheers*]; and yet the right honourable Baronet favours the growth of flax in order to restore the country, which is sinking into this abject and hopeless state for want of agricultural protection. [*Renewed cheers.*] The right honourable Baronet will forgive me—I am sure he will, he looks as if he would [*laughter*]—if I allude a little to the subject of leases. The honourable Gentleman on that occasion, I believe, complained that it was a great pity that farmers did not grow more flax, and I saw it in a Brighton paper a week afterwards. I do not know whether it was true or not that the right honourable Baronet's leases to his own tenants forbade them to grow that article. [*Cheers and laughter.*] Now, it is quite as possible that the right honourable Baronet does not exactly know what covenants or clauses there are in his leases. [*Hear.*] But I know that it is a very common case to preclude the growth of flax; and it just shows the kind of management by which the landed proprietors have carried on their affairs; that actually, I believe, the original source of the error that flax was very pernicious to the ground was derived from Virgil; I believe there is a passage in Virgil to that effect. From that classic authority, no doubt, some learned lawyer put this clause into the lease, and there it has remained ever since. [*Laughter.*]

Now, I have alluded to the condition of the labourers at the present time; but I am bound to say that while the farmers at the present moment are in a worse condition than they have been for the last ten years, I believe the agricultural labourers have passed over the winter with less suffering and distress, although it has been a five-months' winter and a severer one, too, than they endured in the previous year. [*"Hear, hear" from the Ministerial benches.*] I am glad to find that corroborated by honourable Gentlemen opposite, because it bears out in a remarkable degree the opinion that we who are in connexion with the free-trade question entertain. We maintain that a low price of food is beneficial to the labouring classes. We assert, and we can prove it, at least in the manufacturing districts, that whenever provisions are dear wages are low, and whenever food is cheap wages invariably rise. We have had a strike in almost every business in Lancashire since the price of wheat has been down to something like 50*s.*; and I am glad to be corroborated when I state that the agricultural labourers have been in a better condition during the last winter than they were in the previous one. But does not that show that even in your case, though your labourers have in a general way only just as much as will find them a subsistence, they are benefited by a great abundance of the first necessaries of life? Although their wages may rise and fall with the price of food—although they may go up with the advance in the price of corn and fall when it is lowered—still, I maintain that it does not rise in the same proportion as the price of food rises, nor fall to the extent to which food falls. Therefore, in all cases the agricultural labourers are in a better state when food is low than when it is high. [*Hear, hear.*]

Now, I am bound to say that whatever may be the condition of the agricultural labourer, I hold that the farmer is not responsible for that condition while he is placed in the situation in which he now is by the present system. I have seen during the last autumn and winter a great many exhortations made to the farmers that they should employ more labourers. I think that is very unfair towards the farmer; I believe he is the man who is suffering most; he stands between you and your impoverished, suffering peasantry; and it is rather too bad to point to the farmer as the man who should relieve them. [*Cheers.*] I have an extract from Lord Hardwicke's[22] address to the labourers of Haddenham. He says:

> Conciliate your employers, and if they do not perform their duty to you and themselves, address yourselves to the landlords; and I assure you that you will find us ready to urge our own tenants to the proper cultivation of their farms and consequently to the just employment of the labourer.

Now, I hold that this duty begins nearer home, and that the landed proprietors are the parties who are responsible if the labourers have not employment. [*Hear.*] You have absolute power; there is no doubt about that. You can, if you please, legislate for your labourers or yourselves. Whatever you may have done besides, your legislation has been adverse to the labourer, and you have no right to call upon the farmers to remedy the evils which you have caused. [*Cheers.*] I have a very curious proof with regard to what is done for the agricultural labourers by the landlords, which I will read to you. It is a labourer's certificate, seen at Stowupland in Suffolk, in July, 1844, which was placed upon the mantelpiece of a peasant's cottage there:

> West Suffolk Agricultural Association, established 1833, for the advancement of agriculture and the encouragement of industry and skill, and good conduct among labourers and servants in husbandry. President: The Duke of Grafton, Lord Lieutenant of the county. This is to certify that a prize of £2 was awarded to William Burch, aged 82, labourer, of the parish of Stowupland, in West Suffolk, September 25, 1840, for having brought up nine children without relief, *except when flour was very dear*; and for having worked on the same farm twenty-eight years.
> (Signed)   RT. RUSHBROOKE, Chairman.

[*Cheers and laughter.*]

---

[22] Possibly the Earl of Hardwicke, then Lord Lieutenant of Cambridgeshire.

Now, I need not press that point. It is admitted by the honourable Gentlemen opposite—and I am glad it is so—that after a very severe winter, in the midst of great distress among farmers, when there have been a great many able-bodied men wanting employment, still there have been fewer in the streets and workhouses than there had been in the previous year. But the condition of the agricultural labourer is a bad case at the very best. [*Hear.*] You can look before you, and you have to foresee the means of giving employment to those men. I need not tell you that the late census shows that you cannot employ your own increasing population in the agricultural districts. But you say the farmers should employ them. How can they give employment to them? Will not this evil—if evil you call it—press on you more and more every year? What can you do to remedy the mischief? I only appear here now because you have proposed nothing. We all know your system of allotments, and we are all aware of its failure. What other remedy have you? For mark you, that is worse than a plaything, if you were allowed to carry out your own views. [*Hear.*] Ay, it is well enough for some of you that there are wiser heads than your own to lead you, or you would be conducting yourselves into precisely the same condition in which they are in Ireland [*Hear*], but with this difference—this increased difficulty—that there they do manage to maintain the rights of property by the aid of the English Exchequer and 20,000 bayonets; but bring your own country into the same condition, and where would be your rights of property? [*Cheers.*] What do you propose to do now? That is the question. Nothing has been brought forward this year which I have heard, having for its object to benefit the great mass of the English population—nothing I have heard suggested which has at all tended to alleviate their condition.

You admit that the farmer's capital is sinking from under him and that he is in a worse state than ever. Have you distinctly provided some plan to give confidence to the farmer, to cause an influx of capital to be expended upon his land, and so bring increased employment to the labourer? How is this to be met? I cannot believe that you are going to make this a political game. You must set up some specific object to benefit the agricultural interest. It is well said that the last election was an agricultural triumph. There are 200 county Members sitting behind the Prime Minister who prove that it was so.

What, then, is your plan for this distressing state of things? That is what I want to ask you. Do not, as you have done before, follow me and quarrel with me because I have imperfectly stated my case. I have done my best; and I again ask you what have you to do? I tell you that this "protection," as it has been called, is a failure. It was so when you had the prohibition up to 80*s*. You know the state of your farming tenantry in 1821. It was a failure when you had a protection price of 60*s*.; and you know what was the condition of your farm tenantry in 1835. It is a failure now with your last amendment, for you have admitted and proclaimed it to us; and what is the condition of your agricultural population at this time?

I ask, what is your plan? I hope this is not a pretence—a mere political game that has been played throughout the last election—and that you have not all come up here as mere politicians. There are politicians in the House, men who look with an ambition—probably a justifiable one—to the honours of office. There may be men who—with thirty years of continuous service, having been raised into a state from which they can neither escape nor retreat—may be holding office, and high office, maintained there, probably, at the expense of their present convictions, which do not harmonise very well with their early convictions. I make allowances for them; but the great body of the honourable Gentlemen opposite came up to this House not as politicians, but as the farmers' friends and protectors of the agricultural interests. Well, what do you propose to do? You have heard the Prime Minister declare that if he could restore all the protection which you have had, that protection would not benefit agriculturists. Is that your meaning? If so, why not submit to it; and if it is not your conviction, you have falsified your mission in this House by following the right honourable Baronet out into the lobby and opposing inquiry into the condition of the very men who sent you here. [*Cheers.*]

With mere politicians I have no right to expect to succeed in this motion. But I have no hesitation in telling you, that if you give me a Committee of this House, I will explode the delusion of agricultural protection. [*Cheering.*] I will bring forward such a mass of evidence and give you such a preponderance of talent and of authority that when the Blue Book is published and sent forth to the world as we can now send it by our vehicles of information, your system of protection shall not live in the public opinion for two years afterwards. [*Hear, hear.*] Politicians do not want that. This cry of protection has been a very convenient handle for politicians. The cry of protection carried the counties at the last election, and politicians gained honours, emoluments, and place by it; you cannot set up for any such. Now, is that old tattered flag of protection, tarnished and torn as it is already, to be kept hoisted still in the counties for the benefit of politicians, or will you come forward honestly and fairly to inquire into this question? Why, I cannot believe that the gentry of England will be made mere drumheads to be sounded upon by others to give forth unmeaning and empty sounds, and to have no articulate voice of their own. [*"Hear, hear" and cheers.*] No. You are the gentry of England who represent the counties. You are the aristocracy of England. Your fathers led our fathers; you may lead us if you will go the right way. But, although you have retained your influence with this country longer than any other aristocracy, it has not been by opposing popular opinion or by setting yourselves against the spirit of the age.

In other days, when the battle and the hunting fields were the tests of manly vigour, why, your fathers were first and foremost there. The aristocracy of England were not like the aristocracy of France, the mere minions of a court; nor were they like the hidalgos of Madrid, who dwindled into pigmies. You have been Englishmen. You have not shown a want of courage and firmness when any call has been made upon you. This is a new era. It is the age of improvement, it is the age of social advancement, not the age for war or for feudal sports. You live in a mercantile age, when the whole wealth of the world is poured into your lap. You cannot have the advantage of commercial rents and feudal privileges [*Hear, hear*]; but you may be what you always have been if you will identify yourselves with the spirit of the age. The English people look to the gentry and aristocracy of their country as their leaders. [*Hear, hear.*] I, who am not one of you, have no hesitation in telling you that there is a deep-rooted, a hereditary prejudice, if I may so call it, in your favour in this country. But you never got it, and you will not keep it, by obstructing the spirit of the age. If you are indifferent to enlightened means of finding employment for your own peasantry; if you are found obstructing that advance which is calculated to knit nations more together in the bonds of peace by means of commercial intercourse; if you are found fighting against the discoveries which have almost given breath and life to material nature, and setting up yourselves as obstructives of that which the community at large has decreed shall go on—why, then, you will be the gentry of England no longer, and others will be found to take your place. [*Hear, hear.*]

And I have no hesitation in saying that you stand just now in a very critical position. There is a widespread suspicion that you have been tampering with the best feelings and with the honest confidence of your own country in this cause. Everywhere you are doubted and suspected. Read your own organs, and you will see that this is the case. [*Hear, hear.*] Well, now, this is the time to show that you are not the mere Party politicians which you are said to be. I have said that we shall be opposed in this measure by politicians: they do not want inquiry. But I ask you to go into this Committee with me. I will give you a majority of country Members. You shall have a majority of the Central Society in that Committee. I ask you only to go into a fair inquiry as to the causes of the distress of your own population. [*Hear.*] I only ask that this matter may be fairly examined. Whether you establish my principle or yours, good will come out of the inquiry; and I do, therefore, beg and entreat the honourable independent country Gentlemen of this House that they will not refuse, on this occasion, to go into a fair, a full, and an impartial inquiry.[22]

[*The honourable Gentleman resumed his seat amidst loud cheers.*]

---

[22] Cobden's notion lost 121–213.

Benjamin Disraeli

"Against Repeal of the Corn Laws"[*]

Commons, May 15, 1846

Sir, the Secretary of State,[1] in the speech he made on the first night of this discussion, reminded Gentlemen sitting on these benches and professing opinions favourable to the protection of the industry of their country that in the various and prolonged discussions which during late years have occurred with regard to great commercial changes, they have nevertheless found it necessary to abandon many of the opinions they professed and to give up many of those dogmas which they previously upheld.

Sir, I acknowledge the fact. I believe that to be the necessary result of all discussion; nor can I understand the use of public discussion at all if it be not to correct erroneous impressions; or if at the conclusion both parties are to take refuge in the cry that they have not changed a single opinion which they held before the question came under debate. Sir, I do not claim for myself—and I think I may venture to say none of my Friends around me claim—an infallibility in argument. We listen with attention and respect to every argument brought against the opinions which we advocate; and if we find that any argument thus advanced cannot be satisfactorily answered, we feel the necessity of no longer maintaining an opposite and untenable conclusion. But if this rule applies to our Party, I think I could without difficulty show to the Secretary of State that it is a quality not peculiar to us. I rather imagine that some opinions loudly advocated and long ably maintained by honourable Gentlemen opposite—I still address myself to honourable Gentlemen opposite, for, though this discussion was commenced by Her Majesty's Government, I always remember who were really the originators of the ideas—I say I think that some of the opinions formerly advocated by honourable Gentlemen opposite are now no longer upheld

---

[*] The text is from *Hansard's Parliamentary Debates*, Third Series. Vol. LXXXVI. cols. 651–677.

[1] Sir James Graham, who spoke on May 11.

and are therefore to be placed in that category of abandonment to which the Secretary of State referred.

I might begin with cheap bread. We heard a Minister of the Crown, a Member of the Cabinet—even in this year, in this important Session, when all the opinions of Her Majesty's Government must doubtless be so well matured and so well considered with all the advantage of four Cabinet meetings in a week—we heard a Member of Her Majesty's Government announce that the claptrap cry of cheap bread was given up by all parties. The right honourable Gentleman seemed to hold it, as his noble colleague the Secretary for Ireland did a few years back, as the "fugitive cry of a dying faction." Even the honourable Member for Stockport,[2] the highest authority on this point, announced that the cry of cheap bread had never been his. Well, then, that is one great opinion abandoned. We shall presently find that there are others in the same predicament.

I believe it is no longer maintained that our Corn Laws are productive of extraordinary fluctuations in the price of corn. And yet that was an opinion which was once very industriously disseminated in the country—one perpetually introduced into the discussions of this House, and which has unquestionably influenced the existing public opinion on the main question. Yet I believe it is now admitted that the tendency neither of the present nor even of the late Corn Laws has been to produce extraordinary fluctuations in price. Well, that is another great opinion that has been abandoned.

Then we were told that these same Corn Laws were the bane of agriculture. That opinion is certainly given up. We have shown you—and you have admitted the facts—from the evidence of the best authorities, the most intelligent valuers under the Tithe Commutation Act, and the most skilful land agents in the country—we have shown you that in England the average produce of an acre is twenty-eight bushels of wheat. We know by a report prepared by a public commissioner that the average produce per acre in Russia is sixteen bushels, while we have evidence that the average amount in France is fifteen bushels. But I have got a document here which is very much at the service of honourable Members opposite. It is the Report in 1845 of the Agricultural Society of New York, giving the average produce of sixty-nine counties in that State, and it appears from this report that the average produce of wheat per acre in the United States is fourteen bushels. Does it then appear from these figures that protection is indeed the bane of agriculture? These statements show that England produces more corn per acre in a great degree than any other country. This, then, is a third opinion that has been abandoned.

Again, there is another opinion which has been put forward with much pertinacity. It has been long loudly and diligently asserted that the pop-

---

[2] Richard Cobden.

ulation in this country increases in a greater ratio than its production. That opinion has been given up. You came down to the House and told us always that the population was increasing a thousand a day, or 365,000 a year, and after your fashion you assumed the country could not feed the people. We have shown you, or rather you have shown us—for it has been one of the circumstances adduced by the Minister in favour of his measure— that the price of wheat for years has regularly declined. If we divide the current century into three equal portions of fifteen years each, you will find the price of wheat lowest in the last division, so that while the population has been increasing in the ratio you allege, the means of production have been increasing in a still greater ratio; the population has been increasing in this degree, and at the same time the price of the necessaries of life has been decreasing.

There is another dogma which has also much influenced public opinion, and that is that our Corn Laws have produced hostile tariffs. This opinion also is, I believe, now abandoned; every day's experience assures us, whatever may be the policy of the Government of this country, that Continental nations and manufacturing countries are not to be influenced by it. But according to the new school of philosophy, we need not dwell on this; it does not signify whether other nations are influenced by our liberal policy or not; we are quite independent of all such considerations.

There is yet another opinion which I have observed frequently advanced in speeches out of this House—and speeches out of this House, be it remembered, have had much influence on conduct within it. It has been often urged at public meetings by the honourable Member for Stockport, whose speeches I always read with attention, that the amount of freight alone would be a sufficient protection to land. The honourable Member has been in the habit of assuring his audience that the average rate of freight was 10s. 6d. per quarter of corn, and that to this extent a protection was afforded to agriculture. I believe honourable Gentlemen have even made the same declaration in this House; and I believe had it been made in this House a year ago, we should all of us have believed it. Now, I doubt whether there is any freight that amounts to 10s. 6d. I doubt whether at present we pay 10s. 6d. per quarter even from Odessa. But generally speaking, it is now universally admitted that freight is no protection at all, for it is just as expensive to transport a quarter of corn from one English port to another as to bring it from any of the contiguous foreign ports from which your chief supply is anticipated.

I will say one word on a topic which I have already touched upon lightly, because I heard a cheer from an honourable Member opposite when I mentioned that the tendency of the present Corn Laws was not to produce great fluctuations in price. I do not mention these topics merely in retort to the Secretary of State, but because I think it not an inconvenient mode to clear the course of all collateral topics before I address myself to the main question. We maintain, then, with regard to the present and even the late Corn Laws, that they have not produced extraordinary fluctuation in price; on the contrary, we maintain that the fluctuation of price in England has been less than in any other country in the world. I will establish this fact on data that are incontrovertible. Understand, I lay this down as a fact, that every country, rich or poor, in Europe or America, has in respect of the important necessary of life—grain—been subject to much greater fluctuation in price than England.

Mr. Secretary Gladstone recently moved for an important return—a return which I observe is never alluded to by honourable Gentlemen opposite. It is a return from 1834 to 1840 inclusive of the highest and lowest weekly prices of wheat per imperial quarter in most of the principal capitals of the United States. Now, I take one of these capitals, Philadelphia, because the peculiar circumstances of that capital tell the least for my argument. Philadelphia is the capital of one of the wealthiest and most populous states of the American union; and it has this peculiarity —that it is a state that does not commonly produce sufficient corn for the supply of its inhabitants. It should be observed that little or no corn or flour was imported from America into England during the first five years of this period, and that the importation in 1839 and 1840 tended to raise the low prices of those years, and so to diminish the extreme limits of their fluctuation. Philadelphia, too, is a great mart of commerce, communicating freely with every region of the world, and its corn trade is free, being subject only to a moderate fixed duty—a moderate fixed duty of 8s. 8d. per quarter. Now, Sir, what are the facts? It appears by this return of Mr. Secretary Gladstone that the average annual difference between the highest and lowest prices of wheat in Philadelphia is 47 per cent, while during the corresponding period in England it was only 33 per cent; and while the extreme difference between the highest and lowest prices of wheat in this septennial period was 270 per cent in Philadelphia, it was only 227 in England. And yet no septennial period could have been chosen which would have exhibited, under the operation of the Corn Laws, such extensive fluctuation of prices. It may be objected to this return that it only gives the extreme weekly prices of wheat, and it may be possible that local and peculiar causes may have had an effect on those prices. Well, then, here is a return of the average annual prices of wheat in Philadelphia from 1830 to 1838 inclusive; and I find the difference between the highest and lowest price of wheat at Philadelphia to be 121 per cent, while the corresponding difference during the same period in England is only 69 per cent. The returns from every considerable port and corn market in Europe have been analysed, and the result I find to be of exactly the same character.

But it will be urged that the prices of corn abroad are disturbed by the action of our Corn Laws, and that we cannot form a correct idea of the price of grain when trade flows in its natural course. But this will not impair our argument. The noble Lord the Member for Lynn[3] has anticipated this objection, and he says, "I will take rye, because that is the food of the Continental people and cannot be influenced by our Corn Laws, and I will show you equal fluctuations in the price of rye." Now, Sir, I also have a return of the prices of rye at Warsaw and at Dantzic. We have been told tonight that Dantzic is in favour of a fluctuating scale, but that at Warsaw they are devoted to free trade. Yet the difference in the annual price of rye during the years from 1834 to 1839 in the market at Warsaw sometimes amounted to 149 per cent, whereas in Dantzic the difference was only 65 per cent. In all the great Prussian markets the difference during the same period between the annual prices of rye was 100 per cent.

I think, therefore, we may fairly conclude that the objection urged against the system of graduated protection, with regard to its producing fluctuation in prices, is no longer an argument for this House. But I must remind the House that the instances which I have adduced and the inferences which I have drawn from these instances are under the influence of the late law—a law much more tending to fluctuation than the present. The scale of the late law was originally well devised. It was planned by Mr. Canning, but altered for the worse—let it always be remembered, altered for the worse—by the present First Minister.[4] If I had taken the experience of the present scale, the result would have been still more favourable; but the result being favourable enough, I am content with the former scale.

It seems, therefore, that some arguments have been abandoned by honourable Gentlemen opposite as well as by us. It is possible that both sides may have abandoned many important opinions without losing faith in the principles on which their respective systems are upheld. But I defy Gentlemen opposite who have had for years such free warren of sarcasm against the advocates of protection to bring forward a catalogue of renounced opinions on the subject which can compete with the one I have sketched, and yet left imperfect, before the House. What then are we to do with these opinions, these exhausted arguments, these exploded fallacies? Our great poet conceived the existence of a limbo for exploded systems and the phantasies of the schools. I think we ought to invent a limbo for political economists, where we might hang up all those arguments that have served their purpose and which have turned out to be sophistries. Yes; but these are the arguments that have agitated a nation and have converted a Ministry. It is all very well to say, after six or seven years' discussion, "We have discovered them to be false, and there is not a single Gentleman opposite prepared to maintain them"; but these are the agencies by which a certain amount of public opinion has been brought to bear on great economical

[3] Lord George Bentinck.
[4] Sir Robert Peel.

questions; that public opinion has changed the policy of a Government, and, according to our belief, is perilling the destinies of a great people.

Now, Sir, I must fairly acknowledge that one of these fallacies must be resuscitated by myself. Notwithstanding the high authority of the Secretary at War[5]—notwithstanding the influential adhesion to his opinion of the still higher authority of the Member for Stockport—I must raise on this occasion the cry of "cheap bread." I do believe the effect of the present Corn Laws is to raise the price of the necessaries of life to the community. That is my opinion. But I believe and I think I can show that they increase in an infinitely greater ratio the purchasing powers by the community of the necessaries of life. I hope I am meeting the argument fairly. The Secretary of State did me the honour to say that I had on another occasion fairly expressed the question at issue, and I wish strictly to address myself to it.

Now, how am I to prove my proposition? The first witness I shall call is a high authority. It is a work circulated under the immediate influence of that great commercial confederation—the power of which is acknowledged—written, I believe, by a gentleman who was once a Member of this House and, I believe I may add, who would have been a Member of this House now if I had not had the pleasure of beating him in the first election I won—Colonel Thompson.[6] In his *Corn Law Catechism* it is maintained that the Corn Law is a tax upon the community, because, assuming a certain number of quarters of corn are produced every year in this country—say, for instance, fifty millions of quarters—the Corn Law, by artificially raising the price of that corn 8s. or 10s. per quarter on an average, acts as a tax on the community, we will say, of £20,000,000. Another economist, an equally celebrated and more successful free-trader, has fallen foul of the calculations of this work, which is a great authority with the Anti-Corn Law League, and he has shown the gallant calculator that he has omitted to deduct the number of quarters that are required for seed, for the sustenance of the agriculturists themselves, for the support of their horses, and so at once the critic cuts down the estimate of the Colonel to a tax of nine or ten millions on the public.

But I will give, as is my custom, an advantage to my opponents, and take the first calculation. The conclusion of the Colonel and of the school of which he is so distinguished a champion is that it is better for England not to raise a single quarter of corn, and then the whole of this tax might thus be saved. You will say this is an extreme statement; but the statement is not mine, and an extreme case tests the truth of a principle. Let us suppose, then, that England imports fifty millions of quarters of corn—let us suppose

[5] Sidney Herbert, Member for South Wiltshire.
[6] Colonel T. Perronet Thompson's *Catechism*, published in 1827, was an arsenal of information and argument for League speakers.

that she thus saves ten or twenty millions of taxation. We will admit it for the purpose of discussion. But you cannot deny that England has lost the wages of labour that would have produced those fifty millions of quarters; you cannot deny that England has lost the profits of the capital that would have been invested in the production of those fifty millions of quarters; you cannot deny that England has lost the rent that this cultivation would have afforded after paying these wages of labour and furnishing these profits of capital. What is their united amount? It would be a light estimate to place it at twenty times that of the imaginary tax. In the proportion that united amount bears to the assumed tax, the purchasing power of the community created by the law exceeds the tax on the community alleged to be occasioned by the law.

I am ready to acknowledge that the honourable Member for Stockport never addressed any public assembly with these opinions. He is a practical man—he knows very well there is no chance of changing the laws of England with abstract doctrines—and he says very properly, "I don't admit your conclusion—we don't suppose any land will be thrown out of cultivation. There may be a reduction of price or not; but what we say is, you are creating that artificial price for the first necessaries of life in the country, and you are creating that artificial price for the benefit of a class; and, therefore, the reduction of price is, at the worst, the destruction of rent." That is the position he takes up. Now, for my own part, I will admit that I see no difference between a territorial class and the handloom weavers. If you show me that there is a law kept up merely to give a revenue to any class in this country and that by putting an end to that law the great body of the people can be fed better and as well employed, I cannot imagine anything like a Corn Law can be maintained.

Well, then, we are brought to the gist of the question. Will this change occasion a great displacement of labour? And if so, can you supply new employment for those who are displaced? It seems to me, Sir, impossible to arrive at any conclusion on this head, unless we form some estimate of the probable price of corn in this country after the measures of the Ministers have fairly come into play. It is in vain to make this inquiry of the right honourable Gentleman, and therefore we must be thrown on our elements of calculation. If we can show to you that for the future the price of corn must necessarily be such as to render it impossible in the greater part of this country to cultivate wheat or other grain with a profit, you must acknowledge there will be a great displacement of labour. We will endeavour to meet you with facts, and protest against your answering us with assumptions. I will not trouble the House by referring to those countries whose names have been so long familiar in these debates. If I allude to them, it is only because I do not wish the House to suppose that I depreciate the productive power of those countries.

My honourable Friend the Member for Somersetshire[7] said that the surplus produce of Russia was twenty-eight millions of quarters of corn, whereupon the Secretary of State rose to express his incredulity amid the sympathising derision of Gentlemen opposite. Why, Sir, the authority for that statement is the officer of the Government, the functionary who is employed by you to analyse the tariffs and resources of foreign countries; and probably the Secretary of State is the Minister who laid his Report on the Table of the House. The authority is Mr. M'Gregor.[8] I allude to it in passing, not that I value the authority of Mr. M'Gregor a rush; but it is right that it should be known that the statement of my honourable Friend was derived from your own Blue Books and prepared by one of your own officers. What is the object of publishing these Blue Books, except to furnish us with the elements of opinion?

I will not, however, enter into the Empire of all the Russias; I know that it contains about seventy principalities; that more than one of them has an area greater than the United Kingdom; and that every one produces corn. I cannot forget the rich valley of the Wolga, or the exuberant plains of the Ukraine. I won't take you to the valley of the Mississippi, though I have a statement here made by a high authority on this subject, who declares that its produce may be indefinitely extended and that its wheat can be supplied, with a high estimate for freight, in London at 30s. per quarter. But what I wish to bring before the notice of the House are the markets that are never mentioned, but which, I believe, will exercise a great influence on the price of corn.

There is one market which has never been mentioned in the course of these discussions, and that is Hungary. Hungary is a plain which consists of 36,000 English square miles. It is the richest soil in the world—the soil of a garden, varying in depth from one foot to seven feet. You may go hundreds of miles together and not find a stone in it. If you deduct one-third of that area for morasses, there are 24,000 square miles of the most fertile soil in the world, under the influence of a climate admirably adapted to the growth of corn. I have had a return sent to me of the production of one province in 1844, twelve millions of bushels; in Croatia the produce was one and a half millions of quarters. Yet thousands upon thousands of acres are uncultivated. But, honourable Gentlemen will say, how are we to get this corn from Hungary? That is what I am going to tell you.

Here is a letter from the greatest corn merchant in Hungary. He lives at Sissek on the Saave, the great depôt of the corn trade of that country. I will not give you the prices of this year, which is a year of scarcity, but I will give you the average of the last five years. An English quarter of Hungarian wheat—which, it should be remembered, ranks with the highest classes of

---

[7] William Miles.
[8] The evidence of John MacGregor, a renowned compiler of international trade statistics, often was cited in Corn Law debates. He was appointed to the Board of Trade in 1840.

Dantzic wheats—costs in English money from 18s. to 20s. per quarter. It is sent from Sissek by the river Kulpa to Carlstadt for 4d. per quarter, and from Carlstadt by land to Fiume for 1s. 8d. per quarter. The person who gives me this information is a practical man. He says, "Only give me a regular trade with England, and I will send you from Sissek 500,000 quarters in the first year." I will soon show you what is the effect of a steady market on increased supply and decreased price.

I will take another market—a very interesting one—that of the Danubian provinces. In the year 1842, at the two ports of the Danube, Galatz and Ibrail, there were 1,350 ships laden with the produce of those countries, and only eight of them were English. That is a remarkable fact. We are the greatest commercial country in the world; and yet in an active scene of commerce, where an almost absolute freedom of trade is enjoyed, it appears by a return dated since the accession of the present Government to office that out of 1,350 merchant ships laden in the two ports of the Danube, only eight were English. A house at Galatz has written to a house in England on the subject of supplying this country with corn, and the writer says:

> I will undertake to lay down, if secured a price of 18s. per quarter, in any English port, 200,000 quarters of wheat from this particular district, at 28s. to 30s., but if you will secure me a certain market I will double that quantity next year.

From the same place another house asserts that if you will ensure a regular trade they can supply one million of quarters of wheat, at 18s. per quarter; and if this measure passes, they undertake, at the end of seven years, that that quantity shall be doubled and sent to England at a reduced price. I speak of mercantile letters and can give honourable Gentlemen opposite the names of the firms.

I feel I must not dwell too long on this point; but yet, under the head of unenumerated markets which have not been the subject of discussion in the House, I may mention Spain—which will act greatly on this country—Egypt, and Sicily. Each of these countries, when the new measures are fairly in play, will be able, I believe, to furnish this country with as much corn as they have required in years of deficiency. My opinion is that in exact proportion as your demand for wheat and for various kinds of grain increases, in the same proportion the price will diminish. I believe it may be laid down as a principle of commerce that where an article can be progressively produced to an indefinite extent, precisely as the demand increases the price will decrease. I am aware that that is exactly contrary to the opinion of honourable Gentlemen opposite and to the opinion of the Government. We have had it announced from the hustings that exactly as you import a million of quarters of wheat from Continental markets, prices abroad will rise 10s. per quarter. That which was announced by a great authority is only the echo of the Manchester school and has been accepted by the Government. The honourable Member for Montrose[9] stated the other night that the result of these contemplated changes was only to equalise prices—we shall equalise prices by the demand, but we shall not lower prices. The gist of the question is the accuracy of this opinion. Is it true? The question whether England can maintain her character as an agricultural country—the question whether her people can be employed as they have been—the question whether there will be a great displacement of labour—depends upon the accuracy of this opinion.

I referred on a former occasion to the instance of tea. I said in that case that an increased demand had decreased the price. That intimation was received rather incredulously. It was not met by any argument or decided fact; but subsequently it was contradicted and in a very unsatisfactory manner. I will now show the House how far I was justified in that statement. I wrote to a mercantile house which is more largely connected with the China trade than any other house in the country. I placed before them the assertion I had made, and the reply it had met. What was the answer I received? Here it is:

> I hand you enclosed the prices per lb. of sound common congou tea, which is the kind most consumed in this country, from which you will be able to observe that there has been a great fall in the price since the year 1831.

What, then, was that fall in price per pound of congou tea—the sort most consumed in this country? In the year 1831 congou tea was 2s. 2d. per pound; in the year 1846 it is 9d. per pound. I know very well that the price of tea in 1831 was, to a certain degree, artificial. The mercantile influence of the East India Company still prevailed, and the supply was limited. But that influence was not greater than that of the China war, and, it will be observed, those disturbances only affected the market for a couple of years. In 1832, tea was 2s. 1½d.; in 1833, 1s. 11d.; 1834, 1s. 7¼d.; 1835, 1s. 4d.; 1836, 1s. 1d.; 1837, 1s. 7d.; 1838, 1s. 2d. And then we come to the disorders in China, which had the effect of raising the price in 1839 to 2s. 5d.; it then fell in 1842 to 1s. 3½d.; 1843, to 11d.; 1844, to 10d.; in 1845, to 9½d.; until, in 1846, we find it reduced to 9d. per pound; and all this time the import of tea from that country, which, from its being solely produced there, enjoys a *quasi* monopoly, was increasing by millions of pounds. And then, Sir, I am told that by the last accounts from Canton the price of tea is rising; and that is called an answer. Why, Sir, if by the last accounts from Canton the prices of tea had been falling, I should not have adduced that as an argument in favour of the principle I am upholding. The price of tea will fall and will rise according to the circumstance of the market; there must

---

[9] Joseph Hume.

always be undulation in price. But the question is, what, if I may use the expression, is the gradient of price, what the inevitable and unmistakable tendency of price during a series of years?

The next instance I shall take is one which is more favourable to our case, but, at the same time, strictly legitimate. It is one which bears more analogy to corn—namely, cotton. The price of cotton, upland, per pound, in the year 1836 was $10\frac{1}{8}d.$; in 1837, $8d.$; 1838, $8\frac{1}{4}d.$; 1839, $6\frac{3}{4}d.$; 1840, $6\frac{1}{8}d.$; 1841, $5\frac{5}{8}d.$; 1842, $5\frac{1}{4}d.$; 1843, $5\frac{1}{8}d.$; 1844, $4\frac{1}{8}d.$; and in 1845, from $4d.$ to $4\frac{1}{4}d.$ per pound; and in those ten years of progressive fall in price the import of cotton into England had risen from 350,000,000 pounds to 597,000,000 pounds, while during the same period of a falling price other manufacturing countries, including the United States, had increased their consumption of that article from 282,000,000 pounds to 439,000,000 pounds. It seems therefore to be demonstrable that where there is no natural or artificial cause to check the progress of production, price will proportionately fall.

Now, in the article I am about to refer to there are these causes in operation; and the whole state of the sugar trade is so anomalous that I might fairly have omitted it from the application of the test. But it occurred to me that it might be tried with reference to the production of East India sugar since the duties were equalised. What is the result? At the end of the year 1841 the price of brown Bengal sugar was 47s. to 52s.; 1842, 45s. to 51s.; 1843, 47s. to 55s.; 1844, 39s. to 49s.; 1845, 38s. to 42s.; 1846, 37s. to 42s.; and with that falling price the amount imported increased from 24,000 tons in the first year to 62,000 tons in the last year. With respect to the finest kinds of the same sugar, the price fell from 69s. to 74s. down to 52s. to 56s. during the same period. Therefore the instance of sugar is in perfect harmony with the general and ruling principle I have laid down.

The case of coffee I find to be still more satisfactory. I must apply my rule again to East India production in this case, owing to the anomalous state of our West India Colonies. Let us then take Ceylon coffee, and we shall find that the importation has greatly increased. The price of that article in 1840 was, per bag, 90s. to 91s.; in 1846 it fell to 44s.; and in the first year the quantity imported was 53,000 bags; in the last year 133,000 bags. Then take the case of Mysore coffee during the same time. In the first year the price was 70s. to 80s. per cask; in the last year 36s. to 48s. per cask; the quantity imported in the former year being 48,000 casks; in the latter 63,530. There are many other important articles which it would be wearisome to refer to in detail, but which I mention that Gentlemen may have an opportunity of investigating this important principle. Look at the instances of indigo, salt, iron, coal, and fruits, ever since the alteration of the law, and you will find this principle is invariably observed, universally demonstrated.

Well, Sir, is it then unreasonable for me to ask what there is in corn to make it an exception to this general rule? I want that question to be answered. It is a fair question. Why, I repeat, is corn to be an exception to this rule? Is it because corn is produced in every country and under every clime? I want to know where it is you will not produce corn. We have had by late arrivals accounts of the price of wheat in Persia, where we find it is at present 5s. per quarter. True, you can't very easily import corn from Persia; but there are countries lying at each point of the compass from Persia where you may purchase corn at from 10s. to 20s. per quarter. The rest is an affair of the cost of transport, in an age when the principle of locomotion is bringing all articles to a level.

Now, Sir, before I estimate the consequences of these proposed changes, I will first advert to the parallel which has been so often drawn between the importation of foreign corn and foreign cattle in order to show how ill-founded may be our fears. It does not appear to me that there is much analogy between these two instances, which are always treated as the same. In the first place, Continental countries have been corn-growing countries long before England became so. But they have never been to any extent cattle-feeding countries. The very fact of the prevalence in them of the Roman Catholic religion, which prevented the consumption of meat to the same extent as in Protestant countries, alone has discouraged it. Besides, the pastures of England have always, even in old days, been unrivalled. Nor should we forget the difficulty and danger of transport in the commerce of livestock. It appears, therefore, that the analogy between these cases is very imperfect.

I say, then, assuming as I have given you reason to assume that the price of wheat, when this system is established, ranges in England at 35s. per quarter, and other grain in proportion, this is not a question of rent, but it is a question of displacing the labour of England that produces corn, in order on an extensive and even universal scale to permit the entrance into this country of foreign corn produced by foreign labour. Will that displaced labour find new employment? The Secretary of State says that England is no longer an agricultural but a commercial and manufacturing country; and the right honourable Gentleman, when reminded by the noble Lord the Member for Gloucestershire[10] of his words, said, "No, I did not say that; but I said that England was no longer exclusively an agricultural country." Why, Sir, the commerce of England is not a creation of yesterday: it is more ancient than that of any other existing country. This is a novel assumption on the part of the Government to tell us that England has hitherto been a strictly agricultural country, and that now there is a change, and that it is passing into a commercial and manufacturing country. I doubt whether, in the first place, England is a greater commercial country now than she has been at other periods of her history. I do not mean to say that she has not now more commercial transactions, but that

[10] Grantley Berkeley.

with reference to her population and the population of the world, her commerce is not now greater than at other periods of her history; for example, when she had her great Levantine trade, when the riches of the world collected in the Mediterranean, when she had her great Turkey merchants, her flourishing Antilles, and her profitable though in some degree surreptitious trade with the Spanish Main.

But then it is also said that England has become a great manufacturing country. I believe, Sir, if you look to the general distribution of labour in England, you will find she may be less of a manufacturing country now than she has been. Well, I give you my argument; answer it if you can. I say, looking to the employment of the people, manufacturing industry was more scattered over the country a hundred years ago than it is now. Honourable Gentlemen have laid hold of a word uttered in the heat of speaking. I say manufacturing industry was more dispersed over the country then than now—there were more counties in which manufactures flourished then than at the present moment. For instance, in the West of England, manufactures were more flourishing, and your woollen manufacture bore a greater ratio in importance to the industrial skill of Europe 300 years ago than it does to the aggregate industry of Europe at the present moment. That manufacture might not have been absolutely more important; but as a development of the national industry, it bore a greater relative importance to the industry of Europe then than at the present moment. You had then considerable manufactures in various counties— manufactures a hundred years ago which are now obsolete, or but partially pursued. You have no doubt now a gigantic development of manufacturing skill in a particular county which is unprecedented. It is one of those developments which confer the greatest honour on this country, which has been a great source of public wealth, a development of which Englishmen should be justly proud. But, generally speaking, it is confined to one county; and now Ministers tell us we must change our whole system, because, forsooth, England has ceased to be an agricultural country and has become a commercial and manufacturing one. That is to say, that we must change our whole system in favour of one particular county.

Sir, that is an extremely dangerous principle to introduce. I have heard of a repeal of the Union, but we may live to hear of a revival of the Heptarchy[11] if Her Majesty's Ministers pursue this policy; if those portions of the country which are agricultural or suffering under the remains of an old obsolete manufacturing population are to be told that we must change our whole system because one county where there is a peculiar development of one branch of industry demands it. But what are the resources of this kind of industry to employ and support the people, supposing the great depression in agricultural produce occur which is feared—that this great

---

[11] The seven kingdoms established by the Angles and Saxons.

revolution, as it has appropriately been called, takes place—that we cease to be an agricultural people—what are the resources that would furnish employment to two-thirds of the subverted agricultural population—in fact, from three and a half to four millions of people? Assume that the workshop-of-the-world principle is carried into effect; assume that the attempt is made to maintain your system, both financial and domestic, on the resources of the cotton trade; assume that in spite of hostile tariffs that already gigantic industry is doubled—a bold assumption, even if there be no further improvements in machinery, further reducing the necessity of manual labour—you would only find increased employment for 300,000 of your population. Perhaps mechanical invention may reduce the number half, and those only women and children. What must be the consequence? I think we have pretty good grounds for anticipating social misery and political disaster.

But then, I am told, immense things are to be done for the agriculturist by the application of capital and skill. Let us test the soundness of this doctrine. When a man lends his capital, he looks to the security he is to have and to what is to pay the interest. Is the complexion of these measures such as to render men more ready to lend money on landed estates? The mortgagee, when he advances money on land, looks to the margin in the shape of rent for his security. Will any man rise and maintain that the tendency of these measures is to increase that margin? But you are not only diminishing the opportunity of obtaining loans upon your own estates, but you are creating for capital an investment which will be more profitable for it in the estates of the foreigner. Look at the relations in which you will place the foreign merchant with his London correspondent. He has no longer to fear the capricious effects of the sliding scale: he has got a certain market; he goes to his London banker with an increased security for an advance; he obtains his loan with ease; he makes his advances to the country dealers on the Continent as he makes his advance of English capital now in the foreign wool trade, before the clip and the great fairs; and thus, while you diminish the security of the landed proprietor, you are offering to the English capitalist a better and securer investment.

But then you tell us of the aid to be had by the agriculturist from skill. It is not easy to argue on a phrase so indefinite as skill; but I think I can show you that the English agriculturist is far more advanced in respect to skill than even the English manufacturer. I don't mean to say that there are not English farmers who might cultivate their lands better and with more economy than they do; but the same may surely be said in their respective pursuits of many a manufacturer and many a miner; but what I mean to say is that an English farmer produces more effectively and wastes less—is more industrious and more intelligent than the manufacturer. I will prove this by the evidence of a member of the Anti-Corn Law League—Mr.

Greg.[12] Mr. Greg says that the competition is so severe that he almost doubts the possibility of the English manufacturer long maintaining that competition with the Continental or American manufacturer, who approach them nearer every day in the completeness of their fabrics and the economy of their productions. But no such thing can be said of the English agriculturist, who, I have shown you, can produce much more per bushel than the French, Russian, or American agriculturist. So much, then, for the argument with respect to skill.

There is one argument, or rather appeal, which I know has influenced opinion out of this House and also within it. You bring before us the condition of the English peasant. It is too often a miserable condition. My honourable Friend the Member for Shaftesbury[13] has gained and deserves great credit for investigating the condition of the Dorsetshire labourer. He has introduced it into this discussion. Now, the condition of the Dorsetshire labourer is one of the reasons which induce me to support this law. It is very easy to say that the condition of the agricultural labourer, when compared with the general state of our civilisation, is a miserable and depressed one, and that protection has produced it. If I cannot offer you reasons which may induce you to believe that protection has had nothing to do with it, I shall be perfectly ready to go tonight into the same Lobby with Her Majesty's Ministers. I asked you the other night, if protection has produced the Dorsetshire labourer at 7s. per week, how is it that protection has produced the Lincolnshire labourer with double that sum? I do not say that is an argument. It is a suggestive question which I will endeavour to follow up.

Mr. Huskisson[14] made an observation, in conversation with an acquaintance of mine, which has always struck me very forcibly. When Mr. Huskisson first settled in Sussex, his attention was naturally drawn to the extraordinary state of pauperism in that county; and after giving the subject all the meditation of his acute mind, he said that he traced it to the fact that Sussex had formerly been the seat of a great iron trade, and that agriculture had never been able to absorb the manufacturing population. Now, apply that principle to the western counties, and don't you think it will throw some light upon their condition? They also have been the seats of manufactures—many of them obsolete and many of them now only partially pursued. There, too, you will find that the manufacturing population has never been absorbed by the agricultural—that is, agriculture does not bear its ratio in its means of support to the amount of the population which it has to sustain, but which it did not create.

[12] Robert H. Greg, Member for Manchester, was influential in the moderate wing of the League.
[13] Richard Sheridan.
[14] William Huskisson, Member for Liverpool, a great free-trade advocate.

And now go to Lincolnshire. I will rest our case on Lincolnshire. It is a new county; it is a protected county. Lincolnshire is to agriculture what Lancashire is to manufactures. The population there is produced by land and supported by land, in the same manner that the population of Lancashire has been produced and is supported by manufactures. Let us picture to ourselves for a moment that celebrated tower that looks over that city, which my gallant Friend[15] and his ancestors have represented since the time of the last Stuart. Let us picture him for a moment placing the archfiend of political economy in that befitting niche and calling his attention to the surrounding landscape. To the north, extending to the Humber, an endless tract of wolds, rescued from the rabbits, once covered with furze and whins, and now with exuberant crops of grain; to the south, stretching for miles, is what was once Lincoln Heath, where in the memory of living men there used to be a lighthouse for the traveller and which, even in the recollection of the middle-aged, was let to the warrener at 2s. 6d. an acre, now one of the best-farmed and most productive corn districts in the Kingdom. Then turning from the wolds and the heaths eastward, reaching to the sea, he might behold a region of fens, the small ones drained by the steam-engine, with the East and West and Wildmere Fens, once more than half of the year under water, now cleared by large canals and bearing magnificent wheats and oats; with the great Witham and Black Sluice drainage districts, one extending over 60,000 and the other 90,000 acres, admirably reclaimed and drained, and bearing and creating and well sustaining a large and industrious and thriving population. And all under the faith of protective Acts of Parliament. I am told that it is the contiguity of manufactures that makes Lincolnshire so prosperous. But, Sir, the frontiers of Wilts are nearer that great manufacturing district of which Birmingham is the centre than those of Lincolnshire are to Lancashire. Now, see what Lincolnshire has produced under protection. There you see the protective system fairly tested. But when you find the labourers in the western counties wretched and miserable, do not say that protection has been the cause of it, when protection is, perhaps, the reason why they exist at all; but see if you cannot find other causes for their poverty and means to counter-act it. I must say, that nothing astonished me more than when the noble Lord the Member for Falkirk[16] asked the farmers in Newark market, "What has protection done for you?" Why, that market is supplied with the wheat of Lincoln Heath, the intrinsic poverty of whose soil is only sustained by the annual application of artificial manures, but which produces the finest corn in the Kingdom. What has protection done for them? Why, if protection had never existed, Lincolnshire might still have been a wild wold, a barren heath, a plashy marsh.

There are one or two points to which I could have wished to call the

---
[15] Colonel C. D. W. Sibthorp, Member for Lincoln.
[16] Lord Lincoln, a Conservative who supported Peel.

attention of the House, but which time will only permit me to glance at. I will not presume to discuss them. But you cannot decide this question without looking to your Colonies. I am not one of those who think it the inevitable lot of the people of Canada to become annexed to the United States. Canada has all the elements of a great and independent country and is destined, I sometimes believe, to be the Russia of the New World. The honourable and learned Member for Bath,[17] in answering the speech of the noble Lord the Member for Lynn last night, treated our commerce with Canada very lightly, rather as a smuggling traffic than legitimate commerce. That is an argument for keeping the Canadas. I have no desire to see a smuggling trade if we can have any other. But I will ask the gentlemen of Manchester to consider what may become of the trans-Atlantic market for their manufactures if the whole of that continent belong to one power?

But I must not dwell on the Colonies, and I shall scarcely touch the case of Ireland. It is too terrible, especially if there be truth in the opinion of the noble Lord whose conversion has been so much a matter of congratulation to the Government[18] that their measure must be fatal to small farmers. Why, Ireland is a nation of small farmers. There was, however, one observation made with respect to Ireland by the honourable Member for Stockport, which, considering the effect it has had, I cannot help noticing. The honourable Gentleman says, "Ireland an argument in favour of the Corn Laws! Of all countries in the world I never should have supposed that Ireland would have been brought forward in support of the Corn Laws." That is a saucy and gallant sally; but is it an argument? What does it prove? The population is reduced to the lowest sources of subsistence, admitted; but how do they gain even their potatoes except by cultivating the soil and by producing that wheat and those oats which they send to England? I should be very glad if that wheat and those oats remained in Ireland; but I ask, what will be the state of Ireland if the effect of this measure on your markets be such as I have assumed? You say that capital will flow into the country and manufactures will be established. What length of time will elapse before these manufactures are established? Perhaps before that time the iron trade will revive in Sussex, or we shall see the drooping energies of the Dorsetshire labourer revived by his receiving the same wages as are paid at Rochdale and Stockport.

Believing that this measure would be fatal to our agricultural interests; believing that its tendency is to sap the elements and springs of our manufacturing prosperity; believing that in a merely financial point of view it will occasion a new distribution of the precious metals, which must induce the utmost social suffering in every class—I am obliged to ask myself, if the measure be so perilous, why is it produced? Sir, I need not ask what so many

[17] John A. Roebuck responded to Bentinck on commercial policy toward Canada.
[18] Lord Heytesbury, Viceroy of Ireland (1844–1846) in Peel's Administration.

Gentlemen both in and out of this House have already asked: what was there in the circumstances of this country to authorise the change? If we are only a commercial and manufacturing people, all must admit that commerce was thriving and that manufactures flourished. Agriculture was also content; and even had it been suffering and depressed, what does it signify, since England has ceased to be an agricultural country? Obliged, then, to discover some cause for this social revolution, I find that a body of men have risen in this country, eminent for their eloquence, distinguished for their energy, but more distinguished, in my humble opinion, for their energy and their eloquence than for their knowledge of human nature or for the extent of their political information. Sir, I am not one of those who, here or elsewhere, in public or in private, have spoken with that disrespect which some have done of that great commercial confederation which now exercises so great an influence in this country. Though I disapprove of their doctrines—though I believe from the bottom of my heart that their practise will eventually be as pernicious to the manufacturing interest as to the agricultural interests of this country—still I admire men of abilities who, convinced of a great truth and proud of their energies, band themselves together for the purpose of supporting it and come forward, devoting their lives to what they consider to be a great cause.

Sir, this country can only exist by free discussion. If it is once supposed that opinions are to be put down by any other means, then whatever may be our political forms, liberty vanishes. If we think the opinions of the Anti-Corn Law League are dangerous—if we think their system is founded on error, and must lead to confusion—it is open in a free country like England for men who hold opposite ideas to resist them with the same earnestness, by all legitimate means—by the same active organisation, and by all the intellectual power they command. But what happens in this country? A body of Gentlemen,[19] able and adroit men, come forward, and profess contrary doctrines to those of these new economists. They place themselves at the head of that great popular party who are adverse to the new ideas, and professing their opinions, they climb and clamber into power by having accepted or rather by having eagerly sought the trust. It follows that the body whom they represent, trusting in their leaders, not unnaturally slumber at their posts. They conclude that their opinions are represented in the State. It was not for us or the millions out of the House to come forward and organise a power in order to meet the hostile movements of the honourable Member for Stockport. No, we trusted to others—to one who, by accepting or rather by seizing that post, obtained the greatest place in the country and at this moment governs England. Well, Sir, what happens? The right honourable Gentleman the First Minister told his friends that he had given them very significant hints of the change of his

[19] Peel's Conservative Ministry of 1841.

opinions. He said that even last year Lord Grey had found him out, and he was surprised that we could have been so long deluded.

Sir, none of the observations of the right honourable Gentleman applied to me. More than a year ago I rose in my place and said that it appeared to me that protection was in about the same state as Protestantism was in 1828.[20] I remember my friends were very indignant with me for that assertion, but they have since been so kind as to observe that instead of being a calumny it was only a prophecy. But I am bound to say, from personal experience, that with the very humble exception to which I have referred, I think the right honourable Baronet may congratulate himself on his complete success in having entirely deceived his Party, for even the noble Lord the Member for Lynn himself, in a moment of frank conversation, assured me that he had not till the very last moment the slightest doubt of the right honourable Gentleman. The noble Lord, I suppose, like many others, thought that the right honourable Gentleman was, to use a very favourite phrase on these benches in 1842, "only making the best bargain for them." I remember when the Whig Budget was rejected and the right honourable Gentleman was installed into office, the changes which he proposed at the time created some suspicion; but all suspicion was hushed at the moment because the right honourable Gentleman was looked upon as the man who could make the "best bargain" for the Party. I want to know what Gentlemen think of their best bargain now? Suddenly, absolute as was the confidence in the right honourable Gentleman, the announcement was made that there was to be another change; that that was to occur under his auspices, which, only a few months before, he had aptly described as a "social revolution." And how was that announcement made? Were honourable Gentlemen called together or had the influential Members of either House any intimation given to them of the nature of it? No, Sir. It was announced through the columns of a journal[21] which is always careful never to insert important information except on the highest authority. Conceive the effect of that announcement on foreign countries and on foreign Ministers. I can bear witness to it. I happened to be absent from England at the time, and I know of great potentates sending for English Ambassadors and demanding an explanation; and of English Ambassadors waiting on great potentates and officially declaring that there was not the slightest truth in the announcement. And all this time, too, Members of the Government—I have some of them in my eye —were calling on other newspapers devoted to the Government and instructing them to announce that the whole was an "infamous fabrication." How ingenuous was the conduct of Her Majesty's Government—or of that Minister who formed the omnipotent minority of the Cabinet—I

---

[20] The reference is to Peel's reversal of position on Catholic Emancipation in 1828.
[21] *The Times* for December 4, 1845, reported a Cabinet decision to "recommend an immediate consideration of the Corn Laws, preparatory to their total repeal."

leave the House to decide. But was it not strange that, after so much agitation, after all these schemes, after all these Machiavellian manœuvres, when the Minister at last met the House and his Party he acted as if we had deserted him instead of his having left us? Who can forget those tones? Who can forget that indignant glance?

> *Vectabor humeris tunc ego inimicis eques;*
> *Meæque terra cedet insolentiæ;*[22]

which means to say, "I, a protectionist Minister, mean to govern England by the aid of the Anti-Corn Law League. And, as for the country Gentlemen, why, I snap my fingers in their face."

Yet even then the right honourable Gentleman had no cause to complain of his Party. It is very true that on a subsequent occasion, 240 Gentlemen recorded their sense of his conduct.[23] But then he might have remembered the considerable section of converts that he obtained even in the last hour. Why, what a compliment to a Minister—not only to vote for him but to vote for him against your opinions and in favour of opinions which he had always drilled you to distrust. That was a scene, I believe, unprecedented in the House of Commons. Indeed, I recollect nothing equal to it unless it be the conversion of the Saxons by Charlemagne, which is the only historical incident that bears any parallel to that illustrious occasion. Ranged on the banks of the Rhine, the Saxons determined to resist any further movement on the part of the great Cæsar; but when the Emperor appeared, instead of conquering he converted them. How were they converted? In battalions—the old chronicler informs us they were converted in battalions and baptised in platoons. It was utterly impossible to bring these individuals from a state of reprobation to a state of grace with a celerity sufficiently quick. When I saw the 112 fall into rank and file, I was irresistibly reminded of that memorable incident on the banks of the Rhine.

And now, Sir, I must say in vindication of the right honourable Gentleman that I think great injustice has been done to him throughout these debates. A perhaps justifiable misconception has universally prevailed. Sir, the right honourable Gentleman has been accused of foregone treachery—of long meditated deception—of a desire unworthy of a great statesman, even if an unprincipled one—of always having intended to abandon the opinions by professing which he rose to power. Sir, I entirely acquit the right honourable Gentleman of any such intention. I do it for this reason: that when I examine the career of this Minister, which has now filled a great space in the Parliamentary history of this country, I find that for

---

[22] "Then as a horseman I'll ride upon your hated shoulders, and the earth shall yield to my arrogance" (Horace, *Epode* XVII.74–75).

[23] In the Division of February 27, these Members, including 231 Conservatives, opposed the Government's motion to begin discussion of Peel's tariff proposal.

between thirty and forty years, from the days of Mr. Horner[24] to the days of the honourable Member for Stockport, that right honourable Gentleman has traded on the ideas and intelligence of others. His life has been one great appropriation clause. He is a burglar of others' intellect. Search the *Index* of Beatson[25] from the days of the Conqueror to the termination of the last reign, there is no statesman who has committed political petty larceny on so great a scale. I believe, therefore, when the right honourable Gentleman undertook our cause on either side of the House that he was perfectly sincere in his advocacy; but as in the course of discussion the conventionalisms which he received from us crumbled away in his grasp, feeling no creative power to sustain him with new arguments, feeling no spontaneous sentiments to force upon him conviction, the right honourable Gentleman—reduced at last to defending the noblest cause, one based on the most high and solemn principles, upon the "burdens peculiar to agriculture"—the right honourable Gentleman, faithful to the law of his nature, imbibed the new doctrines, the more vigorous, bustling, popular, and progressive doctrines of Mr. Horner—as he had imbibed the doctrines of every leading man in this country for thirty or forty years with the exception of the doctrine of Parliamentary Reform, which the Whigs very wisely led the country upon and did not allow to grow sufficiently mature to fall into the mouth of the right honourable Gentleman.

Sir, the right honourable Gentleman tells us that he does not feel humiliated. Sir, it is impossible for anyone to know what are the feelings of another. Feeling depends upon temperament; it depends upon the idiosyncracy of the individual; it depends upon the organisation of the animal that feels. But this I will tell the right honourable Gentleman, that though he may not feel humiliated, his country ought to feel humiliated. Is it so pleasing to the self-complacency of a great nation, is it so grateful to the pride of England, that one who from the position he has contrived to occupy must rank as her foremost citizen is one of whom it may be said, as Dean Swift said of another Minister, that "he is a Gentleman who has the perpetual misfortune to be mistaken!"

And, Sir, even now, in this last scene of the drama, when the Party whom he unintentionally betrayed is to be unintentionally annihilated—even now, in this the last scene, the right honourable Gentleman, faithful to the law of his being, is going to pass a project which, I believe it is matter of notoriety, is not of his own invention. It is one which may have been modified but which I believe has been offered to another Government and by that Government has been wisely rejected. Why, Sir, these are matters of general notoriety. After the day that the right honourable Gentleman made his first exposition of his scheme, a Gentleman well known in this House

---

[24] Francis Horner, Member for Wendover, an early opponent of protection.
[25] Robert Beatson, *A Political Index to the Histories of Great Britain and Ireland*, 3 vols. (London, 1806).

and learned in all the political secrets behind the scenes met me and said, "Well, what do you think of your chief's plan?" Not knowing exactly what to say, but, taking up a phrase which has been much used in the House, I observed, "Well, I suppose it's a 'great and comprehensive' plan." "Oh!" he replied, "we know all about it! It was offered to us! It is not his plan; it's Popkins's plan!"[26] And is England to be governed by "Popkins's plan?" Will he go to the country with it? Will he go with it to that ancient and famous England that once was governed by statesmen—by Burleighs and by Walsinghams; by Bolingbrokes and by Walpoles; by a Chatham and a Canning—will he go to it with this fantastic scheming of some presumptuous pedant? I won't believe it. I have that confidence in the common sense—I will say the common spirit—of our countrymen that I believe they will not long endure this huckstering tyranny of the Treasury Bench—these political pedlars that bought their Party in the cheapest market and sold us in the dearest.

I know, Sir, that there are many who believe that the time is gone by when one can appeal to those high and honest impulses that were once the mainstay and the main element of the English character. I know, Sir, that we appeal to a people debauched by public gambling—stimulated and encouraged by an inefficient and shortsighted Minister. I know that the public mind is polluted with economic fancies; a depraved desire that the rich may become richer without the interference of industry and toil. I know, Sir, that all confidence in public men is lost. But, Sir, I have faith in the primitive and enduring elements of the English character. It may be vain now, in the midnight of their intoxication, to tell them that there will be an awakening of bitterness; it may be idle now, in the springtide of their economic frenzy, to warn them that there may be an ebb of trouble. But the dark and inevitable hour will arrive. Then, when their spirit is softened by misfortune, they will recur to those principles that made England great and which, in our belief, can alone keep England great. Then, too, perchance they may remember not with unkindness those who, betrayed and deserted, were neither ashamed nor afraid to struggle for the "good old cause"—the cause with which are associated principles the most popular, sentiments the most entirely national—the cause of labour—the cause of the people—the cause of England.

---

[26] The sarcastic reference is to John MacGregor, Assistant Secretary to the Board of Trade. MacGregor, later Member for Glasgow, helped Peel draft the measure for repeal of the Corn Laws.

David Lloyd George

"The Budget and the People"[*]

Limehouse, London, July 30, 1909

A few months ago a meeting was held not far from this hall, in the heart of the City of London, demanding that the Government should launch into enormous expenditure on the Navy. That meeting ended up with a resolution promising that those who passed that resolution would give financial support to the Government in their undertaking. There have been two or three meetings held in the City of London since [*laughter and cheers*] attended by the same class of people, but not ending up with a resolution promising to pay. [*Laughter.*] On the contrary, we are spending the money, but they won't pay. [*Laughter.*] What has happened since to alter their tone? Simply that we have sent in the Bill. [*Laughter and cheers.*] We started our four "Dreadnoughts."[1] They cost £8,000,000. We promised them four more; they cost another £8,000,000. Somebody has to pay, and then these Gentlemen say, "Perfectly true; somebody has to pay, but we would rather that somebody were somebody else." [*Laughter.*] We started building; we wanted money to pay for the building; so we sent the hat around. [*Laughter.*] We sent it round amongst workmen [*Hear, hear*] and the Scotchmen of Dumfries [*cheers*], who, like all their countrymen, know the value of money [*laughter*]; they all dropped in their coppers.[2] We went round Belgravia,[3] and there has been such a howl ever since that it has well-nigh deafened us.

---

[*] This text is taken from Lloyd George's *Better Times* (London, 1910), pp. 144–156. A boisterous audience of 4,000 crowded into the hall in Limehouse, a working-class district in East London, to hear Lloyd George. He was interrupted frequently; more than a dozen persons were arrested for disturbances. Omissions and errors in *The Times*'s report (July 31, 1909, p. 9) suggest the difficulties experienced by their correspondent in hearing the speech. However, *The Times*'s record of audience reactions has been incorporated into this text.

[1] In 1906, England launched the H.M.S. *Dreadnought*, a battleship whose speed and uniform heavy armament made obsolete other capital ships. To keep pace with German naval expansion, eight British "dreadnoughts" were to be constructed, four immediately and four more if needed.

[2] By-elections had been held in these places several days before the speech, returning candidates favorable to the budget.

[3] Then a fashionable, upper-class district in central London.

But they say, "It is not so much the 'Dreadnoughts' we object to, it is pensions." [*Hear, hear.*] If they objected to pensions, why did they promise them? [*Cheers.*] They won elections on the strength of their promises. It is true they never carried them out. [*Laughter.*] Deception is always a pretty contemptible vice, but to deceive the poor is the meanest of all. [*Cheers.*] They go on to say, "When we promised pensions we meant pensions at the expense of the people for whom they were provided. We simply meant to bring in a Bill to compel workmen to contribute to their own pensions." [*Laughter.*] If that is what they meant, why did they not say so? [*Cheers.*] The Budget, as your Chairman has already so well reminded you, is introduced not merely for the purpose of raising barren taxes, but taxes that are fertile, taxes that will bring forth fruit—the security of the country which is paramount in the minds of all. The provision for the aged and deserving poor—was it not time something was done? [*Cheers.*] It is rather a shame that a rich country like ours—probably the richest in the world, if not the richest the world has ever seen—should allow those who have toiled all their days to end in penury and possibly starvation. [*Hear, hear.*] It is rather hard that an old workman should have to find his way to the gates of the tomb, bleeding and footsore, through the brambles and thorns of poverty. [*Cheers.*] We cut a new path for him [*cheers*]—an easier one, a pleasanter one, through fields of waving corn. We are raising money to pay for the new road—aye, and to widen it so that 200,000 paupers shall be able to join in the march. [*Cheers.*] There are many in the country blessed by Providence with great wealth, and if there are amongst them men who grudge out of their riches a fair contribution towards the less fortunate of their fellow-countrymen, they are very shabby rich men. [*Cheers.*]

We propose to do more by means of the Budget. We are raising money to provide against the evils and the sufferings that follow from unemployment. [*Cheers.*] We are raising money for the purpose of assisting our great friendly societies[4] to provide for the sick and the widows and orphans. We are providing money to enable us to develop the resources of our own land. [*Cheers.*] I do not believe any fair-minded man would challenge the justice and the fairness of the objects which we have in view in raising this money.

Some of our critics say, "The taxes themselves are unjust, unfair, unequal, oppressive—notably so the land taxes." [*Laughter.*] They are engaged not merely in the House of Commons but outside the House of Commons in assailing these taxes with a concentrated and a sustained ferocity which will not allow even a comma to escape with its life. [*"Good" and laughter.*] Now, are these taxes really so wicked? Let us examine them; because it is perfectly clear that the one part of the Budget that attracts all this hostility and animosity is that part which deals with the taxation of

---

[4] Private insurance and savings agencies.

land. Well, now, let us examine it. I do not want you to consider merely abstract principles. I want to invite your attention to a number of concrete cases, fair samples to show you how in these concrete illustrations our Budget proposals work. Let us take them. Let us take first of all the tax on undeveloped land and on increment.

Not far from here, not so many years ago, between the Lea and the Thames, you had hundreds of acres of land which was not very useful even for agricultural purposes. In the main it was a sodden marsh. The commerce and the trade of London increased under free trade [*loud cheers*], the tonnage of your shipping went up by hundreds of thousands of tons and by millions; labour was attracted from all parts of the country to cope with all this trade and business which was done here. What happened? There was no housing accommodation. This Port of London became overcrowded, and the population overflowed. That was the opportunity of the owners of the marsh. All that land became valuable building land, and land which used to be rented at £2 or £3 an acre has been selling within the last few years at £2,000 an acre, £3,000 an acre, £6,000 an acre, £8,000 an acre. Who created that increment? [*Cheers.*] Who made that golden swamp? [*More cheers.*] Was it the landlord? ["*No.*"] Was it his energy? Was it his brains [*laughter and cheers*]—a very bad look-out for the place if it were—his forethought? It was purely the combined efforts of all the people engaged in the trade and commerce of the Port of London—trader, merchant, shipowner, dock labourer, workman—everybody except the landlord. [*Cheers.*] Now, you follow that transaction. Land worth £2 or £3 an acre running up to thousands. During the time it was ripening, the landlord was paying his rates and his taxes not on £2 or £3 an acre. It was agricultural land, and because it was agricultural land a munificent Tory Government [*laughter*] voted a sum of £2,000,000 to pay half the rates of those poor distressed landlords [*laughter and "Shame"*], and you and I had to pay taxes in order to enable those landlords to pay half their rates on agricultural land, while it was going up every year by hundreds of pounds through your efforts and the efforts of your neighbours.

That is now coming to an end. [*Loud and long-continued cheering.*] On the walls of Mr. Balfour's[5] meeting last Friday were the words, "We protest against fraud and folly." [*Laughter.*] So do I. [*Great cheering.*] These things I tell you of have only been possible up to the present through the "fraud" of the few and the "folly" of the many. [*Cheers.*] What is going to happen in the future? In future those landlords will have to contribute to the taxation of the country on the basis of the real value [*more cheers*]—only one halfpenny in the pound! [*Laughter.*] Only a halfpenny! And that is what all the howling is about.

There is another little tax called the increment tax. For the future what

[5] Arthur Balfour, Conservative Member for the City of London, opposed the 1909 budget.

will happen? We mean to value all the land in the Kingdom. [*Cheers.*] And here you can draw no distinction between agricultural land and other land, for the simple reason that East and West Ham[6] was agricultural land a few years ago. And if land goes up in the future by hundreds and thousands an acre through the efforts of the community, the community will get 20 per cent of that increment. [*Cheers.*] Ah! what a misfortune it is that there was not a Chancellor of the Exchequer to do this thirty years ago! [*Cheers and "Better late than never."*] We should now have been enjoying an abundant revenue from this source. [*Cheers.*]

I have instanced West Ham. Let me give you a few more cases. Take cases like Golder's Green and others of a similar kind where the value of land has gone up in the course, perhaps, of a couple of years through a new tramway or a new railway being opened. Golder's Green to begin with. A few years ago there was a plot of land there which was sold at £160. Last year I went and opened a tube railway there. What was the result? This year that very piece of land has been sold for £2,100 [*"Shame"*]—£160 before the railway was opened—before I went there [*laughter*]—£2,100 now. My Budget demands 20 per cent of that. [*Laughter.*]

There are many cases where landlords take advantage of the needs of municipalities and even of national needs and of the monopoly which they have got in land in a particular neighbourhood in order to demand extortionate prices. Take the very well-known case of the Duke of Northumberland [*Hear, hear*], when a County Council wanted to buy a small plot of land as a site for a school to train the children who in due course would become the men labouring on his property. The rent was quite an insignificant thing; his contribution to the rates I think was on the basis of 30s. an acre. What did he demand for it for a school? Nine hundred pounds an acre. [*"Hear, hear" and "Shame."*] All we say is this—if it is worth £900, let him pay taxes on £900. [*Cheers.*]

There are several of these cases that I want to give to you. Take the town of Bootle, a town created very much in the same way as these towns in the East of London, by the growth of a great port, in this case Liverpool. In 1879 the rates of Bootle were £9,000 a year—the ground rents were £10,000—so that the landlord was receiving more from the industry of the community than all the rates derived by the municipality for the benefit of the town. In 1898 the rates had gone up to £94,000 a year—for improving the place, constructing roads, laying out parks, and extending lighting and opening up the place. But the ground landlord was receiving in ground rents £100,000. It is time that he should pay for all this value, and the Budget makes him pay. [*Cheers.*]

Another case was given me from Richmond which is very interesting. The Town Council of Richmond recently built some workmen's cottages

---

[6] These suburban areas, along with several others mentioned later, were rapidly being industrialized.

under a housing scheme. The land appeared on the rate-book as of the value of £4, and, being agricultural [*laughter*], the landlord only paid half the rates, and you and I paid the rest for him. [*Laughter.*] It is situated on the extreme edge of the borough, therefore not very accessible, and the Town Council naturally thought they would get it cheap. [*Laughter.*] But they did not know their landlord. They had to pay £2,000 an acre for it. ["*Shame.*"] The result is that instead of having a good housing scheme with plenty of gardens and open space, plenty of breathing space, plenty of room for the workmen at the end of their days, forty cottages had to be crowded on two acres. If the land had been valued at its true value, that landlord would have been at any rate contributing his fair share of the public revenue, and it is just conceivable that he might have been driven to sell at a more reasonable price.

I do not want to weary you with these cases. ["*Go on!*"] But I could give you many. I am a member of a Welsh County Council, and landlords even in Wales are not more reasonable. [*Laughter.*] The Police Committee the other day wanted a site for a police station. [*Laughter.*] Well, you might have imagined that if a landlord sold land cheaply for anything it would have been for a police station. The housing of the working classes—that is a different matter. [*Laughter.*] But a police station means security for property. [*Laughter and cheers.*] Not at all. The total population of Caernarvonshire[7] is not as much—I am not sure it is as great—as the population of Limehouse alone. It is a scattered area; no great crowded populations there. And yet they demanded for a piece of land which was contributing 2*s*. a year to the rates £2,500 an acre! All we say is, "If their land is as valuable as all that, let it have the same value in the assessment book [*cheers*] as it seems to possess in the auction room." [*Cheers.*]

There was a case from Greenock the other day. The Admiralty wanted a torpedo range. Here was an opportunity for patriotism! [*Laughter.*] These are the men who want an efficient Navy to protect our shores, and the Admiralty state that one element in efficiency is straight shooting and say: "We want a range for practise for torpedoes on the coast of Scotland." There was a piece of land there which had a rating value of £11 2*s*., and it was sold to the nation for £27,225. And these are the gentlemen who accuse us of robbery and spoliation! [*Cheers.*]

Now, all we say is this: "In future you must pay one halfpenny in the pound on the real value of your land. In addition to that, if the value goes up, not owing to your efforts—if you spend money on improving it—we will give you credit for it; but if it goes up owing to the industry and the energy of the people living in that locality, one-fifth of that increment shall in future be taken as a toll by the State." [*Cheers.*] They say: "Why should you tax this increment on landlords and not on other classes of the community?" They say: "You are taxing the landlord because the value of his

[7] Lloyd George's home county in Wales.

property is going up through the growth of population, through the increased prosperity of the community. Does not the value of a doctor's business go up in the same way?"

Ah, fancy their comparing themselves for a moment! What is the landlord's increment? Who is the landlord? The landlord is a gentleman—I have not a word to say about him in his personal capacity—the landlord is a gentleman who does not earn his wealth. He does not even take the trouble to receive his wealth. [*Laughter.*] He has a host of agents and clerks to receive it for him. He does not even take the trouble to spend his wealth. He has a host of people around him to do the actual spending for him. He never sees it until he comes to enjoy it. His sole function, his chief pride is stately consumption of wealth produced by others. [*Cheers.*] What about the doctor's income? How does the doctor earn his income? The doctor is a man who visits our homes when they are darkened with the shadow of death; who, by his skill, his trained courage, his genius, wrings hope out of the grip of despair, wins life out of the fangs of the Great Destroyer. [*Cheers.*] All blessings upon him and his divine art of healing that mends bruised bodies and anxious hearts. [*Cheers.*] To compare the reward which he gets for that labour with the wealth which pours into the pockets of the landlord purely owing to the possession of his monopoly is a piece—if they will forgive me for saying so—of insolence which no intelligent man would tolerate. [*Cheers.*]

So much then for the halfpenny tax on unearned increment. Now I come to the reversion tax. What is the reversion tax? You have got a system in this country which is not tolerated in any other country in the world, except, I believe, Turkey [*laughter*]—a system whereby landlords take advantage of the fact that they have got complete control over the land to let it for a term of years, spend money upon it in building; and year by year the value passes into the pockets of the landlord, and at the end of sixty, seventy, eighty, or ninety years the whole of it passes away to the pockets of a man who never spent a penny upon it. In Scotland they have a system of 999-years leases. The Scotsmen have a very shrewd idea that at the end of 999 years there will probably be a better land system in existence [*laughter and cheers*], and they are prepared to take their chance of the millennium coming round by that time. But in this country we have sixty-years leases. I know districts—quarry districts—in Wales where a little bit of barren rock on which you could not feed a goat, where the landlord could not get a shilling an acre for agricultural rent, is let to quarrymen for the purpose of building houses at a ground rent of 30s. or £2 a house. The quarryman builds his house. He goes to a building society to borrow money. He pays out of his hard-earned weekly wage contributions to the building society for ten, twenty, or thirty years. By the time he becomes an old man he has cleared off the mortgage, and more than half the value of the house has passed into the pockets of the landlord.

You have got cases in London here. There is the famous Gorringe case.[8] In that case, advantage was taken of the fact that a man had built up a great business. The landlords said in effect, "You have built up a great business here; you cannot take it away; you cannot move to other premises because your trade and goodwill are here; your lease is coming to an end, and we decline to renew it except on the most oppressive terms." The Gorringe case is a very famous case. It was the case of the Duke of Westminster. ["*Oh, oh*," *laughter, and hisses*.] Oh, these dukes [*loud laughter*], how they harass us! [*More laughter*.]

Mr. Gorringe had got a lease of the premises at a few hundred pounds a year ground rent. He built up a great business there as a very able business man. When the end of the lease came he went to the Duke of Westminster, and he said, "Will you renew my lease? I want to carry on my business here." The reply was, "Oh, yes, I will; but only on condition that the few hundreds a year you pay for ground rent shall in the future be £4,000 a year." [*Groans*.] In addition to that, Mr. Gorringe had to pay a fine of £50,000 and to build up huge premises at enormous expense, according to plans approved by the Duke of Westminster. ["*Oh, oh*."]

All I can say is this—if it is confiscation and robbery for us to say to that Duke that being in need of money for public purposes we will take 10 per cent of all you have got for those purposes, what would you call *his* taking nine-tenths from Mr. Gorringe? [*Cheers*.]

These are the cases we have to deal with. Look at all this leasehold system. This system—it is the system I am attacking, not individuals—is not business, it is blackmail. [*Loud cheers*.] I have no doubt some of you have taken the trouble to peruse some of those leases, and they are really worth reading; and I will guarantee that if you circulate copies of some of these building and mining leases at Tariff Reform meetings [*hisses*], and if you can get the workmen at those meetings and the businessmen to read them, they will come away sadder but much wiser men. [*Cheers*.] What are they? Ground rent is a part of it—fines, fees; you are to make no alteration without somebody's consent. Who is that somebody? It is the agent of the landlord. A fee to him. You must submit the plans to the landlord's architect and get his consent. There is a fee to him. There is a fee to the surveyor; and then, of course, you cannot keep the lawyer out. [*Laughter*.] He always comes in. And a fee to him. Well, that is the system, and the landlords come to us in the House of Commons, and they say: "If you go on taxing reversions we will grant no more leases." Is not that horrible? [*Loud laughter*.]

---

[8] According to *The Times* (August 5, 1909, p. 7), there was nothing famous or remarkable about "the Gorringe case." Information was produced that Frederick Gorringe did pay rent of £4,000 a year, but the rent had grown slowly over a period of years; it had not raised abruptly as Lloyd George suggested. In a letter to *The Times* (August 6, 1909, p. 10), Lloyd George replied that his point at Limehouse had been to show the great increase in ground rent, rather than to imply it had happened precipitously or without Mr. Gorringe's agreement.

No more leases, no more kindly landlords [*laughter*] with all their retinue of good fairies—agents, surveyors, lawyers—ready always to receive [*laughter*] ground rents, fees, premiums, fines, reversions. [*Laughter.*] The landlord has threatened us that if we proceed with the Budget he will take his sack [*loud laughter*] clean away from the hopper, and the grain which we are all grinding in order to fill his sack will go into our own. Oh, I cannot believe it. There is a limit even to the wrath of outraged landlords. We must really appease them; we must offer up some sacrifice to them. Suppose we offer the House of Lords to them? [*Loud and prolonged cheers.*]

Now, unless I am wearying you ["*No, no*"], I have just one other land tax to speak to you about. The landlords are receiving £8,000,000 a year by way of royalties. What for? They never deposited the coal in the earth. [*Laughter.*] It was not they who planted those great granite rocks in Wales. Who laid the foundations of the mountains? Was it the landlord? [*Laughter.*] And yet he, by some divine right, demands as his toll—for merely the right for men to risk their lives in hewing those rocks—£8,000,000 a year!

I went down to a coalfield the other day [*cheers*], and they pointed out to me many collieries there. They said: "You see that colliery. The first man who went there spent £750,000 in sinking shafts, in driving mains and levels. He never got coal, and he lost his £750,000. The second man who came spent £100,000—and he failed. The third man came along and he got the coal." What was the landlord doing in the meantime? The first man failed; but the landlord got his royalty, the landlord got his dead rent —and a very good name for it. The second man failed, but the landlord got his royalty.

These capitalists put their money in, and I asked, "When the cash failed, what did the landlord put in?" He simply put in the bailiffs. [*Loud laughter.*] The capitalist risks, at any rate, the whole of his money; the engineer puts his brains in; the miner risks his life. [*Hear, hear.*] Have you been down a coal mine? ["*Yes.*"] I went down one the other day. We sank down into a pit half a mile deep. We then walked underneath the mountain, and we had about three-quarters of a mile of rock and shale above us. The earth seemed to be straining—around us and above us—to crush us in. You could see the pit-props bent and twisted and sundered, their fibres split in resisting the pressure. Sometimes they give way, and then there is mutilation and death. Often a spark ignites, the whole pit is deluged in fire, and the breath of life is scorched out of hundreds of breasts by the consuming flame. In the very next colliery to the one I descended, just a few years ago, 300 people lost their lives in that way; and yet when the Prime Minister and I knock at the doors of these great landlords and say to them, "Here, you know these poor fellows who have been digging up royalties at the risk of their lives, some of them are old, they have survived the perils of their trade, they are broken, they can earn no more. Won't you give something towards keeping them out of the workhouse?" they scowl at us. We say, "Only a ha'penny, just a copper." They retort, "You thieves!" And they turn their dogs on to us, and you can hear their bark every morning. [*Loud laughter and cheers.*] If this is an indication of the view taken by these great landlords of their responsibility to the people who, at the risk of life, create their wealth, then I say their day of reckoning is at hand. [*Loud cheers.*]

The other day, at the great Tory meeting held at the Cannon Street Hotel, they had blazoned on the walls, "We protest against the Budget in the name of democracy [*loud laughter*], liberty, and justice." Where does the democracy come in in this landed system? Where is the liberty in our leasehold system? Where is the seat of justice in all these transactions? I claim that the tax we impose on land is fair, is just, and is moderate. [*Cheers.*] They go on threatening that if we proceed they will cut down their benefactions and discharge labour. What kind of labour? [*A voice: "Hard labour"; laughter.*] What is the labour they are going to choose for dismissal? Are they going to threaten to devastate rural England by feeding and dressing themselves? Are they going to reduce their gamekeepers? Ah, that would be sad! [*Laughter.*] The agricultural labourer and the farmer might then have some part of the game that is fattened by their labour. Also what would happen to you in the season? No week-end shooting with the Duke of Norfolk or anyone. [*Laughter.*] But that is not the kind of labour they are going to cut down. They are going to cut down productive labour—their builders and their gardeners—and they are going to ruin their property so that it shall not be taxed.

The ownership of land is not merely an enjoyment, it is a stewardship. [*Cheers.*] It has been reckoned as such in the past, and if the owners cease to discharge their functions in seeing to the security and defence of the country, in looking after the broken in their villages and in their neighbourhoods, the time will come to reconsider the conditions under which land is held in this country. [*Loud cheers.*] No country, however rich, can permanently afford to have quartered upon its revenue a class which declines to do the duty which it was called upon to perform since the beginning. [*Hear, hear.*]

I do not believe in their threats. They have threatened and menaced like this before, but in good time they have seen it is not to their interest to carry out their futile menaces. They are now protesting against paying their fair share of the taxation of the land, and they are doing so by saying: "You are burdening industry; you are putting burdens upon the people which they cannot bear." Ah! they are not thinking of themselves. [*Laughter.*] Noble souls! [*Laughter.*] It is not the great dukes they are feeling for, it is the market gardener [*laughter*], it is the builder, and it was, until recently, the small holder. [*Hear, hear.*] In every debate in the House of Commons they said: "We are not worrying for ourselves. We can afford it, with our broad acres; but just think of the little man who has only got a few acres"; and we were so much impressed by this tearful appeal that at last we said: "We will leave him out." [*Cheers.*] And I almost expected to see Mr. Pretyman[9] jump over the table when I said it—fall on my neck and embrace me. [*Loud laughter.*] Instead of that, he stiffened up, his face wreathed with anger, and he said, "The Budget is more unjust than ever." [*Laughter and cheers.*]

We are placing burdens on the broadest shoulders. [*Cheers.*] Why should I put burdens on the people? I am one of the children of the people. [*Loud and prolonged cheering, and a voice: "Bravo, David; stand by the people and they will stand by you."*] I was brought up amongst them. I know their trials; and God forbid that I should add one grain of trouble to the anxieties which they bear with such patience and fortitude. [*Cheers.*] When the Prime Minister did me the honour of inviting me to take charge of the National Exchequer [*a voice: "He knew what he was about"; laughter*] at a time of great difficulty, I made up my mind, in framing the Budget which was in front of me, that at any rate no cupboard should be barer [*loud cheers*], no lot should be harder. [*Cheers.*] By that test, I challenge you to judge the Budget. [*Loud and long-continued cheers, during which the right honourable Gentleman resumed his seat. Afterwards the audience rose and sang, "For he's a jolly good fellow."*]

---

[9] Ernest G. Pretyman, Conservative Unionist Member for Chelmsford, Essex.

Stanley Baldwin

"Industrial Peace"[*]

Commons, March 6, 1925

I beg to move to leave out from the word "That" to the end of the Question, and to add instead thereof the words:

> ... this House, while approving the principle of political liberty embodied in the Trade Union (Political Fund) Bill, is of opinion that a measure of such far-reaching importance should not be introduced as a private Member's Bill.

I very much regret the tendency in this Parliament for Friday to become the principal debating day of the week. Old Members of the House have long looked forward to Friday as a day of comparative leisure. When Bills of great importance are brought in on that day, it is perfectly impossible to provide adequate time in which to discuss them. I apologise to my honourable and learned Friend the Member for Argyllshire[1] for being unable to be in the House at the beginning of his speech. I got here as soon as I could after my engagements elsewhere, and I had the pleasure of hearing quite half his speech and the whole of the speech of my honourable and learned Friend the Member for Norwood.[2] I think those speeches themselves clinch the point I made about the absence of time for discussion of matters of such importance, because it was perfectly obvious from the interruptions which punctuated them, particularly the speech of the Seconder, that there will be a great deal to be said controverting the statements which have been made; and there can be no doubt, in the case of a subject of this importance, that before the House can come to a decision, there ought to be far more time for debate than possibly can be found between eleven and four o'clock.

In my own view, the equity of the case made by my honourable and learned Friend is one of great strength. It will probably be supported in

---

[*] This text is from *Parliamentary Debates (Official Report)*, Fifth Series, Vol. CLXXXI, cols. 833–841.

[1] F. A. Macquisten, who had introduced the Trade Union (Political Fund) Bill.
[2] Walter Greaves-Lord, who seconded the motion.

various quarters of the House and indeed as violently opposed. And I suggest that very much of what I said with reference to the Reform Bill a fortnight ago[3] is equally true of a Bill of this magnitude being brought in by private Members on a Friday. But as I do not wish to detain the House longer than I can, I will do my best now to get away from the direct treatment of the points that have been raised in order to give the House the reasons that have induced me to put down the amendment which stands in my name. In some ways this is a very difficult speech for me to make. The matter of the Bill itself digs right into one of the most difficult and fundamental questions in the country today and touches at various points questions which have interested me during the whole of my working life. I have thought so much about them and I feel that I have so much to say about them that my difficulty will be in choosing the little that I can possibly say today and finding words to express clearly to the House what is in my mind.

I often wonder if all the people in this country realise the inevitable changes that are coming over the industrial system in England. People are apt either to get their knowledge of the industrial system from textbooks, which must inevitably be half a generation behind, or from some circumstances familiar to them at a fixed and static point in their lives; whereas as a matter of fact, ever since the industrial system began in this country, it has been not only in a state of evolution but in a state of evolution which, I think, historians in the centuries to come, when they write its history, will acknowledge to be an evolution that has developed at a far more rapid rate than was visible to the people who lived in these times.

I hope the House will bear with me and forgive me if I draw for a few minutes on my own experience, because it so happens that owing to the peculiar circumstances of my own life, I have seen a great deal of this evolution taking place before my own eyes. I worked for many years in an industrial business[4] and had under me a large number—or what was then a large number—of men. And it so happened, owing to the circumstances of this being an old family business with an old and, I venture to say, a very good tradition, that when I was first in business, I was probably working under a system that was already passing. I doubt if its like could have been found in any of the big modern industrial towns of this country, even at that time. It was a place where I knew and had known from childhood every man on the ground, a place where I was able to talk with the men not only about the troubles in the works but troubles at home where strikes and lock-outs were unknown. It was a place where the fathers and grandfathers of the men then working there had worked and where their

[3] In response to Ramsay MacDonald on February 20, Baldwin expressed regret that the House must consider important measures when debate was limited.
[4] The Baldwin family owned important iron works at Stourport and Wilden in Worcestershire.

sons went automatically into the business. It was also a place where nobody ever "got the sack," and where we had a natural sympathy for those who were less concerned in efficiency than is this generation, and where a number of old gentlemen used to spend their days sitting on the handle of a wheelbarrow, smoking their pipes. Oddly enough, it was not an inefficient community. It was the last survivor of that type of works and ultimately became swallowed up in one of those great combinations towards which the industries of today are tending.

I remember very well the impact of the outside world that came on us which showed how industry was changing in this country. Nothing had interrupted the even tenor of our ways for many years, until one day there came a great strike in the coalfields.[5] It was one of the earlier strikes, and it became a national strike. We tried to carry on as long as we could, but of course it became more and more difficult to carry on, and gradually furnace after furnace was damped down; the chimneys ceased to smoke, and about 1,000 men who had no interest in the dispute that was going on were thrown out of work through no fault of their own, at a time when there was no unemployment benefit. I confess that that event set me thinking very hard. It seemed to me at that time a monstrous injustice to these men, because I looked upon them as my own family, and it hit me very hard—I would not have mentioned this only it got into the press two or three years ago—and I made an allowance to them—not a large one, but something—for six weeks to carry them along, because I felt that they were being so unfairly treated.[6]

But there was more in it really than that. There was no conscious unfair treatment of these men by the miners. It simply was that we were gradually passing into a new state of industry when the small firms and the small industries were being squeezed out. Business was all tending towards great amalgamations on the one side of employers and on the other side of the men, and when we came in any form between these two forces, God help those who stood outside! That has been the tendency of industry. There is nothing that could change it, because it comes largely, if not principally, from that driving force of necessity in the world which makes people combine together for competition and for the protection they need against that competition.

Those two forces with which we have to reckon are enormously strong, and they are the two forces in this country to which now to a great extent, and it will be a greater extent in the future, we are committed. We have to see what wise statesmanship can do to steer the country through this time of evolution until we can get to the next stage of our industrial civilisation.

[5] The coal strike that began March 1, 1912, involved about 850,000 miners; ten days later an estimated 1,300,000 workers in other industries had been made idle.

[6] On March 20, Baldwin announced a weekly wage allowance for all employees of his firm "thrown out of employment through no fault of their own."

It is obvious from what I have said that the organisations of both masters and men—or, if you like, the more modern phrase invented by economists, who always invent beastly words, "employers and employés"—these organisations throw an immense responsibility on the representatives themselves and on those who elect them. And although big men have been thrown up on both sides, there are a great many on both sides who have not got the requisite qualities of head and heart for business. There are many men with good heads and no hearts, and many men with good hearts and no heads.

What the country wants today from the men who sit on this side of the House and on that is to exercise the same care as the men who have to conduct those great organisations from inside. I should like to try to clear our minds of cant on this subject and recognise that the growth of these associations is not necessarily a bad thing in itself, but that whatever associations may call themselves, it is the same human nature in both and exactly the same problems have to be met, although we hear a good deal more of some of those problems than of others. Now, if you look at an employers' organisation for a moment—and we will assume that it has come into being to protect the industry in the world market—we cannot lose sight of the fact that in that organisation, just as much as in the men's organisation, the mere fact of organising involves a certain amount of sacrifice of personal liberty. That cannot be helped. Everybody knows that perfectly well, both employers and employés.

To a certain extent both these organisations must on one side be uneconomic. A trade union is uneconomic in one sense of the word when it restricts output, and when it levels down the work to a lower level. It is an association for the protection of the weaker men, which has often proved uneconomic. Exactly the same thing happens in the employers' organisation. Primarily, it is protective, but in effect it is very often uneconomic, because it keeps in existence works which, if left to the process of competition, would be squeezed out, and whose prolonged existence is really only a weakness to the country. It has also another very curious effect, not at all dissimilar from that of the trade-union reaction, which shows that both those organisations are instinct with English traditions. The workmen's organisation is formed to see that under the conditions a workman cannot get his living in a particular trade unless he belong to that union. An employers' organisation is formed in that particular trade for the protection of the trade, and it has the result of effectively preventing any new man starting in that trade.

In this great problem which is facing the country in years to come, it may be from one side or the other that disaster may come, but surely it shows that the only progress that can be obtained in this country is by those two bodies of men—so similar in their strength and so similar in their weaknesses—learning to understand each other and not to fight each other.

It is perfectly true—every point raised by my honourable and learned Friends is true—that trade unionism has its weak spots. We are primarily discussing trade unions, and that is why I shall content myself to speak about trade unions only. It is perfectly true that my honourable and learned Friends have laid their finger on three points which trade unionists themselves know are their weak spots. That can be seen by the interruptions that came from the Labour benches. Those three points are the question whether in all cases the subject of the levy is treated fairly, the question of the ballot, and the question of bookkeeping. To my mind, it is impossible to dissociate one of these questions from the other, and they really all hang together. The whole tradition of our country has been to let Englishmen develop their own associations in their own way, and with that I agree. But there are limits to that.

I spoke some time ago—and I spoke with a purpose—about the recognition of the change in the industrial situation in those works with which I was connected, when for the first time what was done in the way of organising the coal strike suddenly came and hit thousands of men who had nothing to do with it and had no direct interest in it. As these associations come along and become more powerful, on whichever side they are, there may come a time when not only they may injure their own members—about which probably there would be a good deal of argument—but when they may directly injure the State. It is at that moment any Government should say that whatever freedom and latitude in that field may be left to any kind of association in this free country, nothing shall be done which shall injure the State, which is the concern of all of us and far greater than all of us or of our interests.

I have not very much more to say. I have just tried to put, as clearly as I can in a few words, my conviction that we are moving forward rapidly from an old state of industry into a newer, and the question is: What is that newer going to be? No man, of course, can say what form evolution is taking. Of this, however, I am quite sure, that whatever form we may see, possibly within this generation, or, at any rate, in the time of the next generation, it has got to be a form of pretty close partnership, however that is going to be arrived at. And it will not be a partnership the terms of which will be laid down—at any rate not yet—in Acts of Parliament, or from this Party or that. It has got to be a partnership of men who understand their own work, and it is little help that they can get really either from politicians or from intellectuals. There are few men fitted to judge, to settle, and to arrange the problem that distracts the country today between employers and employed. There are few men qualified to intervene who have not themselves been right through the mill. I always want to see at the head of these organisations on both sides men who have been right through the mill, who themselves know exactly the points where the shoe pinches, who know exactly what can be conceded and what cannot, who can make their reasons plain; and I hope that we shall always find such men trying to steer their respective ships side by side, instead of making for head-on collisions.

Having said what I have said about that, what am I to say about the attitude of the Party of which I have the honour to be the head? I do not know whether the House will forgive me if I speak for a minute or two on a rather personal note. For two years past in the face of great difficulties, perhaps greater than many were aware of, I have striven to consolidate and to breathe a living force into my great Party.[7] Friends of mine who have done me the honour to read my speeches during that time have seen pretty clearly, however ill they may have been expressed, the ideals at which I have been aiming. I spoke on that subject again last night at Birmingham,[8] and I shall continue to speak on it as long as I am where I am. We find ourselves, after these two years in power, in possession of perhaps the greatest majority our Party has ever had, and with the general assent of the country. Now, how did we get there? It was not by promising to bring this Bill in; it was because, rightly or wrongly, we succeeded in creating an impression throughout the country that we stood for stable Government and for peace in the country between all classes of the community.

Those were the principles for which we fought; those were the principles on which we won; and our victory was not won entirely by the votes of our own Party, splendidly as they fought. I should think that the number of Liberals who voted for us at the last election ran into six figures, and I should think that we probably polled more Labour votes than were polled on the other side. That being so, what should our course be at the beginning of a new Parliament? I have not myself the slightest doubt. Last year the Leader of the Labour Party,[9] when he was Prime Minister, suspended what had been settled by the previous Government, and that was further progress for the time being on the scheme of Singapore. He did it on the ground that it was a gesture for peace, and he hoped that it would be taken as such by all the countries in the world. He hoped that a gesture of that kind might play its part in leading to what we all wish to see, that is, a reduction in the world's armaments.

I want my Party today to make a gesture to the country of a similar nature, and to say to them: "We have our majority; we believe in the justice of this Bill which has been brought in today; but we are going to withdraw our hand and we are not going to push our political advantage

---

[7] Baldwin brought into his second Government in 1924 such figures as Austen Chamberlain, Arthur Balfour, and Winston Churchill. His appointments served to forge a united Conservative Party and politically to isolate Lloyd George. In fact, Lloyd George never again held political office.

[8] The speech stressed the roles of labor and industry in promoting economic stability; it was reported in *The Times*, March 6, 1925, p. 10.

[9] Ramsay MacDonald.

home at a moment like this. Suspicion which has prevented stability in Europe is the one poison that is preventing stability at home, and we offer the country today this: we, at any rate, are not going to fire the first shot. We stand for peace. We stand for the removal of suspicion in the country. We want to create an atmosphere, a new atmosphere in a new Parliament for a new age, in which the people can come together. We abandon what we have laid our hands to. We know we may be called cowards for doing it. We know we may be told that we have gone back on our principles. But we believe we know what at this moment the country wants, and we believe it is for us in our strength to do what no other Party can do at this moment, and to say that we at any rate stand for peace."

I know—I am as confident as I can be of anything—that that will be the feeling of all those who sit behind me, and that they will accept the amendment which I have put down in the spirit in which I have moved it. And I have equal confidence in my fellow-countrymen throughout the whole of Great Britain. Although I know that there are those who work for different ends from most of us in this House, yet there are many in all ranks and all parties who will re-echo my prayer:

Give peace in our time, O Lord.[10]

---

[10] From "The Order for Daily Evening Prayer," *Book of Common Prayer*.

Hugh Gaitskell

"Labour Politics and Democratic Socialism"[*]

Blackpool, November 28, 1959

It is not the purpose of this debate to reach final conclusions. We are not discussing any resolution. The Executive is putting forward no proposals. So this afternoon I speak for myself alone.

Since the election I have received many letters, read many articles and listened to many speeches, all concerned with why we lost the election and what we should do now. The vast majority have been constructive and sincere, reflecting the wonderful spirit in which we fought the election itself. To be sure, some explanations were rather remote, like that of the lady who said that it was all because twenty-five years ago we rejected the Douglas social-credit theory[1] owing to the sinister influence of the present Leader of the Party, or that of the man who put it down to our holding meetings on Sundays. Some blamed not the Labour Party but the electorate —"those illiterate women and ignorant men," as one man put it. This reminds me of Oscar Wilde's remark, "The play was a great success but the audience was a failure."

Some put it down wholly to Tory propaganda—including Mr. Hurry and the Institute of Directors.[2] Tory propaganda was undoubtedly exceedingly effective, particularly in the year or two before the election. There was launched against us the most expensive and professional political propaganda campaign ever carried out in Britain. And since it proved highly profitable to those who put up the money, we may be sure they will do it again. The lesson is that we must revise altogether our ideas of how much money we should be raising and spending for posters and other

[*] The text is from *Report of the Fifty-Eighth Annual Conference of the Labour Party* (London, 1960) pp. 105–114.

[1] In the 1930's Major C. H. Douglas advanced a scheme to expand the money supply by issuing paper money that would depreciate weekly.

[2] A firm of management consultants who surveyed political attitudes; the survey was thought to be financed by firms threatened with nationalisation.

forms of propaganda. Twenty thousand pounds, all we could afford for a little poster campaign, is utterly inadequate against the hundreds of thousands if not millions spent by the Tories.

Our programme has been criticised for not being sufficiently idealistic. I do not agree. Is it not idealistic to propose to help old people in hardship, to throw open the doors of educational opportunity, to speed up the granting of political freedom and economic help to colonial peoples, to fight racial injustice?

It has been said that we made too many promises and did not explain how our plans were to be paid for. Certainly this was the main Tory counter-attack against us. But such an argument is inevitable in any election we fight. For the Labour Party is almost certain to want to spend more than the Tories on the social services. We shall always give them a higher priority than reducing taxes on the rich.

For my part, I am convinced that we made no promise that we could not have carried out on the condition clearly expressed—that this country achieved what is well within its capacity, namely, a steady increase in output year by year. And although this was not simple to put across, we made a sustained effort to do so.

No. I must say flatly that I believe our programme was excellent—well thought out, moderate, practical, and yet fully in tune with our Socialist convictions. It produced great enthusiasm amongst our supporters and so, incidentally, disproved the idea that to arouse their spirits we must always adopt an extremist line. I have seen no evidence to suggest that had we done this, we would have won more votes.

I hope we shall not now abandon this programme and start immediately to construct a new one. Such a course would be far too early. We can look at it again in two or three years' time when most of it will probably be out of date. Meanwhile, let us take a holiday from producing streams of new, detailed policy pamphlets. There are other and more important jobs to be done.

There was much less criticism in this election of our organisation. There may have been weak spots here and there, but everybody agrees that on balance it was far better than in 1955.

Nor have I heard much grumbling about our publicity. A special tribute is due to our General Secretary[3] for his masterly handling of the Press; and I should like to hand another bouquet to that sometimes much abused paper, the *Daily Herald*, for the support they gave us. There have been many friendly references to our television programmes. Some say they were too smooth, too slick, too polished. But had they been rough, clumsy, and dull we would have heard much more about it.

Indeed, in all the post-election discussions, our campaign has come in for little criticism. No doubt there were mistakes—I could certainly mention a

[3] Morgan Phillips.

few—but most people agree that the organisation was better, that the publicity was well handled, that the central direction was clear and effective, that the programme was good, and above all, that the spirit and response of our workers and supporters was magnificent. If these facts made the result a greater shock and a more bitter disappointment, as indeed they did, are they not also the silver lining to the dark cloud of defeat? They are the foundation on which we may build our future victory.

Why, then, despite these favourable factors, did we lose? One common answer is that the campaign began too late. Now if this means that until the election was announced the National Executive, the Parliamentary Party, the officials, the agents, the Party members, and all of us were all hibernating, it is nonsense.

Have we forgotten the immense effort made since 1955 to improve our organisation, the long and painstaking study and discussion on the policy documents? The striking improvement in our publications, . . . including the best propaganda pamphlet ever produced by a political party—*The Future Labour Offers You?* No. It is just not true that we did little before the election, though it is true that during it we were able to take effective advantage of the far greater publicity opportunities which the election made available to us.

If, on the other hand, to say that "the campaign began too late" means that the election was to a large extent decided before it was fought, I agree that this was probably so; but there is nothing unusual about that. Most elections are largely decided before they are fought. One must not go too far, however. I believe that on this occasion we made a very real impact during the campaign. Indeed, it seemed for a time as though that impact would carry us forward to victory. But it was not to be. I conclude, then, that it was not bad organisation or a poor programme or too late a start which lost us the election. I believe that we must look for more fundamental influences. And the basic point to remember is this: that we cannot treat the 1959 election result on its own. The stark fact is that this is the third successive General Election we have lost and the fourth in which we have lost seats. This is a grave development which we are bound to take very seriously indeed. For an Opposition to suffer three successive defeats is almost unprecedented in British political history. In the past the pendulum has always swung against the Party in power after one or at most two periods of office. It has not been swinging in these last few years. And this trend is all the more serious for a Party like ours which assumed, and quite naturally, that while there would be ups and downs in the long struggle for power, nevertheless over the years our advance would be inexorable. This is no longer happening today. That is why there is no room at all for complacency.

What has caused this adverse trend? It is, I believe, a significant change in the economic and social background of politics. First, there is the changing character of the labour force. There are fewer miners, more engineers; fewer farmworkers, more shop assistants; fewer manual workers, more clerical workers; fewer railwaymen, more research workers. Everywhere the balance is shifting away from heavy physical work and towards machine maintenance, distribution, and staff jobs. Go to any large works in the country, as I happened to have done a good deal in the last couple of years, and you will find exactly the same story. It is an inevitable result of technological advance. But it means that the typical worker of the future is more likely to be a skilled man in a white overall watching dials in a bright new modern factory than a badly paid cotton operative working in a dark and obsolete nineteenth-century mill. The second great change is the absence of serious unemployment or even the fear of it. True, we had a minor recession and there are still parts of the country which have considerable unemployment. But taking the country as a whole, the contrast with 1939 and still more with 1932 is staggering. Today we talk of unemployment as being serious if it rises above 2 per cent. In the interwar years it was never less than 10 per cent. It permeated the lives of the British people. Serious slumps at more or less regular intervals were a normal part of our existence—and, incidentally, an important cause of the swing of the political pendulum. They were a constant reminder that a system which permitted such misery and waste was a failure; they were part of the practical basis of our Socialist propaganda.

Of course, we not only profoundly welcome the change to full employment but we take great pride in the part we played in bringing it about. For the change would never have occurred but for the insistence by the British Labour Movement that a Government with the will and the power could maintain full employment and that, therefore, the power of the State over the economy must be increased. This is exactly what has happened. But it may be asked, is not this only a temporary phenomenon? Is not another slump just round the corner? This is not an easy question to answer categorically. I can only say that in my opinion capitalism has significantly changed, largely as a result of our own efforts. The capacity of the Government to plan the economy has undeniably substantially increased; the Budget absorbs a quarter of the national income; public investment is now nearly half of total investment; most, if not all, of the basic industries are in public hands. All these are vital changes. They may still not have gone far enough. But in my opinion, they have gone sufficiently far to make it most unlikely that we shall ever again suffer from the great booms and slumps of the prewar period. Minor recessions we shall most certainly have—yes, and for all their boasts the Tories have certainly not achieved the combination of full employment, swift industrial expansion, and price stability at the same time. Any advance under the Tories will surely be both slower and less regular than it need be. Nevertheless, in my judgment—and I must give it—we can probably expect a further improvement in living conditions of the same kind as that experienced in recent years.

To full employment we can add the welfare state—another of our achievements of which we are proud and which has also had profound consequences. We point out rightly how much remains to be done. Indeed, we fought the election to a very large extent on the improvements which are so urgently needed. But this is not to deny that for the majority at least, the protection of the welfare state has already made a profound difference. Unfortunately, gratitude is not a very reliable political asset.

Moreover, the recent improvements in living standards have been of a special kind. There has been a particularly notable increase in comforts, pleasures, and conveniences in the home. Television, whether we like it or not, has transformed the leisure hours of the vast majority of our fellow-citizens. Washing machines, refrigerators, modern cookers have made women's lives a good deal easier. And incidentally, I fancy that our failure this time was largely a failure to win support from the women—and I may say that I wrote this before reading this morning's *Daily Herald's* leading article. I hope that in our deliberations we shall pay special attention to this. It is no use dismissing the problem, as some do, by saying that women are too snobbish or too politically apathetic. They are voters and count just as much as men.

Holidays show another profound change. It is still true that many people do not go away from home. But vastly more do. It is inconceivable that twenty years ago *Reynolds News* could have organised three-week tours for its readers in the United States at £200 per person and in the Soviet Union at £100 per person. Most obviously, perhaps, there is the increase in the cars. Not only have many more got them but many more are expecting to get them. It is a safe bet that before the next General Election there may well be two million more car owners than there are today. I know there will be difficult problems in knowing where they are to go and where they are to be parked, but, in my judgment, that will not affect the purchasing of cars.

Again and again, especially talking to candidates in the Midlands and the South, I have heard the same story of the relatively prosperous younger married couples who, having moved from older houses in solid Labour areas to new attractive housing estates, usually built by Labour councils, then lost their Labour loyalty and voted Conservative. And indeed, it is hard otherwise to explain the fact that in England we did not win a single seat where there is a new town and that we gained much less than we expected in those constituencies where huge new housing estates had been built.

In short, the changing character of labour, full employment, new housing, the new way of living based on the telly, the frig., the car, and the glossy magazines—all these have had their effect on our political strength. Of course, one can exaggerate the importance of the effect, but when we are talking, as we must, of swings of 1, 2, 3, and 5 per cent, even a small change can be of decisive importance.

It is easier to describe these changes and their political effects than to prescribe the remedy. It may be this which has led to what I can only describe as defeatism in some quarters. But defeatism is as bad as complacency. We should firmly reject the idea, even the whisper of it, that perhaps we should be content to remain in permanent Opposition until somehow in twenty or thirty years' time the country comes to its senses and condescends to elect us to power. It is our job to get back into power as quickly as possible so that we may do the things in which we believe for our country and the world. If we lose sight of this we condemn our movement to decay and decrepitude. The British people will not be interested in a party which is no longer concerned with power. They do not take kindly, in politics or war, to those who have given up the will to battle.

What then is the answer? Some rather desperate remedies have been proposed. It has been suggested that we should make a pact with the Liberals. We can toss that one out of the window straight away. It is not just a matter of being prejudiced against it—though most of us probably are. There is no evidence that it would do us any good. No one knows how far the Liberals take votes from us or from the Tories—whether it is to our advantage or disadvantage for Liberal candidates to intervene. Nevertheless, we must expect the Liberals in the next few years to make a strong drive to win votes at our expense. They will probably go for the young voters and the social groups of whom I have just been speaking. We have to be sure we beat them to it. For if they were ever to look like becoming a serious political force again, the process might easily gain momentum. We must not allow it to start.

It has also been proposed that we should change our name. I have had several letters to this effect from people who are alarmed by the snobbery of some of the new suburban voters. We should toss this out of the window, too. Our name is one which evokes the loyalty of many millions of British people. And I doubt if the snobs would be much influenced if we did change it.

There is a third desperate suggestion which also goes out of the window right away—the proposal that the Labour Party should break with the unions. We have heard it before. And from the same quarter we've heard the suggestion that the unions in their own interests should break with the Labour Party. It's not a friendly quarter. And the advice is not disinterested. I have always looked upon the Trades Union Congress and the Labour Party as part of the same great Labour Movement and our close integration as one of our greatest strengths. I see no reason to change my mind. I hope our trade-union friends feel likewise.

Of course, the fact that we are so closely bound together means that what one partner does must be of interest and concern to the other. But surely this argues not for looser ties but for a better co-ordination of our activities. No doubt unofficial strikes have damaged the prospects of the Labour Party as well as the popularity of the trade unions—despite the fact that the trade-union leaders usually condemn these strikes in the strongest terms. There is no doubt too that a most unfair and distorted picture of the trade-union movement is now being deliberately created in the public mind. But these are matters of which the unions themselves are well aware. We can safely leave it to them to take the necessary action.

Now let me be more positive. I do not believe that the social and economic changes of which I have spoken were bound to react against us. They did so simply because we did not take them sufficiently into account. We assumed too readily an instinctive loyalty to Labour which was all the time slowly, gradually being eroded. We failed to appreciate that we should have to make a special conscious effort to win over these younger, newer, social groups.

Sometimes I think we seem to do the opposite and give the idea that clerical, administrative, and other white-collar classes of workers, whose numbers are growing, are not welcome in our ranks. This is a pity and it creates a false impression. If you look at the Parties in the House of Commons today you will see that ours is a far better cross-section of the community than the Tories, who are still overwhelmingly drawn from a single social class. Yet somehow we let the Tories get away with the monstrous falsehood that *we* are a class Party and they are *not*. We must surely now attend to this.

We should put more stress on the issues which specially appeal to younger people. I believe these include the cause of Colonial freedom; the protection of the individual against ham-handed and arrogant bureaucracy; resistance to the squalid commercialism which threatens to despoil our countryside and disfigure our cities; a dislike of bumbledom in all forms; a greater concern for sport and the arts.

It is sometimes said that we appeal too much on behalf of the underdog. True, the underdogs are fewer than they used to be, and consequently they bring us fewer votes. But I cannot accept that we should cease to appeal on their behalf. To me that would be a betrayal of Socialist principles. And I believe too that young people still respond more to idealism than to purely materialistic and selfish causes.

More important still is the way in which we present ourselves and what we stand for. We have to show them that we are a modern, mid-twentieth-century Party looking to the future, not to the past. We must have, for example, modern-looking Party premises situated in the right place—in the centre of the main street, newly painted and decorated brightly, attractive to the public of 1959. They're not all like that today!

We should welcome and encourage newcomers. We should look on them—and again I agree with the man who said this morning that we need not assume that the young people when they come in are necessarily on our side—as friends to be won over, not intruders to be frozen out. Nor should we start by imposing too much heavy political doctrine, particularly on young people. If we get them interested in the general idea, the detail will follow later. The Tory Youth Organisation is largely a social affair. We cannot afford nor would we desire to emulate it. But there is a sound point behind it—that you often win people over more effectively by an indirect approach.

Above all, our object must be to broaden our base, to be in touch always with ordinary people, to avoid becoming small cliques of isolated, doctrine-ridden fanatics, out of touch with the mainstream of social life in our time. We should be missionaries, not monks, a mass Party, not a conspiratorial group.

There are also some handicaps which we must try and eliminate. For example, we still sometimes give an appearance of disunity. This may seem strange, since in fact we were more united than for many years past. But between elections, at least, we do argue with each other a great deal in public, and this tends to give the impression that we're always at sixes and sevens, incapable of ever speaking with a single voice or of managing our own affairs properly, let alone those of the nation. Is it a forlorn hope to suggest that we might all spend more of our time putting over our policy and less in pointing out why we think it should be a different policy? How wonderful it would be if we could always be as united as we generally were in the last General Election.

Another handicap, I'm afraid, was the unpopularity of certain Labour local councils. I do not want to be too critical. I am sure that the public often doesn't know the true circumstances. But the criticisms are too widespread to be ignored, whether it be of the attitude to council-house tenants or of excessively rigid standing orders or, more generally, of apparently arbitrary and intolerant behaviour. It may be largely a matter of public relations. But I think we should examine the question in a friendly way to see if between us we can't make some improvement.

Now I turn to public ownership and nationalisation. There seems no doubt that if we are to accept the majority view of those who fought this election, nationalisation—on balance—lost us votes. No one suggests it was the main cause, but anything which appears to have swung votes against us deserves careful and, as far as possible, dispassionate study.

Why was nationalisation apparently a vote loser? For two reasons, I believe. First, some of the existing nationalised industries are unpopular. This unpopularity is very largely due to circumstances which have nothing to do with nationalisation. London buses are overcrowded and slow—not because the Transport Commission is inefficient but because of the state of

London traffic and the way the Tory Government have neglected it all these years. The backward conditions of the railways are not really the result of bad management but of inadequate investment in the past which has left behind a gigantic problem of modernisation. Coal costs more not because the Coal Board or the miners have done badly, but because in the postwar world we have to pay miners a decent wage to induce them to work in the pits. But all these things are blamed on nationalisation. Tory propaganda has gone all out to achieve precisely this result. Every weakness or grumble is magnified in the Tory press; every success is minimised or ignored.

We must make an even bigger effort to counter this pernicious propaganda. Do not blame it all on to us. Here is a small collection of the pamphlets, leaflets, and other propaganda material put out from Transport House in the last few years. I wonder how many delegates at this Conference could say they had read it all, let alone tried to put it across. But there is something else to be said. The nationalised Boards themselves could help—not for us but in their own interests, for the sake of goodwill with their customers and better morale among their employees. If a private industry had been subjected to a fraction of the hostile propaganda they have had to endure, it would have fought back with violent intensity. This is what the Boards should do. They should stand up for themselves far more.

I am not saying that the trouble is entirely one of public relations; that everything is otherwise perfect. Let us by all means look at the question of structure and accountability again. But let us not give aid and comfort to the Tories by treating the nationalised industries and the workers in them as scapegoats for everything that goes wrong.

Above all we must face the fact that nationalisation as such will not be positively popular until *all* these industries are clearly seen to be performing at least as well as the best firms in the private sector. When this goal has been achieved, then we can face the country with complete confidence on this issue. Our fellow-citizens are more likely to judge the value of the public sector by their experience of it than from theoretical arguments in speeches or Labour Party pamphlets.

The second reason, I believe, why nationalisation was a vote loser was the confusion in the public mind about our future policy. This confusion was again in large part the result of gross misrepresentation. What the voters disliked was not so much our policy but what they came to think our policy was. Our moderate, practical proposals were distorted out of all recognition by our opponents. Thousands and perhaps millions of voters were induced to think that we intended to nationalise any and every private firm, however efficiently it might be operating—a chemical factory in this constituency, an engineering works in that, a motor-car firm in the other. They were led to suppose we were going to take over everything indiscriminately, right and left, when we got back into power, simply out of a doctrinaire belief in public ownership. There was, of course, no relationship between these fears and the actual content of our programme.

But although much of the misunderstanding was due to the campaign of the Institute of Directors and the Tory Central Office, perhaps we gave them some help. Perhaps we were not sufficiently precise about what we were going to do or why we wanted to do it. This brings me to the central problem of future policy on public ownership.

I agree with neither of the two extreme points of view. Some suggest that we should accept for all time the present frontiers between the public and private sectors. We cannot do that. It would imply that everything works so perfectly in the private sector that we shall never want to intervene. But things are far from perfect in the private sector. One industry after another today is begging for Government financial help. Recently there have been critical reports by independent investigators—on the machine-tool, ship-building, shipping, and other industries. I am not saying that we shall want to nationalise all these industries, but I do mean that we can't conceivably commit ourselves to the view that no future Labour Government will ever want to do anything about them. The extension of the public sector will not necessarily take the form of what people call old-style nationalisation—that is, the setting up of huge State monopolies by Act of Parliament. We had better recognise that though large-scale organisations often have technical and economic advantages, they have human and psychological weaknesses; and that though public monopolies are much better than private ones, all monopolies—let us face it—have their drawbacks. We may not be far from the frontier of this kind of giant State monopoly. We may be more concerned in the future with other forms of public ownership—and there are many other forms: public competitive enterprises, State factories in development areas, a greater share of the total trading going to the co-operative movement. I would love to see that happen, and it would make a profound difference to the outlook of the ordinary man on public and private enterprise. All these things are possible, and I hope we shall pursue that path. But I cannot agree that we have reached the frontier of public ownership as a whole.

At the same time I disagree equally with the other extreme view that nationalisation or even public ownership is the be-all and end-all, the ultimate first principle and aim of Socialism. I believe that this view arises from a complete confusion about the fundamental meaning of Socialism and, in particular, a misunderstanding about ends and means.

So I want now to set out what I, at any rate, regard as the basic first principles of British Democratic Socialism. Of course, we have tried to do this on many occasions. I had a go at it in a very few sentences when I last spoke in this hall at the T.U.C.[4] just at the beginning of the General

[4] Trades Union Congress.

Election campaign. But that was off the cuff. I thought that this afternoon I had better be a little more formal.

So I say, first, we express what G. D. H. Cole[5] once called "a broad, human movement on behalf of the bottom dog"—on behalf of all those who are oppressed or in need or hardship. Thus, at home, our first concern is naturally for the less fortunate—the old, the sick, the widowed, the unemployed, the disabled, and the badly housed; abroad, it is reflected in a deep concern for the well-being of peoples much, much poorer than ourselves, badly in need of help.

Secondly, we believe in social justice, in an equitable distribution of wealth and income. We do not demand exact equality. But we do demand that the differences should be related not to the accident of birth and inheritance but on how much of effort, skill, and creative energy we each contribute to the common good.

Thirdly, we believe in a "classless society"—a society without the snobbery, the privilege, the restrictive social barriers which are still far too prevalent in Britain today.

Fourthly, we believe in the fundamental equality of all races and of all peoples, and in the building of an international order which will enable them to live together in peace. We detest equally the arrogant postures of white supremacy and the exercise of unbridled power by large nations over small ones. Suez, Hungary, Hola[6] are words of infamy to us. For we believe quite simply in the brotherhood of man.

Fifthly, British Socialism has always contained an essential element of personal idealism—the belief that the pursuit of material satisfaction by itself without spiritual values is empty and barren and that our relations with one another should be based not on ruthless self-regarding rivalry but on fellowship and co-operation. It is hard to convey this idea in plain language. But we can, surely, agree that without it our Socialism would be the poorer.

Sixthly, we believe that the public interest must come before private interest. We are not opposed to individuals seeking to do the best they can for themselves and their families. But we insist that the pursuit of private gain should not take precedence over the public good. The idea of public planning in the interests of the whole community both for economic and social reasons is certainly a basic principle of Socialism.

Finally, we believe that these things must be achieved with and through freedom and democratic self-government. We intend to maintain this for ourselves and, so far as lies within our power, to help others to enjoy it, too.

These, I believe, constitute the essential first principles of our Democratic

---

[5] Economic historian and guild socialist.

[6] At Hola detention camp in Kenya on March 3, 1959, eleven Mau detainees were beaten to death. Labourites in Commons proposed a motion of censure on the Government for failing to initiate an inquiry into the incident.

Socialism. Everything else—nationalisation, controls, our particular policies on housing or education or old age pensions—constitute only the means to realising these principles in practise. For example, the extension of public ownership may help towards a more equitable distribution of wealth by securing for the community profits and capital gains which would otherwise accrue to wealthy private shareholders. It was for this reason that we decided that the State and other public agencies should be free to hold shares in private industry. But public ownership is not itself the ultimate objective; it is only a means of achieving the objective.

Again, we hold that in order to plan and control the working of the economy, to secure full employment, steady expansion, and rising productivity, there must be an important public sector. To use Mr. Bevan's[7] words, we need to control "the commanding heights of economic power." Though, of course, just how far we have to go at any one time is a matter for discussion. But here again the public sector is a means, not an end.

We have not only ourselves to understand just why public ownership and nationalisation are means to our ultimate ends, but also to explain this convincingly to the electorate. There is no denying the difficulty—and the danger of misrepresentation. We say, for instance, that we need a large public sector to plan for full employment and expanding productivity. But if there is already something like full employment and reasonable prosperity, it is not so easy to convince people that we must nevertheless, on these particular grounds, extend public ownership still further. We say we want public ownership because we think these industries should be made accountable to the people. But the man in the street says, "How is that going to affect me in my home?" and "What about accountability of the existing nationalised industries?"

Again, more public ownership does make in the long run for greater equality in the distribution of wealth. But it is in the long run only.

Yet we must be sure when we adopt a particular policy that it is within our capacity to persuade enough of our fellow-citizens not only that we are right, but that what we intend to do is relevant to their needs and aspirations. And I need hardly say that in this matter the attitude of the workers in the industries concerned is of special importance.

Nor must we forget in all this that public ownership and nationalisation are not the only means to our ends. In the postwar Labour Government we found and sharpened many other weapons for controlling the economy and altering the distribution of wealth.

I conclude that we should make two things clear to the country. First, that we have no intention of abandoning public ownership and accepting for all time the present frontiers of the public sector. Secondly, that we regard public ownership not as an end in itself but as a means—and not

[7] Aneurin Bevan, member for Ebbw Vale and Deputy Leader of the Parliamentary Labour Party.

necessarily the only or most important one to certain ends—such as full employment, greater equality, and higher productivity. We do not aim to nationalise every private firm or to create an endless series of State monopolies. While we shall certainly wish to extend social ownership in particular directions, as circumstances warrant, our goal is not 100 per cent State ownership. Our goal is a society in which Socialist ideals are realised. Our job is to move towards this as fast as we can. The pace at which we can go depends on how quickly we can persuade our fellow-citizens to back us. They will only do this if we pay proper attention to the kind of people they are and the kind of things they want.

As I have already said, I am against starting on a new election programme now. But I do think that we should clear our minds on these fundamental issues and then try to express in the most simple and comprehensive fashion what we stand for in the world today.

The only official document which embodies such an attempt is the Party Constitution, written over forty years ago. It seems to me that this needs to be brought up to date. For instance, can we really be satisfied today with a statement of fundamentals which makes no mention at all of Colonial freedom, race relations, disarmament, full employment, or planning? The only specific reference to our objectives at home is the well-known phrase:

> To secure for the workers by hand or by brain the full fruits of their industry and the most equitable distribution thereof that may be possible, upon the basis of the common ownership of the means of production, distribution, and exchange. . . .

Standing as it does on its own, this cannot possibly be regarded as adequate. It lays us open to continual misrepresentation. It implies that common ownership is an end, whereas in fact it is a means. It implies that the only precise object we have is nationalisation, whereas in fact we have many other Socialist objectives. It implies that we propose to nationalise everything. But do we? Everything?—the whole of light industry, the whole of agriculture, all the shops—every little pub and garage? Of course not. We have long ago come to accept, we know very well, for the foreseeable future, at least in some form, a mixed economy; in which case, if this is our view—as I believe it to be of 90 per cent of the Labour Party—had we better not say so instead of going out of our way to court misrepresentation?

I knew I should say some things that would not be palatable to everybody this afternoon. It would have been very nice in some ways to have made a speech which contained so many bromides and so little controversial matter that it was certain of a very large number of cheers. But I do not conceive that to be my duty today. I would rather forego the cheers now in the hope that we shall get more votes later on. I do not want deliberately to advise a course of action which could only involve me in leading this Party to another electoral defeat, and I will not do so.

I am sure that the Webbs[8] and Arthur Henderson,[9] who largely drafted this Constitution, would have been amazed and horrified had they thought that their words were to be treated as sacrosanct forty years later in utterly changed conditions. Let us remember that we are a Party of the future, not of the past; that we must appeal to the young as well as the old —young people who have very little reverence for the past. It is no use waving the banners of a bygone age. The first need now, in the words of one who has already been quoted today, that great Socialist teacher R. H. Tawney,[10] "is to treat sanctified formulae with judicious irreverence and to start by deciding what precisely is the end in view."

I hope, then, that the Executive will during the next few months try to work out and state the fundamental principles of British Democratic Socialism as we see and as we feel it today, in 1959, not 1918, and I hope that in due course another Conference will endorse what they propose. I hope that the Executive in doing this work will tilt the balance to the future rather than the past, so that what is decided will be and will seem relevant in 1970—even, if you like, in 1980. After that we can have another look at it again.

It is not the only thing the National Executive Committee have to do. I have already mentioned finance and it is going to be a major problem. I have mentioned that the local council organisation will, of course, need looking into. I hope, incidentally, that we shall be able to bring the Parliamentary Labour Party into rather closer touch with Transport House than it has been in the past. There is a bit of a gap here which I should like to see closed. And, of course, there is something to be done in encouraging youth. We had a lively debate on this this morning. I hope we shall have a fine broad-based youth movement. I add only one thing. We must also, if we are to succeed, give younger people their chance in the Party, their chance of responsibility in office, while they are still young.

It is right that we should have had this discussion; not to have had it would have been appallingly complacent. But we must be careful not to overdo it, not to overdo the self-analysis. We must not expend all our time on it, and we must not get it out of perspective. Before I sit down, I would like to remind the Conference of some of the other things in the election. I think of the grand, tumultuous, gay, good-humoured meetings, the passionate, excited longing of the crowds that we should win. I do not think they were all Party members; they jolly well should have been out

---

[8] Sidney and Beatrice Webb, social reformers and historians of the trade-union movement.
[9] Secretary of the Labour Party from 1911 to 1934.
[10] Intellectual socialist; Tawney drafted the Party policy statement, *Labour and the Nation,* in 1927.

canvassing, anyway! But they were certainly supporters. I think of the hundreds of letters I have had since the election, since the defeat. They were not bitter letters, they were warm and enthusiastic, like the crowds at the meetings.

I ask myself what most of these people want of us now. They see the need for our re-thinking; they have been doing some themselves, some of it very sensible stuff, too. But what they wanted above all was that we should win, and why they wanted us to win was so that we could carry out the programme in which both we and they believe. What they want us to do now first of all is to go on fighting for the things we fought for in the election, and they are dead right. We have got to go on fighting for a square deal for the old people, for the widows, the disabled and the sick; we have got to go on fighting for a real proper superannuation plan which will abolish poverty in old age, not the sham thing the Tories put up, which merely distributes the burden more unfairly than before. We have to go on demanding, as we have been, that work should be brought to the workers in the areas of unemployment. We have to go on pressing for the abolition of the eleven-plus; for more, not fewer, council houses; for councils to take over the older rented houses and modernise them. We have to go on pressing for freedom and self-government for the Colonies and an end to the repulsive policies of racial discrimination. We have to go on fighting for an end to nuclear tests, for all-out disarmament and a real effort to stop the hideous danger of the spread of nuclear weapons from one country to another. These things are and must remain our first priority in Parliament and in the country. In Parliament, though our members are fewer, we shall fight all the harder. That I pledge on behalf of the Parliamentary Labour Party. In the country and in the constituencies I know there is the same determination. I have heard accounts up and down the country of people coming in wanting to join and wanting to increase our membership immediately after the election defeat.

Our defeat, comrades, must not be a depressive or a sedative but a supreme challenge, a challenge to keep up the spirit of attack, the spirit of attack again and again and again, until we win. For in this way, and in this way only, we shall keep faith with the millions of people who had faith in us at the last General Election, and the millions of people abroad who still look to us for leadership, because they, like us, believe in the imperishable ideals of Democratic Socialism. [*Prolonged applause.*]

THE LIVE SHELL.

(WHICH OF 'EM WILL THROW IT OVERBOARD?)

4

Religious and Political Liberty for Ireland

Richard Lalor Sheil

"Religious Toleration"*
Penenden Heath, Kent, October 24, 1828

Mr. Sheil . . . presented himself amidst much applause on the one side and tremendous uproar from the opposite quarter.

The Under Sheriff immediately rose and, after having with difficulty obtained a hearing, said, "The High Sheriff feels it his duty to inquire how the Gentleman who is about to address the Meeting is connected with the county?"

MR. SHEIL: I am a freeholder of this county, and as such I have as complete and as perfect a right to address you as the first Peer in your county.[1]

---

* Our text is from *The Sun* (London), October 25, 1828, pp. 2–3. It is the only full account to appear in the English press. Other newspapers, complaining that the uproar was so great their reporters were unable to hear the speech, printed only fragments. The version of Sheil's speech often printed in anthologies bears little resemblance to what is reported in this text. For example, Sheil is usually made to begin:

> Let no man believe that I have come here in order that I might enter the lists of religious controversy and engage with any of you in a scholastic disputation. In the year 1828, the Real Presence does not afford an appropriate subject for debate, and it is not by the shades of a mystery that the rights of a British citizen are to be determined. I do not know whether there are many here by whom I am regarded as an idolater, because I conscientiously adhere to the faith of your forefathers and profess the doctrine in which I was born and bred; but if I am so accounted by you, you ought not to inflict a civil deprivation upon the accident of the cradle.

In subsequent paragraphs Sheil smoothly, without interruption, discourses on the subject of Catholic rights and then concludes:

> The worst foes with which you have to contend are lodged in your own breasts—your prejudices are the most formidable of your antagonists, and to discomfit them will confer upon you a higher honour than if in the shouts of battle you put your enemies to flight. It is over your antipathies, national and religious, that a masterdom should be obtained by you, and you may rest assured that if you shall vanquish your animosities, and bring your passions into subjection, you will, in conquering yourselves, extend your dominion over that country by which you have been so long resisted; your empire over our feelings will be securely established, you will make a permanent acquisition of the affections of Irishmen, and make our hearts your own.

[John Hayward, ed., *Silver Tongues* (London, 1937), pp. 138–151.]

[1] Sheil had purchased a small piece of property in Kent, thus entitling him as a freeholder to speak at this public meeting.

Here there was a great uproar—an individual on the hustings cried out, "That is Sheil, the famous Irish agitator." Another exclaimed, "The traitor, pull him down, turn him out."

MR. COBBETT:[2] Tell them that you bought your freehold and that it is not mortgaged like theirs.

Others cried out, "Ask the cowards if they are afraid to hear the truth." The Under Sheriff then came forward and said that the High Sheriff declared Mr. Sheil had a right to speak; he also requested that, as the day was far advanced, Gentlemen would be as concise as possible in their speeches.

Mr. Sheil attempted to speak again, amidst great uproar. He exclaimed:

Is this fair play? Is this English? Is this just? My country is assailed, my religion is vilified—will you not hear before you condemn? The basest criminal is allowed to plead not guilty; and even when convicted, the judge asks him what he has to say as to why sentence of execution should not be passed upon him. I, on behalf of my country, demand that you should hear why sentence of everlasting thraldom should not be passed against it. I am no intruder; you are adjudicating upon my rights; you shall not put me down; you must, you shall hear me. I bid you defiance. [*Uproar on the left, mixed with cheers from the right.*] You may trample upon my country, but you shall not, as an individual, tread upon me. I have the law of the land on my side. [*Cheers.*] Again I tell you that you shall not, you cannot, put me down. [*Great uproar.*]

What sort of system is this? Lord Winchilsea[3] challenges me to produce evidence from history to show that my religion is not that of a bigot and a slave—he throws down the gauntlet, and you, honourable Brunswickers[4] as you are, rush in to prevent me from taking it up. Even Lord Camden[5] has assailed the Association to which I belong; he has referred distinctly to myself; and when I rise in my own vindication, you try to stifle my voice with your ferocious cries. But I am proud of this. The Brunswickers, the parson-ridden Brunswickers, tremble at the truth. [*Continued uproar.*] Mr. Sheriff, I call upon you to do your duty, and out of respect for yourself let me not be so maltreated.

Here the High Sheriff came forward and said, "I request you will hear Mr. Sheil; particularly as he is a freeholder of the county." A voice: "Pretty freeholder, he got it only yesterday at Maidstone." The High Sheriff: "As you heard one side,

---

[2] William Cobbett, whose *Parliamentary Debates* became the later *Hansard*, was a Radical Member at the time of this meeting.

[3] The Earl of Winchilsea, a principal organizer of Brunswick clubs in England, spoke just before Sheil.

[4] Brunswick clubs were a network of Protestant lodges organized in Ireland to resist Catholic emancipation. While their principal activity was to prepare petitions and hold public meetings, violent confrontations occurred between Brunswickers and members of the Catholic Association.

[5] Camden followed Earl Fitzwilliam in 1795 as Lord Lieutenant of Ireland. Like Lords Kenyon and Newcastle, later mentioned by Sheil, Camden was a powerful opponent of Catholic emancipation.

you ought to hear the other." Cries of "No, no" and "That's illiberal." A third voice: "Apologise for what you have said about the Duke of York." Mr. Sheil proceeded:

It is after this fashion that Ireland is ever treated at your hands; her very complaints are made crimes; you rack her because she groans; and when this is the treatment which we experience, my Lord Camden, forsooth, marvels at our violence. [*Cheers.*] He wonders that we are violent when he has this sample of Brunswick violence before him. But I do not charge the whole of this assembly with this gross and palpable injustice. The vast majority are on my side. [*Loud cheers from the right, mixed with loud cries of disapprobation from the left.*] It is only a faction of fierce and infuriated conspirators that seek to put me down. But they shall not put me down, for I have not only justice on my side, but what is much better: the majority of the meeting.

Applause and disapprobation. Mr. Sheil then proceeded to speak to the following effect amidst the incessant groaning of one side and the applause of the other.

I am a freeholder, but I put my claim to speak not so much upon any ground of strict legal right as upon the title which I derive from your magnanimity and justice. You are bound by your own spirit of fairness and just dealing to hear me in the cause of my religion and of my country, for upon the character of that religion and the interests of that country you are assembled to adjudicate. What is my religion, and what is my country? I am a native of that island which is one of the finest spots upon the sea but which, in place of being the fortunate land which nature intended it to be, exhibits in its distractions and its wretchedness the evidences of that condition to which its rulers—and Englishmen are its rulers—have reduced it. And with respect to my religion, I profess the faith of seven millions of your fellow-citizens and, let me add, the religion of those—your great ancestors—to whom you are indebted for Parliamentary representation, for Magna Carta, and the trial by jury. I am a Roman Catholic; I am therefore deeply concerned in the result of your deliberations, and that concern confers upon me a right to speak. You will act only in consistency with your own character as Englishmen in hearing me, not with favour but with forbearance. I want nothing, to use a simple phrase drawn from your own national habits, but "fair play." That I find you will not refuse me.

But it is right that I should tell you something more touching myself. I am not only an Irishman and a Roman Catholic but I am one of the individuals who have incurred the displeasure of many of you, but for whose vehement language and possibly over-ardent emotion, you would, I think, if you knew the full extent of the grievances of which they complain, find in your own feelings some extenuation. I am a member of that body which you have been so often told is among the chief evils of Ireland, but which is the product and not the cause of its discontents and, instead of giving birth to the public calamities, is indebted to them for its parentage. I am—and I am well aware that in announcing it I do not beseech your partialities—a member of the Roman Catholic Association. You may not much relish me on that account, but still, you owe it to yourselves and not to me to hear why sentence of eternal discord should not be pronounced against my country.

I will tell you more, for with Englishmen, plain and direct dealing is the wisest as it is certainly the honestest course. I am one of the most strenuous of the persons who are designated as the agitators of Ireland; yet however inimical, I am entitled to plead not guilty, and I stand at your bar for the purpose of so doing. I have travelled here with no other view than to raise my voice in this assembly, and I did so in spite of much remonstrance and admonition. I was told that you would consider me guilty of an intrusion, and I answered, "That cannot be where my privileges as a fellow-citizen are so deeply involved, and I must be affected by the issue of their deliberations." I was told that you would treat me with contumely and derision, and I replied that you had too much respect for yourselves to act such a part in my regard. It was said to me that you would not hear me, and I exclaimed, "They are Englishmen, and without hearing they never will condemn." Protestants, Englishmen, was I wrong, when I spoke thus? I am convinced that I judged you rightly; and I am also convinced that I shall persuade you that many of you have judged me and the community to which I belong most wrongfully, in attributing to us many sentiments and opinions which, so far from entertaining, we reject with abhorrence for their detestable character and indignant astonishment that they should be attributed to us. Would to Heaven that Protestants and Catholics more frequently blended and mixed their minds together, for upon a mutual approach they would discover with how much reciprocal injustice they had cast injurious imputations upon each other. If they would but meet calmly and dispassionately and with a little Christianity in their tempers as well as in their creeds, they would part, not perhaps with any change in their religious opinions, but with a great reduction in acrimonious spirit of contention, which vitiates the heart so deeply while it obscures the judgment in the investigation of truth.

It were most desirable that Roman Catholics should often attend assemblies of their Protestant fellow-citizens in order to set them right and to be set right in return; and upon the other hand, but devoutly it were to be wished, that strong zealots in the cause of Protestant liberty, men of worth and honour, like Lord Winchilsea and Lord Kenyon and the Duke of Newcastle, would condescend to visit Ireland and by ocular inspection ascertain the real extent and the substantial cause of the calamities of the country. They would possibly find reason to concur in the opinion which Lord Camden, who administered the Government, and so many other Lords Lieutenant have arrived at, by being actual observers of the condition of that unhappy country. Oh! my good friends (permit me so to call you), would to God that Englishmen and Irishmen were bound in everlasting unity with each other. You do not know the true state of that country whose future destiny is in some measure in your hands. You should actually see Ireland before you take upon yourselves to pronounce upon her fate. How many good and kindly natured as well as eminently gifted individuals have seen cause to change their opinions after having actually visited the country.

I do not speak merely of statesmen and politicians—their minds are engrossed by ambition and clouded too often by passion—but of persons who, occupying the middle class of life, had no motive of personal interest to sway them and were the most credible because the most competent judges. I might cite a thousand examples; but there are two persons who are in themselves most assuredly worth many ordinary authorities. I perceive that a gentleman named Dr. Fry, at a late dinner at Aylesbury, thought it in accordance with his clerical character to indulge in some curious specimens of Bachanalian mirth mingled with Bachanalian savageness at the expense of Ireland. On reading his after-dinner homily, my mind was carried by the identity not indeed of character but of name to the dismal dungeon and to the gloomy prison-house where that incomparable woman, that guardian angel of captivity, that female Howard, exhibited all the elevation of genuine Christianity united with all the charities of a human heart.[6] Yes, we may well contrast her with the Doctor and triumphantly appeal to her counter-testimony in favour of Ireland. She went to that country attended by a relative of the same religious opinions, and she went merely upon a mission of charity, yet the political state of Ireland pressed itself upon her, and in the account which she afterwards published of her journey of benevolence, she stated that she had gone to Ireland with feelings adverse to Roman Catholic emancipation, and having seen the country, that she was persuaded that it was absolutely necessary for its improvement.

But I deviate from the order of observation which I had intended to pursue. It is not so much my office to invite you to visit my country as to apologise for my coming amongst you. My vindication for so doing was in a single sentence. You are called together upon a matter which affects my interests and rights; I am entitled to address you. Englishmen, I am not come here to enter into religious disputation with you. It is not in the year 1828 that we should enter into a scholastic controversy upon the Real Presence. I believe in it, you do not; what matter is it to me what you believe, and what matter is it to you what I believe? I do not want to take down the ponderous folios of disputation in order to blow the dust with

---

[6] The reference is to Elizabeth Fry who continued the work of prison reform that philanthropist John Howard began in the late 1700's. Mrs. Fry made her first visit to Newgate in 1813.

which they are appropriately laden into your eyes and to envelop myself in a cloud of theology. You think me an idolater. I deny it. But supposing I am: I am not the worse citizen; I have a right to be an idolater if I think proper, and my idolatry is no business of yours. It would be very hard indeed because I may have a fancy to holy water that I should be excluded from the benefits of the Constitution.

But it is said that my religion is the religion of slavery. Now this, I admit, calls for an answer, and I must say that with the exception of William Cobbett's reply[7] to the charge, I never read a sufficiently strenuous defence against this accusation. A Protestant in encountering this imputation may reason well, but he will not feel strongly. I as a Catholic feel strongly, and such are the facts in my favour that I should be dull and unskillful indeed if my reasoning were not conclusive. I deny and I decry with a justifiable warmth that there is any foundation for this charge; and although I admit that there have been many Catholic despots, I ask, with a retorting interrogatory, were there never any Protestant despots? Do I attribute a spirit of tyranny to your religion? No such thing. But I claim the same indulgence for my own; and I demand that you should not refer the atrocities of Catholics to their religion when I do not refer the atrocities of Protestants to theirs.

But come, let us go out of theories and speculations and proceed to facts. One fact is worth a hundred arguments, and I have a host of facts upon my side. First, let us open the pages of English history. Where do you find the elements of your Constitution? Alfred gave you the body of your common law: your judges, your magistrates, your sheriffs (you hold your office, Sir, and have called this great assembly by virtue of his institutions), your courts of justice, your elective system, and the grand bulwark of your liberties—the best and most useful as well as the most glorious of your rights, the shield of freedom—the trial by jury. He placed this great ægis in the temple of the Constitution. Does the Duke of Newcastle think that Alfred was a Protestant? Or that the Barons of Runnymede with Archbishop Langton[8] at their head were Protestants?

But to touch upon a case that appertains more nearly to His Grace. Who was it that gave the people the power of self-taxation and fixed, if he did not create, the representation of the people? Edward I. Oh! my Lord Duke, there were no rotten boroughs then. The House of Commons was not returned by a set of nobles who, talking about liberty, opposed all reform. There were no great men in those times of Catholic slavery who sent in ten Members to the House of Commons and, when a corrupt borough was cut off, contrived to get its still more rotten substitute into their pockets.

---

[7] Cobbett's *History of the Protestant Reformation*, begun in 1824, was a famous polemic in the cause of Catholic emancipation.

[8] Stephen Langton, English cardinal and archbishop of Canterbury, was associated with the baronial opposition to King John leading to the Magna Carta.

The House of Commons was then a perfect mirror of the people which was unstained by the breath of an oligarchy. Give up your ten Members, my Lord Duke,[9] and then you will talk of liberty with a better grace, if not to a more useful purpose. It was to the first Edward that England was indebted for her Parliament and her pecuniary control over the Crown; and the third Edward gave perfection to the system by holding annual Parliaments. He, too, passed the great statute against constructive treason. Englishmen, with these facts before you, how can you listen to the men who tell you that popery and slavery are necessarily allied? Englishmen, when you peruse the ancient chronicles of your glory, do not your hearts beat with a sense of exultation, are not your motives deeply stirred, and are not your natures highly kindled? Where is the English boy who reads the story of his own great island whose pulse does not warmly beat at the contemplation of all the renowned names and all the lofty incidents with which the early annals of his country are splendidly studded? Is there one of you all who hath not almost fallen down to adore the memory of Alfred? Have not you turned idolaters in the worship of the immortal Edwards? Who is there that hath not thrilled at the name of Runnymede and whose soul hath not swelled and dilated at the remembrance of the scene when Langton, with a Catholic mitre upon his head, extorted from a tyrant your mighty, and I trust in God that it will prove your eternal, charter? Still little did you think—and yet how could you forget?—when you experienced, as you must, this generous national exultation—little did you think that it was at the altars of the religion which you are instructed to consider as the handmaid of oppression that the great progenitors of liberty knelt down. You may write damnation upon every grave which bears date before the year 1521,[10] but in the face of clear and indisputable evidence, with Alfred and the Edwards, with trial by jury, with Parliament, and with Magna Carta before you, do not denounce the religion of your forefathers as the brother of slavery and visit it with all the execration that should pursue the part of so detestable a child.

Englishmen, I have spoken with warmth; I cannot help it. But that warmth shall not carry me too far—it is enough for me to defend my religion without animadverting on yours. But if I were disposed so to do, might I not turn the leaves of history upon you, and after you had charged my creed with its servile tendencies, might I not ask whether the cradle of the Reformation was not rocked with a bloody and an iron hand? Whether he did not trample upon the press of liberty and his base Parliament did not make him a voluntary release and surrender of the Constitution? Did liberty exist in the reign of that precocious theologian, Edward VI, or under the auspices of the virgin of the Reformation who took infant Protestantism under her maiden auspices? You might say to

[9] Newcastle was notorious as a patron of boroughs in Sussex and Nottinghamshire.
[10] The year Henry VIII became "Defender of the Faith."

me, if I were sufficiently bold to press these considerations, that I should not refer to such remote events. Well, then—but no, I will. It is a fact of much importance —without meaning to offer you the smallest offence I think it only due to honesty to repeat to you—that on the 21st day of 1683, William Lord Russell,[11] one of the martyrs to liberty, perished on the scaffold, and on the very same day (it was a felicitous selection) the University—the Protestant University of Oxford, the seat of reformed Christianity, the throne of English orthodoxy—published its ingenious declaration in favour of passive obedience. I pray you, when you are disposed to fling your projectiles against the Catholic religion, to look round you and consider of how much glass your own house is built.

But let us travel a little out of England. Protestantism, it is said, is the inseparable companion of liberty—they are always found walking arm in arm together in their march for the improvement of mankind. If this be so, how does it happen that Prussia is a Protestant and Prussia is a slave; and Sweden is a Protestant and Sweden is a slave; and Denmark is a Protestant and Denmark is a slave; and half the German states are Protestant and are also slaves; and even Hanover (hear it ye Brunswickers!), even under the moral government of the Duke of Cumberland,[12] is also a slave! Turn now to Catholic Europe. Look at Italy—not as she now is, but as she was long before the name of Luther was ever uttered—look at her when the Catholic was her entire religion and liberty was her glorious practise. I call up her crowd of republics as witnesses in that cause which I am thus daring enough to plead before you. Venice, Catholic Venice, rises up from the ocean with all her republican glory round about her. Venice fell at last into an oligarchy; but Venice was for five hundred years a noble and lofty democratic government. I next produce as witnesses in my favour Genoa and Florence and all the rest of those free states in which popery, liberty, literature, and the arts grew up and flourished together. You think, perhaps, that when Italy is exhausted you can bring Spain against me. Even there, before Ximenes[13] trod upon the rights of Spaniards, the Catholic Cortes were a free assembly and imposed upon the Monarch an oath in which they told him that they were individually as good and taken altogether far better than himself, and his power derived from the people. But if you think that you can turn Spain against us, shall I not find in the country of Switzerland and in the mountains of William Tell

---

[11] Tried and sentenced to death for his opposition to Charles I, Russell refused even after sentence to renounce the position that there are cases in which it is justifiable to resist the Crown. The newspaper report of Sheil's speech incorrectly uses the name "Lord John Russell" and leaves blank the space intended for the date; both name and date are, however, clear from the context.

[12] Ernest Augustus, fifth son of George III, was King of Hanover. In 1799 he was named Duke of Cumberland.

[13] Ximenes de Cisneros (1437–1517), Cardinal of Toledo, who became Grand Inquisitor in 1507.

a glorious testimony in my form? The parental hand that bent the bow and loosed the shaft of Tell was raised in prayer before the altars at church. I am told that none but slaves have ever prayed. But to pass from distant periods and from sequestered valleys, there you may say that simplicity in spite of popery was the source of freedom. I bid you turn your eyes to France, and I ask of you whether with her Charter, with her trial by jury, and with her Chamber of Deputies—and observe also, with her glorious toleration—she is not ascending into competition with yourselves. But no. I will not wound you with the comparison. I will not tell you that Catholic Frenchmen are your competitors in free institutions but will bid you turn to a spectacle upon which every Englishman may well repose with a sort of parental pride. From the Old, I travel to the New World, and I produce to England her glorious pupils, the Catholic democracies of South America. Republic after republic is bursting forth at your bidding through that almost immeasurable continent, and from the summit of the Andes, liberty may be said to unfurl her standard over half the world. It is false, utterly false—never was there calumny more destitute of foundation, and history aids out against it—that Catholicism and a genuine love of freedom cannot exist together.

Have I not made out a case by evidence which cannot be overthrown? And is it not hard—is it not worse than hard, is it not most unjust and cruel—to use such an argument or rather so baseless an assertion as a ground for keeping seven millions of people in their degraded and exasperating condition? Englishmen, I willingly forgive any imputation but this. Heap insult upon insult upon our creed, even that it is idolatrous; write damnation on the graves of your forefathers. Call us image-worshippers, water-sprinklers, sin-whisperers, and God-eaters if you will. I'll bear it all. But do not call me and do not deem me slave; tell me not and deem me not a wretch made to lie prostrate before a tyrant and bow my head into the dust. You do me and you do my country wrong. Where were men animated with a stronger passion for their liberty than the people of Ireland are at this instant? How did the hearts of a whole nation beat for the attainment of freedom with a strange palpitation? Never were men more resolved and never were men more deserving of being free.

Englishmen, look at Ireland—that do you behold—a beautiful country with wonderful agricultural and commercial advantages, the link between America and Europe, the natural resting place of trade in its way to either hemisphere, indented with havens, watered by deep and numerous rivers, with a fortunate climate and a soil teeming with easy fertility, and inhabited by a bold, intrepid, and with all their faults, a generous and enthusiastic people. Such is rational Ireland—what is artificial Ireland? Such is Ireland as God made her—what is Ireland as England made her? For she is your colony, your dependent, and you are as answerable for her faults as a parent is for the education of a child.

What, then, have you made Ireland? Look at her again. This fine country is laden with a population the most miserable in Europe and of whose wretchedness, if you are the authors, you are beginning to be the victims—the poisoned chalice is returned in its just circulation to your lips. Your domestic swine are better housed than the people; harvests, the most abundant, are reaped by men with starvation in their faces; famine covers a fertile soil, and disease inhales a pure atmosphere. All the great commercial facilities of the country are lost. The deep rivers that should circulate opulence and turn the machinery of a thousand manufactures flow on to the ocean without wafting a boat or turning a wheel, and the wave breaks in solitude in the silent magnificence of deserted and shipless harbours. In place of being a source of wealth and revenue to the Empire, Ireland cannot defray its own expenses or pay a single tax; her discontents cost millions of money, and she hangs like a financial millstone round England's neck. In place of being a bulwark and a fortress, she debilitates, exhausts, and endangers England, and offers an allurement to the speculators in universal ruin. The great mass of her enormous population are alienated and dissociated from the State—the influence of the constituted and legitimate authorities is gone. A strange, anomalous, and unexampled kind of government has sprung up from the public passions and exercises a despotic sway over the great mass of the community, while the class, inferior in numbers but accustomed to authority and infuriated at its loss, are thrown into a formidable reaction. The most ferocious passions rage from one extremity of the country to the other. Hundreds of thousands of men, arrayed with badges, gather in the South, and the smaller faction, with discipline and with arms, are marshalled in the North. The country is strewed with the materials of civil commotion and seems like one vast magazine of powder which a spark might ignite into an explosion which would shake the whole fabric of civil society into ruin, and which England would not only feel, but perhaps never recover from the shock. And gracious God!—for I cannot refrain from the exclamation—is this horrid, this appalling, this accursed state of things to be permitted to continue? It is only requisite to present the question in order that all men should answer, "Something must be done."

Well, then, what is to be done? Are you to re-enact the Penal Code?[14] You were obliged to relax the Penal Code when the Catholics were only three millions, and now that they are seven, will you lay on their chains again? Are you to deprive the Catholics of their properties, shut up their schools, drive them from the bar, strip them of the elective franchise, and reduce them to a state of Egyptian bondage? It is easy for some visionary in oppression, in his dreams of tyranny, to imagine these things. Certain parts of the established religion have, in the drunkenness of their

[14] After 1695, Catholics were subject to repressive measures regarding land ownership, education, and office holding; in 1727, they were deprived of the Parliamentary franchise. Restrictions were not relaxed until the 1770's.

sacerdotal debauch, given vent to such sanguinary aspirations; and many are the teachers of the gospel—the ministers of a mild and merciful Redeemer who lift up their hands from the altar to invite peace and tranquillity from Heaven, who distribute the communicative cup and circulate the sacramental chalice—who have recently uttered in the midst of their ferocious wassails the bloody aspiration that the whole country should be covered with massacre, and that upon the pile of carnage the genius of Orange[15] ascendancy should be placed on a secure and appropriate throne. But these men are set down as maniacs in ferocity, whose ravenous appetites for blood you will merely undertake to satiate. I will therefore take it for granted that you are not inclined to renew the system of torture which was once practised in Ireland, and that you will leave no other but those of the imagination to the amiable religionists who previously implored you to indulge them in the luxuries of laceration and the lusts of cruelty again. You would not wish, if you thought that Ireland could be thus treated with impunity, to have recourse to such a dreadful expedient as the extirpation of a whole people, and therefore I will take it as conceded that the recondite theories for the salutary pacification of Ireland will not be adopted. What then is to be done? You have tried a great deal—everything has failed. Surely, when the patient is getting worse and worse you will not have recourse to the same prescriptions—especially when you are told by the great moral leaders, the "Ministers to the mind diseased," that there is a specific which would cure Ireland of her paroxysms and convulsions and restore her to wholesome vigour and to rational strength again.

Englishmen, when you consider, as surely you must consider, what ought to be done in this emergency, surely you will not dismiss from your recollection that the greatest, the wisest, and the best statesmen and legislators, who have for the last fifty years directed your councils and conducted the business of this mighty Empire, all concurred in the opinion that without a concession of the Catholic claims, nothing permanently useful and effectually sanative could be done for Ireland. Without going through the catalogue of splendid names which stand engaged in the cause of emancipation, I shall select only three: Burke, and Pitt, and Fox. They were all different in habit, in character, and in theory, yet on this question their great minds met in a deep conflux. Burke, the foe to revolution; Fox, the assertor of popular right; Pitt, the stay and prop of the Prerogative— the grand triumvirate of legislation concurred in this single opinion. See to what a conclusion you must arrive when you denounce the advocates of emancipation as the foes and the enemies of their country. To whom will your anathema reach? It will take in one-half of Westminster Abbey— and is not the very dust in which the tongues and hearts of Pitt and Burke and Fox have mouldered better than the living hearts and tongues of those who have survived them? Yes. I will put it on this test. If you were to try

[15] William III (Prince of Orange) in 1688 expelled Catholic James II from his throne, and reigned as King of England and Ireland until his death in 1702.

the question by the venerable authorities of the illustrious dead and by these voices which may be said to issue from the grave, how would you decide? If, instead of counting votes in St. Stephen's, you were to count the tombs in the mausoleum beside it, how would the division of the great departed stand? Enter the sacred aisles which contain the ashes of your greatest men and ask yourselves, as you pass, how they felt and spoke when they had emotion and they had utterance in that Senate where they can be heard no more? Write "Emancipation" on the grave of every great advocate and its counter-epitaph on that of every opponent of the peace of Ireland, and will there not be a majority of sepulchres in our favour?

But pass from authority and consider how such a system as that of exclusion ought to work. How did it operate in other countries? You will find a parallel to the state of Ireland in the condition of the Colonies of Spain. Before the revolution, the natives of the country were shut out from all offices of emolument and honour, which were monopolised by Spaniards. They were in possession of all the wealth of the state and of all its distinctions. None but Spaniards were admissible to stations of power and influence—the finances, the Church property, the administration of justice, were all in their hands. And what was the result? That the most ferocious detestation arose from this Spanish ascendancy between monopoly and exclusion, and ended in events which throw a terrific light upon the system. There is this difference between Protestant ascendancy with you and Spanish ascendancy with them—there is indeed this difference—that religion throws additional hatred into the feud, and the contest for pre-eminence on the one side and for equality on the other is embittered by the proverbial animosity of polemics.

But put all comparisons out of the way and look at the matter itself. Can that be a wise and politic course of government which creates not an aristocracy of opulence and rank and talent but an aristocracy in religion, and places seven millions of people at the feet of a few hundred thousand? Try this fashion of government by a very obvious test and make the case your own. If a few hundred thousand Presbyterians stood towards you in the relation in which the Irish Protestants stand towards the Catholics, how would you endure it? How would you brook a system by which Episcopalians should be rendered incapable of holding seats in the House of Commons, by which the oldest nobility in the country should be turned by plebeian Presbyterians out of the House of Lords, should be excluded from sheriffships and from corporate offices and from the bench of justice and from all the higher offices in the administration of the law? And how would you like to pay for the building and repairing of Presbyterian churches and chapels, while you should be deprived of all voice in your own taxation? And how would you like, I pray you, Presbyterian tithes and cesses and ecclesiastical courts? And how would you like to be tried by none but Presbyterian juries, flushed with the insolence of power and infuriated with all the venom of passion? How would you like all this? And more than this, how would you like the degradation which would arise from such a system and the shame and scorn and contumelies and disgrace which would flow from it? Englishmen, would you bear with all this? And above all, would you listen with patience to men who told you that there was no grievance in all this, that your complaints were groundless, and that your language was full of factious menaces, and that the very right of murmuring ought to be taken away from you? Are Irishmen and Roman Catholics so differently constituted from yourselves that they are to behold nothing but blessings in a system which you would look upon as a mass of unendurable wrong?

Protestants and Englishmen, however debased you may deem our country and however slavish you may regard our religion, believe me that we have enough of human nature left within us, we have enough of the spirit of manhood, all Irishmen as we are, to resent a usage of this kind. You would not bear the yoke for a moment. We are gored and galled by it, but we do not throw it off. You are told that there is no national calamity in the exclusion of a few gentlemen from Parliament and a few lawyers from the present list at the bar. How heinous a view of the case is this? Don't you feel that this very exclusion throws degradation over the whole of the disfranchised community, and that the spirit which is derived from that political dishonouring of a whole people must run through all the departments of society and must be baneful indeed? A brand is struck upon the forehead of the country, and it festers there. The nation is divided into two castes. The powerful and privileged few are patricians in religion and oligarchs in creed and trample upon and despise the plebeian Christianity of the millions who are laid prostrate at their feet. Every Protestant thinks himself a Catholic's better, and every Protestant feels himself the member of a privileged corporation which must be protected—their judges, their sheriffs, their Crown counsels, their Crown attorneys, their juries, are Protestant to a man. What confidence can a Catholic have in the administration of public justice?

We have the authority of an eminent Irish judge, the late Mr. Fletcher,[16] who declared that in the southern counties the Protestants guilty were uniformly acquitted, and the Catholics innocent were as undeviatingly condemned. A body of armed Orangemen fall upon and murder a set of defenceless Catholics; they are put upon their trial; and when they raise their eyes and look upon the jury as they are commanded to do, they see twelve of their brethren in massacre impanelled for their trial. And after this, I shall be told that all the evil of Catholic disqualification is in the stuff gowns of lawyers and the disappointed longing of some dozen gentlemen after the House of Commons. No. It is the shame, the disgrace, the bane, the opprobrium, the stigma, the brand, the contumely, the note and

[16] William Fletcher, Justice of the Common Pleas in Ireland.

mark of dishonour, and the scandalous partialities, the flagitious broils, the sacrilegious and perjured leanings, and the monstrous and hydra-headed injustice that constitute the grand and essential evils of the country.

And you think it very wonderful (you, forsooth, that cut off the head of a king for imposing an illegal tax upon you) that we should be indignant at all this. You marvel and are astonished and think it prodigious that we are harried by a sense of these injuries into the use of rash and vehement phrases; but I won't deny that we, and that I myself in particular, have occasionally turned my burning emotions into language the employment of which I may have had reason to regret. But are we the only individuals who have forgotten the dictates of temperance and of chastity? And have our opponents been always distinguished by their meekness and forbearance? And have no exasperating expressions and no galling taunts and no fierce sarcasms and no ferocious menaces ever escaped from them? Look—look, I pray you—to the Brunswick orgies of Ireland, and behold not merely the torturers of ninety-eight[17]—who, like retired butchers, feel the want of their own occupation and long for the political shambles again—but look to the ministers of the Gospel, pouring out their votive libations to the Moloch of ascendancy and cheering their demon with the promise of a hecatomb of blood. Oh! Englishmen—and therefore generous, just, magnanimous, and lofty-minded men—may I implore some allowance for the excess into which with much provocation we may be harried, and pardon for us when you recollect how under the same circumstances you would in all likelihood feel yourselves.

But perhaps you will say that while you are conscious that we have much to suffer, you owe it to your own safety to exclude us from power. Englishmen, we have power already—the power to do mischief. Give us that of doing good. Disarray us, dissolve us, break up our confederacy, take from the law (for it is the great conspirator) its combining and organising quality; make us equal, and we shall no longer be united by the bad chain of slavery with each other but by the natural bonds of allegiance and of contentment with you. But you fear our influence in the House of Commons. Don't you dread our actual influence out of it? We are only Catholics out of the House of Commons, we should be citizens within it. But you say that we are priest-ridden; I do assure you that the priests find us very uneasy and high trotting. We are ready to go at full gallop our own way, but if a priest attempts to curb us or to turn us from the road we like, we straight begin to plunge and rear and throw him off. The priests lately attempted to stop the quiet assemblies of the people in Tipperary, and the people told them to mind their own concerns, to read their breviaries, and to go home. The priests have great influence, you think, at elections. Yes, when they run with the popular passions. But if they endeavour to control

[17] The insurrection of 1798 in Ireland, led by the United Irish movement, was ruthlessly suppressed.

them, the tenant sweeps them away. But really, it is laughable to hear men talking of the influence of priests over Catholic Members of the House of Commons, as if a Catholic Gentleman, before he gave his vote, would not be much more likely to listen to a whisper from a Minister or a shout from the people than to the injunctions at the confessional or the anathemas of the altar. Why, my God! Do you ever hear of the Catholic Deputies of France or Belgium asking their ghostly fathers how they should vote? Or do the Catholic Members of Congress ask the Pope how he would like to have a popish establishment in the United States? Are they not as good citizens as any other members of the community, and do you ever hear one word about popery and despotism being established in America? But supposing that Catholics had the will, would they have the power to overthrow the Constitution? What! Some twenty Catholics overwhelm the British House of Commons! But it is suggested that they will aim at the annihilation of the Church. Why should they be actuated by any such solicitude when the Church will no longer affect their individual interests or stand in the way of their personal ambition? The Presbyterians of Ireland are a powerful body—they have wealth, intelligence, and public spirit, and constitute the Protestant population of the North of Ireland. They have as strong a political nature for distaste towards the Establishment as the Catholics, and before they were emancipated (for they have been long since put upon a level with the members of the Establishment) it was insisted, especially by Swift, that their equalisation would lead to the destruction of the legal religion. The direct contrary has been the result. The Presbyterians are professedly indifferent to the abuses of the Establishment, and they care not one jot whether a Lord or a Bishop—whether an absentee from Ireland or from Heaven—has £20,000 a year at his command.

You allege, however, that we Catholics would be anxious to raise our Church upon the ruins of yours, to strip your clergy of tithes, and to possess ourselves of the gorgeous opulence of an anti-apostolic and antiscriptural establishment. Never was there a more unfounded imputation. The whole body of the Irish Catholics look upon a wealthy priesthood with abhorrence. They not only do not desire that their bishops should be invested with pontifical gorgeousness and prelatic pomp, but when a Bill was introduced in order to make a small, and no more than a decent, provision for the Catholic clergy, did they not themselves repudiate the offer and prefer their honourable poverty and the affections of the people to the directions of the Crown? And how did the people act? Although a provision for the priesthood would relieve them from a burden, did they not deprecate their adulterous connexion with power? The Catholics of Ireland well know that if their clergy were endowed with the wealth of the Establishment, they would become a corrupt and profligate corporation of lazy churchmen, bloated with insolence, tempered with luxury, swelling with sacerdotal pride, and presenting in their lives and persons a monstrous contrast with that simplicity and poverty of which they are now as well the practisers as the teachers. They well know that in place of being the pious, active, and indefatigable instructors of the peasantry—in place of being their consolers in affliction, their resource in calamity, their preceptors and their models in religion, the trustees of their interests, their visitors in sickness, and their companions in their beds of death—they would be a vain, supercilious, reckless, heartless troop of abandoned profligates, equally insolent to the humble, and sycophantic to the greatest flatterers at the noble's table, and grinders in the poor man's hovel—rapacious in extortion, slaves in politics, and tyrants in demeanour, who from the porticoes of palaces would give their instructions in humility—who from the banquets of patricians would prescribe their lessons in obstinacy—who from mitred chariots would pronounce injunctions against the pride and pomp, and from the primrose path of dalliance would point to the steep and thorny way to Heaven. The Catholics of Ireland well know that this would be the character of their priesthood if their Church was ever raised on the ruins of the Establishment. And monstrous as the opulence of that Establishment now is, they would rather behold the wealth of Protestant bishops increased tenfold and another million of acres added to their episcopal territories than behold their pure and simple priesthood degraded from their poverty into opulence, and sunk from their noble humility to that dishonourable and anti-Christian ostentation which, if it were once established, would be sure to characterise their Church. Englishmen, I speak the sentiments of the whole body of my countrymen when I speak this, and I pledge whatever weight and influence I have in the body to which I belong when I solemnly and emphatically reiterate my asseveration that there is nothing which the Roman Catholic body would regard with more abhorrence than the transfer of the enormous and corrupting revenues of the Establishment to a clergy who owe their virtues to their poverty and the attachment of the people to their dignified dependence upon the people for their support.

Protestants, I should have done, and yet before I retire from your presence, indulge me so far as to permit me to press one remaining topic upon you. I have endeavoured to show you that you have mistaken the character and political principles of my religion; I have endeavoured to make you sensible of the miserable condition of my country—to impress upon you the failure of all the means which have been hitherto tried to tranquilise that unhappy country, and the necessity of adopting some expedient to alleviate its evils. I have dwelt upon the concurrence of great authorities in favour of concession, the little danger that is to be apprehended from that concession, and the great benefit which would arise from the establishment (to use an expression of the Duke of Wellington) of religious peace in Ireland. I might enlarge upon those benefits and show you that where factions were reconciled, then the substantial causes of animosity were removed and the fierce passions which agitate the country would be laid at rest. English capital would in all likelihood flow in and fertilise Ireland; English habits would gradually arise; a confidence in the administration of justice would grow up; the people, instead of appealing to arms for redress, would look to the public tribunals as the only arbiters of right. The obstacles which now stand in the way of education would be removed; the fierceness of polemics would be suspended by that charity which a Christian extends to all mankind; a reciprocal sentiment of kindness would take place between the two islands; a real union—not depending upon acts of Parliament but upon mutual interest and affection —would be permanently established; the Empire would be consolidated; and all danger from the enemies of Great Britain would disappear forever.

I might also point out to you what is obvious enough, that if Ireland be allowed to remain as it now is, at no distant period the natural foes of Great Britain may make that unfortunate country the field for some tremendous speculation. I might draw a picture of the dreadful consequences which would arise if an enormous population were to be roused into a concurrent and simultaneous movement. But I forbear from pressing such considerations upon you, because I had much rather rely upon your own magnanimity and lofty-mindedness than upon any ground of possible evil and ostensible contingency. I therefore do put it to you that independently of every consideration of expediency, it is unworthy of you to persevere in a system of practical religious intolerance which Roman Catholic states, who hold out to you a fine example in this regard at least, have abandoned.

I have heard it said that the Catholic religion is a persecuting religion— to be sure it was, and so was every other religion that was ever invested with authority. I might retort on you the charge of persecution—I might remind you that the early reformers who set up a claim to liberty of conscience for themselves did not indulge any others in a similar luxury. I might tell you that Calvin, having obtained a theological masterdom in Geneva, set fire to the faggots to which Servetus[18] was bound and offered up his screams and groans as a sacrifice to that peculiar orthodox of which he was the founder. I might tell you that even your own Cranmer,[19] who was himself a martyr, had first inflicted what he afterwards suffered, and that this father of your Church had even in the reign of Edward VI accelerated the progress of heretics to immortality and sent them through fire to Heaven. But I will not adopt this course of recrimination. The truth is that both parties have, in the paroxysms of religious frenzy, committed

[18] Michael Servetus was burned alive in 1553 after theological correspondence he had with Calvin was adjudged heretical.
[19] Thomas Cranmer, Archbishop of Canterbury, was excommunicated and burned at the stake in 1556.

the most execrable atrocities, and it might be difficult if their misdeeds were to be weighed to adjust the balance of atrocity between them. But both Catholics and Protestants have changed, and with the situation of time we ourselves have undergone a salutary reformation. In the streets where the massacre of St. Bartholomew[20] took place, the Huguenot walks in friendship with the Catholic, and even in Rome itself, the simple ceremonies of your religion are undisturbed by papal intrusion. Through the whole Continent religious distinctions have begun to vanish, and freedom of conscience is almost universally established.

How does it happen that England should be almost the only country where religious disqualifications are maintained? Protestants who accuse the Catholic religion of intolerance, compare the conduct of Roman Catholics with your own. In France, where the religion of the state is that of Rome, all men are admissible to power and no sort of sectarian distinction is instituted by the law. The third article of the French Magna Carta provides that the Catholic religion shall be the established one, but that every French citizen, no matter of what denomination, shall be capable of holding every office in the state. The Chamber of Deputies is filled with Protestants who are elected by Roman Catholics, and Protestants have held places in the Cabinet of France. You charge our religion with intolerance. Encounter these notorious facts if you can—look to other Catholic states. In Hungary, in the year 1791, Protestants were placed by a Roman Catholic government in a perfect level with their fellow-citizens. In Catholic Bavaria the same principle of toleration was adopted. Thus the Catholics of Europe have given you a splendid example, and while they have refuted the imputation of intolerance, have held out to you a practical reproach. Away then with the charge that my religion is the patroness of oppression, and away with the idle boast of tolerating any philosophical Christianity in which you ever vauntingly indulged. You are behind almost every nation in Europe. Protestant Prussia has emancipated her Catholic subjects and Silesia is free. In Germany the churches are used indiscriminately by Protestants and Catholics—the Lutheran service in a happy succession follows the Catholic mass, or the Catholic mass, according to convenience, follows the Lutheran service. Hanover itself, to which England owes an obligation, Protestant Hanover has made a proclamation of religious liberty and the Hanoverian Catholic is free. And shall the Irish Catholic remain the branded and degraded wretch which your penal laws have made him while the Hanoverian Catholic stands before his Elector without a chain? Is this just dealing towards Ireland? And how can our Gracious Sovereign reconcile the tears which he gave to Ireland with Irish oppression and with Hanoverian liberty? How can you reconcile with your

---

[20] On August 24, 1572, the feast of St. Bartholomew, several thousand Huguenots were massacred in Paris by armed bands directed by Catholic nobles of the court of Catherine of Navarre.

own magnanimity this hard and cruel treatment of my unhappy country? And how can you consent to Hanoverian emancipation and to the perpetuation of Irish thraldom? Will you, can you, with such glaring examples before you, bring yourselves to offer up a wanton invocation to the Legislature to rivet the fetters of your Catholic fellow-citizens? Englishmen, do not undertake so ungenerous an office.

I do not call on you to petition for my liberty, but I implore you not to raise up your arms against it. This is all that I ask. Leave the Legislature in the uncontrolled exercise of its discretion, and do not tell the Parliament that the fetters of your fellow-citizens must be more strongly bolted. On behalf of my country, on behalf of unfortunate Ireland, I conjure, I supplicate you, not to interfere for the low-hearted purposes of oppression. It is ungenerous, it is almost unmanly, it is unworthy of you. Men of Kent, you have never been conquered—yet you shall be conquered today but the victory shall be obtained over yourselves. Conquer your prejudices, obtain a masterdom over your antipathies, be victors of your passions, vanquish your animosities, and put your antipathies to flight. Conquer yourselves—and conquer us. This—this is the way to subdue us, this is the way to obtain an empire over our affections, to fill us with gratitude, and to make our hearts your own. Let me go back to Ireland with the power to say that Englishmen and Protestants with all their prejudices, both natural and sectarian, allowed their eyes to be opened to the calamities of Ireland, and when they saw them, had mercy on us.

During Mr. Sheil's speech the greatest confusion prevailed. He entreated the meeting to hear the defence of the statements that had been made against the Roman Catholics of Ireland. Hisses, hooting—"Turn him off," "Go home to your buttermilk"—and the like were thickly interspersed throughout his speech, with frequent applause from all parts of the circle.

Daniel O'Connell

"Speech at Tara"*

Tara Hill, Ireland, August 15, 1843

It would be the extreme of affectation in me to suggest that I have not some claims to be the leader of this majestic meeting. [*Loud cheers.*] It would be worse than affectation—it would be drivelling folly—if I were not to feel the awful responsibility that the part I have taken in this majestic movement imposes upon me. [*Hear, hear.*] I feel responsibility to my country—responsibility to my Creator. [*Hear.*] Yes, I feel the tremulous nature of that responsibility. Ireland is aroused, is aroused from one end to another. Her multitudinous population have but one expression and one wish, and that is the extinction of the Union, the restoration of her nationality. [*Cheers and a voice: "There will be no compromise."*]

Who is that that talks of compromise? [*Cheers.*] I am not here for the purpose of making anything like a schoolboy's attempt at declamatory eloquence; I am not here to revive in your recollection any of those poetic imaginings respecting the spot on which we stand [*Hear, hear*] and which has really become as familiar as household words; I am not here to exaggerate the historical importance of the spot on which we are congregated. But it is impossible to deny that Tara has historical recollections that give to it an importance relatively to other portions of the land and deserves to be so considered by every person who comes to it for political purposes [*Hear*], and gives it an elevation and point of impression in the public mind that no other part of Ireland can possibly have. History may be tarnished by exaggeration, but the fact is undoubted that we are at Tara of the Kings. [*Cheers.*] We are on the spot where the monarchs of Ireland were elected and where the chieftains of Ireland bound themselves by the sacred pledge of honour and the tie of religion to stand by their native land against the Danes or any other stranger. [*Cheers.*] This is emphatically the spot from which emanated the social power—the legal authority—the right to dominion over the furthest extremes of the island, and the power of

---

* This text is from *The Nation* (Dublin), August 19, 1843, pp. 707–708.

concentrating the force of the entire nation for the purpose of national defence. [*Cheers.*]

On this important spot I have an important duty to perform: I here protest in the face of my country, in the face of my Creator, in the face of Ireland and our God—I protest against the continuance of the unfounded and unjust Union. [*Cheers.*] My proposition to Ireland is that the Union is not binding upon us; it is not binding, I mean, upon conscience—it is void in principle, it is void as matter of right, and it is void in constitutional law. [*"Hear, hear, hear" and cheers.*] I have no higher affection for England than for France—they are both foreign authorities to me. The highest legal authority in England[1] has declared us aliens in blood, aliens in religion, and aliens in language from the English. [*Groans.*] Let no person groan him. I thank him for the honesty of his expression. I never heard of any other act of honesty on his part, and the fact of his having committed one act of honesty ought to recommend him to your good graces. [*Laughter.*] I can refer you to the principle of constitutional law and to Locke on government to show that the Irish Parliament had no power or authority to convey itself away. [*Hear, hear, hear.*] I will only detain you on that point by citing the words of Lord Chancellor Plunket.[2] He declared in the Irish House of Commons that the maniacal suicide might as well imagine that the blow by which he destroyed his miserable body could annihilate his immortal soul, as they to imagine they could annihilate the soul of Ireland, her constitutional right. [*"Hear, hear" and loud cheers.*]

I am here the representative of the Irish nation, and in the name of that great, that virtuous, that moral, temperate, brave, and religious nation, I proclaim the Union a nullity [*"Hear" and loud cheers*], for it is a nullity in point of right. Mr. Saurin,[3] who for twenty years was Attorney General to the Tories, made the declaration and distinction. He said, "You have no right to pass the Union. You may make it law, but it will be void in principle; no man's conscience will be bound by it, and it will be the duty of the Irish people to take the first favourable opportunity to repeal the Union and to restore the nationality of Ireland." [*"Hear, hear" and loud cheers.*] I agree with Saurin that they have power to enforce the law, but they have no power to alter the right. [*Hear, hear.*] Never was any measure carried by such iniquitous means as the Union was carried. [*Hear, hear.*] In fact, corruption was never known to have been carried before or since to such excess in any country of the world; and if such a contract—if contract it could be called—was to be binding on the Irish nation, there was no longer any use for honesty or justice in the world. But strong as was

---

[1] Henry Brougham, Lord Chancellor from 1830 to 1834, doubted Ireland's capacity for self-government.

[2] William C. Plunket, Chancellor of Ireland from 1830 to 1841, had approved passage of the Union in 1800.

[3] William Saurin, Attorney General of Ireland from 1807 to 1822.

the influence on the human mind, the victory[4] which the English Ministry achieved was slow and by no means easy of accomplishment, for intimidation to the death upon the one hand and bribery on the other were impotent to procure a majority for them in the Irish House of Commons in the First Session, when the Bill was introduced. On the contrary, when the first attempt was made to prostrate our liberties, there was a majority of eleven against the Union Bill. But the despoiler was not easy to be foiled, nor was he apt to be disheartened by a single failure. The work of corruption was set on foot with redoubled energy, and the wretches who were not so utterly abandoned as to suffer themselves to be bribed for the direct and positive purpose of giving their vote for the Union accepted bribes on the condition of withdrawing from the House altogether, and accordingly they vacated their seats.[5] And in their place stepped in Englishmen and Scotchmen who knew nothing of Ireland and who were not impeded by any conscientious scruple whatever from giving their unqualified sanction to any plot of the English, how infamous soever, to oppress and plunder the country. By these accumulated means the Union was carried and the fate of Ireland sealed. [*Hear, hear.*] But in the name of the great Irish nation I proclaim it a nullity. [*Loud cheers.*]

But the monster evil of the Union is the financial robbery which by its means was practised upon Ireland. The scandalous injustice thus inflicted would be in itself sufficient even in the absence of other arguments— even if other arguments were wanting—to render the Union void and of no effect. At the passing of that fatal Act, badge of our ruin and disgrace, Ireland owed only £20,000,000, England owed £446,000,000, and the equitable terms upon which the contract was based, whereby both countries were to be allied and identified—identified, indeed!—were these: that England was generously to undertake the liability of one-half of our national debt on condition that we would undertake the responsibility of one-half of hers. This is not a befitting time nor season to enter into minute details relative to the particulars of this financial swindle, but I may be permitted to direct your attention to this very obvious fact: that whereas England has only doubled her debt since the passing of the Union, the increase of the national debt of Ireland during the same period cannot with justice be estimated on a different ratio, and that consequently, Ireland, at the very highest calculation, cannot in reality and as of her own account owe a larger sum than £40,000,000; and I will tell you, my friends, that never will we consent to pay one shilling more of a national debt than that. [*Cheers; "Never."*] I say it in the name and on behalf of the Irish nation. [*Loud cheers.*] But I will tell you this as a secret, and you may rely upon it as a

---

[4] Enactment of the Union under the younger Pitt.

[5] The Union was carried by compensation to borough owners of the Irish Parliament and by the acquiescence of Catholics secured through pledges of their emancipation. The Irish Parliament acceded to Union 158–115.

truth, that in point of fact we do not owe one farthing more than £30,000,000; and in proof of the truth of this assertion, I beg leave to refer you to a work published by a very near and dear relative of mine—my third son, the Member for Kilkenny—who, by the most accurate statistical calculations and by a process of argument intelligible to the humblest intellect, has made the fact apparent to the world that according to the terms of honest and equitable dealing as between both countries, Ireland's proportion of the national debt cannot be set down at a larger sum than I state—£30,000,000. [*"Hear, hear"* and *loud cheers for Mr. John O'Connell.*] I am proud that there is a son of mine who, after the Repeal shall have been carried, will be able to meet the cleverest English financier of them all, foot to foot and hand to hand, and prove by arguments the most incontestable how grievous and intolerable is the injustice which was inflicted upon our country in this respect by the Union.

The project of robbing Ireland by joining her legislatively with England was no new scheme which entered the minds of the English for the first time about the year 1800. [*"Hear, hear" and loud cheering.*] It was a project which was a favourite theme of dissertation with all the English essayists for years previous to the period when it was carried into practical effect, and the policy towards Ireland which their literary men were continually urging upon the English people for their adoption was similar to that of the avaricious housewife who killed the goose who laid her golden eggs. [*Laughter.*] Yes, such was the course they pursued towards Ireland, and you will deserve the reputation of being the lineal descendants of that goose if you be such ganders as not to declare in a voice of thunder that no longer shall this system of plunder be permitted to continue. [*Hear.*]

My next impeachment of the Union is founded upon the disastrous effects which have resulted therefrom to our commercial and manufacturing interests, as well as to our general national interests. Previous to the Union, the County Meath was filled with the seats of noblemen and gentlemen. What a contrast does its present state present! I yesterday read at the Association a list of the deserted mansions which are now to be found ruined and desolate in your county. Even the spot where the Duke of Wellington, famed the world over for his detestation of his country, drew his first breath,[6] instead of bearing a noble castle or splendid mansion, presented the aspect of ruin and desolation, and briers and nettles adequately marked the place that produced him. [*Hear.*] The County of Meath was at one time studded thickly with manufactories in every direction, and an enormous sum was expended yearly in wages; but here, as in every other district of the country, the eye was continually shocked with sights which evidenced with but too great eloquence the lamentable decay which has been entailed upon our country by the Union. The linen trade at one time

---

[6] Wellington's birthplace was Dangon Castle in County Meath.

kept all Ulster in a state of affluence and prosperity. [*Hear, hear.*] Kilkenny was for ages celebrated for its extensive blanket manufactures. In Cork also, in Carrick-on-Suir, and in a thousand other localities too numerous to mention, thousands were kept in constant and lucrative employment at various branches of national industry from year's end to year's end, before the passing of the Union. But this is no longer the case, and one man is not now kept in employment for a thousand who were employed before the Union. The report[7] of the English Commissioners themselves has declared this appalling fact to the world: that one-third of our population are in a state of actual destitution; and yet, in the face of all this, men may be found who, claiming to themselves the character of political honesty, stand up and declare themselves in favour of the continuance of the Union.

It was no bargain—it was a base swindle. Had it indeed been a fair bargain, the Irish would have continued faithful to it to the last, regardless of the injuries which it might have entailed upon them. For the Irish people have been invariably faithful to their contracts, whereas England never yet made a promise which she did not violate nor ever entered into a contract which she did not shamelessly and scandalously outrage. [*Hear, hear, hear.*] Even the Union itself, beneficial as it is to England, is but a living lie to Ireland. Everybody now admits the mischief that the Union has produced to Ireland. The very fact of its not being a compact is alone sufficient to nullify the Union; and on that ground I here proclaim, in the name of the Irish nation, that it is null and void. [*Loud cheers.*] But it is no union at all. It is a union of legislators, but not a union of nations. Are you and I one bit more of Englishmen now than we were twenty or forty years ago? [*Cheers and laughter.*] If we had a union, would not Ireland have the same Parliamentary franchise that is enjoyed by England? England, calling it a union, has still had the singular extreme of fraud and injustice and iniquity; and no nation on the face of the earth ever committed so much of injustice, fraud, and iniquity as England. But calling it a union, could anything be more unjust on the part of England than to give her own people a higher and more extensive grade of franchise and to the Irish people a more limited and an extinguishing and perishing franchise? She has given to her people an extended municipal reform and to Ireland a wretched and miserable municipal reform. Even within the last week, a plan was brought forward by Lord Eliot[8] and the sneaking Attorney General, Smith,[9] that will have the effect of depriving one-third of those who now enjoy the franchise of its possession.

No, the Union is void, but it is more peremptorily void on the ground of the ecclesiastical revenues of the country being left to support a church

---

[7] *Poor Inquiry Commission Report* (London, 1836).

[8] Lord Eliot was appointed Chief Secretary of Ireland in 1841 by Peel. His Arms Bill of May 29, 1843, to disarm the Irish gave impetus to the monster meetings that culminated at Tara.

[9] Thomas B. C. Smith became Attorney General late in 1842.

of a small portion of the people. In England the ecclesiastical revenues of the country are given to the clergy that the majority of the people believe to teach the truth. In Scotland the ecclesiastical revenues are, or at least were up to a late period, paid to the majority of the clergy of the people; but the Irish people are compelled to pay the clergy of a small minority not amounting to more than the one-tenth of the people of the entire island. [*Great cheering.*] I contend, therefore, that the Union is a nullity. But do I, on that account, advise you to turn out against it? No such thing. I advise you to act quietly and peaceably, and in no other way. [*A voice: "Any way you like."*] Remember that my doctrine is that "the man who commits a crime gives strength to the enemy," and you should not act in any manner that would strengthen the enemies of your country. [*Hear, hear.*] You should act peaceably and quietly, but firmly and determinedly. You may be certain that your cheers here today will be conveyed to England. [*The vast assemblage here commenced cheering for several minutes.*] Yes, the overwhelming majesty of your multitude will be taken to England and will have its effect there.

The Duke of Wellington began by threatening us. He talked of civil war, but he does not say a single word of that now. [*"Hear, hear" and laughter.*] He is now getting eyelet holes made in the old barracks, and only think of an old general doing such a thing, just as if we were going to break our heads against stone walls. [*Laughter.*] I am glad to find that a great quantity of brandy and biscuits has been latterly imported, and I hope the poor soldiers get some of them. But the Duke of Wellington is not now talking of attacking us, and I am glad of it. But I tell him this: I mean no disrespect to the brave, the gallant, and the good-conducted soldiers that compose the Queen's Army; and all of them that we have in this country are exceedingly well-conducted. [*"Hear, hear" and cheers.*] There is not one of you that has a single complaint to make against any of them. [*"Not one."*] They are the bravest army in the world, and therefore I do not mean to disparage them at all; but I feel it to be a fact that Ireland, roused as she is at the present moment, would, if they made war upon us, furnish women enough to beat the entire of the Queen's forces. [*Great cheers.*] At the last fight for Ireland,[10] when she was betrayed by having confided in England's honour—but oh! English honour will never again betray our land, for the man would deserve to be betrayed who would confide again in England; I would as soon think of confiding in the cousin-german of a certain personage having two horns and a hoof [*laughter*]— at that last battle, the Irish soldiers, after three days' fighting, being attacked by fresh troops, faltered and gave way, and 1,500 of the British Army entered the breach. The Irish soldiers were fainting and retiring

---

[10] The Siege of Limerick in 1691. Irish Catholics held that the Treaty of Limerick (October 3, 1691) was breached by a series of repressive statutes, known as Penal Laws, designed to secure Protestant ascendancy in Irish political, economic, and social life.

when the women of Limerick threw themselves between the contending forces and actually stayed the progress of the advancing enemy. I am stating matter of history to you, and the words I use are not mine but those of Parson Story,[11] the chaplain of King William, who describes the siege and who admits that the Limerick women drove back the English soldiers from fifteen to thirty paces. Several of the women were killed when a shriek of horror resounded from the ranks of the Irish. They cried out, "Let us rather die to the last man than that our women should be injured," and they then threw themselves forward; and made doubly valiant by the bravery of the women, they scattered the Saxon and the Dane before them. [*Loud applause.*] Yes, I have women enough in Ireland to beat them if necessary; but, my friends, it is idle to imagine that any statesman ever existed who could resist the cry that Ireland makes for justice. [*Cheers.*]

But there is one thing that I wish to caution you against. I have ascertained that some scoundrel Ribbon Society[12] swearers are endeavouring to delude the people. I have traced their progress from Manchester, and I have ascertained that some of them even had the audacity to state that they are in my confidence. This is a holy festival[13] in the Roman Catholic Church. It is the anniversary of the blessed day when the Mother of our Redeemer ascended from earth to meet her Son and reign with Him forever. Oh! on such a day I would not tell you a falsehood. I hope I am under Her protection. I hope that our sacred cause has Her prayers for its success. [*Loud cheers.*] The Church within the last year offered prayers throughout the Christian world for the cause of religion in Spain and against the sacrilegious plunderers of the Church in that country, and what happened? The minion of these plunderers had fallen from power, and nobody knows how.[14] He made no effort to return, and nobody can tell why. It seems as if he had been bewildered in his course from on high; and the tyrant of Spain has fallen from his power and his station. Well, by the solemnity of this day, I conjure you to lay hold of any of these fellows[15] you can meet with and take them to the police office, and you will very probably find some of the stipendiary magistrates that they may send here very sorry to see their friend in trouble. [*Laughter and loud cries of "Hear, hear."*] I tell you again that I am afraid of nothing but the establishment of Ribbonism. [*Hear, hear.*]

I told you that the Union did not deprive the people of that right or take away the authority to have self-legislation. It has not lessened the Prerog-

---

[11] George Story, who wrote *A True and Impartial History of the Most Material Occurrences in Ireland* (London, 1693).

[12] A secret revolutionary society that used violent methods to counteract Protestant influence and to protect tenant farmers and agricultural workers.

[13] August 15 is called the Feast of the Assumption of the Blessed Virgin.

[14] A military uprising in 1843 deposed General Baldomero Esparteo, known for his persecution of Catholics.

[15] Ribbonmen.

atives of the Crown or taken away the rights of the Sovereign, and amongst them is the right to call her Parliament wherever the people are entitled to it, and the people of Ireland are entitled to have it in Ireland. [*Cheers.*] And the Queen has only tomorrow to issue her writs and get the Chancellor to seal them, and if Sir Edward Sugden[16] does not sign them she will soon get an Irishman that will to revive the Irish Parliament. Remember, I pronounce the Union to be null—to be obeyed as an injustice must be obeyed when it is supported by law until we have the Royal authority to set the matter right and substitute our own Parliament.

I delight at having this day presided over such an assemblage on Tara Hill. [*Cheers.*] Those shouts that burst from you were enough to recall to life the kings and chiefs of Ireland. I almost fancy that the spirit of the mighty dead are hovering over us—that the ancient kings and chiefs of Ireland are from yonder clouds listening to us. Oh, what a joyous and cheering sound is conveyed in the chirrup for Old Ireland! It is the most beautiful, the most fertile, the most abundant, the most productive country on the face of the earth. It is a lovely land, indented with noble harbours, intersected with transcendant, translucent streams, divided by mighty estuaries. Its harbours are open at every hour for every tide and are sheltered from every storm that can blow from any quarter of Heaven. Oh, yes, it is a lovely land, and where is the coward that would not dare to die for it? Yes, our country exhibits the extreme of civilisation, and your majestic movement is already the admiration of the civilised world. No other country could produce such an amount of physical force coupled with so much decorum and propriety of conduct. Many thousands of persons assembled together, and though they have force sufficient to carry any battle that ever was fought, they separate with the tranquillity of schoolboys breaking up in the afternoon. [*Hear.*] I wish you could read my heart to see how deeply the love of Ireland is engraven upon it. And let the people of Ireland, who stood by me so long, stand by me a little longer, and Ireland shall be a nation again. [*Cheers.*]

---

[16] English Lord Chancellor in 1843. Sugden insisted that the monster meetings posed a danger "to the safety of the State."

Charles S. Parnell

"The Irish Land Question"*
Ennis, Ireland, September 19, 1880

In acknowledging my gratification at this splendid reception which you have given us and at this magnificent meeting, exceeded in size and importance by none which I have had the honour of addressing in Ireland, I wish to say that it gives me additional pleasure to have the opportunity of addressing for the first time after the Session of Parliament a meeting in Ennis, which was the first constituency in Ireland to send me help in the last Parliament. [*Cheers.*] I may, perhaps, also be permitted to point out to you a noteworthy feature connected with this meeting, especially as I think it is a sign of the times and a sign of the progress of our movement. When first I addressed you last July twelve-month, this square was glittering with the bayonets of police [*cheers*]; and I promised you then, pointing to the force, that if we could build up a determined and united Irish Party, in a very few years this military force would be abolished altogether. [*Cheers.*] Today there is not a single constable present at this meeting [*cheers*], and it is the first of Irish land meetings which has not been attended by scores, and some of them by several scores, of constables. Let us look upon this as a happy omen of the future, as the first recognition in our history by the Government of England of the ability of our people to maintain order for themselves [*cheers*] and consequently to govern themselves [*cheers*]; and let me ask you, fellow-countrymen, in return so to bear yourselves during this meeting and after this meeting as to show that you are worthy of practical power and of self-government. [*Cheers.*] Let us see after this meeting no disturbance in the streets, no signs of liquor upon any man, and let us give no excuse to the police who are now confined to their barracks. [*Cheers.*]

* The text is from *The Times*, September 20, 1880, p. 11. It is nearly identical to that printed in *Freeman's Journal* (Dublin) for the same date, but contains audience reaction.

The resolution[1] which has been proposed and seconded is one inculcating the necessity of union among ourselves and independence of every English Ministry, whether it be Tory or Radical. [*Hear.*] I have always believed in the necessity of this, but my convictions have been tenfold strengthened by the experience of the past Session. I have seen that the more independence the Irish Party showed, the more respect it gained for itself and for Ireland. [*Hear.*] I do not complain of our Party. Our Party, on the whole, has been a good and a worthy one. It is true that a very small section followed the Government across the House of Commons [*groans*] and refused to sit with the great majority of their colleagues, and the spectacle was presented of an apparently divided Irish Party, divided, perhaps, forty on one side and some twenty on the other.[2] I regret from the bottom of my heart this appearance of division and disunion, but I trust that those Members, recognising that the overwhelming opinion of their constituents is in favour of union and unity, will retrace their steps and will again join the great body of their colleagues in presenting a solid front to every Government. For ourselves, in the last Parliament, when we had a Tory Government to face, I never at the time hid my convictions that with a Liberal Government in power it would be necessary for us somewhat to change or modify our action. Nothing was to be gained from the Tories, and it was therefore necessary for the Irish Party to punish them without sparing them. [*Cheers.*] Yet this present Liberal Government has made great promises. Up to the present it has absolutely given us not one single performance. But through the mouth of a Chief Secretary of Ireland[3] it has entreated that it be given one year's time in order to see whether it cannot benefit Ireland, and we have been willing to give it the time and trial; but I stand here today to express my conviction that whenever it is necessary for us to resume our ancient policy such as we practised against the Tories, that whenever we find that this Liberal Government falls short of either its professions or its performances, on that day it will be the duty of the present strong Irish Party to show that it can punish the Liberal Government as well as the Tory. [*Cheers.*]

Now, we have had issued a Land Commission,[4] and there has been some difference of opinion as to whether the tenant farmers ought to give evidence before that commission or not. I have not yet had an opportunity of

---

[1] "That we cordially endorse the action of the Irish Party under the guidance of Mr Parnell during the last Session of Parliament; but we view with regret the secession of one section of that Party that followed the Whigs across the floor of the House, and we trust that next Session Irish Members will sit in a body in Parliament in opposition to every English Ministry until the right of Ireland to self-government has been restored."
[2] Irish Members traditionally sat with their Liberal or Conservative colleagues. In 1880, Parnell urged that all Irish Nationalists, regardless of party, should sit together on the Opposition (in this case, Tory) side of the House.
[3] William E. Forster held the office from April, 1880, to May, 1882.
[4] A public inquiry sponsored by Parliament that gathered evidence leading to Gladstone's Land Bill introduced on April 7, 1881.

saying anything in public about this matter, but I may say that in the main my opinions coincide with those of Mr. John Dillon[5] with reference to this Commission. [*Hear.*] At the same time, I only wish to express my opinions and I do not wish to coerce the Irish tenant farmer with reference to this matter one way or the other. I am bound to tell you honestly that I believe this Commission was appointed in order to try and whittle down the demand of the Irish tenantry, to find out for the English Government what was the very least measure of reform that had a chance of being accepted in Ireland, and to a great extent to divert the minds of tenant farmers from agitating and organising to the useless work of going before this Commission and giving evidence. I cannot possibly see what useful effect evidence before this Commission can have. We know that the report, if there is any report, must be of a very one-sided character and against the interests of the people of this country. The composition of the Commission is a guarantee of that. Hence we have to consider whether it is at all probable that the advantage that might be gained by having evidence put down could have any counter-balancing advantages as compared with the demoralisation that the farmers must experience when they turn their eyes with any hope or confidence to a Commission so constituted. What will be said if the tenant farmers come before this Commission in large numbers? It will be said that you have accepted the Commission. It will be said that you will be bound by its report, and if there is very much evidence given it will form a very good excuse for the Government and for the English Tory Party to put off legislation on the land question next Session until they have time to read the evidence and consider its bearing and effect. My opinion, then, decidedly is this: whatever harm you do to your cause by going before the Commission, you certainly will be able to do no good. Depend upon it that the measure of the Land Bill[6] of next Session will be the measure of your activity and energy this winter. [*Cheers.*] It will be the measure of your determination not to pay unjust rents; it will be the measure of your determination to keep a firm grip of your homesteads. [*Cheers.*] It will be the measure of your determination not to bid for farms from which others have been evicted. The land question must be settled, and settled in a way that will be satisfactory to you. It depends, therefore, upon yourselves, and not upon any Commission or any Government. When you have made this question ripe for settlement, then, and not till then, will it be settled. [*Cheers.*] It is very nearly ripe already in many parts of Ireland. It is ripe in Mayo, Galway, Roscommon, Sligo, and portions of this County. [*Cheers.*] But I regret to say that tenant farmers of the County Clare have been backward in organisation up to the present

[5] Dillon, an Irish Member who accompanied Parnell on his American tour, was an ardent Land Leaguer.
[6] The Bill, receiving Royal Assent in August, made some concessions to Irish tenants; especially important was the provision for judicially fixed rents.

time. You must take and band yourselves together in land leagues. Every town and village must have its own branch. You must know the circumstances of the holdings and of the tenures of the district over which the League has jurisdiction. You must see that the principles of the Land League are inculcated, and when you have done this in Clare, then Clare will take her rank with the other active counties, and you will be included in the next Land Bill brought forward by the Government. [*Cheers.*]

Now, what are you to do to a tenant who bids for a farm from which another tenant has been evicted? [*"Shoot him!"*] I think I heard somebody say, "Shoot him." I wish to point out to you a very much better way, a more Christian and charitable way, which will give the lost sinner an opportunity of repenting. [*Laughter and "Hear, hear."*] When a man takes a farm from which another has been evicted, you must shun him on the roadside when you meet him, you must shun him in the streets of the town, you must shun him in the shop, you must shun him in the fair green and in the market place, and even in the place of worship. By leaving him severely alone, by putting him into a moral convent, by isolating him from the rest of his countrymen as if he were the leper of old, you must show him your detestation of the crime he has committed.[7] If you do this you may depend on it that there will be no man so lost to shame as to dare the public opinion of all the right-thinking men in the country and transgress your unwritten code of laws. [*Loud cheers.*]

People are very much engaged at present in discussing the way in which the land question is to be settled, just the same as when a few years since Irishmen were at each other's throats as to the sort of Parliament we would have if we got one. I am always thinking it is better first to catch your hare before you decide how you are going to cook him. [*Laughter.*] I would strongly recommend public men not to waste their breath too much in discussing how the land question is to be settled, but rather to help and encourage the people in making it, as I said just now, ripe for settlement. [*Applause.*] When it is ripe for settlement you will probably have your choice as to how it shall be settled, and I said a year ago that the land question would never be settled until the Irish landlords were just as anxious to have it settled as the Irish tenants. [*Cheers and a voice: "They soon will be."*] There are, indeed, so many ways in which it may be settled that it is almost superfluous to discuss them; but I stand here today to express my opinion that no settlement can be satisfactory or permanent which does not ensure the uprooting of that system of landlordism which has brought the country three times in a century to famine. [*Cheers.*] The feudal system of land tenure has been tried in almost every European country and it has been found wanting everywhere, but nowhere has it

---

[7] Social and economic coercion of this type was used against Captain Charles C. Boycott, an English land agent in County Mayo. The incident (and the term "boycott") became famous in 1880.

wrought more evil, produced more suffering, crime, and destitution than in Ireland. [*Cheers.*] It was abolished in Prussia by transferring the lands from the landlords to the occupying tenants; the landlords were given Government paper as compensation. Let the English Government give the landlords their paper tomorrow as compensation. [*Laughter.*] We want no money; not a single penny of money would be necessary. Why, if they gave the Irish landlords—the bad section of them—the £4,000,000 or £5,000,000 a year that they spend on the police and military [*groans*] in helping them to collect their rents, that would be a solution of it [*cheers*], and a very cheap solution of it. But perhaps, as with other reforms, they will try a little patchwork and tinkering for a while until they learn better. [*Hear, hear.*] Well, let them patch and tinker if they wish. In my opinion, the longer the landlords wait, the worse the settlement they will get. [*Cheers.*] Now is the time for them to settle, before the people learn the power of combination.

We have been accused of preaching communistic doctrines when we told the people not to pay an unjust rent, and the following out of this advice in a few of the Irish counties has shown the English Government the necessity for a radical alteration in the land laws. But how would they like it if we told the people some day or other not to pay any rent until this question is settled? [*Cheers.*] We have not told them that yet, and I hope it may never be necessary for us to speak in that way. [*Hear.*] I hope the question will be settled peaceably, in a friendly manner, and justly to all parties. [*Hear.*] If it should not be settled, we cannot continue to allow this millstone to hang round the neck of our country, throttling its industry and preventing progress. [*Cheers.*] It will be for the consideration of wiser heads than mine whether if the landlords continue obdurate and refuse all just concessions, we shall not be obliged to tell the people of Ireland to strike against rent until this question has been settled [*cheers*], and if the 500,000 tenant farmers of Ireland struck against the 10,000 landlords, I should like to see where they would get police and soldiers enough to make them pay. [*Loud cheers.*]

[*A resolution was also adopted pledging the meeting not to take any farm from which a tenant had been evicted. Mr. T. D. Sullivan, M.P., in supporting it, was cheered for saying that in the whole Irish party there was not a more courageous or resolute man than the Member for Ennis. If the order went from Charles Stewart Parnell to take the mace that lay before the Speaker in the House of Commons and throw it out the window, he would do it. In the evening, crowds carrying torches and tar barrels paraded the streets.*]

William E. Gladstone

"The First Home Rule Bill"[*]
Commons, June 7, 1886

Mr. Speaker—I shall venture to make, Sir, a few remarks on the speech of the right honourable Gentleman[1]; but I will first allow myself the satisfaction of expressing what I believe to be a very widespread sentiment, and saying with what pleasure I listened to two speeches this evening—the singularly eloquent speech of the senior Member for Newcastle[2] and the masterly exposition—for I cannot call it less—of the honourable Member for Cork.[3] Sir, I feel a strong conviction that speeches couched in that tone, marked alike by sound statesmanship and far-seeing moderation, will never fail to produce a lasting effect upon the minds and convictions of the people of England and Scotland.

Sir, with respect to the personal question which has arisen between the honourable Member for Cork and the right honourable Gentleman opposite, I think it no part of my duty to interfere. I have avoided and I shall avoid in the discussion of this question, so far as I can, all matters which are of a purely polemical character between Party and Party. I presume that this subject will be carried further. I understand a distinct allegation to be made by the honourable Member for Cork with regard to some person whose name he does not give but who is one of a limited body. In that limited body it will not be difficult, I conclude, to procure it if it can be given. Upon that I pass no judgment. I simply make this comment upon a subject which is of considerable public interest. The right honourable Gentleman opposite will do me the justice to say that I have not sought before taking office or since taking it to make the conduct which right honourable Gentlemen opposite pursued on their accession to power

[*] The text is from *Hansard's Parliamentary Debates*, Third Series, Vol. CCCVI, cols. 1215–1240. The Home Rule Bill, introduced on April 8, was defeated 343–313.
[1] Sir Michael Hicks Beach, Conservative Member for West Bristol.
[2] Joseph Cowen
[3] Charles Parnell, who stated that a Minister in Salisbury's Government had offered Conservative action on Home Rule in exchange for support from Irish Members. Hicks Beach denied the allegation, challenging Parnell to name the Minister.

matter of reproach against them. [*Opposition laughter.*] If they do not like to do me that justice I shall not ask it. On the speech of the right honourable Gentleman I need not dwell at great length. He began by stating a series of what he succinctly described as simple facts. I will not say his simple facts are pure fictions because that would hardly, perhaps, be courteous. But they are as devoid of foundation as if they had been pure fiction.

The right honourable Gentleman declared—though I do not see that it has much to do with the matter—that this is the Bill of one man. Well, I am amazed that the noble Lord[4] and the right honourable Gentleman speak as if they had been at my elbow all day and every day through the autumn and winter of last year. How can any man know that this is the Bill of one man? [*A laugh.*] How can the honourable Member who laughs know that this is the Bill of one man? Reference is made to the allegations of my right honourable Friend the Member for West Birmingham.[5] My right honourable Friend could only speak within the compass of his knowledge, and if he said that it was the Bill of one man he would know no more about it than the honourable Member opposite. What my right honourable Friend said, and said truly, was to state the time at which the Bill came before the Cabinet. But, Sir, long before that time, the subject of the Bill and its leading details had been matter of anxious consideration between me and my nearest political friends. ["*Name!*"] I never heard a more extraordinary demand in my life, not to say gross impropriety. I refer to those of my colleagues who were most likely to give the most valuable aid and with whom from the first I was in communication. Then, Sir, the right honourable Gentleman says we were installed in office by the help of the honourable Member for Cork. The right honourable Gentleman appears to have forgotten the elementary lessons of arithmetic. It is perfectly true that the energetic assistance of the honourable Member for Cork might have kept the right honourable Gentleman in office. The right honourable Gentleman speaks of the Party behind him and the Liberal Party, as it then was on this side of the House, as if they had been two equal Parties and only required the honourable Member for Cork and his friends to turn the scale.

Lord Randolph Churchill: They were.

Mr. Gladstone: They were, says the noble Lord? The noble Lord's arithmetic is still more defective—335 is by 85 votes a larger Party than 250.

Then the right honourable Gentleman says that with the exception of the customs and excise duties no change was made in the Bill after it was first submitted to the Cabinet. He has no means of knowing that, even if it were true, but it happens to be entirely untrue. Provisions of great importance had never been seen by my right honourable Friend the Member for

[4] Lord Randolph Churchill, Member for South Paddington.
[5] Joseph Chamberlain, who broke from the Liberal Party on the Home Rule issue.

West Birmingham. My right honourable Friend took exception to certain provisions of the Bill without being acquainted with the whole *corpus* of the Bill. That is the fact; so that the right honourable Gentleman is entirely wrong also upon this as well as upon his other "simple facts." Then the right honourable Gentleman says that I had announced that this Bill was not to be reconstructed. I announced nothing of the kind. I announced that I did not promise that it should be reconstructed. [*A laugh.*] There are actually Gentlemen opposite—Members of Parliament chosen to represent the country—who think this a matter of laughter and can see no distinction between promises that a Bill shall not be reconstructed and not having promised that it shall be. I conceive that a person who has promised that a Bill shall be reconstructed is bound to reconstruct it. Is that true? A person who has not promised that a Bill shall be reconstructed is free to reconstruct it, but is not bound to do so. I hope I have made a clear distinction; and I am glad to see that the laughter opposite has ceased as light has flowed in upon the minds of those honourable Gentlemen.

I was struck with another observation of the right honourable Gentleman. He says that this Bill, whatever else may happen, will at any rate be rejected by the votes of a majority of English and Scotch Members [*Opposition cheers*]—and he is cheered by those who teach us that they are, above all things, anxious for the maintenance of an absolutely United Kingdom and an absolutely United Parliament, in which Irish Members are in all respects to be assimilated into and identical with those representing English and Scotch constituencies. The right honourable Gentleman talks about a Dissolution, and I am very glad to find that upon that point he and we are much more nearly associated in our views and expectations than upon almost any other point. After what the right honourable Gentleman has said and the want of acquaintance which he has shown with the history of this Bill, on which he dwelt so long, and after what was said by my right honourable Friend behind me,[6] I must again remind the House, at any rate, in the clearest terms I can use, of the exact position in which we stand with reference to the Bill. In the first place, I take it to be absolutely beyond dispute, on broad and high Parliamentary grounds, that that which is voted upon tonight is the principle of the Bill as distinguished from the particulars of the Bill. [*A laugh.*] What may be the principle of the Bill, I grant you freely, I have no authority to determine. [*A laugh.*] The honourable Member laughs; I am much obliged for his running commentary, which is not usual on my observations, but it is our duty to give our own sense of the construction of the principle of the Bill, and I think I drew a confirmation of that construction from the speech of the right honourable Gentleman, because he himself said this was a Bill for the purpose of establishing a legislative body in Ireland for the manage-

---

[6] George Goschen, Member for East Edinburgh.

ment of Irish affairs. Well, Sir, that—if we have any power or any title to give our view on the subject—is the principle of the Bill. As respects the particulars of the Bill, I apprehend it to be beyond all question that Members voting for the principle of the Bill are in this sense entirely and absolutely free—that if they consider that there is another set of provisions by means of which better and fuller effect may be given to the principle of the Bill, they are at liberty to displace all the particulars they find in it which hinder that better and fuller effect being given to the principle. [*A laugh.*] That does not admit of doubt. I am quite certain the honourable Member who laughs will not rise in his place at any time and say that a Member is not at liberty to remove each and all, if he thinks fit, of the particulars of the Bill if in good faith he believes that the principle of the Bill can be better and more adequately promoted by a different set of provisions. But the Government have taken certain engagements. They have taken an engagement as to taxation for the intervention of Irish Members, to the terms of which I need not refer. They have also taken an engagement on the claim of Ireland to a continued concern through her Members in the treatment of Imperial subjects generally. And that has entailed a positive pledge to reconstruct the twenty-fourth clause and to adopt certain consequential amendments connected with it.

One more question has been raised and has excited a deep interest, and that is with respect to other amendments to the Bill. Of course, as to the freedom of honourable Members to suggest other amendments, I have spoken in terms which, I think, are abundantly large. As respects our duty, there can be no question at all that our duty—if an interval is granted to us and the circumstances of the present Session require the withdrawal of the Bill, and it is to be re-introduced with amendments at an early date in the autumn—of course, it is our duty to amend our Bill with every real amendment and improvement and with whatever is calculated to make it more effective and more acceptable for the attainment of its end. It is as a matter of course and without any specific assurance our duty to consider all such amendments. We are perfectly free to deal with them; but it would be the meanest and the basest act on the part of the Government to pretend that they have a plan of reconstruction ready beforehand, cut and dry, in their minds at a time when from the very nature of the case it must be obvious that they can have no such thing. So much, then, for the situation, for the freedom of Members to propose amendments, for the duty of the Government to consider amendments and improve their Bill, if they can, with the view of a fuller and better application of the principle; but subject, let me add, to conditions, five in number, which have been clearly enumerated on a former occasion and from which there is no intention on our part to recede.

The right honourable Gentleman speaks of Ulster as a question of principle. The question of Ulster, or whatever the common name of the question may be, may be one of great importance; but I must say that while I in no respect recede from the statement made in regard to it at the opening of these debates, yet I cannot see that any certain plan for Ulster has made any serious or effective progress. The honourable and gallant Gentleman the Member for North Armagh[7] emphatically disclaims the severance of Ulster from the rest of Ireland, and the honourable Member for Cork has laid before us a reasoned and elaborate argument on that subject today, which, as it appears to me, requires the careful attention of those who propose such a plan for our acceptance. We retain, however, perfect freedom to judge the case upon its merits.

Now, Sir, I want to say a word upon the subject of Irish loyalism, because we are obliged to use phrases in debates of this kind which cannot be explained from time to time when using them, and it is well that there should be a little understanding beforehand. When I hear the speeches of the honourable Member for South Belfast[8]—and of some other Gentlemen —it always appears to me that he is under the pious conviction that loyalty is innate in the Irish Protestants and disloyalty innate in [*a slight pause*] some other persons. I do believe that he is under the impression that at all times, in all the long generations of Irish history, that has been the distinction to be drawn between Protestants and persons who are not Protestants. ["*No, no!*"] Is Protestant loyalism a thing that has a date and origin, or is it not? Has the honourable Member or the honourable and gallant Member for North Armagh inquired what was the state of Ireland in the eighteenth century with respect to loyalty? As far as regarded the great mass of the population—the Roman Catholic population—they were hardly born into political life until the close of the century, and for a long period in the time of Dean Swift, who describes their incapacity for political action as something beyond belief, it would have been absurd to speak of them as loyal or disloyal. But at the close of the century the Protestants and Roman Catholics of Ireland were described in a short passage by Mr. Burke, which I shall now read to the House. The date of it is 1796, and it is taken from a letter to Mr. Windham.[9] He speaks of the subject of disaffection. "It"—that is to say disaffection

> ... has cast deep roots in the principles and habits of the majority amongst the lower and middle classes of the whole Protestant part of Ireland. The Catholics who are intermingled with them are more or less tainted. In the other parts of Ireland (some in Dublin only excepted), the Catholics, who are in a manner the whole people, are as yet sound; but they may be provoked, as all men easily may be, out of their principles.

What does that mean? That the Protestants, not having grievances to complain of, have become loyal; but in many cases the Roman Catholics,

---

[7] Major Edward Saunderson.
[8] William Johnston.
[9] Burke's letter to Windham was dated March 30, 1797.

as Mr. Burke says, have been provoked, as all men easily may be, out of their principles of loyalty. And these are words and these are ideas which show us what is the way in which to promote loyalty and what is the way in which we can destroy it.

Another subject on which I shall dwell only for a moment is that of federation. Many Gentlemen in this House are greatly enamoured of this idea, and the object they have in view is a noble object. I will not admit the justice of the disparagement cast by the right honourable Gentleman on the British Empire. I do not consider that this is a "loosely connected Empire." But I admit that, if means can be devised of establishing a more active connexion with out distant Colonies, the idea is well worthy the attention of every loyal man. The idea of federation is a popular one. I will give no opinion upon it now; but I suspect that it is beset with more difficulties than have as yet been examined or brought to light. But this Bill, whatever be its rights or wrongs in any other respect, is unquestionably a step—an important step—in that direction. Federation rests essentially upon two things and upon two things alone, as preconditioned. One is the division of legislature and the other is the division of subjects, and both those divisions are among the vital objects of this Bill.

The right honourable Gentleman has referred to the question of supremacy. My own opinion is that this debate has, in a considerable degree, cleared the ground upon that subject. It is most satisfactory to me to hear the statements of the honourable Member for Cork. I own I have heard some astounding doctrines—astounding to an ignorant layman—from learned lawyers; but still, upon the whole, the balance of authority seems to me to have established as a clear and elementary proposition that cannot be denied that this Parliament, be it the Imperial Parliament or not, as long as it continues in its legal identity, is possessed now, as it was possessed before the Union and before the time of Grattan's Parliament, of a supremacy which is absolutely and in the nature of things inalienable, which it could not part with if it would and which it would not part with if it could. There is no doubt a practical question, because it is quite true that in constituting a legislature in Ireland we do what we did when we constituted a legislature for Canada and for Australia. We devolve an important portion of power—we did it in Canada and I hope we shall do it in Ireland—and we devolve it with a view to not a partial, not a nominal, but a real and practical independent management of their own affairs. That is what the right honourable Gentleman objects to doing. That is the thing which we desire and hope and mean to do.

It is obvious that the question may be raised, How are you to deal with the possible cases where the Imperial Government, notwithstanding this general division of affairs, may be compelled by obligations of Imperial interest and honour to interfere? My answer is that this question has received a far better solution from practical politics and from the experience of the last forty or fifty years than could ever have been given to it by the definition of lawyers, however eminent they may be. When the Legislature of Canada was founded this difficulty arose. We had the case of the Canadian Rebellion, where I myself, for one, was of opinion, and Lord Brougham was also of opinion—I know not now whether rightly or wrongly—that the honour of the Crown had been invaded by the proposition to grant compensation for losses in the Rebellion to those who had been rebels and who had incurred those losses as rebels. I say nothing now about our being right or wrong; but in 1849 Lord Brougham brought forward a motion on the subject in the House of Lords, and I myself did the same in the House of Commons. The important part was the declaration which was drawn from Ministers of the Crown. Lord John Russell then, in answer to me, laid down what I conceive to be a true and sound doctrine in terms which, I think, may be described as classical and authoritative in their manner of dealing with this question. Lord Russell, speaking on the 14th of June, 1849, said:

> I entirely concur with the right honourable Gentleman—and it is, indeed, in conformity with the sentiments I expressed in a despatch written, I think, some ten years ago—that there are cases which must be left to the decision of the responsible Ministers of the Crown. There are cases where the honour of the Crown and the safety of this country are concerned, and in such cases it requires the utmost temper in the Colonies and the utmost temper and firmness in this country in order to prevent differences from being pushed to a collision which might be fatal to the connexion between the mother country and the Colonies. I fully admit that there are such cases; but when the right honourable Gentleman goes on to say that he considers the Earl of Elgin has received some instructions from the Government of this country by which he is debarred from asking the advice and direction of the Crown upon questions which affect Imperial policy and the national honour, he is totally mistaken in that unwarranted assumption. [*Hansard's Parliamentary Debates*, Third Series, Vol. CVI, cols. 225–226.]

That passage, as I believe, contains very justly and clearly set forth the practical mode by which this question, difficult in the abstract, will be settled now as it has been settled before, and we shall find that as it has been perfectly easy to reconcile the rights of Canada with the supremacy of the Imperial Parliament, it will not be less easy in practise to reconcile the rights and the autonomy of Ireland with the same supremacy.

I wish now to refer to another matter. I hear constantly used the terms Unionists and Separatists. But what I want to know is, who are the Unionists? I want to know, who are the Separatists? I see this Bill described in newspapers of great circulation and elsewhere as a Separation Bill. Several Gentlemen opposite adopt and make that style of description their own. Speaking of that description, I say that it is the merest slang of vulgar controversy. Do you think this Bill will tend to separation? [*Hear, hear.*] Well, your arguments and even your prejudices are worthy of all consideration and respect; but is it a fair and rational mode of conducting a controversy to attach these hard names to measures on which you wish to argue and on which, I suppose, you desire to convince by argument? Let me illustrate. I go back to the Reform Act of Lord Grey. When that Reform Bill was introduced, it was conscientiously and honestly believed by great masses of men, and intelligent men, too, that the Bill absolutely involved the destruction of the Monarchy. The Duke of Wellington propounded a doctrine very much to this effect; but I do not think that any of those Gentlemen, nor the newspapers that supported them, ever descended so low in their choice of weapons as to call the measure "the Monarchy Destruction Bill." Such language is a mere begging of the question.

Now, I must make a large demand on your patience and your indulgence—we conscientiously believe that there are Unionists and Disunionists; but that it is our policy that leads to union and yours to separation. This involves a very large and deep historical question. Let us try, for a few moments, to look at it historically. The arguments used on the other side of the House appear to me to rest in principle and in the main upon one of two suppositions. One of them, which I will not now discuss, is the profound incompetency of the Irish people; but there is another, and it is this. It is, I believe, the conscientious conviction of honourable Gentlemen opposite that when two or more countries associated but not incorporated together are in disturbed relations with each other, the remedy is to create an absolute legislative incorporation. On the other hand, they believe that the dissolution of such an incorporation is clearly the mode to bring about the dissolution of the political relations of those countries. I do not deny that there may be cases in which legislative incorporation may have been the means of constituting a great country, as in the case of France. But we believe, as proved by history, that where there are those disturbed relations between countries associated but not incorporated, the true principle is to make ample provision for local independence, subject to Imperial unity.

These are propositions of the greatest interest and importance. Gentlemen speak of tightening the ties between England and Ireland as if tightening the tie were always the means to be adopted. Tightening the tie is frequently the means of making it burst, whilst relaxing the tie is very frequently the way to provide for its durability and to enable it to stand a stronger strain; so that it is true, as was said by the honourable Member for Newcastle, that the separation of legislatures is often the union of countries, and the union of legislatures is often the severance of countries. Can you give me a single instance from all your historical inquiries where the acknowledgment of local independence has been followed by the severance of countries? [*"Turkey!" "Servia!"*] I was just going to refer to those countries and to make this admission—that what I have said does not apply where a third power has intervened, and has given liberty in defiance of the sovereign power to the subject state. But do you propose to wait until some third power shall intervene in the case of Ireland, as it intervened in the case of America? [*"We are not afraid."*] I never asked the honourable Gentleman whether he was afraid. It does not matter much whether he is afraid or not; but I would inculcate in him that early and provident fear which, in the language of Mr. Burke, is the mother of safety. I admit that where some third power interferes, as France interfered in the case of America, you can expect nothing to result but severance with hostile feeling on both sides. But I am not speaking of such cases. That is not the case before us.

But I ask you to give me a single instance where, apart from the intervention of a third power, the independence of the legislatures was followed by the severance of the nations. I can give several instances where total severance of countries has been the consequence of an attempt to tighten the bond—in the case of England and America, in the case of Belgium and Holland. The attempt to make Belgians conform to the ways and ideas and institutions of Holland led to the severance of the two countries. In the case of Denmark and the Duchies, they long attempted to do what, perhaps, Gentlemen would wish much to do in Ireland—namely, to force Danish institutions and ideas on the Duchies. Those long attempts ended, as we all know, together with the insufficient acknowledgment of the ancient institutions of those Duchies, in the total loss of those Duchies to Denmark and their incorporation in another political connexion. But let us not look simply to the negative side. Where local independence has been acknowledged and legislative severance has been given, there, in a number of cases, it has been made practicable to hold countries together that otherwise could not have been held together, and the difficulties which existed either have been lessened or altogether removed. The world is full of such cases. [*"Turkey."*] An honourable Gentleman imprudently interrupted me by calling out "Turkey." I am going to tell him that in Turkey, with its imperfect organisation, in cases where there has not been violent interference, where the matter has not been driven to a point to provoke armed interference by a foreign power, local autonomy has been tried and tried with the best effect. In the Island of Crete, which twenty years ago appeared to be almost lost to Turkey, loosening the ties to Constantinople has immensely improved the relations between the Sultan and that Island.

LORD RANDOLPH CHURCHILL: Chronic revolution.

MR. GLADSTONE: Chronic revolution! What are the tests of chronic revolution? Has it paid its tribute? Has it called for the armed force of

Turkey to put down revolt? Then I will take another case, the case of the Lebanon. That was the subject of international arrangement twenty-three or twenty-four years ago. The Lebanon was in chronic revolution and was under the absolute sway of Constantinople. The Lebanon was placed under a system of practical local independence, and from that day to this it has never been a trouble to Turkey. In a case more remarkable, the case of the Island of Samos, which has enjoyed for a length of time, I believe, a complete autonomy and in which, singular as it may seem, it has never been possible to create disorder, a real attachment to the Turkish Empire or at any rate a contentment with the political tie subsists and holds that country in tranquillity. So that even Turkey bears testimony to the principle of which I speak.

There are numbers of other cases. The case of Norway and Sweden is most remarkable, because of these two countries the stronger and more populous can hardly hope to have power to coerce the weaker—two countries completely separate, having absolutely no connexion of legislative or executive government, and united together recently, only sixty years ago. That union has been found practicable, and practicable only by means of granting a just autonomy and independence. Take the case of Denmark and Iceland. [*Laughter.*] Laughter is, with honourable Gentlemen opposite, a very common weapon now, and it is very difficult for me to contend with it at this period of my life. Perhaps twenty, thirty, or forty years ago I could have defended myself against it with more ease. It has been said that the Parliament of Iceland has been dissolved and that there have been difficulties. Well, there have been difficulties between the Parliament of Iceland and the Crown of Denmark. The Crown of Denmark is, unhappily, in difficulties with the Legislative Body of Denmark, but between the Legislative Body of Denmark and the Legislative Body of Iceland there have been, I believe, no difficulties. When my honourable Friend the Under Secretary of State for Foreign Affairs[10] in his admirable speech quoted the case of Iceland, honourable Gentlemen opposite with their usual method of rebuke laughed, and someone endeavouring to dignify, adorn, and decorate that laughter with an idea, called out, "Distance; Iceland is so distant." Well, if it is so distant, I apprehend that that makes it a great deal more difficult for Denmark to hold her down by force and therefore more necessary for her to choose the methods which are most likely to secure contentment and tranquillity. But if you object to the case of Iceland on account of distance, what do you say to the case of Finland? Is that country distant from Russia? Are you aware that the social and political difficulties which have so often threatened the peace of Russia and which were fatal not many years ago to the life of one of the best and worthiest of her sovereigns have no place in Finland? Why? Because

---

[10] James Bryce, Member for South Aberdeen, spoke on May 17.

Finland has perfect legislative autonomy, the management of her own affairs, the preservation of her own institutions. That state of things has given contentment to Finland and might be envied by many better known and more famous parts of the world.

But the case of Austria is, perhaps, the most remarkable of all. I will not refer now to Austria and Hungary further than to say that I believe my right honourable Friend the Member for East Edinburgh is entirely wrong, for all practical purposes, in what he said as to the mixture of executive governments. I may lay down this proposition without fear of contradiction. There is no mixture whatever of executive governments so far as local affairs are concerned. As far as joint affairs are concerned it is a different matter; but there is a perfect independence between Austria and Hungary so far as local affairs are concerned. The case there, I should state, was surrounded with difficulties infinitely transcending any before us. But it is not Austria and Hungary alone. It is not too much to say of Austria that that great Empire, with the multitude of states of which it is composed, is held together by local autonomy and nothing else, and that the man who should attempt to banish local autonomy from Austria and to gather together the representatives of her states in Vienna to deal with the local affairs of the provinces would seal the death warrant of the Empire. Long may she flourish as having based herself upon so just and so enlightened a principle. The most striking instance in the wide circuit of her Empire is Galicia. Galicia is inhabited by Poles. Austria has one of the fragments of that unhappy and dissevered country under her charge. Well, I need not speak of Russia and Poland, while even in Prussia the relations of Prussian Poland are, at this moment, the subject of most serious difficulty. There are no difficulties between Galicia and Austria. Why? Because Austria has treated Galicia upon the principle of placing trust and confidence in her, and has invested her with full practical power over the management of her own affairs.

Now, I do not think that I have thrown out any unfair challenges. I have asked for instances from the other side in which the granting of Home Rule has been attended with evil consequences, but none have been given—whereas I have given a multitude of instances in support of my proposition; which is that the severance which we propose to make for local purposes between the Irish Legislative Body and Parliament meeting in these walls is not a mode of disunion but is a mode of closer union, and is not a mode of separation but is a mode preventing separation.

Before I leave this point I must refer to the case of Canada, because it is so remarkable and because, notwithstanding the multitude of circumstantial differences between Canada and Great Britain, yet still the resemblances in principle are so profound and so significant. My right honourable Friend the Member for West Birmingham said, as I understood him the other day, that he had been investigating the case of Canada. I own I thought I knew something about it, because in the early years of my Parliamentary life I took great interest in it and some part in the great discussions on the disposal of Canada some fifty years ago. My reading of the history of Canada sustains my original propositions. My right honourable Friend announced to the House that he had found that the Legislative Councils in Canada had been established for the purpose of protecting the minority. Where did he find that? I read not long ago the very lengthened and detailed debates in Parliament on the subject of the establishment of those Legislative Councils, and from the beginning to the end of those debates, while the character of the Legislative Councils was abundantly discussed, there is not a word about their being appointed for the protection of minorities. But I will not rest the case of Canada upon that ground. What does the case of Canada show? It shows two things—first, that between 1830 and 1840 there were most formidable differences between Great Britain and Canada and that those differences were completely cured and healed by the establishment of a responsible government with a free executive—that is to say, that those differences were absolutely cured by the very remedy which we now propose to apply in the case or Ireland. But, as I have shown, supremacy was not relinquished; it remained as was stated in the citation from Lord Russell. But after that, what happened? The two Provinces changed most fundamentally in their relative importance, and the stereotyped arrangements of the Union of 1840 were found to be totally inadequate to deal with the altered conditions of the Provinces among themselves. Recollect that these Provinces were united Provinces with one legislature. Discord arose between them. What was the mode adopted of curing that discord? The mode which we now propose of the severance of the legislatures—the establishment of an extended Union under which, at this moment, with the multiplied legislatures of those Provinces, a substantial and perfect political harmony exists. I can understand, then, the disinclination which honourable Gentlemen opposite have to go into history as to these cases; but it will be unfolded more and more as these debates proceed if the controversy be prolonged—it will more and more appear how strong is the foundation upon which we stand now and upon which Mr. Grattan stood over eighty-six years ago when he contended that a union of the legislatures was the way to a moral and a real separation between the two countries.[11]

It has been asked in this debate, why have we put aside all the other business of Parliament and why have we thrown the country into all this agitation for the sake of the Irish Question? [*Hear, hear.*] That cheer is the echo that I wanted. Well, Sir, the first reason is this—because in Ireland the primary purposes of government are not attained. What said the honourable Member for Newcastle in his eloquent speech? That in a considerable

[11] After dissolution of the Irish Parliament in January, 1800, Grattan delivered a series of powerful speeches against union in the House of Commons.

part of Ireland distress was chronic, disaffection was perpetual, and insurrection was smouldering. What is implied by those who speak of the dreadful murder that lately took place in Kerry?[12] And I must quote the Belfast outrage[13] along with it, not as being precisely of the same character, but as a significant proof of the weakness of the tie which binds the people to the law. Sir, it is that you have not got that respect for the law, that sympathy with the law on the part of the people without which real civilisation cannot exist. That is our first reason.

I will not go back at this time on the dreadful story of the Union; but that, too, must be unfolded in all its hideous features if this controversy is to be prolonged—that Union of which I ought to say that, without qualifying in the least any epithet I have used, I do not believe that that Union can or ought to be repealed, for it has made marks upon history that cannot be effaced. But I go on to another pious belief which prevails on the other side of the House, or which is often professed in controversies on the Irish Question. It is supposed that all the abuses of English power in Ireland relate to a remote period of history, and that from the year 1800 onwards—from the time of the Union—there has been a period of steady redress of grievances. Sir, I am sorry to say that there has been nothing of the kind. There has been a period when grievances have been redressed under compulsion, as in 1829, when Catholic Emancipation was granted to avoid civil war. There have been grievances mixed up with the most terrible evidence of the general failure of Government, as was exhibited by the Devon Commission[14] in the year 1843. On a former night I made a quotation from the Report which spoke of the labourer. Now I have a corresponding quotation which is more important and which speaks of the cottier. What was the proportion of the population which more than forty years after the Union was described by the Devon Report as being in a condition worse and more disgraceful than any population in Europe? Mr. O'Connell has estimated it in this House at five million out of seven million, and Sir James Graham, in debate with him, declined to admit that it was five million but did admit that it was three and a half million.

Well, Sir, in 1815 Parliament passed an Act of Irish Legislation. What was the purpose of that Act? The Act declared that from the state of the law in Ireland, the old intertangled usages and provisions containing effectual protection for the tenant against the landlord could not avail. These

---

[12] Probably the murder of an old man on the night of June 3. He was suspected of selling turf taken from property owned by the landlord of Ennis. The incident was reported in *The Times*, June 5, 1886, p. 3.

[13] Probably the serious disturbance at Alexandra dock, Belfast, on June 3. When a Protestant laborer was assaulted by his predominately Roman Catholic coworkers, Protestant workers from a nearby shipyard attacked the Catholics. Many injuries and one death resulted from the riot. See *The Times*, June 5, 1886, p. 13.

[14] The Commission was appointed by Peel to inquire into the Irish land problem. Its report was the beginning of serious attention to a root cause of Irish discontent.

intertangled usages, which had replaced in an imperfect manner the tribal usages on which the tenure of land in Ireland was founded—Parliament swept them away and did everything to expose the tenant to the action of the landlord, but nothing to relieve or to deal with, by any amendment of the law, the terrible distress which was finally disclosed by the Devon Commission. Again, what was the state of Ireland with regard to freedom? In the year 1820 the Sheriff of Dublin and the gentry of that county and capital determined to have a county meeting to make compliments to George IV—the trial of Queen Caroline[15] being just over. They held their county meeting; the people went to the county meeting and a counter-address was moved, warm in professions of loyalty, but setting out the grievances of the country and condemning the trial and proceedings against the Queen. The Sheriff refused to hear it. He put his own motion but refused to put the other motion; he left the meeting, which continued the debate, and he sent in the military to the meeting, which was broken up by force. That was the state of Ireland as to freedom of petition and remonstrance twenty years after the Union. Do you suppose that would have been the case if Ireland had retained her own Parliament? No, Sir. Other cases I will not dwell upon at this late hour, simply on account of the lateness of the hour.

From 1857, when we passed an Act which enabled the landlords of Ireland to sell improvements on their tenants' holdings over their heads, down to 1880, when a most limited and carefully framed Bill, the product of Mr. Forster's benevolence, was passed by this House and rejected by an enormous majority in the House of Lords, thereby precipitating the Land Act of 1881, it is impossible to stand by the legislation of this House as a whole since the Union. I have sometimes heard it said you have had all kinds of remedial legislation. The two chief items are the disestablishment of the Church and the reform of the Land Laws. But what did you say of these? Why, you said the change in the Land Laws was confiscation and the disestablishment of the Church was sacrilege. You cannot at one and the same time condemn these measures as confiscation and sacrilege and at the same time quote them as proofs of the justice with which you have acted to Ireland. I must further say that we have proposed this measure because Ireland wants to make her own laws. It is not enough to say that you are prepared to make good laws. You were prepared to make good laws for the Colonies. You did make good laws for the Colonies according to the best of your light. The Colonists were totally dissatisfied with them. You accepted their claim to make their own laws. Ireland, in our opinion, has a claim not less urgent.

Now, Sir, what is before us? What is before us in the event of the rejection

[15] A public inquiry into the conduct of the Queen preliminary to action of Parliament to dissolve the royal marriage. Commons dropped the action but Queen Caroline was not crowned at the coronation of George IV the following year.

of this Bill? What alternatives have been proposed? Here I must for a moment comment on the fertile imagination of my right honourable Friend the Member for West Birmingham. He has proposed alternatives, and plenty of them. My right honourable Friend says that a Dissolution has no terrors for him. I do not wonder at it. I do not see how a Dissolution can have any terrors for him. He has trimmed his vessel and he has touched his rudder in such a masterly way that in whichever direction the winds of Heaven may blow they must fill his sails. Let me illustrate my meaning. I will suppose different cases. Supposing at the election—I mean that an election is a thing like Christmas, it is always coming—supposing that at an election public opinion should be very strong in favour of the Bill. My right honourable Friend would then be perfectly prepared to meet that public opinion, and tell it, "I declared strongly that I adopted the principle of the Bill." On the other hand, if public opinion was very adverse to the Bill, my right honourable Friend again is in complete armour, because he says, "Yes, I voted against the Bill." Supposing, again, public opinion is in favour of a very large plan for Ireland. My right honourable Friend is perfectly provided for that case also. The Government plan was not large enough for him, and he proposed in his speech on the introduction of the Bill that we should have a measure on the basis of federation, which goes beyond this Bill. Lastly—and now I have very nearly boxed the compass—supposing that public opinion should take quite a different turn, and instead of wanting very large measures for Ireland should demand very small measures for Ireland, still the resources of my right honourable Friend are not exhausted, because then he is able to point out that the last of his plans was four provincial councils controlled from London. Under other circumstances I should, perhaps, have been tempted to ask the secret of my right honourable Friend's recipe; as it is, I am afraid I am too old to learn it. But I do not wonder that a Dissolution has no terrors for him, because he is prepared in such a way and with such a series of expedients to meet all the possible contingencies of the case.

Well, Sir, when I come to look at these practical alternatives and provisions, I find that they are visible creations of the vivid imagination born of the hour and perishing with the hour, totally and absolutely unavailable for the solution of a great and difficult problem, the weight of which and the urgency of which my right honourable Friend himself in other days has seemed to feel. But I should not say now that our plan has possession of the field without a rival. Lord Salisbury has given us a rival plan. My first remark is that Lord Salisbury's policy has not been disavowed. It is, therefore, adopted. What is it? [*A laugh.*] Another laugh? It has not been disavowed; what is it? Great complaints are made because it has been called a policy of coercion; and Lord Salisbury is stated to have explained in "another place" that he is not favourable to coercion, but only to legislative provisions for preventing interference by one man with the liberty of another and for ensuring the regular execution of the law. And that, you say, is not coercion? Was that your view six months ago? What did the Liberal Government propose when they went out of office? They proposed to enact clauses against the—["*No, no!*" *from the Opposition.*]

LORD RANDOLPH CHURCHILL: They never made any proposal.

MR. GLADSTONE: Perhaps not; but it was publicly stated. It was stated by me in a letter to the right honourable Gentleman.

SIR MICHAEL HICKS-BEACH: In October.

MR. GLADSTONE: Certainly; but it was stated in order to correct a rather gross error of the right honourable Gentleman. It was stated as what we had intended when we were going out of office—unless I am greatly mistaken, it was publicly stated in this House long before. However, it is not very important. What were the proposals that we were about to make, or that we were supposed to be about to make? Well, a proposal about "boycotting" to prevent one man interfering with the liberty of another, and a proposal about a change of venue to insure the execution of the ordinary law. And how were these proposals viewed? Did not the Tories go to the elections putting upon their placards "Vote for the Tories and no coercion"?

SIR WALTER B. BARTTELOT:[16] No, no!

MR. GLADSTONE: I do not say that every Tory did it. The honourable and gallant Baronet cries, "No." No doubt he did not do it; but he had no Irish voters.

SIR WALTER B. BARTTELOT: If I had I would have done it.

MR. GLADSTONE: Then it means this—that these proposals which we were about to make were defined as coercion by the Tories at the election and Lord Salisbury now denies them to be coercion; and it is resented with the loudest manifestations of displeasure when anyone on this side of the House states that Lord Salisbury has recommended twenty years of coercion. Lord Salisbury recommended, as he says himself, twenty years of those measures which last year were denounced by the Tories. But what did Lord Salisbury call them himself? What were his own words? His words were: "My alternative policy is that Parliament should enable the Government of England to govern Ireland." What is the meaning of those words? Their meaning, in the first instance, is this: the Government does not want the aid of Parliament to exercise their executive power; it wants the aid of Parliament for fresh legislation. The demand that the Parliament should enable the Government of England to govern Ireland is a demand for fresh legislative power. This fresh legislative power, how are they to use? "Apply that recipe honestly, consistently, and resolutely for twenty years, and at the end of that time you will find Ireland will be fit to accept any gift in the way of local government or repeal of Coercion Laws that you

---

[16] Member for North West Sussex.

may wish to give." And yet objections and complaints of misrepresentation teem from that side of the House when anyone on this side says that Lord Salisbury recommended coercion, when he himself applies that same term in his own words. A question was put to me by my honourable Friend the Member for Bermondsey[17] in the course of his most instructive speech. My honourable Friend had a serious misgiving as to the point of time. Were we right in introducing this measure now? He did not object to the principle; he intimated a doubt as to the moment. I may ask my honourable Friend to consider what would have happened had we hesitated as to the duty before us, had we used the constant efforts that would have been necessary to keep the late Government in office and allowed them to persevere in their intentions. On the 26th of January they proposed what we termed a measure of coercion,[18] and I think we were justified in so terming it, because anything attempting to put down a political association can hardly have another name. Can it be denied that that legislation must have been accompanied by legislation against the press, legislation against public meetings, and other legislation without which it would have been totally ineffective? Would it have been better if a great controversy cannot be avoided—and I am sensible of the evil of this great controversy—I say it is better that Parties should be matched in conflict upon a question of giving a great boon to Ireland, rather than—as we should have been if the policy of the 26th of January had proceeded—that we should have been matched and brought into conflict and the whole country torn with dispute and discussion upon the policy of a great measure of coercion. That is my first reason.

My second reason is this. Let my honourable Friend recollect that this is the earliest moment in our Parliamentary history when we have the voice of Ireland authentically expressed in our hearing. Majorities of Home Rulers there may have been upon other occasions; a practical majority of Irish Members never has been brought together for such a purpose. Now, first, we can understand her; now, first, we are able to deal with her; we are able to learn authentically what she wants and wishes, what she offers and will do; and as we ourselves enter into the strongest moral and honourable obligations by the steps which we take in this House, so we have before us practically an Ireland under the representative system able to give us equally authentic information, able morally to convey to us an assurance the breach and rupture of which would cover Ireland with disgrace.

There is another reason, but not a very important one. It is this. I feel that any attempt to palter with the demands of Ireland, so conveyed in

[17] Thorold Rogers.
[18] Sir Michael Hicks Beach gave notice on behalf of the Chief Secretary for Ireland that on the following Thursday his friend would move "to introduce a Bill for the purpose of suppressing the National League and other dangerous associations, for the prevention of intimidation, and for the protection of life, property, and public order in Ireland."

forms known to the Constitution, and any rejection of the conciliatory policy, might have an effect that none of us could wish in strengthening that party of disorder which is behind the back of the Irish representatives, which skulks in America, which skulks in Ireland, which I trust is losing ground and is losing force, and will lose ground and will lose force in proportion as our policy is carried out, and which I cannot altogether dismiss from consideration when I take into view the consequences that might follow upon its rejection.

What is the case of Ireland at this moment? Have honourable Gentlemen considered that they are coming into conflict with a nation? Can anything stop a nation's demand except its being proved to be immoderate and unsafe? But here are multitudes and, I believe, millions upon millions out-of-doors, who feel this demand to be neither immoderate nor unsafe. In our opinion, there is but one question before us about this demand. It is as to the time and circumstance of granting it. There is no question in our minds that it will be granted. We wish it to be granted in the mode prescribed by Mr. Burke. Mr. Burke said in his first speech at Bristol:[19]

> I was true to my old-standing invariable principle that all things which came from Great Britain should issue as a gift of her bounty and beneficence rather than as claims recovered against struggling litigants, or, at least, if your beneficence obtained no credit in your concessions, yet that they should appear the salutary provisions of your wisdom and foresight—not as things wrung from you with your blood by the cruel gripe of a rigid necessity.

The difference between giving with freedom and dignity on the one side, with acknowledgment and gratitude on the other, and giving under compulsion—giving with disgrace, giving with resentment dogging you at every step of your path—this difference is in our eyes fundamental, and this is the main reason not only why we have acted but why we have acted now.

This, if I understand it, is one of the golden moments of our history—one of those opportunities which may come and may go, but which rarely return or, if they return, return at long intervals and under circumstances which no man can forecast. There have been such golden moments even in the tragic history of Ireland, as her poet says:[20]

> One time the harp of Innisfail
> Was tuned to notes of gladness.

And then he goes on to say:

> But yet did oftener tell a tale
> Of more prevailing sadness.

[19] Given on September 6, 1780.
[20] A paraphrase from Thomas Moore's "Dear Harp of my Country." An ancient poetic name for Ireland is "Inis Fail."

But there was such a golden moment—it was in 1795—it was on the mission of Lord Fitzwilliam.[21] At that moment it is historically clear that the Parliament of Grattan was on the point of solving the Irish problem. The two great knots of that problem were, in the first place, Roman Catholic Emancipation and, in the second place, the Reform of Parliament. The cup was at her lips and she was ready to drink it, when the hand of England rudely and ruthlessly dashed it to the ground in obedience to the wild and dangerous intimations of an Irish faction.

Ex illo fluere ac retro sublapsa referri,
Spes Danaûm.[22]

There has been no great day of hope for Ireland, no day when you might hope completely and definitely to end the controversy till now—more than ninety years. The long periodic time has at last run out, and the star has again mounted into the heavens.

What Ireland was doing for herself in 1795 we at length have done. The Roman Catholics have been emancipated—emancipated after a woeful disregard of solemn promises through twenty-nine years, emancipated slowly, sullenly, not from goodwill but from abject terror, with all the fruits and consequences which will always follow that method of legislation. The second problem has been also solved, and the representation of Ireland has been thoroughly reformed; and I am thankful to say that the franchise was given to Ireland on the re-adjustment of last year with a free heart, with an open hand, and the gift of that franchise was the last act required to make the success of Ireland in her final effort absolutely sure. We have given Ireland a voice; we must all listen for a moment to what she says. We must all listen—both sides, both Parties, I mean as they are divided on this question—divided, I am afraid, by an almost immeasurable gap.

We do not undervalue or despise the forces opposed to us. I have described them as the forces of class and its dependents; and that as a general description—as a slight and rude outline of a description—is, I believe, perfectly true. I do not deny that many are against us whom we should have expected to be for us. I do not deny that some whom we see against us have caused us by their conscientious action the bitterest disappointment. You have power, you have wealth, you have rank, you have station, you have organisation. What have we? We think that we have the people's heart; we believe and we know we have the promise of the harvest of the future. As to the people's heart, you may dispute it and dispute it with

---

[21] Earl Fitzwilliam went to Ireland in December, 1794, as Lord Lieutenant. Prior to Fitzwilliam's departure from London, both he and Grattan believed that Pitt had given assurances that Catholic claims would be granted. Pitt denied he had approved this policy; he recalled Fitzwilliam in March, 1795.

[22] "From that moment, the hopes of the Danaans ebbed and slipped backward out to sea" (Virgil, *Aeneid* II. 169–170).

perfect sincerity. Let that matter make its own proof. As to the harvest of the future, I doubt if you have so much confidence, and I believe that there is in the breast of many a man who means to vote against us tonight a profound misgiving approaching even to a deep conviction that the end will be as we foresee and not as you do—that the ebbing tide is with you and the flowing tide is with us.

Ireland stands at your bar expectant, hopeful, almost suppliant. Her words are the words of truth and soberness. She asks a blessed oblivion of the past, and in that oblivion our interest is deeper than even hers. My right honourable Friend the Member for East Edinburgh asks us tonight to abide by the traditions of which we are the heirs. What traditions? By the Irish traditions? Go into the length and breadth of the world, ransack the literature of all countries, find, if you can, a single voice, a single book; find, I would almost say, as much as a single newspaper article, unless the product of the day in which the conduct of England towards Ireland is anywhere treated except with profound and bitter condemnation. Are these the traditions by which we are exhorted to stand? No; they are a sad exception to the glory of our country. They are a broad and black blot upon the pages of its history; and what we want to do is to stand by the traditions of which we are the heirs in all matters except our relations with Ireland, and to make our relations with Ireland to conform to the other traditions of our country.

So we treat our traditions—so we hail the demand of Ireland for what I call a blessed oblivion of the past. She asks also a boon for the future; and that boon for the future, unless we are much mistaken, will be a boon to us in respect of honour no less than a boon to her in respect of happiness, prosperity, and peace. Such, Sir, is her prayer. Think, I beseech you, think well, think wisely, think not for the moment but for the years that are to come before you reject this Bill.

H. H. Asquith, Sir Edward Carson, and John Redmond

"Debate on the Government of Ireland Bill"[*]

Commons, April 11, 1912

THE PRIME MINISTER:[1] Mr. Speaker—it is nineteen years since Mr. Gladstone, in a memorable speech[2] which is still fresh in the recollection of most of us who heard it, at this Table moved for leave to introduce the second and last of his measures to provide for the better government of Ireland. That speech taken, as it must be, by way of supplement to the speech in which he introduced the earlier Bill of 1886 contains the classic exposition of what I may term the historic case as between Great Britain and Ireland. I shall not attempt today to retraverse the ground which he covered. I do not presume to be able to bend the bow of Ulysses. But it is within my compass and it is germane to the task which I have undertaken today if before I enter upon any explanation of the provisions of the Bill which I am about to introduce, I take up the narrative where Mr. Gladstone was obliged to leave it and ask the House of Commons to consider how far the case for or against what is called Home Rule has been affected one way or another by the course of events since 1893.

That inquiry naturally subdivides itself into two branches, according as the problem is regarded from the point of view of Ireland alone or especially, or from the point of view of the United Kingdom and the Empire at large. Let us then first see how the case stands in regard to Ireland. As Mr. Gladstone pointed out, it was not till the General Election of 1885[3] that the democracy of Ireland was able to give effective utterance to its view as to the way in which it should be governed. From the first moment the Irish people was granted an articulate political voice, it pronounced by a

---

[*] The text is from *Parliamentary Debates (Official Report)*, Fifth Series, Vol. XXXVI, cols. 1399–1454.

[1] H. H. Asquith was Liberal Prime Minister during the period 1908–1916.

[2] Gladstone's speech of February 13, 1893, is reported in *Parliamentary Debates (Authorised Edition)*, Fourth Series, Vol. VIII, cols. 1241–1275.

[3] This election led to the third Reform Bill under Salisbury. The Bill redistributed seats in Commons, giving Ireland 103.

majority of four to one of its representatives in favour of Home Rule. That verdict was repeated substantially in the same proportions in 1886 and in 1892, and when Mr. Gladstone spoke in 1893 he had in support of the proposition that "Ireland demands Home Rule" the evidence of three successive General Elections.

Since then nearly twenty years have passed, and from the date of the extension of the franchise in 1884 we have had eight General Elections. The fortunes of parties in this House have during that time ebbed and flowed; governments have come and gone; great personalities have filled the scene and passed away. We have had as a nation peace and war, adversity and prosperity, shifting issues, changing policies; but throughout the welter and confusion, amid all the varying phases and fields of our electoral and Parliamentary campaigns, one thing has remained constant, subject neither to eclipse nor wane—the insistence and persistence of the Irish demand. It remains today, in April, 1912, what it was in January, 1886, and what in the interval it has never ceased to be: a demand preferred by four-fifths of the elected representatives of the Irish people. Analyse the figures a little more closely and they become even more significant.

Here in Great Britain, with the exception of a few peculiarly situated areas, we are accustomed to see the Parliamentary complexion of particular constituencies change from time to time in correspondence with the changes in public opinion; but over by far the larger part of Ireland, while this great issue of national self-government dominates the scene, you see nothing of the kind. The vast majority of the Nationalists' seats are not even contested by those who differ from them. Eighty per cent at the last election of the Nationalist Members were returned without opposition. In the three provinces of Leinster, Munster, and Connaught, with, I believe, only three exceptions—one of them the borough of Galway in which there was not a serious fight—the only pollings that took place were between rival Nationalist candidates. Ulster is the only province where there were real contests and where opinion is genuinely divided. But look at Ulster. Taking Ulster as a whole, the province of Ulster is represented at this moment how? By seventeen Unionists and sixteen Home Rulers.

These figures in themselves are quite sufficient to show the misleading character of the pretence that Ulster would die rather than accept Home Rule. I have never under-estimated the force and I have never spoken with disrespect of the motives of the strong and determined hostility which is felt to Home Rule by the majority in the northeastern counties of Ulster, reinforced, I agree, by a powerful minority in other parts of that province. It is a factor which sane and prudent statesmanship cannot and ought not leave out of account. I hope presently to show that we have not ignored it in the framing of this Bill. But we cannot admit and we will not admit the right of a minority of the people, and relatively a small minority —particularly when every possible care is being taken to safeguard their special interests and susceptibilities—to veto the verdict of the vast body of their countrymen. That verdict, I say again, is today as emphatic as it was twenty-five years ago. And if you refuse to recognise it, you are refusing to recognise the deliberate constitutional demands of the vast majority of the nation, repeated and ratified—

SIR C. KINLOCH COOKE:[4] What nation?

THE PRIME MINISTER: What nation? The Irish nation—repeated and ratified time after time during the best part of the life of a generation. So far, then, Mr. Gladstone's position is strongly fortified by our later experience. But while Ireland remains constant in her political claim, she has in other respects not stood still. And it is necessary to consider what is the bearing, if any, of these other changes which she has undergone upon the Home Rule case. I am glad to acknowledge that the improvement in the conditions of social order—due to a variety of causes, both material and moral—has deprived one of the arguments which used sometimes to be employed of much of its cogency and appositeness. Home Rule can no longer be represented as it used to be sometimes as a counsel of despair, as a concession to violence, as an appeal to the fears and apprehensions of the British electorate. On the other hand, the social and economic conditions of Ireland and its relations to the United Kingdom have been largely affected since 1893 by Imperial legislation. There are the Local Government Act, the Land Purchase Act, the Labourers Act, the University Act, and last, but not least, the Acts for establishing old-age pensions and national insurance. There are, I know, some critics who say that the mere enumeration of such a catalogue of beneficent measures is in itself a refutation of the supposed necessity for Home Rule and ought to make an irresistible appeal to the gratitude of the Irish people. That is not, to my mind, a very formidable argument. I can, at any rate, imagine an Irishman —if I were an Irishman, talking as an Irishman—saying that there are still two sides to the account, and that measures such as these, even if they had been shaped more nearly than some have been in accordance with Irish wishes and Irish interests, were but a tardy and inadequate set-off against an irreparable past, against the evils wrought, as an Irishman would say and believe, by over-taxation, by depopulation, by the legalised confiscation of the property of the tillers of the soil, which went on unchecked during the forty years that elapsed between the grant of Catholic Emancipation and the first of Mr. Gladstone's great remedial Acts.

But I do not wish to burn my feet in the embers of historical controversy. It is more to my purpose—more, at any rate, to my immediate purpose— to observe that the working of these new laws has already done much to weaken the force and indeed to blunt the point of what twenty years ago were some of the most serviceable arrows in the Unionist quiver. Why

[4] Member for Devonport.

do I say that? First, because the operation of elective bodies, such as the County Councils, which have now been at work for over fifteen years, has not been attended by the jobbery, maladministration, and persecution of minorities which were so glibly predicted as the inevitable incidence of self-government in Ireland. Next—and this is really a more important point—that the implication upon a large, I might say upon a colossal, scale of Imperial credit in the working out of land purchase and in the maintenance of old-age pensions makes the idea of separation between the two islands more unthinkable than it ever was. Carlyle[5] used to speak with a certain amount of contempt of the substitution of a sentimental for a cash *nexus* between employers and employed; but a cash *nexus*—still more, perhaps a credit *nexus*—between two countries in the relative geographical and economic conditions of Great Britain and Ireland is a sensible and measurable addition, if addition were needed, to the countless invisible and immaterial ties which have made them politically one, and which no mutation of time or circumstance can ever put asunder.

I wish now to ask the House to proceed to consider the same problem and make the same survey from a wider point of view—that of the United Kingdom and the Empire at large. I myself, while recognising to the full the priority and paramount urgency of the Irish claim, have always presented the case for Irish Home Rule as the first step and only the first step in a larger and more comprehensive policy. I said so with the utmost distinctness in a speech which I made on the Second Reading of the Bill of 1893,[6] and in the twenty years which have since elapsed there is not one year which has not illustrated and emphasised with ever-growing cogency and clearness the imperative need in the interests of the United Kingdom and of the Empire as a whole for the emancipation from local cares and local burdens of the Imperial Parliament. Look, first of all, at the effect of our present system upon purely domestic legislation and administration. It inflicts every year a double injury upon each of the component parts of the United Kingdom. For the moment I leave Ireland out of the account. In the first place, there is no time or room to deal with their separate needs. It is hardly an exaggeration to say that when the season annually comes round for compiling the King's Speech, the practical question for those concerned with its composition is what is the least instalment of that which is admittedly overdue by which England, Scotland, and Wales can respectively for the Session be bought off. That is what it comes to, and further, not only is our local legislation hopelessly in arrears but under our existing arrangements it is constantly coloured and twisted and warped by the voices and votes of those who have no direct concern in the matter. Local experience, local sentiment, and local interest are over-ridden and set at nought. You will never get—I am speaking the lesson that has been

[5] Thomas Carlyle, Scottish essayist and historian.
[6] Given on April 14.

taught me by a quarter of a century of Parliamentary experience—the separate concerns of the different parts of this United Kingdom treated either with adequate time or with adequate knowledge and sympathy until you have the wisdom and the courage to hand them over to the representatives whom alone they immediately affect.

But scanty and insufficient as is, of necessity, the attention which Parliament has given to local legislation, what is the result in other directions of our honest and strenuous but ineffectual efforts to grapple with a desperate task? Let the House consider for a moment the extent and variety of the field over which we insist upon exercising daily and exclusive supervision. Look at the Question Paper of this House on a Monday or Thursday in any week you like to select. What does it include, or, rather, what does it not include? Delay in the postal service of some hamlet in Connemara, a dispute about trawling in the Moray Firth, a decision perhaps in a poaching case by some rural bench in Wales, a case of deportation in East Africa, the position of the Mahomedan community in the new Presidency of Bengal, the efficiency or inefficiency of the rifle that is served out to the Army or to the Territorial Force, the seaworthiness of the latest type of "Dreadnought," and perhaps the international relations between Great Britain and Germany.

CAPTAIN CRAIG:[7] Is all that to be stopped?

THE PRIME MINISTER: I am sure the House will agree I am not exaggerating when I say that is a typical case, illustrated by the Order Paper of almost any day in a week of the Parliamentary Session. These are but samples of the matters, varying from the infinitely great to the infinitely small, of which the House of Commons under our present system requires and properly requires to be constantly informed. Now I ask this question: Has any deliberative assembly in the history of the world ever taken upon itself such a grotesquely impossible task? People complain both inside and outside the House of the deterioration of the quality of our debates and of their excessive curtailment. These twenty years since 1893 have seen the development in our procedure, stage by stage, both Parties having had a hand in the process, of new accelerating expedients and in particular the closure by what is called the guillotine.

Except as a safeguard, which is not often needed, against wanton repetition or obstruction, does anyone welcome it? Is it satisfactory to anyone, I do not care in what quarter of the House he sits, that large fragments of important legislation should pass without adequate debate or sometimes without debate at all, or that vast sums of public money should at the end of every Session be voted undiscussed, unexamined, silently, and *en bloc*? No; there is no one who cares for the dignity and for the efficiency of the House of Commons who would use this modern

[7] Captain James Craig, Member for East Down.

machinery with anything but reluctance and indeed with repugnance. But it is the creature of our own self-imposed necessities, and so long as you insist upon your present system of centralised impotence, resort to it may be and often is the less of two evils. Meanwhile, how are we doing our duty to the Empire at large, with its ever-increasing appeals to our interests? I do not exaggerate when I say that if you were to sit continuously during the whole twelve months of the year and work through them with unremitting ardour and assiduity, you would find at the end not only that there were still large arrears of legislation which you had not even attempted to overtake, not only enormous sums raised by taxation whose appropriation had never even been discussed, but that there were vast areas of the Empire—I do not now speak of the self-governing Dominions[8] —for which we are still directly responsible as trustees, to whose concerns we had not been able to afford so much as one single night. From the Imperial point of view, that is the case for Home Rule. The claim of Ireland rightly comes first, and must be separately dealt with. [*"Why?"*] Why? Because the task is too large and complex and the conditions too varied.

MR. MALCOLM:[9] Why Ireland first?

THE PRIME MINISTER: That may not seem so to honourable Gentlemen opposite. I say the task is too large and complex and the conditions are too varied to admit of its being accomplished by one blow and by a single measure. What we are doing now—I say this advisedly—we should do with the distinct and direct purpose of these further and fuller applications of the principle.

SIR EDWARD CARSON:[10] Will the right honourable Gentleman put the Question of "Home Rule all round" in the preamble?

THE PRIME MINISTER: That is a very premature interruption. I am going to explain the Bill presently, if the right honourable Gentleman will exercise a little patience.

SIR EDWARD CARSON: I will as long as I can.

THE PRIME MINISTER: Home Rule——

CAPTAIN CRAIG: No Home Rule.

THE PRIME MINISTER: Home Rule in this larger sense, in my opinion, rests upon the necessities, is demanded by the responsibilities, and is indeed due to the honour of the Imperial Parliament.

Let me point out further and finally that such a process is in strict accordance with the spirit and the tendency of our Imperial development. Since 1893 we have seen within the Empire the formation of the Australian

---

[8] At this time they were Australia, Canada, Newfoundland, New Zealand, and South Africa.

[9] Ian Malcolm, Member for Croydon.

[10] Carson, Member for Dublin University, was leader of the Unionist forces in Commons. A famous barrister (he had successfully defended Alfred Douglas in the Oscar Wilde case), Carson was named Solicitor General in 1900, and in 1905 was appointed to the Privy Council.

Commonwealth, the grant of self-government to the Transvaal, and the erection of the Union of South Africa.

CAPTAIN CRAIG: "Union."

THE PRIME MINISTER: The case of the Transvaal—and some of us remember what was said about the Transvaal, and all of us now know how absolutely futile were the predictions which were then made, as futile as will be the predictions that are made in regard to this Bill—the case of the Transvaal is strictly analogous to that of Ireland. He would be a bold man—I do not know whether the noble Lord[11] will undertake to do so—who would assert that the case of Ulster presents more difficulties or ought to be less capable of solution than that of Boer and Britain living side by side in a territory just recovering from the ravages of internecine war. In the cases of Australia and South Africa the object was to provide a central legislative and administrative authority to deal with matters of common interest to a group of separate but adjacent states. In the pursuit of that object the utmost care was taken, as it had already been taken in the previous case of the Dominion of Canada, to keep alive and to preserve for the various states in all its integrity full local autonomy for local purposes. The Dominion started with separate states which needed to be combined and centralised for matters of common concern. We start with a congested centre which needs, if it is to do efficiently that which is common to the whole, to be relieved of everything else and to delegate local interests to local management.

In a word, the great Dominions and ourselves setting out from opposite poles, animated by the same purpose, are going to meet at the same goal. I do not believe there is one of them today of which the vast majority of the inhabitants are not in hearty sympathy with the spirit and purposes of the measure I am introducing. I have said so much—I hope not too much—by way of introduction, because I want to make it quite clear what are the general grounds of policy on which His Majesty's Government are submitting this measure to the Imperial Parliament. I shall now proceed to ask a large measure of the indulgence of the House to explain and so far as I can to elucidate the provisions of the Bill itself. I preface that explanation with the statement that if it is to be at all clear and intelligible, I must of necessity omit a great many matters of detail—such matters, for instance, as the saving clauses for vested rights of judges, civil servants, and other officials, which, although not unimportant, are really uncontroversial. I shall content myself and I ask the House to be content with an exposition of the main governing provisions of the Bill. For convenience of explanation I think it will be desirable if I divide what I have to say into four separate heads or chapters. I will begin with the legislative powers which it is proposed to confer on the new Irish body. I shall then deal with the

---

[11] Lord Hugh Cecil, Unionist Member for Oxford University.

Executive, and then I shall proceed to consider finance. Finally, I shall deal with the position of Ireland after the grants of Home Rule in the Imperial Parliament here.

[*Asquith made these major points on legislative power:*

The supreme power and authority of the Imperial Parliament was to be unaffected.

The Bill was to confer upon Ireland local autonomy with regard to Irish concerns.

An Irish Parliament was to be created, consisting of the King and two Houses—the Irish Senate and the Irish House of Commons—with power to make laws for the peace, order, and good government of Ireland.

In addition to reservations included in the Act of 1893, the services of the Irish Land Purchase Acts, the Old Age Pensions Acts, and the Insurance Act were to remain with the Imperial Parliament. Other reserved services were to be the Royal Irish Constabulary, Post Office Savings Banks, public loans made in Ireland before the passing of the Act, and the collecting of taxes other than duties and excise.

The Irish Parliament could not repeal or alter any provision in the Act itself except in some subsidiary matters. Nor would it have power to affect the right of appeal to the Judicial Committee of the Privy Council in all questions which might arise as to the validity of laws passed by the Irish Parliament.

Special provisions were made for the protection and preservation of religious equality.

Additional safeguards against the Irish Parliament exceeding its Constitutional limits were provided by the veto of the Lord Lieutenant and finally, the overriding force of Imperial legislation.

The Senate was to consist of forty Members nominated by the Imperial Executive, the Members to hold office for eight years and to retire by rotation, and as they retired their places to be filled up by the Irish Executive.

The Lower House was to consist of 164 Members elected by the existing Irish constituencies. The unit of population for each was to be 27,000. Ulster would have fifty-nine Members, Leinster forty-one, Munster thirty-seven, Connaught twenty-five, and Universities two.

When there was a disagreement between the two Houses, the two Houses were to sit and vote together.]

So much for the composition of the Legislature. I now come to the position of the Executive. The head of the Executive will be, as now, the Lord Lieutenant, in whose appointment religious disability will no longer count. The office will be open to any of His Majesty's subjects without distinction of creed, and we propose, following the example of the Bill of 1893, that he shall hold his office for a fixed term of years. The Lord Lieutenant will be advised in regard to Irish matters by an Irish Executive, and I wish to make it perfectly clear that as far as the Executive in Ireland is concerned, the area of its authority will be co-extensive with the legislative power of the Parliament—neither greater nor less. In other words, whatever matters are for the time being within the legislative competence of the Irish Parliament will for administrative purposes be within the ambit of the Irish Executive, and whatever matters are for the time being outside the legislative province of the Irish Parliament will remain under the control and subject to the administration of the Imperial Executive. That is all I need say upon that.

[*Asquith next explained the complicated financial provisions:*

The collection of all taxes other than postal duties was to be Imperial, and the product of all taxes, whether Imperial or Irish, were to be paid into the Imperial Exchequer.

The Irish Parliament was to pay the cost of all Irish services, except the reserved services.

Every year the Imperial would transfer to the Irish Exchequer a sum representing the cost, as determined by the Joint Exchequer Board, to the Exchequer of the United Kingdom at the time of the passing of the Act for the Irish services other than postal.

To set up the new Administration, £500,000 a year would be given by the Imperial Exchequer, to be reduced eventually to £200,000.

The Irish Parliament would have power to reduce or discontinue any Imperial taxes, with the result that the transferred sum would be reduced correspondingly.

The Irish Parliament would have power to impose Irish taxes of their own whereby the transferred sum would be increased correspondingly. This power would be subject to restrictions as to customs but not as to excise.

There was to be set up a Joint Exchequer Board consisting of five persons—two to be appointed by the Imperial Government, two by the Irish Executive, and the chairman nominated by the Crown—to adjust the accounts between the two Exchequers.

Provision was made for future adjustment of the financial relations if and when the Irish revenue exceeded the cost of Irish administration.]

Now I come to the last point, that is, the future representation of Ireland in the Imperial Parliament. The House will remember that under Mr. Gladstone's first Bill in 1886, the Irish Members were entirely excluded from this House. In the Bill of 1893, they were retained, to the number of eighty, that number being fixed as Ireland's proportion according to the population, comparing Ireland with the other parts of the United Kingdom. They were retained, as those who are familiar with the history of this legislation will know, in the first instance with powers to vote only on matters of general concern. That was called the "in and out" clause. Then, when that clause was withdrawn, as it was in deference to criticism in the course of the debates, they were given power to vote on all subjects. That is the history. We regard the retention of the Irish Members at Westminster as essential. [*Cheers.*] Honourable Gentlemen will be wise if they reserve their cheering. There never was a worse calculated cheer than that. I say that we regard the retention of the Irish representatives at Westminster as essential for reasons which I have already indicated and which I will presently sum up; but in regard to numbers, our proposal differs widely from that of 1893.

We do not think that where Ireland has obtained full control of her own affairs either justice or policy requires Ireland to continue to be represented here on the same footing in regard to population as the other component parts of the United Kingdom for whom this House will still continue to be the organ of legislation; nor do we believe that the Irish people themselves are prepared to advance any such claim. Under our plan, the Irish representation at Westminster will be reduced to forty-two; in other words, Ireland will have a Member here, roughly, for every 100,000 of her population. This arrangement does not necessitate any general redistribution, but it involves the merger of some of the Irish boroughs and counties and the grouping together of some counties which at present have separate representations. Three boroughs will be left: Belfast will have four Members, Dublin three, and Cork one. The universities for this purpose will cease to be represented.

There will be eight borough Members and thirty-four county Members. I may point out that on the assumption that the Irish representation here continues for Party purposes to be divided in something like the same proportions as it has been for the last five and twenty years—that, of course, is a mere assumption, but upon that assumption—the forty-two Members will consist roughly of eight Unionists and thirty-four Nationalists, showing a Nationalist majority of twenty-six votes. ["*Very useful.*"] There have been very few Houses of Parliament in my experience of over a quarter of a century—only, I think, one—in which such a number has sufficed to turn the scale of political fortune between the two great British Parties. It may be asked, why do we retain as many as forty-two or indeed any Irish Members at all? Ireland, it may be said, will at first, at any rate, be making no contribution to Imperial expenditure, and why should she have a vote in its determination? That is an argument that may be used with equal truth and with much greater cogency at the present moment. Ireland is not now making any contribution to Imperial expenditure—not a halfpenny—of any sort or kind, yet we have with us 103 Irish Members with the same right of voting as the rest of us. The justification for the retention of a reduced number of Irish Members rests upon much broader grounds. In the first place, the Imperial House of Commons will still continue to tax the whole of the United Kingdom.

Next, for some years at any rate, this House of Commons and the Imperial Executive will be responsible for the administration of all the reserved services in which Ireland is vitally interested. But, further, in our view, whatever other changes may be made and however far the devolution of local affairs to local bodies may be carried, the House of Commons must continue to be the House of Commons of the United Kingdom, fairly representing all its constituent parts and inviting the co-operation of each of them in the supervision of their common interests, the transaction of their common business, and the discharge of their joint and corporate trust to the Empire as a whole. It is true that for a time and until there are further applications of the principle of devolution, Irish Members will be here with an unfettered right to vote. For the reasons I have already given, a very substantial reduction in their number makes that a matter of much less practical importance than it was, and we think it may well be found to be the duty of the House of Commons—after this Bill has become the law of the land—the duty of the House of Commons, which is absolute master of its own procedure, to anticipate in some degree further developments of statutory devolution by so moulding its own Standing Orders as to secure the effective consideration and discussion of legislation affecting only one part of the United Kingdom, by those who, as representing that part, are alone directly interested.

MR. PIRIE:[12] In their own country?

THE PRIME MINISTER: I have detained the House longer than I had hoped. I trust I have succeeded in making plain the proposals of the Government. These are the lines upon which we ask Parliament to proceed in taking the first, the most urgent, and the most momentous step towards the settlement of the controversy which, as between ourselves and Ireland, has lasted for more than a century, and of a problem—and I lay great stress on this—which, even apart from the special circumstances of Ireland, has every year, year by year, become increasingly vital to the efficiency of Parliament itself. We maintain in this Bill unimpaired and beyond the reach of challenge or of question the supremacy, absolute and sovereign, of the Imperial Parliament. The powers which we propose to give to Ireland of taxation, of administration, of legislation, are delegated powers, but within the limits of that delegation they embrace at once, with the exception of the reserved services, all matters of local concern. If, as we believe will be the case, as certainly has been the case elsewhere, power carries with it a sense of responsibility that will give to the Irish people a free and ample field for the development of their own national life and at the same time bind them to us and the Empire by a sense of voluntary co-operation and, as I believe, in sincere and loyal attachment. At the same time this Imperial Parliament will have begun to break its own bonds and will be set free by the process of which this is the first stage for a fuller and more adequate discharge of its Imperial duties. I read a speech of the right honourable Gentleman opposite[13] delivered to an audience in Belfast early in the

[12] Duncan V. Pirie, Member for North Aberdeen.
[13] Bonar Law, Member for Bootle, Lancashire, leader of the Conservative opposition and later Prime Minister (1922–1923).

present week. I gather from that speech that he can see in all the proposals of this Bill, and in the attitude and action of the Government in regard to it, "nothing better," to use his own words, "than the latest move in a conspiracy as treacherous as has ever been formed against the life of a great nation." He tells us, and he told the people of Ulster, "The present Government turned the House of Commons into a marketplace where everything is bought and sold." He added, "In order to remain for a few months longer in office, His Majesty's Government have sold the Constitution."

We have sold ourselves. This, Mr. Speaker, is the new style.

CAPTAIN CRAIG: It is the truth, and you do not like it.

THE PRIME MINISTER: I can understand why the Party opposite are so enthusiastic——

SIR JOHN LONSDALE:[14] Will the right honourable Gentleman finish the quotation?

THE PRIME MINISTER: Presumably because of the completeness of the contrast which it presents to anything to which they or we have hitherto been accustomed. ["*Limehouse.*"] This is all very well for Ulster, but what about the House of Commons?

MR. BONAR LAW: I have said it here.

THE PRIME MINISTER: Am I to understand that the right honourable Gentleman repeats here or is prepared to repeat on the floor of the House of Commons——

MR. BONAR LAW: Yes.

THE PRIME MINISTER: Let us see exactly what it is: it is that I and my colleagues are selling our convictions.

MR. BONAR LAW: You have not got any.

THE PRIME MINISTER: We are getting on with the new style. The right honourable Gentleman said that I and my colleagues are selling our convictions——

CAPTAIN CRAIG: You have sold them to Mr. John Redmond.[15]

THE PRIME MINISTER: That we are producing a Bill which the right honourable Gentleman said, elsewhere in the same speech, does not represent our views——

MR. BONAR LAW: Hear, hear.

THE PRIME MINISTER: In order that for a few months longer we may cling to office. Does he really believe that? What have I to gain? ["*Office.*"] What have my colleagues to gain ["*Office*"] by a transaction to purchase for us——

CAPTAIN CRAIG: Eighty Nationalist votes.

THE PRIME MINISTER: To purchase for us a short further spell of the burdens and responsibilities which we have borne in very difficult and

---

[14] Member for Mid Armagh.
[15] Member for Waterford.

troublous times, now for the best part of seven years, at the price of surrendering our convictions and soiling for all time our personal and political honour? How many people, I wonder, in this House really believe that? We, as the responsible advisers of the Crown, put this Bill forward as the embodiment of our own honest and deliberate judgment. What is your alternative? [*"Tariff Reform."*] Are you satisfied with the present system? [*"Quite."*] Were you satisfied with it two years ago? What do you propose to put in its place? Have you any answer to the demand of Ireland [*"Yes"*] beyond the naked veto of an irreconcilable minority and the promise of a freer and more copious outflow to Ireland of Imperial doles? There are at this moment between twenty and thirty self-governing legislatures under the allegiance of the Crown. They have solved under every diversity of conditions—economic, racial, and religious—the problem of reconciling local autonomy with Imperial unity. Are we going to break up the Empire by adding one more? The claim comes this time not from remote outlying quarters, but from a people close to our own doors, associated with us by every tie of kindred, of interest, of social and industrial intercourse, who have borne and are bearing their share—and a noble share it has been—in the building up and the holding together of the greatest Empire in history. [*"Cheering our defeats in South Africa"; "Did Lynch*[16] *do that?"*] That claim no longer falls on deaf ears. There has been reserved for this Parliament, this House of Commons, the double honour of reconciling Ireland and emancipating herself.

Question proposed, "That leave be given to bring in a Bill to amend the provision for the Government of Ireland."

SIR EDWARD CARSON: I do not mind in the least if I am accused of adopting what the Prime Minister calls the "new style" if I say that in my opinion—and I think there will be many both in the House and outside who will agree with me—more ridiculous or fantastic proposals than those which have been so clearly outlined by the Prime Minister have never been put before this or any other Parliament. I am one of the survivors of the old fight in 1893. I am sorry I have not got the energy I had then, but while the proposals of Mr. Gladstone were difficult and complex, the proposals that we have heard made here today are, as I believe will be shown in the course of the debate we will have, absolutely unworkable and ridiculous. The new Senate, the great safeguard of that contemptible minority which I attempt to represent in this House, is to be a nominated body. That is a radical proposition. Any such proposal as that is a deliberate insult to this House of Commons. What is the use of it? Nominated by whom? Nominated, I suppose, by the Imperial Government. Will it be

---

[16] Colonel Arthur A. Lynch, Member-elect for Galway, Ireland, was prosecuted for treason by Carson for joining the Boer side in the South African war. Sentenced to death in January, 1903, his sentence was commuted; several months later he was released from prison. Lynch sat in Commons for West Clare from 1909 to 1918.

nominated or could it be nominated against the wish of the honourable Members who will be retained in this House and supported by a Parliament in Dublin which you yourselves created? The thing is fantastic. It is worth nothing, like all the other safeguards that you have put forward. Take the safeguard of the supremacy of the Imperial Parliament. Does the right honourable Gentleman really think that he is adding anything by putting that into the Bill? He knows well it adds nothing. It is put there merely as a picture, merely as something of a palliative for those who have some conscience left. I do not think there are any such words in the British North American Act.[17] [*"There are."*] They add nothing there to the Act.

This Parliament which passes an Act has an inherent right necessarily to alter or change or repeal any Act that is passed. Therefore these and the other great safeguards put there and announced by the Prime Minister are simply delusions. At all events, they are nothing to us. We care nothing about them. I rise at the earliest moment to say that so far as I am concerned, I oppose even the introduction of this Bill, and I do so for this reason: that I gather—and with me, at all events, this is the main principle that I have to consider—I gather that we will no longer have in Ireland the protection of an Executive which is responsible to this Parliament. That is what we have now. That is what this country invited us to have. That is what we loyally accepted; that is what, with those matchless phrases but I do not think always with great sincerity, the Prime Minister now asks us to abandon. The Prime Minister waxed very warm and eloquent over the charges made by the Leader of the Opposition at Belfast the other day. I shall put a question in a moment to the Prime Minister. We are now here opposing a policy which has been twice rejected by the electorate. [*"No, no"; "Only once"; "Twice."*] It has been twice rejected by the electorate. More than that, it is a policy which has been rejected upon the only occasions upon which it was ever put into concrete form. The late Duke of Devonshire said,[18] and I think said very truly, speaking on the Home Rule Bill in 1893:

> Before this measure is passed into law we have a right to demand that the judgment of the country shall be given not upon a cry, not upon an aspiration, not upon an impatient impulse, but upon a completed work; and that this measure, the result of the collective wisdom of the Government and Parliament, shall be submitted for the approval of the country aye or no.

The Prime Minister is angry at being charged with selling us to the Irish party. I ask him this question: Is he going to allow this Bill to be submitted to the electorate? [*"Answer."*] Will he assert in this House that that Bill

[17] This Act, passed in 1867, organized the Dominion of Canada.
[18] Devonshire developed this point in the House of Lords in the debate of September 5, 1893.

which he outlined today before this House has even been approved of by the electorate? It was the details of the other Bills that were rejected. [*"Not the principle."*] I am on the question of submitting the Bill to the country at the present time. It was the details of the Bill that were rejected. The details of this Bill are far worse for England and, in my opinion, are far worse for Ireland, but that is not all. What is the moment at which you are bringing in this Bill? You are bringing it in while the Constitution of the country is in suspense. You are bringing it in while the lying Preamble[19] remains unrepealed. We believe that you passed that Bill and certainly that you got the Irish assistance—the Irish Nationalist assistance —to pass it for the purpose of passing Home Rule while the Constitution was suspended. [*Hear, hear.*] Honourable Members opposite cheer that. If that is true, every word that was said by my right honourable Friend as to the disreputable bargain is true also. You cannot plead now that you have no time to carry out the Preamble of the Parliament Bill. [*"Parliament Act."*] Parliament Act—if honourable Members opposite get a little comfort from the fact that it is an Act. You cannot plead that you have no time because you are at the present moment entering upon this controversy which not only sets up two new Houses in Ireland but smashes this House in this country and for the United Kingdom. The truth of the matter is that so far as this Home Rule Bill is concerned, you are compelled to do what you are doing by the necessity of retaining the Irish votes in this House. That is a matter that is demonstrable. As long as you had a majority independent of them, we heard nothing of Home Rule. It was then, as I think the Prime Minister called it, an abstract or academic question.

THE PRIME MINISTER: On the contrary. In the Parliament to which the right honourable Gentleman referred, a resolution in favour of Home Rule was moved by the honourable and learned Member for Waterford and supported by me on behalf of His Majesty's Government.

SIR EDWARD CARSON: That is what I call an academic question. They did not bring in a Bill. No; on the contrary, they said that the proper policy and the one they believed in was a Council Bill. Why did they bring in a Council Bill if they believed in a Home Rule Bill? Are they ever genuine? They brought in a Council Bill; the Council Bill was submitted to an Irish Convention and the Irish Convention rejected it. Then, of course, they toed the line, and we heard no more of the Irish Council Bill. It was not the House of Lords who threw it out; it was something far more important to the right honourable and honourable Gentlemen opposite; it was the Irish Convention. The great Government of England, with the largest majority that any Government has ever had, bowed the knee to the Irish Convention.

---

[19] The reference is to part of the preamble to the Parliament Act of 1911 that reads: "It is intended to substitute for the House of Lords as it at present exists a Second Chamber constituted on a popular instead of hereditary basis, but such substitution cannot be immediately brought into operation."

Then they say, forsooth, that they have always acted upon the highest motives and with the greatest independence, and they repudiate even any kind of transaction or bargain for the sake of votes.

Since these proposals were last before the House, as the right honourable Gentleman has said, a great deal has happened in Ireland. Nearly twenty years have passed. Yes, but all that has passed has gone to show how right we were and how wrong the Government of the day was. The right honourable Gentleman has asked what is our alternative. Our alternative then was to maintain the Union and to do justice to Ireland. That has been done with results which, I venture to think, so great have they been in the direction of the prosperity of Ireland, could not have been contemplated by even the most optimistic Member of this House of either Party. On the other hand, what about the finance of both those Home Rule Bills? Is there any man who, having gone into the subject, will deny what was stated the other day at a meeting of the General County Councils Assembly in Ireland by Mr. Ellis, one of the witnesses before the expert Committee; namely, that if the finance of 1893 had become law in Ireland, Ireland would long since have been in a state of bankruptcy? Surely after twenty years it is something for us to start with this, that you were demonstrably wrong and we were demonstrably right. What has been done since then? County Councils[20] have been set up in Ireland. I am not prepared to join in the panegyric which the right honourable Gentleman has pronounced about them. I think that if he knew a little more about them he would not have been so lavish with his praises of them. The university question has been settled. Primary education has been enormously improved. Above all, land purchase has been brought not to completion—because you for your political purposes have checked it—but a sum of some £115,000,000 raised upon British credit has been either paid over or agreed to be paid over under the land-purchase system. Where would all that have come from if Home Rule had been granted in 1893?

I go further. What are now the outstanding grievances in Ireland? I know of none. I do not say that there are not many things to be remedied there as there are here. Primary education is one of them. But it will want money, and the way we are going to get money—I hope Irish Members will go down and candidly say so in Ireland—is by taxing land subject to instalments and, I suppose, by taxing the industries in the North of Ireland. I noticed an emphatic phrase of the Prime Minister that the Irish Parliament will have the power of taxing everything. That is a pleasant outlook. I shall deal in a few moments with the argument about Ireland not paying its way, but before I do that I should like, because I do not think its importance can be exaggerated, to say a few words more about what has happened under Unionist policy in Ireland since the last

[20] The councils were established to provide local government administration in rural districts.

Home Rule Bill was rejected. Take a speech made by Lord MacDonnell[21] on the 29th of November. He said:

> Within the last eight years he had seen marvellous improvements in the state of Ireland. He had seen confidence growing up. Men looked them in the face. Men were no longer afraid of the future. He put that down not to taxation of this or that; he put it down to land purchase, the first great remedial measure that had been introduced. He himself was a Liberal; but counting the measures that had been introduced into Ireland in the last twenty years, the great majority had been introduced by the Conservative Party. They would give them credit for that. From Mr. Balfour's time in 1891 up to the present day there had been a succession of great things. Consequently they must admit that however Ireland might have suffered in the past, the day of her regeneration had already dawned.

The Vice-President of the Board of Agriculture a short time ago said:

> People talk about poor Ireland, but I have the opinion that relatively Ireland is doing quite as well as any part of the Empire.

I will not trouble the House by going into figures to show that prosperity. The right honourable Gentleman has admitted it. But if anybody likes to go into the matter, they will find that whereas we were always being taunted in the old Home Rule discussions about the illiberality of this county towards Ireland, about the want of development in Ireland and the poverty of her citizens, the one boast of every Irishman now, whatever his political creed may be, is the advancing prosperity of his country and the progress that her citizens have made. It is that moment, when Ireland was progressing—to use the words of the Vice-President of the Board of Agriculture—as fast and as greatly as any other portion of the Empire, when confidence was largely restored, when great differences were dying down, when men of all creeds were meeting each other in a spirit that, I think, has never existed there before—it is that moment that you select, before even these measures of which I have been speaking have reached their full fruition, to pack Ireland into the melting pot of discussion and the melting pot of all those political and religious passions which have in the past so distracted her from true economic progress and co-operation. I was surprised at the Prime Minister's claim today about the cost of Ireland to the Exchequer of the United Kingdom. I think his argument was a false one, and, if I may say so without wishing in the least to say offensive things [*Hear, hear*]—if you like, I will say them—I think the argument was a foolish one. What was his argument? Of course I know what he was leading up to. He was leading up to this. Taking the

---

[21] Lord Antony Patrick MacDonnell was an Irishman who favored greater Irish representation in Parliament and fairer sharing of taxation and benefits.

finance of Ireland, he had to announce to this House that in getting rid of Ireland, or rather in putting Ireland "on its own," so to speak, in the new Parliament, this country would have to give her a free grant of £2,000,000 a year. That is what it comes to; also that forever this country would give up the power under any circumstances or under any difficulties of ever again taxing Ireland for any contribution. I do not envy the Prime Minister who ever tries to do it. When you start with this state of finance, when you advance £2,000,000 a year over which you are to have no control, and you are to ask for no contribution, either towards Imperial purposes or the national debt—not forgetting always that you took over the national debt of Ireland in 1817—or towards the upkeep of the Empire! The Prime Minister affects to think—of course he does not really do so—that it is the same thing to give away £2,000,000 a year to Ireland over which you have no control as Ireland being deficient £2,000,000, when Ireland forms a part of the United Kingdom and you have control of everything. I venture to think that argument will not stand a moment's examination.

What is the object of the United Kingdom? As I understand it, it is that all parts of that Kingdom should be worked together as one whole, under one system, and with the object that the poorer may be helped by the richer, and the richer may be the stronger by the co-operation of the poorer. If you were to take certain counties in England at the present moment—I shall not name any, as it might seem invidious—and work out what their contribution to the United Kingdom is, you will find that many of them do not pay for their upkeep. Is that a reason that they should be deprived of that upkeep? No; and I say this further, that a worse, a more foolish, and a more impossible policy it would be impossible to inaugurate than to suggest that either Ireland or any other part of the United Kingdom, whether large or small, should be allowed to go back in the race of progress and civilisation and not to be kept up to the same standard as you yourselves, or as near thereto as possible. The whole of this argument is based upon a fallacy, because the moment you make a common Exchequer you have no right to segregate any unit paying into that Exchequer towards local or Imperial upkeep. As Ireland pays exactly the same taxes as Great Britain pays, you have no right whatsoever to segregate her. It is not true in argument to say that Ireland contributes nothing at the present time to the Imperial upkeep.

There was one observation made by the right honourable Gentleman to which I must reply somewhat. He says, as I understand, that this Bill is to be the precursor of similar devolution to the other countries of the United Kingdom. [*Hear, hear.*] That is cheered. We also know that a resolution was passed by this House—a pious resolution supported by Members of the Government—calling upon the Government, in the same Parliament, to pass a scheme of Home Rule for Scotland. I am not sure whether poor England was mentioned at all! Just let us look at this for a moment. We are told there was a mandate for this Home Rule Bill at the last election. I believe that to be false myself; but take it so for the moment. Was there a mandate for Home Rule for England? Was there a mandate for Home Rule for Scotland? I believe the whole of this question as regards the giving of "Home Rule all round," as you call it, or federal government, to be absolutely hypocritical as regards this argument. It is put forward simply for the purpose of pretending that you are only giving to Ireland something that you would also give to England and Scotland. You have not the least intention of doing any such thing. You may as well put it in your Preamble; we will then know it is false. I remember all this same pretence years ago. Why, twenty years ago there was even a Scottish Home Rule Association got up. What has it done for the last twenty years? Has it ever produced a scheme?

Sir Henry Dalziel:[22] There is one before the House.

Sir Edward Carson: Has it taken twenty years to grow?

Sir Henry Dalziel: It is produced every year.

Sir Edward Carson: What about Home Rule for England? You will see in a moment how important it is to take the thing together. If you are going to have a federal system, if that is really your view, you are now laying the foundations of these Bills—if you are doing anything at all! Was there a mandate for this at the last election? Was there a mandate for Home Rule for England? Where are the offices of the English Home Rule Association?

Let me in this context try to deal with the argument of the right honourable Gentleman. He says this is to be the foundation of Home Rule all round, including Home Rule for England. The only reason he gives as to why it should be granted is because there is a majority of Irish Members in favour of it, and the congestion of business in this House. Very well. But mainly, he says—and this is the unanswerable argument—it is because a majority of Irish Members are in favour of it. Will the right honourable Gentleman refuse it to England if a majority of the English Members are against it or, as at the present moment, even against this beginning? How do you know you are ever going to have a majority of English Members in favour of English Home Rule? If you do not get it, are you going to force it upon them? Are you going to do exactly the opposite to what you say you are going to do as regards Ireland? If you are going to act upon the principle that you have laid down, this Separatist doctrine, with regard to the majority, and taking each of the three Kingdoms in this way, is the only country that is never going to get Home Rule to be England? And what becomes of your pretence that this is the basis of a great system of devolution all round, for which you have never had even a majority of the constituencies of the country, which you say is necessary before you enter

[22] Member for Kirkcaldy Burghs.

upon it? There is even more than that. If you are going to rely on giving federal government, you must give it in one measure, or you must have it at one and the same time. For this reason: what is the first thing you will have to do? The first thing you will have to do is to lay down what is to be the Imperial system of taxation, not as regards any one of the Kingdoms but as regards all; secondly, you will have to lay down not the relations of one of them but the relations of all of them to this House, or rather to the Imperial Houses; thirdly, you will have to lay down the relations of each of them to the other. Have you done that? Why have you not? Because you are only pretending. I go further.

Does the right honourable Gentleman really tell this House that he is going to have Home Rule all round? Does he say that until the other constitutions are completed the Irish Members are to be here dealing with the local affairs of England and Scotland, and England and Scotland are to have nothing to say about the local affairs of Ireland? No. If you were in earnest you would have these schemes, whether brought in in one Bill or three all operating together. I will put it to the test. I will ask the right honourable Gentleman a question which will test his sincerity upon the subject. Will he agree to hang up this Bill until he has framed the others? Of course he will not. Do honourable Members think he would be allowed? The truth of the matter is that all this is simple hypocrisy. When you are granting to Ireland this system, which is said to be part of the federal system, there is really behind it a much deeper matter than the right honourable Gentleman has dealt with. Before you can grant a federal system at all you must make up your mind as to what is the demand, the real demand, of Ireland. Does Ireland demand national independence —"Ireland a nation"? Is that her demand? If it is, what has a federal system to do with it? It is inconsistent. You say, "We cannot grant you national independence. It would not be safe for this country"—though I do not know how that operates upon the argument as to yielding to the majority of Members—"we cannot have a second independent nation, such as Canada is, practically at our doors." How much of the feeling I have mentioned do you satisfy by the federal system? Nothing. All you do by your federal system—and indeed there is a great deal of confusion of thought upon this matter—is to give a larger and a greater power to the new Parliament—that is, to Ireland—than ever it had before; a power which I believe—and which I think time will show—is irresistible if those concerned persist in their demands in the direction in which they are going—that is of national independence, of "Ireland a nation"!

Just picture what you are setting up. Do picture it in relation to the complicated system of taxation you are setting up, and which I venture to think will not last six months, and try to realise what it is that will then happen. Just think of the Irish Chancellor of the Exchequer bringing in his Budget and explaining to an Irish House of Commons mainly composed of agricultural Members that it is necessary to raise more money and that it must come from the land, or if he had the power, which he never will have, from the industries of Ulster. What will be his argument? He would tell the Irish House of Commons, "This is a very bad system; you have got your instalments to pay to that brutal English Government; they have reserved that to themselves. You have got a great many other taxes to pay. But the one thing we are not allowed to set up is a system of taxation which we know and believe would be best for our own country. We cannot help it. It is the brutal English Government that has done this." You will not find everybody at that time with all sorts of pleasant death-bed repentances like the honourable and learned Member for Waterford, and then in addition to that you will have your forty Irish Members over here. I doubt if you will have one who will be on the side of England. I do not know why you should. You will have your forty Irish Members over here probably holding the balance between both parties in this House, and they will be asking you not paltry questions about a post office at Ballaghadereen or some other place, but they will be directing your serious attention probably to an outbreak against taxation in Ireland which has all been caused by the artificial system of taxation you have set up and by your partial gift which only gives power to ask for more. That is all you are doing by setting up a federal system. Lord Derby in 1887 wrote this, which is mentioned in the *Life of the Duke of Devonshire*:

> I hold, and have held all along, that there is no middle course possible. If Ireland and England are not to be one, Ireland must be treated like Canada or Australia. All between is delusion and fraud.[23]

Yes, Sir, and delusion and fraud is what you are adopting. But whatever limitations you put into your Bill and whatever reservation and whatever limitation of taxation you make in your Bill, believe me, once your Bill passes you will have no power on earth to resist. Will the Irish Members tell us that this is going to be accepted as a final settlement? I venture to think that not one of them will. The honourable and learned Member for Waterford himself was the Member who got up when Mr. Gladstone's "final settlement" was passing its Third Reading and told us this:[24]

> As the Bill now stands, no man in his senses can regard it as a full, final, and satisfactory settlement of the Irish question. Sir, the word "provisional," so to speak, has been stamped in red ink across every page of this Bill.

I venture to say in addition to the word "provisional" the word "fantastic" will be found on every section of this Bill. Anybody who has

---
[23] Quoted in Bernard Holland, *The Life of Spencer Compton, Eighth Duke of Devonshire* (London, 1911), II, 196.
[24] Redmond's speech was given on August 30, 1893.

watched the movement in Ireland will see that at the present moment, even before your Bill is brought in, there is an outcry against the very limitations you are attempting to impose by it. The honourable Member for East Mayo[25] said in 1904:

> I say deliberately that I should never have dedicated my life as I have done to this great struggle if I did not see at the end of this great struggle the crowning and consummation of our work in a free and independent nation.

What has that got to do with federalism? We have had very little discussion of the Bill by English Ministers during the autumn or up to the present. I imagined the reason was they did not know what they would be allowed to put into the Bill. The right honourable Gentleman the First Lord of the Admiralty[26] made a speech at Belfast, and that speech was adopted, as I understand it, by the honourable and learned Member for Waterford. Two or three days afterwards one of his followers, the Member for North Meath,[27] said this:

> On the question of legislative freedom he noticed that Mr. Churchill was silent, but that was no reason why they should be silent. Wherever Irishmen met they must declare they would not be satisfied with anything short of a free and unfettered Parliament. Irishmen had always maintained that Ireland was a nation, but Mr. Churchill was somewhat inconsistent, for subsequently he said the Imperial Parliament could repeal a Bill passed by the Irish Parliament. Was there any free Parliament in the world that would allow an outside Parliament to repeal its laws? If the Irish Parliament is to be dominated by the English Parliament and if the English Parliament has power to repeal a law which is passed, then that Irish Parliament would only be a sham, and in less than twenty years the people of this country will find themselves worse off than they are now.

The extraordinary part of it all is that we are always being told we ought to trust the Irish Nationalist Member. I believe myself it is only in trust, if you can trust them, that any guarantee counts at all. But on what ground are we asked to trust them? Upon the ground that we ought not to believe a single word they have ever said. Now the right honourable Gentleman took some time in developing the guarantees that we are to have. There is not one of them worth the paper it is written on. There can be no guarantees of an administration unless you have confidence in the Parliament to which that administration is to be responsible. The Executive is everything. It is idle to tell us that the Lord Lieutenant is to exercise his veto. Is it upon the advice of his Executive in Ireland or is it upon the advice of the Cabinet in England? Is it upon both, or is it sometimes upon the one and sometimes upon the other? What a farce it is to tell us you are going to

---

[25] John Dillon.
[26] Winston S. Churchill.
[27] Patrick White.

establish a Parliament and all the paraphernalia of an independent Executive answerable alone to that Parliament, and the moment anything arises you are to send over here to Downing Street and say, "Stop the Parliament you set up! Stop the nominated chamber you yourselves have nominated! Over-ride the Lord Lieutenant, and tell him to set at nought your Parliament and your nominative chamber!"

What a position for any country to be in! No, Sir, the veto of the Lord Lieutenant is worth nothing. Instructions from His Majesty are worth nothing in this Bill "to bring about better relations and for the better government of the two countries." And just think, the Lord Lieutenant is to hold office for six years; he cannot be changed when there is a change of Ministers in this House, and he is to receive his directions from the Government of the day in power. The next Government, coming in a few days afterwards, can upset every one of them. What other guarantees are there? If anything is done *ultra vires*, you can go before the Privy Council in England. That is a good thing to tell a man who feels that he has been unfairly dealt with: "What grievance have you—you man in a dockyard or in a factory? Go before the Privy Council of England!" No, Sir, the guarantees are valueless. I do not often agree with the honourable Member for East Mayo, but he said this, speaking in November last at Salford:

> Then there was the question of guarantees. The Irish party were asked if they were willing that guarantees should be inserted in the Home Rule measure to protect the Protestant minority. He attached no importance to those guarantees at all. He did not believe that artificial guarantees in an Act of Parliament were any real protection.

That is why they have allowed the Government so profusely to put them in. Let me take one example of what I mean by administration throwing over any guarantees even under our present system. You passed the University Bill. It was a Bill which Nonconformists opposite were very careful to see had safeguards against it being turned into a denominational Bill. I was under no such delusion. I remember seeing posted up somewhere on one of your organisations or some place that was in sympathy with you a document giving a list of your great aims and bearing the statement that this was the greatest Protestant Parliament that ever existed since the time of Cromwell. That was a great boast, and it did them great credit to pass that Bill; they took great care that there should be safeguards in it to prevent its being turned to denominational purposes. And to follow this you must remember that the Bill provided that County Councils were allowed to give scholarships to the University, and what is the first thing they did? Did they care about your safeguards? Here is what Cardinal Logue[28] said:

---

[28] Michael Cardinal Logue, Primate of Ireland, whose residence was at Armagh in Ulster province.

> No matter what obstacles the Nonconformists of England may have inserted in the Constitution of the University to keep it from being made Catholic we will make it Catholic in spite of them.

I am not blaming him. I am only calling attention to the fact. Then what becomes of your scholarships? When you have made the University Catholic the County Councils give the scholarships, but they tell you they will not allow them to be held unless you go to that University because it has been made Catholic. What becomes of your elaborate provision that they are not to be allowed to endow any religion? They will tell you that there will be no open persecution. Of course not. Nobody suggests that anybody will go and shoot a man because he is a Protestant or a Catholic or *vice versa*. That is not the way it is done, and nobody is afraid of that. That is the kind of thing they represent us as being afraid of. No, Sir, it is the working of the institution for political or for religious purposes and objects, and that no guarantee set up by any Parliament can prevent. What we may look for, too, can be seen by the threats that have already been made. The honourable Member for East Mayo, speaking last October when he wanted to put pressure on certain landlords to compel them to sell their land, said:

> I tell these men that the sands in the hourglass are running out fast. Home Rule is coming and we will get it whether they like it or not, and when Home Rule has come and there is an Irish Parliament sitting in Dublin, I do not think they will get English Ministers to trouble themselves much about their woes in future. They will make their bed with the people of Ireland, and be it short or long, they will have to be on that bed. It is better for them to make friends with their own people while there is yet time.

Yes, we know what "making friends" means. No wonder that the honourable Member for Cork,[29] who has taken so great an interest in land purchase and who was a party to the bargain that has been so disgracefully broken, said in relation to that speech that once the Unionists, aye, or the Liberals, got it into their heads that an Irish Parliament would produce the hell upon earth foreshadowed by Mr. Dillon, there would be an end of any Home Rule Bill for years. It is not possible for me on a motion of this kind to examine all the various proposals that have been indicated by the right honourable Gentleman. I have taken the matter in a general way. All through the Prime Minister's speech I have asked myself what are the benefits that he indicates to Irishmen, and I have not heard one. Does he think his complicated finance will make it easier to raise taxation in Ireland? Does he think the separation of the poorer and the richer country will benefit the poorer country? Does he think that in Ireland, in a country

---

[29] William O'Brien.

torn asunder, unfortunately, by religious dissension and by very grave political differences, the withdrawal of England as the arbitrator between the two will bring about a better state of things? No, Sir. I at all events represent here a minority only and I admit it, but it is a minority which has always been true to the United Kingdom.

Some people say this is really a religious question. I do not see, if it is, that it is any less to be considered or any less important on that ground. But, Sir, it is a religious question added to various other questions. There is no doubt that the broad dividing line in Ireland in relation to this question of the Home Rule Bill can broadly be said to put on one side the Protestants and on the other side the Roman Catholics. I know there are some Protestants, not many I think, who are Home Rulers, just as there are some Catholics, a great many I think, who are not Home Rulers. It is unfortunate that that should be the dividing line, but it is there and you cannot neglect it. The reason this is the dividing line in my opinion is an historical one. In my opinion it is the dividing line because Protestantism has in history been looked upon as the British occupation in Ireland. It is the dividing line because when you attempted to bring home to the people the principles of the Reformation, you did not succeed in Ireland as you did in England and in Scotland. There remains, however, the dividing line, and I would like to know: when a statesman takes up a question he has to solve with that line there, what argument is there that you can raise for giving Home Rule to Ireland that you do not equally raise for giving Home Rule to that Protestant minority in the northeast province? I believe there is none. But in addition, that minority which is there gives an answer to the argument of the failure of the rule of the United Kingdom Parliament in Ireland. The success of Belfast, which has grown from 15,000 or 16,000 people before the Union to a population of 400,000 or thereabouts, the success of the surrounding counties, not at all the most prolific or the most fertile in Ireland, give the lie to those who say that it is English misrule in Ireland, as they call it—though why it should be called English I do not know—that has prevented the other parts of Ireland attaining a similar state of prosperity. Those are the men at all events that I represent here—the men whom you invited into your Parliament when Pitt passed his Bill.

Mr. Swift MacNeill:[30] Bribery.

Sir Edward Carson: You had better not talk of bribery. ["*We shall talk a great deal of it.*"] I do not think there needs much to be said about bribery since the corruption of last year on the Parliament Bill, when you were prepared to buy votes for peerages. You had then a little less to say for corruption, because that was done at your bidding. The Unionist minority in Ireland were invited into your Union. Reading Mr. Gladstone's speech the other day, I noticed he said that they were the men who opposed the

---

[30] Member for South Donegal.

Union. Sir, that seems to me to be the strongest reason why you should not now turn them out of the Union. You ask them into the Union and they asked to be left out. They came in and they got satisfied under your rule and became loyal, and because they did, now you tell them to go out. Sir, that is a policy of cowardice. Where is the precedent in the whole of history for any such action by a Parliament—a Parliament turning out a community who are satisfied to stay under their rule. We used to hear of Norway and Sweden, but that argument has gone, and gone in the direction which it necessarily must go when the tendency is for separation and not for union and co-operation. We, at all events, in this matter have a plain and a ready duty before us. It is to oppose this Bill with all the energy we can at every stage and at every moment that it is before the House. That is our duty. We believe it to be an unnecessary Bill. We believe it to be a fatal Bill for our country and an equally fatal Bill for yours, and above all things, we believe it to be involved in the greatest series of dishonourable transactions that have ever disgraced any country.

MR. JOHN REDMOND:[31] Whatever views may be entertained by honourable Members for or against this Bill as described to us by the Prime Minister, everyone will agree that this is a great historical occasion and that the subject we are called upon to discuss is a vast Constitutional and Imperial issue. Such a theme deserves from opponents, as well as from supporters, calm and serious discussion. It may possibly be considered the interest of some people in this House to engender passion in debates and to endeavour to overwhelm the issue by personal attacks and by insulting and irritating references to the nationality and the cherished aspirations of the Irish people. But I would like to say at the commencement of these discussions that so far as my honourable Friends on these benches are concerned, we will not be tempted to retaliate, and I can assure the House that so far as we are concerned, we will enter on these discussions with a heavy sense of responsibility, and will conduct the debate, so far as we can, with self-restraint and good temper. I have held for a very long time that as a rule First Reading debates[32] are more or less futile. Until honourable Members have in their hands the print of the Bill, no matter how great and lucid the exposition of it may have been, it is impossible to have anything except something very much in the nature of a futile discussion, and I think one of the earliest reforms in the procedure of this House in the future ought to be to abolish First Reading debates altogether.

But with reference to the right honourable Gentleman who has just resumed his seat, this consideration is scarcely a disadvantage at all. He is not in the position of a man objecting to this Bill because of its details; he

---

[31] A close friend and follower of Parnell, Redmond after 1900 led the Irish Nationalist Party in the Parliamentary contest for Home Rule.

[32] The rule was changed. Now, on first reading, the title of the bill is read and the bill ordered printed; debate is not permitted.

stands as an opponent to Home Rule in any shape or form. He said the other day in Belfast that if both Parties in this House united to carry a Home Rule Bill—in fact, if the House of Commons were unanimously in favour of it with the exception of the half of the representatives of Ulster— he would be opposed to it. He stands therefore not as a critic of the details of the Bill but as a root and branch opponent of Home Rule in any shape or form. Although, as the Prime Minister has reminded us, a little over a year ago a number of prominent Unionist politicians in this country and many leading Unionist organs of public opinion were seriously discussing the possibility of making Home Rule, under some different name, perhaps, part of a general settlement of the Constitutional question, and although undoubtedly there are many Members in the Unionist Party today of the same opinion, still, so far as the right honourable Gentleman is concerned, he takes up the clear and frank position that under any circumstances, no matter what the majority of the United Kingdom in favour of Home Rule may be, he will oppose it so long as he has at his back a certain number of the representatives of the constituencies in Ulster.

I will not delay the House by any academic discussion on the principle of this Bill. The principle of devolving on local assemblies the management of local affairs has at its back the sanction of the whole world. It has at its back the sanction of the Empire. Why, it is the foundation of the Empire today, and it is the bond and the only bond of union. I think it is true to say that no community of white men within the Empire has ever asked for this right, and up to this has been refused the exercise of it. The right honourable Gentleman let fall a phrase the exact meaning and significance of which I do not appreciate. He endeavoured to draw a clear line of demarcation between those whom he represents and the rest of the people of Ireland, and he said: If it is right to give Home Rule to the rest of Ireland, is it not right to give it to Ulster? Is that his proposal? Is that his demand?

SIR EDWARD CARSON: Will you agree to it?

MR. JOHN REDMOND: I would like the proposal to be made first. I did not appreciate the importance of that statement, and I do not know that I do now. I do not know whether it is a statement in the air or whether there is anything behind it, but under the circumstances of this case, the onus undoubtedly lies upon those who argue that what has proved to be good and just everywhere else in the world is bad and unjust and mischievous in Ireland. What are the main arguments against the principle of self-government for Ireland? The first of them is the question of separation; and Unionist orators, especially in the country—I notice more in the country than in this House, where they are face to face with their opponents—have constantly been saying that the Irish people want separation and that the Irish leaders are Separatists. I will be perfectly frank on this matter. There always have been and there is today a certain section of Irishmen who would like to see separation from this country. They are a small, a very small, section. They were once a large section. They are a very small section, but these men who hold these views at this moment only desire separation as an alternative to the present system; and if you change the present system and give into the hands of Irishmen the management of purely Irish affairs, even that small feeling in favour of separation will disappear; and, if it survive at all, I would like to know how, under those circumstances, it would be stronger or more powerful for mischief than at the present moment. It is constantly said that the late Mr. Parnell was a Separatist in disguise, and it is one of the commonplaces of the platform of this country that I am a Separatist in disguise, and that my Friends are all Separatists in disguise. Of course, when an assertion of that kind is made, as far as I am concerned I can only deny it. What is Mr. Parnell's record on this matter? In his evidence before the Parnell Commission on the 1st of May, 1889, he said:

> I have never gone further, either in my thought or action, than the restitution of the legislative independence of Ireland,

and in 1886 he specifically accepted as a final settlement of that demand the concession of a strictly statutory subordinate Parliament for Ireland, and that acceptance by him was endorsed by the mass of the Irish people. I came across the other day a really interesting statement by him, made quite early in his career when he was engaged in a violent movement in Ireland, when time had not mellowed his views or turned him into what might be regarded by Englishmen as a matured statesman, and when his views naturally would be more vehement than they were later in his life. What did he say? He said:

> Home Rule would be the introduction of a system which would remove the rankling sting of suppressed but not extinct enmity. Give back to Ireland her nationality, her individual existence, and soothe thereby the wounded pride that goes for so much in history and that often turns the scale in the destinies of nations as well as of individuals. Such a system as that——

——mark these words——

> ——would teach Ireland to regard Imperial affairs with interest, as being the concerns no longer of a master and oppressor but of a dear colleague and sister whose honour and dishonour would be alike hers, whose downfall could never be her profit, and to whom she would be bound by ties sacred because voluntarily assumed. It would be a system that would *de facto* though not *de jure* be an intimately closer union than England has yet brought about by six centuries of coercion or than she could bring about by six centuries more of the same method.

That was not made at a time when Mr. Parnell was endeavouring, as it is said I am endeavouring today, to cajole public opinion in England into giving Home Rule to Ireland. It was made years before Home Rule became a reality in this country. It was made when fighting against both Parties in this country; and I cite those words to show that Parnell was never a Separatist and that his evidence before the Parnell Commission was absolutely true. We on these benches stand precisely where Parnell stood. We want peace with this country. We deny that we are Separatists, and we say we are willing, as Parnell was willing, to accept a subordinate Parliament created by Statute of this Imperial Legislature, as a final settlement of Ireland's claims. If I might be allowed to say so, I was extremely gratified and relieved to find that the right honourable Gentleman who has just spoken put the religious aspect of this question in a very different way from that in which I am sorry to say it is put from the platform and in leaflets and pamphlets. As far as we are concerned, we in Ireland regard no insult so grievous as the insult that we, as a nation, are intolerant in matters of religion. We believe that your Protestant Unionist historian Lecky[33] told the truth when he said that was never a characteristic of the Irish people all through their history. We believe the testimony of John Wesley, who, after his journey in Ireland, recorded in his journal that he was received everywhere with kindness and who spoke in the highest terms of the tolerant spirit of the Catholics of Ireland. Still, there are, we admit, Protestants in Ireland and in this country who do not believe that and who, many of them apparently, entertain honest fears upon this matter. Our position on that point is this: We say, "Put into your Bill any safeguards you like." There are many safeguards in this Bill; and it is idle to tell the House of Commons or to tell any sensible man that these safeguards are of no use. You have got your nominated Senate.

CAPTAIN CRAIG: "Nominated." By whom?

MR. JOHN REDMOND: Nominated, in the first instance, by the Imperial Parliament. Then there is the safeguard of the veto, a most far-reaching safeguard. The right honourable Gentleman apparently thinks the veto makes this Bill such a sham and a fraud from the Nationalist point of view that it is not worth our taking. What free Parliament in the world, he says, would submit to it? Every free Parliament in the Empire is subjected to it. Is it not trifling with the House of Commons to say that we must regard as a humiliation to us and as a degradation to our Parliament a provision with reference to the veto which is in operation in every one of the self-governing Colonies? ["*Is it exercised?*"] Yes, and exercised. It has been exercised and it would be exercised tomorrow if anything in the nature of an unjust and intolerant Bill attacking people because of their religious faith were to be passed; and so it will be exercised in Ireland, and so only. No one suggests

---

[33] William H. Lecky, a distinguished historian, was Unionist Member for Dublin University for the period 1896–1903.

that veto will be exercised every day in the daily life of the Irish Parliament. Of course, if it were, the latter state would be worse than the first and the whole system would break down. I say it is a safeguard to the Protestants and to those who really have a fear for their property or their religion. Any Bill interfering unjustly with them can be reserved for the decision of the King in Council here on the decision of the Imperial Parliament. The right honourable Gentleman did not allude at all to the clause which the Prime Minister read out, and which expressly forbids

> ... making any law interfering with the free exercise of religion, or endowing or giving any preference or privilege to any religion or making any religious belief or religious ceremony a condition of the validity of any marriage in Ireland.

Any law made in contravention of these things would not have to be vetoed by the Crown at all. It would be void by itself. Then, behind that, there is the inherent and inalienable supremacy of the Imperial Parliament. This Parliament has the power to pass legislation for every one of the self-governing Colonies. It has the power to repeal any of their Bills. It has the power to pass concurrent legislation. It will have the same power here, and no more. And how in the name of common sense anybody can say that the small minority in Ireland—and that minority is a very small minority—can entertain really honest fears under these circumstances passes my comprehension. The right honourable Gentleman went into the question of finance and said, "You are not only giving Ireland the management of her own concerns but you are asking England to pay £2,000,000 a year to enable her to have that privilege." You are doing nothing of the kind. You are paying £2,000,000 a year, more or less, at present, for the privilege of misgoverning us and of keeping Ireland discontented and dissatisfied.

This financial business is worth considering for a moment. When the first Home Rule Bill was introduced in 1886, Mr. Gladstone was enabled to provide an Imperial contribution of £3,250,000 sterling. Seven years passed, and when he introduced his second Home Rule Bill, he found he was able to provide an Imperial contribution of only £2,200,000. The contribution has been a decreasing contribution for many years. Its history is extraordinary. In less than a century Ireland has contributed to the upkeep of the Army and Navy, in addition to paying out of her own taxes the whole of her own cost, a sum of £325,000,000 sterling; and it is an extraordinary thing that during the famine years in Ireland, from 1846 onwards, Ireland was still contributing—although you were sending money over to keep her people from starvation—something like £2,000,000 a year to the upkeep of the Empire.

Mr. Gladstone warned England what would happen. In his speech he distinctly pointed out that this contribution was a diminishing quantity, the Bill properly, they may then be abolished or reduced or increased by the Irish Parliament. In fact, Ireland will not have the power to put customs or excise duties on any articles that do not bear such duties in this country. But she may decide for herself, within certain limits as to some taxes and without limit as to others, the amount of those duties and increase them to any amount so far as the excise on beer and spirits is concerned, and under certain limitations with regard to other articles. Old age pensions, insurance, land purchase, and the cost of the Land Commission remain an Imperial charge, the Irish Parliament having the option of taking these charges. That is an important point, the option of taking over old age pensions, the charge still remaining an Imperial charge, but the Irish Parliament being able to take advantage of any savings in the administration which she may be able to effect; and until the deficit has been worked off by means of the increased prosperity and increased taxation of the country, this country will continue, at her own cost, to collect the taxes; but when there is an equilibrium between the expenditure and the taxation, then this new Board—the Joint Exchequer Board—will make a report; and some machinery will be devised whereby an arrangement can be come to, by agreement between the two parties, as to the future, whereby we get back the collection of almost all of the taxes, and some Imperial contribution will be fixed for Ireland in the future, and, in addition, Ireland has authority to put on any new taxes she likes.

On the question of land purchase, I listened very carefully to what the Prime Minister said, and I would like to say to him and his colleagues that so far as the Land Purchase Acts are concerned, we fully and completely accept the principle that the Imperial Government must have the most absolute security for the payment of the loans advanced under those Acts. We believe that this principle involves the consequence that Ireland cannot claim powers to legislate as to the terms on which those loans are to be raised or in any way whatever to interfere with the security for those loans. Subject to these two principles, I have no doubt that it must be quite easy to come to a satisfactory arrangement as to the administration of the Acts. I must not delay the House by going further into the question of police or the question of the judges; we shall have plenty of opportunity for, I hope, frank and friendly discussion of these matters in Committee. What I want to say is this: that, viewing this Bill as a whole, I say here—and in what I say I speak for my colleagues on these benches—it is a great measure, and that it is a measure adequate to carry out the objects of its promoters. It is a great measure and we welcome it. This Bill will be submitted to an Irish National Convention, and I shall without hesitation recommend to that Convention the acceptance of this Bill. I say of this Bill what Parnell said of a Bill which was far worse, in my opinion—the Bill of 1886. Here are the words he used regarding that measure on the night of the First Reading:

House that Mr. Parnell was willing in 1886 to have no Irish Members here, although such serious questions as the police and the judiciary were reserved to this House; and when Mr. Gladstone changed his mind and decided that the Irish Members should be here, Mr. Parnell took the view that they ought to be here in small numbers. I was reading the other day an extremely interesting statement made by him in a published letter on the 5th of February, 1891. It was when he was having an unfortunate controversy with Mr. Gladstone and the Liberal Party. He said:

> But within the last twenty hours, information of a most startling character has reached me from a reliable source. It will be remembered that during the Hawarden communication, the one point upon which the views of the Liberal leaders were not definitely and clearly conveyed to me was that regarding the question of the retention of the Irish Members at Westminster. It was represented to me that the unanimous opinion was in favour of permanently retaining a reduced number—thirty-four—as the symbol of Imperial unity, but not with a view of affording grounds, occasions, or pretexts for Imperial interference in Irish national concerns, it being held most properly that the permanent retention of a large number would afford such grounds.

And he goes on to say:

> But from the information recently conveyed to me, it would appear that this decision has been reconsidered and that it is now most probable that the Irish Members in their full strength will be permanently retained.

From that point of view we certainly have authority for the position we take up in order to meet the anomaly which will exist and prevent a manifest injustice by calling on Irishmen to manage their own affairs and come over here in such numbers as to dominate your affairs. We desire to be here only under such condition as to make it practically impossible for us to govern decisions on Scotch, Welsh, or English Bills. We are brought here at all only because, pending a final settlement, it is necessary that this symbol of Imperial unity should be, at any rate, maintained.

On the question of finance I desire to express my strong opinion that this is a far better Bill than either the Bill of 1886 or that of 1893. As I understand the Bill—the Prime Minister will correct me if I am wrong—the Irish Exchequer will have at its disposal the proceeds of all existing Irish taxes, and the balance between that amount and the expenditure on Irish services—that is to say, the deficit—will be met, and over and above that there will be a surplus of £500,000 a year. The customs and excise duties, I understand, are to be fixed in the first instance on Imperial authority, but once they are fixed by Imperial authority, if I understand

Victoria, where they are elected, there has been an intermittent struggle for five-and-twenty years by the elected Upper House to exercise financial powers which on principle and by nearly universal practice are reserved for the popular chamber.

Only the other day—and this will interest honourable Members on the Labour benches opposite—we had a most extraordinary instance of the danger of an elected upper chamber—elected on a narrow franchise. It occurred in Australia. In South Australia the Labour party was returned to office and introduced a number of what seemed to them and to a large majority of the elected Members valuable measures. They were all rejected by the upper elected chamber. Then the Labour Government dissolved Parliament and came back a second time with a majority and sent their measures up again. Again they were all rejected, and then they introduced and passed a Parliament Bill like the one passed here last year. They sent that up, and that was rejected. They had no Royal Prerogative to fall back upon, and the result was an absolute deadlock. That is an instance which I give to my honourable Friends opposite of the danger of an elected upper chamber when it is on a narrow franchise, and it is a proof, I submit, that a nominated upper chamber is more valuable.

Let me take another point. Let me say a word on the reduction of Irish Members at Westminster. On this question of—I will not call it federalism, because that is a word which is very much misunderstood—on this question of local bodies managing their own affairs at home and sending local representatives to this House, I personally have a perfectly consistent record. In the debate on the Second Reading of the Home Rule Bill in 1886, when a proposal to exclude all the Irish Members was made, I stated in my speech that while, of course, I agreed, as Mr. Parnell had agreed, to accept it, I agreed only with great reluctance, and I said I looked forward to the time when if Irish Members were entirely excluded, they would be called back in very fair numbers to take part as representatives with other portions of the United Kingdom in what would be a real Imperial Parliament. I entirely share the hope and belief of the Prime Minister that this Bill will be the first great step in a movement which will end by giving local control over local affairs to the other parts of the United Kingdom. But until that is completed, I admit the presence of Irish Members here in any numbers is an anomaly. Your Constitution is full of anomalies—and full of inconsistencies, which is worse. The point I want to make is this: that until the system is completed you must have a certain amount of abnormality in your proceedings here. What is the best way of dealing with it? The best way is that taken by the Government in reducing the numbers. For my part, they might reduce them considerably more. I would not complain.

On this question of reduction of the Irish Members, may I remind the and if Home Rule were refused, it would speedily disappear. I think he said it would do so in fifteen years, and as a matter of fact, in practically fifteen years it has disappeared. You are not asked to finance the Government. You are not asked to pay anything in addition to what you are paying already or what you will be paying if this system goes on for the next two or three years. I therefore think myself, from the financial point of view alone, that this Home Rule Bill ought to commend itself to the judgment of the people of this country. But, after all, is not that a rather unworthy standpoint from which to view a question of this kind? Is it not an unworthy standpoint for a great, powerful, and wealthy country like England to take up? Think what it cost to settle the Transvaal. You forgave them a loan of £30,000,000. You gave them £3,000,000 or £4,000,000 sterling for other purposes. I say nothing about what you spent on the war, but if instead of £30,000,000 the sum had been £300,000,000, do you think there is any Englishman who will say it was not worth it in order to have cemented the races as it has done and turned South Africa into a loyal portion of the Empire? It is unworthy of the people of this country to talk in this way about terms. If Home Rule is unjust and wrong, refuse it; if it is just and right, what consistent argument can you put forward which is founded upon the question of a few paltry pounds, shillings, and pence?

I want to pass from this general subject to the proposals of the Bill. The House will naturally expect to hear from me some definite views upon those proposals and upon the Bill as a whole. Take first the case of the nominated Senate. I personally have for many years taken the view that from a democratic point of view, a nominated Senate—nominated not for life but for a short term—is a far safer body than a Senate elected on a narrow franchise. The late Sir Charles Gavan Duffy,[34] who was one of the most experienced men in the working of free institutions in your Empire, was a standing object lesson of the value of Home Rule in his own person, because having been tried for treason in Dublin, he went to the other end of the world and became one of the most loyal, wise, and honoured statesmen of the Queen in Australia. In a remarkable pamphlet issued a few years ago, he said:

> Nomination and not election is a method by which an Upper House is commonly chosen in free countries. Teuton, Celt, and Magyar, Catholic and Protestant, large and small states, have equally preferred deliberate selection to the hazard of the hustings. Senators are nominated in Italy, Germany, Austria, Hungary, Prussia, Portugal, Bavaria, and several smaller states, and among British Colonies in Canada, New Zealand, and New South Wales. In

---

[34] Irish nationalist and editor of *The Nation* (Dublin) from 1842 to 1848, Duffy emigrated to Australia in 1855. He was prominent in Australian politics and was Prime Minister for Victoria in 1871–1872.

The Prime Minister has truly said that it ought not to proceed unless it is cheerfully welcomed not only by the Irish Members but by the Irish people. I cordially agree in that proposition, and I am convinced . . . that it will be cheerfully accepted by the Irish people and their representatives as a solution of the long-standing dispute between the two countries, and that it will lead to the prosperity and peace of Ireland and the satisfaction of England.

On the Second Reading of the Bill, after discussion had gone on all over the country about it, Mr. Parnell said this:

I now repeat what I have already said on the First Reading of the measure immediately after I heard the statement of the Prime Minister, that we look upon the provisions of this Bill as a final settlement of this question, and that I believe the Irish people have accepted it as such a settlement.

I beg leave to apply every syllable of those two statements on behalf of my colleagues and myself to this Bill. If I may say so reverently, I personally thank God that I have lived to see this day. I believe this Bill will pass into law. I believe it will result in the greater unity and strength of the Empire; I believe it will put an end once and for all to ["*Cattle-driving*"] the wretched ill-will, suspicion, and disaffection that have existed in Ireland and to the suspicion and misunderstanding that have existed between this country and Ireland. I believe it will have the effect of turning Ireland in time—of course, it will take time—into a happy and prosperous country, with a united, loyal, and contented people. I well remember the night when the Home Rule Bill of 1886 was introduced to this House. It seems to me only yesterday that there stood at that box the venerable figure of that grand old statesman, who, with an eloquence that moved every heart of friend or foe alike, extended the hand of friendship to Ireland for the first time; and it seems only yesterday to me that the figure rose up of that great Irishman whose work had made the scene of 1886 possible and whose career has made this scene of today possible, and who accepted the proffered hand of friendship and accepted the Bill. These two great figures have disappeared, but their spirit dominates this scene today; and the memory of these two great men will be forever cherished in the grateful hearts of their countrymen respectively in England and in Ireland.

Twenty-six years afterwards, tonight, another Prime Minister, with magnificent power and eloquence, has again extended the hand of friendship to Ireland; but under what happier auspices! No one can realise better than he himself how happier the auspices are today. Since 1886 the two peoples have learned to know each other far better. Ireland today is peaceful beyond record. She has almost entirely, I believe, cast aside her suspicions and her rancour towards this country; and England, on her side, is, I believe, today more willing than ever she was in her past history to admit Ireland on terms of equality, liberty, and loyalty into that great sisterhood of nations that makes up the British Empire. Have Members of this House read the cabled messages which were published in the papers of London this morning? One paper publishes a whole page of them from the leading statesmen of every one of your self-governing Colonies—from Canada, from Australia, and last, but not least, from General Louis Botha[35] —all in favour of Home Rule for Ireland and giving their blessings to this Bill and encouragement to the right honourable Gentleman who introduced it. In addition there is this happy auspice, that England has witnessed that great experiment to which the Prime Minister referred of self-government in local affairs in Ireland; and England has admired the wisdom and efficiency of the Irish people in the management of their own local concerns. [*"Oh, oh!"*] The right honourable Gentleman the Member for the University of Dublin threw some doubt upon the efficiency and good working of those boards. If it were worthwhile, I could read to him the testimony of the right honourable Gentleman the Member for Dover,[36] the testimony of Mr. Gerald Balfour;[37] and in addition to that, I could read to him the Reports of the Local Government Board for Ireland year after year, showing that the conduct of these boards has been efficient and pure; and I could quote the figures showing that on the whole in Ireland, their work has been economic and has led to the reduction of taxation. Therefore, I believe that the right honourable Gentleman today is introducing this Bill under far more happy auspices, and the portents, in my belief, point in the direction of a settlement now of this Irish question. I pray earnestly that this Bill may pass; that it may achieve all the objects which its promoters have in view; and that, in the beautiful words of the prayer with which the proceedings of this House of Commons are opened every day:

> ... the result of all our counsels may be the maintenance of true religion and justice, the safety, honour, and happiness of the King, the public health, peace, and tranquility of the realm, and the uniting and knitting together therein of the hearts of all persons and estates within the same, in true Christian love and charity.

---

[35] Prime Minister of the Union of South Africa.
[36] George Wyndham.
[37] In 1898, Balfour, former Chief Secretary for Ireland, sponsored the legislation establishing county and district councils in Ireland.

MAN·IS·BVT·A·WORM·

5

Faith,
Reason,
and
Knowledge

John Henry Cardinal Newman

"Christianity and Scientific Investigation"[*]

Catholic University of Ireland, Dublin, 1855

This is a time, Gentlemen, when not only the classics, but much more the sciences, in the largest sense of the word, are looked upon with anxiety, not altogether ungrounded, by religious men; and whereas a university such as ours professes to embrace all departments and exercises of the intellect, and since I for my part wish to stand on good terms with all kinds of knowledge, and have no intention of quarrelling with any, and would open my heart, if not my intellect (for that is beyond me), to the whole circle of truth, and would tender at least a recognition and hospitality even to those studies which are strangers to me, and would speed them on their way—therefore, as I have already been making overtures of reconciliation, first between polite literature and religion and next between physics and theology, so I would now say a word by way of deprecating and protesting against the needless antagonism which sometimes exists in fact between divines and the cultivators of the sciences generally.

Here I am led at once to expatiate on the grandeur of an institution which is comprehensive enough to admit the discussion of a subject such as this. Among the objects of human enterprise—I may say it surely without extravagance, Gentlemen—none higher or nobler can be named than that which is contemplated in the erection of a university. To set on foot and to maintain in life and vigour a real university, is confessedly, as soon as the word "university" is understood, one of those greatest works, great in their difficulty and their importance, on which are deservedly expended the rarest intellects and the most varied endowments. For, first of all, it professes to teach whatever has to be taught in any whatever department of human knowledge, and it embraces in its scope the loftiest subjects of

---

[*] This lecture was written late in 1855 for presentation during the spring of 1856. It was never delivered as a speech. Probably published first in Newman's *Lectures and Essays on University Subjects* (1859), it was included later as part of *The Idea of a University*. The text is taken from this work (London, 1875), pp. 456–479.

human thought and the richest fields of human inquiry. Nothing is too vast, nothing too subtile, nothing too distant, nothing too minute, nothing too discursive, nothing too exact, to engage its attention.

This, however, is not the reason why I claim for it so sovereign a position; for, to bring schools of all knowledge under one name and call them a university may be fairly said to be a mere generalization; and to proclaim that the prosecution of all kinds of knowledge to their utmost limits demands the fullest reach and range of our intellectual faculties is but a truism. My reason for speaking of a university in the terms on which I have ventured is not that it occupies the whole territory of knowledge merely, but that it is the very realm; that it professes much more than to take in and to lodge as in a caravanserai[1] all art and science, all history and philosophy. In truth, it professes to assign to each study which it receives its own proper place and its just boundaries; to define the rights, to establish the mutual relations, and to effect the intercommunion of one and all; to keep in check the ambitious and encroaching and to succour and maintain those which from time to time are succumbing under the more popular or the more fortunately circumstanced; to keep the peace between them all and to convert their mutual differences and contrarieties into the common good.

This, Gentlemen, is why I say that to erect a university is at once so arduous and beneficial an undertaking, viz., because it is pledged to admit without fear, without prejudice, without compromise, all comers, if they come in the name of Truth; to adjust views and experiences and habits of mind the most independent and dissimilar; and to give full play to thought and erudition in their most original forms and their most intense expressions, and in their most ample circuit. Thus to draw many things into one is its special function; and it learns to do it not by rules reducible to writing but by sagacity, wisdom, and forbearance, acting upon a profound insight into the subject matter of knowledge and by a vigilant repression of aggression or bigotry in any quarter.

We count it a great thing, and justly so, to plan and carry out a wide political organization. To bring under one yoke after the manner of old Rome a hundred discordant peoples; to maintain each of them in its own privileges within its legitimate range of action; to allow them severally the indulgence of national feelings and the stimulus of rival interests; and yet withal to blend them into one great social establishment and to pledge them to the perpetuity of the one imperial power—this is an achievement which carries with it the unequivocal token of genius in the race which effects it.

Tu regere imperio populos, Romane, memento.[2]

[1] A shelter or resting place for caravans.
[2] "Remember, Roman, to rule peoples by your empire" (Virgil, *Aeneid* VI. 851).

This was the special boast, as the poet considered it, of the Roman; a boast as high in its own line as that other boast, proper to the Greek nation, of literary preëminence, of exuberance of thought, and of skill and refinement in expressing it.

What an empire is in political history, such is a university in the sphere of philosophy and research. It is, as I have said, the high protecting power of all knowledge and science, of fact and principle, of inquiry and discovery, of experiment and speculation; it maps out the territory of the intellect and sees that the boundaries of each province are religiously respected, and that there is neither encroachment nor surrender on any side. It acts as umpire between truth and truth and, taking into account the nature and importance of each, assigns to all their due order of precedence. It maintains no one department of thought exclusively, however ample and noble, and it sacrifices none. It is deferential and loyal, according to their respective weight, to the claims of literature, of physical research, of history, of metaphysics, of theological science. It is impartial towards them all and promotes each in its own place and for its own object.

It is ancillary certainly, and of necessity, to the Catholic Church, but in the same way that one of the Queen's judges is an officer of the Queen and nevertheless determines certain legal proceedings between the Queen and her subjects. It is ministrative to the Catholic Church first because truth of any kind can but minister to truth; and next, still more, because nature ever will pay homage to grace, and reason cannot but illustrate and defend revelation; and thirdly, because the Church has a sovereign authority and when she speaks *ex cathedra* must be obeyed. But this is the remote end of a university; its immediate end (with which alone we have here to do) is to secure the due disposition, according to one sovereign order, and the cultivation in that order of all the provinces and methods of thought which the human intellect has created.

In this point of view, its several professors are like the ministers of various political powers at one court or conference. They represent their respective sciences and attend to the private interests of those sciences respectively; and should dispute arise between those sciences, they are the persons to talk over and arrange it, without risk of extravagant pretensions on any side, of angry collision, or of popular commotion. A liberal philosophy becomes the habit of minds thus exercised; a breadth and spaciousness of thought, in which lines seemingly parallel may converge at leisure, and principles recognised as incommensurable may be safely antagonistic.

And here, Gentlemen, we recognise the special character of the philosophy I am speaking of, if philosophy it is to be called, in contrast with the method of a strict science or system. Its teaching is not founded on one idea or reducible to certain formulæ. Newton might discover the great law of motion in the physical world and the key to ten thousand phenomena, and a similar resolution of complex facts into simple principles may be possible in other departments of nature; but the great universe itself, moral and material, sensible and supernatural, cannot be gauged and meted by even the greatest of human intellects, and its constituent parts admit indeed of comparison and adjustment, but not of fusion. This is the point which bears directly on the subject which I set before me when I began and towards which I am moving in all I have said or shall be saying.

I observe, then, and ask you, Gentlemen, to bear in mind that the philosophy of an imperial intellect—for such I am considering a university to be—is based not so much on simplification as on discrimination. Its true representative defines, rather than analyses. He aims at no complete catalogue or interpretation of the subjects of knowledge, but a following out, as far as man can, what in its fullness is mysterious and unfathomable. Taking into his charge all sciences, methods, collections of facts, principles, doctrines, truths, which are the reflexions of the universe upon the human intellect, he admits them all, he disregards none, and, as disregarding none, he allows none to exceed or encroach. His watchword is, Live and let live. He takes things as they are; he submits to them all, as far as they go; he recognises the insuperable lines of demarcation which run between subject and subject; he observes how separate truths lie relatively to each other, where they concur, where they part company, and where, being carried too far, they cease to be truths at all. It is his office to determine how much can be known in each province of thought; when we must be contented not to know; in what direction inquiry is hopeless or on the other hand full of promise; where it gathers into coils insoluble by reason, where it is absorbed in mysteries or runs into the abyss. It will be his care to be familiar with the signs of real and apparent difficulties, with the methods proper to particular subject matters, what in each particular case are the limits of a rational scepticism, and what the claims of a peremptory faith. If he has one cardinal maxim in his philosophy, it is that truth cannot be contrary to truth; if he has a second, it is that truth often *seems* contrary to truth; and if a third, it is the practical conclusion that we must be patient with such appearances and not be hasty to pronounce them to be really of a more formidable character.

It is the very immensity of the system of things, the human record of which he has in charge, which is the reason of this patience and caution; for that immensity suggests to him that the contrarieties and mysteries which meet him in the various sciences may be simply the consequences of our necessarily defective comprehension. There is but one thought greater than that of the universe, and that is the thought of its Maker. If, Gentlemen, for one single instant, leaving my proper train of thought, I allude to our knowledge of the Supreme Being, it is in order to deduce from it an illustration bearing upon my subject. He, though One, is a sort of world of worlds in Himself, giving birth in our minds to an indefinite number of distinct truths, each ineffably more mysterious than anything that is found in this universe of space and time. Any one of His attributes, considered by itself, is the object of an inexhaustible science; and the attempt to reconcile any two or three of them together—love, power, justice, sanctity, truth, wisdom—affords matter for an everlasting controversy. We are able to apprehend and receive each divine attribute in its elementary form, but still we are not able to accept them in their infinity, either in themselves or in union with each other. Yet we do not deny the first because it cannot be perfectly reconciled with the second, nor the second because it is in apparent contrariety with the first and the third. The case is the same in its degree with His creation material and moral. It is the highest wisdom to accept truth of whatever kind wherever it is clearly ascertained to be such, though there be difficulty in adjusting it with other known truth.

Instances are easily producible of that extreme contrariety of ideas, one with another, which the contemplation of the universe forces upon our acceptance, making it clear to us that there is nothing irrational in submitting to undeniable incompatibilities which we call apparent only because if they were not apparent but real, they could not co-exist. Such, for instance, is the contemplation of space, the existence of which we cannot deny, though its idea is capable, in no sort of posture, of seating itself (if I may so speak) in our minds; for we find it impossible to say that it comes to a limit anywhere, and it is incomprehensible to say that it runs out infinitely; and it seems to be unmeaning if we say that it does not exist till bodies come into it, and thus is enlarged according to an accident.

And so again in the instance of time. We cannot place a beginning to it without asking ourselves what was before that beginning; yet that there should be no beginning at all, put it as far back as we will, is simply incomprehensible. Here again, as in the case of space, we never dream of denying the existence of what we have no means of understanding.

And passing from this high region of thought (which, high as it may be, is the subject even of a child's contemplations), when we come to consider the mutual action of soul and body, we are specially perplexed by incompatibilities which we can neither reject nor explain. How it is that the will can act on the muscles is a question of which even a child may feel the force, but which no experimentalist can answer.

Further, when we contrast the physical with the social laws under which man finds himself here below, we must grant that physiology and social science are in collision. Man is both a physical and a social being; yet he cannot at once pursue to the full his physical end and his social end, his physical duties (if I may so speak) and his social duties, but is forced to sacrifice in part one or the other. If we were wild enough to fancy that there were two creators, one of whom was the author of our animal frames, the other of society, then indeed we might understand how it comes to pass that labour of mind and body, the useful arts, the duties of a statesman, government, and the like, which are required by the social system, are so destructive of health, enjoyment, and life. That is, in other words, we cannot adequately account for existing and undeniable truths except on the hypothesis of what we feel to be an absurdity.

And so in mathematical science, as has been often insisted on, the philosopher has patiently to endure the presence of truths which are not the less true for being irreconcileable with each other. He is told of the existence of an infinite number of curves which are able to divide a space into which no straight line, though it be length without breadth, can even enter. He is told, too, of certain lines which approach to each other continually with a finite distance between them, yet never meet; and these apparent contrarieties he must bear as he best can without attempting to deny the existence of the truths which constitute them in the science in question.

Now, let me call your attention, Gentlemen, to what I would infer from these familiar facts. It is to urge you with an argument *a fortiori*: viz., that as you exercise so much exemplary patience in the case of the inexplicable truths which surround so many departments of knowledge, human and divine, viewed in themselves; as you are not at once indignant, censorious, suspicious, difficult of belief, on finding that in the secular sciences one truth is incompatible (according to our human intellect) with another or inconsistent with itself; so you should not think it very hard to be told that there exists, here and there, not an inextricable difficulty, not an astounding contrariety, not (much less) a contradiction as to clear facts, between revelation and nature, but a hitch, an obscurity, a divergence of tendency, a temporary antagonism, a difference of tone, between the two—that is, between Catholic opinion on the one hand, and astronomy, or geology, or physiology, or ethnology, or political economy, or history, or antiquities on the other. I say that as we admit because we are Catholics that the Divine Unity contains in it attributes which, to our finite minds, appear in partial contrariety with each other; as we admit that in His revealed nature are things which, though not opposed to reason, are infinitely strange to the imagination; as in His works we can neither reject nor admit the ideas of space and of time and the necessary properties of lines without intellectual distress or even torture; really, Gentlemen, I am making no outrageous request when, in the name of a university, I ask religious writers, jurists, economists, physiologists, chemists, geologists, and historians to go on quietly and in a neighbourly way in their own respective lines of speculation, research, and experiment, with full faith in the consistency of that multiform truth which they share between them in a generous confidence that they will be ultimately consistent, one and all, in their combined results, though there may be momentary collisions, awkward appearances, and many forebodings and prophecies of contrariety, and at all times things hard to the imagination, though not, I repeat, to the reason. It surely is not asking them a great deal to beg of them—since they are forced to admit mysteries in the truths of revelation, taken by themselves, and in the truths of reason, taken by themselves—to beg of them, I say, to keep the peace, to live in good will, and to exercise equanimity, if, when nature and revelation are compared with each other, there be, as I have said, discrepancies—not in the issue, but in the reasonings, the circumstances, the associations, the anticipations, the accidents, proper to their respective teachings.

It is most necessary to insist seriously and energetically on this point for the sake of Protestants, for they have very strange notions about us. In spite of the testimony of history the other way, they think that the Church has no other method of putting down error than the arm of force or the prohibition of inquiry. They defy us to set up and carry on a school of science. For their sake, then, I am led to enlarge upon the subject here. I say, then, he who believes revelation with that absolute faith which is the prerogative of a Catholic is not the nervous creature who startles at every sudden sound and is fluttered by every strange or novel appearance which meets his eyes. He has no sort of apprehension, he laughs at the idea, that anything can be discovered by any other scientific method which can contradict any one of the dogmas of his religion. He knows full well there is no science whatever, but, in the course of its extension, runs the risk of infringing without any meaning of offence on its own part the path of other sciences; and he knows also that if there be any one science which, from its sovereign and unassailable position can calmly bear such unintentional collisions on the part of the children of earth, it is theology. He is sure and nothing shall make him doubt that if anything seems to be proved by astronomer, or geologist, or chronologist, or antiquarian, or ethnologist, in contradiction to the dogmas of faith, that point will eventually turn out first, *not* to be proved, or secondly, not *contradictory*, or thirdly, not contradictory to anything *really revealed*, but to something which has been confused with revelation. And if, at the moment, it appears to be contradictory, then he is content to wait, knowing that error is like other delinquents: give it rope enough and it will be found to have a strong suicidal propensity. I do not mean to say he will not take his part in encouraging, in helping forward the prospective suicide; he will not only give the error rope enough but show it how to handle and adjust the rope; he will commit the matter to reason, reflection, sober judgment, common sense; to time, the great interpreter of so many secrets. Instead of being irritated at the momentary triumph of the foes of revelation, if such a feeling of triumph there be, and of hurrying on a forcible solution of the difficulty which may in the event only reduce the inquiry to an inextricable tangle, he will recollect that in the order of Providence, our seeming dangers are often our greatest gains; that in the words of the Protestant poet,[3]

> The clouds you so much dread
> Are big with mercy, and shall break
> In blessings on your head.

[3] The Protestant poet is William Cowper; the lines are from the third verse of the hymn "God Moves in a Mysterious Way."

To one notorious instance indeed it is obvious to allude here. When the Copernican system first made progress, what religious man would not have been tempted to uneasiness or at least fear of scandal from the seeming contradiction which it involved to some authoritative tradition of the Church and the declaration of Scripture? It was generally received as if the Apostles had expressly delivered it both orally and in writing, as a truth of revelation, that the earth was stationary and that the sun, fixed in a solid firmament, whirled round the earth. After a little time, however, and on full consideration, it was found that the Church had decided next to nothing on questions such as these, and that physical science might range in this sphere of thought almost at will, without fear of encountering the decisions of ecclesiastical authority. Now, besides the relief which it afforded to Catholics to find that they were to be spared this addition, on the side of cosmology, to their many controversies already existing, there is something of an argument in this very circumstance in behalf of the divinity of their religion. For it surely is a very remarkable fact, considering how widely and how long one certain interpretation of these physical statements in Scripture had been received by Catholics, that the Church should not have formally acknowledged it. Looking at the matter in a human point of view, it was inevitable that she should have made that opinion her own. But now we find, on ascertaining where we stand in the face of the new sciences of these latter times, that in spite of the bountiful comments which from the first she has ever been making on the sacred text, as it is her duty and her right to do, nevertheless she has never been led formally to explain the texts in question or to give them an authoritative sense which modern science may question.

Nor was this escape a mere accident, but rather the result of a providential superintendence, as would appear from a passage of history in the dark age itself. When the glorious St. Boniface,[4] Apostle of Germany, great in sanctity though not in secular knowledge, complained to the Holy See that St. Virgilius[5] taught the existence of the Antipodes, the Holy See was guided what to do; it did not indeed side with the Irish philosopher, which would have been going out of its place, but it passed over in a manner not revealed, a philosophical opinion.

Time went on; a new state of things intellectual and social came in; the Church was girt with temporal power; the preachers of St. Dominic[6] were in the ascendant; now at length we may ask with curious interest, did the Church alter her ancient rule of action and proscribe intellectual activity? Just the contrary; this is the very age of universities; it is the classical period of the schoolmen; it is the splendid and palmary instance of the wise policy and large liberality of the Church as regards philosophical

[4] English missionary monk (ca. 675—ca. 754).
[5] St. Virgilius (Virgile), Archbishop of Arles (died ca. 610).
[6] Castilian churchman (1170—ca. 1221), founder of the Dominicans.

inquiry. If there ever was a time when the intellect went wild and had a licentious revel, it was at the date I speak of. When was there ever a more curious, more meddling, bolder, keener, more penetrating, more rationalistic exercise of the reason than at that time? What class of questions did that subtle, metaphysical spirit not scrutinise? What premiss was allowed without examination? What principle was not traced to its first origin and exhibited in its most naked shape? What whole was not analysed? What complex idea was not elaborately traced out and, as it were, finely painted for the contemplation of the mind till it was spread out in all its minutest portions as perfectly and delicately as a frog's foot shows under the intense scrutiny of the microscope?

Well, I repeat, here was something which came somewhat nearer to theology than physical research comes; Aristotle was a somewhat more serious foe then, beyond all mistake, than Bacon has been since. Did the Church take a high hand with philosophy then? No, not though that philosophy was metaphysical. It was a time when she had temporal power and could have exterminated the spirit of inquiry with fire and sword; but she determined to put it down by *argument*; she said: "Two can play at that, and my argument is the better." She sent her controversialists into the philosophical arena. It was the Dominican and Franciscan doctors, the greatest of them being St. Thomas,[7] who in those medieval universities fought the battle of revelation with the weapons of heathenism. It was no matter whose the weapon was; truth was truth all the world over. With the jawbone of an ass, with the skeleton philosophy of pagan Greece, did the Samson of the schools put to flight his thousand Philistines.

Here, Gentlemen, observe the contrast exhibited between the Church herself, who has the gift of wisdom, and even the ablest, or wisest, or holiest of her children. As St. Boniface had been jealous of physical speculations, so had the early Fathers shown an extreme aversion to the great heathen philosopher whom I just now named, Aristotle. I do not know who of them could endure him; and when there arose those in the middle age who would take his part, especially since their intentions were of a suspicious character, a strenuous effort was made to banish him out of Christendom. The Church the while had kept silence; she had as little denounced heathen philosophy in the mass as she had pronounced upon the meaning of certain texts of Scripture of a cosmological character. From Tertullian[8] and Caius[9] to the two Gregories of Cappadocia,[10] from them to Anastasius Sinaita,[11] from him to the school of Paris, Aristotle was a word of offence; at length St. Thomas made him a hewer of wood and

---

[7] St. Thomas Aquinas (1225–1275) is considered the "patron of Catholic universities."
[8] Roman theologian and apologist (ca. 160—ca. 230).
[9] Bishop of Rome from 283 to 296.
[10] St. Gregory I (ca. 540–604) was Pope from 590 to 604; St. Gregory II (died 731) was Pope from 715 to 731.
[11] St. Anastasius the Sinaite (died ca. 700).

drawer of water to the Church. A strong slave he is, and the Church herself has given her sanction to the use in theology of the ideas and terms of his philosophy.

Now, while this free discussion is, to say the least, so safe for religion, or rather so expedient, it is on the other hand simply necessary for progress in science; and I shall now go on to insist on this side of the subject. I say, then, that it is a matter of primary importance in the cultivation of those sciences in which truth is discoverable by the human intellect that the investigator should be free, independent, unshackled in his movements; that he should be allowed and enabled without impediment to fix his mind intently, nay, exclusively, on his special object, without the risk of being distracted every other minute in the process and progress of his inquiry by charges of temerariousness or by warnings against extravagance or scandal. But in thus speaking I must premise several explanations, lest I be misunderstood.

First, then, Gentlemen, as to the fundamental principles of religion and morals and again as to the fundamental principles of Christianity, or what are called the *dogmas* of faith—as to this double creed, natural and revealed—we none of us should say that it is any shackle at all upon the intellect to maintain these inviolate. Indeed, a Catholic cannot put off his thought of them; and they as little impede the movements of his intellect as the laws of physics impede his bodily movements. The habitual apprehension of them has become a second nature with him, as the laws of optics, hydrostatics, dynamics, are latent conditions which he takes for granted in the use of his corporeal organs. I am not supposing any collision with dogma; I am speaking of opinions of divines or of the multitude parallel to those in former times of the sun going round the earth, or of the last day being close at hand, or of St. Dionysius[12] the Areopagite being the author of the works which bear his name.

Nor secondly, even as regards such opinions, am I supposing any direct intrusion into the province of religion or of a teacher of science actually laying down the law *in a matter of religion,* but of such unintentional collisions as are incidental to a discussion pursued on some subject of his own. It would be a great mistake in such a one to propose his philosophical or historical conclusions as the formal interpretation of the sacred text, as Galileo is said to have done, instead of being content to hold his doctrine of the motion of the earth as a scientific conclusion and leaving it to those whom it really concerned to compare it with Scripture. And, it must be confessed, Gentlemen, not a few instances occur of this mistake at the present day, on the part not indeed of men of science, but of religious men who, from a nervous impatience lest Scripture should for one moment seem inconsistent with the results of some speculation of the hour, are

[12] The first-century Bishop of Athens. He is often confused with St. Dionysius of Paris (St. Denis) or Dionysius the "pseudo-Areopagite," an ecclesiastical writer of the fifth century.

ever proposing geological or ethnological comments upon it, which they have to alter or obliterate before the ink is well dry, from changes in the progressive science which they have so officiously brought to its aid.

And thirdly, I observe that when I advocate the independence of philosophical thought, I am not speaking of any *formal teaching* at all, but of investigations, speculations, and discussions. I am far indeed from allowing in any matter which even borders on religion what an eminent Protestant divine has advocated on the most sacred subjects—I mean "the liberty of prophesying." I have no wish to degrade the professors of science, who ought to be prophets of the truth, into mere advertisers of crude fancies or notorious absurdities. I am not pleading that they should at random shower down upon their hearers ingenuities and novelties, or that they should teach even what has a basis of truth in it in a brilliant, off-hand way to a collection of youths who may not perhaps hear them for six consecutive lectures and who will carry away with them into the country a misty idea of the half-created theories of some ambitious intellect.

Once more, as the last sentence suggests, there must be great care taken to avoid scandal or shocking the popular mind or unsettling the weak, the association between truth and error being so strong in particular minds that it is impossible to weed them of the error without rooting up the wheat with it. If, then, there is the chance of any current religious opinion being in any way compromised in the course of a scientific investigation, this would be a reason for conducting it not in light ephemeral publications which come into the hands of the careless or ignorant, but in works of a grave and business-like character, answering to the medieval schools of philosophical disputation, which, removed as they were from the region of popular thought and feeling, have, by their vigorous restlessness of inquiry, in spite of their extravagances, done so much for theological precision.

I am not, then, supposing the scientific investigator (1) to be *coming into collision with dogma;* nor (2) venturing by means of his investigations upon any interpretation of *Scripture* or upon other conclusion *in the matter of religion;* nor (3) of his *teaching* even in his own science religious paradoxes, when he should be investigating and proposing; nor (4) of his recklessly *scandalizing the weak;* but these explanations being made, I still say that a scientific speculator or inquirer is not bound in conducting his researches to be every moment adjusting his course by the maxims of the schools or by popular traditions or by those of any other science distinct from his own, or to be ever narrowly watching what those external sciences have to say to him, or to be determined to be edifying, or to be ever answering heretics and unbelievers; being confident, from the impulse of a generous faith, that however his line of investigation may swerve now and then and vary to and fro in its course or threaten momentary collision or embarrassment with any other department of knowledge, theological or not; yet, if he lets it alone, it will be sure to come home, because truth never can really be contrary to truth and because often what at first sight is an *exceptio* in the event most emphatically *probat regulam*.[13]

This is a point of serious importance to him. Unless he is at liberty to investigate on the basis and according to the peculiarities of his science, he cannot investigate at all. It is the very law of the human mind in its inquiry after and acquisition of truth to make its advances by a process which consists of many stages and is circuitous. There are no short cuts to knowledge; nor does the road to it always lie in the direction in which it terminates, nor are we able to see the end on starting. It may often seem to be diverging from a goal into which it will soon run without effort, if we are but patient and resolute in following it out; and as we are told in ethics to gain the mean merely by receding from both extremes, so in scientific researches error may be said, without a paradox, to be in some instances the way to truth, and the only way. Moreover, it is not often the fortune of any one man to live through an investigation; the process is one of not only many stages but of many minds. What one begins another finishes; and a true conclusion is at length worked out by the co-operation of independent schools and the perseverance of successive generations. This being the case, we are obliged, under circumstances, to bear for a while with what we feel to be error, in consideration of the truth in which it is eventually to issue.

The analogy of locomotion is most pertinent here. No one can go straight up a mountain; no sailing vessel makes for its port without tacking. And so, applying the illustration, we can indeed, if we will, refuse to allow of investigation or research altogether; but if we invite reason to take its place in our schools, we must let reason have fair and full play. If we reason, we must submit to the conditions of reason. We cannot use it by halves; we must use it as proceeding from Him who has also given us revelation; and to be ever interrupting its processes and diverting its attention by objections brought from a higher knowledge is parallel to a landsman's dismay at the changes in the course of a vessel on which he has deliberately embarked, and argues surely some distrust either in the powers of reason on the one hand or the certainty of revealed truth on the other. The passenger should not have embarked at all if he did not reckon on the chance of a rough sea, of currents, of wind and tide, of rocks and shoals; and we should act more wisely in discountenancing altogether the exercise of reason than in being alarmed and impatient under the suspense, delay, and anxiety which, from the nature of the case, may be found to attach to it. Let us eschew secular history and science and philosophy for good and all if we are not allowed to be sure that revelation is so true that the altercations and perplexities of human opinion cannot really or eventually injure its authority. That is no intellectual triumph of any truth of religion which has not been preceded

---

[13] The exception proves the rule.

by a full statement of what can be said against it; it is but the *ego vapulando, ille verberando*[14] of the comedy.

Great minds need elbow-room, not indeed in the domain of faith, but of thought. And so indeed do lesser minds and all minds. There are many persons in the world who are called, and with a great deal of truth, geniuses. They had been gifted by nature with some particular faculty or capacity; and while vehemently excited and imperiously ruled by it, they are blind to everything else. They are enthusiasts in their own line and are simply dead to the beauty of any line *except* their own. Accordingly, they think their own line the only line in the whole world worth pursuing, and they feel a sort of contempt for such studies as move upon any other line. Now, these men may be and often are very good Catholics and have not a dream of anything but affection and deference towards Catholicity, nay, perhaps are zealous in its interests. Yet, if you insist that in their speculations, researches, or conclusions in their particular science it is not enough that they should submit to the Church generally and acknowledge its dogmas, but that they must get up all that divines have said or the multitude believed upon religious matters, you simply crush and stamp out the flame within them and they can do nothing at all.

This is the case of men of genius. Now, one word on the contrary in behalf of master minds gifted with a broad philosophical view of things and a creative power and a versatility capable of accommodating itself to various provinces of thought. These persons perhaps, like those I have already spoken of, take up some idea and are intent upon it—some deep, prolific, eventful idea, which grows upon them till they develop it into a great system. Now, if any such thinker starts from radically unsound principles or aims at directly false conclusions, if he be a Hobbes[15] or a Shaftesbury[16] or a Hume[17] or a Bentham,[18] then, of course, there is an end of the whole matter. He is an opponent of revealed truth, and he means to be so; nothing more need be said. But perhaps it is not so; perhaps his errors are those which are inseparable accidents of his system or of his mind and are spontaneously evolved, not pertinaciously defended. Every human system, every human writer, is open to just criticism. Make him shut up his portfolio; good! and then perhaps you lose what, on the whole and in spite of incidental mistakes, would have been one of the ablest

---

[14] "I by being beaten, he by beating"—we are both exhausted (Terence, *Adelphi*, Act II, Scene ii, line 213).

[15] Thomas Hobbes (1588–1679), English philosopher, insisted on the complete separation of theology and philosophy and the subordination of church to state.

[16] Probably Anthony Ashley Cooper, Third Earl of Shaftesbury (1671–1713), who found true morality in a balance of egoism and altruism.

[17] Scottish philosopher and historian, David Hume (1711–1776). His skeptical views were opposed to metaphysics as a legitimate field of knowledge.

[18] Jeremy Bentham (1748–1832), English philosopher, held that the greatest happiness of the greatest number was the fundamental and self-evident principle of morality.

defences of revealed truth (directly or indirectly, according to his subject) ever given to the world.

This is how I should account for a circumstance which has sometimes caused surprise that so many great Catholic thinkers have in some points or other incurred the criticism or animadversion of theologians or of ecclesiastical authority. It must be so in the nature of things; there is indeed an animadversion which implies a condemnation of the author; but there is another which means not much more than the *pie legendum*[19] written against passages in the Fathers. The author may not be to blame, yet the ecclesiastical authority would be to blame if it did not give notice of his imperfections. I do not know what Catholic would not hold the name of Malebranche[20] in veneration, but he may have accidentally come into collision with theologians or made temerarious assertions notwithstanding. The practical question is whether he had not much better have written as he has written than not have written at all. And so fully is the Holy See accustomed to enter into this view of the matter that it has allowed of its application not only to philosophical but even to theological and ecclesiastical authors who do not come within the range of these remarks. I believe I am right in saying that in the case of three great names in various departments of learning, Cardinal Noris,[21] Bossuet,[22] and Muratori,[23] while not concealing its sense of their having propounded each what might have been said better, nevertheless it has considered that their services to religion were on the whole far too important to allow of their being molested by critical observation in detail.

And, now, Gentlemen, I bring these remarks to a conclusion. What I would urge everyone, whatever may be his particular line of research —what I would urge upon men of science in their thoughts of theology— what I would venture to recommend to theologians, when their attention is drawn to the subject of scientific investigations—is a great and firm belief in the sovereignty of truth. Error may flourish for a time, but truth will prevail in the end. The only effect of error ultimately is to promote truth. Theories, speculations, hypotheses, are started; perhaps they are to die; still, not before they have suggested ideas better than themselves. These better ideas are taken up in turn by other men, and if they do not yet lead to truth, nevertheless they lead to what is still nearer to truth than themselves; and thus knowledge on the whole makes progress. The errors of

---

[19] The expression may be interpreted in various ways, but "sympathetic critique" would seem best to convey the intended meaning.

[20] Nicolas Malebranche (1638–1715), French philosopher, author of *De la recherche de la vérité*.

[21] Henry Cardinal Noris (1631–1704), professor of church history at Padua and author of *The History of Pelagianism*. He was named head of the Vatican Library in 1700.

[22] Jacques Benigne Bossuet (1627–1704), French bishop, author, and one of the greatest pulpit orators of his day.

[23] Luigi Antonio Muratori (1672–1760), Italian scholar.

some minds in scientific investigation are more fruitful than the truths of others. A science seems making no progress but to abound in failures, yet imperceptibly all the time it is advancing, and it is of course a gain to truth even to have learned what is not true, if nothing more.

On the other hand, it must be of course remembered, Gentlemen, that I am supposing all along good faith, honest intentions, a loyal Catholic spirit, and a deep sense of responsibility. I am supposing in the scientific inquirer a due fear of giving scandal, of seeming to countenance views which he does not really countenance, and of siding with parties from whom he heartily differs. I am supposing that he is fully alive to the existence and the power of the infidelity of the age; that he keeps in mind the moral weakness and the intellectual confusion of the majority of men; and that he has no wish at all that any one soul should get harm from certain speculations today, though he may have the satisfaction of being sure that those speculations will, as far as they are erroneous or misunderstood, be corrected in the course of the next half-century.

Thomas Huxley

"Science and Culture"[*]
Mason College, Birmingham, October, 1, 1880

Six years ago, as some of my present hearers may remember, I had the privilege of addressing a large assemblage of the inhabitants of this city who had gathered together to do honour to the memory of their famous townsman, Joseph Priestley;[1] and if any satisfaction attaches to posthumous glory, we may hope that the manes of the burnt-out philosopher were then finally appeased.[2]

No man, however, who is endowed with a fair share of common sense and not more than a fair share of vanity will identify either contemporary or posthumous fame with the highest good; and Priestley's life leaves no doubt that he, at any rate, set a much higher value upon the advancement of knowledge and the promotion of that freedom of thought which is at once the cause and the consequence of intellectual progress.

Hence, I am disposed to think that if Priestley could be amongst us today, the occasion of our meeting would afford him even greater pleasure than the proceedings which celebrated the centenary of his chief discovery. The kindly heart would be moved, the high sense of social duty would be satisfied, by the spectacle of well-earned wealth, neither squandered in tawdry luxury and vainglorious show nor scattered with the careless charity which blesses neither him that gives nor him that takes, but expended in the execution of a well-considered plan for the aid of present and future generations of those who are willing to help themselves.

We shall all be of one mind thus far. But it is needful to share Priestley's keen interest in physical science, and to have learned, as he had learned,

---

[*] This text is taken from Thomas Huxley's *Science and Culture and Other Essays* (London, 1881), pp. 1–23.

[1] Eighteen-century scientist and philosopher. For Priestley's views on rhetoric, see Joseph Priestley, *A Course of Lectures on Oratory and Criticism*, ed. Vincent M. Bevilacqua and Richard Murphy (Carbondale, Illinois, 1965).

[2] The reference is to a speech given August 1, 1874, on the occasion of the presentation of a statue of Joseph Priestley. See "Joseph Priestley," in Thomas Huxley's *Science and Education* (New York, 1895), pp. 1–37.

the value of scientific training in fields of inquiry apparently far remote from physical science, in order to appreciate, as he would have appreciated, the value of the noble gift which Sir Josiah Mason[3] has bestowed upon the inhabitants of the Midland district.

For us children of the nineteenth century, however, the establishment of a college under the conditions of Sir Josiah Mason's Trust has a significance apart from any which it could have possessed a hundred years ago. It appears to be an indication that we are reaching the crisis of the battle, or rather of the long series of battles, which have been fought over education in a campaign which began long before Priestley's time and will probably not be finished just yet.

In the last century, the combatants were the champions of ancient literature on the one side and those of modern literature on the other; but, some thirty years[4] ago, the contest became complicated by the appearance of a third army ranged round the banner of physical science. I am not aware that anyone has authority to speak in the name of this new host. For it must be admitted to be somewhat of a guerilla force composed largely of irregulars, each of whom fights pretty much for his own hand. But the impressions of a full private who has seen a good deal of service in the ranks, respecting the present position of affairs and the conditions of a permanent peace, may not be devoid of interest; and I do not know that I could make a better use of the present opportunity than by laying them before you.

From the time that the first suggestion to introduce physical science into ordinary education was timidly whispered until now, the advocates of scientific education have met with opposition of two kinds. On the one hand, they have been pooh-poohed by the men of business who pride themselves on being the representatives of practicality, while on the other hand, they have been excommunicated by the classical scholars in their capacity of Levites in charge of the ark of culture and monopolists of liberal education.

The practical men believed that the idol whom they worship—rule of thumb—has been the source of the past prosperity and will suffice for the future welfare of the arts and manufactures. They were of opinion that science is speculative rubbish; that theory and practice have nothing to do with one another; and that the scientific habit of mind is an impediment rather than an aid in the conduct of ordinary affairs.

I have used the past tense in speaking of the practical men—for although they were very formidable thirty years ago, I am not sure that the pure species has not been extirpated. In fact, so far as mere argument goes, they

[3] Manufacturer and philanthropist. Mason College became the University of Birmingham.
[4] In a footnote to this text of his speech, Huxley states: "The advocacy of the introduction of physical science into general education by George Combe and others commenced a good deal earlier; but the movement had acquired hardly any practical force before the time to which I refer."

have been subjected to such a *feu d'enfer*[5] that it is a miracle if any have escaped. But I have remarked that your typical practical man has an unexpected resemblance to one of Milton's angels. His spiritual wounds, such as are inflicted by logical weapons, may be as deep as a well and as wide as a church door, but beyond shedding a few drops of ichor, celestial or otherwise, he is no whit the worse. So, if any of these opponents be left, I will not waste time in vain repetition of the demonstrative evidence of the practical value of science; but knowing that a parable will sometimes penetrate where syllogisms fail to effect an entrance, I will offer a story for their consideration.

Once upon a time, a boy with nothing to depend upon but his own vigorous nature was thrown into the thick of the struggle for existence in the midst of a great manufacturing population. He seems to have had a hard fight inasmuch as by the time he was thirty years of age, his total disposable funds amounted to twenty pounds. Nevertheless, middle life found him giving proof of his comprehension of the practical problems he had been roughly called upon to solve, by a career of remarkable prosperity. Finally, having reached old age with its well-earned surroundings of "honour, troops of friends," the hero of my story bethought himself of those who were making a like start in life and how he could stretch out a helping hand to them.

After long and anxious reflexion, this successful practical man of business could devise nothing better than to provide them with the means of obtaining "sound, extensive, and practical scientific knowledge," and he devoted a large part of his wealth and five years of incessant work to this end. I need not point the moral of a tale which, as the solid and spacious fabric of the scientific college assures us, is no fable, nor can anything which I could say intensify the force of this practical answer to practical objections.

We may take it for granted, then, that in the opinion of those best qualified to judge, the diffusion of thorough scientific education is an absolutely essential condition of industrial progress, and that the college which has been opened today will confer an inestimable boon upon those whose livelihood is to be gained by the practise of the arts and manufactures of the district.

The only question worth discussion is whether the conditions under which the work of the college is to be carried out are such as to give it the best possible chance of achieving permanent success.

Sir Josiah Mason, without doubt most wisely, has left very large freedom of action to the trustees, to whom he proposes ultimately to commit the administration of the college, so that they may be able to adjust its arrangements in accordance with the changing conditions of the future. But with respect to three points, he has laid most explicit injunctions upon both

[5] Hellfire.

administrators and teachers. Party politics are forbidden to enter into the minds of either, so far as the work of the college is concerned; theology is as sternly banished from its precincts; and finally, it is especially declared that the college shall make no provision for "mere literary instruction and education."

It does not concern me at present to dwell upon the first two injunctions any longer than may be needful to express my full conviction of their wisdom. But the third prohibition brings us face to face with those other opponents of scientific education, who are by no means in the moribund condition of the practical man, but alive, alert, and formidable. It is not impossible that we shall hear this express exclusion of "literary instruction and education" from a college which nevertheless professes to give a high and efficient education sharply criticised. Certainly the time was that the Levites of culture would have sounded their trumpets against its walls as against an educational Jericho.

How often have we not been told that the study of physical science is incompetent to confer culture; that it touches none of the higher problems of life; and what is worse, that the continual devotion to scientific studies tends to generate a narrow and bigoted belief in the applicability of scientific methods to the search after truth of all kinds. How frequently one has reason to observe that no reply to a troublesome argument tells so well as calling its author a "mere scientific specialist." And, as I am afraid it is not permissible to speak of this form of opposition to scientific education in the past tense, may we not expect to be told that this not only omission but prohibition of "mere literary instruction and education" is a patent example of scientific narrow-mindedness?

I am not acquainted with Sir Josiah Mason's reasons for the action which he has taken; but if, as I apprehend is the case, he refers to the ordinary classical course of our schools and universities by the name of "mere literary instruction and education," I venture to offer sundry reasons of my own in support of that action. For I hold very strongly by two convictions. The first is that neither the discipline nor the subject matter of classical education is of such direct value to the student of physical science as to justify the expenditure of valuable time upon either; and the second is that for the purpose of attaining real culture, an exclusively scientific education is at least as effectual as an exclusively literary education.

I need hardly point out to you that these opinions, especially the latter, are diametrically opposed to those of the great majority of educated Englishmen, influenced as they are by school and university traditions. In their belief, culture is obtainable only by a liberal education, and a liberal education is synonymous not merely with education and instruction in literature, but in one particular form of literature, namely, that of Greek and Roman antiquity. They hold that the man who has learned Latin and Greek, however little, is educated, while he who is versed in other branches of knowledge, however deeply, is a more or less respectable specialist, not admissible into the cultured caste. The stamp of the educated man, the university degree, is not for him. I am too well acquainted with the generous catholicity of spirit, the true sympathy with scientific thought, which pervades the writings of our chief apostle of culture to identify him with these opinions; and yet one may cull from one and another of those epistles to the Philistines, which so much delight all who do not answer to that name, sentences which lend them some support.

Mr. Arnold tells us that the meaning of culture is "to know the best that has been thought and said in the world."[6] It is the criticism of life contained in literature. That criticism regards "Europe as being for intellectual and spiritual purposes one great confederation bound to a joint action and working to a common result, and whose members have for their common outfit a knowledge of Greek, Roman, and Eastern antiquity, and of one another. Special local and temporary advantages being put out of account, that modern nation will in the intellectual and spiritual sphere make most progress which most thoroughly carries out this programme. And what is that but saying that we too, all of us as individuals, the more thoroughly we carry it out, shall make the more progress?"

We have here to deal with two distinct propositions, the first, that a criticism of life is the essence of culture; the second, that literature contains the materials which suffice for the construction of such a criticism. I think that we must all assent to the first proposition. For culture certainly means something quite different from learning or technical skill. It implies the possession of an ideal and the habit of critically estimating the value of things by comparison with a theoretic standard. Perfect culture should supply a complete theory of life based upon a clear knowledge alike of its possibilities and of its limitations.

But we may agree to all this and yet strongly dissent from the assumption that literature alone is competent to supply this knowledge. After having learnt all that Greek, Roman, and Eastern antiquity have thought and said, and all that modern literatures have to tell us, it is not self-evident that we have laid a sufficiently broad and deep foundation for that criticism of life which constitutes culture. Indeed, to anyone acquainted with the scope of physical science, it is not at all evident. Considering progress only in the "intellectual and spiritual sphere," I find myself wholly unable to admit that either nations or individuals will really advance if their common outfit draws nothing from the stores of physical science. I should say that an army without weapons of precision and with no particular base of operations might more hopefully enter upon a campaign on the Rhine

---

[6] This is an idea Matthew Arnold often expressed. Huxley is apparently referring to Arnold's essay, "The Function of Criticism at the Present Time." See Arnold's *Essays in Criticism*, First Series (London, 1865).

than a man devoid of a knowledge of what physical science has done in the last century upon a criticism of life.

When a biologist meets with an anomaly, he instinctively turns to the study of development to clear it up. The rationale of contradictory opinions may with equal confidence be sought in history. It is, happily, no new thing that Englishmen should employ their wealth in building and endowing institutions for educational purposes. But five or six hundred years ago, deeds of foundation expressed or implied conditions as nearly as possible contrary to those which have been thought expedient by Sir Josiah Mason. That is to say, physical science was practically ignored while a certain literary training was enjoined as a means to the acquirement of knowledge which was essentially theological.

The reason of this singular contradiction between the actions of men alike animated by a strong and disinterested desire to promote the welfare of their fellows is easily discovered. At that time, in fact, if anyone desired knowledge beyond such as could be obtained by his own observation or by common conversation, his first necessity was to learn the Latin language, inasmuch as all the higher knowledge of the western world was contained in works written in that language. Hence, Latin grammar, with logic and rhetoric studied through Latin, were the fundamentals of education. With respect to the substance of the knowledge imparted through this channel, the Jewish and Christian Scriptures as interpreted and supplemented by the Romish Church were held to contain a complete and infallibly true body of information.

Theological dicta were, to the thinkers of those days, that which the axioms and definitions of Euclid are to the geometers of these. The business of the philosophers of the middle ages was to deduce from the data furnished by the theologians conclusions in accordance with ecclesiastical decrees. They were allowed the high privilege of showing by logical process how and why that which the Church said was true must be true. And if their demonstrations fell short of or exceeded this limit, the Church was maternally ready to check their aberrations, if need be, by the help of the secular arm.

Between the two, our ancestors were furnished with a compact and complete criticism of life. They were told how the world began and how it would end; they learned that all material existence was but a base and insignificant blot upon the fair face of the spiritual world, and that nature was, to all intents and purposes, the playground of the devil; they learned that the earth is the centre of the visible universe and that man is the cynosure of things terrestrial; and more especially was it inculcated that the course of nature had no fixed order, but that it could be and constantly was altered by the agency of innumerable spiritual beings, good and bad, according as they were moved by the deeds and prayers of men. The sum and substance of the whole doctrine was to produce the conviction that the only thing really worth knowing in this world was how to secure that place in a better which, under certain conditions, the Church promised.

Our ancestors had a living belief in this theory of life and acted upon it in their dealings with education, as in all other matters. Culture meant saintliness—after the fashion of the saints of those days; the education that led to it was, of necessity, theological; and the way to theology lay through Latin. That the study of nature—further than was requisite for the satisfaction of everyday wants—should have any bearing on human life was far from the thoughts of men thus trained. Indeed, as nature had been cursed for man's sake, it was an obvious conclusion that those who meddled with nature were likely to come into pretty close contact with Satan. And, if any born scientific investigator followed his instincts, he might safely reckon upon earning the reputation and probably upon suffering the fate of a sorcerer.

Had the western world been left to itself in Chinese isolation, there is no saying how long this state of things might have endured. But happily, it was not left to itself. Even earlier than the thirteenth century, the development of Moorish civilisation in Spain and the great movement of the Crusades had introduced the leaven which, from that day to this, has never ceased to work. At first through the intermediation of Arabic translations, afterwards by the study of the originals, the western nations of Europe became acquainted with the writings of the ancient philosophers and poets and, in time, with the whole of the vast literature of antiquity.

Whatever there was of high intellectual aspiration or dominant capacity in Italy, France, Germany, and England spent itself for centuries in taking possession of the rich inheritance left by the dead civilisations of Greece and Rome. Marvellously aided by the invention of printing, classical learning spread and flourished. Those who possessed it prided themselves on having attained the highest culture then within the reach of mankind. And justly. For saving Dante on his solitary pinnacle, there was no figure in modern literature at the time of the Renaissance to compare with the men of antiquity; there was no art to compete with their sculpture; there was no physical science but that which Greece had created. Above all, there was no other example of perfect intellectual freedom—of the unhesitating acceptance of reason as the sole guide to truth and the supreme arbiter of conduct.

The new learning necessarily soon exerted a profound influence upon education. The language of the monks and schoolmen seemed little better than gibberish to scholars fresh from Virgil and Cicero, and the study of Latin was placed upon a new foundation. Moreover, Latin itself ceased to afford the sole key to knowledge. The student who sought the highest thought of antiquity found only a second-hand reflexion of it in Roman literature and turned his face to the full light of the Greeks. And after a battle not altogether dissimilar to that which is at present being fought over the teaching of physical science, the study of Greek was recognised as an essential element of all higher education. Thus the Humanists, as they were called, won the day, and the great reform which they effected was of incalculable service to mankind. But the Nemesis of all reformers is finality, and the reformers of education, like those of religion, fell into the profound, however common, error of mistaking the beginning for the end of the work of reformation.

The representatives of the Humanists in the nineteenth century take their stand upon classical education as the sole avenue to culture as firmly as if we were still in the age of Renaissance. Yet surely the present intellectual relations of the modern and the ancient worlds are profoundly different from those which obtained three centuries ago. Leaving aside the existence of a great and characteristically modern literature, of modern painting, and especially of modern music, there is one feature of the present state of the civilised world which separates it more widely from the Renaissance than the Renaissance was separated from the middle ages.

This distinctive character of our own times lies in the vast and constantly increasing part which is played by natural knowledge. Not only is our daily life shaped by it, not only does the prosperity of millions of men depend upon it, but our whole theory of life has long been influenced, consciously or unconsciously, by the general conceptions of the universe which have been forced upon us by physical science. In fact, the most elementary acquaintance with the results of scientific investigation shows us that they offer a broad and striking contradiction to the opinions so implicitly credited and taught in the middle ages.

The notions of the beginning and the end of the world entertained by our forefathers are no longer credible. It is very certain that the earth is not the chief body in the material universe and that the world is not subordinated to man's use. It is even more certain that nature is the expression of a definite order with which nothing interferes and that the chief business of mankind is to learn that order and govern themselves accordingly. Moreover, this scientific "criticism of life" presents itself to us with different credentials from any other. It appeals not to authority nor to what anybody may have thought or said, but to nature. It admits that all our interpretations of natural fact are more or less imperfect and symbolic and bids the learner seek for truth not among words but among things. It warns us that the assertion which outstrips evidence is not only a blunder but a crime.

The purely classical education advocated by the representatives of the Humanists in our day gives no inkling of all this. A man may be a better scholar than Erasmus[7] and know no more of the chief causes of the present intellectual fermentation than Erasmus did. Scholarly and pious persons worthy of all respect favour us with allocutions upon the sadness of the

---

[7] Renaissance Dutch scholar, author of *The Praise of Folly*.

antagonism of science to their mediæval way of thinking, which betray an ignorance of the first principles of scientific investigation, an incapacity for understanding what a man of science means by veracity, and an unconsciousness of the weight of established scientific truths which is almost comical.

There is no great force in the *tu quoque* argument,[8] or else the advocates of scientific education might fairly enough retort upon the modern Humanists that they may be learned specialists but that they possess no such sound foundation for a criticism of life as deserves the name of culture. And, indeed, if we were disposed to be cruel, we might urge that the Humanists have brought this reproach upon themselves not because they are too full of the spirit of the ancient Greek, but because they lack it.

The period of the Renaissance is commonly called that of the "Revival of Letters," as if the influences then brought to bear upon the mind of Western Europe had been wholly exhausted in the field of literature. I think it is very commonly forgotten that the revival of science, effected by the same agency, although less conspicuous was not less momentous. In fact, the few and scattered students of nature of that day picked up the clue to her secrets exactly as it fell from the hands of the Greeks a thousand years before. The foundations of mathematics were so well laid by them that our children learn their geometry from a book written for the schools of Alexandria two thousand years ago. Modern astronomy is the natural continuation and development of the work of Hipparchus and of Ptolemy; modern physics of that of Democritus and of Archimedes; it was long before modern biological science outgrew the knowledge bequeathed to us by Aristotle, by Theophrastus, and by Galen.

We cannot know all the best thoughts and sayings of the Greeks unless we know what they thought about natural phenomena. We cannot fully apprehend their criticism of life unless we understand the extent to which that criticism was affected by scientific conceptions. We falsely pretend to be the inheritors of their culture unless we are penetrated, as the best minds among them were, with an unhesitating faith that the free employment of reason in accordance with scientific method is the sole method of reaching truth.

Thus I venture to think that the pretensions of our modern Humanists to the possession of the monopoly of culture and to the exclusive inheritance of the spirit of antiquity must be abated, if not abandoned. But I should be very sorry that anything I have said should be taken to imply a desire on my part to depreciate the value of classical education as it might be and as it sometimes is. The native capacities of mankind vary no less than their opportunities, and while culture is one, the road by which one man may best reach it is widely different from that which is most advantageous to

---

[8] A response to *ad hominem* attack; the "you also" argument.

another. Again, while scientific education is yet inchoate and tentative, classical education is thoroughly well organised upon the practical experience of generations of teachers. So that given ample time for learning and destination for ordinary life or for a literary career, I do not think that a young Englishman in search of culture can do better than follow the course usually marked out for him, supplementing its deficiencies by his own efforts.

But for those who mean to make science their serious occupation or who intend to follow the profession of medicine or who have to enter early upon the business of life—for all these, in my opinion, classical education is a mistake; and it is for this reason that I am glad to see "mere literary education and instruction" shut out from the curriculum of Sir Josiah Mason's College, seeing that its inclusion would probably lead to the introduction of the ordinary smattering of Latin and Greek. Nevertheless, I am the last person to question the importance of genuine literary education, or to suppose that intellectual culture can be complete without it. An exclusively scientific training will bring about a mental twist as surely as an exclusively literary training. The value of the cargo does not compensate for a ship's being out of trim, and I should be very sorry to think that the scientific college would turn out none but lop-sided men.

There is no need, however, that such a catastrophe should happen. Instruction in English, French, and German is provided, and thus the three greatest literatures of the modern world are made accessible to the student.

French and German, and especially the latter language, are absolutely indispensable to those who desire full knowledge in any department of science. But even supposing that the knowledge of these languages acquired is not more than sufficient for purely scientific purposes, every Englishman has in his native tongue an almost perfect instrument of literary expression, and in his own literature, models of every kind of literary excellence. If an Englishman cannot get literary culture out of his Bible, his Shakespeare, his Milton, neither, in my belief, will the profoundest study of Homer and Sophocles, Virgil and Horace, give it to him. Thus, since the constitution of the college makes sufficient provision for literary as well as for scientific education and since artistic instruction is also contemplated, it seems to me that a fairly complete culture is offered to all who are willing to take advantage of it.

But I am not sure that at this point the "practical" man, scotched but not slain, may ask what all this talk about culture has to do with an institution the object of which is defined to be "to promote the prosperity of the manufactures and the industry of the country." He may suggest that what is wanted for this end is not culture nor even a purely scientific discipline, but simply a knowledge of applied science.

I often wish that this phrase "applied science" had never been invented. For it suggests that there is a sort of scientific knowledge of direct practical use which can be studied apart from another sort of scientific knowledge which is of no practical utility and which is termed "pure science." But there is no more complete fallacy than this. What people call applied science is nothing but the application of pure science to particular classes of problems. It consists of deductions from those general principles established by reasoning and observation which constitute pure science. No one can safely make these deductions until he has a firm grasp of the principles, and he can obtain that grasp only by personal experience of the operations of observation and of reasoning on which they are founded.

Almost all the processes employed in the arts and manufactures fall within the range either of physics or of chemistry. In order to improve them one must thoroughly understand them, and no one has a chance of really understanding them unless he has obtained that mastery of principles and that habit of dealing with facts which is given by long-continued and well-directed purely scientific training in the physical and the chemical laboratory. So that there really is no question as to the necessity of purely scientific discipline, even if the work of the college were limited by the narrowest interpretation of its stated aims.

And as to the desirableness of a wider culture than that yielded by science alone, it is to be recollected that the improvement of manufacturing processes is only one of the conditions which contribute to the prosperity of industry. Industry is a means and not an end, and mankind work only to get something which they want. What that something is depends partly on their innate and partly on their acquired desires. If the wealth resulting from prosperous industry is to be spent upon the gratification of unworthy desires, if the increasing perfection of manufacturing processes is to be accompanied by an increasing debasement of those who carry them on, I do not see the good of industry and prosperity.

Now, it is perfectly true that men's views of what is desirable depend upon their characters and that the innate proclivities to which we give that name are not touched by any amount of instruction. But it does not follow that even mere intellectual education may not, to an indefinite extent, modify the practical manifestation of the characters of men in their actions by supplying them with motives unknown to the ignorant. A pleasure-loving character will have pleasure of some sort, but if you give him the choice, he may prefer pleasures which do not degrade him to those which do. And this choice is offered to every man who possesses in literary or artistic culture a never-failing source of pleasures which are neither withered by age nor staled by custom nor embittered in the recollection by the pangs of self-reproach.

If the institution opened today fulfills the intentions of its founder, the picked intelligences among all classes of the population of this district will pass through it. No child born in Birmingham, henceforward, if he have the capacity to profit by the opportunities offered to him first in the primary and other schools and afterwards in the scientific college, need fail to obtain not merely the instruction but the culture most appropriate to the conditions of his life.

Within these walls, the future employer and the future artisan may sojourn together for a while and carry through all their lives the stamp of the influences then brought to bear upon them. Hence, it is not beside the mark to remind you that the prosperity of industry depends not merely upon the improvement of manufacturing processes, not merely upon the ennobling of the individual character, but upon a third condition—namely, a clear understanding of the conditions of social life on the part of both the capitalist and the operative and their agreement upon common principles of social action. They must learn that social phenomena are as much the expression of natural laws as any others; that no social arrangements can be permanent unless they harmonise with the requirements of social statics and dynamics; and that in the nature of things, there is an arbiter whose decisions execute themselves.

But this knowledge is only to be obtained by the application of the methods of investigation adopted in physical researches to the investigation of the phenomena of society. Hence, I confess I should like to see one addition made to the excellent scheme of education propounded for the college, in the shape of provision for the teaching of sociology. For though we are all agreed that party politics are to have no place in the instruction of the college, yet in this country, practically governed as it is now by universal suffrage, every man who does his duty must exercise political functions. And if the evils which are inseparable from the good of political liberty are to be checked—if the perpetual oscillation of nations between anarchy and despotism is to be replaced by the steady march of self-restraining freedom—it will be because men will gradually bring themselves to deal with political as they now deal with scientific questions; to be as ashamed of undue haste and partisan prejudice in the one case as in the other; and to believe that the machinery of society is at least as delicate as that of a spinning-jenny and as little likely to be improved by the meddling of those who have not taken the trouble to master the principles of its action.

In conclusion, I am sure that I make myself the mouthpiece of all present in offering to the venerable founder of the institution, which now commences its beneficent career, our congratulations on the completion of his work; and in expressing the conviction that the remotest posterity will point to it as a crucial instance of the wisdom which natural piety leads all men to ascribe to their ancestors.

Matthew Arnold

"Literature and Science"*
Cambridge University, June 14, 1882

No wisdom, nor counsel, nor understanding, against the Eternal! says the Wise Man. Against the natural and appointed course of things there is no contending. Ten years ago I remarked[1] on the gloomy prospect for letters in this country, inasmuch as while the aristocratic class, according to a famous dictum of Lord Beaconsfield, was totally indifferent to letters, the friends of physical science on the other hand, a growing and popular body, were in active revolt against them. To deprive letters of the too great place they had hitherto filled in men's estimation and to substitute other studies for them was now the object, I observed, of a sort of crusade with the friends of physical science—a busy host important in itself, important because of the gifted leaders who march at its head, important from its strong and increasing hold upon public favour.

I could not help, I then went on to say—I could not help being moved with a desire to plead with the friends of physical science on behalf of letters and in deprecation of the slight which they put upon them. But from giving effect to this desire I was at that time drawn off by more pressing matters. Ten years have passed, and the prospects of any pleader for letters have certainly not mended. If the friends of physical science were in the morning sunshine of popular favour even then, they stand now in its meridian radiance. Sir Josiah Mason founds a college at Birmingham to exclude "mere literary instruction and education"; and at its opening a brilliant and charming debater, Professor Huxley, is brought down to pronounce their funeral oration.[2] Mr. Bright, in his zeal for the United

---

* This text is from *The Nineteenth Century*, XII (August, 1882), 216–230. Arnold revised the lecture and gave it during his American tour, 1883–1884. It is reprinted in Arnold's *Discourses in America* (London, 1885).

[1] It is difficult to be sure which remarks Arnold had in mind in this reference, because he expressed his concern about letters, physical science, and education in a variety of publications. However, exactly ten years prior to this speech, he published his views in *A Bible Reading for Schools* (London, 1872); see, for instance, pp. vi–vii.

[2] The reference is to the speech that precedes this one. Arnold's "Literature and Science" is a direct reply to Huxley's "Science and Literature."

States, exhorts young people to drink deep of "Hiawatha"; and *The Times*—which takes the gloomiest view possible of the future of letters and thinks that a hundred years hence there will only be a few eccentrics reading letters and almost everyone will be studying the natural sciences—*The Times,* instead of counselling Mr. Bright's young people rather to drink deep of Homer, is forgiving them above all "the works of Darwin and Lyell[3] and Bell[4] and Huxley" and for nourishing them upon the voyage of the "Challenger."[5] Stranger still, a brilliant man of letters in France, M. Renan,[6] assigns the same date of a hundred years hence as the date by which the historical and critical studies in which his life has been passed and his reputation made will have fallen into neglect and deservedly so fallen. It is the regret of his life, M. Renan tells us, that he did not himself originally pursue the natural sciences, in which he might have forestalled Darwin in his discoveries.

What does it avail, in presence of all this, that we find one of your own prophets, Bishop Thirlwall,[7] telling his brother who was sending a son to be educated abroad that he might be out of the way of Latin and Greek: "I do not think that the most perfect knowledge of every language now spoken under the sun could compensate for the want of them"? What does it avail, even, that an august lover of science, the great Goethe, should have said: "I wish all success to those who are for preserving to the literature of Greece and Rome its predominant place in education"? Goethe was a wise man, but the irresistible current of things was not then manifest as it is now. *No wisdom, nor counsel, nor understanding, against the Eternal!*

But to resign oneself too passively to supposed designs of the Eternal is fatalism. Perhaps they are not really designs of the Eternal at all, but designs —let us for example say—of Mr. Herbert Spencer.[8] Still, the design of abasing what is called "mere literary instruction and education" and of exalting what is called "sound, extensive, and practical scientific knowledge" is a very positive design and makes great progress. The universities are by no means outside its scope. At the recent congress in Sheffield of elementary teachers—a very able and important body of men whose movements I naturally follow with strong interest—at Sheffield one of the principal speakers proposed that the elementary teachers and the universities should come together on the common ground of natural science. On the ground of the dead languages, he said, they could not possibly come

---

[3] Sir Charles Lyell, geologist. His work facilitated the acceptance of Darwin's theories.

[4] Sir Charles Bell, Scottish anatomist and surgeon, was author of *The Nervous System of the Human Body* (1830).

[5] The Challenger was a corvette used for a scientific expedition led by Professor C. Wyville Thompson to survey physical and biological data in the Atlantic and Pacific Oceans. The voyage lasted four years.

[6] Ernest Renan, French historian and critic.

[7] Connop Thirwall, Bishop of St. David's Church in Wales.

[8] English philosopher whose work supported the theory of evolution.

together; but if the universities would take natural science for their chosen and chief ground instead, they easily might. Mahomet was to go to the mountain, as there was no chance of the mountain's being able to go to Mahomet.

The Vice-Chancellor[9] has done me the honour to invite me to address you here today, although I am not a member of this great university. Your liberally conceived use of Sir Robert Rede's lecture leaves you free in the choice of a person to deliver the lecture founded by him, and on the present occasion the Vice-Chancellor has gone for a lecturer to the sister university. I will venture to say that to an honour of this kind from the University of Cambridge no one on earth can be so sensible as a member of the University of Oxford. The two universities are unlike anything else in the world, and they are very like one another. Neither of them is inclined to go hastily into raptures over her own living offspring or over her sister's; each of them is peculiarly sensitive to the good opinion of the other. Nevertheless they have their points of dissimilarity. One such point in particular cannot fail to arrest notice. Both universities have told powerfully upon the mind and life of the nation. But the University of Oxford, of which I am a member and to which I am deeply and affectionately attached, has produced great men indeed, but has above all been the source or the centre of great movements. We will not now go back to the middle ages; we will keep within the range of what is called modern history. Within this range, we have the great movements of Royalism, Wesleyanism, Tractarianism, Ritualism, all of them having their source or their centre in Oxford. You have nothing of the kind. The movement taking its name from Charles Simeon[10] is far, far less considerable than the movement taking its name from John Wesley. The movement attempted by the Latitude men[11] in the seventeenth century is next to nothing as a movement; the men are everything. And this is, in truth, your great, your surpassing distinction: not your movements, but your men. From Bacon to Byron, what a splendid roll of great names you can point to! We at Oxford can show nothing equal to it. Yours is the university not of great movements but of great men. Our experience at Oxford disposes us, perhaps, to treat movements, whether our own or extraneous movements such as the present movement for revolutionising education, with too much respect. That disposition finds a corrective here. Masses make movements, individualities explode them. On mankind in the mass, a movement, once started, is apt to impose itself by routine; it is through the insight, the independence, the self-confidence of

---

[9] The Rev. James Porter was Vice-Chancellor of Cambridge University in 1882.

[10] Influential evangelical leader, one of the founders of the Church Missionary Society.

[11] The latitudinarians were churchmen who advocated the union of dissenters with the established church on the basis of doctrines held in common, but tolerated differences in opinions concerning worship and the relations of church and state.

powerful single minds that its yoke is shaken off. In this university of great names, whoever wishes not to be demoralised by a movement comes into the right air for being stimulated to pluck up his courage and to examine what stuff movements are really made of.

Inspirited, then, by this tonic air in which I find myself speaking, I am boldly going to ask whether the present movement for ousting letters from their old predominance in education and for transferring the predominance in education to the natural sciences—whether this brisk and flourishing movement ought to prevail and whether it is likely that in the end it really will prevail. My own studies have been almost wholly in letters, and my visits to the field of the natural sciences have been very slight and inadequate, although those sciences strongly move my curiosity. A man of letters, it will perhaps be said, is quite incompetent to discuss the comparative merits of letters and natural science as means of education. His incompetence, however, if he attempts the discussion but is really incompetent for it, will be abundantly visible; nobody will be taken in; he will have plenty of sharp observers and critics to save mankind from that danger. But the line I am going to follow is, as you will soon discover, so extremely simple that perhaps it may be followed without failure even by one who for a more ambitious line of discussion would be quite incompetent.

Some of you may have met with a phrase of mine which has been the object of a good deal of comment; an observation to the effect that in our culture, the aim being to know ourselves and the world, we have, as the means to this end, to know the best which has been thought and said in the world. Professor Huxley, in his discourse at the opening of Sir Josiah Mason's college, laying hold of this phrase, expanded it by quoting some more words of mine, which are these: "Europe is to be regarded as now being for intellectual and spiritual purposes one great confederation bound to a joint action and working to a common result, and whose members have for their common outfit a knowledge of Greek, Roman, and Eastern antiquity, and of one another. Special local and temporary advantages being put out of account, that modern nation will in the intellectual and spiritual sphere make most progress which most thoroughly carries out this programme."

Now, on my phrase thus enlarged, Professor Huxley remarks that I assert literature to contain the materials which suffice for making us know ourselves and the world. But it is not by any means clear, says he, that after having learnt all which ancient and modern literatures have to tell us, we have laid a sufficiently broad and deep foundation for that criticism of life which constitutes culture. On the contrary, Professor Huxley declares that he finds himself "wholly unable to admit that either nations or individuals will really advance if their common outfit draws nothing from the stores of physical science. An army without weapons of precision and with no particular base of operations might more hopefully enter upon a campaign on the Rhine than a man devoid of a knowledge of what physical science has done in the last century upon a criticism of life."

This shows how needful it is for those who are to discuss a matter together to have a common understanding as to the sense of the terms they employ—how needful and how difficult. What Professor Huxley says implies just the reproach which is so often brought against the study of *belles lettres,* as they are called: that the study is an elegant one, but slight and ineffectual; a smattering of Greek and Latin and other ornamental things of little use for anyone whose object is to get at truth. So, too, M. Renan talks of the "superficial humanism" of a school course which treats us as if we were all going to be poets, writers, orators, and he opposes this humanism to positive science, or the critical search after truth. And there is always a tendency in those who are remonstrating against the predominance of letters in education to understand by letters *belles lettres,* and by *belles lettres* a superficial humanism, the opposite of science or true knowledge.

But when we talk of knowing Greek and Roman antiquity, for instance, which is what people have called Humanism, we mean a knowledge which is something more than a superficial humanism, mainly decorative. "I call all teaching *scientific,*" says Wolf,[12] the critic of Homer, "which is systematically laid out and followed up to its original sources. For example: a knowledge of classical antiquity is scientific when the remains of classical antiquity are correctly studied in the original languages." There can be no doubt that Wolf is perfectly right—that all learning is scientific which is systematically laid out and followed up to its original sources and that a genuine Humanism is scientific.

When I speak of knowing Greek and Roman antiquity, therefore, as a help to knowing ourselves and the world, I mean more than a knowledge of so much vocabulary, so much grammar, so many portions of authors, in the Greek and Latin languages. I mean knowing the Greeks and Romans and their life and genius and what they were and did in the world—what we get from them and what is its value. That, at least, is the ideal, and when we talk of endeavouring to know Greek and Roman antiquity as a help to knowing ourselves and the world, we mean endeavouring so to know them as to satisfy this ideal, however much we may still fall short of it.

The same as to knowing our own and other modern nations with the aim of getting to understand ourselves and the world. To know the best that has been thought and said by the modern nations is to know, says Professor Huxley, "only what modern *literatures* have to tell us; it is the criticism of life contained in modern literature." And yet "the distinctive character of our times," he urges, "lies in the vast and constantly increasing part which

---

[12] Friedrich August Wolf, German classical scholar.

is played by natural knowledge." And how, therefore, can a man devoid of knowledge of what physical science has done in the last century enter hopefully upon a criticism of modern life?

Let us, I say, be agreed about the meaning of the terms we are using. I talk of knowing the best which has been thought and uttered in the world; Professor Huxley says this means knowing *literature*. Literature is a large word; it may mean everything written with letters or printed in a book. Euclid's *Elements* and Newton's *Principia* are thus literature. All knowledge that reaches us through books is literature. But by literature Professor Huxley means *belles lettres*. He means to make me say that knowing the best which has been thought and said by the modern nations is knowing their *belles lettres* and no more. And this is no sufficient equipment, he argues, for a criticism of modern life. But as I do not mean by knowing ancient Rome knowing merely more or less of Latin *belles lettres*, and taking no account of Rome's military and political and legal and administrative work in the world; and as by knowing ancient Greece I understand knowing her as the giver of Greek art and the guide to a free and right use of reason and to scientific method and the founder of our mathematics and physics and astronomy and biology—I understand knowing her as all this and not merely knowing certain Greek poems, histories, and speeches—so as to the knowledge of modern nations also. By knowing modern nations, I mean not merely knowing their *belles lettres* but knowing also what has been done by such men as Copernicus, Galileo, Newton, Darwin. "Our ancestors learned," says Professor Huxley, "that the earth is the centre of the visible universe and that man is the cynosure of things terrestrial; and more especially was it inculcated that the course of nature had no fixed order, but that it could be and constantly was altered." But for us now, says Professor Huxley, "the notions of the beginning and the end of the world entertained by our forefathers are no longer credible. It is very certain that the earth is not the chief body in the material universe and that the world is not subordinated to man's use. It is even more certain that nature is the expression of a definite order with which nothing interferes. And yet," he cries, "the purely classical education advocated by the representatives of the Humanists in our day gives no inkling of all this!"

In due place and time we will perhaps touch upon the question of classical education, but at present the question is as to what is meant by knowing the best which modern nations have thought and said. It is not knowing their *belles lettres* merely that is meant. To know Italian *belles lettres* is not to know Italy, and to know English *belles lettres* is not to know England. Into knowing Italy and England there comes a great deal more, Galileo and Newton amongst it. The reproach of being a superficial humanism, a tincture of *belles lettres*, may attach rightly enough to some other disciplines, but to the particular discipline recommended when I proposed knowing the best that has been thought and said in the world, it does not apply. In that best I certainly include what in modern times has been thought and said by the great observers and knowers of nature.

There is, therefore, really no question between Professor Huxley and me as to whether knowing the results of the scientific study of nature is not required as a part of our culture, as well as knowing the products of literature and art. But to follow the processes by which those results are reached ought, say the friends of physical science, to be made the staple of education for the bulk of mankind. And here there does arise a question between those whom Professor Huxley calls with playful sarcasm "the Levites of culture" and those whom the poor Humanist is sometimes apt to regard as its Nebuchadnezzars.

The great results of the scientific investigation of nature we are agreed upon knowing, but how much of our study are we bound to give to the processes by which those results are reached? The results have their visible bearing on human life. But all the processes, too, all the items of fact by which those results are established, are interesting. All knowledge is interesting to a wise man, and the knowledge of nature is interesting to all men. It is very interesting to know that from the albuminous white of the egg the chick in the egg gets the materials for its flesh, bones, blood, and feathers, while from the fatty yolk of the egg it gets the heat and energy which enable it at length to break its shell and begin the world. It is less interesting, perhaps, but still it is interesting, to know that when a taper burns, the wax is converted into carbonic acid and water. Moreover, it is quite true that the habit of dealing with facts which is given by the study of nature is, as the friends of physical science praise it for being, an excellent discipline. The appeal is to observation and experiment; not only is it said that the thing is so, but we can be made to see that it is so. Not only does a man tell us that when a taper burns the wax is converted into carbonic acid and water, as a man may tell us, if he likes, that Charon is in his boat on the Styx, or that Victor Hugo is a truly great poet; but we are made to see that the conversion into carbonic acid and water does really happen. This reality of natural knowledge it is which makes the friends of physical science contrast it, as a knowledge of things, with the Humanist's knowledge, which is, say they, a knowledge of words. And hence Professor Huxley is moved to lay it down that "for the purpose of attaining real culture, an exclusively scientific education is at least as effectual as an exclusively literary education." And a certain President of the Section for Mechanical Science in the British Association[13] is, in Scripture phrase, "very bold," and declares that if a man in his education "has substituted literature and history for natural science, he has chosen the less useful alternative." Whether we go these lengths or not, we must all admit that in natural science the habit

[13] The British Association for the Advancement of Science was founded in 1831 as a meeting ground for scientists belonging to different societies.

gained of dealing with facts is a most valuable discipline and that everyone should have some experience of it.

But it is proposed to make the training in natural science the main part of education, for the great majority of mankind, at any rate. And here I confess I part company with the friends of physical science, with whom up to this point I have been agreeing. In differing from them, however, I wish to proceed with the utmost caution and diffidence. The smallness of my acquaintance with the disciplines of natural science is ever before my mind, and I am fearful of doing them injustice. The ability of the partisans of natural science makes them formidable persons to contradict. The tone of tentative inquiry, which befits a being of dim faculties and bounded knowledge, is the tone I would wish to take and not to depart from. At present it seems to me that those who are for giving to natural knowledge, as they call it, the chief place in the education of the majority of mankind leave one important thing out of their account—the constitution of human nature. But I put this forward on the strength of some facts not at all recondite—very far from it; facts capable of being stated in the simplest possible fashion and to which, if I so state them, the man of science will, I am sure, be willing to allow their due weight.

Deny the facts altogether, I think he hardly can. He can hardly deny that when we set ourselves to enumerate the powers which go to the building up of human life and say that they are the power of conduct, the power of intellect and knowledge, the power of beauty, and the power of social life and manners—he can hardly deny that this scheme, though drawn in rough and plain lines and not pretending to scientific exactness, does yet give a fairly true account of the matter. Human nature is built up by these powers; we have the need for them all. This is evident enough, and the friends of physical science will admit it. But perhaps they may not have sufficiently observed another thing—namely, that these powers just mentioned are not isolated, but there is in the generality of mankind a perpetual tendency to relate them one to another in divers ways. With one such way of relating them I am particularly concerned here. Following our instinct for intellect and knowledge, we acquire pieces of knowledge; and presently, in the generality of men, there arises the desire to relate these pieces of knowledge to our sense for conduct, to our sense for beauty, and there is weariness and dissatisfaction if the desire is balked. Now, in this desire lies, I think, the strength of that hold which letters have upon us.

All knowledge is, as I said just now, interesting; and even items of knowledge which from the nature of the case cannot well be related but must stand isolated in our thoughts have their interest. Even lists of exceptions have their interest. If we are studying Greek accents, it is interesting to know that *pais* and *pas* and some other monosyllables of the same form of declension do not take the circumflex upon the last syllable of the genitive plural, but vary, in this respect, from the common rule. If we are studying physiology, it is interesting to know that the pulmonary artery carries dark blood and the pulmonary vein carries bright blood, departing in this respect from the common rule for the division of labour between the veins and the arteries. But everyone knows how we seek naturally to combine the pieces of our knowledge together, to bring them under general rules, to relate them to principles—and how unsatisfactory and tiresome it would be to go on forever learning lists of exceptions or accumulating items of fact which must stand isolated.

Well, that same need of relating our knowledge which operates here within the sphere of our knowledge itself we shall find operating also outside that sphere. We feel, as we go on learning and knowing—the vast majority of mankind feel the need of relating what we have learnt and known to the sense which we have in us for conduct, to the sense which we have in us for beauty.

The prophetess Diotima explained to Socrates that love is, in fact, nothing but the desire in men that good should be forever present to them. This primordial desire it is, I suppose—this desire in men that good should be forever present to them—which causes in us the instinct for relating our knowledge to our sense for conduct and to our sense for beauty. At any rate, with men in general the instinct exists. Such is human nature. Such is human nature, and in seeking to gratify the instinct, we are following the instinct of self-preservation in humanity.

Knowledges which cannot be directly related to the sense for beauty, to the sense for conduct, are instrument knowledges; they lead on to other knowledge which can. A man who passes his life in instrument knowledges is a specialist. They may be invaluable as instruments to something beyond, for those who have the gift thus to employ them, and they may be disciplines in themselves wherein it is useful to everyone to have some schooling. But it is inconceivable that the generality of men should pass all their mental life with Greek accents or with formal logic. My friend Professor Sylvester,[14] who holds transcendental doctrines as to the virtue of mathematics, is far away in America; and therefore, if in the Cambridge Senate House one may say such a thing without profaneness, I will hazard the opinion that for the majority of mankind a little of mathematics, also, goes a long way. Of course this is quite consistent with their being of immense importance as an instrument to something else, but it is the few who have the aptitude for thus using them, not the bulk of mankind.

The natural sciences do not stand on the same footing with these instrument knowledges. Experience shows us that the generality of men will find more interest in learning that when a taper burns the wax is converted into carbonic acid and water, or in learning the explanation of the phenomenon of dew, or in learning how the circulation of the blood is carried on,

[14] James Joseph Sylvester taught at major universities in England and America, including Oxford and Johns Hopkins.

than they find in learning that the genitive plural of *pais* and *pas* does not take the circumflex on the termination. And one piece of natural knowledge is added to another and others to that, and at last we come to propositions so interesting as the proposition that "our ancestor was a hairy quadruped furnished with a tail and pointed ears, probably arboreal in his habits." Or we come to propositions of such reach and importance as those which Professor Huxley brings us, when he says that the notions of our forefathers about the beginning and the end of the world were all wrong, and that nature is the expression of a definite order with which nothing interferes.

Interesting, indeed, these results of science are, important they are, and we should all be acquainted with them. But what I now wish you to mark is that we are still, when they are propounded to us and we receive them—we are still in the sphere of intellect and knowledge. And for the generality of men there will be found, I say, to arise, when they have duly taken in the proposition that their ancestor was "a hairy quadruped furnished with a tail and pointed ears, probably arboreal in his habits"—there will be found to arise an invincible desire to relate this proposition to the sense within them for conduct and to the sense for beauty. But this the men of science will not do for us and will hardly even profess to do. They will give us other pieces of knowledge, other facts, about other animals and their ancestors, or about plants, or about stones, or about stars, and they may finally bring us to those "general conceptions of the universe which have been forced upon us," says Professor Huxley, "by physical science." But still it will be knowledge only which they give us; knowledge not put for us into relation with our sense for conduct, our sense for beauty, and touched with emotion by being so put—not thus put for us, and therefore, to the majority of mankind, after a certain while unsatisfying, wearying.

Not to the born naturalist, I admit. But what do we mean by a born naturalist? We mean a man in whom the zeal for observing nature is so strong and eminent that it marks him off from the bulk of mankind. Such a man will pass his life happily in collecting natural knowledge and reasoning upon it and will ask for nothing, or hardly anything, more. I have heard it said that the sagacious and admirable naturalist whom we have lately lost, Mr. Darwin, once owned to a friend that for his part he did not experience the necessity for two things which most men find so necessary to them—poetry and religion; science and the domestic affections, he thought, were enough. To a born naturalist, I can well understand that this should seem so. So absorbing is his occupation with nature, so strong his love for his occupation, that he goes on acquiring natural knowledge and reasoning upon it and has little time or inclination for thinking about getting it related to the desire in man for conduct, the desire in man for beauty. He relates it to them for himself as he goes along, so far as he feels the need, and he draws from the domestic affections all the additional solace necessary. But then Darwins are very rare. Another great and admirable master of natural knowledge, Faraday,[15] was a Sandemanian.[16] That is to say, he related his knowledge to his instinct for conduct and to his instinct for beauty by the aid of that respectable Scottish sectary, Robert Sandeman. And for one man amongst us with the disposition to do as Darwin did in this respect, there are fifty, probably, with the disposition to do as Faraday.

Professor Huxley holds up to scorn mediæval education, with its neglect of the knowledge of nature, its poverty of literary studies, its formal logic devoted to "showing how and why that which the Church said was true must be true." But the great mediæval universities were not brought into being, we may be sure, by the zeal for giving a jejune and contemptible education. Kings have been our nursing fathers, and queens have been our nursing mothers, but not for this. Our universities came into being because the supposed knowledge delivered by Scripture and the Church so deeply engaged men's hearts and so simply, easily, and powerfully related itself to the desire for conduct, the desire for beauty—the general desire in men, as Diotima said, that good should be forever present to them. All other knowledge was dominated by this supposed knowledge and was subordinated to it, because of the surpassing strength of the hold which it gained upon men's affections by allying itself profoundly with their sense for conduct and their sense for beauty.

But now, says Professor Huxley, conceptions of the universe fatal to the notions held by our forefathers have been forced upon us by physical science. Grant to him that they are thus fatal, that they must and will become current everywhere, and that everyone will finally perceive them to be fatal to the beliefs of our forefathers. The need of humane letters, as they are truly called, because they serve the paramount desire in men that good should be forever present to them—the need of humane letters to establish a relation between the new conceptions and our instinct for beauty, our instinct for conduct, is only the more visible. The middle age could do without humane letters as it could do without the study of nature, because its supposed knowledge was made to engage its emotions so powerfully. Grant that the supposed knowledge disappears, its power of being made to engage the emotions will of course disappear along with it—but the emotions will remain. Now if we find by experience that humane letters have an undeniable power of engaging the emotions, the importance of humane letters in man's training becomes not less but greater in proportion to the success of science in extirpating what it calls "mediæval thinking."

Have humane letters, have poetry and eloquence, the power here attributed to them of engaging the emotions, and how do they exercise it? And if they have it and exercise it, how do they exercise it in relating the results of natural science to man's sense for conduct, his sense for beauty?

---

[15] Michael Faraday, scientist, professor of chemistry at the Royal Institution.

[16] A religious sect founded by John Glas, a Scottish minister, which held that national churches and civil interference in religious matters are not authorized in the Scriptures. Robert Sandeman led the movement to extend these beliefs in England and America.

All these questions may be asked. First, have poetry and eloquence the power of calling out the emotions? The appeal is to experience. Experience shows us that for the vast majority of men, for mankind in general, they have the power. Next, how do they exercise it? And this is perhaps a case for applying the Preacher's words: "Though a man labour to seek it out, yet he shall not find it; yea, further, though a wise man think to know it, yet shall he not be able to find it." Why should it be one thing in its effect upon the emotions to say, "Patience is a virtue," and quite another thing in its effect upon the emotions to say with Homer, "for an enduring heart have the destinies appointed to the children of men"? Why should it be one thing in its effect upon the emotions to say with Spinoza,[17] *Felicitas in eo consistit quod homo suum esse conservare potest*—"Man's happiness consists in his being able to preserve his own essence"—and quite another thing in its effect upon the emotions to say, "What is a man advantaged if he gain the whole world and lose himself, forfeit himself?" How does this difference of effect arise? I cannot tell and I am not much concerned to know; the important thing is that it does arise and that we can profit by it. But how, finally, are poetry and eloquence to exercise the power of relating the results of natural science to man's instinct for conduct, his instinct for beauty? And here again I answer that I do not know how they will exercise it, but that they can and will exercise it, I am sure. I do not mean that modern philosophical poets and modern philosophical moralists are to relate for us the results of modern scientific research to our need for conduct, our need for beauty. I mean that we shall find, as a matter of experience, if we know the best that has been thought and uttered in the world—we shall find that the art and poetry and eloquence of men who lived perhaps long ago, who had the most limited natural knowledge, who had the most erroneous conceptions about many important matters—we shall find that they have in fact not only the power of refreshing and delighting us, they have also the power—such is the strength and worth, in essentials, of their authors' criticism of life—they have a fortifying and elevating and quickening and suggestive power capable of wonderfully helping us to relate the results of modern science to our need for conduct, our need for beauty. Homer's conceptions of the physical universe were, I imagine, grotesque; but really, under the shock of hearing from modern science that "the world is not subordinated to man's use and that man is not the cynosure of things terrestrial," I could desire no better comfort than Homer's line which I quoted just now: "τλητὸν γὰρ Μοῖραι θυμὸν θέσαν ἀνθρώποισιν"—"for an enduring heart have the destinies appointed to the children of men."

And the more that men's minds are cleared, the more that the results of science are frankly accepted, the more that poetry and eloquence come to be studied as what they really are—the criticism of life by gifted men, alive

[17] Baruch (Benedict) Spinoza, Dutch philosopher of the seventeenth century.

and active with extraordinary power at an unusual number of points—so much the more will the value of humane letters and of art also, which is an utterance having a like kind of power with theirs, be felt and acknowledged and their place in education be secured.

Let us, all of us, avoid as much as possible any invidious comparison between the merits of humane letters as means of education and the merits of the natural sciences. But when some President of a Section for Mechanical Science insists on making the comparison and tells us that "he who in his training has substituted literature and history for natural science has chosen the less useful alternative," let us say to him that the student of humane letters only will at least know also the great general conceptions brought in by modern physical science; for science, as Professor Huxley says, forces them upon us all. But the student of the natural sciences only will, by our very hypothesis, know nothing of humane letters; not to mention that in setting himself to be perpetually accumulating natural knowledge, he sets himself to do what only specialists have the gift for doing genially. And so he will be unsatisfied, or at any rate incomplete, and even more incomplete than the student of humane letters.

I once mentioned in a school report how a young man in a training college, having to paraphrase the passage in *Macbeth* beginning "Can'st thou not minister to a mind diseased?" turned this line into "Can you not wait upon the lunatic?" And I remarked what a curious state of things it would be if every pupil of our primary schools knew that when a taper burns the wax is converted into carbonic acid and water and thought at the same time that a good paraphrase for "Can'st thou not minister to a mind diseased?" was "Can you not wait upon the lunatic?" If one is driven to choose, I think I would rather have a young person ignorant about the converted wax but aware that "Can you not wait upon the lunatic?" is bad than a young person whose education had left things the other way.

Or to go higher than the pupils of our primary schools. I have in my mind's eye a Member of Parliament who goes to travel in America, who relates his travels, and who shows a really masterly knowledge of the geology of the country and of its mining capabilities, but who ends by gravely suggesting that the United States should borrow a prince from our Royal Family and should make him their king and should create a House of Lords of great landed proprietors after the pattern of ours—and then America, he thinks, would have her future happily secured.[18] Surely, in this case, the President of the Section for Mechanical Science would himself hardly say that our Member of Parliament, by concentrating himself upon geology and mining and so on and not attending to literature and history, had "chosen the more useful alternative."

If, then, there is to be separation and option between humane letters on

---

[18] The reference is to Hussey Vivian, Member for Glamorganshire.

the one hand and the natural sciences on the other, the great majority of mankind, all who have not exceptional and overpowering aptitudes for the study of nature, would do well, I cannot but think, to choose to be educated in humane letters rather than in the natural sciences. Letters will call out their being at more points, will make them live more.

And indeed, to say the truth, I cannot really think that humane letters are in danger of being thrust out from their leading place in education, in spite of the array of authorities against them at this moment. So long as human nature is what it is, their attractions will remain irresistible. They will be studied more rationally, but they will not lose their place. What will happen will rather be that there will be crowded into education other matters besides, far too many; there will be, perhaps, a period of unsettlement and confusion and false tendency; but letters will not in the end lose their leading place. If they lose it for a time, they will get it back again. We shall be brought back to them by our wants and aspirations. And a poor Humanist may possess his soul in patience, neither strive nor cry, admit the energy and brilliancy of the partisans of physical science and their present favour with the public to be far greater than his own, and still have a happy faith that the nature of things works silently on behalf of the studies which he loves, and that while we shall all have to acquaint ourselves with the great results reached by modern science and to give ourselves as much training in its disciplines as we can conveniently carry, yet the majority of men will always require humane letters and so much the more as they have the more and the greater results of science to relate to the need in man for conduct and to the need in him for beauty.

And so we have turned in favour of the humanities the *No wisdom, nor understanding, nor counsel, against the Eternal!* which seemed against them when we started. The "hairy quadruped furnished with a tail and pointed ears, probably arboreal in his habits," carried hidden in his nature, apparently, something destined to develop into a necessity for humane letters. The time warns me to stop; but most probably, if we went on, we might arrive at the further conclusion that our ancestor carried in his nature also a necessity for Greek. The attackers of the established course of study think that against Greek, at any rate, they have irresistible arguments. Literature may perhaps be needed in education, they say, but why on earth should it be Greek literature? Why not French or German? Nay, "has not an Englishman models in his own literature of every kind of excellence?" As before, it is not on any weak pleadings of my own that I rely for convincing the gainsayer; it is on the constitution of human nature itself and on the instinct of self-preservation in humanity. The instinct for beauty is set in human nature as surely as the instinct for knowledge is set there or the instinct for conduct. If the instinct for beauty is served by Greek literature as it is served by no other literature, we may trust to the instinct of self-preservation in humanity for keeping Greek as part of our culture. We may trust to it for even making this study more prevalent than it is now. As I said of humane letters in general, Greek will come to be studied more rationally than at present; but it will be increasingly studied as men increasingly feel the need in them for beauty; and how powerfully Greek art and Greek literature can serve this need! Women will again study Greek, as Lady Jane Grey did; perhaps in that chain of forts with which the fair host of the Amazons is engirdling this university they are studying it already.[19] *"Defuit una mihi symmetria prisca,"*[20] said Leonardo da Vinci, and he was an Italian. What must an Englishman feel as to his deficiencies in this respect, as the sense for beauty, whereof symmetry is an essential element, awakens and strengthens within him! What will not one day be his respect and desire for Greece and its *symmetria prisca,* when the scales drop from his eyes as he walks the London streets and he sees such a lesson in meanness as the Strand, for instance, in its true deformity! But here I have entered Mr. Ruskin's[21] province, and I am well content to leave not only our street architecture but also letters and Greek under the care of so distinguished a guardian.

[19] Arnold is referring to the movement to establish institutions of higher learning for women. Girton College in 1869 and Newnham College in 1875 were founded near Cambridge University.

[20] "Only old-fashioned symmetry was lacking for me."

[21] Professor, artist, and author of prose and poetry. In 1853, he delivered a series of lectures on "Architecture and Painting" at Edinburgh. He also published *Seven Lamps of Architecture* (1849) and *Stones of Venice* (1851–1853).

Alfred North Whitehead

"Technical Education and its Relation to Science and Literature"[*]

London, January 5, 1917

The subject of this address is technical education. I wish to examine its essential nature and also its relation to a liberal education. Such an enquiry may help us to realise the conditions for the successful working of a national system of technical training. It is also a very burning question among mathematical teachers, for mathematics is included in most technical courses.

Now it is unpractical to plunge into such a discussion without forming in our minds the best ideal result towards which we desire to work, however modestly we may frame our hopes as to the result which in the near future is likely to be achieved.

People are shy of formulated ideals, and accordingly we find formulation of the ideal state of mankind placed by a modern dramatist[1] in the mouth of a mad priest: "In my dreams it is a country where the State is the Church and the Church the people: three in one and one in three. It is a commonwealth in which work is play and play is life: three in one and one in three. It is a temple in which the priest is the worshipper and the worshipper the worshipped: three in one and one in three. It is a godhead in which all life is human and all humanity divine: three in one and one in three. It is, in short, the dream of a madman."

Now the part of this speech to which I would direct attention is embodied in the phrase "It is a commonwealth in which work is play and play is life." This is the ideal of technical education.

---

[*] This text is taken from *The Mathematical Gazette*, IX (March, 1917), 20–33. The address was reprinted in Whitehead's *The Organisation of Thought: Educational and Scientific* (London, 1917) and *The Aims of Education and Other Essays* (New York, 1929).

[1] George Bernard Shaw, *John Bull's Other Island* (London, 1907).

It sounds very mystical when we confront it with the actual facts, the toiling millions, tired, discontented, mentally indifferent, and then the employers—I am not undertaking a social analysis, but I shall carry you with me when I admit that the present facts of society are a long way off this ideal. Furthermore, we are agreed that an employer who conducted his workshop on the principle that "work should be play" would be ruined in a week.

The curse that has been laid on humanity, in fable and in fact, is that by the sweat of its brow shall it live. But reason and moral intuition have seen in this curse the foundation for advance. The early Benedictine monks rejoiced in their labours because they were thereby made fellow-workers with Christ. Stripped of its theological trappings, the essential idea remains that work should be transfused by intellectual and moral vision and thereby turned into a joy triumphing over its weariness and its pain.

Each of us will restate this abstract formulation in a more concrete shape in accordance with his private outlook. State it how you like, so long as you do not lose the main point in your details. However you phrase it, it remains the sole real hope of toiling humanity; and it is in the hands of technical teachers and of those who control their spheres of activity so to mould the nation that daily it may pass to its labours in the spirit of the monks of old.

The immediate need of the nation is a large supply of skilled efficient workmen, of men with inventive genius, and of employers alert in the development of new ideas. Another essential condition is industrial peace.

There is only one way to obtain these admirable results. It is by producing workmen, men of science, and employers who enjoy their work. View the matter practically, in the light of our knowledge of average human nature. Is it likely that a tired, bored workman, however skillful his hands, will produce a large output of first-class work? He will limit his production and be an adept at evading inspection; he will be slow in adapting himself to new methods; he will be a focus of discontent, full of impractical revolutionary ideas, controlled by no sympathetic apprehension of the real working of trade conditions. If, in the troubled times which may be before us, you wish appreciably to increase the chance of some savage upheaval, introduce widespread technical education and ignore the Benedictine ideal. Society will then get what it deserves. Again, inventive genius requires pleasurable mental activity as a condition for its vigorous exercise. "Necessity is the mother of invention" is a silly proverb. "Necessity is the mother of futile dodges" is much nearer to the truth. The basis of the growth of modern invention is science, and science is almost wholly the outgrowth of pleasurable intellectual curiosity.

The third class are the employers, who are to be enterprising. Now, it should be observed that it is the successful employers who are the important people to get at, the men with business connexions all over the world, men who are already rich. No doubt there will always be a continuous process of rise and fall of businesses. But it is futile to expect flourishing trade, if in the mass the successful businesses are suffering from atrophy. Now, if the successful men conceive their businesses as merely indifferent means for acquiring other disconnected opportunities of life, they have no spur to alertness. They are already doing very well; the mere momentum of their business engagements will carry them on for their time. They are not at all likely to bother themselves with the doubtful chances of new methods. Their real soul is in the other side of their life. Desire for money will produce hardfistedness and no enterprise. There is much more hope for humanity from manufacturers who enjoy their work than from those who continue in irksome business with the object of founding hospitals.

Finally, there can be no prospect of industrial peace so long as masters and men in the mass conceive themselves as engaged in a soulless operation of extracting money from the public. Enlarged views of the work performed and of communal service thereby rendered can be the only basis on which to found sympathetic co-operation.

The conclusion to be drawn from this discussion is that, alike for masters and for men, a technical or technological education which is to have any chance of satisfying the practical needs of the nation must be conceived in a liberal spirit as a real intellectual enlightenment as to principles applied and the services rendered. In such an education, geometry and poetry are as essential as turning-lathes.

The mythical figure of Plato may stand for modern liberal education as does that of St. Benedict[2] for technical education. We need not entangle ourselves in the qualifications necessary for a balanced representation of the actual thoughts of the actual men. They are used here as symbolic figures typical of antithetical notions. We consider Plato in the light of the type of culture he now inspires. In its essence a liberal education is an education for thought and for æsthetic appreciation. It proceeds by imparting a knowledge of the masterpieces of thought, of imaginative literature, and of art. The action which it contemplates is command. It is an aristocratic education, implying leisure. This Platonic ideal has rendered imperishable services to European civilisation. It has encouraged art, it has fostered that spirit of disinterested curiosity which is the origin of science, it has maintained the dignity of mind in the face of material force, a dignity which claims freedom of thought. Plato did not, like St. Benedict, bother himself to be a fellow-worker with his slaves; but he must rank with Benedict among the emancipators of mankind. His type of culture is the peculiar inspiration of the liberal aristocrat, the class from which Europe derives what ordered liberty it now possesses. For centuries, from Pope Nicholas V to the schools of the Jesuits and from the Jesuits to the modern headmasters of English schools, this educational ideal has had the strenuous support of the clergy.

---

[2] Founder of the Benedictines, a Catholic order honoring manual labor and worship.

For certain people it is a very good education. It suits their type of mind and the circumstances amid which their life is passed. But more has been claimed for it than this. It has been represented as the ideal education, and every curriculum has been judged adequate or defective according to its approximation to this sole type.

The essence of the type is a large discursive knowledge of the best literature. The ideal product of the type is the man who is acquainted with the best that has been written such a man will have acquired the chief languages, he will have considered the histories of the rise and fall of nations, the varied poetic expression of human feeling, and have read the great dramas and novels. He will also be well-grounded in the chief philosophies and have attentively read those philosophic authors who are distinguished for lucidity of style.

It is obvious that, except at the close of a long life, he will not have much time for anything else, if any approximation is to be made to the fulfilment of this programme. One is reminded of the calculation in a dialogue of Lucian[3] that before a man could be justified in practising any one of the current ethical systems, he should have spent 150 years in examining their credentials.

Such ideals are not for human beings. What is meant by a liberal culture is nothing so ambitious as a full acquaintance with the varied literary expression of civilised mankind from Asia to Europe and from Europe to America. A small selection only is required, but then, as we are told, it is a selection of the very best. I have my doubts of a selection which includes Xenophon and omits Confucius, but then I have read neither in the original. The ambitious programme of a liberal education really shrinks to a study of some fragments of literature, included in a couple of important languages.

But the expression of the human spirit is not confined to literature. There are the other arts and there are the sciences. Also, education must pass beyond the passive reception of the ideas of others. Powers of initiative must be strengthened. Unfortunately, initiative does not mean just one acquirement. There is initiative in thought, initiative in action, and the imaginative initiative of art; and these three categories require many subdivisions.

The field for acquirement is large, and the individual so fleeting and so fragmentary. Classical scholars, scientists, headmasters, are all equally ignoramuses.

There is a curious illusion that a more complete culture was possible when there was less to know. Surely the only gain was that it was more possible to remain unconscious of ignorance. It cannot have been a gain to Plato to have read neither Shakespeare, nor Newton, nor Darwin. The

---

[3] Second-century author of *Dialogues of the Gods* and *Dialogues of the Dead*.

achievements of a liberal education have in recent times not been worsened. The change is that its pretensions have been found out.

My point is that no course of study can claim any position of ideal completeness. Nor are the omitted factors of subordinate importance. The insistence in the Platonic culture on disinterested intellectual appreciation is a psychological error. Action and the transition of events amid the inevitable bond of cause to effect are fundamental. An education which strives to divorce intellectual or æsthetic life from these fundamental facts carries with it the decadence of civilisation. Essentially, culture should be for creative action, and its effect should be to divest labour of the associations of aimless toil. Art exists in order that we may know the deliverances of our senses as good. It heightens the sense-world.

Again, disinterested scientific curiosity is a passion for an ordered intellectual vision of the connexions of events. But the goal of such curiosity is the marriage of action to thought. This essential intervention of action even in abstract science is often overlooked. No man of science wants merely to know. He acquires knowledge to appease his passion for discovery. He does not discover in order to know, he knows in order to discover. The pleasure which art and science can give to toil is the pleasure which arises from successfully directed intention. Also, it is this same pleasure which is yielded to the scientist and to the artist.

The antithesis between a technical and a liberal education is fallacious. There can be no adequate technical education which is not liberal, and no liberal education which is not technical; that is, no education which does not impart both technique and intellectual vision. In simpler language, education should turn out the pupil with some things he knows well and and some things he can do well. This intimate union of practise and theory aids both. The intellect does not work best in a vacuum; the stimulation of creative impulse requires, especially in the case of a child, the quick natural transition to practise. Geometry and mechanics, followed by workshop practise, gain that reality without which mathematics is verbiage.

There are three main methods which are required in a national system of education: the literary curriculum, the scientific curriculum, the technical curriculum.

But each one of these curricula should include the other two. What I mean is that every form of education should give the pupil a technique, a science, an assortment of general ideas, an æsthetic appreciation, and that each of these sides of his training should be illuminated by the others. Lack of time, even for the most favourable pupil, makes it impossible to develop fully each curriculum. Always there must be a dominant emphasis. The most direct æsthetic training naturally falls in the technical curriculum, in those cases when the technique is that requisite for some art or artistic craft. But it is of high importance in both a literary and a scientific education.

The educational method of the literary curriculum is the study of language; that is, the study of our most habitual method of conveying to others our states of mind. The technique which should be acquired is the technique of verbal expression; the science is the study of the structure of language and the analysis of the relations of language to the states of mind conveyed. Furthermore, the subtle relations of language to feeling and the high development of the sense organs to which spoken and written words appeal lead to keen æsthetic appreciations being aroused by the successful employment of language.

Finally, the wisdom of the world is preserved in the masterpieces of linguistic composition.

This curriculum has the merit of homogeneity. All its various parts are co-ordinated and play into each other's hands. We can hardly be surprised that such a curriculum, when once broadly established, should have claimed the position of the sole perfect type of education.

Its defect is unduly to emphasise the importance of language. Indeed, the varied importance of verbal expression is so overwhelming that its sober estimation is difficult. Recent generations have been witnessing the retreat of literature and of literary forms of expression from their position of unique importance in intellectual life. In order truly to become a servant and a minister of nature something more is required than literary aptitudes.

A scientific education is primarily a training in the art of observing natural phenomena and in the knowledge and deduction of laws concerning the sequence of such phenomena. But here, as in the case of a liberal education, we are met by the limitations imposed by shortness of time. There are many types of natural phenomena, and to each type there corresponds a science with its peculiar modes of observation and with its peculiar types of thought employed in the deduction of laws. A study of science in general is impossible in education; all that can be achieved is the study of two or three allied sciences. Hence the charge of narrow specialism urged against any education which is primarily scientific. It is obvious that the charge is apt to be well-founded; and it is worth considering how, within the limits of a scientific education and to the advantage of such an education, the danger can be avoided.

Such a discussion requires the consideration of technical education. A technical education is in the main a training in the art of utilising knowledge for the manufacture of material products. Such a training emphasises manual skill, and the co-ordinated action of hand and eye, and judgment in the control of the process of construction. But judgment necessitates knowledge of those natural processes of which the manufacture is the utilisation. Thus somewhere in technical training, an education in scientific knowledge is required. If you minimise the scientific side, you will confine it to the scientific experts; if you maximise it, you will also impart it in some measure to the men and—what is of no less importance—to the directors and managers of businesses.

Technical education is not necessarily allied exclusively to science on its mental side. It may be an education for an artist or for apprentices to an artistic craft. In that case æsthetic appreciation will have to be cultivated in connexion with it.

An evil side of the Platonic culture has been its total neglect of technical education as an ingredient in the complete development of ideal human beings. This neglect has arisen from two disastrous antitheses; namely, that between mind and body and that between thought and action. I will here interject, solely to avoid criticism, that I am well aware that the Greeks highly valued physical beauty and physical activity.

I lay it down as an educational axiom that in teaching you will come to grief as soon as you forget that your pupils have bodies. This is exactly the mistake of the post-Renaissance Platonic curriculum. But nature can be kept at bay by no pitchfork; so in English education, being expelled from the classroom, she returned with a cap and bells in the form of all-conquering athleticism.

The connexions between intellectual activity and the body, though diffused in every bodily feeling, are focussed in the eyes, the ears, the voice, and the hands. There is a co-ordination of senses and thought, and also a reciprocal reaction between brain activity and material creative activity. In this reaction the hands are peculiarly important. It is a moot point whether the human hand created the human brain, or the brain created the hand. Certainly the connexion is intimate and reciprocal. Such deep-seated relations are not widely atrophied by a few hundred years of disuse in exceptional families.

The disuse of hand-craft is a contributory cause to the brain-lethargy of aristocracies, which is only mitigated by sport where the concurrent brain activity is reduced to a minimum, and the hand-craft lacks subtlety. The necessity for constant writing and vocal exposition is some slight stimulus to the thought-power of the professional classes. Great readers, who exclude other activities, are not distinguished by subtilety of brain. They tend to be timid conventional thinkers. No doubt this is partly due to their excessive knowledge outrunning their powers of thought; but partly it is due to the lack of brain-stimulus from the productive activities of hand or voice.

In estimating the importance of technical education we must rise above the exclusive association of learning with book learning. Firsthand knowledge is the ultimate basis of intellectual life. To a large extent book learning conveys secondhand information, and as such can never rise to the importance of immediate practise. Our goal is to see the immediate events of our lives as instances of our general ideas. What the learned world tends to offer is one secondhand scrap of information illustrating an idea derived from another secondhand scrap of information. The secondhandedness of the learned world is the secret of its mediocrity. It is tame because it has never been scared by facts. The main importance of Francis Bacon's influence does not lie in any peculiar theory of inductive reasoning which he happened to express, but in the revolt against secondhand information of which he was a leader.

The peculiar merit of a scientific education should be that it bases thought upon firsthand observation; and the corresponding merit of a technical education is that it follows our deep natural instinct to translate thought into manual skill, and manual activity into thought.

We are a mathematical association, and it is natural to ask, "Where do we come in?" We come in just at this point.

The thought which science evokes is logical thought. Now, logic is of two kinds: the logic of discovery and the logic of the discovered.

The logic of discovery consists in the weighing of probabilities, in discarding details deemed to be irrelevant, in divining the general rules according to which events occur, and in testing hypotheses by devising suitable experiments. This is inductive logic.

The logic of the discovered is the deduction of the special events which under certain circumstances would happen in obedience to the assumed laws of nature. Thus, when the laws are discovered or assumed, their utilisation entirely depends on deductive logic. Without deductive logic, science would be entirely useless. It is merely a barren game to ascend from the particular to the general, unless afterwards we can reverse the process and descend from the general to the particular, ascending and descending like the angels on Jacob's ladder. When Newton had divined the law of gravitation, he at once proceeded to calculate the earth's attractions on an apple at its surface and on the moon. We may note in passing that inductive logic would be impossible without deductive logic.

Now, mathematics is nothing else than the more complicated parts of the art of deductive reasoning, especially where it concerns number, quantity, and space. In the teaching of science, the art of thought should be taught: namely, the art of forming clear conceptions applying to firsthand experience, the art of divining the general truths which apply, the art of testing divinations, and the art of utilising general truths by reasoning to more particular cases of some peculiar importance. Furthermore, a power of scientific exposition is necessary so that the relevant issues from a confused mass of ideas can be stated clearly, with due emphasis on important points.

By the time a science or small group of sciences has been taught thus amply, with due regard to the general art of thought, we have gone a long way towards correcting the specialism of science. The worst of a scientific education based, as is necessarily the case, on one or two particular branches of science is that the teachers under the influence of the examination system are apt merely to stuff their pupils with the narrow results of those special sciences. It is essential that the generality of the method be continually brought to light and contrasted with the speciality of the particular application. A man who knows only his own science, as a routine peculiar to that science, does not even know that. He has no fertility of thought, no power of quickly seizing the bearing of alien ideas. He will discover nothing and will be stupid in every practical application.

This exhibition of the general in the particular is extremely difficult to effect, especially in the case of younger pupils. The art of education is never easy. To surmount its difficulties, especially those of elementary education, is a task worthy of the highest genius. It is the training of human souls.

Mathematics, well taught, should be the most powerful instrument in gradually implanting this generality of idea. The essence of mathematics is perpetually to be discarding more special in favour of more general ideas, and special methods in favour of general methods. We express the conditions of a special problem in the form of an equation, but that equation will serve for a hundred other problems scattered through diverse sciences. The general reasoning is always the powerful reasoning, because deductive cogency is the property of abstract form. There again we must be careful. We shall ruin mathematical education if we use it merely to impress general truths. The general ideas are the means of connecting particular results. After all, it is the concrete special cases which are important. Thus, in the handling of mathematics, in your results you cannot be too concrete, and in your methods you cannot be too general. The essential course of reasoning is to generalise what is particular and then to particularise what is general. Without generality there is no reasoning, without concreteness there is no importance.

Concreteness is the strength of technical education. I would remind you that truths which lack the highest generality are not necessarily concrete facts. For example, $x + y = y + x$ is an algebraic truth more general than $2 + 2 = 4$. But "two and two make four" is itself a highly general proposition lacking any element of concreteness. To obtain a concrete proposition, immediate intuition of a truth concerning particular objects is requisite; for example, "these two apples and those two apples together make four apples" is a concrete proposition, if you have direct perception or immediate memory of the apples.

In order to obtain the full realisation of truths as applying, and not as empty formulae, there is no alternative to technical education. Mere passive observation is not sufficient. In creation only is there vivid insight into the properties of the object produced. "If you want to understand anything, make it yourself" is a sound rule. Your faculties will be alive, your thoughts gain vividness by an immediate translation into acts. Your ideas gain that reality which comes from seeing the limits of their application.

In elementary education this doctrine has long been put into practise. Young children are taught to familiarise themselves with shapes and colours by simple manual operations of cutting out and of sorting. But good though this is, it is not quite what I mean. That is practical experience before you think, experience antecedent to thought in order to create the ideas, a very excellent discipline. But technical education should be much more than that; it is creative experience while you think, experience which realises your thought, experience which teaches you to co-ordinate act and thought, experience leading you to associate thought with foresight and foresight with achievement. Technical education gives theory and a shrewd insight as to where theory fails.

A technical education is not to be conceived as a maimed alternative to the perfect Platonic culture, namely, as a defective training unfortunately made necessary by cramped conditions of life. No human being can attain to anything but fragmentary knowledge and a fragmentary training of his capacities. There are, however, three main roads along which we can proceed with good hope of advancing towards the best balance of intellect and character: these are the way of literary culture, the way of scientific culture, the way of technical culture. No one of these methods can be exclusively followed without grave loss of intellectual activity and of character. But a mere mechanical mixture of the three curricula will produce bad results in the shape of scraps of information never interconnected or utilised. We have already noted as one of the strong points of the traditional literary culture that all its parts are co-ordinated. The problem of education is to retain the dominant emphasis, whether literary, scientific, or technical, and without loss of co-ordination to infuse into each way of education something of the other two.

To make definite the problem of technical education, fix attention on two ages, one thirteen when elementary education ends and the other seventeen when technical education ends, so far as it is comprised in a school training. These dates give four years for a technical course. I am aware that for artisans in junior technical schools a three years' course would be more usual. On the other hand, for naval officers and for the directing classes generally a longer time can be afforded. We want to consider the principles to govern a curriculum which shall land these children at the age of seventeen in the position of having technical skill useful to the community.

Their technical manual training should start at thirteen bearing a modest proportion to the rest of their work and should increase in each year, finally to attain to a substantial proportion. Above all things it should not be too specialised. Workshop finish and workshop dodges adapted to one particular job should be taught in the commercial workshop and should form no essential part of the school course. A properly trained worker would pick them up in no time. In all education the main cause of failure is staleness. Technical education is doomed if we conceive it as a a system for catching children young and for giving them one highly specialised manual aptitude. The nation has need of a fluidity of labour, not merely from place to place, but also, within the reasonable limits of allied aptitudes, from one special type of work to another special type. I know that here I am on delicate ground, and I am not claiming that men while they are specialising on one sort of work should spasmodically be set to other kinds. That is a question of trade organisation with which educationalists have no concern. I am only asserting the principles that the training should be broader than the ultimate specialisation, and that the resulting power of adaptation to varying demands is advantageous to the workers, to the employers, and to the nation.

In considering the intellectual side of the curriculum, we must be guided by the principle of the co-ordination of studies. In general, the intellectual studies most immediately related to the manual training will be some branches of science. More than one branch will, in fact, be concerned, and even if that be not the case, it is impossible to narrow down scientific study to a single thin line of thought. It is possible, however, provided that we do not press the classification too far, roughly to classify technical pursuits according to the dominant science involved. We thus find a sixfold division, namely: (1) geometrical techniques; (2) mechanical techniques; (3) physical techniques; (4) chemical techniques; (5) biological techniques; (6) techniques of commerce and of social service.

By this division it is meant that, apart from auxiliary sciences, some particular science requires emphasis in the training for most occupations. We can, for example, reckon carpentry, ironmongery, and many artistic crafts among geometrical techniques. Similarly, agriculture is a biological technique. Probably cookery, if it includes food catering, would fall midway between biological, physical, and chemical sciences, though of this I am not sure.

The sciences associated with commerce and social service would be partly algebra, including arithmetic and statistics, and partly geography and history. But their section is somewhat heterogeneous in its scientific affinities. Anyhow, the exact way in which technical pursuits are classified in relation to science is a detail. The essential point is that with some thought it is possible to find scientific courses which illuminate most occupations. Furthermore, the problem is well understood and has been brilliantly solved in many of the schools of technology and junior technical schools throughout the country.

In passing from science to literature in our review of the intellectual elements of technical education, we note that many studies hover between the two, for example, history and geography. They are both of them very essential in education, provided that they are the right history and right geography. Also, books giving descriptive accounts of the general results and trains of thought in various sciences fall in the same category. Such books should be partly historical and partly expository of the main ideas which have finally arisen. Prof. R. A. Gregory's recent book, *Discovery*,[4] and the Home University Library series illustrate my meaning. Their value in education depends on their quality as mental stimulants. They must not be inflated with gas on the wonders of science and must be informed with a broad outlook.

It is unfortunate that the literary element in education has rarely been considered apart from grammatical study. The historical reason is that, when the modern Platonic curriculum was being formed, Latin and Greek were the sole keys which rendered great literature accessible. But there is no necessary connection between literature and grammar. The great age of Greek literature was already past before the arrival of the grammarians of Alexandria. Of all types of men today existing, classical scholars are the most remote from the Greeks of the Periclean times.

Mere literary knowledge is of slight importance. The only thing that matters is how it is known. The facts related are as nothing. Literature exists only to express and develop that imaginative world which is our life, the kingdom which is within us.

It follows that the literary side of a technical education should consist in an effort to make the pupils enjoy literature. It does not matter what they know, but the enjoyment is vital. The great English universities, under whose direct authority school children are examined in plays of Shakespeare to the certain destruction of their enjoyment, should be prosecuted for soul-murder.

Now, there are two kinds of mental enjoyment, the enjoyment of creation and the enjoyment of relaxation. They are not necessarily separated. A change of occupation may give the full tide of happiness which comes from the concurrence of both forms of pleasure.

The appreciation of literature is really creation. The written word, its music, and its associations are only the stimuli. The vision which they evoke is our own doing. No one, no genius other than our own, can make our own life live. But except for those engaged in literary occupations, literature is also a relaxation. It gives exercise to that other side which any occupation must suppress during working hours. It also has the same function in life as has literature.

To obtain the pleasure of relaxation requires no help. The pleasure is merely to cease doing. Some such pure relaxation is a necessary condition of health. Its dangers are notorious, and to the greater part of the necessary pure relaxation, nature has affixed not enjoyment but the oblivion of sleep.

Creative enjoyment is the outcome of successful effort and requires help for its initiation. Such enjoyment is necessary for high-speed work and for original achievement. To speed up production with unrefreshed workmen

---

[4] Sir Richard A. Gregory's book was subtitled *The Spirit and Service of Science*; it was published in 1916.

is a disastrous economic policy. Temporary success will be at the expense of the nation, which for long years of their lives will have to support worn-out artisans, unemployables. Equally disastrous is the alternation of spasms of effort with periods of pure relaxation. Such periods are the seed time of degeneration, unless rigorously curtailed. The normal recreation should be change of activity satisfying the cravings of other instincts. Games afford such activity. Their disconnexion emphasises the relaxation, but their excess leaves us empty.

It is here that literature and popular art should play an essential part in a healthily organised nation. Their services to economic production would be only second to those of sleep or of food. I am not now talking of the training of an artist but of the use of art as a condition of healthy life. It is analogous to sunshine in the physical world.

When we have once rid our minds of the idea that knowledge is to be exacted, there is no special difficulty or expense involved in helping the growth of artistic enjoyment. All school children could be sent at regular intervals to neighbouring theatres where suitable plays could be subsidised. Similarly for concerts and kinema films. Pictures are more doubtful in their popular attraction. But interesting representations of scenes or ideas which the children have read about would probably appeal. The pupils themselves should be encouraged in artistic efforts. Above all, the art of reading aloud should be cultivated. The Roger de Coverley essays of Addison are perfect examples of readable prose.[5]

Art and literature have not merely an indirect effect on the main energies of life. Directly, they give vision. The world spreads wide beyond the deliverances of material sense, with subtleties of reaction and with pulses of emotion. Vision is the necessary antecedent to control and to direction. In the contest of races, which in its final issues will be decided in the workshops and not on the battlefield, the victory will belong to those who are masters of stores of trained nervous energy, working under conditions favourable to growth. One such essential condition is art.

If there had been time, there are other things which I should like to have said: for example, to advocate the inclusion of one foreign language in all education. From direct observation, I know this to be possible for artisan children. But enough has been put before you to make plain the principles with which we should undertake national education.

In conclusion, I recur to the thought of the Benedictines who saved for mankind the vanishing civilisation of the ancient world by linking together knowledge, labour, and moral energy. Our danger is to conceive practical affairs as the kingdom of evil, in which success is only possible by the extrusion of ideal aims. I believe that such a conception is a fallacy, directly negatived by experience. In education this error takes the form of a mean

---

[5] Joseph Addison depicted Sir Roger de Coverley, a Tory country squire, in a series of essays in the *Spectator*. For example, see Nos. 106, 269, 329, 335, and 383.

view of technical training. Our forefathers in the dark ages saved themselves by embodying high ideals in great organisations. It is our task, without servile imitation, boldly to exercise our creative energies, remembering amid discouragements that the coldest hour immediately precedes the dawn.

C. P. Snow

"The Two Cultures"*
Cambridge University, May 7, 1959

It is about three years since I made a sketch in print of a problem which had been on my mind for some time[1]. It was a problem I could not avoid just because of the circumstances of my life. The only credentials I had to ruminate on the subject at all came through those circumstances, through nothing more than a set of chances. Anyone with similar experience would have seen much the same things and I think made very much the same comments about them. It just happened to be an unusual experience. By training I was a scientist; by vocation I was a writer. That was all. It was a piece of luck, if you like, that arose through coming from a poor home.

But my personal history isn't the point now. All that I need say is that I came to Cambridge and did a bit of research here at a time of major scientific activity. I was privileged to have a ringside view of one of the most wonderful creative periods in all physics. And it happened through the flukes of war—including meeting W. L. Bragg[2] in the buffet on Ket-

---

* The text is taken from *The Two Cultures and A Second Look* (Cambridge, Eng., 1964), pp. 1–18.

[1] See C. P. Snow, "The Two Cultures," *New Statesman*, LII (October 6, 1956), 413–414.

[2] Snow mentions many of the outstanding scientists, writers, and statesmen of English history, especially of the twentieth century. Among those who might need to be identified are Edgar Douglas Adrian, physiologist; Kingsley Amis, writer, one of the original English "angry young men"; John Anderson, Viscount Waverley, Minister of the Civil Scientific Departments, 1940–1943; Arthur Balfour, Prime Minister, 1902–1905, who also served as President of the British Association; John D. Bernal, physicist; Patrick M. S. Blackett, physicist; Sir William L. Bragg, physicist; Prince Louis de Broglie, French physicist; Alan Bullock, historian; Robert A. Cecil, Marquess of Salisbury, Prime Minister 1900–1902, a student of science and President of the British Association; Arthur H. Compton, American physicist; Paul Adrien Maurice Dirac, English physicist; Sir Arthur S. Eddington, astronomer and physicist; Michael Faraday, British chemist and physicist; Robert Greene, sixteenth-century pamphleteer, poet, and dramatist; Godfrey Harold Hardy, mathematician; Sir James H. Jeans, mathematician, theoretical physicist, and astronomer; Thomas Kyd, sixteenth-century dramatist; Wyndham Lewis, writer and artist; Frederick A. Lindemann, Viscount Cherwell, physicist; John E. Littlewood, mathematician; Sir Thomas Ralph Merton, physicist; J. H. Plumb, historian; Ezra Pound, American poet; Rainer Maria Rilke, German lyric poet and writer; Nathaniel Victor Rothschild, British zoologist; Ernest Rutherford, physicist; A. L. Smith, Master of Balliol College, Oxford; Sir Joseph J. Thomson, physicist; William Butler Yeats, Irish poet and playwright.

tering station on a very cold morning in 1939, which had a determining influence on my practical life—that I was able, and indeed morally forced, to keep that ringside view ever since. So for thirty years I have had to be in touch with scientists not only out of curiosity but as part of a working existence. During the same thirty years I was trying to shape the books I wanted to write, which in due course took me among writers.

There have been plenty of days when I have spent the working hours with scientists and then gone off at night with some literary colleagues. I mean that literally. I have had, of course, intimate friends among both scientists and writers. It was through living among these groups and much more, I think, through moving regularly from one to the other and back again that I got occupied with the problem of what, long before I put it on paper, I christened to myself as the "two cultures." For constantly I felt I was moving among two groups—comparable in intelligence, identical in race, not grossly different in social origin, earning about the same incomes—who had almost ceased to communicate at all; who in intellectual, moral, and psychological climate had so little in common that instead of going from Burlington House or South Kensington to Chelsea, one might have crossed an ocean.

In fact, one had travelled much further than across an ocean—because after a few thousand Atlantic miles, one found Greenwich Village talking precisely the same language as Chelsea, and both having about as much communication with M.I.T. as though the scientists spoke nothing but Tibetan. For this is not just our problem; owing to some of our educational and social idiosyncrasies it is slightly exaggerated here; owing to another English social peculiarity it is slightly minimised; by and large this is a problem of the entire West.

By this I intend something serious. I am not thinking of the pleasant story of how one of the more convivial Oxford greats dons—I have heard the story attributed to A. L. Smith—came over to Cambridge to dine. The date is perhaps the 1890's. I think it must have been at St. John's, or possibly Trinity. Anyway, Smith was sitting at the right hand of the President—or Vice-Master—and he was a man who liked to include all round him in the conversation, although he was not immediately encouraged by the expressions of his neighbours. He addressed some cheerful Oxonian chit-chat at the one opposite to him and got a grunt. He then tried the man on his own right hand and got another grunt. Then, rather to his surprise, one looked at the other and said, "Do you know what he's talking about?" "I haven't the least idea." At this, even Smith was getting out of his depth. But the President, acting as a social emollient, put him at his ease, by saying, "Oh, those are mathematicians! We never talk to *them*."

No, I intend something serious. I believe the intellectual life of the whole of Western society is increasingly being split into two polar groups. When I say the intellectual life, I mean to include also a large part of our practical life, because I should be the last person to suggest the two can at the deepest level be distinguished. I shall come back to the practical life a little later. Two polar groups: at one pole we have the literary intellectuals, who incidentally while no one was looking took to referring to themselves as "intellectuals" as though there were no others. I remember G. H. Hardy once remarking to me in mild puzzlement, some time in the 1930's, "Have you noticed how the word 'intellectual' is used nowadays? There seems to be a new definition which certainly doesn't include Rutherford or Eddington or Dirac or Adrian or me. It does seem rather odd, don't y' know."

Literary intellectuals at one pole—at the other, scientists, and as the most representative, the physical scientists. Between the two a gulf of mutual incomprehension—sometimes (particularly among the young) hostility and dislike, but most of all lack of understanding. They have a curious distorted image of each other. Their attitudes are so different that even on the level of emotion they can't find much common ground. Non-scientists tend to think of scientists as brash and boastful. They hear Mr. T. S. Eliot, who just for these illustrations we can take as an archetypal figure, saying about his attempts to revive verse drama that we can hope for very little, but that he would feel content if he and his co-workers could prepare the ground for a new Kyd or a new Greene. That is the tone, restricted and constrained, with which literary intellectuals are at home: it is the subdued voice of their culture. Then they hear a much louder voice, that of another archetypal figure, Rutherford, trumpeting: "This is the heroic age of science! This is the Elizabethan age!" Many of us heard that and a good many other statements beside which that was mild, and we weren't left in any doubt whom Rutherford was casting for the role of Shakespeare. What is hard for the literary intellectuals to understand, imaginatively or intellectually, is that he was absolutely right.

And compare "this is the way the world ends, not with a bang but a whimper"—incidentally, one of the least likely scientific prophecies ever made—compare that with Rutherford's famous repartee: "Lucky fellow, Rutherford, always on the crest of the wave." "Well, I made the wave, didn't I?"

The non-scientists have a rooted impression that the scientists are shallowly optimistic, unaware of man's condition. On the other hand, the scientists believe that the literary intellectuals are totally lacking in foresight, peculiarly unconcerned with their brother men, in a deep sense anti-intellectual, anxious to restrict both art and thought to the existential moment. And so on. Anyone with a mild talent for invective could produce plenty of this kind of subterranean back-chat. On each side there is some of it which is not entirely baseless. It is all destructive. Much of it rests on misinterpretations which are dangerous. I should like to deal with two of the most profound of these now, one on each side.

First, about the scientists' optimism. This is an accusation which has been made so often that it has become a platitude. It has been made by some of the acutest non-scientific minds of the day. But it depends upon a confusion between the individual experience and the social experience, between the individual condition of man and his social condition. Most of the scientists I have known well have felt—just as deeply as the non-scientists I have known well—that the individual condition of each of us is tragic. Each of us is alone; sometimes we escape from solitariness, through love or affection or perhaps creative moments, but those triumphs of life are pools of light we make for ourselves while the edge of the road is black; each of us dies alone. Some scientists I have known have had faith in revealed religion. Perhaps with them the sense of the tragic condition is not so strong; I don't know. With most people of deep feeling, however high-spirited and happy they are, sometimes most with those who are happiest and most high-spirited, it seems to be right in the fibres, part of the weight of life. That is as true of the scientists I have known best as of anyone at all.

But nearly all of them—and this is where the colour of hope genuinely comes in—would see no reason why, just because the individual condition is tragic, so must the social condition be. Each of us is solitary; each of us dies alone; all right, that's a fate against which we can't struggle—but there is plenty in our condition which is not fate and against which we are less than human unless we do struggle.

Most of our fellow human beings, for instance, are underfed and die before their time. In the crudest terms, *that* is the social condition. There is a moral trap which comes through the insight into man's loneliness; it tempts one to sit back, complacent in one's unique tragedy, and let the others go without a meal.

As a group, the scientists fall into that trap less than others. They are inclined to be impatient to see if something can be done, and inclined to think that it can be done until it's proved otherwise. That is their real optimism, and it's an optimism that the rest of us badly need.

In reverse, the same spirit, tough and good and determined to fight it out at the side of their brother men, has made scientists regard the other culture's social attitudes as contemptible. That is too facile; some of them are, but they are a temporary phase and not to be taken as representative.

I remember being cross-examined by a scientist of distinction. "Why do most writers take on social opinions which would have been thought distinctly uncivilised and démodé at the time of the Plantagenets?[3] Wasn't that true of most of the famous twentieth-century writers? Yeats, Pound, Wyndham Lewis—nine out of ten of those who have dominated literary sensibility in our time—weren't they not only politically silly, but politically wicked? Didn't the influence of all they represent bring Auschwitz that much nearer?"

I thought at the time and I still think that the correct answer was not to defend the indefensible. It was no use saying that Yeats, according to

[3] The English kings from Henry II to the accession of the Tudors, descended from French medieval rulers (the Angevins), are called the Plantagenets.

friends whose judgment I trust, was a man of singular magnanimity of character, as well as a great poet. It was no use denying the facts, which are broadly true. The honest answer was that there is, in fact, a connexion, which literary persons were culpably slow to see, between some kinds of early twentieth-century art and the most imbecile expressions of anti-social feeling. That was one reason, among many, why some of us turned our backs on the art and tried to hack out a new or different way for ourselves.

But though many of those writers dominated literary sensibility for a generation, that is no longer so, or at least to nothing like the same extent. Literature changes more slowly than science. It hasn't the same automatic corrective, and so its misguided periods are longer. But it is ill-considered of scientists to judge writers on the evidence of the period 1914-1950.

Those are two of the misunderstandings between the two cultures. I should say, since I began to talk about them—the two cultures, that is—I have had some criticism. Most of my scientific acquaintances think that there is something in it, and so do most of the practising artists I know. But I have been argued with by non-scientists of strong down-to-earth interests. Their view is that it is an over-simplification, and that if one is going to talk in these terms there ought to be at least three cultures. They argue that though they are not scientists themselves, they would share a good deal of the scientific feeling. They would have as little use—perhaps, since they knew more about it, even less use—for the recent literary culture as the scientists themselves. J. H. Plumb, Alan Bullock, and some of my American sociological friends have said that they vigorously refuse to be corralled in a cultural box with people they wouldn't be seen dead with, or to be regarded as helping to produce a climate which would not permit of social hope.

I respect those arguments. The number 2 is a very dangerous number; that is why the dialectic is a dangerous process. Attempts to divide anything into two ought to be regarded with much suspicion. I have thought a long time about going in for further refinements; but in the end I have decided against. I was searching for something a little more than a dashing metaphor, a good deal less than a cultural map; and for those purposes the two cultures is about right, and subtilising any more would bring more disadvantages than it's worth.

At one pole, the scientific culture really is a culture, not only in an intellectual but also in an anthropological sense. That is, its members need not and of course often do not always completely understand each other; biologists more often than not will have a pretty hazy idea of contemporary physics; but there are common attitudes, common standards and patterns of behaviour, common approaches and assumptions. This goes surprisingly wide and deep. It cuts across other mental patterns, such as those of religion or politics or class.

Statistically, I suppose slightly more scientists are in religious terms unbelievers, compared with the rest of the intellectual world—though there are plenty who are religious, and that seems to be increasingly so among the young. Statistically also, slightly more scientists are on the Left in open politics—though again, plenty always have called themselves conservatives, and that also seems to be more common among the young. Compared with the rest of the intellectual world, considerably more scientists in this country and probably in the U.S. come from poor families. Yet, over a whole range of thought and behaviour, none of that matters very much. In their working and in much of their emotional life, their attitudes are closer to other scientists than to non-scientists who in religion or politics or class have the same labels as themselves. If I were to risk a piece of shorthand, I should say that naturally they had the future in their bones.

They may or may not like it, but they have it. That was as true of the conservatives J. J. Thomson and Lindemann as of the radicals Einstein or Blackett; as true of the Christian A. H. Compton as of the materialist Bernal; of the aristocrats de Broglie or Russell as of the proletarian Faraday; of those born rich, like Thomas Merton or Victor Rothschild, as of Rutherford, who was the son of an odd-job handyman. Without thinking about it, they respond alike. That is what a culture means.

At the other pole, the spread of attitudes is wider. It is obvious that between the two, as one moves through intellectual society from the physicists to the literary intellectuals, there are all kinds of tones of feeling on the way. But I believe the pole of total incomprehension of science radiates its influence on all the rest. That total incomprehension gives, much more pervasively than we realise, living in it, an unscientific flavour to the whole "traditional" culture, and that unscientific flavour is often, much more than we admit, on the point of turning anti-scientific. The feelings of one pole become the anti-feelings of the other. If the scientists have the future in their bones, then the traditional culture responds by wishing the future did not exist. It is the traditional culture, to an extent remarkably little diminished by the emergence of the scientific one, which manages the western world.

This polarisation is sheer loss to us all. To us as people, and to our society. It is at the same time practical and intellectual and creative loss, and I repeat that it is false to imagine that those three considerations are clearly separable. But for a moment I want to concentrate on the intellectual loss.

The degree of incomprehension on both sides is the kind of joke which has gone sour. There are about 50,000 working scientists in the country and about 80,000 professional engineers or applied scientists. During the war and in the years since, my colleagues and I have had to interview somewhere between 30,000 and 40,000 of these—that is, about 25 per cent. The number is large enough to give us a fair sample, though of the men we talked to, most would still be under forty. We were able to find out a certain amount of what they read and thought about. I confess that even I, who am fond of them and respect them, was a bit shaken. We hadn't quite expected that the links with the traditional culture should be so tenuous, nothing more than a formal touch of the cap.

As one would expect, some of the very best scientists had and have plenty of energy and interest to spare, and we came across several who had read everything that literary people talk about. But that's very rare. Most of the rest, when one tried to probe for what books they had read, would modestly confess, "Well, I've *tried* a bit of Dickens," rather as though Dickens were an extraordinarily esoteric, tangled, and dubiously rewarding writer, something like Rainer Maria Rilke. In fact that is exactly how they do regard him; we thought that discovery, that Dickens had been transformed into the type-specimen of literary incomprehensibility, was one of the oddest results of the whole exercise.

But of course in reading him, in reading almost any writer whom we should value, they are just touching their caps to the traditional culture. They have their own culture, intensive, rigorous, and constantly in action. This culture contains a great deal of argument, usually much more rigorous and almost always at a higher conceptual level than literary persons' arguments; even though the scientists do cheerfully use words in senses which literary persons don't recognise, the senses are exact ones, and when they talk about "subjective," "objective," "philosophy," or "progressive," they know what they mean, even though it isn't what one is accustomed to expect.

Remember, these are very intelligent men. Their culture is in many ways an exacting and admirable one. It doesn't contain much art, with the exception—an important exception—of music. Verbal exchange, insistent argument. Long-playing records. Colour-photography. The ear, to some extent the eye. Books, very little, though perhaps not many would go so far as one hero—who perhaps I should admit was further down the scientific ladder than the people I've been talking about—who, when asked what books he read, replied firmly and confidently: "Books? I prefer to use my books as tools." It was very hard not to let the mind wander —what sort of tool would a book make? Perhaps a hammer? A primitive digging instrument?

Of books, though, very little. And of the books which to most literary persons are bread and butter—novels, history, poetry, plays—almost nothing at all. It isn't that they're not interested in the psychological or moral or social life. In the social life they certainly are, more than most of us. In the moral, they are by and large the soundest group of intellectuals we have; there is a moral component right in the grain of science itself, and almost all scientists form their own judgments of the moral life. In the psychological they have as much interest as most of us, though occasionally I fancy they come to it rather late. It isn't that they lack the interests. It is much more that the whole literature of the traditional culture doesn't seem to them relevant to those interests. They are, of course, dead wrong. As a result, their imaginative understanding is less than it could be. They are self-impoverished.

But what about the other side? They are impoverished, too—perhaps more seriously, because they are vainer about it. They still like to pretend that the traditional culture is the whole of "culture," as though the natural order didn't exist. As though the exploration of the natural order was of no interest either in its own value or its consequences. As though the scientific edifice of the physical world was not, in its intellectual depth, complexity and articulation, the most beautiful and wonderful collective work of the mind of man. Yet most non-scientists have no conception of that edifice at all. Even if they want to have it, they can't. It is rather as though, over an immense range of intellectual experience, a whole group was tone-deaf. Except that this tone-deafness doesn't come by nature but by training, or rather the absence of training.

As with the tone-deaf, they don't know what they miss. They give a pitying chuckle at the news of scientists who have never read a major work of English literature. They dismiss them as ignorant specialists. Yet their own ignorance and their own specialisation is just as startling. A good many times I have been present at gatherings of people who, by the standards of the traditional culture, are thought highly educated and who have with considerable gusto been expressing their incredulity at the illiteracy of scientists. Once or twice I have been provoked and have asked the company how many of them could describe the Second Law of Thermodynamics.[4] The response was cold; it was also negative. Yet I was asking something which is about the scientific equivalent of "Have you read a work of Shakespeare's?"

I now believe that if I had asked an even simpler question—such as "What do you mean by mass, or acceleration?" which is the scientific equivalent of saying, "Can you read?"—not more than one in ten of the highly educated would have felt that I was speaking the same language. So the great edifice of modern physics goes up, and the majority of the cleverest people in the Western world have about as much insight into it as their neolithic ancestors would have had.

Just one more of those questions that my non-scientific friends regard as being in the worst of taste. Cambridge is a university where scientists and non-scientists meet every night at dinner. About two years ago, one of the most astonishing discoveries in the whole history of science was brought off. I don't mean the Sputnik—that was admirable for quite

---

[4] The second law states that when a free exchange of heat takes place between two bodies as a self-sustaining and continuous process, the heat must always be transferred from the hotter to the colder body.

different reasons, as a feat of organisation and a triumphant use of existing knowledge. No, I mean the discovery at Columbia by Yang and Lee.[5] It is a piece of work of the greatest beauty and originality, but the result is so startling that one forgets how beautiful the thinking is. It makes us think again about some of the fundamentals of the physical world. Intuition, common sense—they are neatly stood on their heads. The result is usually known as the non-conservation of parity. If there were any serious communication between the two cultures, this experiment would have been talked about at every High Table in Cambridge. Was it? I wasn't here, but I should like to ask the question.

There seems then to be no place where the cultures meet. I am not going to waste time saying that this is a pity. It is much worse than that. Soon I shall come to some practical consequences. But at the heart of thought and creation we are letting some of our best chances go by default. The clashing point of two subjects, two disciplines, two cultures—of two galaxies, so far as that goes—ought to produce creative chances. In the history of mental activity, that has been where some of the breakthroughs came. The chances are there now. But they are there, as it were, in a vacuum, because those in the two cultures can't talk to each other. It is bizarre how very little of twentieth-century science has been assimilated into twentieth-century art. Now and then one used to find poets conscientiously using scientific expressions and getting them wrong—there was a time when "refraction" kept cropping up in verse in a mystifying fashion, and when "polarised light" was used as though writers were under the illusion that it was a specially admirable kind of light.

Of course, that isn't the way that science could be any good to art. It has got to be assimilated along with and as part and parcel of the whole of our mental experience, and used as naturally as the rest.

I said earlier that this cultural divide is not just an English phenomenon; it exists all over the Western world. But it probably seems at its sharpest in England, for two reasons. One is our fanatical belief in educational specialisation, which is much more deeply ingrained in us than in any country in the world, West or East. The other is our tendency to let our social forms crystallise. This tendency appears to get stronger, not weaker, the more we iron out economic inequalities, and this is specially true in education. It means that once anything like a cultural divide gets established, all the social forces operate to make it not less rigid but more so.

The two cultures were already dangerously separate sixty years ago; but a Prime Minister like Lord Salisbury could have his own laboratory at Hatfield, and Arthur Balfour had a somewhat more than amateur

[5] Chen Ning Yang and Tsung-Dao Lee received the Nobel Prize for physics in 1957. They proposed a theory, the principle of space reflection symmetry, leading to experiments that disproved the parity conservation hypothesis, which concerns the distinction between right- and left-handedness.

interest in natural science. John Anderson did some research in inorganic chemistry in Leipzig before passing first into the Civil Service, and incidentally took a spread of subjects which is now impossible. None of that degree of interchange at the top of the Establishment is likely or indeed thinkable now.

In fact, the separation between the scientists and non-scientists is much less bridgeable among the young than it was even thirty years ago. Thirty years ago the cultures had long ceased to speak to each other; but at least they managed a kind of frozen smile across the gulf. Now the politeness has gone, and they just make faces. It is not only that the young scientists now feel that they are part of a culture on the rise while the other is in retreat. It is also, to be brutal, that the young scientists know that with an indifferent degree they'll get a comfortable job, while their contemporaries and counterparts in English or History will be lucky to earn 60 per cent as much. No young scientist of any talent would feel that he isn't wanted or that his work is ridiculous, as did the hero of *Lucky Jim;* and in fact, some of the disgruntlement of Amis and his associates is the disgruntlement of the under-employed arts graduate.

There is only one way out of all this: it is, of course, by rethinking our education.

.   .   .   .   .

POLITICAL PARROTS.

Mr. B. "OH! THIS DREADFUL SCREECHING!!"

6

Politics and Party Principles

Benjamin Disraeli

"Conservative and Liberal Principles"[*]
Crystal Palace, London, June 24, 1872

My Lord Duke[1] and Gentlemen—I am very sensible of the honour which you have done me in requesting that I should be your guest today, and still more for your having associated my name with the important toast which has been proposed by the Lord Mayor.[2] In the few observations that I shall presume to make on this occasion, I will confine myself to some suggestions as to the present state of the Constitutional cause and the prospects which, as a great Constitutional party, are before us. Some years ago—not indeed an inconsiderable period, but within the memory of many who are present—the Tory Party experienced a great overthrow.[3] I am here to admit that in my opinion it was deserved. A long course of power and prosperity had induced it to sink into a state of apathy and indifference, and it had deviated from the great principle of that political association which had so long regulated the affairs and been identified with the glory of England. Instead of those principles which were professed by Mr. Pitt and Lord Grenville and which those great men inherited from Tory statesmen who had preceded them not less illustrious, the Tory system had degenerated into a policy which found its basis on the principles of exclusiveness and restriction.[4]

A body of public men distinguished by their capacity took advantage of these circumstances. They seized the helm of affairs in a manner the honour of which I do not for a moment question, but they introduced a new system into our political life. Influenced in a great degree by the philosophy

---

[*] This text is from *The Times*, June 25, 1872, pp. 7–8.

[1] The Duke of Abercorn presided over the dinner meeting of delegates to the annual conference of the National Union of Conservative and Constitutional Associations.

[2] Sir James C. Lawrence, Lord Mayor of London, proposed "The Constitutional Cause."

[3] An allusion to the Tory defeat of 1830. This defeat ushered in the Whig Ministry that passed the Reform Bill of 1832.

[4] Disraeli is criticizing the administration of Lord Liverpool (1812–1827).

and the politics of the Continent, they endeavoured to substitute cosmopolitan[5] for national principles, and they baptised the new scheme of politics with the plausible name of Liberalism. [*Cheers.*] Far be it from me for a moment to intimate that a country like England should not profit by the political experience and science of Continental nations of not inferior civilisation. Far be it from me for a moment to maintain that the Party which then obtained power and which has since generally possessed it did not make many suggestions for our public life that were of great value and bring forward many measures which, though changes, were nevertheless improvements. But the tone and tendency of Liberalism cannot be concealed. It is to attack the institutions of the country under the name of reform [*cheers*], and to make war on the manners and customs of the people of this country under the pretext of progress. [*Cheers.*] During the forty years that have elapsed since the commencement of this new system—although the superficial have seen upon its surface only the contentions of political parties—the real state of affairs has been this: the attempt of one party to establish in this country cosmopolitan ideas, and the efforts of another—unconscious efforts sometimes, but always continued—to recur to and resume the national principles to which we attribute the greatness and glory of the country. [*Hear, hear.*]

The Liberal Party cannot complain that they have not had fair play. Never had a political party such advantages, never such opportunities. They are still in power; they have been for a long period in power. And yet what has been the result? I speak not, I am sure, the language of exaggeration when I say that they are viewed by the community with mistrust and, I might even say, with repugnance. [*Cheers.*] I have said it was a great mistake that those who succeeded statesmen like Mr. Pitt and Lord Grenville should have so conducted affairs that they built up their policy on the most contracted basis. Gentlemen, the Tory Party, unless it is a national party, is nothing. [*Cheers.*] Is it not a confederacy of nobles, it is not a democratic multitude; it is a party formed from all the numerous classes of the realm—classes alike and equal before the law, but whose different conditions and different aims give vigour and variety to our national life. I propose briefly to consider what is the present prospect of that national party. I have ventured to say that in my opinion, Liberalism from its essential elements—notwithstanding all the energy and ability with which its tenets have been advocated by its friends—notwithstanding the advantage which has accrued to them, as I will confess, from all the mistakes of their opponents—Liberalism, its true and inevitable tendency being recognised by the country, is viewed with mistrust. Now in what light is the Party of which we are members viewed by the country,

[5] For contemporary listeners, the term would connote "continental," "radical," or "equalitarian." Carlyle, Macaulay, and Mill, for example, use the term with similar meaning.

and what relation does public opinion bear to our opinions and our policy? That appears to me to be an instructive query; and on an occasion like the present, it is better that we should enter into its investigation than to pay mutual compliments to each other, which may in the end, perhaps, prove futile.

Now, I have always been of opinion that the Tory Party has three great objects. The first is to maintain the institutions of the country—not from any sentiment of political superstition, but because we believe that the principles upon which a community like England can alone safely rest— the principles of liberty, of order, of law, and of religion [*cheers*]—ought not to be entrusted to individual opinion or to the caprice and passion of multitudes, but should be embodied in a form of permanence and power. [*Hear, hear.*] We associate with the Monarchy the ideas which it represents —the majesty of law, the administration of justice, the fountain of mercy and of honour. We know that the Estates of the Realm,[6] by the privileges they enjoy, are the best security for public liberty and good government. We believe that a national profession of faith can only be attained by maintaining an Established Church [*cheers*], and that no society is safe unless there is a public recognition of the Providential government of the world and of the future responsibility of man. [*Cheers.*]

Well, it is a curious circumstance that during all these same forty years of triumphant Liberalism, every one of those institutions has been attacked and assailed—I say continuously attacked and assailed. And what, Gentlemen, has been the result? For the last forty years the most depreciating comparisons have been instituted between the sovereignty of England and the sovereignty of a great republic. We have been called upon in every way, in Parliament, in the press, by articles in newspapers, by pamphlets, by every means which can influence opinion, to contrast the simplicity and economy of the Government and sovereignty of the United States with the cumbrous cost of the sovereignty of England. [*Laughter and cheers.*]

Gentlemen, I need not in this company enter into any vindication of the sovereignty of England on that head. I have recently enjoyed the opportunity, before a great assemblage of my countrymen, of speaking upon that subject.[7] [*Cheers.*] I have made a statement upon it which has not been answered either on this side of the Atlantic or the other. [*Hear, hear.*] And only six months ago the advanced guard of Liberalism,[8] acting in entire

---

[6] The three estates of Britain are the Lords Spiritual, the Lords Temporal, and the Commons. The press is popularly termed the "fourth estate."

[7] On April 3, 1872, Disraeli spoke at Manchester, announcing that "the programme of the Conservative Party is to maintain the Constitution of the country."

[8] Sir Charles Dilke, Radical Member for Chelsea, initiated a republican campaign in a speech at Newcastle-on-Tyne on November 6, 1871, associating his cause with accusations of extravagance against the monarchy. On March 2, 1872, he proposed in the Commons that an audit be made of royal income and expenses since Queen Victoria's accession. The motion received only two "Aye" votes.

unison with that spirit of assault upon the Monarchy which the literature and the political confederacies of Liberalism have for forty years maintained, announced itself flatly as republican and appealed to the people of England on that distinct issue. Gentlemen, what was the answer? I need not dwell upon it. It is fresh in your memories and hearts. The people of England have expressed, in a manner which cannot be mistaken,[9] that they will uphold the ancient Monarchy of England—the Constitutional Monarchy of England, limited by the co-ordinate authority of the Estates of the Realm, but limited by nothing else. [*Cheers.*] Now, if you consider the state of public opinion with regard to those Estates of the Realm, what do you find? Take the case of the House of Lords. The House of Lords has been assailed during the reign of Liberalism in every manner and unceasingly. Its Constitution has been denounced as anomalous, its influence declared pernicious. But what has been the result of this continued criticism of forty years? Why, the people of England, in my opinion, have discovered that the existence of a second chamber is necessary to Constitutional government [*cheers*], and while necessary to Constitutional government, is at the same time, of all political inventions, the most difficult to secure. Therefore, the people of this country have congratulated themselves that by the aid of an ancient and famous history, there has been developed in this country an assembly which possesses all the virtues which a senate should possess—independence, great local influence, eloquence, all the accomplishments of political life, and a public training which no theory could supply. [*Cheers.*]

The assault of Liberalism upon the House of Lords has been mainly occasioned by the prejudice of Liberalism against the land laws of this country. [*Hear, hear.*] But in my opinion and in the opinion of wiser men than myself and of men in other countries besides this, the liberty of England depends much upon the landed tenure of England—upon the fact that there may be a class which can alike defy despots and mobs around which the people may always rally, and which must be patriotic from its intimate connexion with the soil. [*Cheers.*] Well, Gentlemen, as far as the institutions of the country—the Monarchy and the Lords Spiritual and Temporal—are concerned, I think we may fairly say, without exaggeration, that public opinion is in favour of those institutions, the maintenance of which is one of the principal tenets of the Tory Party.

Now, let me say a word about the other Estate of the Realm, which was first attacked by Liberalism. The most distinguishing feature or at least one of the most distinguishing features of the great change effected in 1832 was that those who effected it at once abolished all the franchises of the working classes. They were franchises as ancient as those of the Baronage of England; and, while they abolished them, they offered and proposed no

[9] A reference to popular enthusiasm on the occasion of the Royal Procession to St. Paul's on February 27, 1872, celebrating the recovery of the Prince of Wales from typhoid fever.

substitute.[10] [*Hear, hear.*] The discontent upon the subject of the representation which afterwards more or less pervaded our society dates from that period, and that discontent, all will admit, has now ceased. It was terminated by the Act of Parliamentary Reform of 1867-1868. [*Cheers.*] That Act was founded on a confidence that the great body of the people of this country were "conservative." I use the word in its purest and loftiest sense. I mean that the people of England, and especially the working classes of England, are proud of belonging to a great country and wish to maintain its greatness—that they are proud of belonging to an imperial country and are resolved to maintain, if they can, the Empire of England—that they believe, on the whole, that the greatness and the Empire of England are to be attributed to the ancient institutions of the land.

I venture to express my opinion, long entertained and which has never for a moment faltered, that that is the conviction and disposition of the great mass of our people; and I am not misled for a moment by wild expressions and eccentric conduct which may occur in the metropolis of this country. [*Laughter.*] There are people who may be or who at least affect to be working men, and who, no doubt, have a certain influence with a certain portion of the metropolitan working class, who talk Jacobinism. [*Laughter.*] But, Gentlemen, that is no novelty. That is not the consequence of recent legislation or of any political legislation of this century. There always has been a Jacobinical section in the city of London. [*Laughter.*] I don't mean that most distinguished and affluent portion of the metropolis which is ruled by my right honourable Friend the Lord Mayor. [*Laughter.*] Mr. Pitt complained of and suffered by it. There has always been a certain portion of the working class in London who have sympathised —perverse as we may deem the taste—with the Jacobin feelings of Paris. Well, Gentlemen, we all know now, after eighty years' experience, in what the Jacobinism of Paris has ended [*cheers*], and I hope I am not too sanguine when I express my conviction that the Jacobinism of London will find a very different result. [*Hear, hear.*]

I say with confidence that the great body of the working class of England utterly repudiate such sentiments. [*Cheers.*] They have no sympathy with them. They are English to the core. They repudiate cosmopolitan principles. They adhere to national principles. They are for maintaining the greatness of the Kingdom and the Empire, and they are proud of being subjects of our Sovereign and members of such an empire. Well, then, as regards the political institutions of this country, the maintenance of which is one of the chief tenets of the Tory Party, so far as I can read public opinion, the feeling of the nation is in accordance with the Tory Party. [*Cheers.*] It was not always so. There was a time when the institutions of this country were decried. They have passed through a scathing criticism of

---

[10] The 1832 Act disfranchised 80,000 ancient right electors, mainly from the artisan class.

forty years; they have passed through that criticism when their political upholders have, generally speaking, been always in opposition. They have been upheld by us when we were unable to exercise any of the lures of power to attract force to us, and the people of this country have arrived at these conclusions from their own thought and their own experience. [*Cheers.*]

Let me say one word upon another institution, the position of which is most interesting at this time. No institution of England, since the advent of Liberalism, has been so systematically, so continuously assailed, as the Established Church. [*Hear, hear.*] Gentlemen, we were first told that the Church was asleep, and it is very possible—as everybody, civil and spiritual, was asleep forty years ago—that that might have been the case. [*Laughter.*] Now we are told that the Church is too active and that it will be destroyed by its internal restlessness and energy. [*Laughter.*] I see in all these efforts of the Church to represent every mood of the spiritual mind of man no evidence that it will fail, no proof that any fatal disruption is at hand. I see in the Church, as I believe I see in England, an immense effort to rise to national feelings and recur to national principles. [*Cheers.*] The Church of England, like all our institutions, feels that it must be national, and it knows that to be national it must be comprehensive. [*Hear.*] Gentlemen, I have referred to what I look upon as the first object of the Tory Party— namely, to maintain the institutions of the country—and reviewing what has occurred and referring to the present temper of the times upon these subjects, I think that the Tory Party, or, as I will venture to call it, the National Party [*cheers*], has everything to encourage it. I think that the nation, tested by many and severe trials, has arrived at the conclusion which we have always maintained, that it is the first duty of England to maintain its institutions, because to them we principally ascribe the power and prosperity of the country.

If the first great object of the Tory Party is to maintain the institutions of the country, the second is, in my opinion, to maintain the Empire of England. [*Hear, hear.*] If you look to the history of this country since the advent of Liberalism forty years ago, you will find that there has been no effort so continuous, so subtle, supported by so much energy, and carried on with so much ability and acumen as the attempts of Liberalism to effect the disintegration of the Empire. And, Gentlemen, of all its efforts, this is the one which has been the nearest to success. Statesmen of the highest character, writers of the most distinguished ability, the most organised and efficient means have been employed in this endeavour. It has been proved to all of us that we have lost money by our Colonies. It has been shown with precise, with mathematical demonstration that there never was a jewel in the Crown of England that was so truly costly as the possession of India. How often has it been proposed that we should at once emancipate ourselves from this incubus. [*A laugh.*] Well, that result was nearly accomplished. When those subtle views were adopted by the country under the plausible plea of granting self-government to the Colonies,[11] I confess that I myself thought that the tie was broken. Not that I, for one, object to self-government. I cannot conceive how our distant Colonies can have their affairs administered except by self-government. But self-government, in my opinion, when it was conceded, ought to have been conceded as part of a great policy of Imperial consolidation. [*Hear.*] It ought to have been accompanied by an Imperial tariff, by securities for the people of England for the enjoyment of the unappropriated lands which belonged to the Sovereign as their trustee, and by a military code which should have precisely defined the means and the responsibilities by which the Colonies should have been defended and by which, if necessary, this country, should call for aid from the Colonies themselves. [*Hear, hear.*] It ought, further, to have been accompanied by the institution of some representative council in the metropolis, which would have brought the Colonies into constant and continuous relations with the Home Government. All this, however, was omitted, because those who advised that policy—and I believe their convictions were sincere—looked upon the Colonies of England, looked even upon our connexion with India, as a burden upon this country, viewing everything in a financial aspect and totally ignoring those moral and political considerations which make nations great and by the influence of which alone men are distinguished from animals. [*Cheers.*]

Well, what has been the result of this attempt during the reign of Liberalism for the disintegration of the Empire? It has entirely failed. But how has it failed? By the sympathy of the Colonies with the mother country. They have decided that the Empire shall not be destroyed, and in my opinion no Minister in this country will do his duty who neglects any opportunity of reconstructing as much as possible our Colonial Empire and of responding to those distant sympathies which may become the source of incalculable strength and happiness to this land. Therefore, Gentlemen, with respect to the second great object of the Tory Party also —the maintenance of the Empire—public opinion appears to be in favour of our principles—that public which, I am bound to say, thirty years ago was not favourable to our principles and which, during a long interval of controversy, had been doubtful.

Gentlemen, another great object of the Tory Party, and one not inferior to the maintenance of the Empire or the upholding of our institutions, is the elevation of the condition of the people. Let us see in this great struggle between Toryism and Liberalism during the last forty years what are the salient features. It must be obvious to all who consider the condition of the people with a desire to improve and elevate it that no important step

[11] The first experiments in self-government in the Empire were made in Canada (1848), Newfoundland (1854), New Zealand (1854), and New South Wales (1855).

can be gained unless you can effect some reduction of their hours of labour and humanise their toil. [*Hear, hear.*] The great problem is to be able to achieve such results without violating those principles of economic truth upon which the prosperity of all states depends. You recollect well that many years ago the Tory Party believed that these results might be obtained—that you might elevate the condition of the people by the reduction of their toil and the mitigation of their labour and at the same time inflict no injury on the wealth of the nation. You know how that effort was encountered—how these views and principles were met by the triumphant statesmen of Liberalism. [*Laughter.*] They told you that the inevitable consequence of your policy was to diminish capital, that that, again, would lead to the lowering of wages, to a great diminution of the employment of the people, and ultimately to the impoverishment of the Kingdom.

These were not merely the opinions of Ministers of State but those of the most blatant and loud-mouthed leaders of the Liberal Party.[12] [*Laughter and cheers.*] And what has been the result? Those measures were carried, but carried, as I can bear witness, with great difficulty and after much labour and a long struggle. Yet they were carried; and what do we now find? That capital was never enriched so quickly, that wages were never higher, that the employment of the people was never greater and the country never wealthier. [*Cheers.*] I ventured to say a short time ago, speaking in one of the great cities of this country, that the attention of public men should be directed to the condition of the people; that the health of the people was a most important question for a statesman. [*Cheers.*] It is, Gentlemen, a large subject. It has many branches. It concerns the state of the dwellings of the people, the moral consequences of which are not less important than the physical. It concerns their enjoyment of some of the chief elements of nature—air, light, and water. It concerns the regulation of their industry, the inspection of their toil. It concerns the purity of their provisions, and it touches upon all the means by which you may wean them from habits of excess and of brutality. [*Hear, hear.*] Now, what is the feeling upon these subjects of the Liberal Party—that Liberal Party who opposed the Tory Party when, even in their weakness, they advocated a diminution of the toil of the people and introduced and supported those Factory Laws the principles of which they extended in the brief period when they possessed power to every other trade in the country? [*Cheers.*] What is the opinion of the great Liberal Party—the Party that seeks to substitute cosmopolitan for national principles in the government of this country—on this subject? Why, the views which I expressed in the great capital of the County of Lancaster have been held

---

[12] Probably a reference to Cobden and Bright, who opposed factory legislation.

up to derision by the Liberal press.[13] [*Hear, hear.*] A leading Member—a very rising Member, at least, among the new Liberal Members—denounced them the other day as the "policy of sewage." [*Laughter.*]

Well, it may be the "policy of sewage" to a Liberal Member of Parliament. [*Laughter and cheers.*] But to one of the labouring multitude of England who has found fever always to be one of the inmates of his household—who has, year after year, seen stricken down the children of his loins, on whose sympathy and material support he has looked with hope and confidence—it is not a "policy of sewage" but a question of life and death. [*Cheers.*] And I can tell you this, Gentlemen, from personal conversation with some of the most intelligent of the class—and I think there are many of them in this room who can bear witness to what I say—that the policy of the Tory Party—the hereditary, the traditionary policy of the Tory Party, that would improve the condition of the people—is more appreciated by the people than the ineffable mysteries and all the pains and penalties of the Ballot Bill.[14] [*Laughter and cheers.*] Gentlemen, is that wonderful? Consider the condition of the great body of the working classes of this country. They are in possession of personal privileges—of personal rights and liberties—which are not enjoyed by the aristocracies of any other country. Recently they have obtained—and wisely obtained—a great enjoyment of political right; and when the people of England see that under the Constitution of this country, by means of the Constitutional cause which my right honourable Friend the Lord Mayor has proposed, they possess every personal right of freedom and, according to the conviction of the whole country, also an adequate concession of political rights, is it at all wonderful that they should wish to elevate and improve their condition, and is it unreasonable that they should ask the Legislature to assist them in that behest as far as it is consistent with the general welfare of the Realm? [*Cheers.*]

Why, the people of England would be greater idiots than the Jacobinical leaders of London even suppose if, with their experience and acuteness, they had not long seen that the time had arrived when social and not political improvement is the object at which they should aim. [*Cheers.*] I have touched, Gentlemen, on the three great objects of the Tory Party. I have told you what I believe to be the position of that Party in reference to public opinion. I have told you also with frankness what I believe the position of the Liberal Party to be. Notwithstanding their proud position, I believe they are viewed by the country with mistrust and repugnance. But on all the three great objects which are now sought by Toryism—the maintenance of our institutions, the preservation of our Empire, and the

---

[13] In his speech at Manchester on April 3, Disraeli urged that public attention be concentrated on sanitary legislation then before Parliament.

[14] The Ballot Act was passed in 1872, insuring that voting should be secret.

improvement of the condition of the people—I find a rising opinion in the country sympathising with our tenets and prepared, if the opportunity offers, to uphold them until they prevail. [*Cheers.*]

Before sitting down, I would make one remark particularly applicable to those whom I am now addressing. This is a numerous assembly; this is an assembly influential individually; but it is not on account of its numbers, it is not on account of its individual influence, that I find it to me deeply interesting. It is because I know that I am addressing a representative assembly. [*Cheers.*] It is because I know that there are men here who come from all districts and all quarters of England, who represent classes and powerful societies, and who meet here not merely for the pleasure of a festival, but because they believe that our assembling together may lead to national advantage. Yes, I tell all who are here present that there is a responsibility which you have incurred today and which you must meet like men. When you return to your homes, to your counties and your cities, you must tell to all those whom you can influence that the time is at hand—that at least it cannot be far distant [*loud and continued cheers*]—when England will have to decide between national and cosmopolitan principles. The issue is not a mean one. It is whether you will be content to be a comfortable England, modelled and moulded upon Continental principles and meeting in due course an inevitable fate, or whether you will be a great country—an imperial country—a country where your sons, when they rise, will rise to paramount positions and obtain not merely the respect of their countrymen but command the respect of the world. [*Loud cheers.*]

Upon you depends the issue. Whatever may be the general feeling, you must remember that in fighting against Liberalism or the Continental system you are fighting against those who have the advantage of power—against those who have been in high places for nearly half a century. You have nothing to trust to but your own energy and the sublime instinct of an ancient people. [*Cheers.*] You must act as if everything depended on your individual efforts. The secret of success is constancy of purpose. Go to your homes, teach them these truths, which will soon be imprinted on the conscience of the land. Make each man feel how much rests on his own exertions. The highest, like my noble Friend the Chairman, may lend us his great aid. But rest assured that the assistance of the humblest is not less efficient. [*Hear, hear.*] Act in this spirit and you will succeed. You will maintain your country in its present position. But you will do more than that—you will deliver to your posterity a land of liberty, of prosperity, of power, and of glory. [*Loud and continued cheering.*]

Lord Randolph Churchill

"Trust the People"*
Birmingham, April 16, 1884

Gentlemen, members of the Midland Conservative Club—I believe it is my duty this evening, in accordance with the rules of your institution, to deliver an inaugural address, and I imagine that I shall be expressing your unanimous sentiments when I assert that the Midland Conservative Club would gladly take this opportunity of recording a vote of thanks to its late president, Lord Windsor [*cheers*], who is a nobleman well acquainted with you all, ardently devoted to the cause of the Tory Party, and eminent for devoting his abilities and his resources to the promotion of the institutions of the locality in which he finds himself. I have also another task, much more difficult, and that is to express to you, or to endeavour to express to you, my very deep sense of the high honour which you have done me in electing me as president for the year. [*Cheers.*] I feel that honour greatly, and I wish it was in my power to express to you adequately my feelings on the point. You are a young club, but you have all the vigour of youth; and, although young, you have in a very short time made prodigious strides. [*Cheers.*] You are all united together not only for the ordinary purposes of a club—constant friendly conversation or convivial intercourse —but you have resolved and determined to make use of the friendship and the intercourse promoted by the club in order to forward the political cause. [*Cheers.*] You have banded yourselves together to do all that lies in your power to support the interests of the Tory Party in the Midland counties, and to support it in the most effectual way in which you can: by supplying what has been up to now and still is to a certain extent the great want of Conservative organisation—namely, voluntary assistance.

The organisation of a great political party is a matter of very intense interest. You are aware that in the old days, before the Reform Bill of 1867, organisation—political organisation—was a very different thing to what it is now. You had, as a rule, the leader of the party, who was not often or very directly concerned in electoral matters. The management of

---

* This text is from *The Times*, April 17, 1884, p. 10.

electoral organisation was generally left to the person who was known as the Parliamentary Whip, and he was assisted by a paid agent in the metropolis who was generally a person of legal attainments. Between them they disposed of certain funds which were known by the name of the Carlton Fund,[1] and they were in correspondence with certain agents in the constituencies in the country who also, as a rule, possessed legal attainments. Those parties possessed each other's confidence and were well qualified to carry on delicate or secret negotiations, and the concomitant—the ordinary concomitant—of those parties, which appears generally at election times, was a species of individual who has, I am happy to say, I believe almost vanished from this country, who was generally known as the "man in the moon." [*Laughter.*] And you had also those other individuals who were generally known as the "free and independent electors," who always carefully deliberated so long over their votes that they rarely recorded them until just at the close of the poll. [*Laughter.*] That was the old organisation, not at all confined to the Conservative Party, but equally the organisation of the Whig Party; and no doubt it may have been suited to the morality of that day, and it may have been suited to £10 householders. But that organisation has long been quite obsolete; it has utterly passed out of use on account of the great change which has taken place in the dimensions of our modern constituencies. Formerly the organiser had to deal with classes and with cliques; now he has to deal with great masses —and, moreover, intelligent, instructed, and independent masses—of electors. [*Hear, hear.*] Now those masses cannot be dictated to; they cannot be driven; they cannot be wire-pulled [*Hear, hear*]; they must be argued with and persuaded [*cheers*], and that is the first duty which, I imagine, devolves upon a member of the Midland Conservative Club. [*Cheers.*]

Now, I do not think that there will be any indiscretion if I admit that as regards party organisation the Liberals have been a little ahead of the Conservative Party. [*Hear, hear.*] They have been the first to adopt a peculiar form of organisation which is known as the caucus. [*Groans and cheers.*] I hope you will not be shocked at all if I tell you that I see nothing whatever objectionable in that form of organisation which is known as the caucus. [*Hear, hear.*] The caucus as a form of political organisation simply means this: that great masses of people, thinking that they are too unwieldy to manage their own affairs directly, confide the management of their affairs to certain elected persons in whom they have confidence, and those elected persons are responsible to the masses who have elected them. [*Hear, hear.*] That is the organisation which is known in America as the caucus. But the Radicals always push things to extremes [*Hear, hear*], and they have pushed the caucus to extremes to which it was never meant to be pushed, and they have used it for things which are undoubtedly mischievous and dangerous to the freedom of our political life. [*Cheers.*]

[1] The name probably came from the Carlton Club. Founded by the Duke of Wellington, the Club was the recognized social citadel of Toryism.

The caucus, as you know it here in Birmingham, has not been content to limit its work to party organisation but has endeavoured to interfere more or less—and more rather than less ["*Hear, hear*" *and laughter*]—tyrannically in dictating a policy which should be pursued on political questions by our public men. [*Hear, hear.*] I say that when the Birmingham caucus assumes to decide for itself public questions of the highest interest and of the greatest delicacy, to issue its mandates to the other associations in the country, and to issue its mandates even to Members of Parliament—I say the caucus has altogether transgressed the limits of its functions. [*Cheers.*]

Well, Gentlemen, the Conservative Party, although perhaps it does not move so rapidly, moves more surely than the Liberals. [*Hear, hear.*] We have our popular organisations. They are known by the name of Conservative Associations [*Hear, hear*], and so far as I know, they have always confined themselves to the duties of strict Party organisation and have not attempted to follow the evil examples which have been set them by your friends in Birmingham. [*Cheers.*] But our organisation is quite as popular as the Liberal organisation. [*Hear, hear.*] Your organisation in Birmingham is essentially a popular organisation. [*Cheers.*] In Lancashire and Yorkshire and in some parts of the South of England, these Conservative Associations have spread and flourished; but there still remains, I am able to tell you, a very great field of work which is yet untouched. Now, perhaps I may take this opportunity of saying what I have for some time wished to say to a public meeting—that the National Union of Conservative Associations is the centre and the nucleus of all—of many, not all—of the Conservative Associations throughout the country [*cheers*], and the aim and ambition of the National Union and of their council—and in this you, the members of the Midland Conservative Club, can render them great assistance—is to extend all over England—not only in our great towns but in our counties and also in our hamlets and villages—the popular principles of Conservative organisation. [*Cheers.*] The National Union is making great efforts in that direction. It does not meet with quite as much encouragement at headquarters as I should like to see. There is still a small knot of people whose minds dwell affectionately on the past and who look back with some longing to the happy days when organisation was conducted on non-elementary principles, which I described to you at the beginning [*laughter*], and they seem to look with some amount of apprehension on the popular voice. But I have no doubt myself that all that will soon subside, and I look to intelligent and experienced men like yourselves who form this club to assist those who are endeavouring to popularise the organisation of the Conservative Party. [*Cheers.*] Our object is to have a popular organisation by the election by those who are voters of the executive, who shall manage their Party affairs. Our object is to obtain, if possible, the representative executive and to obtain, if possible, an executive which shall hold itself responsible to those who have elected it. [*Hear, hear.*] In fact, my idea would be—and it is the idea, I am happy to say, of many of my friends—that the Tory Party should be like the English people—a self-governed party. That, I believe myself, is the only form of organisation by which you can attract and get the masses of the people to support the political opinions which you profess. [*Hear.*]

Now, all of you who belong to this club can undoubtedly, each of you, render immense service to the Conservative Party. Most of you are men well acquainted with business, commerce, and trade; and it is in your power to give most enlightened instruction to the masses of the people on subjects which undoubtedly most intimately concern their welfare. [*Hear, hear.*] I will especially urge upon you the importance of taking steps for the forwarding of clubs for the artisan classes. [*Cheers.*] Many of you, from the position which you hold, have sufficient time on your hands, which the artisan classes do not have, in which you may be able to devote yourselves to the most useful work. All I say is, make a trial. Let one of you or three of you or five of you settle among yourselves that you will take this subject up and start one or two or three clubs for the use of the artisan classes. [*Renewed cheers.*] My idea, if I may say so without presumption, in politics or in political organisation, is always to try a thing. You may fail, but at any rate, till you fail you do not know whether anything is good or bad. [*Cheers.*] In the great County of Lancashire there are numbers of these artisans' clubs in all the large towns, and I believe myself that that is one of the reasons why the Tory Party is so strong in the County of Lancashire. [*Cheers.*] Now, I say to you, let Birmingham also lead the way in this matter. [*Hear, hear.*] Birmingham has done good services to the Liberal Party in political organisation; let Birmingham be a little impartial and do good services to the Conservative Party [*cheers*], and let the extension and the popularising of the organisation of the Conservative Party be the aim and the object of every member of the Midland Conservative Club. [*Hear, hear.*]

That, Gentlemen, is my respectful and humble advice to you as your president for the year. [*Cheers.*] But, above all, let us be stirring; do not let us go to sleep. [*Hear, hear.*] I have a sort of idea that an election is not far off. [*Loud cheers.*] I do not know how it will come, and I do not quite know to a week when it will come. [*Laughter.*] But I can scent it in the air [*loud and continued cheers*], and my opinions on this subject, which a day or two ago only partook of the nature of suspicion, have almost deepened into absolute certainty from a curious act which is now being done by a certain Minister. Sir William Harcourt[2] [*groans and hisses*] has gone down to his constituents at Derby. [*Laughter.*] Now, since the year 1880, when owing to a consultation between Mr. Plimsoll[3] and his family [*laughter*] a vacancy

[2] Home Secretary in Gladstone's Cabinet.
[3] Samuel Plimsoll, Member for Derby, during debate on the Merchant Shipping Bill in 1875, spoke with such violence that Disraeli moved that he be reprimanded for disorderly behavior. During the 1880 Session, he posted placards denouncing his principal opponents in their constituencies. He avoided censure when the House decided that action against Plimsoll might set a precedent for abridgments of free speech.

was found for the wandering Home Secretary [*renewed laughter*], Sir William Harcourt has not been near his constituents to address them on public affairs [*"Shame" and laughter*]; and my idea is that Sir William Harcourt would not have gone near his constituents if he had not had certain reasons for knowing that he might have to meet them in a disagreeable way before long. But of this I think it my duty to remind you that the last election of 1880, which was undoubtedly disastrous to the Conservative Party [*"Hear, hear" and some cheers*], was lost by them principally and chiefly on account of their defective and neglected organisation. [*Hear.*] I can tell you as a matter of fact that that was the opinion of Lord Beaconsfield [*cheers*], and no better judge of politics has ever existed in this country. [*Cheers.*] Now, for Heaven's sake, don't let us be caught napping again [*Hear, hear*]; and I am certain of this: that if every Conservative in the country—and those who profess Conservative principles—would take the trouble to endeavour to realise to himself for a moment the immense political questions which will be involved in the next election [*Hear*], he would not lose a moment [*Hear*] before plunging into the fray and offering his services to the Conservative Association or the Conservative candidate of his locality. [*Hear.*] Why, in the election that is going to come off before long, the first principles of our English policy—of our English politics—are involved. [*Hear.*] The Radical Party of the present day are so numerous, so bold, and so enterprising [*cheering and groans*] that if we, the Tory Party, are not on our guard and are not equal to them in activity, we shall wake up one morning to find that the English Constitution has entirely disappeared [*laughter and cheers*] and that some Pinchbeck[4] American arrangement [*laughter*] has been substituted in its stead. [*Hear, hear.*]

Now, may I say a few words to you this evening on what I may call the first principles of our politics [*Hear, hear*], and endeavour to impress upon you the topics and the nature of the topics which you ought not to be afraid of dealing with when you are endeavouring to persuade to your views the masses of the electors. [*Hear, hear.*] After all, what is the great and wide difference which distinguishes the two great political parties who endeavour to attract the support of the English people? It has been often well and wisely stated, but I do not think it can be too often repeated. [*Hear, hear.*] The Tory Party clings with veneration and affection to the institutions of our country [*cheers*]; the Radicals regard them with aversion [*"Hear, hear" and "No"*] and will always give multitudinous and specious reasons for their unhappy frame of mind. [*Laughter.*] But can we, the Tory Party, give no good reasons, no good and convincing reasons, to the people for the faith that is in us? We do not defend the Constitution from any silly sentiment for the past or from any infatuated superstition about divine right or hereditary excellence. [*Hear, hear.*] We defend the Constitution

---

[4] Christopher Pinchbeck, an inventor who died in 1732. The term was used to mean spurious or counterfeit.

solely on the ground of its utility to the people. [*Cheers.*] It is on the ground of utility alone that we come to you, and if we fail to make good our ground on utilitarian arguments and for utilitarian ends, then let the present combination of Throne, Lords, and Commons be forever swept away. [*Cheers.*] The hereditary Throne is the surest device which has ever been imagined or invented for the perpetuation of civil order and for that first necessity of civilised society, the continuity of governments [*cheers*]; and he would be a bold man in argument who would assert that the hereditary character of the British Throne is a defect. [*Hear, hear.*] When we remember that the English Monarchy has endured for upwards of a thousand years, what device, may I ask you, of the wisest philosopher or the most acute mathematician could have discovered a monarchy more perfect, for all the purposes of a monarchy, than the one which the hereditary descent of a thousand years provided for us? [*Loud cheers.*] There are, I believe, many in this town who glibly tell you that the Monarchy is too expensive and is not worth the price. To them I would reply that it would be impossible to devise a form of government as effectual and yet cheaper and more simple. [*Hear, hear.*] And if in an evil hour you were to listen to those silly talkers [*Hear, hear*], the sums of money which you would have to pay for police and military in times of administrative change, the fluctuation of credit, the displacement of capital, the loss to the interests of industry and labour which constant and inevitable administrative change would produce, and the destruction of property in the absence of any recognised centre of authority—instead of being counted by the few hundred thousands which are the cost of an hereditary throne, would be counted by millions and millions. [*Loud cheers.*]

So much for the estate and the institution which the Radical Party glibly threaten. It is as well to remind ourselves from time to time of its history, its nature, and its uses. The immediate object of the Radical detestation is the House of Lords, in which they pretend to discover all the most unreasonable forms of class prejudice and privilege. I have no doubt myself that much of the enthusiasm with which the Radical Party clamour for the Reform Bill is due to the hope which they entertain that the passage of that Bill may possibly provoke a conflict between the Lords and the Commons, and that the Lords may forever come down. I am not concerned myself nor need you be concerned to defend all the actions of the House of Lords in modern times; but I could, if I liked, point to many bright instances of statesmanship and liberality on their part. [*Cheers.*] The House of Lords makes mistakes at times, I have no doubt, but even in this respect they will compare very favourably with Mr. Gladstone's Government or even with the Radical Party. I maintain that the House of Lords should be preserved solely on the hard ground of its utility to the people. [*Cheers.*] I do not put forward as an argument for its preservation its long history, in order to show you that it possesses great merits as an institution; I do not argue, as some do, that it has acquired stability from the reason that it is rooted in the soil.[5] I content myself with the fact of its existence at the present time, and I find in it not only a powerful check on popular impulses arising from imperfect information, not only an aggregation of political wisdom and experience such as no other country can produce [*cheers*], but above all because I find in it literally the only effectual barrier against that most fatal foe to freedom, the one-man power [*cheers*]—that power, Gentlemen, which has more than once prostrated and enslaved the liberties of France and which every moment terrifies the defenceless citizens of the United States. I hope I shall give no offence to anyone here if I suggest that you in Birmingham, on a small and limited scale, have had some little experience of one-man power.[6] [*Laughter and cheers.*] From a national and Imperial point of view you need never be alarmed about the dangers of one-man power so long as the House of Lords endures. [*Cheers.*] Be he Minister, be he capitalist, be he demagogue, be he Mr. Gladstone or Mr. Chamberlain [*hisses and cheers*] or even Mr. Schnadhorst[7] [*loud groans*] or Mr. Bradlaugh[8] [*groans*] or the Claimant[9] [*laughter*], against that bulwark of popular liberty and civil order he will dash himself in vain. [*Cheers.*] The House of Lords may perhaps move slowly; they may perhaps be over-cautious about accepting the merits of the legislation of the House of Commons; they may perhaps at times regard with some exaggeration the sentiment of extreme rights of property —that is the price which you have to pay, and a small price it is for so valuable a possession which guards you against great dangers. The House of Lords are essentially of the people; year by year they are recruited from the people. Every privilege, every franchise, every liberty which is gained by the people is treasured up and guarded by those who, animated by tradition and by custom, by long descent and by lofty name, fear neither monarchs nor ministers nor men, but fear only the people whose trustees they are. [*Cheers.*] It is recorded of the Sultan Saladin[10] that he always had a shroud carried before him in state processions to remind him of the perils and of the destination of monarchs. In like manner, I would advise

---

[5] Disraeli expressed this view in his speech at the Crystal Palace, June 24, 1872.

[6] A reference to Joseph Chamberlain, three times elected Mayor of Birmingham, now Liberal Member for Birmingham.

[7] Francis Schnadhorst helped to form the National Liberal Federation in 1877 and became its Secretary.

[8] Radical Member for Northampton from 1880 to 1891. Bradlaugh was denied his seat until 1886 for refusing on religious grounds to take the Parliamentary oath. The persecution was ended by judicial decision in the Court of Appeal. Churchill gained public notice through his opposition to Bradlaugh.

[9] The reference is to a celebrated case involving Arthur Orton's claim that he was the long-missing heir to the Tichborne fortune. After a prolonged trial, Orton was found to be an imposter; the case excited a great popular interest and was discussed in Parliament. He was released from prison in 1884.

[10] Sultan of Egypt and Syria, Saladin (1138–1193) took Jerusalem from the Crusaders in 1187.

the English people when speculating on or deciding political questions to bear always before their minds this great Constitutional fabric of the House of Lords, and to continually inquire into the reasons for its existence and preservation so that they may be perpetually and forever reminded of the dangers to which democracies are prone. [*Cheers.*]

I cannot pass from the subject of the House of Lords without alluding to the other bugbear of the Radical Party, the Church of England and its connexion with the State. [*Cheers.*] Now this question will be more or less directly before you at the next election. Again, I adhere to my utilitarian line of defence, and I would urge upon you not to lend yourselves hastily to any projects for the demolition of the Established Church. [*Cheers.*] But I would also, in dealing with this question, mingle a little of the wine of sentiment with the cold, clear spring water of utilitarianism. I see in the Church of England an immense and omnipresent ramification of machinery working without any expense to the people and daily and hourly lifting the masses of the people, rich and poor alike, up from the dead and dreary level of the lowest and most material views of life to the contemplation of higher and serener forms of existence and of destiny. [*Cheers.*] I see in the Church of England a centre, a source, and a guide of charitable effort, mitigating by its mendicant importunity the violence of human misery, whether mental or physical, and contributing to that work an alleviation from its not superfluous resources. [*Cheers.*] And I urge upon you not to throw that source of charity upon the haphazard almsgiving of a busy and a selfish world. I see the Church of England eagerly co-operating in the work of national education [*Hear, hear*], not only benefiting your children but saving your pockets. And I remember that it has been the work of the Church to pour forth floods of knowledge, secular and scientific as well as religious. But my chief reason for supporting the Church of England I find in the fact that when compared with other creeds and other sects, it is essentially the Church of religious liberty. [*Loud cheers.*] Whether in one direction or another, it is continually possessed by the ambition not of excluding but of including all shades of religious thought, all sorts and conditions of men. [*Hear, hear.*] And in standing out like a lighthouse over a stormy ocean, it marks the entrance to a port where those who are wearied at times with the woes of the world and troubled often by the trials of existence may search for and may find that "peace which passeth all understanding."[11] [*Loud cheers; "Babble"; "Bravo."*] I cannot and will not allow myself to believe that the English people, who are not only naturally religious but also eminently practical, will ever consent, for the purpose of gratifying sectarian animosities or for the wretched purpose of pandering to infidel proclivities [*Hear*], to deprive themselves of so abundant a fountain of aid and consolation or acquiesce in the demolition of a Constitution which elevates the life of a nation and consecrates the acts of a state. [*Cheers.*]

[11] Philippians 4:7.

Gentlemen, last, but not least—nay, rather first—in the scheme of Tory politics come the Commons of England [*cheers*] with their marvellous history and their ancient descent, combining the blood of many nations, their unequalled liberties, and, I believe, their splendid future. [*Cheers.*] The social progress of the Commons by means of legislative reforms on the lines and carried on under the protection of the Constitution whose utilities I have endeavoured to describe to you—that must be the policy of the Tory Party. [*Cheers.*] Their industries must be stimulated and protected by a lightening of the load of taxation and by a large redistribution of the incidence of taxation. [*Hear, hear.*] Their efforts to emancipate their brethren from the vices of an undeveloped civilisation—such as intemperence, crime, and a weak standard of morality—must be encouraged and facilitated. [*Cheers.*] No class interest should be allowed to stand in the way of those mighty movements, and with those movements the Tory Party must not only sympathise but identify themselves. [*Cheers.*] Social reform producing direct and immediate benefit to the Commons—that must be our cry, as opposed to the Radicals who foolishly scream for organic change and waste their energies and their time in attacking institutions whose destruction would only endanger popular freedom [*cheers*], while they would leave the social condition of the people precisely where it was before. [*Cheers.*] Apply this test to every legislative proposal, to every political movement, to every combination of circumstances and phenomena, and you will know what course to take, what line of action to adopt. I was much struck the other day in the House of Commons by a sentence which fell from the Prime Minister[12] when, leaning over the table and addressing the Tory Party, he said to them, "Trust the people." I have long tried to make that my motto [*cheers*], but I know and would not conceal that there are some—a few—in our Party who have that lesson yet to learn [*Hear, hear*] and who have not yet understood that the Tory Party of today is no longer identified with the small and narrow class which is connected with the ownership of land [*Hear, hear*], but that its great strength can be found and must be developed in our large towns as well as in our country districts. [*Cheers.*] Yes, trust the people. You who are the guardians, who are ambitious and rightly ambitious of being the guardians of the English Constitution, trust the people and they will trust you [*cheers*] and follow you. They will follow you and join you in the defence of that Constitution against any and every foe. [*Cheers.*]

Now, I dare say some of our Radical friends, who are always ready to sneer at any remark of that kind made by a Tory, will say, "Well, if you trust the people, why did you vote against the Reform Bill?" Well, that question sounds very plausible, but in reality it is a very foolish question. [*Hear, hear.*] In the first place, the Government of England is government by party, and under that system it is the general duty of the followers of Sir

---

[12] Gladstone.

Stafford Northcote[13] [*cheers*] to resist the legislation which may be proposed by Mr. Gladstone. [*Hear, hear.*] But my actual reason for voting against the Reform Bill was the omission of redistribution. [*"Hear, hear" and cheers.*] As I said last night,[14] the extension of the franchise and redistribution are one and indivisible [*"Hear, hear" and cheers*], and any attempt to divorce them one from the other is unnatural and portentous. [*Cheers.*] I did not vote against the Reform Bill from any distrust of the people. [*Hear, hear.*] The agricultural labourer will never destroy the British Constitution. [*Cheers.*] I have no fear of democracy. I don't fear for minorities. I don't care for those checks and securities which Mr. Goschen[15] seems to think of such importance. Modern checks and securities are not worth a brass farthing. [*Cheers.*] Give me a fair arrangement of the constituencies, and one part of England will correct and balance the other. [*Hear, hear.*] I don't think that electoral reform is a matter of national urgency. I should have been glad to see Parliament devote its attention and its time to other matters, such as finance, local taxation [*"Hear, hear" and applause*], commerce, Ireland, and Egypt. [*Hear, hear.*] I think that electoral reform is a matter of Ministerial urgency, of party urgency [*Hear, hear*], and that it is being treated as a question of party tactics [*Hear, hear*] and for the purpose of uniting and stimulating the already shattered Liberal majority. [*Cheers.*] And it was for these reasons that I voted against the Reform Bill, and I defy any person in this room to give better. [*Cheers.*] But you may be sure that the English Constitution will endure and thrive whether you add two millions or 200 to the electoral roll. So long as the Tory Party is true to its trust [*Hear, hear*], mindful of its history, faithful to the policy which was bequeathed to it by Lord Beaconsfield [*loud cheers*], the future of the Constitution, the destinies of the Empire, are in the hands of the Tory Party. [*"Hear, hear", "Oh, oh," and cheers.*] And if only the leaders of the Party in Parliament will have the courage of their convictions, grasp their responsibilities, and adapt their policy to those responsibilities, and if they are supported and stimulated by you who are here tonight and others like you in our large towns, that future and those destinies are great and assured. [*Hear, hear.*] To rally the people round the Throne, to unite the Throne with the people [*Hear, hear*]—a loyal Throne and a patriotic people [*Hear, hear*]—that is our policy and that is our faith. [*Loud and prolonged cheering.*]

[13] Conservative Leader in the House of Commons from 1876 (when Disraeli went to the Lords as Earl of Beaconsfield) to 1885.

[14] Churchill announced his candidacy the previous evening in Birmingham Town Hall. Challenging John Bright in his own stronghold, Churchill was narrowly beaten (4,989 votes for Bright to 4,216 for Churchill); but he was elected the following day for the London constituency of South Paddington.

[15] George Goschen, Member for Edinburgh, then a Liberal. When Churchill abruptly resigned as Chancellor of the Exchequer in late 1886, Goschen accepted the position. Churchill's action and the willingness of Goschen to accept office in Salisbury's Cabinet marked the political decline of Lord Randolph, who had seemed destined to become Prime Minister.

J. Keir Hardie

"Socialist Commonwealth"*

Commons, April 23, 1901

I rise to move the motion that stands in my name.[1] After the discussion to which we have just listened, in which one section of the community has claimed support from the State and shown that German steamship lines have an advantage over British lines because they are subsidised by the State, I trust the House will listen to the logical outcome of these arguments. I make no apology for bringing the question of Socialism before the House of Commons. It has long commanded the attention of the best minds in the country. It is a growing force in the thought of the world, and whether men agree or disagree with it, they have to reckon with it, and may as well begin by understanding it. In the German Empire, Socialism is the one section of political thought which is making headway, and to an extent which is, I believe, alarming the powers that be. Over fifty Socialist members occupy seats in the German Reichstag, between forty and fifty in the Chamber of Deputies in France, and between thirty and forty in the Belgian Parliament. Socialism on the Continent therefore is an established and recognised fact so far as its entry into politics is concerned, and if it be argued that while that may be true of the Continent it is not true of this country, I reply that the facts and conditions now existing in this country are such as to make it extremely probable that the progress of Socialism in this country will be at a more rapid pace than in any other country in Europe.

* The text is from *Parliamentary Debates (Authorised Edition)*, Fourth Series, Vol. XCII, cols. 1176–1180.

[1] "That, considering the increasing burden which the private ownership of land and capital is imposing upon the industrious and useful classes of the community, the poverty and destitution and general moral and physical deterioration resulting from a competitive system of wealth production which aims primarily at profit making, the alarming growth of trusts and syndicates able by reason of their great wealth to influence Governments and plunge peaceful Nations into war to serve their interests, this House is of opinion that such a condition of affairs constitutes a menace to the well-being of the Realm, and calls for legislation designed to remedy the same by inaugurating a Socialist Commonwealth founded upon the common ownership of land and capital, production for use and not for profit, and equality of opportunity for every citizen."

Needless to say, at this hour of the evening[2] it is impossible for me to treat this subject adequately, and I will therefore summarise briefly the principal arguments that it was my intention to submit to the House had time permitted. I begin by pointing out that the growth of our national wealth, instead of bringing comfort to the masses of the people, is imposing additional burdens on them. We are told on high authority that some 300 years ago the total wealth of the English nation was £100,000,000 sterling. At the beginning of the last century it had increased to £2,000,000,000, and this year it is estimated to be £13,000,000,000. While our population during the last century increased three and a half times, the wealth of the community increased over six times. But one factor in our national life remained with us all through the century and is with us still, and that is that at the bottom of the social scale there is a mass of poverty and misery equal in magnitude to that which obtained 100 years ago. I submit that the true test of progress is not the accumulation of wealth in the hands of a few, but the elevation of a people as a whole. I admit frankly that a considerable improvement was made in the condition of the working people during the last century. At the beginning of the nineteenth century the nation industrially was sick almost unto death. It was at that time passing from the old system of handicraft, under which every man was his own employer and his own capitalist and traded direct with his customer, to the factory system which the introduction of machinery brought into existence. During these 100 years the wealth of the nation accumulated, and the condition of the working classes as compared with the early years of the century improved, but I respectfully submit to the House that there was more happiness, more comfort, and more independence before machinery began to accumulate wealth. ["*No.*"] "No" is not an argument. I ask honourable Gentlemen opposite to listen and refute my statements if they are incorrect. I will quote an authority on this point whose words deserve respect. I mean the late Professor Thorold Rogers, who supports that view in his *Six Centuries of Work and Wages*.[3] The high standard of comfort reached by the labouring classes at the end of the last century has not brought them that happiness which obtained in England 300 years ago when there was no machinery, no large capitalists, no private property in land as we know it today, and when every person had the right to use the land for the purpose of producing food for himself and his family. I said that an improvement was made during the last century, but I would qualify that statement in this respect—that practically the whole of that improvement was made during the first seventy-five years. During the last quarter of the century the condition of the working classes has been practi-

---

[2] Hardie secured the floor at twenty-five minutes to midnight, the time for adjournment. Despite the hour and his limited time, he felt the opportunity was too great to be lost. Hardie's motion was the first Socialist resolution to come before the Commons.

[3] Published in 1884.

cally stationary. There have been slight increases of wages here and reductions of hours there, but the landlord with his increased rent has more than absorbed any advantage that may have been gained. I could quote figures, if that statement is disputed, showing that in all the industrial parts of the country rents during the past twenty years have been going up by leaps and bounds. I will refer to one authority whom even honourable Gentlemen opposite will not dare to call into question. Viscount Goschen,[4] when First Lord of the Admiralty, in defending the Government for refusing to give increased wages to labourers at Woolwich Arsenal, said on the 14th of April, 1899:

> If the position of the labourers at Woolwich and Deptford was as described, it was rather due to sweating landlords than to the rate of wages. The wages had been raised 20 per cent in the last ten years, and the house rents 50 per cent. It was constantly the case in those districts that the increase of wages only led to a larger sum going into the pockets of the landlords, and he was even told that some of the men who were locally the loudest in the cry for justice to the labourers were owners of cottage property who would benefit if the wages were raised.

In view of a statement of that kind, made by such an authority, I submit that my assertion is not without substance.

I come now to the causes which have forced thinking people of all ranks of society to reconsider their attitude towards Socialism. I refer particularly to the great and alarming growth of what are known as trusts and syndicates in connexion with industry. We have hitherto been accustomed to regard a trust as a distinctively American product. That cannot be said any longer. Let me name a few of the trusts and combinations which have been formed in this country within recent years. Amongst others there are the Cotton Thread Trust, with capital of £9,750,000; the Fine Cotton Spinners and Doublers, with a capital of over £5,000,000; the Bradford Dyers, £3,750,000; the Bleachers' and Calico Printers' Association, £14,000,000; Cory and Co., London, £2,600,000; Rickett and Co., London, £900,000; Armstrong, Whitworth, and Co., engineers, over £4,000,000; the Associated Cement Makers, over £7,000,000; the well-known Castle Line, £2,000,000; the Wilson, Furness, and Leyland Line and the Leyland Line, between them, £3,450,000. These are figures which might well give the House of Commons pause and cause it to reconsider its attitude towards the whole question of political economy. So long as industry is conducted by individuals competing one with another there is a chance of the article produced being supplied at an approximation to its market value, but competition has been found to be destructive of

---

[4] George Goschen, Member for Edinburgh, was made Viscount in 1901. He served as First Lord of the Admiralty from 1895 to 1900.

the interests of the owners and possessors of capital in this as in every other country. Three or four firms which formerly entered one market and competed with each other find it conducive to their interests to combine, thereby creating a monopoly which enables them to charge whatever price they like and to treat their workpeople in any way that seems good to them.

I approach this question of trusts from two points of view: first, from that of the consumer, who is at the mercy of an uncontrolled and, it may be, perfectly unscrupulous combination which cares only for dividends; and secondly—and this is to me of greater concern—from that of the worker. The consumer may protect himself, but the worker is helpless. I could quote instance after instance of the most scandalous and shameless persecution of workmen by these big trusts and combinations, railway monopolies and the like. I will refer only to one case, which occurred last year in connexion with the Great Eastern Railway. An employee was elected to serve on the Poplar Borough Council, exercising a right conferred upon him by this House, and being elected to a body created by this House. He was dismissed from his employment because he had permitted himself to be elected to apply a part of his own time to the public welfare without having obtained the leave of his employers. As John Stuart Mill—himself a convert to Socialism, despite the fact that as a political economist of the older school he had written against the system before he understood its full meaning and the necessity for it—wrote:

> The social problem of the future we [referring to himself and his wife] consider to be how to unite the greatest liberty of action with a common ownership in the raw material of the globe and an equal participation in all the benefits of combined labour.[5]

We are rapidly approaching a point when the nation will be called upon to decide between an uncontrolled monopoly, conducted for the benefit and in the interests of its principal shareholders, and a monopoly owned, controlled, and manipulated by the State in the interests of the nation as a whole. I do not require to go far afield for arguments to support that part of my statement concerning the danger which the aggregation of wealth in a few hands is bringing upon us. This House and the British nation knows to their cost the danger which comes from allowing men to grow rich and permitting them to use their wealth to corrupt the press, to silence the pulpit, to degrade our national life, and to bring reproach and shame upon a great people, in order that a few unscrupulous scoundrels might be able to add to their ill-gotten gains. The war in South Africa is a millionaires' war. Our troubles in China are due to the desire of the

---

[5] The quotation is from Mill's *Autobiography* (London, 1873), p. 232. The report changes slightly Mill's last sentence that reads, "and an equal participation of all in the benefits of combined labour."

capitalists to exploit the people of that country as they would fain exploit the people of South Africa. Much of the jealousy and bad blood existing between this country and France is traceable to the fact that we went to war in Egypt to suppress a popular uprising seeking freedom for the people, in order that the interest of our bondholders might be secured.

Socialism, by placing land and the instruments of production in the hands of the community, eliminates only the idle, useless class at both ends of the scale. Half a million of the people of this country benefit by the present system; the remaining millions of toilers and businessmen do not. The pursuit of wealth corrupts the manhood of men. We are called upon at the beginning of the twentieth century to decide the question propounded in the Sermon on the Mount as to whether or not we will worship God or Mammon. The present day is a Mammon-worshipping age. Socialism proposes to dethrone the brute-god Mammon and to lift humanity into its place. I beg to submit in this very imperfect fashion the resolution on the Paper, merely premising that the last has not been heard of the Socialist movement either in the country or on the floor of this House, but that, just as sure as Radicalism democratised the system of Government politically in the last century, so will Socialism democratise the country industrially during the century upon which we have just entered.

John Maynard Keynes

"Am I A Liberal?"*
Liberal Summer School, Cambridge, August 1, 1925

If one is born a political animal, it is most uncomfortable not to belong to a party; cold and lonely and futile it is. If your party is strong and its programme and its philosophy sympathetic, satisfying the gregarious, practical, and intellectual instincts all at the same time, how very agreeable that must be!—worth a large subscription and all one's spare time—that is, if you are a political animal.

So the political animal, who cannot bring himself to utter the contemptible words, "I am no party man," would almost rather belong to any party than to none. If he cannot find a home by the principle of attraction, he must find one by the principle of repulsion and go to those whom he dislikes least, rather than stay out in the cold.

Now, take my own case—where am I landed on this negative test? How could I bring myself to be a Conservative? They offer me neither food nor drink—neither intellectual nor spiritual consolation. I should not be amused or excited or edified. That which is common to the atmosphere, the mentality, the view of life of—well, I will not mention names—promotes neither my self-interest nor the public good. It leads nowhere; it satisfies no ideal; it conforms to no intellectual standard; it is not even safe, or calculated to preserve from spoilers that degree of civilisation which we have already attained.

Ought I, then, to join the Labour Party? Superficially that is more attractive. But looked at closer, there are great difficulties. To begin with, it is a class party, and the class is not my class. If I am going to pursue sectional interests at all, I shall pursue my own. When it comes to the class struggle as such, my local and personal patriotisms, like those of everyone else except certain unpleasant zealous ones, are attached to my own surroundings. I can be influenced by what seems to me to be justice and

* Our text is from *The Nation and the Athenaeum*, XXXVII (August 8, 1925), 563–564, and XXXVII (August 15, 1925), 587–588.

good sense; but the class war will find me on the side of the educated bourgeoisie.

But, above all, I do not believe that the intellectual elements in the Labour Party will ever exercise adequate control; too much will always be decided by those who do not know *at all* what they are talking about; and if—which is not unlikely—the control of the party is seized by an autocratic inner ring, this control will be exercised in the interests of the extreme Left wing—the section of the Labour Party which I shall designate the party of catastrophe.

On the negative test, I incline to believe that the Liberal Party is still the best instrument of future progress—if only it had strong leadership and the right programme.

But when we come to consider the problem of party positively—by reference to what attracts rather than to what repels—the aspect is dismal in every party alike, whether we put our hopes in measures or in men. And the reason is the same in each case. The historic party questions of the nineteenth century are as dead as last week's mutton; and whilst the questions of the future are looming up, they have not yet become party questions, and they cut across the old party lines.

Civil and religious liberty, the franchise, the Irish question, Dominion self-government, the power of the House of Lords, steeply graduated taxation of incomes and of fortunes, the lavish use of the public revenues for "social reform"—that is to say, social insurance for sickness, unemployment, and old age, education, housing, and public health—all these causes for which the Liberal Party fought are successfully achieved or are obsolete or are the common ground of all parties alike. What remains? Some will say—the land question. Not I—for I believe that this question in its traditional form has now become by reason of a silent change in the facts of very slight political importance. I see only two planks of the historic Liberal platform still seaworthy—the drink question and free trade. And of these two free trade survives as a great and living political issue by an accident. There were always two arguments for free trade—the *laissez-faire* argument which appealed and still appeals to the Liberal individualists, and the economic argument based on the benefits which flow from each country's employing its resources where it has a comparative advantage. I no longer believe in the political philosophy which the doctrine of free trade adorned. I believe in free trade because, in the long run and in general, it is the only policy which is technically sound and intellectually tight.

But take it at the best, can the Liberal Party sustain itself on the land question, the drink question, and free trade alone, even if it were to reach a united and clear-cut programme on the two former? The *positive* argument for being a Liberal is, at present, very weak. How do the other parties survive the positive test?

The Conservative Party will always have its place as a die-hard home. But constructively, it is in just as bad case as the Liberal Party. It is often no more than an accident of temperament or of past associations, and not a real difference of policy or of ideals, which now separates the progressive young Conservative from the average Liberal. The old battle-cries are muffled or silent. The Church, the aristocracy, the landed interests, the rights of property, the glories of Empire, the pride of the services, even beer and whisky, will never again be the guiding forces of British politics.

The Conservative Party ought to be concerning itself with evolving a version of individualistic capitalism adapted to the progressive change of circumstances. The difficulty is that the capitalist leaders in the City and in Parliament are incapable of distinguishing novel measures for safeguarding capitalism from what they call Bolshevism. If old-fashioned capitalism was intellectually capable of defending itself, it would not be dislodged for many generations. But, fortunately for Socialists, there is little chance of this.

I believe that the seeds of the intellectual decay of individualistic capitalism are to be found in an institution which is not in the least characteristic of itself, but which it took over from the social system of feudalism which preceded it—namely, the hereditary principle. The hereditary principle in the transmission of wealth and the control of business is the reason why the leadership of the capitalist cause is weak and stupid. It is too much dominated by third-generation men. Nothing will cause a social institution to decay with more certainty than its attachment to the hereditary principle. It is an illustration of this that by far the oldest of our institutions, the Church, is the one which has always kept itself free from the hereditary taint.

Just as the Conservative Party will always have its die-hard wing, so the Labour Party will always be flanked by the party of catastrophe—Jacobins, Communists, Bolshevists, whatever you choose to call them. This is the party which hates or despises existing institutions and believes that great good will result merely from overthrowing them—or at least that to overthrow them is the necessary preliminary to any great good. This party can only flourish in an atmosphere of social oppression or as a reaction against the rule of die-hard. In Great Britain it is, in its extreme form, numerically very weak. Nevertheless its philosophy in a diluted form permeates, in my opinion, the whole Labour Party. However moderate its leaders may be at heart, the Labour Party will always depend for electoral success on making some slight appeal to the widespread passions and jealousies which find their full development in the party of catastrophe. I believe that this secret sympathy with the policy of catastrophe is the worm which gnaws at the seaworthiness of any constructive vessel which the Labour Party may launch. The passions of malignity, jealousy, hatred of those who have wealth and power (even in their own body), ill consort with ideals to build up a true social republic. Yet it is necessary for a successful Labour leader to be, or at least to appear, a little savage. It is not enough that he should love his fellow-men; he must hate them too.

What then do I want Liberalism to be? On the one side, Conservatism is a well-defined entity—with a Right of die-hards to give it strength and passion, and a Left of what one may call "the best type" of educated, humane, conservative free-traders to lend it moral and intellectual respectability. On the other side, Labour is also well-defined—with a Left of catastrophists to give it strength and passion, and a Right of what one may call "the best type" of educated, humane, Socialistic reformers to lend it moral and intellectual respectability. Is there room for anything between? Should not each of us here decide whether we consider ourselves to be "the best type" of Conservative free-traders or "the best type" of Socialistic reformers, and have done with it?

Perhaps that is how we shall end. But I still think that there is room for a party which shall be disinterested as between classes and which shall be free in building the future both from the influences of die-hardism and from those of catastrophism, which will spoil the constructions of each of the others. Let me sketch out in the briefest terms what I conceive to be the philosophy and practice of such a party.

To begin with, it must emancipate itself from the dead-wood of the past. In my opinion there is now no place, except in the Left Wing of the Conservative Party, for those whose hearts are set on old-fashioned individualism and *laissez-faire* in all their rigour—greatly though these contributed to the success of the nineteenth century. I say this not because I think that these doctrines were wrong in the conditions which gave birth to them (I hope that I should have belonged to this Party if I had been born a hundred years earlier), but because they have ceased to be applicable to modern conditions. Our programme must deal not with the historic issues of Liberalism, but with those matters—whether or not they have already become Party questions—which are of living interest and urgent importance today. We must take risks of unpopularity and derision. *Then* our meetings will draw crowds and our body be infused with strength.

I divide the questions of today into five headings:

1. Peace questions
2. Questions of government
3. Sex questions
4. Drug questions
5. Economic questions

On peace questions let us be pacifist to the utmost. As regards the Empire, I do not think that there is any important problem except in India. Elsewhere, so far as problems of government are concerned, the process of friendly disintegration is now almost complete—to the great benefit of all. But as regards pacifism and armaments we are only just at the beginning. I should like to take risks in the interests of peace, just as in the past we have taken risks in the interests of war. But I do not want these risks to assume the form of an undertaking to make war in various hypothetical circumstances. I am against pacts. To pledge the whole of our armed forces to defend disarmed Germany against an attack by France in the plenitude of the latter's military power is foolish; and to assume that we shall take part in every future war in Western Europe is unnecessary. But I am in favour of giving a very good example, even at the risk of being weak, in the direction of arbitration and of disarmament.

I turn next to questions of government—a dull but important matter. I believe that in the future the Government will have to take on many duties which it has avoided in the past. For these purposes Ministers and Parliament will be unserviceable. Our task must be to decentralise and devolve wherever we can, and in particular to establish semi-independent corporations and organs of administration to which duties of government, new and old, will be entrusted—without, however, impairing the democratic principle or the ultimate sovereignty of Parliament. These questions will be as important and difficult in the future as the franchise and the relations of the two Houses have been in the past.

The questions which I group together as sex questions have not been party questions in the past. But that was because they were never or seldom the subject of public discussion. All this is changed now. There are no subjects about which the big general public is more interested, few which are the subject of wider discussion. They are of the utmost social importance; they cannot help but provoke real and sincere differences of opinion. Some of them are deeply involved in the solution of certain economic questions. I cannot doubt that sex questions are about to enter the political arena. The very crude beginnings represented by the suffrage movement were only symptoms of deeper and more important issues below the surface.

Birth control and the use of contraceptives, marriage laws, the treatment of sexual offences and abnormalities, the economic position of women, the economic position of the family—in all these matters the existing state of the law and of orthodoxy is still mediæval—altogether out of touch with civilised opinion and civilised practise and with what individuals, educated and uneducated alike, say to one another in private. Let no one deceive himself with the idea that the change of opinion on these matters is one which only affects a small educated class on the crust of the human boiling. Let no one suppose that it is the working women who are going to be shocked by ideas of birth control or of divorce reform. For them these things suggest new liberty, emancipation from the most intolerable of tyrannies. A party which would discuss these things openly and wisely at its meetings would discover a new and living interest in the electorate—because politics would be dealing once more with matters about which everyone wants to know and which deeply affect everyone's own life.

These questions also interlock with economic issues which cannot be evaded. Birth control touches on one side the liberties of women and on the other side the duty of the State to concern itself with the size of the population just as much as with the size of the army or the amount of the Budget. The position of wage-earning women and the project of the family wage affect not only the status of women—the first in the performance of paid work and the second in the performance of unpaid work—but also raise the whole question whether wages should be fixed by the forces of supply and demand in accordance with the orthodox theories of *laissez-faire*, or whether we should begin to limit the freedom of those forces by reference to what is "fair" and "reasonable" having regard to all the circumstances.

Drug questions in this country are practically limited to the drink question; though I should like to include gambling under this head. I expect that the prohibition of alcoholic spirits and of bookmakers would do good. But this would not settle the matter. How far is bored and suffering humanity to be allowed, from time to time, an escape, an excitement, a stimulus, a possibility of change? That is the important problem. Is it possible to allow reasonable licence, permitted Saturnalia,[1] sanctified carnival, in conditions which need ruin neither the health nor the pockets of the roysterers and will shelter from irresistible temptation the unhappy class who, in America, are called addicts?

I must not stay for an answer, but must hasten to the largest of all political questions, which are also those on which I am most qualified to speak—the economic questions.

An eminent American economist, Professor Commons,[2] who has been one of the first to recognise the nature of the economic transition amidst the early stages of which we are now living, distinguishing three epochs, three economic orders, upon the third of which we are entering.

The first is the era of scarcity, "whether due to inefficiency or to violence, war, custom, or superstition." In such a period "there is the minimum of individual liberty and the maximum of communistic, feudalistic, or governmental control through physical coercion." This was, with brief intervals in exceptional cases, the normal economic state of the world up to, say, the fifteenth or sixteenth century.

Next comes the era of abundance. "In a period of extreme abundance there is the maximum of individual liberty, the minimum of coercive control through government, and individual bargaining takes the place of

---

[1] The festival of Saturn celebrated in ancient Rome.
[2] John R. Commons, Professor of Economics at the University of Wisconsin. His *Legal Foundations of Capitalism* (New York) appeared in 1924.

rationing." During the seventeenth and eighteenth centuries we fought our way out of the bondage of scarcity into the free air of abundance, and in the nineteenth century this epoch culminated gloriously in the victories of *laissez-faire* and historic liberalism. It is not surprising or discreditable that the veterans of the Party cast backward glances on that easier age.

But we are now entering on a third era, which Professor Commons calls the period of stabilisation and truly characterises as "the actual alternative to Marx's communism." In this period, he says, "there is a diminution of individual liberty, enforced in part by governmental sanctions, but mainly by economic sanctions through concerted action, whether secret, semi-open, open, or arbitrational, of associations, corporations, unions, and other collective movements of manufacturers, merchants, labourers, farmers, and bankers."

The abuses of this epoch in the realms of government are Fascism on the one side and Bolshevism on the other. Socialism offers no middle course, because it also is sprung from the presuppositions of the era of abundance, just as much as *laissez-faire* individualism and the free play of economic forces, before which latter, almost alone amongst men, the city editors, all bloody and blindfolded, still piteously bow down.

The transition from economic anarchy to a regime which deliberately aims at controlling and directing economic forces in the interests of social justice and social stability will present enormous difficulties both technical and political. I suggest, nevertheless, that the true destiny of New Liberalism is to seek their solution.

It happens that we have before us today, in the position of the coal industry, an object-lesson of the results of the confusion of ideas which now prevails. On the one side the Treasury and the Bank of England are pursuing an orthodox nineteenth-century policy based on the assumption that economic adjustments can and ought to be brought about by the free play of the forces of supply and demand. The Treasury and the Bank of England still believe—or at any rate did until a week or two ago—that the things which would follow on the assumption of free competition and the mobility of capital and labour actually occur in the economic life of today.

On the other side, not only the facts but public opinion also have moved a long distance away in the direction of Professor Commons's epoch of stabilisation. The trade unions are strong enough to interfere with the free play of the forces of supply and demand, and public opinion, albeit with a grumble and with more than a suspicion that the trade unions are growing dangerous, supports the trade unions in their main contention that coalminers ought not to be the victims of cruel economic forces which *they* never set in motion.

The idea of the old-world party, that you can, for example, alter the value of money and then leave the consequential adjustments to be brought about by the forces of supply and demand, belongs to the days of fifty or a hundred years ago when trade unions were powerless, and when the economic juggernaut was allowed to crash along the highway of progress without obstruction and even with applause. Half the copybook wisdom of our statesmen is based on assumptions which were at one time true or partly true, but are now less and less true day by day. We have to invent new wisdom for a new age. And in the meantime we must, if we are to do any good, appear unorthodox, troublesome, dangerous, disobedient to them that begat us.

In the economic field this means, first of all, that we must find new policies and new instruments to adapt and control the working of economic forces, so that they do not intolerably interfere with contemporary ideas as to what is fit and proper in the interests of social stability and social justice.

It is not an accident that the opening stage of this political struggle, which will last long and take many different forms, should centre about monetary policy. For the most violent interferences with stability and with justice, to which the nineteenth century submitted in due satisfaction of the philosophy of abundance, were precisely those which were brought about by changes in the price level. But the consequences of these changes, particularly when the authorities endeavour to impose them on us in a stronger dose than even the nineteenth century ever swallowed, are intolerable to modern ideas and to modern institutions.

We have changed, by insensible degrees, our philosophy of economic life, our notions of what is reasonable and what is tolerable, and we have done this without changing our technique or our copybook maxims. Hence our tears and troubles.

A party programme must be developed in its details day by day under the pressure and the stimulus of actual events; it is useless to define it beforehand, except in the most general terms.[3] But if the Liberal Party is to recover its forces, it must have an attitude, a philosophy, a direction. I have endeavoured to indicate my own attitude to politics, and I leave it to others to answer, in the light of what I have said, the question with which I began—Am I a Liberal?

---

[3] Liberals seemed to discuss political doctrine or creed less than did Tories and Labourites; instead, they tended to address themselves to policies and proposals. See, for instance, speeches in this volume representing Liberal views: Asquith, Bright, Cobden, Gladstone, Lloyd George, Macaulay, Mill, Palmerston, and Russell.

Winston S. Churchill

"The Conservative Programme"[*]
BBC Broadcast, June 4, 1945

I am sorry to have lost so many good friends who served with me in the five years' Coalition. It was impossible to go on in a state of "electionitis" all through the summer and autumn. This election will last quite long enough for all who are concerned in it, and I expect many of the general public will be sick and tired of it before we get to polling day. My sincere hope was that we could have held together until the war against Japan was finished. On the other hand, there was a high duty to consult the people after all these years. I could be relieved of that duty only by the full agreement of the three Parties, and in addition, perhaps, fortified by a kind of official Gallup Poll, which I am sure would have resulted in an overwhelming request that we should go on to the end and finish the job. That would have enabled me to say at once: "There will be no election for a year"—or words to that effect.

I know that many of my Labour colleagues would have been glad to carry on. On the other hand, the Socialist Party, as a whole, had been for some time eager to set out upon the political warpath, and when large numbers of people feel like that, it is not good for their health to deny them the fight they want. We will therefore give it to them to the best of our ability. Party, my friends, has always played a great part in our affairs. Party ties have been considered honourable bonds, and no one could doubt that when the German war was over and the immediate danger to this country, which had led to the Coalition, had ceased, conflicting loyalties would arise. Our Socialist and Liberal friends felt themselves forced, therefore, to put party before country. They have departed and we have been left to carry the nation's burden. I have therefore formed, exactly as I said I would two years ago, another form of national government, resting no longer on the agreement of the three official Party machines but on the Conservative Party, with all the men of good will of any party, or no party, who would have been ready to give their services. I claim the

[*] The text is from *The Listener*, XXXIII (June 7, 1945), 629, 632.

support of all throughout the country who sincerely put the nation first in their thoughts. This is a national government. I shall stand myself as a Conservative and National candidate. Others may choose to call themselves National or Liberal National, and those who give us their support should vote National rather than Party on polling day.

Why do I claim the right to call this government "National?" First of all, because those who have left us have left us on party grounds alone. Secondly, because the Conservative Party, which has for many years been the strongest in this country, has been willing to abandon party feeling to such an extent that more than one-third of the members of Cabinet rank in this new government are not members of the Conservative Party. Many of these very able men, without whose aid we could not have got through the war, would prefer not to call themselves Conservative in a party sense; they stand as Nationals. And many Conservatives who might have looked forward to high office in the ordinary course have accepted cheerfully the interruption of their political careers in order to aid the nation in its time of trouble.

Particularly do I regret the conduct of the Liberal Party. Between us and the orthodox Socialists there is a great doctrinal gulf which yawns and gapes. Of this Continental[1] conception of human society called Socialism, or in its more violent form, Communism, I shall say more later; there is no such gulf between the Conservative and National government I have formed and the Liberals. There is scarcely a Liberal sentiment which animated the great Liberal leaders of the past which we do not inherit and defend. Above all, there is our championship of freedom at home and abroad. All the guiding principles of the British Constitution are proclaimed and enforced by us in their highest degree. When could any Liberal Party in the past have been offered a political programme of social reform so massive, so warm, so adventurous as that which is contained in our Four-Years' Plan?[2] Indeed, I feel that Mr. Gladstone would have recoiled from a great deal of it. He would have thought that it was going too far. But we still have a Rosebery and a Lloyd George to carry forward the flags of their fathers.[3]

Why, then, should the Liberal Party spurn us? Why, then, should they leave the fighting line? Why could not they at any rate stay with us until we have beaten down the cruel domination of Japan, and until we have set on foot some tolerable way of life for agonised Europe? I am sorry to tell you that they have yielded to the tactical temptation, natural to politicians, to acquire more seats in the House of Commons if they can at

[1] The term was used in a similar sense by Disraeli. See p. 432, footnote 5.
[2] The program, announced by Churchill in a radio broadcast on March 22, 1943, advanced a plan of postwar social and economic reconstruction. It stressed national insurance, price stabilization, full employment, improvements in health and education, and town planning and rebuilding.
[3] The reference is to the sixth Earl of Rosebery and Gwilym Lloyd-George.

all costs. It is also obvious that the more equally the two large parties can be brought together at the polls, the greater will be the Liberal bargaining power in the ensuing Parliament. That is, no doubt, why all the criticisms of the Sinclair-Beveridge Liberals[4]—you have to be very accurate about these things—are directed upon us; it is us they abuse.

I am sorry indeed to see such a line developed by men and women who are my friends, by a party many of whose ideals I cherish and will always strive to achieve or guard to the best of my strength. I do not wonder at all that a very large part of the Liberal Party have chosen the National course and still remain in office with us bearing our heavy burden. But I appeal also to Liberals in all parts of the land and I call upon them to search their hearts as to whether their differences with the British Government which will put through the Four-Years' Plan—a Government which is animated by the love of freedom, which is vowed to that harmonious medium of justice and generosity so befitting to the conqueror—has not more claim on their ancestral loyalties than has a Socialist Party Administration whose principles are the absolute denial of traditional Liberalism. Let them think it out carefully in the light of the speeches of the famous Liberal leaders of the past. Let them think it out carefully in the warmth which may come to the weary Liberal combatant when he sees his ideas increasingly accepted by enlightened peoples and victorious nations.

My friends, I must tell you that a Socialist policy is abhorrent to the British ideas of freedom. Although it is now put forward in the main by people who have a good grounding in the Liberalism and Radicalism of the early part of this century, there can be no doubt that Socialism is inseparably interwoven with totalitarianism and the abject worship of the State. It is not alone that property in all its forms is struck at, but that liberty in all its forms is challenged by the fundamental conceptions of Socialism. Look how, even today, they hunger for controls of every kind, as if these were delectable foods instead of wartime inflictions and monstrosities. There is to be one State to which all are to be obedient in every act of their lives. This State is to be the arch-employer, the arch-planner, the arch-administrator and ruler, and the arch-caucus-boss. How is an ordinary citizen or subject of the King to stand up against this formidable machine, which once it is in power will prescribe for every one of them where they are to work, what they are to work at, where they may go and what they may say, what views they are to hold and within what limits they may express them, where their wives are to go to queue up for the State ration and what education their children are to receive to mould their views of human liberty and conduct in the future.

---

[4] Sir Archibald Sinclair was Leader of the Liberal Party. In December, 1942, the famous Report of Sir William Beveridge proposed a comprehensive national program of health services and social security.

A Socialist state, once thoroughly completed in all its details and its aspects—and that is what I am speaking of—could not afford to suffer opposition. Here in old England, in Great Britain, of which old England forms no inconspicuous part, here in this glorious island, the cradle and citadel of free democracy throughout the world, we do not like to be regimented and ordered about and have every action of our lives prescribed for us. In fact we punish criminals by sending them to Wormwood Scrubs and Dartmoor[5] where they get full employment and whatever board and lodging is appointed by the Home Secretary. Socialism is in its essence an attack not only upon British enterprise, but upon the right of an ordinary man or woman to breathe freely without having a harsh, clumsy, tyrannical hand clapped across their mouths and nostrils. A free Parliament—look at that—a free Parliament is odious to the Socialist doctrinaire. Have we not heard Mr. Herbert Morrison[6] descant upon his plans to curtail Parliamentary procedure and pass laws simply by resolutions of broad principle in the House of Commons, afterwards to be left by Parliament to the Executive and to the bureaucrats to elaborate and enforce by departmental regulations? As for Sir Stafford Cripps[7] on "Parliament in the Socialist State," I have not time to read you what he said, but perhaps it will meet the public eye during the election campaign.

But I will go further. I declare to you from the bottom of my heart that no Socialist system can be established without a political police. Many of those who are advocating Socialism or voting Socialist today will be horrified at this idea. That is because they are short-sighted; that is because they do not see where their theories are leading them. No Socialist government conducting the entire life and industry of the country could afford to allow free, sharp, or violently worded expressions of public discontent. They would have to fall back on some form of Gestapo,[8] no doubt very humanely directed in the first instance. And this would nip opinion in the bud as it formed; it would stop criticism as it reared its head; and it would gather all the power to the supreme party and the party leaders rising like stately pinnacles above their vast bureaucracies of civil servants—no longer servants and no longer civil. And where would be the ordinary simple folk, the "common people," as they like to call them in America? Where would they be once this mighty organism had got them in its grip? I stand for the sovereign freedom of the individual,

---

[5] Maximum security prisons for criminals serving long terms.
[6] Labour Member for Hackney, Secretary of State for Home Affairs and Home Security in the War Cabinet.
[7] Member for East Bristol, Cripps resigned as Lord Privy Seal in October, 1942. The relation of Socialism and Parliament was a recurring theme in his speeches and writings.
[8] This expression proved damaging to Churchill in the campaign. The *Annual Register* for 1945 (p. 50) recorded that "he astounded multitudes of his hearers by declaring in all seriousness that if the Labour Party got into power they would use Gestapo methods to introduce Socialism into the country."

within the laws which freely elected parliaments have freely passed. I stand for the rights of the ordinary man to say what he thinks of the government of the day, however powerful, and to turn them out neck and crop if he thinks he can better his temper or his home thereby, and if he can persuade enough others to vote with him.

But you will say, "Look at what has been done in this war. Have not many of those evils which you have depicted been the constant companions of our daily life?" It is quite true that the horrors of war do not end with the fighting line; they spread far away to the base and to the homeland, and everywhere people give up their rights and liberties for the common cause. But this is because the life of their country is in mortal peril, or for the sake of the cause of freedom in some other land. They give them freely as a sacrifice. It is quite true that the conditions of Socialism no doubt play a great part in wartime; they are, as it were, a foretaste of what would happen under a complete Socialist system. We all submit to being ordered about to save our country, but when the war is over and the imminent danger to our existence is removed, we cast off these shackles and burdens which we imposed upon ourselves in times of dire and mortal peril, and quit the gloomy caverns of war and march out into the breezy fields where the sun is shining and where all may walk joyfully in its warm and golden rays.

Our present opponents, or assailants, will be, I am sure, very many of them, shocked to see where they are going and where they are trying to lead us. So they adopt temporary expedients; they say, "Just let us nationalise anything we can get hold of according to the size of our majority. And let us get the Bank of England into the hands of trustworthy Socialist politicians and we will go ahead and see what happens next." Indeed you would see what happened next. But let me tell you that once a Socialist government begins monkeying with the credit of Britain and trying, without regard to facts, figures, or confidence, to manipulate it to Socialist requirements, there is no man or woman in this country, who has, by their thrift or toil, accumulated a nest-egg, however small, who will not run the risk of seeing it shrivel before their eyes.

Mr. Greenwood[9] said two years ago—and I rebuked him for it then—"pounds, shillings, and pence are meaningless symbols." All this "meaningless symbol" talk is very dangerous and would enable a Socialist government which had got control of the Bank of England to issue notes that would destroy the value of any scrap of savings or nest-egg that anyone had accumulated in this country. The new National Government stands decisively for the maintenance of the purchasing power of the pound sterling, and we would rather place upon all classes, rich and poor alike, the heaviest burden of taxation they could bear than slide into the delirium

---

[9] Arthur Greenwood, Labour Member for Wakefield, Minister without Portfolio in the War Cabinet from 1940 to 1942.

of inflation. I warn you that if you vote for me and those who are acting with me, we give no guarantee of lush and easy times ahead. On the other hand, you need not expect pounds, shillings, and pence to become a meaningless symbol. On the contrary, our resolve will be that what has been earned by sweat, toil, and skill, or saved by self-denial, shall command the power to buy the products of peace at an equal value in sweat, toil, and skill. We will also take good care against unfair rake-offs and monopolies, and we will protect the common man by law against them, by controlling monopolies whose operations are any restraint on trade or oppressive to the smaller producer or distributor.

My friends, I have been forced into a discussion between the Socialist and individualist theories of life and government. That is because, for the first time, the challenge has been made in all formality, "Socialism *versus* the Rest." But now I must come back to the job which stands in front of us. What have we got to do—what have we got to do now? We have to bring home the soldiers who have borne the brunt of the war, and make sure by every scrap of strength and brains we possess that they find waiting for them food, homes, and work. The demobilisation scheme has been drawn up with all the advantages of seeing what mistakes were made last time. Mr. Bevin[10] has worked out a scheme which aims at being fair and square between one soldier and another, besides avoiding undue complications. But what a terrific business he has left us to carry through! And then you have to add to it that out of this demobilising army has got to be formed at the same time a new army to go out and finish off, at the side of our American brothers, the Japanese tyrants at the other side of the world. Here is a tremendous task.

And then come along serious people who say that we have got to get our mills going to provide new clothes and articles of all kinds for home and for our export trade—and what about our food, of which we grow only about two-thirds even under wartime pressure? We have got anyhow to buy food and raw materials overseas, and how are we going to pay for these? We gave our foreign investments largely to the common cause. We sold every asset we could lay our hands on in that year—that memorable grim year when we stood alone against the might of Hitler with Mussolini at his tail. We gave all—and we have given all throughout to the prosecution of this war—and we have reached one of the great victorious halting-posts.

Then we have our Four-Years' Plan, with all its hopes and benefits, with all the patient work that it means to pass it into law and bring it into action; all these are definite, practical, gigantic tasks; they will take every scrap of strength, good management, and above all, good comradeship, that we can possibly screw out of ourselves. What a mad thing it would be to slash across this whole great business of resettlement and reorganisation,

[10] Ernest Bevin, Labour Member for Central Wandsworth, was Minister of Labour in the War Cabinet.

with these inflaming controversies of Socialistic agitation! How foolish to plunge us into the bitter political and party fighting which must accompany the attempt to impose a vast revolutionary change in the whole daily life and structure of Britain! Surely at least we can wait till another election. The world is not coming to an end in the next few weeks or years. The progress of free discussion can show whose fears or whose hopes are well-founded.

Can we not get Europe settled up and Britain settled down before we plunge out on this hateful internal struggle? Let us, I say, concentrate on practical and immediate action and make sure that in gazing at the stars, we do not fail in our duty to our fellow mortals. On with the forward march! Leave these Socialist dreamers to their Utopias or their nightmares, let us be content to do the heavy job that is right on top of us, and let us make sure that the cottage home to which the warrior will return is blessed with modest but solid prosperity, well-fenced and guarded against misfortune, and that Britons remain free to plan their lives for themselves and for those they love.

Clement Attlee

"The Labour Programme"*
BBC Broadcast, June 5, 1945

When I listened to the Prime Minister's speech last night in which he gave such a travesty of the policy of the Labour Party, I realised at once what was his object. He wanted the electors to understand how great was the difference between Winston Churchill the great leader in war of a united nation, and Mr. Churchill the Party Leader of the Conservatives. He feared lest those who had accepted his leadership in war might be tempted out of gratitude to follow him further. I thank him for having disillusioned them so thoroughly. The voice we heard last night was that of Mr. Churchill, but the mind was that of Lord Beaverbrook.[1]

I am also addressing you tonight on the wireless for the first time for five years as a party leader, but before turning to the issues that divide parties, I would like to pay my tribute to my colleagues in the late Government of all parties or of none, with whom I have had the privilege of serving under a great leader in war, the Prime Minister. No political differences will efface the memory of our comradeship in this tremendous adventure: of the anxiety shared, of the tasks undertaken together, and of the spirit of friendly co-operation in a great cause which prevailed. I know well the contributions made by one and all to the achievement of victory. The fact that men of diverse political views, backed by the continuous support of Parliament and the country, were able to work together for five years is a great testimony to British democracy and the political maturity of this country. We concentrated our energies on the supreme need of winning the war and were able to agree on all the practical measures required. The plan for the immediate post-war period was more difficult, but here again, on such matters as social insurance, we were able to submit to the country proposals supported by us all. It was, however, inevitable

---

* This text is from *The Listener*, XXXIII (June 14, 1945), 656–657, 660.

[1] Beaverbrook, a prominent newspaper publisher, was a Tory leader and Churchill's principal adviser. During the war he served as Minister of Aircraft Production.

that when an approach was made to long-term policy in relation to the economic organisation of the country there would be a divergence of view on the principles to be applied, which necessitated an appeal to the country. The issues involved had sooner or later to be put to the people by the rival parties in order that they might be decided.

I should like to deal for a minute or two with the reason for having this election, for I notice there is some misunderstanding and some deliberate misrepresentation. We have fought a great war for democracy. It is the essence of the democratic system that the people should from time to time have the opportunity of deciding by what persons and on what principles they should be governed. In the United States of America, for instance, there must be an election of a President, war or no war, every four years. In this country the system is more elastic—but five years is the fixed limit for the continuance of a Parliament. The life of the present House of Commons has lasted nearly ten years. Parliament has again and again extended its own life. Here, fortunately, our elastic system allowed it to be done because we could not have had a proper election in the conditions of the war against Germany. But it would be contrary to the spirit of the Constitution for Parliament to extend its life unless there was some compelling reason. The point was very well put by the Prime Minister himself in introducing the Prolongation of Parliament Bill in 1944. He said, "I could not blame anyone who claimed that there should be an appeal to the people once the German peril is removed. I have myself a clear view that it would be wrong"—note that word *wrong*—"to continue this Parliament beyond the period of the German war. I can assure the House that in the absence of most earnest representations from the Labour and Liberal Parties, I could not refrain from making a submission to the Crown in respect of a Dissolution after the German war is effectively and officially finished."

Well, the Labour Party did not make a representation. But I received from the Prime Minister a proposal that we should continue until the war with Japan was ended, a period that might last more than a year. I could not accept, because I agree with the Prime Minister that it would be wrong to continue this Parliament, and I could not adopt his suggestion that instead of an election we should have a referendum. It would have been quite contrary to the spirit of the Constitution for a ten-years-old Parliament to have introduced such an exotic novelty in order to prolong its own life. The Labour Ministers offered to continue until the end of the session in the autumn, when the life of Parliament ended. An election then would have afforded a more accurate register and would have given to fighting men a fairer opportunity of voting. The Prime Minister, however, refused our offer, and under heavy pressure from his Party and the Party press, decided to have an election now. I am sorry that the Prime Minister, who after all owed his position as Prime Minister to the Labour Party, should have accused us of putting party before country. His proposal to carry on for another year would have meant a Conservative majority in the House during the crucial period of reconstruction.

The calling of a General Election involved a break-up of the Government but has not in any way altered the firm resolve of the Labour Party to do its utmost to win the war against Japan. While Labour Ministers were still in office, all preparations had been made to ensure that the men and materials necessary for this purpose should be made available. Equally, we are resolved to maintain as long as it is necessary the forces required elsewhere to deal with the aftermath of war. Everyone wants the fighting men home again as soon as possible, and I know that some have been away a very long time, but the job has got to be done. Plans for the re-allocation to help in the demobilisation of the forces have been carefully worked out to be as fair as possible. Hard cases are inevitable, but it is essential that the general plan should not be disturbed. There are many other matters which the late Government dealt with in order to provide for the immediate situation after the ending of the war against Germany on which there is no difference between parties. They are not in issue at this election. I hope, too, there may be continued agreement among us all on the main lines of foreign policy.

After the last war, the League of Nations was formed to maintain peace and the rule of law and to prevent aggression. My generation, that fought in the last war, hoped much from it. It failed, but the idea was right. The development of modern long-range weapons has made still more cogent the reasons for creating a world organisation charged with the maintenance of peace. The Labour Party, unlike the majority of the Conservatives, gave wholehearted support to the League through the inter-war period; and it welcomes the attempt now being made at San Francisco to create a world organisation armed with the power to deter the aggressor. It is, we believe, vital to world peace that the close co-operation of the British Commonwealth, the United States, and Russia should continue, but with the other peace-loving powers, they should take measures to prevent any would-be aggressor from disturbing the peace of the world. Germany and Japan must be deprived of the power to make war again. We must now recognise that if we wish for peace, we must take our share in providing the armed forces necessary to give power to the new organisation. Only when world security is fully established and war has become a thing of the past can we be rid of the burden of armaments.

But it is not enough to prevent war. There must be constructive action to remove the causes of war. World economic anarchy between the wars gave Hitler his chance. I hold that it should be a principal object of the United Nations to wage war on hunger, poverty, disease, and ignorance, and to promote the greatest measure of economic co-operation between all nations in order to raise the standard of life of the masses of the people. I welcome the conferences that have been held with this object and particularly the general acceptance now of the view always held by the Labour Party, though derided by our opponents, that the interests of this country and of the world demand the utilisation of abundance and not the artificial creation of scarcity. Holding strongly these views, a Labour Government will bring to the task of world economic co-operation an enthusiasm and a drive impossible to those who are so closely bound to private interests, especially where we seek to advance the standards of life of the less-developed peoples of the world, holding that economic progress, education, and increasing self-government must go forward together. It is in the light of these world problems that we must consider our domestic policy, for our prosperity depends on the prosperity of other nations.

It is here on domestic policy that we get the main clash between parties. The Prime Minister spent a lot of time painting to you a lurid picture of what would happen under a Labour Government in pursuit of what he called "a Continental conception." He has forgotten that Socialist theory was developed by Robert Owen[2] in Britain long before Karl Marx. He has forgotten that Australia and New Zealand, whose peoples have played so great a part in the war, and the Scandinavian countries have had Socialist governments for years, to the great benefit of their peoples, with none of these dreadful consequences. There are no countries in the world more free and democratic. When he talks of a danger of secret police and all the rest of it, he forgets that these things were actually experienced in this country only under the Tory Government of Lord Liverpool[3] in the years of repression when the British people, who had saved Europe from Napoleon, were suffering deep distress. He has forgotten many things, including—when he talks of the danger of Labour mismanaging finance—his own disastrous record at the Exchequer over the Gold Standard. I shall not waste time on this theoretical stuff which seems to me to be a second-hand version of the academic views of an Austrian professor, Friedrich August von Hayek,[4] who is very popular just now with the Conservative Party. Any system can be reduced to absurdity by this kind of theoretical reasoning, just as German professors showed theoretically that British democracy must be beaten by German dictatorship. In fact it was not.

The men and women of this country, who have endured great hardships in the war, are asking what kind of life awaits them in peace. They seek for the opportunity of leading reasonably secure and happy lives, and they deserve to have it. They need good homes, sufficient food, clothing, the amenities of life, employment and leisure, and social provision for accident,

[2] A Manchester industrialist and social reformer, Owen promoted the development of trade unions, model communities, and the cooperative movement.
[3] Liverpool's Administration (1812–1827) is associated with a period of social discontent and political reaction.
[4] An Austrian economist living in England who was critical of collectivist economic planning. The reference is to von Hayek's book, *The Road to Serfdom*, published in 1944.

sickness, and old age. For their children they desire an educational system that will give them the chance to develop all their faculties. How are we to provide our people with what they desire? Here rises the disagreement between parties. The Conservative Party believes that the basis of our economic activities must be what they call "private enterprise" inspired by the motive of private profit. They would reduce direction by and for the nation to the minimum. They seem to hold that if every individual seeks his own interest, somehow or other the interests of all will be served. It is a pathetic faith resting on no foundation of experience. The country has been run on these principles, though with inevitable modifications, for years. Yet a great number of people in this country have always been badly housed, badly fed and clothed, and denied very often the opportunity of working. While our agriculture has languished, finance has been misdirected and many of our most vital industries have, as recent inquiries have shown, been inefficiently and wastefully managed. The Labour Party, on the contrary, believes that if you want certain results you must plan to secure them, but in peace as in war the public interest must come first; and that if in war, despite the diversion of most of our energies to making instruments of destruction and despite the shortage of supply imposed by war conditions, we were able to provide food, clothing, and employment for all our people, it is not impossible to do the same in peace, provided the Government has the will and the power to act.

During the war the Government, in the national interest, imposed many restrictions on the right of the individual to do as he pleased. Some of these, though necessary, were very irksome. They should be removed as soon as the necessity for them has passed away. But others are still vitally needed to protect the public from profiteers and monopolists, yet strong elements in the Conservative Party clamour as their predecessors did successfully in 1918 for their abolition. There is a world shortage of many kinds of food and of most consumable goods, while there is in the hands of the public a large volume of purchasing power. If controls are removed there will be a rush for the available commodities; prices would soar, profiteers would have a good time, while the general public would lose. Wage and salary earners, pensioners, and investors in war savings would find that their money would purchase much less than they expected. The late Government, wisely and firmly, by strict control, maintained prices fairly steady. The Labour Party is determined not to countenance inflation. We want a stable price level. Inflation is no imaginary danger; it is just what happened after the last war where in a hurry-in election the country was rushed in to return a huge reactionary majority at the instance of the war leader, Mr. Lloyd George. Similarly, if controls are removed from rents, the present shortage would mean that the community would pay an immense toll to the landlords. I am sure that the wiser Conservatives would agree with all this. So, no doubt, did their predecessors in 1918; but they yielded to the clamour of private interests.

We believe that it is essential to maintain the economic controls necessary to give direction to our national life. We must ensure that the natural resources of the country are fully utilised. Private interest must not be allowed to stand in the way of national welfare. For some time to come the raw materials will be scarce, and they must be used to the best advantage. The savings of the nation must be directed into those channels where they will produce the things that are most needed, not those that will give the most immediate profit. It is obvious to all that building materials and labour must be employed on providing the urgently needed houses, schools, factories, and not on luxury buildings and non-essentials. But the same principle of first things first should be applied to other things than building. We cannot afford to waste the land of this country. We need a prosperous agriculture. We need well-planned, well-built cities with parks and playing fields, homes and schools, factories and shops in their right relationship. We do not want our beautiful country spoilt by haphazard development, dictated only by the hope of gain. Enough damage has already been done in the past. Therefore we must control the use of the land and have power to acquire what the nation or the local council need, paying a fair price, but not an extravagant ransom extorted on account of the needs of the community.

We need a planned location of industry to give a balance to the country and to preserve social capital. We must have no more distressed areas. No one of these things can be effected without giving power to the Government. The Prime Minister made much play last night with the rights of the individual and the danger of people being ordered about by officials. I entirely agree that people should have the greatest freedom compatible with the freedom of others. But there was a time when employers were free to work little children sixteen hours a day. I remember when employers were free to employ sweated women working on finishing trousers at a penny-ha'penny a pair. There was a time when people were free to neglect sanitation, so that thousands died of preventable disease. For years every attempt to remedy these crying evils was blocked by the same plea of freedom for the individual. It was, in fact, freedom for the rich and slavery for the poor. Make no mistake, it has only been through the power of the State, given to it by Parliament, that the general public has been protected against the greed of ruthless profit-makers and profiteers.

No one supposes that all the industries of this country can or should be socialised forthwith, but there are certain great basic industries which, from their nature, are ripe for conversion into public services. Inland transport is tending more and more towards monopoly, and it is unsafe to leave a monopoly in private hands. A Conservative Government has bought out the owners of coal and proposes to leave the getting and distributing of it in the hands of the same people whose inefficiency has been condemned by every impartial inquiry. Much of the production of gas and electricity is in public hands, to the great advantage of the consumers. Labour's policy is to transform the whole business of providing fuel and power and light into a public service, a similar policy to be pursued in relation to iron and steel. In every case there must be a suitable organisation which, while protecting the public interest, will give scope for business organisation and the application of scientific methods. There will be plenty of scope for the technician and for that enterprise which is so often lacking in private industry today; fair but not excessive compensation will be paid. Wherever there is danger of monopolies and cartels, there must be public supervision to prevent exploitation. Those who cry out against state control are generally the loudest in demanding subsidies, tariffs, and other state aids for themselves. It is Labour's policy to stimulate industry, especially to help our export trade, but that help will only be given on condition that industry and trade are efficient.

I have not time tonight to deal with other points in Labour's programme. In particular, there are proposals for the social services, for health, education, for the application of science to the problems that face us. My colleagues who will be speaking later in the campaign will deal in more detail with subjects to which I have only referred in passing. It has been my purpose to give you the general principles of Labour's policy, with some illustrations of particular points. You may ask, "Can these things be done? Can we give to our returned fighting men and to all our people the kind of life which they so richly deserve? Can we have the Britain we desire?" My answer is that in the war, we accomplished far harder tasks than this. I speak on the eve of the anniversary of D-Day. The people who planned and carried through the Normandy landings will not be daunted by any difficulties. The British people can do these things if they will them and work for them.

In the ranks of the Labour Party are men with vision, enthusiasm, and varied experience. My Labour colleagues have shown that they can administer great departments, accept heavy responsibilities, and plan and carry out far-reaching policies. We are confident that if you give Labour the power it can and will lead this country through the dangers and difficulties of the time into a happier and securer future. Forty years ago the Labour Party might, with some justice, have been called a "class" party representing almost exclusively the wage earners. It is still based on organised labour but has steadily become more and more inclusive. In the ranks of the Parliamentary Party and among our candidates, you find numbers of men and women drawn from every class and occupation in the community. Wage and salary earners form the majority, but there are many from other walks of life—from the professions, from the business world—giving a wide range of experience. More than 120 of our candidates come from the fighting services, so that youth is well represented. The present Government is Conservative; I do not suppose that the Prime Minister expected anyone to take seriously his claim that the addition to the Conservative majority of a few Independents who were staying on as temporary caretakers, and some tame Liberals who owe their seats to Tory votes and obey strictly the Tory Whip, really makes his Government National; it is Conservative.

The Conservative Party remains, as always, a "class" party. In twenty-three years in the House of Commons, I cannot recall more than half a dozen Conservatives from the ranks of the wage-earners; it represents today, as in the past, the forces of property and privilege. The Labour Party is in fact the one party which most nearly reflects in its representation and composition all the main streams which flow into the great river of our national life. Our appeal to you, therefore, is not narrow or sectional. We are proud of the fact that our country in the hours of its greatest danger stood firm and united, setting an example to the world of how a great people rose to the heights of the occasion and saved democracy and liberty. We are proud of the self-sacrifice and devotion displayed by men and women in every walk of life in this great adventure.

We call you to another great adventure which will demand the same high qualities as those shown in the war—the adventure of civilisation. We have seen a great and powerful nation return to barbarism. We have seen European civilisation almost destroyed, an attempt made to set aside the moral principles on which it has been built. It is for us to help to reknit the fabric of civilised life woven through the centuries and with the other nations to seek to create a world in which free peoples living their own distinctive lives in a society of nations co-operate free from the fear of war. We have to plan the broad lines of our national life so that all may have the duty and the opportunity of rendering service to the nation, everyone in his or her own sphere, and that all may help to create and share in an increasing material prosperity free from the fear of want. We have to preserve and enhance the beauty of our country, to make it a place where men and women may live finely and happily, free to worship God in their own way, free to speak their minds, free citizens of a great country.

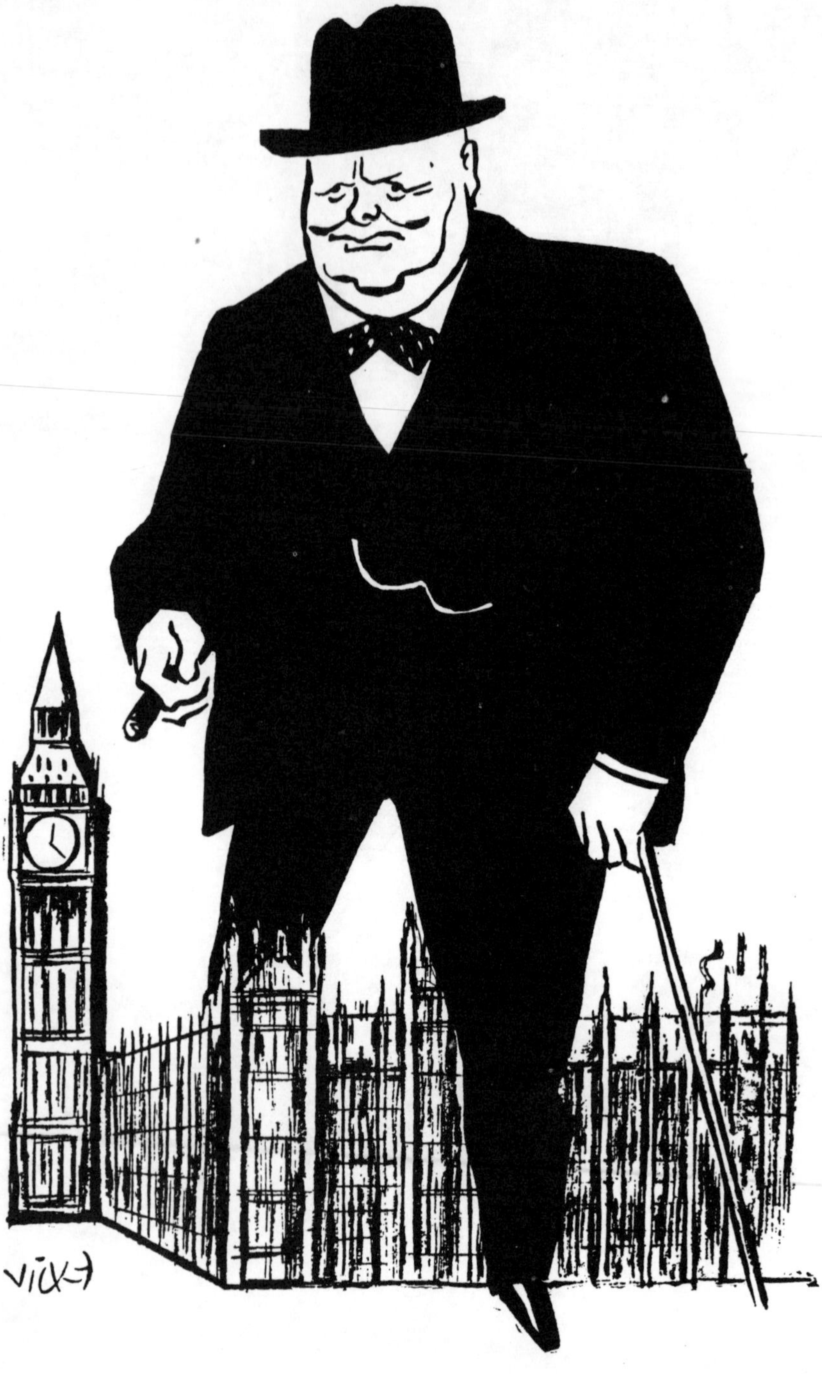
VICKY

7

World Wars and Unstable Peace

David Lloyd George

"Appeal to the Nation"*
London, September 19, 1914

I have come here this afternoon to talk to my fellow-countrymen about this great war and the part we ought to take in it. I feel my task is easier after we have been listening to the greatest battle-song in the world.[1] [*Cheers.*] There is no man in this room who has always regarded the prospects of engaging in a great war with greater reluctance, with greater repugnance than I have done throughout the whole of my political life.[2] There is no man either inside or outside of this room more convinced that we could not have avoided it without national dishonour. [*Cheers.*] I am fully alive to the fact that whenever a nation has engaged in any war she has always invoked the sacred name of honour. Many a crime has been committed in its name; there are some crimes being committed now. But all the same, national honour is a reality, and any nation that disregards it is doomed. Why is our honour as a country involved in this war? Because in the first place we are bound in an honourable obligation to defend the independence, the liberty, the integrity of a small neighbour that has lived peaceably, but she could not have compelled us because she was weak. [*"Quite right!"*] The man who declines to discharge his debt because his creditor is too poor to enforce it is a blackguard. [*Cheers.*]

We entered into this treaty, a solemn treaty, a full treaty, to defend Belgium and her integrity. Our signatures are attached to the document. Our signatures do not stand alone. This was not the only country to defend the integrity of Belgium. Russia, France, Austria, and Prussia [*hisses*]— they are all there. Why did they not perform the obligation? It is suggested that this treaty is purely an excuse on our part. It is our low craft and cunning, just to cloak our jealousy of a superior civilisation which we are

---

* This text is taken from *The Times*, September 20, 1914, pp. 3–4.

[1] The reference is to "March of the Men of Harlech." Harlech was the last fortress in England and Wales to surrender to the Yorkists in 1468.

[2] Early in his career, Lloyd George was primarily interested in domestic rather than foreign policy. He was opposed to war and hoped that "the world would ultimately abandon war as a tribunal for adjudicating international disputes." He was appointed Minister of Munitions on May 26, 1915, by Prime Minister Asquith.

attempting to destroy. Our answer is the action we took in 1870.[3] Mr. Gladstone was then Prime Minister. Lord Granville, I think, was Foreign Secretary. I have never heard it alleged to their charge that they were ever jingos.[4] That treaty bond was this: we called upon the belligerent powers to respect that treaty. We called upon France, we called upon Germany. At that time, bear in mind, the greatest danger to Belgium came from France and not from Germany. We intervened to protect Belgium against France exactly as we are doing now to protect her against Germany. We are proceeding exactly in the same way. We invited both the belligerent powers to state that they had no intention of violating Belgian territory. What was the answer given by Bismarck? He said it was superfluous to ask Prussia such a question in view of the treaties in force. France gave a similar answer. We received the thanks at that time of the Belgian people for our intervention in a very remarkable document. This is a document addressed by the Municipality of Brussels to Queen Victoria after that intervention:

> The great and noble people over whose destinies you preside have just given a further proof of its benevolent sentiments towards this country. The voice of the English nation has been heard above the din of arms. It has asserted the principles of justice and right. Next to the unalterable attachment of the Belgian people to their independence, the strongest sentiment which fills their hearts is that of an imperishable gratitude to the people of Great Britain.

[*Loud cheers.*]

That was in 1870. Three or four days after that document of thanks, the French Army was wedged up against the Belgian frontier, every means of escape shut up by a ring of flame from Prussian cannon. There was one way of escape—by violating the neutrality of Belgium. The French on that occasion preferred ruin and humiliation to the breaking of their bond. The French Emperor,[5] French marshals, 100,000 gallant Frenchmen in arms preferred to be carried captive to the strange land of their enemy rather than dishonour the name of their country. It was the last French Army defeat. Had they violated Belgian neutrality the whole history of that war would have been changed. And yet it was to the interest of France to break the treaty. She did not do it. It is to the interest of Prussia to break the treaty, and she has done it. ["*Shame.*"] She avowed it with cynical contempt for every principle of justice. She says treaties only bind you when it is to

---

[3] During the Franco-Prussian War, Gladstone proposed a treaty to France and Germany providing that if either country invaded Belgium, Britain would assist the other in defending Belgian interests. Both France and Germany signed the document.

[4] "Jingos" was first used to designate supporters of war, according to G. M. Trevelyan, in 1876 during the Russian incursions against Bulgaria. A popular song ran:

> We don't want to fight,
> But by Jingo, if we do,
> We've got the men, we've got the ships,
> We've got the money too.

[5] Napoleon III.

your interest to keep them. "What is a treaty?" says the German Chancellor. "A scrap of paper."[6] Have you any £5 notes about you? I am not calling for them. [*Laughter.*] Have you any of those neat little Treasury £1 notes? [*Laughter.*] If you have, burn them; they are only scraps of paper. [*Cheers.*] What are they made of? Rags. [*Laughter.*] What are they worth? The whole credit of the British Empire. [*Cheers.*]

Scraps of paper. I have been dealing with scraps of paper within the last month. We suddenly found the commerce of the world coming to a standstill. The machine had stopped. I will tell you why. We discovered, many of us for the first time, that the machinery of commerce was moved by bills of exchange. I have seen some of them [*laughter*]—wretched, crinkled, scrawled over, blotched, frowsy—and yet wretched little scraps of paper move great ships, laden with thousands of tons of precious cargo from one end of the world to the other. [*Cheers.*] What was the motive power behind them? The honour of commercial men. [*Cheers.*] Treaties are the currency of international statesmanship. Let us be fair. German merchants and German traders have the reputation of being as upright and straightforward as any traders in the world; but if the currency of German commerce is to be debased to the level of that of her statesmanship, no trader from Shanghai to Valparaiso will ever look at a German signature again. [*Cheers.*]

This doctrine of the scrap of paper, this doctrine which is proclaimed by Bernhardi[7] that treaties bind a nation only as long as it is to its interest, goes under the root of all public law. It is the straight road to barbarism. It is just as if you removed the magnetic pole whenever it was in the way of a German cruiser. [*Laughter.*] The whole navigation of the seas would become dangerous, difficult, impossible, and the whole machinery of civilisation will break down if this doctrine wins in this war. We are fighting against barbarism, and there is only one way of putting it right. If there are nations that say they will respect treaties only when it is to their interests to do so, we must make it to their interests to do so for the future. [*Cheers.*]

Just look at the interview which took place between our Ambassador and great German officials. When their attention was called to this treaty to which they were parties, they said, "We cannot help that." Rapidity of action was the great German asset. There is a greater asset for a nation than rapidity of action, and that is honest dealing. [*Cheers.*] What are her excuses? She says that Belgium was plotting against her, that Belgium was engaged in a great conspiracy with Britain and with France to attack her. Not merely is it not true, but Germany knows it is not true. What is her other excuse? France meant to invade Germany through Belgium. Absolutely untrue. France offered Belgium five Army corps to defend her if

---

[6] Theobald von Bethmann-Hollweg, in a dispatch to Sir Edward Goschen, British Ambassador to Germany, on August 4, 1914, declared: "Just for a scrap of paper, Great Britain is going to make war on a kindred nation who desires nothing better than to be friends with her."

[7] Friedrich von Bernhardi, Prussian general and military writer.

she were attacked. Belgium said, "I don't require them; I have got the word of the Kaiser. Shall Cæsar send a lie?"

All these tales about conspiracy have been vamped up since. A great nation ought to be ashamed to behave like a fraudulent bankrupt. It is not true what she says. She has deliberately broken this treaty, and we were in honour bound to stand by Belgium. [*Cheers.*] Belgium has been treated brutally—how brutally we shall not yet know. We know already too much. What had she done? Had she sent an ultimatum to Germany? Had she challenged Germany? Was she preparing to make war on Germany? Had she inflicted any wrong upon Germany which the Kaiser was bound to redress? She was one of the most unoffending little countries in Europe. There she was: peaceable, industrious, thrifty, hard-working, giving offence to no one. Her cornfields have been trampled down. Her villages have been burned to the ground. Her art treasures have been destroyed. Her men have been slaughtered; yes, and her women and her children, too. What had she done? Hundreds and thousands of her people, their neat, comfortable little homes burnt to the dust, wandering homeless in their own land. What was their crime? Their crime was that they trusted to the word of a Prussian king.

I do not know what the Kaiser hopes to achieve by this war. I have a shrewd idea what he will accomplish. I am not depending on them. It is enough for me to have the story which the Germans themselves avow, admit, defend, proclaim. The burning and massacring, the shooting down of harmless people. Why? Because according to the Germans, they fired on German soldiers. What business had German soldiers there at all? [*Cheers.*] Belgium was acting in pursuance of a most sacred right, the right to defend your own home. But they were not in uniform when they shot. If a burglar broke into the Kaiser's palace at Potsdam, destroyed his furniture, shot down his servants, ruined his art treasures, especially those he made himself [*laughter and cheers*], burned his precious manuscripts—do you think he would wait until he got into uniform before he shot him down? [*Laughter.*] They were dealing with those who had broken into their households. But their perfidy has already failed. They entered Belgium to save time. They have not gained time, but they have lost their good name.

But Belgium was not the only little nation that has been attacked in this war, and I make no excuse for referring to the case of the other little nation—the case of Servia. The history of Servia is not unblotted. What history in the category of nations is unblotted? The first nation that is without sin, let her cast a stone at Servia, a nation trained in a horrible school. But she won her freedom with her tenacious valour, and she has maintained it by the same courage. If any Servians were mixed up in the assassination of the Grand Duke,[8] they ought to be punished. Servia admits that. The Servian Government had nothing to do with it. Not even Austria claimed that. The

[8] Austrian Archduke Francis Ferdinand.

Servian Prime Minister[9] is one of the most capable and honoured men in Europe. Servia was willing to punish any one of her subjects who had been proved to have any complicity in that assassination. What more could you expect?

What were the Austrian demands? She sympathised with her fellow-countrymen in Bosnia. That was one of her crimes. She must do so no more. Her newspapers were saying nasty things about Austria. They must do so no longer. That is the Austrian spirit. You had it in Zabern.[10] How dare you criticise a customs official, and if you laugh, it is a capital offence. The colonel threatened to shoot them if they repeated it. Servian newspapers must not criticise Austria. I wonder what would have happened had we taken up the same line about German newspapers. Servia said, "Very well, we will give orders to the newspapers that they must not criticise Austria in future, neither Austria, nor Hungary, nor anything that is theirs." [*Laughter.*] Who can doubt the valour of Servia when she undertook to tackle her newspaper editors? [*Laughter.*] She promised not to sympathise with Bosnia, promised to write no critical articles about Austria. She would have no public meetings at which anything unkind was said about Austria. That was not enough. She must dismiss from her Army officers whom Austria should subsequently name. But these officers had just emerged from a war where they were adding lustre to the Servian arms—gallant, brave, efficient. [*Cheers.*] I wonder whether it was their guilt or their efficiency that prompted Austria's action. Servia was to undertake in advance to dismiss them from the Army, the names to be sent on subsequently. Can you name a country in the world that would have stood that? Supposing Austria or Germany had issued an ultimatum of that kind to this country. [*Laughter.*] "You must dismiss from your Army and from your Navy all those officers whom we shall subsequently name." Well, I think I could name them now. Lord Kitchener[11] [*cheers*] would go, Sir John French[12] [*cheers*] would be sent about his business, General Smith-Dorrien[13] [*cheers*] would be no more, and I am sure that Sir John Jellicoe[14] [*cheers*] would go. [*Laughter.*] And there was another gallant old warrior who would go—Lord Roberts.[15] [*Cheers.*]

[9] Nikola Pasic (Pashitch) was Premier of Serbia (now part of Yugoslavia) from 1906 to 1926.

[10] Saverne, France. The reference is to series of incidents involving German troops and local citizens between November and December, 1913. A German officer, Lieutenant von Forstner, was responsible for the major clashes.

[11] Sir Herbert Kitchener, famous for his campaign at Khartoum, was Secretary of War in the Coalition Ministry of Asquith.

[12] Commander-in-Chief, British Expeditionary Force in France.

[13] Sir Horace L. Smith-Dorrien commanded the II Corps in key battles at Mons and LeCateau and later headed the Second Army.

[14] Admiral Jellicoe was Commander-in-Chief of the Grand Fleet in 1914.

[15] Nineteenth-century army hero. Lord Frederick Sleigh Roberts held many important posts during his career, including Commander-in-Chief in India and later in Ireland, and Commander-in-Chief of the Armies from 1900 to 1905. He died in 1914.

It was a difficult situation for a small country. Here was a demand made upon her by a great military power who could put five or six men in the field for every one she could; and that power supported by the greatest military power in the world. How did Servia behave? It is not what happens to you in life that matters; it is the way in which you face it. [*Cheers.*] And Servia faced the situation with dignity. [*Loud cheers.*] She said to Austria, "If any officers of mine have been guilty and are proved to be guilty I will dismiss them." Austria said, "That is not good enough for me." It was not guilt she was after, but capacity. [*Laughter.*]

Then came Russia's turn. Russia has a special regard for Servia. She has a special interest in Servia. Russians have shed their blood for Servian independence many a time. Servia is a member of her family, and she cannot see Servia maltreated. Austria knew that. Germany knew that, and Germany turned round to Russia and said, "I insist that you shall stand by with your arms folded whilst Austria is strangling your little brother to death." [*Laughter.*] What answer did the Russian Slav give? He gave the only answer that becomes a man. [*Cheers.*] He turned to Austria and said, "You lay hands on that little fellow and I will tear your ramshackle Empire limb from limb." [*Prolonged cheers.*] And he is doing it. [*Renewed cheers.*]

That is the story of the little nations. The world owes much to little nations [*cheers*] and to little men. [*Laughter and cheers.*] This theory of bigness—you must have a big empire and a big nation and a big man—well, long legs have their advantage in a retreat. [*Laughter.*] Frederick the Great chose his warriors for their height, and that tradition has become a policy in Germany. Germany applies that ideal to nations. She will allow only six-feet-two nations to stand in the ranks. But all the world owes much to the little five-feet-high nations. [*Cheers.*] The greatest art of the world was the work of little nations. The most enduring literature of the world came from little nations. The greatest literature of England came from her when she was a nation of the size of Belgium fighting a great empire. The heroic deeds that thrill humanity through generations were the deeds of little nations fighting for their freedom. Ah, yes, and the salvation of mankind came through a little nation. God has chosen little nations as the vessels by which he carries the choicest wines to the lips of humanity to rejoice their hearts, to exalt their vision, to stimulate and to strengthen their faith; and if we had stood by when two little nations were being crushed and broken by the brutal hands of barbarism, our shame would have rung down the everlasting ages. [*Cheers.*]

But Germany insists that this is an attack by a low civilisation upon a higher. Well, as a matter of fact, the attack was begun by the civilisation which calls itself the higher one. Now, I am no apologist for Russia. She has perpetrated deeds of which I have no doubt her best sons are ashamed. But what empire has not? And Germany is the last empire to point the finger of reproach at Russia. [*Hear, hear.*] But Russia has made sacrifices for freedom—great sacrifices. You remember the cry of Bulgaria when she was torn by the most insensate tyranny that Europe has ever seen.[16] Who listened to the cry? The only answer of the higher civilisation was that the liberty of Bulgarian peasants was not worth the life of a single Pomeranian soldier. But the rude barbarians of the north, they sent their sons by the thousands to die for Bulgarian freedom. [*Cheers.*]

What about England? You go to Greece, the Netherlands, Italy, Germany, and France, and all these lands could point out to you places where the sons of Britain have died for the freedom of these countries. [*Cheers.*] France has made sacrifices for the freedom of other lands than her own. Can you name a single country in the world for the freedom of which the modern Prussian has ever sacrificed a single life? [*Cheers.*] The test of our faith, the highest standard of civilisation, is the readiness to sacrifice for others. [*Cheers.*] I would not say a word about the German people to disparage them. They are a great people; they have great qualities of head, of hand, and of heart. I believe, in spite of recent events, there is as great a store of kindness in the German peasant as in any peasant in the world, but he has been drilled into a false idea of civilisation [*Hear, hear*]—efficiency, capability. But it is a hard civilisation; it is a selfish civilisation; it is a material civilisation. They could not comprehend the action of Britain at the present moment. They say so. "France," they say, "we can understand. She is out for vengeance, she is out for territory—Alsace-Lorraine. [*Cheers.*] Russia, she is fighting for mastery; she wants Galicia." They can understand vengeance, they can understand you fighting for mastery, they can understand you fighting for greed of territory; they cannot understand a great empire pledging its resources, pledging its might, pledging the lives of its children, pledging its very existence to protect a little nation that seeks for its defence. [*Cheers.*]

God made man in His own image, high of purpose, in the region of the spirit. German civilisation would re-create him in the image of a Diesel machine—precise, accurate, powerful, with no room for the soul to operate. That is the higher civilisation. What is their demand? Have you read the Kaiser's speeches? If you have not a copy, I advise you to buy it; they will soon be out of print—and you won't have any more of the same sort again. [*Laughter and cheers.*] They are full of the clatter and bluster of German militarists—the mailed fist, the shining armour. Poor old mailed fist—its knuckles are getting a little bruised. Poor shining armour—the shine is being knocked out of it. [*Laughter.*] But there is the same swagger and boastfulness running through the whole of the speeches. You saw that remarkable speech which appeared in the *British Weekly* this week.[17] It is

---

[16] The reference is to the Bulgarian revolt against Turkish rule in 1876–1878.

[17] Excerpts of two speeches by the Kaiser were reported in the *British Weekly*, LVI (September 17, 1914), 585.

a very remarkable product as an illustration of the spirit we have got to fight. It is his speech to his soldiers on the way to the front.

> Remember that the German people are the chosen of God. On me, on me as German Emperor, the Spirit of God has descended. I am his weapon, His sword, and His Vicegerent. Woe to the disobedient. Death to cowards and unbelievers.

There has been nothing like it since the days of Mahomet.[18] Lunacy [*laughter*] is always distressing, but sometimes it is dangerous, and when you get it manifested in the head of the state and it has become the policy of a great empire it is about time it should be ruthlessly put away. [*Cheers.*] I do not believe he meant all these speeches; it was simply the martial straddle which he had acquired. But there were men around him who meant every word of it. This was their religion. Treaties: they tangle the feet of Germany in her advance; cut them with the sword. Little nations: they hinder the advance of Germany; trample them in the mire under the German heel. The Russian Slav: he challenges the supremacy of Germany in Europe; hurl your legions at him and massacre him. Britain: she is a constant menace to the predominancy of Germany in the world; wrest the trident out of her hand.

More than that, the new philosophy of Germany is to destroy Christianity—sickly sentimentalism about sacrifice for others, poor pap for German mouths. We will have the new diet, we will force it on the world. It will be made in Germany [*laughter*]—a diet of blood and iron. What remains? Treaties have gone; the honour of nations gone; liberty gone. What is left? Germany—Germany is left—*Deutschland über alles*. That is all that is left. That is what we are fighting, that claim to predominancy of a civilisation, a material one, a hard one, a civilisation which, if once it rules and sways the world, liberty goes, democracy vanishes, and unless Britain comes to the rescue, and her sons, it will be a dark day for humanity. [*Loud cheers.*]

We are not fighting the German people. The German people are just as much under the heel of this Prussian military caste—and more so, thank God, than any other nation in Europe. It will be a day of rejoicing for the German peasant and artisan and trader when the military caste is broken. [*Cheers.*] You know his pretensions. He gives himself the airs of a demi-god walking the pavement—civilians and their wives swept into the gutter; they have no right to stand in the way of the great Prussian Junker. Men, women, nations—they have all got to go. He thinks all he has got to say is, "We are in a hurry." [*Laughter.*] That is the answer he gave to Belgium. "Rapidity of action is Germany's greatest asset," which means, "I am in a hurry. Clear out of my way." You know the type of motorist, the terror of

---

[18] Mohammed, the Prophet of Islam (570–632).

the roads, with a 60-h.p. car. He thinks the roads are made for him, and anybody who impedes the action of his car by a single mile is knocked down. The Prussian Junker is the road hog of Europe. [*Loud cheers.*] Small nations in his way hurled to the roadside, bleeding and broken; women and children crushed under the wheels of his cruel car; Britain ordered out of his road. All I can say is this. If the old British spirit is alive in British hearts, that bully will be torn from his seat. [*Prolonged cheers.*] Were he to win it would be the greatest catastrophe that befell democracy since the days of the Holy Alliance and its ascendancy.

They think we cannot beat them. It will not be easy. It will be a long job. It will be a terrible war. But in the end we shall march through terror to triumph. [*Cheers.*] We shall need all our qualities, every quality that Britain and its people possess—prudence in council, daring in action, tenacity in purpose, courage in defeat, moderation in victory [*cheers*], in all things faith—and we shall win. [*Cheers.*] It has pleased them to believe and to preach the belief that we are a decadent, degenerated nation. They proclaim it to the world, through their professors [*laughter*], that we are an unheroic nation skulking behind our mahogany counters whilst we are egging on more gallant races to their destruction. This is a description given to us in Germany: "a timorous, craven nation, trusting to its fleet." I think they are beginning to find their mistake out already, and there are half a million of young men of Britain who have already registered the vow to their King that they will cross the seas and hurl that insult against British courage against its perpetrators in the battlefields of France and of Germany too. And we want half a million more, and we shall get them. [*Cheers.*]

But Wales must continue doing her duty. I should like to see a Welsh Army in the field. [*Cheers.*] I should like to see the race who faced the Normans for hundreds of years in a struggle for freedom, the race that helped to win Crécy,[19] the race that fought for a generation under Glendower against the greatest captain in Europe[20]—I should like to see that race go and give a taste of its quality in this great struggle in Europe. And they are going to do it. I envy you young people your opportunity. They have put up the age limit for the Army. But I have marched, I am sorry to say, a good many years even beyond that. But still, our turn will come. It is a great opportunity. It comes only once in many centuries to the children of men. For most generations sacrifice comes in drab weariness of spirit to men. It has come today to you—it has come today to us all in the form of the glory and thrill of a great movement for liberty that compels millions throughout Europe to the same noble end. It is a great war for

[19] Crécy-en-Ponthieu, site of the defeat of Philip VI by Edward III in the "Hundred-Year's War" on August 26, 1346.

[20] The reference is to Owen Glendower (1359?–1416?), a Welsh nationalist leader who headed a courageous but unsuccessful revolt against Henry IV. He was proclaimed Prince of Wales by his followers.

the emancipation of Europe from the thraldom of a military caste which has thrown its shadows upon two generations of men and which has now plunged the world into a welter of bloodshed and terror.

Some have already given their lives. There are some who have given more than their lives, they have given the lives of those who are dear to them. I honour their courage, and may God be their comfort and their strength. Those who have fallen have died consecrated deaths. They have taken their part in the making of a new Europe—a new world. I can see signs of it coming through the glare of the battlefield. The people of all lands will gain more by this struggle than they comprehend at the present moment. They will be rid of the greatest menace to their freedom.

That is not all. There is another blessing, infinitely greater and more enduring, which is already emerging out of this great contest—a new patriotism, richer, nobler, more exalted than the old. I see a new recognition amongst all classes high and low, shedding themselves of selfishness—a new recognition that the honour of a country does not depend merely upon the maintenance of its glory in the stricken field but in protecting its homes from distress as well. It is a new patriotism which is bringing a new outlook over all classes. The great flood of luxury and of sloth which had submerged the land is receding, and a new Britain is appearing. We can see for the first time the fundamental things that matter in life and that had been obscured from our vision by the tropical growth of prosperity.

May I tell you in a simple parable what I think this war is doing for us? I know a valley in the North of Wales between the mountains and the sea—a beautiful valley, snug, comfortable, sheltered by the mountains from all the bitter blast. It was very enervating, and I remember how the boys were in the habit of climbing the hill above the village to have a glimpse of the great mountains in the distance and to be stimulated and freshened by the breezes which came from the hilltops and by the great spectacle of that valley. We have been living in a sheltered valley for generations. We have been too comfortable, too indulgent, many, perhaps, too selfish; and the stern hand of fate has scourged us to an elevation where we can see the great everlasting things that matter for a nation—the great peaks of honour we had forgotten—duty, patriotism, and—clad in glittering white—the great pinnacle of sacrifice, pointing like a rugged finger to Heaven. We shall descend into the valleys again, but as long as the men and women of this generation last, they will carry in their hearts the image of these great mountain peaks, whose foundations are not shaken though Europe rock and sway in the convulsions of a great war. [*Prolonged cheers.*]

Winston S. Churchill

"Blood, Toil, Tears, and Sweat"[*]

Commons, May 13, 1940

I beg to move,

> That this House welcomes the formation of a Government representing the united and inflexible resolve of the nation to prosecute the war with Germany to a victorious conclusion.

On Friday evening last I received His Majesty's Commission to form a new Administration. It was the evident wish and will of Parliament and the nation that this should be conceived on the broadest possible basis and that it should include all parties, both those who supported the late Government and also the parties of the Opposition. I have completed the most important part of this task. A War Cabinet[1] has been formed of five Members, representing, with the Opposition Liberals, the unity of the nation. The three Party Leaders[2] have agreed to serve either in the War Cabinet or in high executive office. The three fighting services have been filled. It was necessary that this should be done in one single day, on account of the extreme urgency and rigour of events. A number of other positions, key positions, were filled yesterday, and I am submitting a further list to His Majesty tonight. I hope to complete the appointment of the principal Ministers during tomorrow. The appointment of the other Ministers usually takes a little longer, but I trust that when Parliament meets again, this part of my task will be completed and that the Administration will be complete in all respects.

. . . . .

---

[*] This text is taken from *Parliamentary Debates (Official Report)*, Fifth Series, Vol. CCCLX, cols. 1501–1502.

[1] The War Cabinet included Winston S. Churchill as Minister of Defense as well as Prime Minister; Neville Chamberlain as Lord President of the Council; Clement Attlee as Lord Privy Seal; Lord Halifax as Secretary of State for Foreign Affairs; and Arthur Greenwood as Minister without Portfolio.

[2] Neville Chamberlain, Conservative; Clement Attlee, Labour; and Sir Archibald Sinclair, Liberal, Secretary for Air.

To form an Administration of this scale and complexity is a serious undertaking in itself, but it must be remembered that we are in the preliminary stage of one of the greatest battles in history, that we are in action at many other points in Norway and in Holland, that we have to be prepared in the Mediterranean, that the air battle is continuous and that many preparations, such as have been indicated by my honourable Friend below the Gangway,[3] have to be made here at home. In this crisis I hope I may be pardoned if I do not address the House at any length today. I hope that any of my friends and colleagues or former colleagues who are affected by the political reconstruction will make allowance, all allowance, for any lack of ceremony with which it has been necessary to act. I would say to the House, as I said to those who have joined this Government, "I have nothing to offer but blood, toil, tears, and sweat."[4]

We have before us an ordeal of the most grievous kind. We have before us many, many long months of struggle and of suffering. You ask: What is our policy? I will say: It is to wage war, by sea, land, and air, with all our might and with all the strength that God can give us; to wage war against a monstrous tyranny, never surpassed in the dark, lamentable catalogue of human crime. That is our policy. You ask: What is our aim? I can answer in one word: It is victory, victory at all costs, victory in spite of all terror, victory, however long and hard the road may be; for without victory, there is no survival. Let that be realised: no survival for the British Empire, no survival for all that the British Empire has stood for, no survival for the urge and impulse of the ages that mankind will move forward towards its goal. But I take up my task with buoyancy and hope. I feel sure that our cause will not be suffered to fail among men. At this time I feel entitled to claim the aid of all, and I say, "Come then, let us go forward together with our united strength."

---

[3] The reference is most likely to Herbert Morrison, whom Churchill appointed Secretary for the Home Office and Home Security. See Morrison's speech on the conduct of the war, May 8, 1940, *Parliamentary Debates (Official Report)*, Fifth Series, Vol. CCCLX, cols. 1251–1265.

[4] A paraphrase of Giuseppe Garibaldi's famous exhortation to Romans to follow his lead into battle against the French who threatened Rome in 1849: "I offer neither pay, nor quarters, nor provisions; I offer hunger, thirst, forced marches, battles, and death. Let him who loves his country and not with lips only, follow me."

Winston S. Churchill

"Be Ye Men of Valour"[*]

BBC Broadcast, May 19, 1940

I speak to you for the first time as Prime Minister in a solemn hour for the life of our country, of our Empire, of our Allies, and, above all, of the cause of freedom.

A tremendous battle is raging in France and Flanders. The Germans, by a remarkable combination of air bombing and heavily armoured tanks, have broken through the French defence north of the Maginot Line, and strong columns of their armoured vehicles are ravaging the open country, which for the first day or two was without defenders. They have penetrated deeply and spread alarm and confusion in their track. Behind them there are now pouring infantry in lorries, and behind them again large masses are moving forward. Regroupment of the French armies, to make head against and to strike at this intruding wedge, has been proceeding for several days, largely assisted by the magnificent efforts of the Royal Air Force.

We must not allow ourselves to be intimidated by the presence of these armoured vehicles in unexpected places behind our lines. If they are behind our front, the French are also at many points fighting actively behind theirs. Both sides are therefore in an extremely dangerous position. If the French Army and our own are well handled, as I believe they will be; if the French retain their genius for recovery and counter-attack, for which they have so long been famous; and if the British Army shows the dogged endurance and solid fighting powers of which there have been so many examples in the past—then a sudden transformation of the scene might spring into being.

It would be foolish, however, to disguise the gravity of the hour. It would be still more foolish to lose heart and courage or to suppose that well-trained, well-equipped armies numbering three or four millions of men can be overcome in the space of a few weeks or even months by a scoop or raid by mechanised vehicles, however formidable. We may look with con-

---

[*] This text is from *The Times*, May 20, 1940, p. 6.

fidence to the stabilisation of the front in France and to the general engagement of the masses which will enable the qualities of French and British soldiers to be matched squarely against those of their adversaries.

For myself I have invincible confidence in the French Army and its leaders. Only a very small part of that splendid Army has yet been heavily engaged, and only a very small part of France has yet been invaded. There is good evidence to show that practically the whole of the mechanised and specialised forces of the enemy have already been thrown into the battle, and we know that very heavy losses have been inflicted on them. No officer or man, no brigade or division which grapples at close quarters with the enemy, wherever encountered, can fail to make a worthy contribution to the general results. The armies must cast away the idea of resisting attack behind concrete lines or natural obstacles and must realise that mastery can be regained only by furious, unrelenting assault. And this spirit must not only animate the High Command but must inspire every fighting man.

In the air, often at serious odds, even at odds hitherto thought overwhelming, we have been clawing down three or four to one of our enemies, and the relative balance of the British and German Air Forces is now considerably more favourable to us than at the beginning of the battle. In cutting down the German bombers we are fighting our own battle, as well as that of France. My confidence in our ability to fight it out to the finish with the German Air Force has been strengthened by the fierce encounters which have taken place and are taking place. At the same time our heavy bombers are striking nightly at the tap root of German mechanised power, and have already inflicted serious damage on the oil refineries on which the Nazi effort to dominate the world directly depends.

We must expect that as soon as stability is reached on the Western Front, the bulk of that hideous apparatus of aggression which dashed Holland into ruins and slavery in a few days will be turned on us. I am sure I speak for all when I say we are ready to face it, to endure it, and to retaliate against it to any extent that the unwritten laws of war permit. There will be many men and women in this island who, when the ordeal comes on them, as come it will, will feel a comfort and even a pride that they are sharing the peril of our lads at the front—soldiers, sailors, and airmen, God bless them —and are drawing away from them a part, at least, of the onslaught they have to bear. Is not this the appointed time for all to make the utmost exertions in their power? If the battle is to be won, we must provide our men with ever-increasing quantities of the weapons and ammunition they need. We must have and we must have quickly more tanks, more aeroplanes, more shells, and more guns. There is an imperious need for these vital munitions. They increase our strength against the powerfully armed enemy; they replace the wastage of the obstinate struggle; and the knowledge that wastage will speedily be replaced enables us to draw more readily on our reserves and throw them in now when everything means so much. Our task is not only to win the battle but to win the war.

After this battle in France abates its force, there will come a battle for our island, for all that Britain is and all that Britain means. That will be the struggle. In that supreme emergency, we shall not hesitate to take every step, even the most drastic, to call forth from our people the last ounce of effort of which they are capable. The interests of property and the hours of labour are nothing compared with the struggle for life and honour and freedom to which we have vowed ourselves. I have received from the Chiefs of the French Republic, and in particular from its indomitable Prime Minister, M. Reynaud, the most sacred pledges that whatever happens, they will fight to the end, be it bitter or be it glorious. Nay, if we fight to the end it can only be glorious.

Having received His Majesty's Commission, I have formed an Administration of every party and almost every point of view. We have differed and quarrelled in the past, but now one bond unites us all—to wage war until victory is won and never to surrender ourselves to servitude and shame, whatever the cost and whatever the agony may be.

If this is one of the most awe-striking periods in the history of France and Britain, it is also beyond doubt the most sublime. Side by side, unaided except by their kith and kin in the great Dominions and the wide Empires which rest beneath their shield, the British and French have advanced to rescue not only Europe but mankind from the foulest and most soul-destroying tyranny that has ever darkened and stained the pages of history. Behind them, behind us, behind the armies and fleets of Britain and France gather a group of shattered states and bludgeoned races—the Czechs, the Poles, the Norwegians, the Danes, the Dutch, the Belgians—on all of whom the long night of barbarism will descend unbroken even by a star of hope unless we conquer, as conquer we must, as conquer we shall.

Today is Trinity Sunday. Centuries ago words were written to be a call and a spur to faithful servants of truth and justice:

> Arm yourselves, and be ye men of valour, and be in readiness for the conflict, for it is better for us to perish in battle than to look on the outrage of our nation and our altars. As the will of God is in Heaven, even so let Him do.[1]

---

[1] The original source of Churchill's quotation is I Maccabees 3:58–60. It was often used as an antiphon during church services after Trinity Sunday.

Winston S. Churchill

"Dunkirk: 'A Miracle of Deliverance'"*

Commons, June 4, 1940

From the moment that the French defences at Sedan and on the Meuse[1] were broken at the end of the second week of May, only a rapid retreat to Amiens and the south could have saved the British and French Armies who had entered Belgium at the appeal of the Belgian King,[2] but this strategic fact was not immediately realised. The French High Command hoped they would be able to close the gap, and the Armies of the North were under their orders. Moreover, a retirement of this kind would have involved almost certainly the destruction of the fine Belgian Army of over twenty divisions and the abandonment of the whole of Belgium. Therefore, when the force and scope of the German penetration were realised and when a new French Generalissimo, General Weygand, assumed command in place of General Gamelin,[3] an effort was made by the French and British Armies in Belgium to keep on holding the right hand of the Belgians and to give their own right hand to a newly created French Army which was to have advanced across the Somme in great strength to grasp it.

However, the German eruption swept like a sharp scythe around the right and rear of the Armies of the North. Eight or nine armoured divisions, each of about 400 armoured vehicles of different kinds, but carefully assorted to be complementary and divisible into small self-contained units, cut off all communications between us and the main French Armies. It severed our own communications for food and ammunition, which ran first to Amiens and afterwards through Abbéville, and it shore its way up

---

* This text is taken from *Parliamentary Debates (Official Report)*, Fifth Series, Vol. CCCLXI, cols. 787–795.

[1] On May 14, 1940, German forces made their major break through French lines at Sedan and across the Meuse River.

[2] King Leopold.

[3] General Maxime Weygand, French Commander-in-Chief at Algiers, replaced General Maurice Gamelin as Commander-in-Chief of French Armies on May 19, 1940.

the coast to Boulogne and Calais and almost to Dunkirk. Behind this armoured and mechanised onslaught came a number of German divisions in lorries, and behind them again there plodded comparatively slowly the dull brute mass of the ordinary German Army and German people, always so ready to be led to the trampling down in other lands of liberties and comforts which they have never known in their own.

I have said this armoured scythe-stroke almost reached Dunkirk—almost but not quite. Boulogne and Calais were the scenes of desperate fighting. The Guards defended Boulogne for a while and were then withdrawn by orders from this country. The Rifle Brigade, the 60th Rifles, and the Queen Victoria's Rifles, with a battalion of British tanks and 1,000 Frenchmen, in all about 4,000 strong, defended Calais to the last. The British Brigadier was given an hour to surrender. He spurned the offer, and four days of intense street fighting passed before silence reigned over Calais, which marked the end of a memorable resistance. Only thirty unwounded survivors were brought off by the Navy and we do not know the fate of their comrades. Their sacrifice, however, was not in vain. At least two armoured divisions, which otherwise would have been turned against the British Expeditionary Force, had to be sent for to overcome them. They have added another page to the glories of the Light Division, and the time gained enabled the Graveline waterlines[4] to be flooded and to be held by the French troops.

Thus it was that the port of Dunkirk was kept open. When it was found impossible for the Armies of the north to reopen their communications to Amiens with the main French Armies, only one choice remained. It seemed, indeed, forlorn. The Belgian, British, and French Armies were almost surrounded. Their sole line of retreat was to a single port and to its neighbouring beaches. They were pressed on every side by heavy attacks and far outnumbered in the air.

When a week ago today I asked the House to fix this afternoon as the occasion for a statement, I feared it would be my hard lot to announce the greatest military disaster in our long history. I thought—and some good judges agreed with me—that perhaps 20,000 or 30,000 men might be reembarked. But it certainly seemed that the whole of the French First Army and the whole of the British Expeditionary Force north of the Amiens-Abbéville gap would be broken up in the open field or else would have to capitulate for lack of food and ammunition. These were the hard and heavy tidings for which I called upon the House and the nation to prepare themselves a week ago. The whole root and core and brain of the British Army, on which and around which we were to build and are to build the great British Armies in the later years of the war, seemed about to

---

[4] Canals near Calais whose defense was critical to British evacuation. If this waterway protecting the southern front of retreating troops had fallen, the short sea route between Dunkirk and Dover would have been within range of German artillery.

perish upon the field or to be led into an ignominious and starving captivity.

That was the prospect a week ago. But another blow which might well have proved final was yet to fall upon us. The King of the Belgians had called upon us to come to his aid. Had not this ruler and his government severed themselves from the Allies who rescued their country from extinction in the late war, and had they not sought refuge in what has proved to be a fatal neutrality, the French and British Armies might well at the outset have saved not only Belgium but perhaps even Poland. Yet at the last moment, when Belgium was already invaded, King Leopold called upon us to come to his aid, and even at the last moment we came. He and his brave, efficient army, nearly half a million strong, guarded our eastern flank and thus kept open our only line of retreat to the sea. Suddenly, without prior consultation, with the least possible notice, without the advice of his Ministers and upon his own personal act, he sent a plenipotentiary to the German Command, surrendered his army, and exposed our whole flank and means of retreat.

I asked the House a week ago to suspend its judgment because the facts were not clear, but I do not feel that any reason now exists why we should not form our own opinions upon this pitiful episode. The surrender of the Belgian Army compelled the British at the shortest notice to cover a flank to the sea more than thirty miles in length. Otherwise all would have been cut off, and all would have shared the fate to which King Leopold had condemned the finest army his country had ever formed. So, in doing this and in exposing this flank, as anyone who followed the operations on the map will see, contact was lost between the British and two out of the three corps forming the First French Army, who were still further from the coast than we were, and it seemed impossible that any large number of Allied troops could reach the coast.

The enemy attacked on all sides with great strength and fierceness, and their main power, the power of their far more numerous air force, was thrown into the battle or else concentrated upon Dunkirk and the beaches. Pressing in upon the narrow exit both from the east and from the west, the enemy began to fire with cannon upon the beaches by which alone the shipping could approach or depart. They sowed magnetic mines in the channels and seas. They sent repeated waves of hostile aircraft, sometimes more than 100 strong in one formation, to cast their bombs upon the single pier that remained and upon the sand dunes upon which the troops had their eyes for shelter. Their U-boats, one of which was sunk, and their motor launches took their toll of the vast traffic which now began. For four or five days an intense struggle reigned. All their armoured divisions—or what was left of them—together with great masses of German infantry and artillery, hurled themselves in vain upon the ever-narrowing, ever-contracting appendix within which the British and French Armies fought.

Meanwhile, the Royal Navy, with the willing help of countless merchant seamen, strained every nerve to embark the British and Allied troops. Two hundred and twenty light warships and 650 other vessels were engaged. They had to operate upon the difficult coast, often in adverse weather, under an almost ceaseless hail of bombs and an increasing concentration of artillery fire. Nor were the seas, as I have said, themselves free from mines and torpedoes. It was in conditions such as these that our men carried on, with little or no rest, for days and nights on end, making trip after trip across the dangerous waters, bringing with them always men whom they had rescued. The numbers they have brought back are the measure of their devotion and their courage. The hospital ships, which brought off many thousands of British and French wounded, being so plainly marked, were a special target for Nazi bombs; but the men and women on board them never faltered in their duty.

Meanwhile, the Royal Air Force, which had already been intervening in the battle, so far as its range would allow, from home bases, now used part of its main metropolitan fighter strength and struck at the German bombers and at the fighters which in large numbers protected them. This struggle was protracted and fierce. Suddenly the scene has cleared, the crash and thunder has for the moment—but only for the moment—died away. A miracle of deliverance, achieved by valour, by perseverance, by perfect discipline, by faultless service, by resource, by skill, by unconquerable fidelity, is manifest to us all. The enemy was hurled back by the retreating British and French troops. He was so roughly handled that he did not harry their departure seriously. The Royal Air Force engaged the main strength of the German Air Force and inflicted upon them losses of at least four to one; and the Navy, using nearly 1,000 ships of all kinds, carried over 335,000 men, French and British, out of the jaws of death and shame, to their native land and to the tasks which lie immediately ahead. We must be very careful not to assign to this deliverance the attributes of a victory. Wars are not won by evacuations. But there was a victory inside this deliverance which should be noted. It was gained by the Air Force. Many of our soldiers coming back have not seen the Air Force at work; they saw only the bombers which escaped its protective attack. They underrate its achievements. I have heard much talk of this; that is why I go out of my way to say this. I will tell you about it.

This was a great trial of strength between the British and German Air Forces. Can you conceive a greater objective for the Germans in the air than to make evacuation from these beaches impossible and to sink all these ships which were displayed, almost to the extent of thousands? Could there have been an objective of greater military importance and significance for the whole purpose of the war than this? They tried hard, and they were beaten back; they were frustrated in their task. We got the Army away; and they have paid fourfold for any losses which they have inflicted. Very large formations of German aeroplanes—and we know that they are a very brave race—have turned on several occasions from the attack of one-quarter of their number of the Royal Air Force, and have dispersed in different directions. Twelve aeroplanes have been hunted by two. One aeroplane was driven into the water and cast away by the mere charge of a British aeroplane which had no more ammunition. All of our types—the Hurricane, the Spitfire, and the new Defiant—and all our pilots have been vindicated as superior to what they have at present to face.

When we consider how much greater would be our advantage in defending the air above this island against an overseas attack, I must say that I find in these facts a sure basis upon which practical and reassuring thoughts may rest. I will pay my tribute to these young airmen. The great French Army was very largely, for the time being, cast back and disturbed by the onrush of a few thousands of armoured vehicles. May it not also be that the cause of civilisation itself will be defended by the skill and devotion of a few thousand airmen? There never had been, I suppose, in all the world, in all the history of war, such an opportunity for youth. The Knights of the Round Table, the Crusaders, all fall back into a prosaic past—not only distant but prosaic; but these young men, going forth every morn to guard their native land and all that we stand for, holding in their hands these instruments of colossal and shattering power, of whom it may be said that

> When every morning brought a noble chance,
> And every chance brought out a noble knight,[5]

deserve our gratitude, as do all of the brave men who, in so many ways and on so many occasions, are ready and continue ready to give life and all for their native land.

I return to the Army. In the long series of very fierce battles, now on this front, now on that, fighting on three fronts at once, battles fought by two or three divisions against an equal or somewhat larger number of the enemy, and fought fiercely on some of the old grounds that so many of us knew so well—in these battles our losses in men have exceeded 30,000 killed, wounded, and missing. I take occasion to express the sympathy of the House to all who have suffered bereavement or who are still anxious. The President of the Board of Trade[6] is not here today. His son has been killed, and many in the House have felt the pangs of affliction in the sharpest form. But I will say this about the missing. We have had a large number of wounded come home safely to this country—the greater part—but I would say about the missing that there may be very many reported missing who will come back home, some day, in one way or another. In the confusion of this fight it is inevitable that many have been left in positions where honour required no further resistance from them.

[5] The lines are from Alfred Lord Tennyson's "The Passing of Arthur."
[6] Sir Andrew Duncan.

Against this loss of over 30,000 men we can set a far heavier loss certainly inflicted upon the enemy. But our losses in material are enormous. We have perhaps lost one-third of the men we lost in the opening days of the battle of the 21st of March, 1918,[7] but we have lost nearly as many guns—nearly 1,000 guns—and all our transport—all the armoured vehicles that were with the Army in the North. This loss will impose a further delay on the expansion of our military strength. That expansion had not been proceeding as fast as we had hoped. The best of all we had to give had gone to the British Expeditionary Force, and although they had not the numbers of tanks and some articles of equipment which were desirable, they were a very well and finely equipped army. They had the first fruits of all that our industry had to give, and that is gone. And now here is this further delay. How long it will be, how long it will last, depends upon the exertions which we make in this island. An effort the like of which has never been seen in our records is now being made. Work is proceeding everywhere, night and day, Sundays and week-days. Capital and labour have cast aside their interests, rights, and customs and put them into the common stock. Already the flow of munitions has leapt forward. There is no reason why we should not in a few months overtake the sudden and serious loss that has come upon us, without retarding the development of our general programme.

Nevertheless, our thankfulness at the escape of our Army and so many men, whose loved ones have passed through an agonising week, must not blind us to the fact that what has happened in France and Belgium is a colossal military disaster. The French Army has been weakened, the Belgian Army has been lost, a large part of those fortified lines upon which so much faith had been reposed is gone, many valuable mining districts and factories have passed into the enemy's possession, the whole of the Channel ports are in his hands, with all the tragic consequences that follow from that, and we must expect another blow to be struck almost immediately at us or at France. We are told that Herr Hitler has a plan for invading the British Isles. This has often been thought of before. When Napoleon lay at Boulogne for a year with his flat-bottomed boats and his Grand Army, he was told by someone,[8] "There are bitter weeds in England." There are certainly a great many more of them since the British Expeditionary Force returned.

The whole question of home defence against invasion is, of course, powerfully affected by the fact that we have for the time being in this island incomparably more powerful military forces than we have ever had at any moment in this war or the last. But this will not continue. We shall not be content with a defensive war. We have our duty to our Ally. We have to reconstitute and build up the British Expeditionary Force once again, under its gallant Commander-in-Chief, Lord Gort. All this is in train; but in the

---

[7] This day was the beginning of a German offensive on a fifty-mile front. In eight days, the Germans claimed to have captured 40,000 men and 600 guns.

[8] Probably Talleyrand, Napoleon's Minister of Foreign Affairs.

interval we must put our defences in this island into such a high state of organisation that the fewest possible numbers will be required to give effective security and that the largest possible potential of offensive effort may be realised. On this we are now engaged. It will be very convenient, if it be the desire of the House, to enter upon this subject in a secret Session. Not that the Government would necessarily be able to reveal in very great detail military secrets, but we like to have our discussions free, without the restraint imposed by the fact that they will be read the next day by the enemy, and the Government would benefit by views freely expressed in all parts of the House by Members with their knowledge of so many different parts of the country. I understand that some request is to be made upon this subject, which will be readily acceded to by His Majesty's Government.

We have found it necessary to take measures of increasing stringency not only against enemy aliens and suspicious characters of other nationalities, but also against British subjects who may become a danger or a nuisance should the war be transported to the United Kingdom. I know there are a great many people affected by the orders which we have made who are the passionate enemies of Nazi Germany. I am very sorry for them, but we cannot, at the present time and under the present stress, draw all the distinctions which we should like to do. If parachute landings were attempted and fierce fighting attendant upon them followed, these unfortunate people would be far better out of the way, for their own sakes as well as for ours. There is, however, another class, for which I feel not the slightest sympathy. Parliament has given us the powers to put down fifth-column activities[9] with a strong hand, and we shall use those powers, subject to the supervision and correction of the House, without the slightest hesitation until we are satisfied and more than satisfied that this malignancy in our midst has been effectively stamped out.

Turning once again, and this time more generally, to the question of invasion, I would observe that there has never been a period in all these long centuries of which we boast when an absolute guarantee against invasion, still less against serious raids, could have been given to our people. In the days of Napoleon, of which I was speaking just now, the same wind which would have carried his transports across the Channel might have driven away the blockading fleet. There was always the chance, and it is that chance which has excited and befooled the imaginations of many Continental tyrants. Many are the tales that are told. We are assured that novel methods will be adopted, and when we see the originality of malice, the ingenuity of aggression, which our enemy displays, we may certainly

---

[9] "Fifth column" is an expression coined by General Emilio Mola during the Spanish Civil War. He led his troops in four columns against Madrid. He called those who committed espionage, sabotage, and other subversive activities behind enemy lines his fifth column. The term was used in World War II to describe an enemy working within one's own home territory.

prepare ourselves for every kind of novel stratagem and every kind of brutal and treacherous manœuvre. I think that no idea is so outlandish that it should not be considered and viewed with a searching, but at the same time, I hope, with a steady eye. We must never forget the solid assurances of sea power and those which belong to air power if it can be locally exercised.

I have, myself, full confidence that if all do their duty, if nothing is neglected, and if the best arrangements are made, as they are being made, we shall prove ourselves once again able to defend our island home, to ride out the storm of war, and to outlive the menace of tyranny, if necessary for years, if necessary alone. At any rate, that is what we are going to try to do. That is the resolve of His Majesty's Government—every man of them. That is the will of Parliament and the nation. The British Empire and the French Republic, linked together in their cause and in their need, will defend to the death their native soil, aiding each other like good comrades to the utmost of their strength. Even though large tracts of Europe and many old and famous states have fallen or may fall into the grip of the Gestapo and all the odious apparatus of Nazi rule, we shall not flag or fail. We shall go on to the end. We shall fight in France, we shall fight on the seas and oceans, we shall fight with growing confidence and growing strength in the air, we shall defend our island, whatever the cost may be. We shall fight on the beaches, we shall fight on the landing grounds, we shall fight in the fields and in the streets, we shall fight in the hills. We shall never surrender, and even if, which I do not for a moment believe, this island or a large part of it were subjugated and starving, then our Empire beyond the seas, armed and guarded by the British Fleet, would carry on the struggle, until, in God's good time, the new world, with all its power and might, steps forth to the rescue and the liberation of the old.

Winston S. Churchill

"Their Finest Hour"[*]

Commons, June 18, 1940

I spoke the other day of the colossal military disaster which occurred when the French High Command failed to withdraw the Northern Armies from Belgium at the moment when they knew that the French front was decisively broken at Sedan and on the Meuse. This delay entailed the loss of fifteen or sixteen French divisions and threw out of action for the critical period the whole of the British Expeditionary Force. Our Army and 120,000 French troops were indeed rescued by the British Navy from Dunkirk but only with the loss of their cannon, vehicles, and modern equipment. This loss inevitably took some weeks to repair, and in the first two of those weeks the battle in France has been lost. When we consider the heroic resistance made by the French Army against heavy odds in this battle, the enormous losses inflicted upon the enemy, and the evident exhaustion of the enemy, it may well be thought that these twenty-five divisions of the best-trained and best-equipped troops might have turned the scale. However, General Weygand had to fight without them. Only three British divisions or their equivalent were able to stand in the line with their French comrades. They have suffered severely, but they have fought well. We sent every man we could to France as fast as we could re-equip and transport their formations.

I am not reciting these facts for the purpose of recrimination. That I judge to be utterly futile and even harmful. We cannot afford it. I recite them in order to explain why it was we did not have, as we could have had, between twelve and fourteen British divisions fighting in the line in this great battle instead of only three. Now I put all this aside. I put it on the shelf, from which the historians, when they have time, will select their documents to tell their stories. We have to think of the future and not of the past. This also applies in a small way to our own affairs at home. There are many who would hold an inquest in the House of Commons on the conduct of the Governments—and of Parliaments, for they are in it, too—during the

[*] This text is taken from *Parliamentary Debates (Official Report)*, Fifth Series, Vol. CCCLXII, cols. 51–61.

years which led up to this catastrophe. They seek to indict those who were responsible for the guidance of our affairs. This also would be a foolish and pernicious process. There are too many in it. Let each man search his conscience and search his speeches. I frequently search mine.

Of this I am quite sure, that if we open a quarrel between the past and the present, we shall find that we have lost the future. Therefore, I cannot accept the drawing of any distinctions between Members of the present Government. It was formed at a moment of crisis in order to unite all the parties and all sections of opinion. It has received the almost unanimous support of both Houses of Parliament. Its Members are going to stand together, and subject to the authority of the House of Commons, we are going to govern the country and fight the war. It is absolutely necessary at a time like this that every Minister who tries each day to do his duty shall be respected, and their subordinates must know that their chiefs are not threatened men, men who are here today and gone tomorrow, but that their directions must be punctually and faithfully obeyed. Without this concentrated power we cannot face what lies before us. I should not think it would be very advantageous for the House to prolong this debate this afternoon under conditions of public stress. Many facts are not clear that will be clear in a short time. We are to have a secret Session on Thursday, and I should think that would be a better opportunity for the many earnest expressions of opinion which Members will desire to make and for the House to discuss vital matters, as I have said before, without having everything read the next morning by our dangerous foes.

The military events which have happened during the past fortnight have not come to me with any sense of surprise. Indeed, I indicated a fortnight ago, as clearly as I could, to the House that the worst possibilities were open, and I made it perfectly clear then that whatever happened in France would make no difference to the resolve of Britain and the British Empire to fight on, "if necessary for years, if necessary alone."[1] During the last few days we have successfully brought off the great majority of the troops we had on the lines of communication in France—a very large number, scores of thousands—and seven-eighths of the troops we have sent to France since the beginning of the war—that is to say, about 350,000 out of 400,000 men—are safely back in this country. Others are still fighting with the French, and fighting with considerable success in their local encounters with the enemy. We have also brought back a great mass of stores, rifles, and munitions of all kinds which had been accumulated in France during the last nine months.

We have, therefore, in this island today a very large and powerful military force. This force includes all our best-trained and finest troops and includes scores of thousands of those who have already measured their

---

[1] The expression comes from Churchill's "Dunkirk" speech, page 505.

quality against the Germans and found themselves at no disadvantage. We have under arms at the present time in this island over a million and a quarter men. Behind these we have the Local Defence Volunteers, numbering half a million, only a portion of whom, however, are yet armed with rifles or other firearms. We have incorporated into our Defence Forces every man for whom we have a weapon. We expect a very large addition to our weapons in the near future, and in preparation for this we intend to call up, drill, and train further large numbers at once. Those who are not called up or employed upon the vast business of munitions production in all its branches—and it runs through every kind of grade—serve their country best by remaining at their ordinary work until they are required.

We also have Dominions Armies here. The Canadians had actually landed in France but have now been safely withdrawn, much disappointed but in perfect order, with all their artillery and equipment. These very high-class forces from the Dominions will now take part in the defence of the mother country. Lest the account which I have given of these very large forces should raise the question why they did not take part in the great battle in France, I must make it clear that apart from the divisions training and organising at home, only twelve divisions were equipped to fight upon a scale which justified their being sent abroad. This was fully up to the number which the French had been led to expect would be available in France at the ninth month of the war. The rest of our forces at home have a fighting value for home defence which will, of course, steadily increase every week that passes. Thus, the invasion of Great Britain would at this time require the transportation across the sea of hostile armies upon a very large scale, and after they had been so transported, they would have to be continually maintained with all the masses of munitions and supplies which are required for continuous battle, as continuous battle it would be.

Here is where we come to the Navy. After all, we have a navy. Some people seem to forget that. We must remind them. For the last thirty years I have been concerned in discussions about the possibilities of oversea invasion, and I took the responsibility on behalf of the Admiralty, at the beginning of the last war, of allowing all regular troops to be sent out of the country, although our territorials had only just been called up and were quite untrained. Therefore, this island was for several months practically denuded of fighting troops. The Admiralty had confidence at that time in their ability to prevent a mass invasion, even though at that time the Germans had a magnificent battle fleet in the proportion of ten to sixteen, even though they were capable of fighting a general engagement every day and any day, whereas now they have only a couple of heavy ships worth speaking of. We are also told that the Italian Navy is to come to gain sea superiority in these waters. If they seriously intend it, I shall only say that we shall be delighted to offer Signor Mussolini a free and safeguarded passage through the Straits of Gibraltar in order that he may play the part which he aspires to do. There is general curiosity in the British Fleet to find out whether the Italians are up to the level they were at in the last war or whether they have fallen off at all.

Therefore, it seems to me that as far as seaborne invasion on a great scale is concerned, we are far more capable of meeting it today than we were at many periods in the last war and during the early months of this war, before our other troops were trained and while the B.E.F.[2] was already abroad and still abroad. The Navy have never pretended to be able to prevent raids by bodies of 5,000 or 10,000 men flung suddenly across and thrown ashore at several points on the coast some dark night or foggy morning. The efficacy of sea power, especially under modern conditions, depends upon the invading force being of large size. It has to be of large size, in view of our military strength, to be of any use. If it is of large size, then the Navy have something they can find and meet and, as it were, bite on. Now we must remember that even five divisions, however lightly equipped, would require 200 to 250 ships, and with modern air reconnaissance and photography, it would not be easy to collect such an armada, marshal it, and conduct it across the sea without any powerful naval forces to escort it, and with the very great possibility that it would be intercepted long before it reached the coast and the men all drowned in the sea or, at the worst, blown to pieces with their equipment while they were trying to land. We also have a great system of minefields, recently strongly reinforced, through which we alone know the channel. If the enemy tries to sweep passages through these minefields, it will be the task of the Navy to destroy the minesweepers and any other forces employed to protect them. There should be no difficulty in this, owing to our great superiority at sea.

Those are the regular, well-tested, well-proved arguments on which we have relied during many years in peace and war. But the question is whether there are any new methods by which those solid assurances can be circumvented. Odd as it may seem, some attention has been given to this by the Admiralty, whose prime duty and responsibility it is to destroy any large seaborne expedition before it reaches or at the moment when it reaches these shores. It would not be useful to go into details. It might even suggest ideas to other people which they have not thought of, and they would not be likely to give us any of their ideas in exchange. All I will say is that untiring vigilance and mind-searching must be devoted to the subject, because the enemy is crafty and cunning and full of novel treacheries and stratagems. The House may be assured that the utmost ingenuity is being displayed and imagination is being evoked from large numbers of competent officers, well trained in tactics and thoroughly up to date, to measure and counter-work novel possibilities, of which many are suggested, some very absurd and some by no means utterly irrational.

[2] British Expeditionary Force.

Some people will ask why, then, was it that the British Navy was not able to prevent the movement of a large army from Germany into Norway across the Skaggerak? But the conditions in the Channel and in the North Sea are in no way like those which prevail in the Skaggerak. In the Skaggerak, because of the distance, we could give no air support to our surface ships, and consequently, lying as we did close to the enemy's main air power, in those waters we were compelled to use only our submarines. We could not enforce the decisive blockade or interruption which is possible from surface vessels. Our submarines took a heavy toll but could not, by themselves, prevent the invasion of Norway. In the Channel and in the North Sea, on the other hand, our superior naval surface forces, aided by our submarines, will operate with close and effective air assistance.

This brings me, naturally, to the great question of invasion from the air and of the impending struggle between the British and German Air Forces. It seems quite clear that no invasion on a scale beyond the capacity of our land forces to crush speedily is likely to take place from the air until our Air Force has been definitely overpowered. In the meantime, there may be raids by parachute troops and attempted descents of airborne soldiers. We should be able to give those gentry a warm reception both in the air and if they reach the ground in any condition to continue the dispute. But the great question is, can we break Hitler's air weapon? Now, of course, it is a very great pity that we have not got an air force at least equal to that of the most powerful enemy within striking distance of these shores. But we have a very powerful air force which has proved itself far superior in quality, both in men and in many types of machine, to what we have met so far in the numerous fierce air battles which have been fought. In France, where we were at a considerable disadvantage and lost many machines on the ground, we were accustomed to inflict losses of as much as two to two and a half to one. In the fighting over Dunkirk, which was a sort of no man's land, we undoubtedly beat the German Air Force, and this gave us the mastery locally in the air and we inflicted losses of three or four to one. Anyone who looks at the photographs which were published a week or so ago of the re-embarkation, showing the masses of troops assembled on the beach and forming an ideal target for hours at a time, must realise that this re-embarkation would not have been possible unless the enemy had resigned all hope of recovering air superiority at that point.

In the defence of this island the advantages to the defenders will be very great. We hope to improve on the rate of three or four to one which was realised at Dunkirk, and in addition all our injured machines and their crews which get down safely—and, surprisingly, a very great many injured machines and men do get down safely in modern air fighting—all of these will fall, in an attack upon these islands, on friendly soil and live to fight another day, whereas all injured enemy machines and their complements will be total losses as far as the war is concerned. During the great battle in

France, we gave very powerful and continuous aid to the French Army both by fighters and bombers, but in spite of every kind of pressure we never would allow the entire metropolitan strength of the Air Force, in fighters, to be consumed. This decision was painful, but it was also right, because the fortunes of the battle in France could not have been decisively affected even if we had thrown in our entire fighter force. The battle was lost by the unfortunate strategical opening, by the extraordinary and unforeseen power of the armoured columns, and by the great preponderance of the German Army in numbers. Our fighter Air Force might easily have been exhausted as a mere accident in that great struggle, and we should have found ourselves at the present time in a very serious plight. But, as it is, I am happy to inform the House that our fighter air strength is stronger at the present time, relatively to the Germans, who have suffered terrible losses, than it has ever been, and consequently we believe ourselves to possess the capacity to continue the war in the air under better conditions than we have ever experienced before. I look forward confidently to the exploits of our fighter pilots, who will have the glory of saving their native land, their island home, and all they love from the most deadly of all attacks.

There remains the danger of bombing attacks, which will certainly be made very soon upon us by the bomber forces of the enemy. It is true that the German bomber force is superior in numbers to ours, but we have a very large bomber force also which we shall use to strike at military targets in Germany without intermission. I do not at all under-rate the severity of the ordeal which lies before us, but I believe our countrymen will show themselves capable of standing up to it, like the brave men of Barcelona,[3] and will be able to stand up to it and carry on in spite of it at least as well as any other people in the world. Much will depend upon this, and every man and every woman will have the chance to show the finest qualities of their race and render the highest service to their cause. For all of us at this time, whatever our sphere, our station, our occupation, our duties, it will be a help to remember the famous lines:

> He nothing common did, or mean,
> Upon that memorable scene.[4]

I have thought it right upon this occasion to give the House and the country some indication of the solid, practical grounds upon which we base our inflexible resolve to continue the war, and I can assure them that our professional advisers of the three services unitedly advise that we should do so, and that there are good and reasonable hopes of final victory. We

---

[3] A key battle during the Spanish Civil War; Loyalist forces resisted Franco's troops at Barcelona for two weeks. On January 26, 1939, Franco took the city.
[4] These lines are from Andrew Marvell's "An Horatian Ode on Cromwell's Return from Ireland." The reference is to the behavior of Charles I on the occasion of his beheading.

have also fully informed and consulted all the self-governing Dominions, and I have received from their Prime Ministers, Mr. Mackenzie King,[5] Mr. Menzies,[6] Mr. Fraser,[7] and General Smuts,[8] messages couched in the most moving terms in which they endorse our decision and declare themselves ready to share our fortunes and to persevere to the end.

We may now ask ourselves, in what ways is our position worsened since the beginning of the war? It is worsened by the fact that the Germans have conquered a large part of the coastline of Western Europe, and many small countries have been over-run by them. This aggravates the possibilities of air attack and adds to our naval preoccupations. It in no way diminishes, but on the contrary definitely increases, the power of our long-distance blockade. Should military resistance come to an end in France, which is not yet certain though it will in any case be greatly diminished, the Germans can concentrate their forces, both military and industrial, upon us. But for the reasons I have given to the House these will not be found so easy to apply. If invasion becomes more imminent, we, being relieved from the task of maintaining a large army in France, have far larger and more efficient forces here to meet them. If Hitler can bring under his despotic control the industries of the countries he has conquered, this will add greatly to his already vast armament output. On the other hand, this will not happen immediately, and we are now assured of immense, continuous, and increasing support in supplies and munitions of all kinds from the United States, and especially of aeroplanes and pilots from the Dominions and across the oceans, coming from regions which are beyond the reach of enemy bombers.

I do not see how any of these factors can operate to our detriment on balance before the winter comes, and the winter will impose a strain upon the Nazi régime, with almost all Europe writhing and starving under their heel—which, for all their ruthlessness, will run them very hard. We must not forget that from the moment when we declared war on the 3rd of September, it was always possible for Germany to turn all her Air Force upon this country together with any other devices of invasion she might conceive, and that France could do little or nothing to prevent her doing so. We have, therefore, lived under this danger, in principle and in a slightly modified form, during all these months. In the meanwhile, however, we have enormously improved our methods of defence, and we have learned what we had no right to assume at the beginning, namely, the individual superiority of our aircraft and pilots.

Therefore, in casting up this dread balance sheet, contemplating our dangers with a disillusioned eye, I see great reason for intense vigilance and exertion, but none whatever for panic or despair. During the first four

---

[5] William Mackenzie King, Prime Minister of Canada.
[6] Robert Gordon Menzies, Prime Minister of Australia.
[7] Peter Fraser, Prime Minister of New Zealand.
[8] General Jan Christian Smuts, Prime Minister of the Union of South Africa.

years of the last war, the Allies experienced, as my right honourable Friend opposite the Member for Caernarvon Boroughs[9] will remember, nothing but disaster and disappointment, and yet at the end their morale was higher than that of the Germans, who had moved from one aggressive triumph to another. During that war we repeatedly asked ourselves the question, "How are we going to win?" and no one was able ever to answer it with much precision until at the end, quite suddenly, quite unexpectedly, our terrible foe collapsed before us, and we were so glutted with victory that in our folly we cast it away.

We do not yet know what will happen in France or whether the French resistance will be prolonged, both in France and in the French Empire overseas. The French Government will be throwing away great opportunities and casting away their future if they do not continue the war in accordance with their treaty obligations, from which we have not felt able to release them. The House will have read the historic declaration in which, at the desire of many Frenchmen and of our own hearts, we have proclaimed our willingness to conclude at the darkest hour in French history a union of common citizenship.[10] However matters may go in France or with the French Government or with another French Government, we in this island and in the British Empire will never lose our sense of comradeship with the French people. If we are now called upon to endure what they have suffered, we shall emulate their courage, and if final victory rewards our toils, they shall share the gains, aye, and freedom shall be restored to all. We abate nothing of our just demands—Czechs, Poles, Norwegians, Dutch, Belgians, all who have joined their causes to our own shall be restored.

What General Weygand called the "Battle of France" is over. I expect that the Battle of Britain is about to begin. Upon this battle depends the survival of Christian civilisation. Upon it depends our own British life and the long continuity of our institutions and our Empire. The whole fury and might of the enemy must very soon be turned on us. Hitler knows that he will have to break us in this island or lose the war. If we can stand up to him, all Europe may be free and the life of the world may move forward into broad, sunlit uplands; but if we fail, then the whole world, including the United States, and all that we have known and cared for, will sink into the abyss of a new dark age made more sinister and perhaps more prolonged by the lights of a perverted science. Let us therefore brace ourselves to our duty and so bear ourselves that if the British Commonwealth and Empire lasts for a thousand years men will still say, "This was their finest hour."

[9] David Lloyd George.
[10] In mid-June, 1940, Paul Reynaud, French Premier, encouraged Churchill and his Cabinet to proclaim a "Declaration of Union" between France and England. The offer was made but the French Cabinet, largely influenced by Marshal Henri Pétain, refused to consider the proposal. Reynaud resigned; Pétain formed a government; an armistice was signed with Germany (June 22, 1940) and Italy (June 24, 1940). Reynaud established a government-in-exile and appointed Charles de Gaulle Under-Secretary for War.

Winston S. Churchill

"Never in the Field of Human Conflict"*

Commons, August 20, 1940

Almost a year has passed since the war began, and it is natural for us, I think, to pause on our journey at this milestone and survey the dark, wide field. It is also useful to compare the first year of this second war against German aggression with its forerunner a quarter of a century ago. Although this war is in fact only a continuation of the last, very great differences in its character are apparent. In the last war millions of men fought by hurling enormous masses of steel at one another. "Men and shells" was the cry, and prodigious slaughter was the consequence. In this war nothing of this kind has yet appeared. It is a conflict of strategy, of organisation, of technical apparatus, of science, mechanics, and morale. The British casualties in the first twelve months of the Great War amounted to 365,000. In this war, I am thankful to say, British killed, wounded, prisoners, and missing, including civilians, do not exceed 92,000, and of these a large proportion are alive as prisoners of war. Looking more widely around, one may say that throughout all Europe, for one man killed or wounded in the first year perhaps five were killed or wounded in 1914–1915.

The slaughter is but a fraction, but the consequences to the belligerents have been even more deadly. We have seen great countries with powerful armies dashed out of coherent existence in a few weeks. We have seen the French Republic and the renowned French Army beaten into complete and total submission with less than the casualties which they suffered in any one of half a dozen of the battles of 1914–1918. The entire body—it might almost seem at times the soul—of France has succumbed to physical effects incomparably less terrible than those which were sustained with fortitude and undaunted will power twenty-five years ago. Although up to the present the loss of life has been mercifully diminished, the decisions

* Our text is taken from *Parliamentary Debates (Official Report)*, Fifth Series, Vol. CCCLXIV, cols. 1159–1171.

reached in the course of the struggle are even more profound upon the fate of nations than anything that has ever happened since barbaric times. Moves are made upon the scientific and strategic boards, advantages are gained by mechanical means, as a result of which scores of millions of men become incapable of further resistance or judge themselves incapable of further resistance, and a fearful game of chess proceeds from check to mate by which the unhappy players seem to be inexorably bound.

There is another more obvious difference from 1914. The whole of the warring nations are engaged, not only soldiers but the entire population—men, women, and children. The fronts are everywhere. The trenches are dug in the towns and streets. Every village is fortified. Every road is barred. The front line runs through the factories. The workmen are soldiers with different weapons but the same courage. These are great and distinctive changes from what many of us saw in the struggle of a quarter of a century ago. There seems to be every reason to believe that this new kind of war is well suited to the genius and the resources of the British nation and the British Empire, and that once we get properly equipped and properly started, a war of this kind will be more favourable to us than the sombre mass slaughters of the Somme and Passchendaele.[1] If it is a case of the whole nation fighting and suffering together, that ought to suit us, because we are the most united of all the nations, because we entered the war upon the national will and with our eyes open, and because we have been nurtured in freedom and individual responsibility and are the products not of totalitarian uniformity but of tolerance and variety. If all these qualities are turned, as they are being turned, to the arts of war, we may be able to show the enemy quite a lot of things that they have not thought of yet. Since the Germans drove the Jews out and lowered their technical standards, our science is definitely ahead of theirs. Our geographical position, the command of the sea, and the friendship of the United States enable us to draw resources from the whole world and to manufacture weapons of war of every kind, but especially of the superfine kinds, on a scale hitherto practised only by Nazi Germany.

Hitler is now sprawled over Europe. Our offensive springs are being slowly compressed, and we must resolutely and methodically prepare ourselves for the campaigns of 1941 and 1942. Two or three years are not a long time even in our short, precarious lives. They are nothing in the history of the nation, and when we are doing the finest thing in the world and have the honour to be the sole champion of the liberties of all Europe, we must not grudge these years or weary as we toil and struggle through them. It does not follow that our energies in future years will be exclusively confined to defending ourselves and our possessions. Many opportunities

[1] The Somme and Passchendaele were sites of disastrous battles during World War I. It is estimated that the British lost 420,000 men during the Somme campaign and 324,000 during the battle of Ypres; Passchendaele was the final scene of this battle.

may lie open to amphibious power, and we must be ready to take advantage of them. One of the ways to bring this war to a speedy end is to convince the enemy, not by words but by deeds, that we have both the will and the means not only to go on indefinitely but to strike heavy and unexpected blows. The road to victory may not be so long as we expect. But we have no right to count upon this. Be it long or short, rough or smooth, we mean to reach our journey's end.

It is our intention to maintain and enforce a strict blockade not only of Germany but of Italy, France, and all the other countries that have fallen into the German power. I read in the papers that Herr Hitler has also proclaimed a strict blockade of the British islands. No one can complain of that. I remember the Kaiser doing it in the last war. What indeed would be a matter of general complaint would be if we were to prolong the agony of all Europe by allowing food to come in to nourish the Nazis and aid their war effort, or to allow food to go in to the subjugated peoples which certainly would be pillaged off them by their Nazi conquerors.

There have been many proposals, founded on the highest motives, that food should be allowed to pass the blockade for the relief of these populations. I regret that we must refuse these requests. The Nazis declare that they have created a new unified economy in Europe. They have repeatedly stated that they possess ample reserves of food and that they can feed their captive peoples. In a German broadcast of the 27th of June, it was said that while Mr. Hoover's plan[2] for relieving France, Belgium, and Holland deserved commendation, the German forces had already taken the necessary steps. We know that in Norway when the German troops went in, there were food supplies to last for a year. We know that Poland, though not a rich country, usually produces sufficient food for her people. Moreover, the other countries which Herr Hitler has invaded all held considerable stocks when the Germans entered and are themselves in many cases very substantial food producers. If all this food is not available now, it can only be because it has been removed to feed the people of Germany and to give them increased rations—for a change—during the last few months. At this season of the year and for some months to come, there is the least chance of scarcity as the harvest has just been gathered in. The only agencies which can create famine in any part of Europe now and during the coming winter will be German exactions or German failure to distribute the supplies which they command.

There is another aspect. Many of the most valuable foods are essential to the manufacture of vital war material. Fats are used to make explosives. Potatoes make the alcohol for motor spirit. The plastic materials now so

[2] Ex-President Herbert Hoover, assuming the role he had played following World War I, proposed in a series of speeches given throughout 1940 that the Red Cross and other such organizations immediately attempt to get food to suffering Europeans. He was head of the Belgian Relief Organization.

largely used in the construction of aircraft are made of milk. If the Germans used these commodities to help them to bomb our women and children, rather than to feed the populations who produce them, we may be sure that imported foods would go the same way, directly or indirectly, or be employed to relieve the enemy of the responsibilities he has so wantonly assumed. Let Hitler bear his responsibilities to the full and let the peoples of Europe who groan beneath his yoke aid in every way the coming of the day when that yoke will be broken. Meanwhile, we can and we will arrange in advance for the speedy entry of food into any part of the enslaved area when this part has been wholly cleared of German forces and has genuinely regained its freedom. We shall do our best to encourage the building up of reserves of food all over the world, so that there will always be held up before the eyes of the peoples of Europe, including—I say it deliberately—the German and Austrian peoples, the certainty that the shattering of the Nazi power will bring to them all immediate food, freedom, and peace.

Rather more than a quarter of a year has passed since the new Government came into power in this country. What a cataract of disaster has poured out upon us since then: the trustful Dutch overwhelmed; their beloved and respected sovereign driven into exile; the peaceful city of Rotterdam the scene of a massacre as hideous and brutal as anything in the Thirty Years' War;[3] Belgium invaded and beaten down; our own fine Expeditionary Force, which King Leopold called to his rescue, cut off and almost captured, escaping, as it seemed, only by a miracle and with the loss of all its equipment; our Ally, France, out; Italy in against us; all France in the power of the enemy, all its arsenals and vast masses of military material converted or convertible to the enemy's use; a puppet government set up at Vichy which may at any moment be forced to become our foe; the whole western seaboard of Europe from the North Cape to the Spanish frontier in German hands; all the ports, all the airfields on this immense front, employed against us as potential springboards of invasion. Moreover, the German air power, numerically so far outstripping ours, has been brought so close to our island that what we used to dread greatly has come to pass and the hostile bombers not only reach our shores in a few minutes and from many directions, but can be escorted by their fighting aircraft. Why, Sir, if we had been confronted at the beginning of May with such a prospect, it would have seemed incredible that at the end of a period of horror and disaster, or at this point in a period of horror and disaster, we should stand erect, sure of ourselves, masters of our fate and with the conviction of final victory burning unquenchable in our hearts. Few would have believed we could survive; none would have believed that we should today not only feel stronger but should actually be stronger than we have ever been before.

[3] On May 14, 1940, the German air force destroyed much of the city and port of Rotterdam.

Let us see what has happened on the other side of the scales. The British nation and the British Empire, finding themselves alone, stood undismayed against disaster. No one flinched or wavered; nay, some who formerly thought of peace now think only of war. Our people are united and resolved as they have never been before. Death and ruin have become small things compared with the shame of defeat or failure in duty. We cannot tell what lies ahead. It may be that even greater ordeals lie before us. We shall face whatever is coming to us. We are sure of ourselves and of our cause, and here, then, is the supreme fact which has emerged in these months of trial.

Meanwhile, we have not only fortified our hearts but our island. We have rearmed and rebuilt our armies in a degree which would have been deemed impossible a few months ago. We have ferried across the Atlantic in the month of July, thanks to our friends over there, an immense mass of munitions of all kinds—cannon, rifles, machine guns, cartridges and shell—all safely landed without the loss of a gun or a round. The output of our own factories, working as they have never worked before, has poured forth to the troops. The whole British Army is at home. More than 2,000,000 determined men have rifles and bayonets in their hands tonight and three-quarters of them are in regular military formations. We have never had armies like this in our island in time of war. The whole island bristles against invaders from the sea or from the air. As I explained to the House in the middle of June,[4] the stronger our Army at home, the larger must the invading expedition be, and the larger the invading expedition, the less difficult will be the task of the Navy in detecting its assembly and in intercepting and destroying it on passage; and the greater also would be the difficulty of feeding and supplying the invaders if ever they landed, in the teeth of continuous naval and air attack on their communications. All this is classical and venerable doctrine. As in Nelson's[5] day, the maxim holds: "Our first line of defence is the enemy's ports." Now air reconnaissance and photography have brought to an old principle a new and potent aid.

Our Navy is far stronger than it was at the beginning of the war. The great flow of new construction set on foot at the outbreak is now beginning to come in. We hope our friends across the ocean will send us a timely reinforcement to bridge the gap between the peace flotillas of 1939 and the war flotillas of 1941. There is no difficulty in sending such aid. The seas and oceans are open. The U-boats are contained. The magnetic mine is, up to the present time, effectively mastered. The merchant tonnage under the British flag, after a year of unlimited U-boat war, after eight months of intensive mining attack, is larger than when we began. We have in addition under our control at least four million tons of shipping from the

[4] The reference is to Churchill's speech "Their Finest Hour," pages 507–509.
[5] Famous naval hero, Lord Horatio Nelson (1758–1805).

captive countries, which has taken refuge here or in the harbours of the Empire. Our stocks of food of all kinds are far more abundant than in the days of peace and a large and growing programme of food production is on foot.

Why do I say all this? Not assuredly to boast; not assuredly to give the slightest countenance to complacency. The dangers we face are still enormous, but so are our advantages and resources. I recount them because the people have a right to know that there are solid grounds for the confidence which we feel, and that we have good reason to believe ourselves capable, as I said in a very dark hour two months ago, of continuing the war "if necessary alone, if necessary for years."[6] I say it also because the fact that the British Empire stands invincible and that Nazidom is still being resisted will kindle again the spark of hope in the breasts of hundreds of millions of downtrodden or despairing men and women throughout Europe and far beyond its bounds, and that from these sparks there will presently come a cleansing and devouring flame.

The great air battle which has been in progress over this island for the last few weeks has recently attained a high intensity. It is too soon to attempt to assign limits either to its scale or to its duration. We must certainly expect that greater efforts will be made by the enemy than any he has so far put forth. Hostile air fields are still being developed in France and the Low Countries, and the movement of squadrons and material for attacking us is still proceeding. It is quite plain that Herr Hitler could not admit defeat in his air attack on Great Britain without sustaining most serious injury. If, after all his boastings and blood-curdling threats and lurid accounts trumpeted round the world of the damage he has inflicted, of the vast numbers of our Air Force he has shot down, so he says, with so little loss to himself; if after tales of the panic-stricken British crouched in their holes cursing the plutocratic Parliament which has led them to such a plight; if after all this his whole air onslaught were forced after a while tamely to peter out, the Führer's reputation for veracity of statement might be seriously impugned. We may be sure, therefore, that he will continue as long as he has the strength to do so and as long as any preoccupations he may have in respect of the Russian Air Force allow him to do so.

On the other hand, the conditions and course of the fighting have so far been favourable to us. I told the House two months ago[7] that whereas in France our fighter aircraft were wont to inflict a loss of two or three to one upon the Germans, and in the fighting at Dunkirk, which was a kind of no man's land, a loss of about three or four to one, we expected that in an attack on this island we should achieve a larger ratio. This has certainly come true. It must also be remembered that all the enemy machines and pilots which are shot down over our island, or over the seas which surround

---

[6] The expression comes from Churchill's "Dunkirk" speech, page 505.
[7] The reference is to Churchill's "Their Finest Hour" address, page 510.

it, are either destroyed or captured; whereas a considerable proportion of our machines and also of our pilots are saved and soon again in many cases come into action.

A vast and admirable system of salvage, directed by the Ministry of Aircraft Production, ensures the speediest return to the fighting line of damaged machines and the most provident and speedy use of all the spare parts and material. At the same time the splendid— nay, astounding—increase in the output and repair of British aircraft and engines which Lord Beaverbrook has achieved by a genius of organisation and drive, which looks like magic, has given us overflowing reserves of every type of aircraft and an ever-mounting stream of production both in quantity and quality. The enemy is, of course, far more numerous than we are. But our new production already, as I am advised, largely exceeds his, and the American production is only just beginning to flow in. It is a fact, as I see from my daily returns, that our bomber and fighter strengths now, after all this fighting, are larger than they have ever been. We hope—we believe—that we shall be able to continue the air struggle indefinitely and as long as the enemy pleases, and the longer it continues the more rapid will be our approach first towards that parity and then into that superiority in the air upon which in a large measure the decision of the war depends.

The gratitude of every home in our island, in our Empire, and indeed throughout the world, except in the abodes of the guilty, goes out to the British airmen who, undaunted by odds, unwearied in their constant challenge and mortal danger, are turning the tide of world war by their prowess and by their devotion. Never in the field of human conflict was so much owed by so many to so few. All hearts go out to the fighter pilots whose brilliant actions we see with our own eyes day after day, but we must never forget that all the time, night after night, month after month, our bomber squadrons travel far into Germany, find their targets in the darkness by the highest navigational skill, aim their attacks—often under the heaviest fire, often with serious loss—with deliberate, careful discrimination, and inflict shattering blows upon the whole of the technical and war-making structure of the Nazi power. On no part of the Royal Air Force does the weight of the war fall more heavily than on the daylight bombers who will play an invaluable part in the case of invasion and whose unflinching zeal it has been necessary in the meanwhile on numerous occasions to restrain.

We are able to verify the results of bombing military targets in Germany not only by reports which reach us through many sources, but also, of course, by photography. I have no hesitation in saying that this process of bombing the military industries and communications of Germany and the air bases and storage depots from which we are attacked—which process will continue upon an ever-increasing scale until the end of the war and may in another year attain dimensions hitherto undreamed of—affords one, at least, of the most certain, if not the shortest, of all the roads to victory. Even if the Nazi legions stood triumphant on the Black Sea or indeed upon the Caspian, even if Hitler was at the gates of India, it would profit him nothing if at the same time the entire economic and scientific apparatus of German war power lay shattered and pulverised at home.

The fact that the invasion of this island upon a large scale has become a far more difficult operation with every week that has passed since we saved our Army at Dunkirk and our very great preponderance of sea power enable us to turn our eyes and to turn our strength increasingly towards the Mediterranean and against that other enemy who, without the slightest provocation, coldly and deliberately for greed and gain stabbed France in the back in the moment of her agony and is now marching against us in Africa. The defection of France has, of course, been deeply damaging to our position in what is called, somewhat oddly, the Middle East. In the defence of Somaliland, for instance, we had counted upon strong French forces attacking the Italians from Jibuti.[8] We had counted also upon the use of the French naval and air bases in the Mediterranean, and particularly upon the North African shore. We had counted upon the French Fleet. Even though metropolitan France was temporarily over-run there was no reason why the French Navy, substantial parts of the French Army, the French Air Force, and the French Empire overseas should not have continued the struggle at our side.

Shielded by overwhelming sea power, possessed of invaluable strategic bases and of ample funds, France might have remained one of the great combatants in the struggle. By so doing, France would have preserved the continuity of her life, and the French Empire might have advanced with the British Empire to the rescue of the independence and integrity of the French motherland. In our own case, if we had been put in the terrible position of France—a contingency now happily impossible, although, of course, it would have been the duty of all war leaders to fight on here to the end—it would also have been their duty, as I indicated in my speech of the 4th of June,[9] to provide as far as possible for the naval security of Canada and our Dominions and to make sure they had the means to carry on the struggle from beyond the oceans. Most of the other countries that have been over-run by Germany for the time being have persevered valiantly and faithfully. The Czechs, the Poles, the Norwegians, the Dutch, the Belgians are still in the field, sword in hand, recognised by Great Britain and the United States as the sole representative authorities and lawful governments of their respective states.

That France alone should lie prostrate at this moment is the crime not of a great and noble nation, but of what are called "the men of Vichy."[10]

[8] Now Djibouti, port city and capital of Afars and Issas, formerly French Somaliland.
[9] The "Dunkirk" speech, page 505.
[10] The Pétain government of "Unoccupied France."

We have profound sympathy with the French people. Our old comradeship with France is not dead. In General de Gaulle and his gallant band, that comradeship takes an effective form. These free Frenchmen have been condemned to death by Vichy, but the day will come as surely as the sun will rise tomorrow when their names will be held in honour, and their names will be graven in stone in the streets and villages of a France restored in a liberated Europe to its full freedom and its ancient fame.

But this conviction which I feel of the future cannot affect the immediate problems which confront us in the Mediterranean and in Africa. It had been decided some time before the beginning of the war not to defend the Protectorate of Somaliland, and when our small forces there, a few battalions, a few guns, were attacked by all the Italian troops—nearly two divisions, which had formerly faced the French at Jibuti—it was right to withdraw our detachments virtually intact for action elsewhere. Far larger operations no doubt impend in the Middle East theatre, and I shall certainly not attempt to discuss or prophesy about their probable course. We have large armies and many means of reinforcing them. We have the complete sea command of the Eastern Mediterranean. We intend to do our best to give a good account of ourselves and to discharge faithfully and resolutely all our obligations and duties in that quarter of the world. More than that I do not think the House would wish me to say at the present time.

A good many people have written to me to ask me to make on this occasion a fuller statement of our war aims and of the kind of peace we wish to make after the war than is contained in the very considerable declaration which was made early in the autumn. Since then we have made common cause with Norway, Holland, and Belgium. We have recognised the Czech Government of Dr. Benes,[11] and we have told General de Gaulle that our success will carry with it the restoration of France. I do not think it would be wise at this moment, while the battle rages and the war is still perhaps only in its earlier stage, to embark upon elaborate speculations about the future shape which should be given to Europe or the new securities which must be arranged to spare mankind the miseries of a third world war. The ground is not new, it has been frequently traversed and explored, and many ideas are held about it in common by all good men and all free men. But before we can undertake the task of rebuilding, we have not only to be convinced ourselves but we have to convince all other countries that the Nazi tyranny is going to be finally broken. The right to guide the course of world history is the noblest prize of victory. We are still toiling up the hill; we have not yet reached the crestline of it; we cannot survey the landscape or even imagine what its condition will be when that longed-for morning comes. The task which lies before us immediately is at once more practical, more simple, and more stern. I hope—indeed I pray—that we shall not be found unworthy of our victory if after toil and tribula-

[11] Eduard Benes, President of Czechoslovakia.

tion it is granted to us. For the rest, we have to gain the victory. That is our task.

There is, however, one direction in which we can see a little more clearly ahead. We have to think not only for ourselves but for the lasting security of the cause and principles for which we are fighting and of the long future of the British Commonwealth of Nations. Some months ago, we came to the conclusion that the interests of the United States and of the British Empire both required that the United States should have facilities for the naval and air defence of the Western Hemisphere against the attack of a Nazi power which might have acquired temporary but lengthy control of a large part of Western Europe and its formidable resources. We had therefore decided spontaneously and without being asked or offered any inducement to inform the Government of the United States that we would be glad to place such defence facilities at their disposal by leasing suitable sites in our transatlantic possessions[12] for their greater security against the unmeasured dangers of the future. The principle of association of interests for common purposes between Great Britain and the United States had developed even before the war. Various agreements had been reached about certain small islands in the Pacific Ocean which had become important as air fuelling points. In all this line of thought we found ourselves in very close harmony with the Government of Canada.

Presently we learned that anxiety was also felt in the United States about the air and naval defence of their Atlantic seaboard, and President Roosevelt has recently made it clear that he would like to discuss with us and with the Dominion of Canada and with Newfoundland the development of American naval and air facilities in Newfoundland and in the West Indies. There is, of course, no question of any transference of sovereignty—that has never been suggested—or of any action being taken without the consent or against the wishes of the various Colonies concerned, but for our part, His Majesty's Government are entirely willing to accord defence facilities to the United States on a ninety-nine-years' leasehold basis, and we feel sure that our interests no less than theirs and the interests of the Colonies themselves and of Canada and Newfoundland will be served thereby. These are important steps. Undoubtedly this process means that these two great organisations of the English-speaking democracies, the British Empire and the United States, will have to be somewhat mixed up together in some of their affairs for mutual and general advantage. For my own part, looking out upon the future, I do not view the process with any misgivings. I could not stop it if I wished; no one can stop it. Like the Mississippi, it just keeps rolling along. Let it roll. Let it roll on full flood, inexorable, irresistible, benignant, to broader lands and better days.

[12] Britain granted rights to bases in Newfoundland and Bermuda, and traded the West Indian and South African base sites on the Bahamas, Jamaica, St. Lucia, Trinidad, Antigua, and British Guiana for a fleet of destroyers.

Aneurin Bevan

"Change the Direction of the War"*
Commons, July 2, 1942

I beg to second the motion.[1]

The honourable Members who put their names to this motion and I were rebuked yesterday by honourable Members in some parts of the House for having done so. They rebuked us on two grounds—one, that a motion of this nature moved at this time would have a bad effect upon the morale of the troops; and the other that it would have a bad effect upon the morale of the country. I want to reply to these two charges at the beginning. I believe it would have been a very bad thing indeed for the reputation of the House of Commons if this motion had not been moved. It is the duty, as I understand it, of Members of Parliament to try and reproduce in the House of Commons the psychology which exists in the country, and there can be no doubt that the country is deeply disturbed by the movement of events at the present time. Having put the motion on the Order Paper, it would have been a great disservice to the country if we had withdrawn it. I do not know whether honourable Members have received many letters in the last few days, but if they have they will have realised that there are far more people supporting the motion outside the House than are represented by the names on the Order Paper.

With regard to the morale of the troops, my honourable Friends and I would be loath indeed to do anything here which might have the effect of undermining the courage and resolution of our troops in battle. It is not, however, what we say in this House, it is not the speeches we make, that bring home to the soldiers the defects in the direction of the war; it is what

---

* This text is taken from *Parliamentary Debates (Official Report)*, Fifth Series, Vol. CCCLXXXI, cols. 527–541.

[1] Sir John Wardlaw-Milne, Member for Kidderminster, moved "That this House, while paying tribute to the heroism and endurance of the Armed Forces of the Crown in circumstances of exceptional difficulty, has no confidence in the central direction of the war."

they experience themselves in battle. It would be a serious thing if the soldiers in the field could not hear any voices raised in their behalf in the House of Commons. I believe that nothing would more nerve our forces to greater efforts and arouse their enthusiasm than the knowledge that their representatives in the House of Commons were doing their best to see that they are given the right weapons with which to fight. It will never be possible for us in this war to move a Vote of Censure on the Government at a time when no battle is in progress. Battles are going to be continuous throughout the war, and therefore we must take the opportunity when we think it is proper to move a Vote of Censure upon the Government, although it may happen that at that very moment a series of grave battles is in progress.

The Prime Minister has decided to wind up the debate, and I understand he proposes to talk for something like an hour and a half. I am bound to point out to the House that I think a very serious disservice is being done to the House and the country by the fact that the Prime Minister did not see fit to open the debate. He has the right to choose when he will speak. Of course he has. But the Prime Minister is also Minister of Defence, and the House had the right to be put in possession of the facts of the case so that the debate might have proceeded upon an examination of those facts. I know that it is better debating tactics for the Prime Minister to wind up the debate. In that way he will win the debate. But the country is now more concerned with the Prime Minister winning the war than with his winning a debate in the House of Commons. The Prime Minister wins debate after debate and loses battle after battle. The country is beginning to say that he fights debates like a war and the war like a debate. It would have been much more dignified for the Prime Minister and of much greater service to the House if he had opened the debate yesterday and allowed one of his Ministers to wind up. Indeed, the Prime Minister could have opened the debate and wound it up as well. He has done so before. But that would have been undignified for other Members of the Government, because it would give the impression once more to the world that there was only one man in the Government.

So, because of that situation, the House of Commons is in the difficulty of having to await the Prime Minister's reply before it is able to consider the merits of the Government's case. Furthermore, yesterday we were at a disadvantage in having had a speech from the Minister of Production.[2] Rather it was the Government's disadvantage, not ours. I have heard some Members of the Government complain about the right honourable Gentleman's speech. I do not see why they should complain, because had the right honourable Gentleman made himself more clear, the Government's case would have suffered more damage. What, in fact, did the right honourable Gentleman say? What was the main case made by him? It was that

[2] Oliver Lyttelton.

we had had no time in which to produce new weapons, and that therefore our troops in Libya had to fight with weapons which were designed before the war. That was his main case—that we could not change the designs in time; that there are new designs in production, but that they could not be put on the battlefield because we had to continue with the old types. What then becomes of the Prime Minister's statement last December[3] that at last we were meeting the enemy on equal terms with modern weapons?

I would also refer to a speech which was made yesterday in another place.[4] Ministers are all concerned to prove that they were right and that they made no mistakes when in office. I recommend honourable Members to read the speech made in another place, because that is another answer to the Government. Ministers are trying to absolve themselves by putting the blame somewhere else. I hope to show that the blame rests squarely upon the Government's own shoulders. I therefore believe that it is the duty of honourable Members to state their minds clearly and independently upon this matter. The House may not agree with me, but when I sit down, there should be no misunderstanding about what I think.

It seems to me that there are three things wrong. First, the main strategy of the war has been wrong; second, the wrong weapons have been produced; and third, those weapons are being managed by men who are not trained in the use of them and who have not studied the use of modern weapons. As I understand it, it is strategy that dictates the weapon and tactics that dictate the use of the weapon. The Government have conceived the war wrongly from the very beginning, and no one has more misconceived it than the Prime Minister himself. The nature of the weapons used by the enemy has not been understood by the Prime Minister ever since the beginning of the war. I will read to the House what the right honourable Gentleman said on the 19th of May, 1940:

> It would be foolish . . . to disguise the gravity of the hour. It would be still more foolish to lose heart and courage or to suppose that well-trained, well-equipped armies numbering three or four millions of men can be overcome in the space of a few weeks or even months by a scoop or raid of mechanised vehicles, however formidable.[5]

That is precisely what did happen in a few weeks. No one was more Maginot-minded than the Prime Minister himself. I have read all his speeches very carefully, and I say that no one has thought of this war in terms of the last war more than the Prime Minister himself. That is contained in the statement to which I refer. He also said: "We may look forward

---

[3] The reference is to Churchill's "Man-Power and Woman-Power" speech of December 2, 1941.

[4] Probably Lord Beaverbrook's address to the House of Lords on the "Conduct of the War." See *Parliamentary Debates (Official Report)*, Fifth Series, Vol. CXXIII, cols. 570–582.

[5] The quotation is from Churchill's "Be Ye Men of Valour" speech, page 495.

with confidence to the stabilisation of the front in France . . . ." Fancy, after Poland and in the opening weeks of the Battle of France, speaking about stabilisation of the front in France. No Russian general, no German general, speaks about the stabilisation of the front. The front cannot be stabilised in modern war, and Rommel[6] is proving it today. The Prime Minister went on to say: ". . . and to the general engagement of the masses which will enable the qualities of French and British soldiers to be matched squarely against those of their adversaries. For myself, I have invincible confidence in the French Army and its leaders."

THE PRIME MINISTER: Ought I to have said the opposite?

MR. BEVAN: It is a case of what the right honourable Gentleman ought not to have said. He ought not to have used language which, on the face of it, reveals quite clearly that the Prime Minister had not penetrated to the heart of the methods that were being used by the Germans or were going to be used in this war. It is that primary misconception of the war which has been responsible for the wrong strategy of the Government, and the strategy being wrong, the wrong weapons were produced. The chief evidence of that is the case of the dive-bomber. The second chief evidence of that is the complete failure to equip the British Army with transport planes. Take the situation in Libya. The right honourable Gentleman the Minister of Production yesterday said that according to modern methods of warfare, "islands" of troops had been made in the desert behind fortifications. We had one in Bir Hacheim, fought with distinguished gallantry by the Free French. This has been one of the most heroic episodes in the whole war, and I am informed that they had not even two-pounder guns in Bir Hacheim. Having seen for more than two years that we should be fighting a desert war in Libya, we still have not provided any transport planes and had to send a tank brigade through with supplies, whereas the Germans have supplied strong points and islands of resistance in Russia right throughout the winter by transport planes.

I say that if the war had been properly conceived, if the Prime Minister had understood it, we should have had both dive-bombers and transport planes, so that wherever we organised a strong point, whether in the desert or elsewhere, transport planes would have been available to supply our troops. Further, had we produced transport planes in any quantity, we should have been able right through the campaign there to use them for carrying a great deal of material, instead of having to send all supplies 14,000 miles by sea. I ask the House seriously whether that condition of affairs reveals any deep penetration by the Government into the nature of the war we have to fight. A lot has been said about dive-bombers. Even now the Government have not made up their minds upon them. The

---

[6] Marshal Erwin Rommel, Commander-in-Chief in North Africa.

Secretary of State for War[7] says that discussions are proceeding. I would remind honourable Members of a letter from Mr. Westbrook,[8] which they have probably read for themselves, which was published in *The Times*. He was at the Ministry of Aircraft Production and went out to the Near East in charge of supplies, or at least as one of the higher officials, and he came home from the Near East for reasons that it is not politic to state in public. He says:

> Just lately many confusing and conflicting statements have been made about the lack of dive-bombers. The true facts are that the Air Ministry decided before the war against the use of them.

Against the use of them before the war. Where was our Intelligence Service? For the last five or six years I have heard the Prime Minister making eloquent speeches about the German military preparations. His reputation to this day rests upon those speeches. The affectionate regard the country still has for him arises out of gratitude because he warned the country at that time. But he warned the country about them quantitatively; the qualitative position he left aside. He gave us the figures, but there was no insight behind the figures. He has been in charge of this war really for three years. He must have known the nature of the weapons that the Germans were making. Dive-bombers were not a secret. The Czechs knew of them and had prepared to resist them. Czech military strategy was based upon the use of the dive-bomber. The letter from Mr. Westbrook goes on:

> Probably this was correct until we had the mastery of the air or sufficient capacity to enable their production without detriment to the more important types.

There, of course, is the official defending his decisions. The fact remains that a prototype was never developed, that the Government could not even make up their mind then, because they fell between two stools. Mr. Westbrook says further:

> Both Lord Beaverbrook and I thought they were necessary, so he obtained a request from Mr. Eden, then at the War Office, and a quantity to a new design were ordered from America in the summer of 1940. These are now in production. There were, however, delivery delays, as the British Air Commission in America were never allowed to give them any form of priority.

That is a most serious statement. We have no right to complain against America. If America did not want to give them priority, why should

---

[7] Sir James Grigg, Member for East Cardiff.
[8] One of Lord Beaverbrook's earliest appointments in the Ministry of Air Production. T. C. L. Westbrook's letter appeared in the issue of June 27, 1942, p. 5.

America do so when we ourselves said they were no use? We did not ask for priority for them. The result is that after three years of war the British Army is not equipped with dive-bombers. I say that at once reveals that the Prime Minister and his Government have not gone to the heart of this modern war-making, and I say that it is disgraceful that the lives of British soldiers should be lost because of the absence of this elementary knowledge at the top.

We ourselves, here, must accept responsibility for it. After all, the Government are responsible to us, and if the House of Commons refuses to exercise its independence against the Government, the House of Commons must accept responsibility for the result. It is we—not party machines, not secret meetings upstairs of Members on any side of the House—but we in this House who are responsible for sending British soldiers on to the battlefield with improper weapons; and honourable Members, when they go back to their constituencies, should not hide behind any formality of Parliamentary debate but face squarely up to the facts. When the mothers and fathers of British soldiers ask why their boys go into battle worse equipped than the enemy, for Heaven's sake say, "We are responsible, and nobody else."

SIR GRANVILLE GIBSON:[9] The honourable Member was for seven years. He always voted against any increase in armaments for seven years.

EARL WINTERTON:[10] What about the Government? What about the Home Secretary?[11]

MR. BEVAN: I will face the issue squarely. I do not run away from it. This House of Commons gave the Government unlimited power to rearm this country in 1935, and Ministers still in this Government were responsible at that time. The right honourable Gentleman has picked them for his Government. Do not throw the jeer back at me; it belongs over there. It is the Prime Minister who has cast the mantle of his benediction on the shoulders of those guilty Ministers. They are still there sitting on that front bench, so do not throw the jeer at me. In any case, even if the rearmament of Britain before the war was quantitatively lacking, there is no excuse for its having been qualitatively inefficient. There may be an excuse for a lack of will, but not for a lack of brains, and our brains were wrong and the brains are still wrong.

I will not talk about guns, because they were exploded yesterday—almost all day. We know the situation as regards guns. We know that the guns supplied to our troops did not answer the Prime Minister's description. They were not modern weapons. The Spanish Republicans were using an eight-pounder anti-tank gun in 1936. The Germans learned the lesson in Spain and made the gun immediately afterwards in Germany. We were rearming then—we were supposed to be rearming. We had two White

---

[9] Member for Pudsey and Otley.
[10] Member for Horsham and Worthing.
[11] Herbert Morrison.

Papers on rearmament. But of course the Government of that day were too much occupied in trying to destroy the Republican Government in Spain to learn any military lessons from the campaign in Spain. That was the situation. I shall not deal further with that aspect of it, because I am going on to another matter.

Why is the strategy wrong? I say, first, that it is because the Prime Minister, although possessing many other qualities, sometimes conceives of the war, it seems to me, in mediæval terms, because he talks of it as if it were a tourney. But the strategy is wrong because the Prime Minister has a wrong instrument of government. We have been at war for three years. Over and over again I have heard the Prime Minister speak most eloquently about the defects of the machinery of government. Look at it for a moment. There is a War Cabinet of seven.[12] One of them I rule out, the Lord President of the Council. I do not want to be offensive—he is a most distinguished man—but I have always looked upon him rather as a civil servant than as a politician. So I rule him out. I do not believe that the guidance of the right honourable Gentleman on matters of high political principle differs from that he would get from any government department. Then there is the Secretary of State for Foreign Affairs, burdened by a complicated office. There is the Minister of Labour, with a most distinguished career, a most dynamic personality. He has a most complicated department, a huge department with a large staff. Also, he speaks every week-end. How can he master documents about the war? I do not think the right honourable Gentleman has ever claimed to understand much about war—this is a serious matter—and in any case he has not got the time.

There is the Minister of Production. He is a member of the War Cabinet. The Minister of Production was, I understand, a businessman of distinction, but he has no political experience worth speaking about, as was revealed yesterday. I say with all respect that in his own sphere he is a most eminent man. [*"And a soldier."*] This place is full of soldiers. Stalin was not a soldier, but he is a very good general. The Minister of Production is at the head of the most vital department of all. He has no time to attend to matters of strategy, so he is no use in the War Cabinet for this purpose. Then there is the Deputy Prime Minister. We had a debate the other day. There was no Vote of Censure then. The Government had an overwhelming Vote of Confidence. Every newspaper in the country, every critic in the House of Commons, including men of long standing such as the right honourable Member for Caernarvon Boroughs,[13] all advised that we

[12] In July, 1942, John Anderson (nonparty) was Lord President of the Council; Sir Stafford Cripps (Labour) was Lord Privy Seal; Anthony Eden (Conservative) was Secretary of State for Foreign Affairs; Clement Attlee (Labour) was Deputy Prime Minister and Secretary for Dominion Affairs; Oliver Lyttelton (Conservative) was Minister of Production; Ernest Bevin (Labour) was Minister of Labour and National Service; and Richard Gardiner Casey (Liberal) was Minister of State (for Middle Eastern Affairs).

[13] David Lloyd George.

should have a small War Cabinet of six Ministers without Portfolio. The Prime Minister made a few changes. He threw out the only Minister in the War Cabinet who did not have a portfolio[14] and gave a portfolio to the Deputy Prime Minister.[15] Before then the Deputy Prime Minister did not have a department. Now he has one.

That foolish instrument exaggerates all the natural weaknesses which are the accompaniments of the Prime Minister's strategy. The Prime Minister has qualities of greatness—everybody knows that—but the trouble is that he has too much to do. He has not around him colleagues to whom he can delegate any of this matter concerning the central direction of the war. The result is that all these defects which he possesses are made dangerous, because the Prime Minister, among all his other qualities, has a gift of expression which is exceedingly dangerous. He very often mistakes verbal felicities for verbal inspiration. The Prime Minister will, in the course of an evening, produce a whole series of brilliant improvisations, but he has not the machinery to carry them through.

It is the absence of support as much as anything else which is responsible for the situation. I seriously suggest to the House that whatever they may do about this motion, they should for Heaven's sake insist, at this grave hour, that the Prime Minister be kept under the clamp of strong men who have got no departmental interests. The House knows that that is the correct thing to do, the country knows it, and every responsible man in public affairs in this country outside the Government knows that it is the right thing to do. Why does not the House of Commons exert its dignity and force the Prime Minister to do it? Even an inadequate man giving his full attention is better than a clever man who cannot give any attention. It would be a most improper thing for me to suggest that the members of the War Cabinet are men of no stature. But in this matter the country is entitled to their full services in the central direction of the war, and I suggest that we should insist upon that being done.

Under the War Cabinet I suggest that you must have a far better co-ordination between the Services than now exists. There must be a central staff, presided over by one man who can have immediate access to the War Cabinet and who can ultimately be responsible for central strategy. I do not disagree with the Prime Minister having no Minister of Defence; I do not see how on earth, in wartime, the Prime Minister could delegate responsibility for the war to anybody else. He could not do that, but what he could do would be to have around him a number of Ministers who could assist him in that matter, and the War Cabinet as a whole could see the Chiefs of Staff instead of the Prime Minister—

THE PRIME MINISTER: They do.

MR. BEVAN:—instead of the Prime Minister seeing them before the War

[14] Arthur Greenwood.
[15] Clement Attlee.

Cabinet sees them, because then the Prime Minister goes into the War Cabinet defending his own decisions.

THE PRIME MINISTER: That is not true.

MR. BEVAN: I am sorry, but the right honourable Gentleman will have his opportunity of correcting me later. It is the strategy that is wrong, and the production of weapons. Again, I should like to remind honourable Members that this is not a new story; we have been saying this for two years. All over the country the working classes have been deeply disturbed by the failures of production. Talk about not being able to change over to new types—even now there are aircraft factories idle in this country, changing over to new long-range bombers which may be available in two years' time. The country is bored with hearing of the production of long-range bombers. They know very well that the long-range bomber is not a decisive weapon of war, whatever else it may be. Therefore it is foolish at this moment to be changing to new types of long-range bombers which may not be available at the decisive moment.

On Tuesday, the right honourable Gentleman the Minister of Production told us that he had now appointed regional controllers. The Trades Union Congress, the trade unions of Britain separately, the Production Engineers Institute, and this House of Commons asked for regional boards over two years ago. We have been trying to get the decentralisation of production controls for over two years, and the Prime Minister fought a successful rearguard action against us. He has been fighting rearguard actions against the House of Commons all the time, making concessions all the while to buy off the political situation, not to create a machine for war-making.

So much for production. Then there is the actual use of the weapons in the field. I speak in this matter without authority at all; I have never fought in a battle, I do not know what it is to use weapons in the field, so I have to speak with diffidence in this. Nevertheless, we are responsible, we have to make up our minds. We are as responsible as the Government. I am informed—the Prime Minister will correct me if I am wrong—that even today the staff colleges of the Army have no textbook on the co-ordination of air and land forces. Even today, our Chiefs of Staff and our war captains are not being educated in the co-ordination of those two weapons. I do not know what honourable Members think of that, but it frightens me. It frightens me to think that after three years of war there is no textbook in our staff colleges on this most urgent and important matter. Why, even the small nations of Europe had it years ago, and we have not got it yet.

We have in this country five or six generals, members of other nations—Czechs, Poles, and French—all of them trained in the use of these German weapons and this German technique. I know it is hurtful to our pride, but would it not be possible to put some of those men temporarily in charge in the field until we can produce trained men of our own? Is there anything wrong in sending out these men, of equal rank with General Ritchie?[16] Why should we not put them in the field in charge of our troops? They know how to fight this war; our people do not, and I say that it is far better to win battles and save British soldiers' lives under the leadership of other members of the United Nations than to lose them under our own inefficient officers. The Prime Minister must realise that in this country there is a taunt on everyone's lips that if Rommel had been in the British Army, he would still have been a sergeant. Is that not so? It is a taunt right through the Army. There is a man in the British Army—and this shows how we are using our trained men—who flung 150,000 men across the Ebro in Spain: Michael Dunbar. He is at present a sergeant in an armoured brigade in this country. He was chief of staff in Spain; he won the battle of the Ebro; and he is a sergeant in the British Army. The fact of the matter is that the British Army is ridden by class prejudice. You have got to change it, and you will have to change it. If the House of Commons has not the guts to make the Government change it, events will. Although the House may not take any notice of me today, you will be doing it next week; remember my words next Monday and Tuesday. It is events which are criticising the Government. All that we are doing is giving them a voice, inadequately perhaps, but we are trying to do it.

Therefore, you have to change that business; you have to purge the Army at the top. It will have to be a drastic purge, because the spirit of the British Army has to be regained. I have spoken to men from other nations who have been around the British Army, and they say that never in the history of Great Britain has better human material been provided in the British Army. But it is badly led, not by men without courage—there is no lack of courage in the British Army at any point, at the top or at the bottom —but it is not trained, or is wrongly trained. Therefore, if you are going to give the new weapons which the Minister of Production talked about yesterday, you must give them into the hands of men who know how to use them and who believe in them. You must do that with the dive-bombers; if you have dive-bombers, you must purge from the Air Ministry those men who do not believe in dive-bombers, because the man who does not believe in his own weapon cannot use it. So you will have to purge them.

Furthermore—and I said I was going to be quite frank—if the Prime Minister wants to restore confidence in the British Army, he will have to change his Secretary of State for War. Why on earth he appointed him I do not know. I am not trying to be offensive; the right honourable Gentleman has been in the War Office for five years, and he is picked out of a respectable obscurity and is pushed into an office. Nobody, no soldier in the British Army, knows him. All they know is that he has been at the War

---

[16] General Neil M. Ritchie headed the Eighth Army in Libya; his forces were defeated in a key battle at Tobruk.

Office for five years, and they have no confidence in the War Office. They do not believe in the War Office, and the Prime Minister's political sagacity is so great that he picks out an official from the War Office and makes him Secretary of State for War. I say that the Prime Minister has great qualities, but obviously picking men is not one of them, and he does not know what the reaction is to these men in the country as a whole.

Now I come to my conclusion. Here is our situation; how are we going to face it? If this debate resulted in causing demoralisation in the country in the slightest degree, I would have preferred to cut my tongue out. We do not want to do that. I believe that there is only one way in which we can recover ourselves. Our weapons are not what they ought to be, but they are the weapons we have got, and Hitler is not going to call the war off until we produce better ones; the war is going on, and we shall have to fight with the weapons we have. This country can fight. If the Government think that there is any dismay in the country, they are wrong; there is anger in the country. This is a proud and brave race, and it is feeling humiliated. It cannot stand the holding out of Sevastopol[17] for months and the collapse of Tobruk[18] in twenty-six hours. It cannot stand the comparison between these lost battles, not lost by lack of courage but by lack of vision at the top. It cannot stand this; it is a proud and valiant country, and it wants leadership. It is getting words, not leadership, at the moment from the Government. There is only one way: fight the enemy in Libya; for Heaven's sake fight him wherever you can get at him.

The country expects, and declarations have been made—I can speak freely about this, though I understand that the Prime Minister cannot—that in a very short time at a time and place to be decided by the Government, we shall launch an attack upon the enemy in a theatre of war nearer to this country. I do beg and pray the Government, when they make that decision, to make it out of considerations of strategical propriety and not as a consequence of political propaganda. Nevertheless, we have to do it. We cannot postpone it until next year. Stalin expects it; please do not misunderstand me—for Heaven's sake do not let us make the mistake of betraying those lion-hearted Russians. Speeches have been made, the Russians believe them and have broken the champagne bottles on them. They believe that this country will act this year on what they call the second front. Molotov said so; they expect it and the British nation expects it. I say it is right, it is the correct thing to do, and the Government have practically said so. Do not on these high matters speak with a twisted tongue; do not use words with double meanings; do not use sentences with

---

[17] Sevastopol, scene of a year-long siege (1854–1855) by British and French forces against Russian troops during the Crimean War, was defended from October, 1941, until July 3, 1942, against German attack.

[18] Libyan port taken and retaken by British and German forces between January, 1941, and late 1942. Rommel's troops took Tobruk on June 21, 1942, in a one-day assault.

hidden purposes. On these high matters, speak truthfully and simply, so that the people can understand and trust. Let the Government, for Heaven's sake, make their political dispositions. In the meantime, let them change the direction of the war. Purge the Army and the Air Force of the elements which are not trusted at the moment. Get at the enemy where he really is—twenty-one miles away, not 14,000 miles away. Get him by the throat. If this country at this moment were downhearted, it would be a very good thing. Send some politicians out. It has been done before: it was done in the Afghanistan campaign. Send some of us out, and let us risk our lives. When the troops land in Europe, and you go to rouse Europe, as Europe can be roused, send some of us out with the landing troops.

PETTY-OFFICER ALAN HERBERT:[19] You must be trained first.

MR. BEVAN: If, by the deaths of some of us, we can rouse the British nation, is it not worthwhile? Some went out to Spain untrained. Training is needed; but we have grand human material, and there is an opportunity in Europe for us. Let us get rid of this defeatist complex. This nation can win; but it must be properly led, it must be properly inspired, and it must have confidence in its military leadership. Give us that, and we can win the war in a fashion which will surprise Hitler and at the same time hearten our friends.

---

[19] Member for Oxford University.

Clement R. Attlee

"A Common Endeavour"[*]
Westminster, London, January 10, 1946

I have the honour today of welcoming to London this great assembly of delegates of the United Nations.[1] I would like in the first place to thank you, Mr. President,[2] for your speech and also to place on record the appreciation which I am sure we all feel for the successful manner in which you have carried out the arduous and important duties of President of the Preparatory Commission. I know well from my colleagues how much that Commission has owed to your guidance. Without your sense of business, readiness to accept responsibility, and the influence which you have exerted on your colleagues, we might not have been able to meet at this time with the procedure and programme ready to hand. I hope that the proceedings of this Conference will be animated by the same sense of urgency, the same practical spirit, and the same co-operative atmosphere as has characterised the work of the Preparatory Commission. I know that great questions were debated frankly and even passionately, but at the same time there was a lively spirit of conciliation and goodwill which led eventually to almost complete unanimity.

I have said that we welcome you here to London, and it will be our endeavour to make you feel at home in this our capital city so that you may speak as freely and frankly as if you were meeting in some special territory under international control. We shall do our best to make your stay here pleasant within the limit of our means. We wish we could do more, but I am sure that all of you in the course of your stay will realise that anything that is lacking in your entertainment is not due to any absence of goodwill, but to the effect of the malice of our enemies wreaked upon this ancient city. The evidences of this you will see around you.

Last night we listened to an inspiring speech by His Majesty the King in which he set before us in a few words the nature of the task which we

[*] The text is from the *Journal of the General Assembly*, I (January 10, 1946—March 7, 1946), 22–26.

[1] Delegates representing fifty-one nations were in attendance.
[2] Dr. Eduardo Zuleta Angel of Colombia.

have to accomplish, the vital importance of the issues at stake, and the keen desire of all the nations of the British Commonwealth, for whom he spoke, to make this first meeting of the United Nations Organisation a complete success.

I had the privilege of taking part in the discussions at San Francisco from which was evolved the Charter of the United Nations. The initiation of these discussions, while our enemies were still in the field against us, was at once an act of faith in our victory and an acknowledgment of the cause for which we were fighting. The purposes and principles set down in the Preamble and in Article I of the Charter[3] have the whole-hearted support of

---

[3] The Preamble reads:

WE THE PEOPLES
OF THE UNITED NATIONS
DETERMINED
to save succeeding generations from the scourge of war, which twice in our lifetime has brought untold sorrow to mankind, and to reaffirm faith in fundamental human rights, in the dignity and worth of the human person, in the equal rights of men and women and of nations large and small, and to establish conditions under which justice and respect for the obligations arising from treaties and other sources of international law can be maintained, and to promote social progress and better standards of life in larger freedom,
AND FOR THESE ENDS
to practice tolerance and live together in peace with one another as good neighbors, and to unite our strength to maintain international peace and security, and to ensure, by the acceptance of principles and the institution of methods, that armed force shall not be used, save in the common interest, and to employ international machinery for the promotion of the economic and social advancement of all peoples,
HAVE RESOLVED TO
COMBINE OUR EFFORTS TO
ACCOMPLISH THESE AIMS.
Accordingly, our respective Governments, through representatives assembled in the city of San Francisco, who have exhibited their full powers found to be in good and due form, have agreed to the present Charter of the United Nations and do hereby establish an international organization to be known as the United Nations.

Article I specifies:

The Purposes of the United Nations are:
1. To maintain international peace and security, and to that end: to take effective collective measures for the prevention and removal of threats to the peace, and for the suppression of acts of aggression or other breaches of the peace, and to bring about by peaceful means, and in conformity with the principles of justice and international law, adjustment or settlement of international disputes or situations which might lead to a breach of the peace;
2. To develop friendly relations among nations based on respect for the principle of equal rights and self-determination of peoples, and to take other appropriate measures to strengthen universal peace;
3. To achieve international cooperation in solving international problems of an economic, social, cultural, or humanitarian character, and in promoting and encouraging respect for human rights and for fundamental freedoms for all without distinction as to race, sex, language, or religion; and
4. To be a center for harmonizing the actions of nations in the attainment of these common ends.

His Majesty's Government and, I believe, of the whole of the people of this country to whatever political party they belong.

We realise that as perhaps never before a choice is offered to mankind. Twice in my lifetime a war has brought untold sorrow to mankind. Should there be a third world war, the long upward progress towards civilisation may be halted for generations, and the work of myriads of men and women through the centuries be brought to nought.

The Preamble to the Charter of the United Nations admirably sets out the ideals for which men and women laid down their lives during the war. But the affirmation of principles is easy; the translation into action, the making of a working reality out of an ideal, is very difficult. In the stress and strain of war it is possible to fuse the ideal aim with practical effort. When in the summer of 1940 this country was left open to the imminent danger of invasion, the whole of the people were animated by one single aim, and that aim was immediately translated into action. Every man and woman leaped forward to serve wherever needed, and the strength of that purpose endured through five years of war. During those five years, as nation after nation joined in the struggle, the efforts of the fighting forces, of the workers behind the line, of the resistance movements in so many countries, were all co-ordinated and directed to the single purpose of victory. Private interests and individual national aspirations were sunk in the common endeavour. Now today, when victory has crowned our arms, we have to bring to the task of creating permanent conditions of peace the same sense of urgency, the same self-sacrifice, and the same willingness to subordinate sectional interests to the common good as brought us through the crisis of war. We all, therefore, must approach our work with a realisation of its outstanding and vital importance.

The United Nations Organisation must become the over-riding factor in foreign policy. After the First World War there was a tendency to regard the League of Nations as something outside the ordinary range of foreign policy. Governments continued on the old lines pursuing individual aims and following the path of power politics, not understanding that the world had passed into a new epoch. In just such a spirit in times past in these islands, great nobles and their retainers used to practise private war in disregard of the authority of the central government. The time came when private armies were abolished, when the rule of law was established throughout the length and breadth of this island. What has been done in Britain and in other countries on a small stage has now to be effected throughout the whole world. We must all now today recognise the truth proclaimed by the Foreign Minister of the USSR at Geneva: "Peace is indivisible."[4]

---

[4] The statement was made at a meeting of delegates to negotiations concerning the League of Nations by Maxim Litvinov, Russian Foreign Minister, in a speech, "On the Indivisibility of Peace," on July 1, 1936.

Looking back on past years, we can trace the origins of the late war to acts of aggression, the significance of which was not fully realised at the time. Failure to deal with the Japanese adventure in the Far East and with the acts of aggression of the Fascist rulers of Germany and Italy led inevitably to the breakdown of the rule of law and to the Second World War. In the last five years the aggression of Hitler in Europe drew eventually into the contest men from all the continents and from the islands of the sea. It should make us all realise that the welfare of every one of us is bound up with the welfare of the world as a whole, and that we are truly all members one of another.

I am glad that the Charter of the United Nations does not deal only with governments and states or with politics and war but with the simple elemental needs of human beings whatever be their race, their colour, or their creed. In the Charter we reaffirm our faith in fundamental human rights. We see the freedom of the individual in the state as an essential complement to the freedom of the state in the world community of nations. We stress too that social justice and the best possible standards of life for all are essential factors in promoting and maintaining the peace of the world.

I have said that the solution of the problem of establishing peace and preventing war is urgent and vital as never before. We, perhaps, in these islands, which were for so long immune from attack behind the barrier of the sea, feel more than any others that we are living in a new age. The development of powerful weapons of destruction operating from distant bases has destroyed the illusion of isolationism. The coming of the atomic bomb was only the last of a series of warnings to mankind that unless the powers of destruction could be controlled, immense ruin and almost annihilation would be the lot of the most highly civilised portions of mankind. I welcome, therefore, the decision to remit the whole problem of the control of atomic energy to a Commission of the United Nations Organisation. In this discovery we can see set clearly before us in tangible form the question that faces the modern world. Here is an invention fraught with immense possibilities—on the one hand of danger and on the other of advantage to the human race. It is for the peoples of the world through their representatives to make their choice between life and death.

I hope and believe that every delegate who is here today has come not only in a spirit of determination but in a spirit of hope. We have always with us the sceptics and the pessimists who will tell us that there always has been war and that there always will be war, who point to the failure of the League of Nations as the reason for scepticism as to the success of the United Nations Organisation. But the progress of civilisation has been one of continual failure and of learning by experience. To take an example, the history of the trade-union movement is marked by failure after failure. After every defeat, the sceptics and the timorous said, "You cannot get the workers to combine; the self-interest of the individual is too strong." But eventually unity was achieved.

I have intense faith that we will make the United Nations Organisation a success. We have learnt from past mistakes. The old League of Nations suffered from many disabilities, most of all perhaps because two great nations, the United States of America and the Union of Socialist Soviet Republics, were not present in its formative stages. Today as never before the world is united. Further, the Constitution of the new organisation is essentially realist, in that it provides for the sanction of force to support the rule of law. I think, too, that at the present time the ordinary men and women in every nation have a greater realisation of what is at stake. To make this organisation a living reality we must enlist the support not only of governments but of the masses of the people throughout the world. They must understand that we are building a defence for the common people. In the purposes of the United Nations, we have linked with the achievement of freedom from fear the delivery of mankind from the peril of want. To the individual citizen, the spectre of economic insecurity is more constant, more imminent, than the shadow of war. Every individual can be brought to realise that the things that are discussed in conference here are the concern of all and affect the home life of every man, woman, and child. Without social justice and security, there is no real foundation for peace, for it is among the socially disinherited and those who have nothing to lose that the gangster and aggressor recruit their supporters.

I believe, therefore, that important as is the work of the Security Council, no less vital is it to make the Economic and Social Council an effective international instrument. A police force is a necessary part of a civilised community, but the greater the social security and contentment of the population the less important is the police force.

Finally, let us be clear as to what is our ultimate aim. It is not just the negation of war, but the creation of a world of security and freedom, of a world which is governed by justice and the moral law. We desire to assert the pre-eminence of right over might and the general good against selfish and sectional aims. We who are gathered here today in this ancient home of liberty and order are able to meet together because thousands of brave men and women have suffered and died that we may live. It is for us today, bearing in mind the great sacrifices that have been made, to prove ourselves no less courageous in approaching our great task—no less patient, no less self-sacrificing. We must and will succeed.

Winston S. Churchill

"The Sinews of Peace"[*]
Westminster College, Fulton, Missouri, March 5, 1946

President McCluer,[1] Ladies and Gentlemen, and last but certainly not least, the President of the United States—I am very glad indeed to come to Westminster College this afternoon and I am complimented that you should give me a degree from an institution whose reputation has been so solidly accepted. It is the name "Westminster," somehow or other, which seems familiar to me. I feel as if I had heard of it before. Indeed, now that I come to think of it, it was at Westminster that I received a very large part of my education in politics, dialectics, rhetoric, and one or two other things. In fact, we have both been educated at the same, or similar, or at any rate kindred, establishments.

It is also an honour, Ladies and Gentlemen, perhaps almost unique, for a private visitor to be introduced to an academic audience by the President of the United States. Amid his heavy burdens, duties, and responsibilities —unsought but not recoiled from—the President has traveled a thousand miles to dignify and magnify our meeting here today and to give me an opportunity of addressing this kindred nation, as well as my own countrymen across the ocean and perhaps some other countries too. The President has told you that it is his wish, as I am sure it is yours, that I should have full liberty to give my true and faithful counsel in these anxious and baffling times. I shall certainly avail myself of this freedom and feel the more right to do so because any private ambitions I may have cherished in my younger days have been satisfied beyond my wildest dreams. Let me, however, make it clear that I have no official mission or status of any kind and that I speak only for myself. There is nothing here but what you see. I can, therefore, allow my mind, with the experience of a lifetime, to play over the problems which beset us on the morrow of our absolute victory in

---

[*] This text is taken from the *New York Times*, March 6, 1946, p. 4. The address is commonly called the "Iron Curtain Speech" or "A Shadow Has Fallen on Europe and Asia."

[1] Dr. Franc Lewis McCluer was President of Westminster College. Churchill was introduced by President Harry S. Truman, who was also awarded an honorary Doctor of Laws degree. Clement Attlee replaced Churchill as Prime Minister on July 5, 1945.

arms; and to try to make sure, with what strength I have, that what has been gained with so much sacrifice and suffering shall be preserved for the future glory and safety of mankind.

Ladies and Gentlemen, the United States stands at this time at the pinnacle of world power. It is a solemn moment for the American democracy. For with this primacy in power is also joined an awe-inspiring accountability to the future. As you look around you, you must feel not only the sense of duty done, but also you must feel anxiety lest you fall below the level of achievement. Opportunity is here now, clear and shining, for both our countries. To reject it or ignore it or fritter it away will bring upon us all the long reproaches of the after-time. It is necessary that constancy of mind, persistency of purpose, and the grand simplicity of decision shall rule and guide the conduct of the English-speaking peoples in peace as they did in war. We must and I believe we shall prove ourselves equal to this severe requirement.

President McCluer, when American military men approach some serious situation they are wont to write at the head of their directive the words, "Overall Strategic Concept." There is wisdom in this, as it leads to clarity of thought. What, then, is the overall strategic concept which we should inscribe today? It is nothing less than the safety and welfare, the freedom and progress, of all the homes and families of all the men and women in all the lands. And here I speak particularly of the myriad cottage or apartment homes, where the wage-earner strives amid the accidents and difficulties of life to guard his wife and children from privation and bring the family up in the fear of the Lord or upon ethical conceptions which often play their potent part.

To give security to these countless homes they must be shielded from the two gaunt marauders—war and tyranny. We all know the frightful disturbance in which the ordinary family is plunged when the curse of war swoops down upon the bread-winner and those for whom he works and contrives. The awful ruin of Europe with all its vanished glories and of large parts of Asia glares us in the eyes. When the designs of wicked men or the aggressive urge of mighty states dissolve over large areas the frame of civilised society, humble folk are confronted with difficulties with which they cannot cope. For them all is distorted, all is broken or is even ground to pulp.

When I stand here this quiet afternoon, I shudder to visualise what is actually happening to millions now and what is going to happen in this period when famine stalks the earth. None can compute what has been called "the unestimated sum of human pain." Our supreme task and duty is to guard the homes of the common people from the horrors and miseries of another war. We are all agreed on that.

Our American military colleagues, after having proclaimed their overall strategic concept and computed available resources, always proceed to the next stop—namely the method. Here again there is widespread agreement. A world organisation has already been erected for the prime purpose of preventing war. UNO, the successor of the League of Nations, with the decisive addition of the United States and all that that means, is already at work. We must make sure that its work is fruitful, that it is a reality and not a sham, that it is a force for action and not merely a frothing of words, that it is a true temple of peace, in which the shields of many nations can some day be hung up, and not merely a cockpit in a tower of Babel. Before we cast away the solid assurances of national armaments for self-preservation, we must be certain that our temple is built not upon shifting sands or quagmires, but upon the rock. Anyone can see, with his eyes open, that our path will be difficult and also long, but if we persevere together as we did in the two world wars—though not, alas, in the interval between them—I cannot doubt that we shall achieve our common purpose in the end. I have, however, a definite and practical proposal to make for action. Courts and magistrates may be set up but they cannot function without sheriffs and constables. The United Nations Organisation must immediately begin to be equipped with an international armed force. In such a matter we can only go step by step; but we must begin now. I propose that each of the powers and states should be invited to dedicate a certain number of air squadrons to the service of the world organisation. These squadrons would be trained and prepared in their own countries but would move around in rotation from one country to another. They would wear the uniform of their own countries with different badges. They would not be required to act against their own nation, but in other respects they would be directed by the world organisation. This might be started on a modest scale and it would grow as confidence grew. I wished to see this done after the First World War and I devoutly trust that it may be done forthwith.

It would, nevertheless, Ladies and Gentlemen, be wrong and imprudent to entrust the secret knowledge or experience of the atomic bomb, which the United States, Great Britain, and Canada now share, to the world organisation while it is still in its infancy. It would be criminal madness to cast it adrift in this still agitated and un-united world.

No one in any country has slept less well in their beds because this knowledge and the method and the raw materials to apply it are at present largely retained in American hands. I do not believe we should all have slept so soundly had the positions been reversed and some Communist or neo-Fascist state monopolised, for the time being, these dread agents. The fear of them alone might easily have been used to enforce totalitarian systems upon the free democratic world, with consequences appalling to human imagination. God has willed that this shall not be, and we have at least a breathing space to set our house in order before this peril has to be encountered, and even then, if no effort is spared, we should still possess so formidable a superiority as to impose effective deterrents upon its employment or threat of employment by others. Ultimately, when the essential brotherhood of man is truly embodied and expressed in a world organisation, with all the necessary practical safeguards to make it effective, these powers would naturally be confided to that organisation.

Now I come to the second of the two marauders, to the second danger which threatens the cottage home and ordinary people—namely, tyranny. We cannot be blind to the fact that the liberties enjoyed by individual citizens throughout the United States and throughout the British Empire are not valid in a considerable number of countries, some of which are very powerful. In these states, control is enforced upon the common people by various kinds of all-embracing police governments, to a degree which is overwhelming and contrary to every principle of democracy. The power of the state is exercised without restraint, either by dictators or by compact oligarchies operating through a privileged party and a political police. It is not our duty at this time, when difficulties are so numerous, to interfere forcibly in the internal affairs of countries which we have not conquered in war, but we must never cease to proclaim in fearless tones the great principles of freedom and the rights of man which are the joint inheritance of the English-speaking world and which, through Magna Carta, the Bill of Rights, the *habeas corpus*, trial by jury, and the English common law, find their most famous expression in the American Declaration of Independence.

All this means that the people of any country have the right and should have the power by constitutional action, by free, unfettered elections with secret ballot, to choose or change the character or form of government under which they dwell, that freedom of speech and thought should reign, that courts of justice independent of the executive, unbiased by any party, should administer laws which have received the broad assent of large majorities or are consecrated by time and custom. Here are the title deeds of freedom which should lie in every cottage home. Here is the message of the British and American peoples to mankind. Let us preach what we practise, let us practise what we preach.

I have now stated the two great dangers which menace the homes of the people—war and tyranny. I have not yet spoken of poverty and privation, which are in many cases the prevailing anxiety. But if the dangers of war and tyranny are removed, there is no doubt that science and co-operation can bring in the next few years—certainly in the next few decades—to the world, newly taught in the sharpening school of war, an expansion of material well-being beyond anything that has yet occurred in human experience.

Now, at this sad and breathless moment, we are plunged in the hunger and distress which are the aftermath of our stupendous struggle; but this will pass and may pass quickly, and there is no reason except human folly or subhuman crime which should deny to all the nations the inauguration and enjoyment of an age of plenty. I have often used words which I learned fifty years ago from a great Irish-American orator, a friend of mine, Mr. Bourke Cockran:[2] "There is enough for all. The earth is a generous mother; she will provide in plentiful abundance food for all her children if they will but cultivate her soil in justice and in peace." So far, I feel that we are in full agreement. Now, while still pursuing the method of realising our overall strategic concept, I come to the crux of what I have travelled here to say.

Neither the sure prevention of war nor the continuous rise of world organisation will be gained without what I have called the fraternal association of the English-speaking peoples. This means a special relationship between the British Commonwealth and Empire and the United States of America. Ladies and Gentlemen, this is no time for generalities and I will venture to be precise. Fraternal association requires not only the growing friendship and mutual understanding between our two vast but kindred systems of society, but the continuance of the intimate relationships between our military advisers leading to common study of potential dangers, the similarity of weapons and manuals of instruction, and the interchange of officers and cadets at technical colleges. It should carry with it the continuance of the present facilities for mutual security by the joint use of all naval and air force bases in the possession of either country all over the world. This would perhaps double the mobility of the American Navy and Air Force, it would greatly expand that of the British Empire forces, and it might well lead, if and as the world calms down, to important financial savings. Already we use together a large number of islands; more may well be entrusted to our joint care in the near future. The United States has already a permanent defence agreement with the Dominion of Canada, which is so devotedly attached to the British Commonwealth and Empire. This agreement is more effective than many of those which have often been made under formal alliances. This principle should be extended to all the British Commonwealths with full reciprocity. Thus, whatever happens, and thus only, shall we be secure ourselves and able to work together for the high and simple causes that are dear to us and bode no ill to any. Eventually there may come—I feel eventually there will come—the principle of common citizenship, but that we may be content to leave to destiny, whose outstretched arm so many of us can already clearly see.

There is, however, an important question we must ask ourselves. Would a special relationship between the United States and the British Commonwealth be inconsistent with our over-riding loyalties to the world organisation? I reply that on the contrary, it is probably the only means by

[2] William Bourke Cockran, lawyer and Democratic politician, was considered by many of his contemporaries the most eloquent spokesman of his day.

which that organisation will achieve its full stature and strength. There are already the special United States relations with Canada, which I just mentioned, and there are the relations between the United States and the South American republics. We British have also our twenty-years' treaty of collaboration and mutual assistance with Soviet Russia. I agree with Mr. Bevin,[3] the Foreign Secretary of Great Britain, that it might well be a fifty-years' treaty so far as we are concerned. We aim at nothing but mutual assistance and collaboration with Russia. We have an alliance, the British with Portugal, unbroken since the year 1384[4] and which produced fruitful results at a critical moment in the recent war. None of these clash with the general interest of a world agreement or a world organisation. On the contrary, they help it. "In my father's house are many mansions."[5] Special associations between members of the United Nations which have no aggressive point against any other country, which harbour no design incompatible with the Charter of the United Nations, far from being harmful, are beneficial and, as I believe, indispensable.

I spoke earlier, Ladies and Gentlemen, of the temple of peace. Workmen from all countries must build that temple. If two of the workmen know each other particularly well and are old friends, if their families are intermingled and if they have faith in each other's purpose, hope in each other's future, and charity toward each other's shortcomings, to quote some good words I read here the other day, why cannot they work together at the common task as friends and partners? Why can they not share their tools and thus increase each other's working powers? Indeed they must do so or else the temple may not be built, or being built, it may collapse, and we shall all be proved again unteachable and have to go and try to learn again for a third time, in a school of war incomparably more rigorous than that from which we have just been released. The dark ages may return, the Stone Age may return on the gleaming wings of science, and what might now shower immeasurable material blessings upon mankind may even bring about its total destruction. Beware, I say; time is plenty short. Do not let us take the course of allowing events to drift along until it is too late. If there is to be a fraternal association of the kind I have described, with all the extra strength and security which both our countries can derive from it, let us make sure that that great fact is known to the world and that it plays its part in steadying and stabilising the foundations of peace. There is the path of wisdom. Prevention is better than cure.

A shadow has fallen upon the scenes so lately lighted by the Allied victory. Nobody knows what Soviet Russia and its Communist international

---

[3] Ernest Bevin, Labour Member for Central Wandsworth.

[4] The date of the Treaty of Windsor was May 9, 1386. It was an agreement by Richard II and John of Avis of Portugal providing British support in the case of a threat to Portuguese security. The treaty was ratified by Henry IV in 1403.

[5] John 14:2.

organisation intends to do in the immediate future, or what are the limits, if any, to their expansive and proselytising tendencies. I have a strong admiration and regard for the valiant Russian people and for my wartime comrade, Marshal Stalin. There is deep sympathy and goodwill in Britain —and I doubt not here also—toward the peoples of all the Russias and a resolve to persevere through many differences and rebuffs in establishing lasting friendships. We understand the Russian need to be secure on her western frontiers by the removal of all possibility of German aggression. We welcome Russia to her rightful place among the leading nations of the world. We welcome her flag upon the seas. Above all, we welcome or should welcome constant, frequent, and growing contacts between the Russian people and our own peoples on both sides of the Atlantic. It is my duty, however—and I am sure you would not wish me not to state the facts as I see them to you—it is my duty to place before you certain facts about the present position in Europe.

From Stettin in the Baltic to Trieste in the Adriatic, an iron curtain[6] has descended across the Continent. Behind that line lie all the capitals of the ancient states of central and eastern Europe. Warsaw, Berlin, Prague, Vienna, Budapest, Belgrade, Bucharest, and Sofia—all these famous cities and the populations around them lie in what I might call the Soviet sphere, and all are subject, in one form or another, not only to Soviet influence but to a very high and in some cases increasing measure of control from Moscow. Police governments are pervading from Moscow. But Athens alone, with its immortal glories, is free to decide its future at an election under British, American, and French observation. The Russian-dominated Polish Government has been encouraged to make enormous and wrongful inroads upon Germany, and mass expulsions of millions of Germans on a scale grievous and undreamed-of are now taking place. The Communist Parties, which were very small in all these eastern states of Europe, have been raised to pre-eminence and power far beyond their numbers and are seeking everywhere to obtain totalitarian control. Police governments are prevailing in nearly every case, and so far, except in Czechoslovakia, there is no true democracy. Turkey and Persia are both profoundly alarmed and disturbed at the claims which are being made upon them and at the pressure being exerted by the Moscow Government. An attempt is being made by the Russians in Berlin to build up a quasi-Communist Party in their zone of occupied Germany by showing special favors to groups of Left-wing German leaders. At the end of the fighting last June, the American and British armies withdrew westward, in accord-

---

[6] The expression "iron curtain" apparently did not originate with Churchill. George W. Crile used it in *A Mechanistic View of War and Peace* (p. 69), a book edited by Amy Rowland (London, 1916); Joseph Goebbels used it in a speech on February 23, 1945; and Senator Arthur Vandenburg used it in a Senate speech on November 15, 1945. Churchill did, however, use it in a message to President Truman on May 12, 1945.

ance with an earlier agreement, to a depth at some points of 150 miles upon a front of nearly 400 miles, in order to allow our Russian allies to occupy this vast expanse of territory which the western democracies had conquered. If now the Soviet Government tries, by separate action, to build up a pro-Communist Germany in their areas, this will cause new serious difficulties in the American and British zones and will give the defeated Germans the power of putting themselves up to auction between the Soviets and the Western democracies. Whatever conclusions may be drawn from these facts—and facts they are—this is certainly not the liberated Europe we fought to build up. Nor is it one which contains the essentials of permanent peace.

The safety of the world, Ladies and Gentlemen, requires a unity in Europe from which no nation should be permanently outcast. It is from the strong parent races in Europe that the world wars we have witnessed or which occurred in former times have sprung.

Twice in our own lifetime we have seen the United States—against her wishes and her traditions, against arguments the force of which it is impossible not to comprehend—twice we have seen them drawn by irresistible forces into these wars in time to secure the victory of the good cause, but only after frightful slaughter and devastation have occurred. Twice the United States has had to send several millions of its young men across the Atlantic to find the war. But now we all can find any nation, wherever it may dwell, between dusk and dawn. Surely we should work with conscious purpose for a grand pacification of Europe within the structure of the United Nations and in accordance with its Charter. That, I feel, opens a course of policy of very great importance.

In front of the iron curtain which lies across Europe are other causes for anxiety. In Italy, the Communist Party is seriously hampered by having to support the Communist-trained Marshal Tito's claims to former Italian territory at the head of the Adriatic.[7] Nevertheless, the future of Italy hangs in the balance.

Again, one cannot imagine a regenerated Europe without a strong France. All my public life I have worked for a strong France and I have never lost faith in her destiny, even in the darkest hours. I will not lose faith now.

However, in a great number of countries far from the Russian frontiers and throughout the world, Communist fifth columns[8] are established and work in complete unity and absolute obedience to directions they receive from the Communist centre. Except in the British Commonwealth and in the United States, where Communism is in its infancy, the Communist Parties or fifth columns constitute a growing challenge and peril to Christian civilisation. These are sombre facts for anyone to have to recite

[7] Trieste.
[8] See page 504, footnote 9.

on the morrow of a victory gained by so much splendid comradeship in arms and in the cause of freedom and democracy, but we should be most unwise not to face them squarely while time remains.

The outlook is also anxious in the Far East and especially in Manchuria. The agreement which was made at Yalta, to which I was party, was extremely favorable to Soviet Russia, but it was made at a time[9] when no one could say that the German war might not extend all through the summer and autumn of 1945, and when the Japanese war was expected by the best judges to last for a further eighteen months from the end of the German war. In this country you are so well-informed about the Far East and such devoted friends of China that I do not need to expatiate on the situation there.

I had, however, felt bound to portray the shadow which, alike in the West and in the East, falls upon the world. I was a Minister[10] at the time of the Versailles treaty and a close friend of Mr. Lloyd George, who was the head of the British delegation at that time. I did not myself agree with many things that were done, but I have a very vague impression in my mind of that situation, and I find it painful to contrast it with that which prevails now. In those days there were high hopes and unbounded confidence that the wars were over and that the League of Nations would become all-powerful. I do not see or feel that same confidence or even the same hopes in the haggard world at the present time.

On the other hand, Ladies and Gentlemen, I repulse the idea that a new war is inevitable, still more that it is imminent. It is because I am sure that our fortunes are still in our hands, in our own hands, and that we hold the power to save the future that I feel the duty to speak out now that I have the occasion and opportunity to do so.

I do not believe that Soviet Russia desires war. What they desire is the fruits of war and the indefinite expansion of their power and doctrines. But what we have to consider here today, while time remains, is the permanent prevention of war and the establishment of conditions of freedom and democracy as rapidly as possible in all countries. Our difficulties and dangers will not be removed by closing our eyes to them. They will not be removed by mere waiting to see what happens. Nor will they be removed by a policy of appeasement. What is needed is a settlement, and the longer this is delayed, the more difficult it will be and the greater our dangers will become.

From what I have seen of our Russian friends and allies during the war, I am convinced that there is nothing they admire so much as strength, and there is nothing for which they have less respect than weakness, especially military weakness. For that reason, the old doctrine of a balance of

---

[9] February 4–11, 1945. Russia won $10,000,000,000 in reparations and virtual control of Eastern Europe.
[10] Churchill was Secretary of State for War.

power is unsound. We cannot afford, if we can help it, to work on narrow margins, offering temptations to a trial of strength.

If the Western democracies stand together in strict adherence to the principles of the United Nations Charter, their influence for furthering those principles will be immense and no one is likely to molest them. If, however, they become divided or falter in their duty, and if these all-important years are allowed to slip away, then indeed catastrophe may overwhelm us all.

Last time I saw it all coming and cried aloud to my own fellow-countrymen and to the world, but no one paid any attention. Up till the year 1933 or even 1935,[11] Germany might have been saved from the awful fate which has overtaken her, and we might all have been spared the miseries Hitler let loose upon mankind.

There never was a war in history easier to prevent by timely action than the one which has just desolated such great areas of the globe. It could have been prevented, in my belief, without the firing of a single shot, and Germany might be powerful, prosperous, and honoured today; but no one would listen, and one by one we were all sucked into the awful whirlpool.

We surely, Ladies and Gentlemen, I put it to you, but surely we must not let that happen again. This can only be achieved by reaching now, in 1946, this year 1946, by reaching a good understanding on all points with Russia under the general authority of the United Nations Organisation and by the maintenance of that good understanding through many peaceful years by the world instrument, supported by the whole strength of the English-speaking world and all its connexions. There is the solution which I respectfully offer to you in this address, to which I have given the title "The Sinews of Peace."

Let no man underrate the abiding power of the British Empire and Commonwealth. Because you see the forty-six millions in our island harassed about their food supply, of which they only grow one-half even in wartime, or because we have difficulty in restarting our industries and export trade after six years of passionate war effort, do not suppose that we shall not come through these dark years of privation as we have come through the glorious years of agony, or that half a century from now you will not see seventy or eighty millions of Britons spread about the world and united in defence of our traditions, and our way of life and of the world causes which you and we espouse.

If the population of the English-speaking Commonwealth be added to that of the United States, with all such co-operation implies in the air, on the sea, all over the globe, and in science and in industry, and in moral force, there will be no quivering, precarious balance of power to offer its

---

[11] Churchill's speeches of warning from 1932 to 1938 are collected in *While England Slept* (New York, 1938).

temptation to ambition or adventure. On the contrary, there will be an overwhelming assurance of security.

If we adhere faithfully to the Charter of the United Nations and walk forward in sedate and sober strength, seeking no one's land or treasure, seeking to lay no arbitrary control upon the thoughts of men—if all British moral and material forces and convictions are joined with your own in fraternal association—the high roads of the future will be clear, not only for us but for all, not only for our time, but for a century to come.

RESEARCH MATERIALS

GENERAL REFERENCES

The editors assume familiarity with standard international guides to research materials; for example, Theodore Besterman, *A World Bibliography of Bibliographies*; Constance M. Winchell, *Guide to Reference Books*; *Keesing's Contemporary Archives*; *Facts on File*; *Guide to Historical Literature*; *Readers' Guide to Periodical Literature*; *Poole's Index to Periodical Literature*; *Ulrich's Periodicals Directory*; the various general encyclopedias; James W. Cleary and Frederick W. Haberman, *Rhetoric and Public Address: A Bibliography, 1947–1961*. We have chosen guides of special usefulness to researchers into the ideas, arguments, and issues of British speech-making in the nineteenth and twentieth centuries.

A. BIBLIOGRAPHIES OF BIBLIOGRAPHIES

Collison, Robert L. *Bibliographies, Subject and National: A Guide to Their Contents, Arrangement, and Use*. 3rd ed. rev. London, 1968.
Courtney, William P. *Register of National Bibliography*. 3 vols. London, 1905–1912.
Eager, Alan R. *A Guide to Irish Bibliographical Material*. London, 1964.
Hewitt, A. R. *Guide to Resources for Commonwealth Studies*. London, 1957.
Howard-Hill, Trevor H. *Bibliography of British Literary Bibliographies*. Oxford, 1969.
Walford, A. J. (ed.). *Guide to Reference Material*. 2nd ed. 2 vols. London, 1966 and 1968.

B. BASIC RESEARCH SOURCES

The Annual Register. London, 1759– . Annual. Subtitle varies.
Burke's Peerage, Baronetage and Knightage. Ed. Peter Townend. 105th ed. London, 1970.
Butler, David and Jennie Freeman. *British Political Facts, 1900–1960*. London, 1963.
Dod's Parliamentary Companion. London, 1832– . Annual. Title varies.
Judd, Gerrit P. *Members of Parliament, 1734–1852*. New Haven, Conn., 1955.
Low, Sir Sidney and F. S. Pulling. *The Dictionary of English History*. New ed. London, 1928.
Powicke, Sir F. Maurice and E. B. Fryde. *Handbook of British Chronology*. 2nd ed. London, 1961.
Statesman's Yearbook: Statistical and Historical Annual of the States of the World. London, 1864– . Annual.
Whitaker, Joseph. *Almanack*. London, 1869– . Annual.
Wilding, Norman and Philip Laundy. *An Encyclopedia of Parliament*. 3rd ed. rev. New York, 1968.

554 RESEARCH MATERIALS

C. British History Sources

Carty, James. *Bibliography of Irish History, 1870–1911.* Dublin, 1940.

Chrimes, S. B. and I. A. Roots. *English Constitutional History: A Select Bibliography.* London, 1958.

Clark, Sir George (ed.). *The Oxford History of England.* 14 vols. Oxford, 1937–1965. Each volume contains an excellent bibliography for its period.

Douglas, David C. (ed.). *English Historical Documents.* 12 vols. projected. New York, 1955– . A distinguished collection of fundamental sources of English history. Each volume contains comprehensive bibliographies.

Historical Manuscripts Commission. *Guide to the Reports of the Royal Commission on Historical Manuscripts, 1870–1911.* 2 vols. London, 1935 and 1938.

Historical Manuscripts Commission. *Guide to the Reports of the Royal Commission on Historical Manuscripts, 1911–1957.* 3 vols. London, 1966.

Gross, Charles. *A Bibliography of British Municipal History.* 2nd ed. Leicester, 1966.

Historical Association. *Annual Bulletin of Historical Literature, 1911–* . London, 1912– . Each volume is a critical review of history publications of the year.

Johnston, Edith M. (ed.). *Irish History: A Select Bibliography.* London, 1969.

Kellaway, W. (comp.). *Bibliography of Historical Works Issued in the United Kingdom, 1961–1965.* London, 1967. See also previous surveys bearing the same title.

Milne, Alexander Taylor (comp.). Royal Historical Society. *Writings on British History, 1934–* . London, 1937– . Books and articles on British history to 1914 published during the year; an appendix includes writings on British history since 1914.

Mitchell, Brian R. and Phyllis Dean. *Abstract of British Historical Statistics.* Cambridge, 1962.

Mowat, Charles L. *British History Since 1926: A Select Bibliography.* London, 1960.

Palmer, H. J. *Government and Parliament in Britain: A Bibliography.* 2nd ed. London, 1964.

Williams, Judith Blow. *A Guide to the Printed Materials for English Social and Economic History, 1750–1850.* New York, 1926.

D. Guides to Biographies and Diaries

Boase, Frederic. *Modern English Biography.* 6 vols. Truro, 1892–1921. Includes only persons whose deaths occurred after 1850.

Dictionary of National Biography. 63 vols. London, 1885–1901. Standard source for information on deceased British subjects. Supplements include entries through 1950. The *Concise DNB* summarizes all entries in the main work.

Kunitz, Stanley J. (ed.). *British Authors of the Nineteenth Century.* New York, 1936. Contains about 1000 biographies.

Matthews, William (comp.). *British Autobiographies: An Annotated Bibliography of British Autobiographies Published or Written Before 1951.* Los Angeles, 1955.

——— (comp.). *British Diaries: An Annotated Bibliography of British Diaries Written Between 1442 and 1942.* Berkeley, Calif., 1950.

Plarr, Victor G. (ed.). *Men and Women of the Time.* 15th ed. London, 1899.

Ward, Thomas H. (ed.). *Men of the Reign*. London, 1885. Biographical dictionary of eminent persons who died during Queen Victoria's reign.

Who's Who: An Annual Biographical Dictionary (With Which Is Incorporated "Men and Women of the Time"). London, 1849–   . Annual.

Who Was Who: A Companion to "Who's Who" Containing the Biographies of Those Who Died During the Period. 5 vols. London, 1929–1961. Covers the period 1897–1960. Volumes are published at ten-year intervals.

E. CATALOGUES OF PRINTED PUBLICATIONS

British Books in Print. London, 1969. Annual. Records over 200,000 titles with publishers and prices.

British Museum. *General Catalogue of Printed Books*. Photolith. ed. 263 vols. London, 1959–1966.

British Museum. *General Catalogue of Printed Books: Ten-Year Supplement, 1956–1965*. 50 vols. London, 1968.

*The British National Bibliography 1950–   *. London, 1951–   . Annual. Classifies by subject.

The English Catalogue of Books, 1835–1863. London, 1864. Subsequent volumes bring to date this record of books published in Britain.

Whitaker's Cumulative Book List. London, 1924–   . Quarterly. A list of titles published or reissued each year.

F. GUIDES TO NEWSPAPERS AND PERIODICALS

British Museum. *Catalogue of Printed Books. Supplement: Newspapers Published in Great Britain and Ireland, 1801–1900*. London, 1905.

British Union-Catalogue of Periodicals: A Record of the Periodicals of the World, From the Seventeenth Century to the Present Day, In British Libraries. 4 vols. London, 1955–1958. Supplement, 1962.

Grobson, Walter J. *English Literary Periodicals*. New York, 1930.

Houghton, Walter E. (ed.). *The Wellesley Index to Victorian Periodicals, 1824–1900*. Toronto, 1966. Contains tables of contents, identification of contributors, and bibliographies of their articles.

Muddiman, J. G. (comp.). *Tercentenary Handlist of English and Welsh Newspapers, Magazines and Reviews, 1620–1920*. London, 1920.

Subject Index to Periodicals, 1915–1961. London, 1919–1962. Annual. Known as the *Athenaeum Subject Index*, 1915–1918.

The Times (London). *Index to The Times*. London, 1907–   . 1906 to present.

———. *Palmer's Index to The Times Newspaper*. London, 1868–1943. 1790 to June, 1941.

Toase, Mary (ed.). *Guide to Current British Periodicals*. London, 1962.

University Microfilms. *English Literary Periodicals, 17th, 18th, and 19th Centuries*. Ann Arbor, Mich., 1951.

Willing's Press Guide: A Comprehensive Index and Handbook of the Press of the United Kingdom of Great Britain, Northern Ireland, and the Irish Republic. London, 1874–   . Annual.

G. Guides to Government Documents and Parliamentary Reports

Barrow, John Henry (comp.). *Mirror of Parliament.* 60 vols. London, 1828–1841. A superior source for Parliamentary debates of the period covered.

A Bibliography of Parliamentary Debates of Great Britain. House of Commons Library Document No. 2. London, 1956.

Catalogue of Parliamentary Papers, 1801–1900. Comp. H. V. Jones. London, 1904. Supplements covered the periods 1901–1910 and 1910–1920.

Ford, Percy and Grace Ford. *A Breviate of Parliamentary Papers, 1900–1954.* 3 vols. Oxford, 1957–1961.

———. *A Guide to Parliamentary Papers: What They Are; How to Find Them; How to Use Them.* Oxford, 1956.

———. *Select List of British Parliamentary Papers, 1833–1899.* Oxford, 1953.

Great Britain. *Government Publications: Catalogue.* London, 1923–   . Annual.

Great Britain. *Government Publications: Official Indexes, Lists, Guides, Catalogues.* Rev. ed. London, 1955.

Hansard, Thomas C. (comp.). *Parliamentary Debates, 1803–   .* London, 1804–   . This principal source for Parliamentary speechmaking has an uninterrupted sequence of publication:

    First Series, 1803–1820, 41 vols., beginning as *Cobbett's Parliamentary Debates* (1804) and becoming with Vol. XXIII (1812) *The Parliamentary Debates from the Year 1803 to the Present Time.*

    New (Second) Series, 1820–1830, 25 vols., entitled *The Parliamentary Debates,* and becoming with Vol. XXI (1829) *Hansard's Parliamentary Debates.*

    Third Series, 1830–1891, 356 vols., entitled *Hansard's Parliamentary Debates.*

    Fourth Series, 1892–1909, 199 vols., entitled *The Parliamentary Debates (Authorised Edition).*

    Fifth Series, 1909 to present date, entitled *The Parliamentary Debates (Official Report),* and becoming with Vol. CCCXCV (1943) *Parliamentary Debates (Hansard).*

H. Miscellaneous Guides and Indexes

British Museum. *The Catalogues of the Manuscript Collections.* Rev. ed. London, 1962.

Chapman, Robert W., et al. (eds.). *Annals of English Literature, 1475–1950.* 2nd ed. Oxford, 1961.

Hale, Richard W. Jr. (ed.). *Guide to Photocopied Historical Materials in the United States and Canada.* Ithaca, N. Y., 1961.

Index to Theses Accepted for Higher Degrees in the Universities of Great Britain and Ireland, 1950–   . London, 1953–   . Annual.

Institute of Advanced Legal Studies. *A Bibliographical Guide to the Law of the United Kingdom, the Channel Islands and the Isle of Man.* London, 1956.

Kendall, Maurice G. (ed.). *The Sources and Nature of the Statistics of the United Kingdom.* 2 vols. London, 1952 and 1957.

A London Bibliography of the Social Sciences. 14 vols. London, 1931–1968.

Maxwell, W. Harold, Leslie F. Maxwell, et al. *A Legal Bibliography of the British Commonwealth of Nations.* 2nd ed. 7 vols. London, 1955–1964.

Notes and Queries. London, 1850–   . Monthly. Subtitle varies.
Social Sciences and Humanities Index. London, 1916–   . Formerly *International Index.* Covers scholarly journals in the humanities and social sciences.

BACKGROUND READINGS

A. GENERAL HISTORY

Aspinall, A. and E. Anthony Smith (eds.). *English Historical Documents: 1783–1832.* New York, 1959.
Churchill, Sir Winston S. *A History of the English-Speaking Peoples.* 4 vols. New York and London, 1956–1958.
Cole, G. D. H. and Raymond Postgate. *The British People, 1746–1946.* New York, 1947.
Creevey, Thomas. *The Creevey Papers.* Ed. Sir Herbert Maxwell. 2nd ed. London, 1904.
Croker, John W. *The Croker Papers, 1808–1857.* Ed. Bernard Pool. London, 1967.
Davis, H. W. C. *The Age of Grey and Peel.* Oxford, 1929.
Ensor, Sir Robert. *England, 1870–1914.* Oxford, 1936.
Gash, Norman. *The Age of Peel.* London, 1968.
Greville, Charles. *The Greville Memoirs, 1814–1860.* Ed. Lytton Strachey and Roger Fulford. 8 vols. London, 1938.
Halévy, Elie. *A History of the English People in the Nineteenth Century.* Trans. E. I. Watkin. 6 vols. New York, 1961.
Havighurst, Alfred F. *Twentieth-Century Britain.* Evanston, Ill., 1962.
Jephson, Henry. *The Platform: Its Rise and Progress.* 2nd ed. 2 vols. London, 1892.
Marriott, Sir John A. R. *England Since Waterloo.* 15th ed. London, 1959.
———. *Modern England, 1855–1945: A History of My Own Times.* 4th ed. London and New York, 1960.
Marwick, Arthur. *Britain in the Century of Total War.* London, 1968.
Medlicott, W. N. *Contemporary England, 1914–1964.* New York, 1967.
Mendelssohn, Peter de. *The Age of Churchill, 1874–1911.* London, 1961.
Mowat, Charles L. *Britain Between the Wars, 1918–1940.* Chicago, 1955.
Sampson, Anthony. *Anatomy of Britain Today.* London, 1965.
Seaman, L. C. B. *Post-Victorian Britain, 1902–1951.* London, 1966.
Smellie, K. B. *Great Britain Since 1688.* Ann Arbor, Mich., 1962.
Somervell, D. C. *English Thought in the Nineteenth Century.* London, 1929.
Stephen, Sir Leslie. *History of English Thought in the Eighteenth Century.* 3rd ed. 2 vols. London, 1902.
Taylor, A. J. P. *English History, 1914–1945.* New York and Oxford, 1965.
Trevelyan, George M. *English History in the Nineteenth Century and After.* Rev. ed. New York and London, 1937.
Turberville, A. S. *English Men and Manners in the Eighteenth Century.* 2nd ed. Oxford, 1929.

Walpole, Sir Spencer. *History of England from the Conclusion of the Great War in 1815*. Rev. ed. 6 vols. London, 1890.

Woodward, Sir Llewellyn. *The Age of Reform, 1815–1870*. 2nd ed. Oxford, 1962.

Young, G. M. and W. D. Handcock (eds.). *English Historical Documents: 1833–1874*. London, 1956.

B. Constitution and Government

Adams, George B. *Constitutional History of England*. Rev. R. L. Schuyler. London, 1963.

Allyn, Emily. *Lords versus Commons: A Century of Conflict and Compromise, 1830–1930*. New York and London, 1931.

Amery, Leopold C. M. S. *Thoughts on the Constitution*. 2nd ed. New York and London, 1956.

Anson, Sir William R. *The Law and Custom of the Constitution*. Ed. M. L. Gwyer and A. B. Keith. 2 vols. Oxford, 1922 and 1935.

Bagehot, Walter. *The English Constitution*. 6th ed. London, 1891.

Berkeley, Humphry. *The Power of the Prime Minister*. London, 1968.

Bromhead, P. A. *The House of Lords and Contemporary Politics, 1911–1957*. London, 1958.

Butler, David E. *The Electoral System in Britain Since 1918*. 2nd ed. Oxford, 1963.

Butler, J. R. M. *The Passing of the Great Reform Bill*. London, 1914.

Butt, Ronald. *The Power of Parliament*. New York, 1967.

Campion, Gilbert F. M. *An Introduction to the Procedure of the House of Commons*. 3rd ed. London and New York, 1958.

Carter, Byrum E. *The Office of Prime Minister*. Princeton, N. J., 1956.

Chrimes, Stanley B. *English Constitutional History*. 2nd ed. London, 1953.

Costin, William C. and J. Steven Watson. *The Law and Working of the Constitution: Documents, 1660–1914*. 2nd ed. 2 vols. London, 1961–1964.

Cowling, Maurice. *1867: Disraeli, Gladstone and Revolution*. Cambridge, Eng., 1967.

Dicey, Albert V. *Lectures on the Relation between Law and Public Opinion in England*. Reissue. London, 1962.

Emden, Cecil S. *The People and the Constitution*. 2nd ed. London, 1956.

Gash, Norman. *Politics in the Age of Peel*. London, 1953.

Greaves, Harold R. G. *The British Constitution*. 3rd ed. London, 1955.

Ilbert, Sir Courtenay P. *Parliament: Its History, Constitution and Practice*. 3rd ed. Rev. Sir Cecil Carr. London and New York, 1956.

Jennings, Sir W. Ivor. *Cabinet Government*. 3rd ed. Cambridge, Eng., 1959.

———. *Parliament*. 2nd ed. Cambridge, Eng., 1957.

———. *The British Constitution*. 5th ed. Cambridge, Eng., 1966.

Keir, Sir David L. *The Constitutional History of Modern Britain*. 5th ed. London, 1953.

Keith, A. Berriedale. *The British Cabinet System, 1830–1938*. 2nd ed. London, 1952.

———. *The Constitution of England from Queen Victoria to George VI*. 2 vols. London, 1940.

LeMay, G. H. L. (ed.). *British Government, 1914–1953: Select Documents*. London, 1955.

Lovell, Colin R. *English Constitutional and Legal History: A Survey*. New York, 1962.

Mackintosh, John P. *The British Cabinet*. 2nd ed. London, 1968.

May, Thomas Erskine. *The Constitutional History of England Since the Accession of George the Third, 1760–1860.* Ed. Francis Holland. 3 vols. London, 1912.
———. *Sir Thomas Erskine May's Treatise on the Law, Privileges, Proceedings and Usage of Parliament.* Ed. Sir Barnett Cocks. 17th ed. London, 1964.
Namier, Sir Lewis B. *Monarchy and the Party System.* Oxford, 1952.
Park, Joseph H. *The English Reform Bill of 1867.* New York, 1920.
Plucknett, T. F. T. *A Concise History of the Common Law.* 5th ed. London, 1956.
Porritt, Edward. *The Unreformed House of Commons.* 2 vols. London, 1903.
Smellie, K. B. *A Hundred Years of English Government.* 2nd ed. London, 1950.
Smith, F. B. *The Making of the Second Reform Bill.* Cambridge, Eng., 1966.
Stankiewicz, W. J. *Crisis in British Government: The Need for Reform.* London, 1967.
Stewart, Michael. *The British Approach to Politics.* 5th ed. rev. London, 1965.
Turberville, A. S. *The House of Lords in the Age of Reform, 1784–1837.* London, 1958.
Wade, E. C. S. and G. Godfrey Phillips. *Constitutional Law.* 6th ed. London, 1960.

C. Sociology and Economics

Abrams, Mark. *The Condition of the British People, 1911–1945.* London, 1945.
Ashton, Thomas S. *The Industrial Revolution, 1760–1830.* London, 1948.
Ashworth, William. *An Economic History of England, 1870–1939.* New York and London, 1960.
Barnes, Donald G. *A History of the English Corn Laws from 1660–1846.* London, 1930.
Brady, Robert A. *Crisis in Britain: Plans and Achievements of the Labour Government.* Berkeley, Calif., 1950.
Briggs, Asa. *The Age of Improvement.* London and New York, 1959.
Cheyney, Edward P. *An Introduction to the Industrial and Social History of England.* Rev. ed. New York, 1920.
Clapham, Sir John H. *An Economic History of Modern Britain.* 2nd ed. 3 vols. Cambridge, Eng., 1950–1952.
Clark, G. Kitson. *The Making of Victorian England.* Cambridge, Mass., 1962.
Cole, G. D. H. *The Post-War Condition of Britain.* London, 1956.
Court, W. H. B. *A Concise Economic History of Britain from 1750 to Recent Times.* Cambridge, Eng., 1954.
Fay, Charles R. *Great Britain from Adam Smith to the Present Day.* 5th ed. London, 1950.
———. *The Corn Laws and Social England.* Cambridge, Eng., 1932.
———. *Life and Labour in the Nineteenth Century.* 4th ed. Cambridge, Eng., 1947.
Finlayson, Geoffrey. *Decade of Reform: England in the Eighteen Thirties.* New York, 1970.
Grove, J. W. *Government and Industry in Britain.* London, 1962.
Hanson, A. H. *Parliament and Public Ownership.* London, 1961.
Hovell, Mark. *The Chartist Movement.* Manchester, 1925.
Knowles, L. C. A. *The Industrial and Commercial Revolutions in Great Britain during the Nineteenth Century.* 4th ed. rev. London and New York, 1926.
Lindsey, Almont. *Socialized Medicine in England and Wales.* Chapel Hill, N. C., 1962.
McCord, Norman. *The Anti-Corn Law League, 1838–1846.* London, 1958.
Pool, A. G. and G. P. Jones. *A Hundred Years of Economic Development in Great Britain.* London, 1940.

Prentice, Archibald. *History of the Anti-Corn Law League.* 2 vols. London, 1853.
Robson, William A. *Nationalized Industry and Public Ownership.* 2nd ed. London, 1962.
Webb, Sidney and Beatrice. *The History of Trade Unionism.* Rev. ed. London, 1920.
Young, George M. *Victorian England: Portrait of an Age.* 2nd ed. London, 1953.

D. POLITICS

Aspinall, A. *Lord Brougham and the Whig Party.* Manchester, 1927.
Beer, Samuel H. *Modern British Politics.* London, 1965.
Black, Eugene C. (ed.). *British Politics in the Nineteenth Century.* New York, 1969.
Boyd, Francis. *British Politics in Transition, 1945–1963.* New York and London, 1964.
Brand, Carl F. *The British Labour Party.* Stanford, Calif., 1964.
Brinton, Crane. *English Political Thought in the Nineteenth Century.* 2nd ed. London, 1949.
Bulmer-Thomas, Ivor. *The Growth of the British Party System.* 2 vols. London, 1965.
Butler, David and Donald Stokes. *Political Change in Britain: Forces Shaping Electoral Choice.* New York, 1969.
Clark, G. Kitson. *Peel and the Conservative Party: A Study in Party Politics, 1832–1841.* London, 1929.
Cole, G. D. H. *A History of the Labour Party from 1914.* London, 1948.
Crosland, C. A. R. *The Future of Socialism.* London, 1956.
Cross, Colin. *The Liberals in Power, 1905–1914.* London, 1963.
Derry, John W. *The Radical Tradition: Tom Paine to Lloyd George.* London and New York, 1967.
Feiling, Sir Keith G. *The Second Tory Party, 1714–1832.* London, 1938.
Feuchtwanger, E. J. *Disraeli, Democracy and the Tory Party.* Oxford, 1968.
Gash, Norman. *Reaction and Reconstruction in English Politics, 1832–1852.* Oxford, 1965.
Gwyn, William B. *Democracy and the Cost of Politics in Britain.* London, 1962.
Jennings, Sir Ivor. *Party Politics.* 3 vols. Cambridge, Eng., 1960–1962.
Maccoby, Simon. *English Radicalism.* 6 vols. London, 1935–1961.
McKenzie, R. T. *British Political Parties.* London, 1955.
Miliband, Ralph. *Parliamentary Socialism: A Study in the Politics of Labour.* London, 1961.
Morrison, Herbert. *Government and Parliament: A Survey from Inside.* London, 1954.
Namier, Sir Lewis B. *The Structure of Politics at the Accession of George III.* 2nd ed. London, 1965.
Pelling, Henry. *The Origins of the Labour Party, 1880–1900.* 2nd ed. Oxford, 1965.
——— . *Popular Politics and Society in Late Victorian Britain.* London, 1968.
——— . *Social Geography of British Elections, 1885–1910.* New York, 1967.
Rasmussen, Jorgen S. *Retrenchment and Revival: A Study of the Contemporary British Liberal Party.* Tucson, Ariz., 1964.
Seymour, Charles. *Electoral Reform in England and Wales.* New Haven, Conn., 1915.
Somervell, D. C. *British Politics Since 1900.* London, 1950.
Vincent, John. *The Formation of the British Liberal Party.* New York, 1966.
Wilson, Trevor. *The Downfall of the Liberal Party, 1914–1935.* Ithaca, N. Y., 1966.

E. Colonial and Foreign Policy

Adams, E. D. *Great Britain and the American Civil War*. London, 1925.
Beloff, Max. *Imperial Sunset: Britain's Liberal Empire, 1897–1921*. New York, 1970.
Calder, Angus. *The People's War: Britain 1939–1945*. New York, 1969.
Carrington, C. E. *The British Overseas*. 2nd ed. Cambridge, Eng., 1968.
Gordon, Donald C. *The Moment of Power: Britain's Imperial Epoch*. Englewood Cliffs, N. J., 1970.
Koebner, Richard and H. D. Schmidt. *Imperialism: The Story and Significance of a Political Word, 1840–1960*. Cambridge, Eng., 1964.
Mansergh, Nicholas. *The Commonwealth Experience*. New York, 1969.
McIntyre, W. D. *Colonies into Commonwealth*. London, 1966.
Morrell, William P. *British Colonial Policy in the Age of Peel and Russell*. Oxford, 1930.
Morris, James. *Pax Britannica: The Climax of an Empire*. London, 1968.
Rose, J. Holland, A. P. Newton, and E. A. Benians. *The Cambridge History of the British Empire*. 9 vols. Cambridge, Eng., 1929–1959.
Seton-Watson, Robert W. *Disraeli, Gladstone and the Eastern Question*. London, 1935.
Snyder, Louis L. (ed.). *The Imperialism Reader: Documents and Readings on Modern Expansionism*. Princeton, N. J., 1962.
Spender, John A. *Great Britain, Empire and Commonwealth, 1886–1935*. London, 1936.
Strang, William S. *Britain in World Affairs*. London, 1961.
Taylor, A. J. P. *The Troublemakers: Dissent Over Foreign Policy, 1792–1939*. London, 1957.
Temperley, H. W. V. and L. M. Penson. *Foundations of British Foreign Policy*. Cambridge, Eng., 1938.
Thornton, A. P. *The Imperial Idea and Its Enemies*. London and New York, 1959.
Ward, Sir A. W. and G. P. Gooch (eds.). *The Cambridge History of British Foreign Policy, 1783–1919*. 3 vols. New York, 1922–1923.
Williamson, James A. *A Short History of British Expansion*. 4th ed. London, 1953.

F. Ireland

Beckett, James C. *The Making of Modern Ireland, 1603–1923*. London, 1966.
Bolton, Geoffrey C. *The Passing of the Irish Act of Union: A Study in Parliamentary Politics*. London, 1966.
Costigan, Giovanni. *A History of Modern Ireland*. New York, 1970.
Curtis, Edmund. *A History of Ireland*. 6th ed. rev. London, 1950.
Edwards, R. Dudley and T. Desmond Williams (eds.). *The Great Famine: Studies in Irish History, 1845–1852*. Dublin, 1956.
Hammond, John L. *Gladstone and the Irish Nation*. London, 1938.
Lecky, William E. H. *A History of Ireland in the Eighteenth Century*. New ed. 5 vols. London, 1892.
Lyons, F. S. L. *The Irish Parliamentary Party, 1890–1910*. London, 1951.
Mansergh, Nicholas. *The Irish Question, 1840–1921*. Rev. ed. London, 1965.
MacCarthy, Michael J. F. *The Irish Revolution*. London, 1912.
MacDowell, Robert B. *The Irish Administration, 1801–1914*. London, 1964.
Norman, E. R. *The Catholic Church and Ireland in the Age of Rebellion, 1859–1873*. Ithaca, N. Y., 1965.

Nowlan, Kevin B. *The Politics of Repeal*. London, 1965.
O'Hegarty, P. S. *A History of Ireland under the Union, 1801–1922*. London, 1952.
Pomfret, John E. *The Struggle for Land in Ireland, 1800–1923*. Princeton, N. J., 1930.
Senior, Hereward. *Orangeism in Ireland and Britain, 1795–1836*. London and Toronto, 1966.

G. RELIGION, EDUCATION, AND LITERATURE

Altick, Richard D. *The English Common Reader: A Social History of the Mass Reading Public, 1800–1900*. Chicago, 1957.
Bamford, T. W. *Rise of the Public Schools*. London, 1967.
Baugh, Albert C. (ed.) *A Literary History of England*. 2nd ed. New York, 1967.
Caine, Sir Sydney. *British Universities: Purpose and Prospects*. London, 1969.
Carpenter, Spencer C. *Church and People, 1789–1899*. London, 1933.
Chadwick, Owen (ed.). *The Mind of the Oxford Movement*. Stanford, Calif., 1960.
———. *The Victorian Church*. 2 parts. New York, 1966 and 1970.
Chew, Samuel C. and Richard D. Altick. *The Nineteenth Century and After, 1789–1939*. 2nd ed. Vol. 4: *A Literary History of England*. New York, 1967.
Church, Richard W. *The Oxford Movement: Twelve Years, 1833–1845*. London, 1891.
Clark, G. Kitson. *The English Inheritance*. London, 1950.
Cockshutt, A. O. J. *Anglican Attitudes: A Study of Victorian Religious Controversies*. London, 1959.
Curtis, S. J. *History of Education in Great Britain*. 7th ed. London, 1967.
Dent, H. C. *The Educational System of England and Wales*. London, 1961.
Elliott-Binns, L. E. *Religion in the Victorian Era*. London, 1936.
Himmelfarb, Gertrude. *Darwin and the Darwinian Revolution*. London, 1959.
Houghton, Walter E. *The Victorian Frame of Mind, 1830–1870*. New Haven, Conn., 1957.
Irvine, William. *Apes, Angels and Victorians*. London, 1956.
Jack, Ian. *English Literature, 1815–1832*. Oxford, 1963.
Lowndes, G. A. N. *The Silent Social Revolution*. 2nd ed. Oxford, Eng., 1969.
Maclure, J. Stuart. *Educational Documents: England and Wales, 1816–1967*. 2nd ed. London, 1968.
Mathieson, William L. *English Church Reform, 1815–1840*. London, 1923.
Nicholls, David. *Church and State in Britain Since 1820*. London and New York, 1967.
Nicoll, Allardyce. *A History of English Drama, 1660–1900*. 6 vols. Cambridge, Eng., 1955 and 1959.
Osgood, Charles G. *The Voice of England: A History of English Literature*. 2nd ed. New York, 1952.
Smith, Warren S. *The London Heretics, 1870–1914*. New York, 1968.
Willey, Basil. *Nineteenth Century Studies: Coleridge to Matthew Arnold*. London, 1949.

MINISTRIES, 1828–1960

Formed	Party	Prime Minister	Chancellor of the Exchequer
Jan., 1828	Tory	Duke of Wellington	Henry Goulburn
Nov., 1830	Whig	Earl Grey	Viscount Althorp
July, 1834	Whig	Viscount Melbourne [I]	Viscount Althorp
Dec., 1834	Conservative	Sir Robert Peel [I]	Sir Robert Peel
April, 1835	Whig	Viscount Melbourne [II]	Thomas Spring-Rice Sir Francis T. Baring, 1839
Sept., 1841	Conservative	Sir Robert Peel [II]	Henry Goulburn
July, 1846	Whig	Lord John Russell [I]	Sir Charles Wood
Feb., 1852	Conservative	Earl of Derby [I]	Benjamin Disraeli
Dec., 1852	Peelites and Whigs	Earl of Aberdeen	William E. Gladstone
Feb., 1855	Whig	Viscount Palmerston [I]	Sir G. Cornewall Lewis
Feb., 1858	Conservative	Earl of Derby [II]	Benjamin Disraeli
June, 1859	Whigs, Peelites, and Liberals	Viscount Palmerston [II]	William E. Gladstone
Oct., 1865	Liberal	Earl Russell [II]	William E. Gladstone
June, 1866	Conservative	Earl of Derby [III]	Benjamin Disraeli

Home Secretary	Foreign Secretary	Other Important Ministers
(Sir) Robert Peel (Bt., 1830)	Earl of Dudley Earl of Aberdeen, 1828	Lord Lyndhurst (Lord Chancellor)
Viscount Melbourne	Viscount Palmerston	Lord Brougham (Lord Chancellor)
Viscount Duncannon	Viscount Palmerston	Thomas Spring-Rice (War and Colonies)
Henry Goulburn	Duke of Wellington	Earl of Aberdeen (War and Colonies)
Lord John Russell Marquess of Normanby, 1839	Viscount Palmerston	Thomas B. Macaulay (War, 1839)
Sir James R. Graham	Earl of Aberdeen	William E. Gladstone; (Board of Trade, 1843; War and Colonies, 1845)
Sir George Grey	Viscount Palmerston Earl Granville, 1851	Marquess of Lansdowne (Lord President of the Council)
Spencer H. Walpole	Earl of Malmesbury	Marquess of Salisbury (Lord Privy Seal)
Viscount Palmerston	Lord John Russell Earl of Clarendon, 1853	Sidney Herbert (War)
Sir George Grey	Earl of Clarendon	Earl Granville (Lord President of the Council)
Spencer H. Walpole Thomas H. S. Sotheron Estcourt, 1859	Earl of Malmesbury	Marquess of Salisbury (Lord President of the Council)
Sir G. Cornewall Lewis Sir George Grey, 1861	Lord John Russell (Earl, 1861)	Sidney Herbert (War) Charles P. Villiers (Poor Law Board, 1859)
Sir George Grey	Earl of Clarendon	Thomas Milner Gibson (Board of Trade)
Spencer H. Walpole Gathorne Hardy, 1867	Lord Stanley	Sir Stafford Northcote (Board of Trade; India, 1867)

Formed	Party	Prime Minister	Chancellor of the Exchequer
Feb., 1868	Conservative	Benjamin Disraeli [I]	George Ward Hunt
Dec., 1868	Liberal	William E. Gladstone [I]	Robert Lowe William E. Gladstone, 1873
Feb., 1874	Conservative	Benjamin Disraeli [II] (became Earl of Beacons- field, 1876)	Sir Stafford Northcote
April, 1880	Liberal	William E. Gladstone [II]	William E. Gladstone Hugh C. E. Childers, 1882
June, 1885	Conservative	Marquess of Salisbury [I]	Sir Michael Hicks Beach
Feb., 1886	Liberal	William E. Gladstone [III]	Sir Wiliam Harcourt
Aug., 1886	Conservative supported by Liberal Unionists	Marquess of Salisbury [II]	Lord Randolph Churchill George J. Goschen, 1887
Aug., 1892	Liberal	William E. Gladstone [IV]	Sir William Harcourt
Mar., 1894	Liberal	Earl of Rosebery	Sir William Harcourt
June, 1895	Unionist	Marquess of Salisbury [III]	Sir Michael Hicks Beach
July, 1902	Unionist	Arthur J. Balfour	Charles T. Ritchie Austen Chamberlain, 1903
Dec., 1905	Liberal	Sir Henry Campbell- Bannerman	H. H. Asquith

MINISTRIES, 1828–1960 567

Home Secretary	Foreign Secretary	Other Important Ministers
athorne Hardy	Lord Stanley	Earl of Malmesbury (Lord Privy Seal)
enry A. Bruce obert Lowe, 1873	Earl of Clarendon Earl Granville, 1870	John Bright (Board of Trade, to 1870) William E. Forster (Education, 1870)
ichard A. Cross	Earl of Derby (formerly Lord Stanley) Marquess of Salisbury, 1878	Sir Michael Hicks Beach (Colonies, 1878)
r William Harcourt	Earl Granville	Joseph Chamberlain (Board of Trade) Marquess of Hartington (India, to 1882; War, 1882)
r Richard A. Cross	Marquess of Salisbury	Lord Randolph Churchill (India) Lord Halsbury (Lord Chancellor)
ugh C. E. Childers	Earl of Rosebery	John Morley (Ireland)
enry Matthews	Earl of Iddesleigh (formerly Sir Stafford Northcote) Marquess of Salisbury, 1887	Sir Michael Hicks Beach (Ireland, to 1887) Arthur J. Balfour (Ireland, 1887)
. H. Asquith	Earl of Rosebery	Henry Campbell-Bannerman (War) John Morley (Ireland)
. H. Asquith	Earl of Kimberley	Henry Campbell-Bannerman (War) John Morley (Ireland)
ir Matthew White Ridley harles T. Ritchie, 1900	Marquess of Salisbury Marquess of Lansdowne, 1900	Joseph Chamberlain (Colonies) Arthur J. Balfour (First Lord of the Treasury)
retas Akers-Douglas	Marquess of Lansdowne	Joseph Chamberlain (Colonies) Earl of Halsbury (Lord Chancellor)
Herbert J. Gladstone	Sir Edward Grey	David Lloyd George (Board of Trade) James Bryce (Ireland)

568 MINISTRIES, 1828–1960

Formed	Party	Prime Minister	Chancellor of the Exchequer
April, 1908	Liberal	H. H. Asquith [I]	David Lloyd George
May, 1915	Coalition	H. H. Asquith [II]	Reginald McKenna
Dec., 1916	Coalition	David Lloyd George	Andrew Bonar Law Austen Chamberlain, 1919 Sir Robert S. Horne, 1921
Oct., 1922	Conservative	Andrew Bonar Law	Stanley Baldwin
May, 1923	Conservative	Stanley Baldwin [I]	Neville Chamberlain
Jan., 1924	Labour	J. Ramsay MacDonald [I]	Philip Snowden
Nov., 1924	Conservative	Stanley Baldwin [II]	Winston S. Churchill
June, 1929	Labour	J. Ramsay MacDonald [II]	Philip Snowden
Aug., 1931	National	J. Ramsay MacDonald [III]	Philip Snowden Neville Chamberlain, 1931
June, 1935	National	Stanley Baldwin [III]	Neville Chamberlain
May, 1937	National	Neville Chamberlain	Sir John Simon
May, 1940	Coalition	Winston S. Churchill [I]	Sir Kingsley Wood Sir John Anderson, 1943
May, 1945	Conservative	Winston S. Churchill [II]	Sir John Anderson
July, 1945	Labour	Clement R. Attlee	Hugh Dalton Sir Stafford Cripps, 1947 Hugh Gaitskell, 1950

MINISTRIES, 1828–1960   569

Home Secretary	Foreign Secretary	Other Important Ministers
Herbert J. Gladstone Winston S. Churchill, 1910 Reginald McKenna, 1911	Sir Edward Grey	Viscount Morley (India) Winston S. Churchill (Board of Trade; Admiralty, 1911) Earl Kitchener (War, 1914)
Sir John Simon Herbert Samuel, 1916	Sir Edward Grey (Viscount, 1916)	David Lloyd George (Munitions) Sir Edward Carson (Attorney General)
Sir George Cave Edward Shortt, 1919	Arthur J. Balfour Earl Curzon, 1919 (Marquess, 1921)	Winston S. Churchill (Munitions, 1917; War and Air, 1918; Colonies, 1921) Stanley Baldwin (Board of Trade, 1921)
W. C. Bridgeman	Marquess Curzon	Viscount Cave (Lord Chancellor)
W. C. Bridgeman	Marquess Curzon	Lord Robert Cecil (Lord Privy Seal)
Arthur Henderson	J. Ramsay MacDonald	Sidney Webb (Board of Trade)
Sir William Joynson-Hicks	(Sir) Austen Chamberlain (K.G., 1925)	Neville Chamberlain (Health) Viscount Hailsham (Lord Chancellor, 1928)
John R. Clynes	Arthur Henderson	Herbert Morrison (Transportation)
Sir Herbert Samuel Sir John Gilmour, 1932	Marquess of Reading Sir John Simon, 1931	Stanley Baldwin (Lord President of the Council)
Sir John Simon	Sir Samuel Hoare Anthony Eden, 1935	J. Ramsay MacDonald (Lord President of the Council)
Sir Samuel Hoare Sir John Anderson, 1939	Anthony Eden Viscount Halifax, 1938	Winston S. Churchill (Admiralty, 1939)
Sir John Anderson Herbert Morrison, 1940	Viscount Halifax Anthony Eden, 1940	Clement Attlee (Deputy Prime Minister, 1942) Lord Beaverbrook (Aircraft Production; Supply, 1941; War Production, to 1942) Ernest Bevin (Labour)
Sir Donald Somervell	Anthony Eden	Harold Macmillan (Air)
Chuter Ede	Ernest Bevin Herbert Morrison, 1951	Sir Stafford Cripps (Board of Trade, to 1947) Aneurin Bevan (Health)

Formed	Party	Prime Minister	Chancellor of the Exchequer
Oct., 1951	Conservative	(Sir) Winston S. Churchill (K.G., 1953) [III]	Richard A. Butler
April, 1955	Conservative	Sir Anthony Eden	Richard A. Butler Harold Macmillan, 1955
Jan., 1957	Conservative	Harold Macmillan	Peter Thorneycroft D. Heathcoat Amory, 1958 Selwyn Lloyd, 1960

Home Secretary	Foreign Secretary	Other Important Ministers
Sir David Maxwell Fyfe Gwilym Lloyd-George, 1954	(Sir) Anthony Eden (K.G., 1954)	Harold Macmillan (Housing and Local Government)
Gwilym Lloyd-George	Harold Macmillan Selwyn Lloyd, 1955	Iain Macleod (Labour and National Service, 1955) Marquess of Salisbury (Lord President of the Council)
Richard A. Butler	Selwyn Lloyd Earl of Home, 1960	Duncan Sandys (Defence) Edward Heath (Labour, 1959)

BIOGRAPHICAL SKETCHES

ARNOLD, MATTHEW (1822–1888). Poet, essayist, and critic. Prominent as an inspector of schools, an assistant commissioner on foreign education, and a professor of poetry at Oxford, Arnold was the foremost spokesman of his day for cultural arts. His social views are expressed in *Culture and Anarchy* and *Friendship's Garland;* his religious views are represented by *Literature and Dogma* and *God and the Bible.* He was probably the most exacting literary critic of the nineteenth century; *Essays in Criticism* reveals his values and methods.

ASQUITH, HERBERT HENRY, 1st Earl of Oxford and Asquith (1852–1928). Liberal Member for East Fife. President of the Oxford Union; later a prominent barrister. Asquith's Parliamentary career began in 1886 and included the offices of Home Secretary, Chancellor of the Exchequer, and Prime Minister. His term of office, 1908–1916, was the longest of any Prime Minister since Lord Liverpool and also one of the most productive. Created Earl in 1925.

ATTLEE, CLEMENT R. (1883–1967). Labour Member for Limehouse. An early convert to socialism, he worked with Beatrice and Sidney Webb in activities of the Fabian Society, led the Labour Party from 1935 to 1955, and wrote *The Labour Party in Perspective.* Before becoming Prime Minister in 1945, he served in Churchill's Coalition Government as Lord Privy Seal, Deputy Prime Minister, Secretary of State for Dominion Affairs, and Lord President of the Council. He was elevated to an earldom in 1955.

BALDWIN, STANLEY (1867–1947). Conservative Member for Bewdley and three times Prime Minister. He also served as President of the Board of Trade, Chancellor of the Exchequer, and Lord President of the Council. He led the Conservative Party from 1923 to 1937. Created Earl Baldwin of Bewdley in 1937. In March, 1948, G. M. Trevelyan made this Baldwin's epitaph: "In a world of voluble hates, he plotted to make men like, or at least tolerate, one another.... He remains the most human and lovable of all the Prime Ministers."

BEVAN, ANEURIN (1897–1960). Elected to Parliament from Ebbw Vale in 1929. His membership in the Labour Party was marked by controversy. Expelled briefly in 1939 and again in 1955, he became leader of the "Bevanites," a left-wing group of dissidents. He was the most active critic of the Government throughout World War II. Minister of Health in Attlee's Administration, 1945–1951, he served for four months in 1951 as Minister of Labour.

BRIGHT, JOHN (1811–1889). Although he held only two offices during his Parliamentary career, President of the Board of Trade and Chancellor of the Duchy of Lancaster, Bright was significant in public affairs. He is noted for his speaking on questions of free trade, reform of franchise laws, disestablishment of the Irish Church, the American Civil War, and the Crimean War. With Richard Cobden, he was a leader of "the Manchester School" of politics. Elected Lord Rector of the University of Glasgow, 1883.

CARSON, SIR EDWARD HENRY (1854–1935). Conservative Member for Dublin University for twenty-six years. A prominent legal advocate, Carson became Solicitor-General in 1900. Appointed Attorney-General in Asquith's Administration of May, 1915. Leader of Ulster Unionists, he fought long and successfully for exclusion of Northern Ireland from Home Rule. Knighted in 1900, he left the House in 1921 on appointment as a Lord of Appeal in Ordinary and took the title of Baron Carson.

CHAMBERLAIN, JOSEPH (1836–1914). Began his Parliamentary career in 1876 as a colleague of John Bright, representing Birmingham. President of the Board of Trade in 1880. Led Unionists from the Liberal Party in 1886. Strong advocate of social reform but best known for his work as Secretary of State for the Colonies, 1895–1903. He has been called the "most spectacular and probably most influential imperialist among British statesmen" of his era.

CHURCHILL, LORD RANDOLPH (1849–1895). In 1874 elected Conservative Member for Woodstock. Prominent among the founders of the Primrose League, dedicated to upholding church, constitution, and traditional national virtues. Appointed by Salisbury to the Exchequer and to Leadership of the House, Churchill attempted to be a decisive force in the Government. He offered his resignation in 1886; to his surprise, it was immediately accepted. Churchill captured public imagination with his advocacy of the Disraelian notion of Tory democracy.

CHURCHILL, WINSTON S. (1874–1965). Statesman, historian, soldier, and journalist. Started his political career as a Liberal and ended it as a Conservative. Held numerous offices, including Under Secretary of State for the Colonies, President of the Board of Trade, Home Secretary, Lord of the Admiralty (twice), Minister of Munitions, Secretary of War, and Prime Minister (twice). His writings earned the Nobel Prize for literature in 1953. In 1963, he was made an honorary citizen of the United States. An outstanding statesman of this century.

COBDEN, RICHARD (1804–1865). Manchester merchant and a founder of the Anti-Corn Law League. Entered Parliament in 1841 as Member for Stockport. Of Cobden's speech of March 13, 1845, Peel reportedly said to Sidney Herbert, "You may answer this, for I cannot." After the Corn Law victory, he turned to matters of peace and disarmament. Joined Palmerston's Cabinet in 1859 as President of the Board of Trade. Along with Bright, he declared for the North in the American Civil War.

CURZON OF KEDLESTON, GEORGE NATHANIEL (1859–1925). Created Earl in 1911, Marquess in 1921. During 1899–1924, served as Viceroy of India, Lord Privy Seal, Lord President of the Council, and Foreign Secretary. Curzon staunchly supported Lord Lansdowne and the "Hedgers" in the Parliament crisis of 1911 and was Lansdowne's chief lieutenant in Lords during party conflicts of the next several years. He was appointed Chancellor of Oxford University in 1907 and devoted much time and attention to university affairs.

DISRAELI, BENJAMIN, 1st Earl of Beaconsfield (1804–1881). After three unsuccessful attempts, he was elected to Parliament in 1837 as Member for Maidstone. Breaking with Peel on the protection issue, he built a new Conservative Party. Chancellor of the Exchequer in Derby's Cabinets of 1852, 1858, and 1866. Twice Prime Minister, he entered Lords in 1876. Of his novels, *Coningsby*, *Sybil*, and *Tancred* are probably best known. Queen Victoria termed the death of her "dear Lord Beaconsfield a national calamity."

GAITSKELL, HUGH T. N. (1906–1963). Leader of the Labour Party, 1955–1963. Formerly Head of the Economics Department at London University, Gaitskell entered Commons in 1945 as Member for South Leeds after wartime service in the Ministry for Economic Warfare and with the Board of Trade. Minister of Fuel and Power and Minister for Economic Affairs before succeeding Sir Stafford Cripps as Chancellor of the Exchequer in 1950. Upon Attlee's resignation in 1955, he was elected Leader of the Labour Opposition. His sudden death in 1963 came at the height of his influence.

GLADSTONE, WILLIAM EWART (1809–1898). For almost sixty three years a member of Commons. Held a variety of important posts, including Secretary for War and Colonies and President of the Board of Trade, but was particularly distinguished in his terms as Chancellor of the Exchequer. Leader of the Liberal Party and four times Prime Minister. Ardent high churchman. Author of religious and classical works, most notably, *Studies on Homer and the Homeric Age*. Morley said Gladstone "conquered the House, because he was saturated with a subject and its arguments." Declined an earldom.

HALSBURY, EARL OF (1823–1921). Born Hardinge Stanley Giffard, he became Baron Halsbury in 1885 on appointment as Lord Chancellor, and in 1898 was created Earl. His reputation in criminal law led to appointment by Disraeli in 1875 as Solicitor-General. In 1877, he entered Commons as Conservative Member for Launceston. Halsbury became Lord Chancellor for a second time in 1886, and again from 1895 to 1905 during the Ministries of Salisbury and Balfour. He supervised production of a noted legal work, *The Laws of England*.

HARDIE, JAMES KEIR (1856–1915). Member for Merthyr Burghs. Founded and edited the *Labour Leader* in 1889, and in 1892 was elected M.P. for South West Ham. Was active in formation of the Labour Representation Committee, forerunner to the Labour Party. In 1906, Hardie became first Leader of the Labour Party in Commons. In his day, according to the *D.N.B.*, he was "perhaps the best-hated and best-loved man in Great Britain."

HUXLEY, THOMAS HENRY (1825–1895). Although he was a first-rate scientist in his own right, Huxley is probably best known for his efforts to make science meaningful to nonscientists. After Charles Darwin published *Origin of the Species* in 1859, Huxley was the foremost advocate and defender of Darwinism. Typical of his work were *Man's Place in Nature*, *Science and Morals*, and his Romanes lecture, *Evolution and Ethics*. To describe his theological/philosophical position, he coined the term "agnostic."

KEYNES, JOHN MAYNARD (1883–1946). Economist and political essayist; a major contributor to modern economic thought. Fellow in economics at Cambridge after 1908. Editor of the *Economic Journal*. Best known of his many works: *Economic Consequences of the Peace; A Treatise on Money; The General Theory of Employment, Interest, and Money;* and *Essays in Biography*. Devised Lloyd George's election program, 1929. Chief Treasury Adviser, 1940–1946. Created Baron Keynes in 1942.

LANSDOWNE, MARQUESS OF (1845–1927). Conservative Leader in the House of Lords. As a Liberal, he held minor offices in Gladstone's administrations (1868–1883); in 1883, he was named Governor-General of Canada. An Irish landlord, he broke with Gladstone on the Home Rule issue. Salisbury appointed him Viceroy of India in 1888. From 1895 to 1905 he served as Secretary of State for War and Foreign Secretary in Salisbury's Cabinets. Lansdowne led the Lords in rejecting Lloyd George's budget of 1909.

LLOYD GEORGE, DAVID (1863–1945). Liberal Member for Caernarvon Boroughs in Wales, 1890–1945. Prime Minister, 1916–1922; earlier had served as President of the Board of Trade, Chancellor of the Exchequer, Minister of Munitions, and Secretary for War. Leader of the Liberal Party, 1926–1931. In 1940 declined Churchill's invitation to join the Coalition Cabinet. Created Earl Lloyd-George of Dwyfor on New Year's Day, 1945.

LOWE, ROBERT, 1st Viscount Sherbrooke (1811–1892). Liberal Member for Calne. His record of public service included Joint Secretary of the Board of Control, Vice-President of the Board of Trade, Chancellor of the Exchequer, and Home Secretary. A fellow in classics at Oxford, he later spent eight years in Australian politics. A man of brilliant intellect, Lowe was a dominant force in the House. His speeches on reform, said Asa Briggs, "set out the most comprehensive case against democracy expressed in the House of Commons in the nineteenth century."

MACAULAY, THOMAS BABINGTON (1800–1859). Historian, essayist, and politician, Macaulay became Whig Member for the pocket borough of Calne in 1830. He rendered distinguished service in the Supreme Council of India, where he inaugurated the system of national education and drafted the basic Indian criminal code. After 1847, he devoted most of his attention to research and writing. His *History of England*, published between 1849 and 1861, enjoyed great success. Created Baron Macaulay in 1857.

MACMILLAN, (Maurice) HAROLD (1894–   ). Conservative Member for Bromley, he replaced Sir Anthony Eden as Prime Minister in 1957 and remained in office until 1963. During and immediately following World War II, he served as Under Secretary of State in the Colonial Office, Minister of Housing and Local Government, Minister of Defense, Secretary of State for Foreign Affairs, and Chancellor of the Exchequer.

MILL, JOHN STUART (1806–1873). Political philosopher and reformer. Liberal Member for Westminster, 1866–1868. Mill was well known as editor of the *London and Westminster Review* and author of *A System of Logic, Principles of Political Economy, On Liberty, Thoughts on Parliamentary Reform, Utilitarianism*, and other works. Lord Rector of Saint Andrews University.

MORLEY, JOHN, VISCOUNT (1838–1923). His career included editorships of the *Literary Gazette*, the *Fortnightly Review*, *Macmillan's Magazine*, and the *Pall Mall Gazette*. Elected to Commons in 1883 as Liberal Member for Newcastle-upon-Tyne. In 1886 and again in 1892 Gladstone appointed him Secretary for Ireland. Later he was Secretary for India. In 1908 he entered Lords as Viscount Morley of Blackburn and defended Lloyd George's budget of 1909 and the Parliament Bill two years later. His *Life of Gladstone* is a masterly biography.

NEWMAN, JOHN HENRY, Cardinal (1801–1890). Author of more than forty works, the most famous of which are *Apologia pro Vita Sua* and *The Idea of a University*. Newman converted to Catholicism from Anglicanism after leaving the Oxford Movement, which opposed governmental interference with the Church of England and reasserted high-church ideals. Appointed Rector of the new Catholic University in Dublin in 1852. Created Cardinal in 1879. The most articulate defender of traditional Christianity in Victorian England.

O'CONNELL, DANIEL (1775–1847). Member for Cork. Lifelong spokesman for Catholic rights and Irish independence. Founder of the Catholic Association. Elected to Parliament in 1828 for County Clare, but denied his seat for refusing to take the oath of supremacy; re-elected, he was seated in February, 1830. Organized the famous "monster meetings" in 1843, concluding at Tara Hill, where the audience was estimated to be nearly one million persons. Popularly called "the Liberator."

PALMERSTON, LORD (Henry John Temple), 3rd Viscount (1784–1865). Prominent in various offices: Lord of the Admiralty, Secretary for War, Secretary of State for Foreign Affairs, Secretary for Home Office, and twice Prime Minister. At the height of his career, Palmerston was considered "the embodiment of John Bull," was called "the Minister for England" by Lord John Russell, and was pronounced in his newspaper obituary "the most English minister that ever governed England."

PARNELL, CHARLES STEWART (1846–1891). Entered Commons in 1875 for County Meath. Led Irish Members in an attempt to discredit the House. In 1879 named President of the newly formed National Land League of Ireland. After Gladstone's Home Rule Bill of 1886, Parnell formed an alliance with the Parliamentary Liberal Party. But the Liberal leadership dissociated itself from Parnell in late 1890, dividing Irish Nationalists into Parnellites and anti-Parnellites. Gladstone said that Parnell did "for Home Rule something like what Cobden did for Free Trade—set the argument on its legs."

PEEL, SIR ROBERT, 2nd Baronet (1788–1850). Tory Member for Tamworth. Served as Chief Secretary for Ireland and Home Secretary before being named Prime Minister. His conversion to free trade in 1846 marked the triumph of anti-Corn Law forces and caused an historic split in the Conservative Party. Peelites then joined Liberals in advancing reform legislation. To Cobden, Peel represented "the idea of the age."

REDMOND, JOHN EDWARD (1856–1918). Member for Waterford. Supported Parnell's policy of independence of Irish Members from British parties. In 1900 became Chairman of the United Irish Party. Marshalled Irish support for Asquith's

Parliament Bill in 1911 and for England's war effort three years later. Redmond's Home Rule policy was moderate, aiming at a united Ireland within the Empire.

ROSEBERY, EARL OF (1847–1929). Born Archibald Philip Primrose, he was created 5th Earl at the death of his father in 1868. In 1878 elected Lord Rector of Aberdeen University and in 1880 of Edinburgh University. In the Gladstone Governments of 1886 and 1892, he was Foreign Secretary. Liberal Prime Minister, 1894–1895. He voted for the Parliament Bill in 1911 and never entered the House of Lords again.

RUSSELL, LORD JOHN, 1st Earl Russell (1792–1878). Entered Commons in 1813 as Whig Member for Tavistock and represented successively Hunts, Bandon, Devon, Stroud, and the City of London. Paymaster of the Forces in 1831. He later served as Home Secretary, Leader of the House of Commons, and Secretary for War and the Colonies. Supported Peel in seeking abolition of the Corn Laws. Upon Peel's resignation in 1846, he became Prime Minister. Palmerston's Foreign Secretary during the U. S. Civil War; he was again Prime Minister in 1865.

SEELEY, JOHN R. (1834–1895). Historian and essayist. Professor of modern history at Cambridge University from 1869 until his death. His work, in particular *The Expansion of England*, gave theoretical support for the imperialist policies of such leaders as Chamberlain, and earned him a knighthood. According to J. A. Hobson, Seeley was, more than any other writer, the one who "is justly accredited with the stimulation of large ideas of the destiny of England."

SHEIL, RICHARD LALOR (1791–1851). Dramatic writer and barrister, Sheil joined O'Connell's agitation for Catholic emancipation in the early 1820's. Entered Parliament in 1831 as Member for the borough of Milborne Port in Dorset. Subsequently sat for County Louth, County Tipperary, and Dungarvan. Vice-President of the Board of Trade, Master of the Mint, and Minister at the Court of Tuscany were his public offices.

SNOW, SIR CHARLES PERCY (1905–   ). Holder of a doctorate in physics from Cambridge, fellow at Christ's College from 1930 to 1950, chief of scientific personnel for the Ministry of Labour, and member of the Civil Service Commission, Snow is regarded as a leading scientist. For his work as a reviewer for the London *Sunday Times* and as a novelist, he is considered an author of first rank. His dual interests led him to publish *The Two Cultures and the Scientific Revolution* and *Science and Government*.

WHITEHEAD, ALFRED NORTH (1861–1947). An internationally honored philosopher, mathematician, and educator. With his student, Bertrand Russell, he wrote the monumental *Principia Mathematica*. In 1924, he moved from England and Imperial College to Harvard University, where he remained until his retirement in 1937. Among his more popular works: *Science and the Modern World*, *Adventures of Ideas*, and *The Aims of Education*.

DATE DUE